D1410589

Structure and Function of Northern Coniferous Forests – An Ecosystem Study

T. Persson (Editor)

Suggested citation:

**Author's name. 1980. Title of paper. – In: Persson, T. (ed.)
Structure and Function of Northern Coniferous Forests – An Ecosystem Study,
Ecol. Bull. (Stockholm) 32: 000–000.**

Cover:
The 120-year-old Scots pine stand at Ivantjärnsheden, Jädraås.
(Photo: T. Persson, 10 May 1979)

ISSN 0346-6868
ISBN 91-546-0288-2
Production and distribution: NFR Editorial Service
LF/ALLF 209 80 001
Printed in Sweden by Berlings, Arlöv 1980, 7634

List of contents

THEORETICAL APPROACHES TO FOREST FUNCTIONING

Preface

This volume is the first comprehensive documentation of the studies conducted within the Swedish Coniferous Forest Project. It consists of 37 individual papers which all deal with aspects of the structure and function of Scots pine forests. The studies have been concentrated upon subsystems or subprocesses within the pine forest ecosystem, whereas limited work so far has been devoted to the ecosystem as a unit. Most papers concern plant and vegetation processes, but particular interest is also given to soil processes, consumption processes and energy and water exchange in the canopy and the soil. These apparently diverse studies are all linked by the central interest in obtaining a deepened understanding of plant biomass dynamics and factors regulating plant growth. For fulfilling this aim, mathematical modelling has provided an important tool in organizing the knowledge and identifying areas of ignorance.

The present volume predominantly consists of original publications. However, some synopses of reports already published and summaries of studies still in progress are also included to give a more complete picture of the project and the ecosystem studied.

Many persons have contributed to the realization of this volume. I especially wish to thank Lena Heiwall, Berit Lundén, Anita Stålhammar and Ingrid Åslin for typing the manuscripts, Nigel Rollison for all linguistic revisions, and Gudrun Sunnerstrand for her extensive work with the illustrations. I am also most grateful to the referees who, in anonymity, proposed valuable improvements to the papers.

Financial support for publication was given by the Swedish Natural Science Research Council, which is hereby gratefully acknowledged.

Uppsala
December 1980

Tryggve Persson

INTRODUCTION

Persson, T. (ed) 1980
Structure and Function of Northern
Coniferous Forests – An Ecosystem Study
Ecol. Bull (Stockholm) 32:11–23.

ECOSYSTEM RESEARCH WITHIN THE SWEDISH CONIFEROUS FOREST PROJECT

F. Andersson[1]

Abstract

This paper is an introduction to a long-term ecosystem study of Swedish coniferous forests. The general objective of this study was to deepen our knowledge of plant growth interpreted in an ecosystem context. The realization of this aim by investigating energy exchange, water turnover, consumption by insects, decomposition of organic matter, mineralization of nutrients, uptake by roots, gas exchange and assimilate dynamics, etc. is outlined. Mathematical simulation models were developed. These models were used for problem formulation and, besides being tools for integrating knowledge, they were also useful for organizing the research.

Project history – raison d'être

The exploitation of natural resources today often leads to unexpected consequences. Politicians mostly call for answers to explain or predict these consequences. During the 1960's the ecological awareness increased, which also influenced the authorities responsible for basic ecological research. In 1970 the Swedish Natural Science Research Council, NFR, found that the basic research in ecology could not meet the requirements from the community, neither in terms of knowledge nor in terms of research methodology. With respect to the situation in the country and the international development, it was suggested that a basic research project on the structure and function of our terrestrial environment ought to start. In this way basic ecology could serve the applied sciences and the society.

After two years of discussion and planning, an integrated project, the Swedish Coniferous Forest Project (SWECON), was started in July 1972 (Andersson, 1972). The coniferous forest was chosen as an object of study. This choice was made as conifer forests cover more than 40% of Sweden. Further reasons were that forest products make up approximately 20% of Swedish export income, and that Sweden had experience of and tradition in forest ecology research.

---

[1] Dept. of Ecology and Environmental Research, Swedish University of Agricultural Sciences, S-750 07 Uppsala, Sweden

Ecosystem research and a systems approach

Ecosystem research is a rather new branch of ecology. Its roots may however be considered as old. Research in agriculture and forestry can often be considered as ecosystem research. Previous studies have dealt with special parts of the systems or specific aspects of the function. The studies often suffered from the fact that simultaneous observations did not take place. Further, a sufficient degree of multidisciplinarity was seldom established. An ecosystem study focuses its interest on the structure and function of the ecosystem. The function is characterized by processes responsible for the flow of energy as well as the formation and turnover of matter. An ecosystem study fulfilling the meaning of the concept requires a coordinated effort with participation of several disciplines in order to depict processes such as energy exchange, plant production including photosynthesis, respiration and growth, decomposition, mineral cycling and activity of soil organisms.

The development of a theoretical and practical terminology of ecosystems and ecosystem functioning started off with Tansley (1935) and Lindeman (1942). Later, the science of ecosystem ecology was consolidated in the textbooks of Odum (1959, 1971). With the research in the International Biological Programme, IBP, carried out during the period 1964–74, a new area of ecosystem research was introduced. Classical investigations during that time were the Belgian Virelles project (Froment *et al.*, 1971), the English Meathop Wood project (Satchell, 1971) and the West-German Solling project (Ellenberg, 1971). The next generation of ecosystem projects were those started in the United States at the end of the 1960's, the biome studies, dealing with deserts, deciduous and coniferous forests, grasslands and tundra (e.g., Van Dyne, 1975).

The development of ecosystem research from the end of the 1960's introduced a methodology with a systems analysis approach. Systems analysis can be considered as an orderly and logical way of organizing data and information into models (Van Dyne, 1975). A systems approach also implies an overall view of the whole rather than separated views of the parts. Models of various parts are developed from the structure and function of the (eco)system. Generally mathematical models and frequently simulation models are utilized in this process. In developing the models it is possible to use isolated data from other investigations, times and places as well as literature data. When adequate models are developed they are supposed to be validated (falsified) with independent data.

By the use of mathematical models it was hoped to provide a deeper understanding of the system and processes investigated as well as enabling experimentation by simulation of possible influences on the system. A systems approach was also considered to be a tool in facilitating research priorities and project management.

The introduction of the systems approach was also suggested for SWECON. It was introduced with great expectations but also with some misgivings.

General objectives – aims

The general formulation to deal with the structure and function of coniferous forests is a very broad objective. With limited funding, priorities must be given, as it is not possible to pay attention to all aspects of a forest ecosystem. Among the items that may be listed as important properties or values of the forest, its ability of plant growth was chosen as the prime object. With this choice the following aims were agreed upon:

– To study the dynamics of the plant biomass and simultaneously to follow important ecosystem processes connected with energy exchange, turnover of water, organic material and mineral nutrients at the main sites of the project (age series including clear-fellings of Scots pine, *Pinus sylvestris* L., stands of dry dwarf shrub type on sandy soils at Ivantjärnsheden, Jädraås, Gästrikland, and an old, mixed coniferous forest stand of mesic dwarf-shrub type on glacial till at Siljansfors, Dalarna). Results are presented as mathematical simulation models.

– To test and transfer the basic models from the main localities to other representative coniferous forest environments.

– To study how the dynamics of the plant biomass and linked ecosystem processes are influenced directly and indirectly by certain human activities.

The first of these aims shows that it is the production by green plants in an ecological sense, i.e., not only stem production but also other plant parts above- and below-ground, as well as the processes within energy exchange, water and mineral turnover, which guide the research. The dynamics of the plant biomass and the resulting litter and humus, and the factors that influence their changes are not only of interest to basic science but are also of fundamental importance in practical silviculture. The first objective is only one of the stages towards the main objective, which aims at obtaining general knowledge about different types of forest, and on this basis the effects of environmental changes can be studied.

Research organization and management

An ecosystem study can be defined as a study of the flow of energy and matter. From a crude flow chart (Fig. 1) of the ecosystem with the compartments of stand atmosphere, plant biomass above-ground, plant biomass below-ground, litter and soil, the flows of energy, water, carbon and the main mineral elements were identified (Table 1) as well as some additional properties (Table 2). From this analysis necessary subprojects were derived. The flow chart was also used for the organisation of the project. Six "problem areas" were identified and within these small working groups "process groups" were established. In the beginning of the project the latter played an important role in strengthening the cooperation between scientists of different disciplines. The field and laboratory research established created an effective investigation system, which initially operated rather independently from the modelling efforts.

The initial problem areas (PA) and process groups (PG) were focused on:

PA 1. Energy exchange and microclimate
      PG 1.1 Energy exchange, atmosphere – stand
      PG 1.2 Energy exchange, stand – ground
      PG 1.3 Microclimate

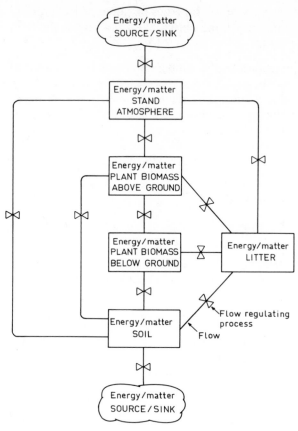

Figure 1. Basic structure used for analyses of structures and processes in a forest ecosystem.

PA 2. Water turnover
    PG 2.1 Water transport outside plant biomass
    PG 2.2 Water transport in plant biomass
    PG 2.3 Transpiration

PA 3. Dynamics of above-ground plant biomass
    PG 3.1 CO_2 exchange
    PG 3.2 Growth and litter formation
    PG 3.3 Consumption

PA 4. Dynamics of assimilates and NPK in plant biomass
    PG 4.1 NPK dynamics
    PG 4.2 Assimilate dynamics

PA 5. Dynamics of below-ground plant biomass
    PG 5.1 Growth and respiration
    PG 5.2 Litter formation and consumption

Table 1. Matrix of studied processes of energy exchange, turnover of water, carbon, and mineral elements, primarily nitrogen. The numbers given after the processes refer to the list of subprojects in the Appendix.

Flow between:	Flow of: Energy	Water	Carbon	Mineral elements
Stand atmosphere – Source/Sink	Energy exchange 1.1.02–03	Water exchange 1.1.01–03	CO_2-exchange 3.1.01–02	NPK-exchange 4.1.01–02
Stand atmosphere – Plant biomass above ground	Energy exchange 1.3.02	Interception 2.1.01, 04, 09; Evaporation 1.3.02, 2.3.05; Transpiration 2.3.02–04	Photosynthesis 3.1.03–04; Respiration 3.1.04–05	Deposition 4.1.01–02; Absorption 4.1.04; N-fixation 4.1.03
Stand atmosphere – Litter	Energy exchange 1.2.02–03	Throughfall 2.1.01; Interception 2.1.04, 09		Deposition 4.1.01–02
Stand atmosphere – Soil	Energy exchange 1.2.02–03	Throughfall 2.1.01; 2.1.09	CO_2-exchange 6.2.02	N-exchange 6.2.03
Plant biomass above-ground – Plant biomass below-ground	–	Water transport 2.2.01, 05	Translocation 4.1.07; 4.2.01–02	Translocation 4.1.06
Plant biomass above-ground – Litter	–	Crown drip 2.1.01; Interception 2.1.04, 09	Litterfall 3.2.09; 3.3.03–05	Litterfall 3.2.09
Plant biomass above-ground – Soil	–	Stem flow 2.1.01; Crown drip 2.1.09	Leaching 4.1.02; 4.2.03	Leaching 4.1.02; 4.2.03
Litter – Plant biomass below-ground	–	–	Litter formation 5.1.01–03; 5.2.01	Litter formation 5.1.02
Litter – Soil	–	Water transport 2.1.09	Leaching 6.1.01; Decomposition 6.2.01	Leaching 6.1.01; Decomposition 6.2.01
Plant biomass below-ground – Soil	–	Water uptake 2.2.01, 05	Respiration 5.1.04; 4.2.01; Exudation	Uptake 4.1.06; 6.3.01
Soil – Source/Sink	Energy exchange 1.2.02	Percolation 2.1.07; Run-off 2.1.10	Leaching 6.1.01	Leaching 6.1.01

Table 2. Matrix of additional properties and processes of the main system components. The numbers given after the properties and processes refer to the list of subprojects in the Appendix.

System component	Subprocess and state variable			
	Energy	Water	Carbon	Mineral elements
Atmosphere	Stored energy 1.3.01 Distribution of radiation 1.3.03	–	–	–
Plant biomass above-ground	Stored energy 1.3.01	Interception water 2.1.04 Distribution of water in plant biomass above-ground 2.2.07 Water transport 2.2.07	Growth 3.2.01–07, 10 Transport of assimilates 4.2.01 Effects of animals on assimilate transport 4.2.02 Consumption 3.3.01–02 Death 3.2.08, 05, 07	Transport of NPK 4.1.05 Transport of assimilates 4.2.01 Effects of animals on assimilate transport 4.2.02 Death 3.2.08
Plant biomass below-ground	–	–	Growth 5.1.01, 03 Consumption 5.2.01	–
Litter	–	Interception water 2.1.04 Infiltration 2.1.09	Decomposition 6.2.01	Decomposition 6.2.01
Soil	Heat conduction in soil 1.2.01 Energy transport in soil atmosphere 1.2.02	Water contents 2.1.05–06 Percolation 2.1.07 Infiltration 2.1.09 Stored energy 1.3.01	Leaching 6.1.01 Decomposition 6.2.01 Respiration 6.2.02 C in soil organisms 6.2.04 Interaction 6.2.05	Leaching 6.1.01 Decomposition 6.2.01 Mineralization 6.2.02 N-fixation 6.2.03 Denitrification 6.2.03 NPK in soil organisms 6.2.04 Immobilization 6.2.04 Interaction 6.2.05

PA 6. Soil processes

    PG 6.1 Leaching

    PG 6.2 Decomposition/mineralization

    PG 6.3 Mineralization/uptake by plants

    PG 6.4 Biomass dynamics of soil organisms

    PG 6.5 N-fixation, nitrification and NH_3-absorption

This management structure was developed during 1973 and was pertaining during the investigation phase (1974–77). In order to focus the activities on specific ecosystem problems the research was focused on ten different subprogrammes from 1978 onwards:

(1) Stand growth – pine
(2) Stand growth – spruce
(3) Ground vegetation – size and effects of plant growth, turnover of nutrients and water
(4) Plant production and production of forest products
(5) Biogeochemical cycling of the ecosystem
(6) Effect of consumption on primary production
(7) Plant production, carbon and nitrogen turnover during a stand rotation
(8) Turnover of water in forests with different site conditions
(9) Variation of climate in stands with different site conditions
(10) Regional evapotranspiration

More details on the development, coordination and administration of the project are given in Andersson (1977).

Problems – models

Dealing with the forest as an ecosystem requires consideration of a more long-term perspective, but in order to have a satisfactory biological background on ecosystem processes there is a need for information valid for a time domain of 1 to 10 years. The field and laboratory efforts have therefore mainly been made with respect to this time domain. There is also a need for information on shorter time domains, as 10 minutes to a day, especially when dealing with physiological properties.

The aims stated earlier are to be considered as general. A more precise description of the aims and problems of the project, as summarized in 1975, is given in a series of models regarding different components and time domains of the forest ecosystem (Fig. 2).

The aims of these models were:

– Stand development model – DEVS
To describe the development of the tree stand and its production as well as the accumulation and decomposition of the organic matter and nitrogen in the soil during a tree generation. The ground vegetation is modelled as a layer competitive to the tree layer. A nitrogen model and a water model will be linked to the main model. The water model, however, will be very crude. Time domain: 150 years.

17

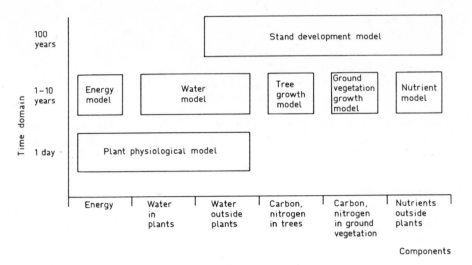

Figure 2. Basic models of a forest ecosystem – the basis for the modelling efforts of the Swedish Coniferous Forest Project since 1975.

– Tree layer production model – PT 1/10
To give the production of tree biomass (mass per unit area and unit time) assorted by the most important components of the trees as a function primarily of climate, tree biomass and physiological status. The model and its information are intended to be used for generalizations and serve as a background to the stand development model. Time domain: 1–10 years.

– Ground layer production model – PGL 1/10
To describe the production, nutrient uptake and water balance of the ground vegetation in such a way that the ground vegetation is competitive to the tree layer regarding the items mentioned. Time domain: 1–10 years.

– 24-hour-model – FAST
To describe on the one hand the dependence of allocation of assimilates and growth on climatic and biotic factors (assimilates, water and nutrient status), and on the other hand, the relation between gas exchange, water balance and climate. The model will be used as an evaluation and test instrument in order to form different types of mean values representing days and weeks (relevant for use in other models). Time domain: 24 hours.

– Nutrient model – N 1/10
To describe the decomposition of soil organic matter within and between years with different climatic conditions; and to describe the release of nutrients, their transport within and between horizons as well as the uptake by plants (mainly nitrogen). The model includes inputs and outputs to and from the soil. The main output to the other models is the uptake of nutrients by plants, mainly nitrogen. Time domain: 1–10 years.

- Water model – W 1
  To describe the flow of water in the ecosystem, in order to provide input data for the production, nutrient and energy models. Time domain: 1 year.

- Energy model – E 1
  To develop models to determine the different terms of the energy exchange equation, in order to derive inputs to the models of the project from common meteorological data (on a monthly basis) with a restricted number of additional measurements (on a daily basis). Time domain: 1 year.

The development or the fate of the modelling work – syntheses – can partly be followed in this volume, especially the work dealing with shorter time perspectives (Ågren & Axelsson, 1980; Bosatta, 1980; Bosatta *et al.*, 1980; Halldin *et al.*, 1980; Lohammar *et al.*, 1980). The use of systems analysis and modelling in ecosystem research is further considered in Ågren *et al.* (1980).

Subprojects

Construction and development of ecosystem related models requires information on compartment sizes, flow rates and driving variables. A number of subprojects were identified to fulfill this need. It was felt urgent to relate the collection of basic data to meaningful investigations for the individual scientist. In this way it was hoped to avoid the often mentioned phenomena that ecosystem research is dominated by collection of data – donkey work – seldom dealing with basic biological relationships. The subprojects have been orientated towards processes, also including experimental elements. A comprehensive field experiment with irrigation and fertilization was established. Other minor field experiments were established, such as trenching (control of root competition), artificial defoliation and isotope experiments.

An introduction to the field and laboratory investigations and subprojects is given for the abiotic studies (Perttu *et al.*, 1980), plant and vegetation processes (Falk, 1980) and soil processes (Lohm, 1980). A listing of the subprojects is given in the Appendix.

Acknowledgements

Without the devoted work of several persons the establishment, development and management of the project would not have been possible. The efforts of the Ecological Committee of the Swedish National Science Research Council are particularly appreciated and especially those of its secretary, Bengt Lundholm, who in an efficient way launched the project. Bo Nilsson-Lindborg has taken part of all the phases of the project and acted as a link between the project and the Natural Science Research Council. In the first planning group during 1970–72 the following persons took part: Carl Olof Tamm, Ulrik Lohm, Thomas Rosswall and Torgny Schütt. Over the years several persons have taken part in the development and management of the project. Especially the following persons must be mentioned:

Abiotic studies:	Kurth Perttu and Swen Halldin
Plant processes:	Björn Axelsson, Jeremy Flower-Ellis, Stig O. Falk and Sune Linder
Consumption:	Olle Tenow
Soil processes:	Ulf Granhall, Ulrik Lohm, Börje Norén and Bengt Nihlgård
Modelling:	Torbjörn Fagerström, Torgny Schütt and Göran I. Ågren
Computer section:	Jan Svensson

Ulf Granhall has also been responsible for the development and management of a subproject on biological effects of clear-felling. Several other persons have from time to time taken part in the management of the project. Among the persons mentioned, the work carried out by Carl Olof Tamm is especially appreciated. His broad and deep knowledge of forest ecology has been of the uttermost importance during all phases of the project.

Several other colleagues have contributed to the success of the project – none mentioned, none forgotten. However, the important role played by Bertil Andersson, director of the field station at Jädraås, cannot be neglected. He has effectively participated in generating applications and developing the field station and research sites. Further, he has provided for both our energetical and nocturnal needs. Finally, Tryggve Persson has our full appreciation for his careful editing of this volume.

References

Ågren, G. I. & Axelsson, B. 1980. PT – a tree growth model. – In: Persson, T. (ed.) Structure and Function of Northern Coniferous Forests – An Ecosystem Study, Ecol. Bull. (Stockholm) 32: 525–536.

Ågren, G. I., Andersson, F. & Fagerström, T. 1980. Experiences of ecosystem research in the Swedish Coniferous Forest Project. – In: Persson, T. (ed.) Structure and Function of Northern Coniferous Forests – An Ecosystem Study, Ecol. Bull. (Stockholm) 32: 591–596.

Andersson, F. (ed.). 1972. Ecology of the Swedish Coniferous Forest Landscape – A Research Programme, Ecol. Bull. (Stockholm) 15, 70 pp.

Andersson, F. 1977. Development, coordination and administration of an ecosystem project. – In: Training in Research Programme Planning and Administration, pp. 36–47. Stockholm: NOS Joint Committee of the Nordic Science Research Councils.

Bosatta, E. 1980. Modelling of soil processes – an introduction. – In: Persson, T. (ed.) Structure and Function of Northern Coniferous Forests – An Ecosystem Study, Ecol. Bull. (Stockholm) 32: 553–564.

Bosatta, E., Bringmark, L. & Staaf, H. 1980. Nitrogen transformations in a Scots pine forest mor – model analysis of mineralization, uptake by roots and leaching. – In: Persson, T. (ed.) Structure and Function of Northern Coniferous Forests – An Ecosystem Study, Ecol. Bull. (Stockholm) 32: 565–589.

Ellenberg, H. 1971. The Solling project, an IBP/PT integrated project in the Federal Republic of Germany. – In: Duvigneaud, P. (ed.) Productivity of Forest Ecosystems, Ecology and Conservation, pp. 667–670. Paris: Unesco.

Falk, S. O. 1980. Studies of plant and vegetation processes within the Swedish Coniferous Forest Project – an introduction. – In: Persson, T. (ed.) Structure and Function of Northern Coniferous Forests – An Ecosystem Study, Ecol. Bull. (Stockholm) 32: 123–124.

Froment, A., Tanghe, M., Duvigneaud, P., Galoux, A., Denaeyer-De Smet, S., Schnock, G., Grubois, J., Mommaerts-Billiet, F. & Vanséveren, J. P. 1971. La chênaie mélangée calcicole de Virelles-Blaimont, en haute Belgique. – In: Duvigneaud, P. (ed.) Productivity of Forest Ecosystems, Ecology and Conservation, pp. 635–665. Paris: Unesco.

Halldin, S., Grip, H., Jansson, P.-E. & Lindgren, Å. 1980. Micrometeorology and hydrology of pine forest ecosystems. II. Theories and models. – In: Persson, T. (ed.) Structure and Function of Northern Coniferous Forests – An Ecosystem Study, Ecol. Bull. (Stockholm) 32: 463–503.

Lindeman, R. L. 1942. The trophic-dynamic aspect of ecology. – Ecology 23: 399–418.

Lohammar, T., Larsson, S., Linder, S. & Falk, S. O. 1980. FAST – simulation models of gaseous exchange in Scots pine. – In: Persson, T. (ed.) Structure and Function of Northern Coniferous Forests – An Ecosystem Study, Ecol. Bull. (Stockholm) 32: 505–523.

Lohm, U. 1980. Soil process studies within the Swedish Coniferous Forest Project – an introduction. – In: Persson, T. (ed.) Structure and Function of Northern Coniferous Forests – An Ecosystem Study, Ecol. Bull. (Stockholm) 32: 329–332.

Odum, E. P. 1959. Fundamentals of Ecology, 2nd ed. Philadelphia–London: W. B. Saunders Company, 546 pp.

Odum, E. P. 1971. Fundamentals of Ecology, 3rd ed. Philadelphia–London: W. B. Saunders Company, 574 pp.

Perttu, K., Bischof, W., Grip, H., Jansson, P.-E., Lindgren, Å., Lindroth, A. & Norén, B. Micrometeorology and hydrology of pine forest ecosystems. I. Field studies. – In: Persson, T. (ed.) Structure and Function of Northern Coniferous Forests – An Ecosystem Study, Ecol. Bull. (Stockholm) 32: 75–121.

Satchell, J. E. 1971. Feasibility study of an energy budget for Meathop Wood. – In: Duvigneaud, P. (ed.) Productivity of Forest Ecosystems, Ecology and Conservation, pp. 619–630. Paris: Unesco.

Tansley, A. G. 1935. The use and abuse of vegetational concepts and terms. – Ecology 16: 284–307.

Van Dyne, G. M. 1975. Some procedures, problems, and potentials of systems-oriented, ecosystem-level research programs. – In: Van Dyne, G. M., Gay, L. W., Stewart, J. B., Eriksson, E., Bischof, W., Waring, R. H., Heal, O. W., Ulrich, B., Khanna, P. K., Mayer, R. & Prenzel, J. Procedures and Examples of Integrated Ecosystem Research – Papers presented to the SWECON seminar in May 1973, Swed. Conif. For. Proj. Tech. Rep. 1: 6–58.

Appendix

List of initial subprojects

Subproject		Responsible

Problem area 1. Energy exchange and microclimate

1.1.01	Evaporation-semiempirical estimations	H. Grip
1.1.02	Energy exchange atmosphere-stand by the energy balance method	K. Perttu
1.1.03	Energy exchange atmosphere-stand by the vertical profile method	K. Perttu
1.2.01	Heat conduction in the soil	P.-E. Jansson
1.2.02	Energy transport in the soil/air phase	P.-E. Jansson
1.2.03	Energy transport by precipitation	H. Grip
1.3.01	Energy storage in a forest stand, Velen	B. Bringfelt
1.3.02	Evapotranspiration from soil and vegetation by the energy balance method	K. Perttu
1.3.03	Quantitative and qualitative dispersion and change of radiation in a stand	K. Perttu
1.3.04	Bioclimate	A. Lindroth

Problem area 2. Water turnover

2.1.01	Throughfall, stem flow, and interception of the tree canopy	H. Grip
2.1.04	Interception in ground vegetation and litter	H. Grip
2.1.05–06	Variation of the water content in the unsaturated zone. Laboratory and field studies	P.-E. Jansson
2.1.07	Percolation and its time variation in the soil profile	P.-E. Jansson
2.1.09	Storage and melting of snow	H. Grip

2.1.10	Run-off	H. Grip
2.2.01	Water transport in the soil-root-needle system in young pines	L.-Å. Andersson
2.2.02	Daily and annual variations in the water uptake of pine. Field investigations	J. Hellkvist
2.2.05	Daily and annual variations in the root-needle water transport of pine. Field investigations	J. Hellkvist
2.2.07	Daily and annual variations in dispersion of water between various ages of needles and various heights of pine. Field investigations	J. Hellkvist
2.3.02	Water transport in the needle-atmosphere system of young pine plants	S. Larsson
2.3.03	Daily and annual variations in transpiration and leaf resistance of pine. Field investigations	J. Hellkvist
2.3.04	Daily and annual variations in transpiration of the ground vegetation of 15 and 120 year-old stands of pine. Field investigations	J. Hellkvist
2.3.05	Evaporation from pine needles. Laboratory investigations	S. Elowson
2.3.08	Water uptake, transport, dispersion and transpiration in trees	J. Hellkvist

Problem area 3. Dynamics of above-ground plant biomass

3.1.01–02	The distribution and flow of CO_2 within stands	W. Bishof
3.1.03	CO_2-exchange of the green plant biomass in stands of pine	S. Linder
3.1.04	CO_2-exchange of pine. Laboratory investigations	S. Linder
3.1.05	CO_2-exchange of the non-green plant biomass	S. Linder
3.2.01	Length and diameter growth of pine	J. G. K. Flower-Ellis
3.2.02–04	Changes in the needle biomass	J. G. K. Flower-Ellis
3.2.05	Biomass changes of *Calluna*	H. Persson
3.2.06	Biomass changes of other vascular plants	H. Persson
3.2.07	Biomass changes of cryptogams	H. Persson
3.2.08	Plant death	J. G. K. Flower-Ellis
3.2.09	Litterfall	J. G. K. Flower-Ellis
3.2.10	Methods for measuring stem diameter and shoot length	H. Odin
3.3.01–02	Consumption and abundance of insect consumers. Field investigations	O. Tenow
3.3.03	Litter fall caused by attacks of bark beetles	O. Tenow
3.3.04	Production of faeces by insects in the field	O. Tenow
3.3.05	Consumption and defaecation by insects in the laboratory	O. Tenow
3.3.06	Model of pine shoot beetle based on published data	O. Tenow
3.3.07	Influence of grazing insects on primary production. Process studies	O. Tenow

Problem area 4. Dynamics of assimilates and NPK in plant biomass

4.1.01	Dry deposition	B. Nihlgård
4.1.02	Wet deposition and leaching from plant biomass above-ground	B. Nihlgård
4.1.03	Nitrogen fixation in the tree and dwarf shrub layers	U. Granhall
4.1.04	Uptake of NPK by absorption of needles	B. Nihlgård
4.1.05	Transport of NPK in plant biomass above-ground showing relationships between NPK and growth	T. Ingestad
4.1.06	Uptake in roots and transport of NPK in plant biomass	S. Pettersson
4.1.07	Effects of invertebrates on the dynamics of mineral elements and assimilates in plant biomass	B. Axelsson

Problem area 5. Dynamics of below-ground plant biomass

5.1.01	Dynamics and production of the root biomass	H. Persson
5.1.02	Ingrowth and death of roots	H. Persson
5.1.03	Root chamber investigations	H. Persson
5.1.04	Root respiration. Pilot studies	H. Staaf
5.2.01	Root consumption	B. Sohlenius

Problem area 6. Soil processes

6.1.01	Leaching of CNPK	L. Bringmark
6.2.01	Decomposition of litter – disappearance and changes of substrates	B. Berg
6.2.02	Mineralization of CNP	H. Staaf
6.2.03	Nitrogen fixation, denitrification	U. Granhall
6.2.04	Biomass of soil organisms, content and assimilation of CNPK	T. Persson
6.2.05	Influence on the mineralization by interaction between soil organisms	B. Sohlenius
6.3.01	Mineralization – uptake by roots	U. Lohm

Persson, T. (ed) 1980
Structure and Function of Northern
Coniferous Forests – An Ecosystem Study
Ecol. Bull. (Stockholm) 32: 25–64.

INVESTIGATION SITES OF THE SWEDISH CONIFEROUS FOREST PROJECT – BIOLOGICAL AND PHYSIOGRAPHICAL FEATURES

B. Axelsson[1] and S. Bråkenhielm[2]*

Abstract

The two intensive research sites of the Swedish Coniferous Forest Project (SWECON) are described. The main sites, a lichen Scots pine heath on sand (Ivantjärnsheden), and a mixed mature stand of Scots pine and Norway spruce on till (Nickobacken) within Siljansfors Experimental Forest, are both situated in Central Sweden near latitude 60°50'N.

Ivantjärnsheden is located just north of the border between the Boreal zone or taiga of Northern Sweden and the Boreo-nemoral zone of Southern Sweden. The basically climatic transition is narrow due to topography and geology. It contains both northern and southern plant and animal species. The research area is a level sedimentary sandy plain at 185 m above mean sea level (M.S.L.). Mean annual air temperature is 3.8°C and mean annual precipitation ca. 600 mm. The vegetation belongs to the *Cladonio-Pinetum (boreale)* K-L 1967 association or the lichen to lichen-dwarf-shrub forest type growing on an ordinary iron podzol. The research plots represent an age-series of pine forest stands from a clear-felled area to a 120-year-old stand.

Siljansfors Experimental Forest has a slightly more continental temperature climate but is distinctly more humid. The forest is situated in a strongly undulating till area with altitudes between 210 m and 425 m above M.S.L. Mean annual air temperature is 3.6°C and annual precipitation ca. 700 mm. On the bouldery, sloping research plot the plant community belongs to a mesic to moist dwarf-shrub forest type with mosses and *Vaccinium myrtillus* on the ground and a tree stand comprising ca. 150-year-old pines and ca. 100-year-old spruces. The nearby Gusseltjärn drainage area is used for hydrological studies.

Introduction

During the introductory stage of the Swedish Coniferous Forest Project (SWE-CON), when the research effort was directed towards developing process models for the forest ecosystem, it was considered necessary to select a site which by homogeneity would simplify the work. Glacifluvial and marine/lacustrine deposits offer rather homogeneous substrates, which greatly facilitates soil sampling. Homogeneity also reduces deviations in the calculation of different soil properties. The dominant ecosystem on these dry and sandy plains is usually lichen-pine forest which occurs with comparatively small variation throughout Sweden.

[1] Dept. of Ecology and Environmental Research, Swedish University of Agricultural Sciences, S-750 07 Uppsala, Sweden
[2] Swedish National Environment Protection Board, Box 1302, S-171 25 Solna, Sweden
* Authors given alphabetically. See also Acknowledgements.

The water movements in these areas are chiefly vertical, with fairly even percolation in contrast to most till soils, and without any influence of ground water close to the soil surface. As an example of such a locality, Ivantjärnsheden, a lichen pine heath on sand at Jädraås in Central Sweden, was chosen as the main research site.

An ecosystem study of the coniferous forest complex also requires access to till soil with well delimited drainage areas. Siljansfors, one of the five experimental forests run by the Swedish University of Agricultural Sciences, has the advantage of having its stand history known for at least a period of 50 years. Within the experimental forest, both individual stands and defined catchment areas are available for investigation. The study was made on a till area typical of Swedish and boreal forest conditions. Nickobacken, a mature stand of pine and spruce within the experimental forest, was chosen as an intensive research area. The nearby Gusseltjärn drainage area was selected for hydrological studies.

Besides the two main sites, other investigation areas used within the project are shown in Fig. 1.

Ivantjärnsheden

Geography, geomorphology, and geology

Ivantjärnsheden is situated at latitude 60°49'N, longitude 16°30'E and at an altitude of about 185 m above M.S.L. The area is inside the so-called Norrland terrain area (Magnusson & Lundqvist, 1957) of undulating hilly land with altitude differences more than 100 m (Rudberg, 1970) but close to the coastal plain of the Bothnian Sea.

The bedrock is part of the Sveco-Fenno-Karelian older granites, sediments and volcanic rocks which are widespread in Fennoscandia (Magnusson, 1967; Magnusson et al., 1963). In the area of investigation they consist mainly of leptite, gneiss-granites and sedimentary gneiss. The bedrock of most of the surroundings of the area, except for a few small outcrops, is covered with sandy till soil mainly with a moderate content of boulders, the material of which was transported various distances by the ice from the northwest.

Ivantjärnsheden, however, is a sandy plain, adjacent to the esker Järboåsen, which is about 75 km long and runs along the valley of the River Jädraån in a northwest-southeast direction (Figs. 2 and 3). At Ivantjärnsheden the esker is very broad, filling most of the valley and consisting of sand with an admixture of gravel. On both sides of the Ivantjärnsheden plain are heights of 200–300 m altitude. The surface of the heath is largely level, but there are some shallow depressions and low ridges, the differences being less than 10 m. As a whole, the heath slopes gently to the southeast.

The origin of the heath sediments is glacifluvial east of the River Jädraån and marine and lacustrine west of it (Fig. 3). Both types were formed during deglaciation under the water. The highest sea shore limit (Fig. 4) reached 205–210 m above the present sea level (at Kungsberget 204 m, Vettåsen 205 m and Rönnåsen near Ockelbo 216 m). After the water had retreated and before vegetation had covered the sandy plain, the wind redeposited the sand into dunes, which were later immobilized and fixed by plants, as they are today.

26

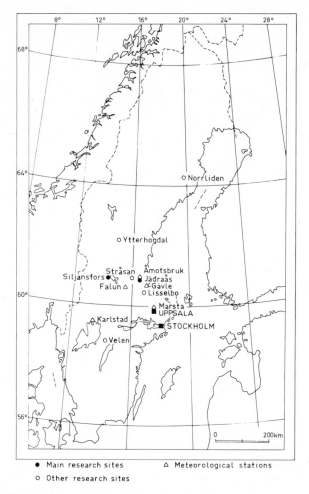

Figure 1. Geographical locations of research sites and meteorological stations used by the Swedish Coniferous Forest Project.

Biogeography and history of land use

The Jädraås district is just north of the border between the Boreal (Northern coniferous) and the Boreo-nemoral (Southern coniferous) zones (Figs. 5 and 6). The border is usually called *Limes norrlandicus* (cf. Fries, 1948). In the vicinity of Jädraås the transition is comparatively narrow with regard to topography, geography, climate and biogeography. It is characterized biologically as a transitional gradient where a number of species and communities become less abundant and others more abundant from south to north. Some species with a northern or southern distribution in Sweden make a halt at or near the *Limes*.

Ahlner (1950) reported that in the province of Gästrikland 50 plant species reached their northern limit in Sweden and 6 their southern limit. Oak (*Quercus*

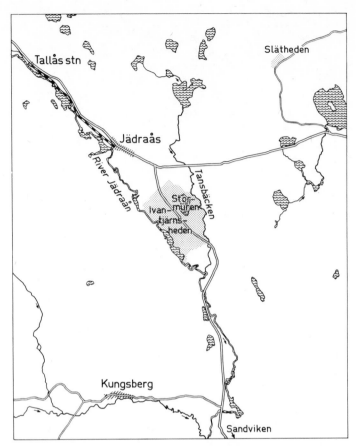

Figure 2. Location of Ivantjärnsheden and Slätheden, the SWECON research areas in the region of Jädraås. The mire Stormuren is used by the EFP (Energy Forestry Project). – Permission for distribution approved by the Security Officer, the National Land Survey of Sweden, 1979-09-24.

robur) and ash (*Fraxinus excelsior*) are absent at Jädraås and other deciduous trees and shrubs such as *Acer platanoides, Corylus avellana, Tilia cordata* and *Ulmus glabra* have ceased to be conspicuous elements in the forest.

The forests of the till soil areas around Ivantjärnsheden mainly consist of mixed Norway spruce (*Picea abies*) and Scots pine (*Pinus sylvestris*) with *Vaccinium myrtillus*, low herbs, grasses and mosses. In the research area the vegetation is mainly a dry pine – dwarf-shrub – lichen heath of the association *Cladonio-Pinetum (boreale)* K-L 1967 (Kielland-Lund, 1973) or the lichen and lichen-dwarf-shrub forest types (Ebeling, 1978).

Curry-Lindahl (1950) reported that birds were represented by 14 northern and 20 southern species in the province. Of mammals, the wood lemming (*Myopus schisticolor*) was the only representative of the exclusively northern group. The southern group was represented by, e.g., badger (*Meles meles*), field hare (*Lepus europaeus*) (introduced) and hedgehog (*Erinaceus europaeus*). The same applies

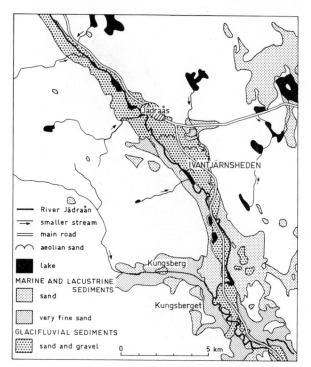

Figure 3. Aquatic sediments in the Jädraås region. Blank areas are chiefly covered with till soil or peat (redrawn from Lundqvist, 1963). – Permission for distribution approved by the Security Officer, the National Land Survey of Sweden, 1979-09-24.

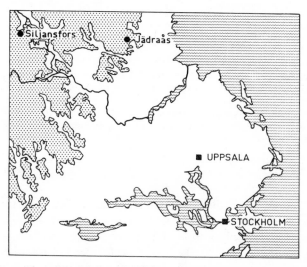

Figure 4. Areas above (dotted) and below the highest post-glacial sea shore limit in East Central Sweden. Note that Jädraås in reality is just below the limit. (Redrawn from Lundqvist & Nilsson, 1959)

29

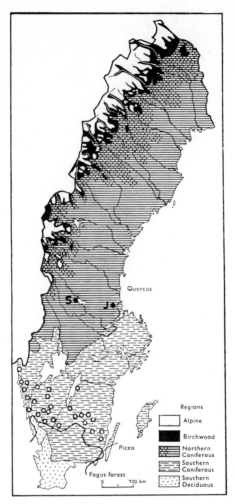

Figure 5. The forest regions of Sweden (from Sjörs, 1965). The birchwood region (subalpine belt) and the northern coniferous forest region form a sector of the Boreal zone. The stippled parts are the areas with predominance, more or less, of the upper, prealpine (montane) subzone, corresponding to the Subarctic or Northern Taiga further east. The southern coniferous forest region (with oak) is a sector of the Boreo-nemoral and the southern deciduous forest region is part of the Nemoral zone. Seemingly spontaneous beech groves above the beech forest limit are approximately indicated by rings, but many more exist. Locations of Siljansfors (S) and Jädraås (J) are indicated.

to the insect fauna, since there are very few exclusive representatives of the Boreal group, somewhat more of the Boreo-nemoral group and a majority of species with a wide distribution in Scandinavia. The area is marginal for both northern and southern pine forest insect pests, the hazard to forest economy probably being comparatively small (Axelsson *et al.*, 1974).

Historical land use in Central Sweden includes such measures as intentional burning of the forest for crops and improved grazing, forest grazing without

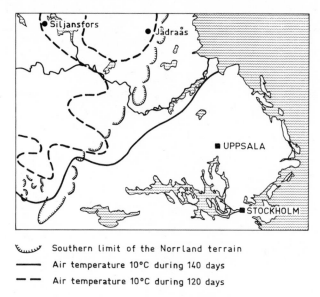

<figure>

~~~~~ Southern limit of the Norrland terrain

───── Air temperature 10°C during 140 days

── ── Air temperature 10°C during 120 days

Figure 6. Map of *Limes norrlandicus* in East Central Sweden as indicated by the southern limit of the Norrland terrain and isolines of a mean air temperature of 10°C during 140 days and 120 days, respectively. The northern limit of oak (*Quercus robur*) and the isoline for 140 days more or less coincide (cf. Fig. 5).

</figure>

burning, felling for charcoal burning, use of stumps and trees killed by intentional damage for tar-burning, logging, silvicultural measures and felling for paper-pulp (e.g., E. Persson, 1950; Tenow, 1974). Thus practically every hectare of land, though sparsely populated, has undergone some type of management which has changed the natural conditions of the forest. At Ivantjärnsheden, where the production of grazing for domestic cattle is very low, charcoal-burning and tar-burning were probably the most important types of land use in recent history. From the age structure of the tree stands it is probable that most of the heath was clear of trees around the middle of the 19th century, apparently a consequence of the large consumption of charcoal for the smeltery at Jädraås, founded in 1858. Around 1960 the tree stands were thinned and the trunks removed by vehicles which produced lasting tracks in the low-productive vegetation.

Soil

Within the research site the dominant soil particle sizes at 15 cm depth are fine and medium sand (0.125–0.5 mm) (Fig. 7), much of which is aeolian in origin. At 70 cm depth the textural composition varies more between subareas, the dominant sizes ranging more broadly from fine to coarse sand (0.125–1 mm) (Figs. 8 and 9). In most places the mineral soil is layered which, for instance, causes differences in its capacity to store water. In places the surface soil is fine to about 40 cm and the subsoil coarse, in others the conditions are reversed.

Porosity and amount of plant-available water in soil profiles at three research

31

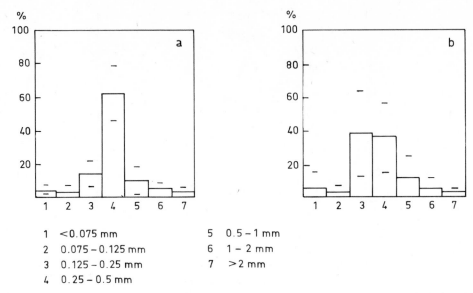

1	<0.075 mm	5	0.5 – 1 mm
2	0.075 – 0.125 mm	6	1 – 2 mm
3	0.125 – 0.25 mm	7	>2 mm
4	0.25 – 0.5 mm		

Figure 7. Frequency distribution of particle size classes (mean value and standard deviation) for Ivantjärnsheden as a whole at a depth of (a) 15 and (b) 70 cm. (From Jansson, 1977)

Table 1. Amount of plant-available water in soil profiles at research plots Ih 0, Ih II and Ih V at different levels of tension (location see Fig. 19). All values are in mm. (From P-E. Jansson, unpubl.)

Level (cm)	Ih 0		Ih II		Ih V	
	Porosity	Tension 150 m–100 cm	Porosity	Tension 150 m–50 cm	Porosity	Tension 150 m–50 cm
0–30	180	50	164	55	171	56
30–60	123	45	130	26	126	25

plots at Ivantjärnsheden are given in Table 1. It should be noted that different levels of tension were applied, reflecting the different layering in the soil profile in different parts of the research area (cf. Figs. 8–11). At Ivantjärnsheden the physical root zone corresponds approximately to the 0–30 cm level, while the effective root zone according to soil water measurements (Jansson, pers. comm.) is somewhat extended into the subjacent soil.

Ivantjärnsheden is situated in an area of podzolized soils although it is fairly close to an area of transition towards brown podzolic soils. The soil of the heath is an ordinary iron podzol and in some dry places a lichen podzol (Jansson, 1977). The mean thickness in the subareas varies between 1 and 7 cm for the humus layer (A_0), between 0.2 and 1.6 cm for the mixed humus-mineral soil (A_1) and between 2 and 7 cm for the bleached layer (A_2). The litter layer (A_{00}) stays around 1 cm. Where Norway spruce forms an important part of the tree stand, e.g., along the

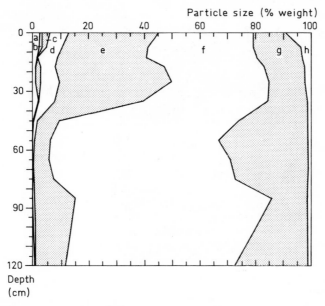

Figure 8. The variation with depth of different particle size classes (not the same as in Fig. 7) and loss on ignition: <0.002 (a), 0.002–0.006 (b), 0.006–0.02 (c), 0.02–0.06 (d), 0.06–0.2 (e), 0.2–0.6 (f), >0.6 (g), and loss on ignition (h). The particle size distribution is representative for soil profiles from research stands Ih II and Ih V. (From Jansson, 1977)

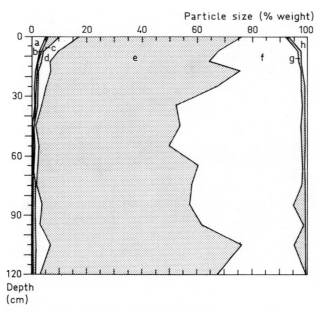

Figure 9. The particle size distribution at Ivantjärnsheden research area with the exception of stands Ih II and Ih V. For full explanation see Fig. 8. (From Jansson, 1977)

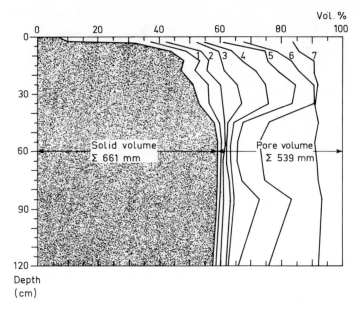

Figure 10. Soil profile diagramme, representative for stand Ih V, showing the variation with depth of material volume and water content at seven different levels of tension. The tensions are 150 m (1), 800 cm (2), 100 cm (3), 50 cm (4), 30 cm (5), 20 cm (6) and 5 cm (7) (From Jansson, 1977). "Solid" and "pore" volumes refer to share of vertical sections as measured down to 1200 mm.

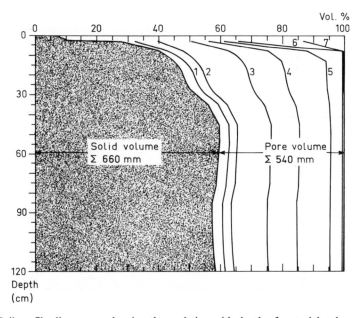

Figure 11. Soil profile diagramme showing the variation with depth of material volume and water content at seven different levels of tension. The tensions from 1 to 7 as in Fig. 10. The profile is from plot Ih 0 but also indicate the site conditions in general. (From P-E. Jansson, unpubl.)

Table 2. Tree stand and soil characteristics of the research plots at Ivantjärnsheden. 95% confidence intervals within parentheses. * = no data, – = absent.

	Ih 0 (1975)	Ih 0 (1977) With slash[1]	Ih 0 (1977) Without slash[1]	Ih I	Ih II	Ih III	Ih IV	Ih V	Data source
Stand age (1979) (years)	100[1]	clear-felling 1976	1976	10	20[2]	23	60	125	Albrektson (1976), Flower-Ellis et al. (1976), Flower-Ellis & Olsson (1978)
No. of trees ha^{-1} (1973)	453	–	–	~2 000 (planted)	1 095[2]	2 933	1 176	393	
Mean tree height (m) (1973)	19	–	–	*	2.1	2.8	12.6	15.8	Albrektson (1976), Flower-Ellis & Olsson (1978)
Mean live crown height (m) (1973)	*	–	–	*	*	2.3	6.8	7.9	Flower-Ellis & Olsson (1978)
Mean diameter at bh o.b. (cm) (1973)	23.1	–	–	*	2.5	3.7	13.6	21.9	Albrektson (1976), Flower-Ellis & Olsson (1978), B. Andersson (unpubl.)
Basal area (m^{-2} ha^{-1}) (1973)	19.3	–	–	*	2.15	5.04	19.98[3]	15.05	Albrektson (1976), Flower-Ellis et al. (1976)
Soil profile	iron-podzol	iron-podzol	iron-podzol	iron-podzol	iron-podzol	iron-podzol	iron-podzol	iron-podzol	Jansson (1977)
Soil texture (dominant fractions)									
–15 cm depth	fine sand	fine sand	fine sand	fine sand	medium sand	medium sand	fine sand	medium sand	Jansson (1977)
–70 cm depth	fine sand	fine sand	fine sand	fine sand	coarse & medium sand	medium & fine sand	fine sand	medium & coarse sand	Jansson (1977)
– Depth (cm)									
A_{00}–A_{02}	7	8	7	7	4–6	*	7–8	6–7	Bringmark & Petersson (1975), Jansson (1977), H. Staaf (unpubl.)
A_1	*	*	*	–	≤ 0.4	*	–	≤ 1.5	
A_2	*	*	*	5	4–6	*	5–12	5–7	
B	*	*	*	6	*	*	8–10	20	
– Dry wt (kg m^{-2})									
Litter layer (A_{00})	1.1	1.7 (0.3)	0.9 (0.1)	1.2 (0.2)	1.5 (0.7)	*	*	0.7 (0.1)	Staaf & Berg (1977), H. Staaf (unpubl.)
Humus layer (A_{01}–A_{02})	3.6	2.9 (0.5)	2.6 (0.3)	*	6.3 (1.6)	*	*	2.0 (0.3)	
Humus, ash free	2.3	2.0 (0.3)	1.8 (0.3)	*	2.2 (0.6)	*	*	1.5 (0.2)	
Mineral layer, 0–10 cm	94.3	93.9 (6.0)	97.5 (3.5)	102 (4.2)	97.8 (2.3)	*	*	99.4 (2)	
Mineral layer, 10–20 cm	113.1	114 (4.6)	113 (3.6)	108 (4.5)	116 (4.9)	*	*	121 (2)	
– pH									
Litter layer	*	4.4	4.4	4.0	*	*	*	4.2	Popović (1976), Popović (1977), Lindberg & Popović (1978)
Humus layer	*	4.3	4.1	4.2	4.3	*	*	4.0	
Mineral layer, 0–10 cm	*	4.6	4.6	5.1	5.0	*	*	4.6	
Mineral layer, 10–20 cm	*	5.0	5.2	5.2	5.1	*	*	5.2	
– Base saturation									
A_2	*	*	*	10.1	*	*	1.5	*	Bringmark & Petersson (1975)
B	*	*	*	2.6	*	*	2.4	*	Bringmark & Petersson (1975)

[1] Stand Ih 0 was 100 years old when clear-felled in 1976.
[2] Stand Ih II has a 20-year-old tree population (1095 trees ha^{-1}) with an understorey of younger pines, the mean stand age being considerably lower than 20 years.
[3] Excluding 0.28 m^2 ha^{-1} of spruce.

Table 3. Cloudiness as percentage cover of sky at Åmotsbruk and incoming shortwave radiation (MJ m^{-2} $month^{-1}$) at Jädraås. All values are means for the period 1965–75, with standard deviation within parentheses. The radiation values were estimated from a comparison between the cloudiness at Åmotsbruk and the radiation measurements at Jädraås. (From K. Perttu, unpubl.)

Month	Cloudiness (%)	Radiation (MJ m^{-2} $month^{-1}$)	Month	Cloudiness (%)	Radiation (MJ m^{-2} $month^{-1}$)
Jan.	71 (8)	3 095 (516)	July	62 (8)	56 571 (5 159)
Febr.	65 (13)	9 542 (1 836)	Aug.	59 (7)	46 223 (3 237)
March	60 (11)	22 606 (2 410)	Sept.	68 (6)	25 557 (1 962)
April	63 (8)	35 895 (3 198)	Oct.	65 (12)	11 931 (4 111)
May	59 (9)	52 178 (4 269)	Nov.	69 (10)	3 888 (779)
June	52 (8)	62 561 (4 451)	Dec.	65 (9)	1 359 (228)
Mean value per year 1965–75:				63 (3)	332 250 (10 450)

ravines, the organic layers and the bleached layer are thicker. Data on soil properties for the different research plots are summarized in Table 2. More information of chemical characteristics of the soil is given by Bringmark (1977) and Staaf & Berg (1977).

Climate

The monthly global radiation at Ivantjärnsheden is given in Table 3, and the daylength at Ivantjärnsheden in Fig. 12. The normal mean monthly temperatures of the nearby meteorological station at Åmotsbruk indicate that the coldest month in the Jädraås district is January (about $-7°C$ mean temperature) and the warmest is July (about 16°C) (Table 4).

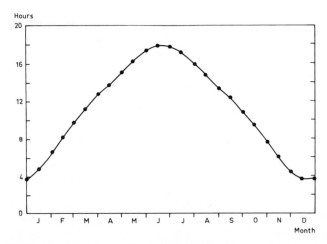

Figure 12. Day-length at Ivantjärnsheden calculated as the time from sunrise to sunset at sea level and adjusted to actual longitude and latitude. (A. Lindroth, unpubl.)

36

Table 4. Normal mean monthly air temperature (°C) 1931–60 at Stockholm, Falun (60°37' N, 15°38' E), Åmotsbruk (60°58' N, 16°27' E) and Siljansfors (60°53' N, 14°23' E). (SMHI referensnormaler, 1931–60)

Month	Stockholm	Falun	Åmotsbruk	Siljansfors
January	-2.9	-7.0	-7.0	-8.7
February	-3.1	-6.3	-6.9	-7.2
March	-0.7	-2.6	-3.4	-3.0
April	4.4	3.4	2.9	2.8
May	10.1	9.7	8.6	8.8
June	14.9	14.1	13.0	13.4
July	17.8	16.7	15.8	15.4
August	16.6	14.9	14.1	13.8
September	12.2	10.1	9.2	9.0
October	7.1	4.8	3.9	3.6
November	2.8	0.4	-0.5	-1.2
December	0.1	-3.4	-3.8	-5.0
Year	6.6	4.6	3.8	3.6

Occurrence of frost during the growing season is very frequent in the research area. During the last few years more than 50% of the nights during the growing season had frost in the clear-felled parts of Ivantjärnsheden. The corresponding figure for the mature stand is about 20% (Perttu et al., 1979). The variation between years in monthly mean temperatures based on day-time, night-time and whole day (24 h) is sometimes rather large (Fig. 13). The length of the growing season (mean daily air temperature above $+6°C$) is around 160 days, the start and end dates of the season being very variable (Table 5).

The normal precipitation in the Jädraås district (1931–60) is about 600 mm (Table 6), but amounts ranging between 413 and 746 have been measured at Åmotsbruk. The yearly variation in precipitation is thus considerable (Fig. 14).

The most frequent wind directions at Gävle, about 50 km SE of Jädraås, are southwest, west and north (Fig. 15), which is common at these latitudes (about 55–65° N). The wind speed may vary locally depending on topography and exposure. On average, however, Ivantjärnsheden probably does not differ much from Åmotsbruk, where mean monthly values are between 2.8 and 3.4 m s^{-1} for the period 1965–75.

The "humidity of the climate", according to O. Tamm (1959), is given as the difference between mean yearly precipitation and mean yearly evapotranspiration. For Jädraås this difference is estimated at about 400 mm, i.e., corresponding to "humidity region" 3 (Fig. 16). Walter & Lieth diagrammes (Fig. 17) can also be used to obtain an idea of the continentality, humidity, probability of frost, etc., of a place. Conditions at Åmotsbruk are similar to those at Jädraås. As a result of the sandy soil the hydrological cycle is characterized by a fairly small storage capacity in the root zone in relation to annual precipitation, indicating an ecosystem which is sensitive to periods of drought (Fig. 18).

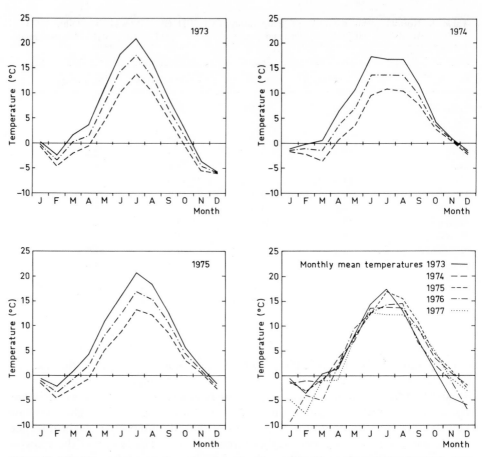

Figure 13. Monthly mean temperatures based on day-time, night-time and whole day for 1973, 1974 and 1975 together with temperature regimes for the period 1973–77 at the research site.

Table 5. Duration of growing season (=mean daily temperature above 6°C) and heat sums of daily mean and maximum temperatures above 6°C during the growing season as mean for the period 1961–74 at Åmotsbruk, Siljansfors and Falun. (From Perttu & Huszár, 1976)

Station	Mean duration		Range of variation		Heat sum	
	Date	No. of days	Start	End	Daily mean	Daily max
Åmotsbruk	May 4– Oct. 10	161	Apr. 20– May 23	Sept. 26– Oct. 31	950	2787
Siljansfors	May 2– Oct. 9	160	Apr. 17– May 23	Sept. 17– Oct. 30	908	2769
Falun	Apr. 26– Oct. 15	172	Apr. 5– May 10	Sept. 28– Oct. 31	1 110	3063

Table 6. Mean monthly precipitation 1931–60 at Stockholm, Falun, Åmotsbruk and Siljansfors. (SMHI referensnormaler, 1931–60)

Month	Stockholm	Falun	Åmotsbruk	Siljansfors
January	46	39	45	47
February	32	27	29	32
March	27	22	27	26
April	33	31	36	40
May	36	41	36	42
June	45	58	57	70
July	61	58	73	92
August	77	80	77	92
September	59	63	68	76
October	50	47	50	56
November	56	53	61	60
December	50	44	48	58
Year	572	579	607	691

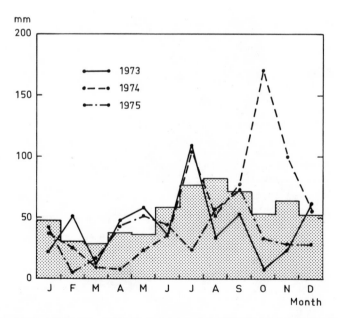

Figure 14. Monthly precipitation at Jädraås for the period 1973–75. The shaded columns show the precipitation during 1931–60 measured at the meteorological station at Åmotsbruk, with an annual mean of 607 mm.

39

GÄVLE   N

11.9

9.1   9.7

12.4   CALM 12.2   7.9

6.1

9.7

21.O

Figure 15. Mean frequency of wind directions in Gävle 1931–60. (From SMHI referensnormaler, 1931–60.)

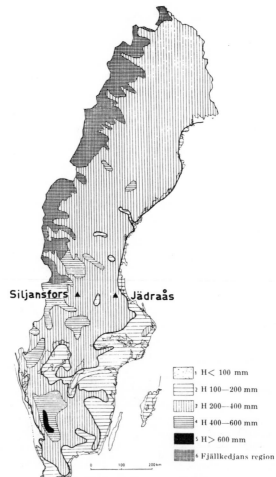

1 H< 100 mm

2 H 100—200 mm

3 H 200—400 mm

4 H 400—600 mm

5 H> 600 mm

6 Fjällkedjans region

Figure 16. Humidity (run-off) regions of Sweden. (1) subarid, (2) weakly humid, (3) normal humid, (4) strongly humid, (5) superhumid, (6) mountain range where degree of humidity changes strongly from 400 mm (in the extreme north 300 mm) to about 1500 mm. (From O. Tamm, 1959)

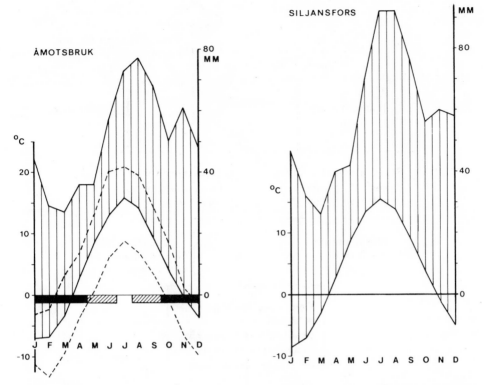

Figure 17. Climate diagrammes for Åmotsbruk, ca. 14 km north of Jädraås, and Siljansfors (cf. Walter & Lieth, 1960–67). Upper solid curve = mean precipitation, lower = mean temperature for 1931–60 and broken curves = mean maximum and minimum temperatures for the period 1965–75. Vertical hatching = humid period; black field = months with daily minimum temperature below 0°C; oblique hatching = months with frost possible. (From SMHI referensnormaler, 1931–60, and Å. Lindgren, unpubl.)

Research plots and sampling layout at Ivantjärnsheden

The general situation of the Ivantjärnsheden research area was shown in Fig. 2, which also showed the adjacent area Slätheden that has been used for a limited number of investigations. With reference to the national grid and the international UTM-system, the location of the research plots at Ivantjärnsheden (Fig. 19) is given with an accuracy of about ± 50 m.

Plot	Situation (UTM)	National grid
Ih 0	WH-819444	6745.5 1538.1
Ih I	WH-814443	6745.5 1537.6
Ih II	WH-819434	6644.5 1538.2
Ih III	WH-812440	6745.1 1537.1
Ih IV	WH-816441	6745.2 1537.8
Ih V	WH-818436	6644.7 1538.0

The research plots were selected so as to represent different stages in the rotation period of a pine forest stand. They were divided into regular grids of 50 × 50 or

41

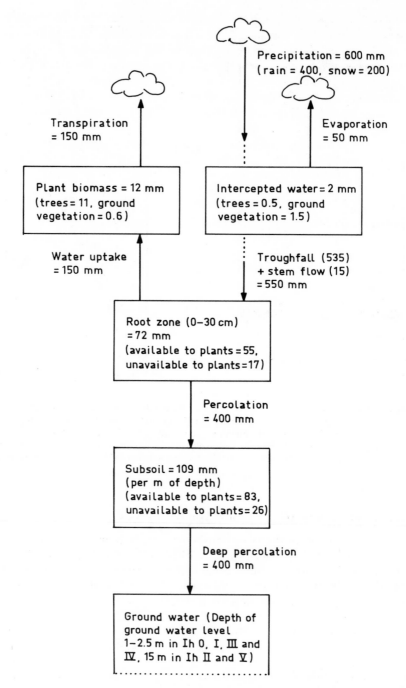

Figure 18. The hydrologic cycle for the Ivantjärnsheden research area at Jädraås. Annual flows and storage capacities within the system are indicated (B. Axelsson & P-E. Jansson, unpubl.).

30×30 m quadrats which were further subdivided into 10×10 m quadrats. In some cases entire large quadrats were left unoccupied to serve as reserve areas. The small quadrats were either allotted to the various sub-projects for their particular research purposes or left alone for use as controls. At Ih II, IV and V bridges of untreated wood were placed along the most frequent pathways in order to prevent damage to vegetation and compaction of soil. Plots Ih 0 and Ih V were surrounded by low fences, and Ih II and Ih III by high ones in order to prevent browsing by moose.

Due to tree stand properties and land use a total of 24 different stands are found within the area. Usually they are coniferous stands but also mixed deciduous-coniferous in age-classes ranging from newly planted areas to 160-year-old stands (see Fig. 20). General characteristics of the different research pine stands are presented in Table 2. For further information on vegetation and stand structure reference should be made to Bråkenhielm (1974), Flower-Ellis et al. (1976) and Flower-Ellis & Olsson (1978).

Within the area, common forest insects generally fluctuate on low population levels (Larsson & Tenow, 1980). According to their seasonal occurrence, defoliating insects within the older pine stands of the area (Ih IV, Ih V) may be grouped into three categories, one early summer group, one late summer group and one autumn group, the first represented mainly by the pine moth (*Panolis flammea* Schiff.) and a solitary diprionid sawfly species, the second by solitary diprionids, and the third dominated by the pine looper (*Bupalus piniarius* L.), an outbreak species in southeastern Sweden. Another outbreak species, occurring at low population levels within the area, is the European pine sawfly (*Neodiprion sertifer* Geoffr.), used in field defoliation experiments in the project. Among tunnelling insects, a chronic pest like the common pine shoot beetle, *Tomicus (Blastophagus) piniperda* L., is kept on a low population level by forestry management practices. In young pine stands, e.g., Ih II, sucking insects seem to be comparatively important, for example, aphids of the genus *Cinara*. The pine bark bug (*Aradus cinnamomeus* Panz.), a sucking insect known to be harmful to young trees (Brammanis, 1975), occurs in moderate numbers on Ih II. A qualitative and quantitative survey of the fauna (above and below ground) at Ivantjärnsheden is presented by Axelsson et al. (1974), the soil inhabiting arthropods in the research area are extensively treated by Wirén (1975) and T. Persson (1975), and the nematodes by Sohlenius (1977). Soil bacteria were studied by Clarholm (1977), mycelial lengths and fungal biomasses in different soil horizons are described by Bååth & Söderström (1977a), who also estimated the annual production of basidiomycete fruitbodies (Bååth & Söderström, 1977b). Finally, use was made of the soil washing technique in a survey of soil microfungi (Söderström & Bååth, 1978).

Ih 0

The plot (Figs. 21–23) is situated in a depression, about 1 m lower than a bog 100 m to the east. It is surrounded to the east, north and west by sand dunes. The ground-water table, at 1–3 m depth, is closer to the surface than at the other plots. The soil is a fine-medium sand and the profile homogeneous. Before the experimental clear-cutting in March 1976 the plant community was intermediate between *Cladonio-Pinetum (boreale)* and *Vaccinio-Pinetum (boreale)* (Kielland-

43

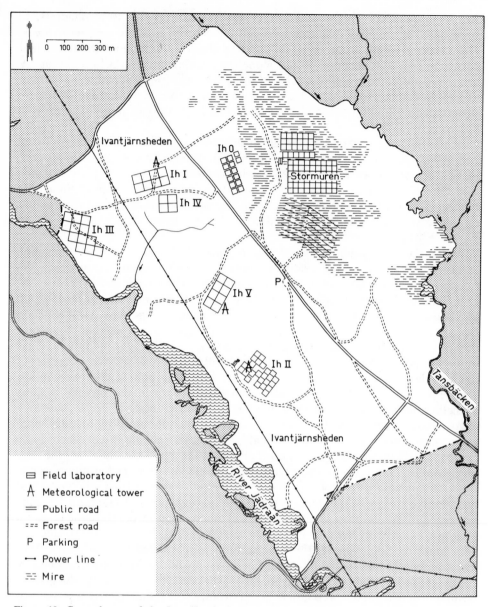

Figure 19. General map of the Ivantjärnsheden and Stormuren research area. Roman numerals indicate research plots within pine stands. – Permission for distribution approved by the Security Officer, the National Land Survey of Sweden, 1979-09-24.

44

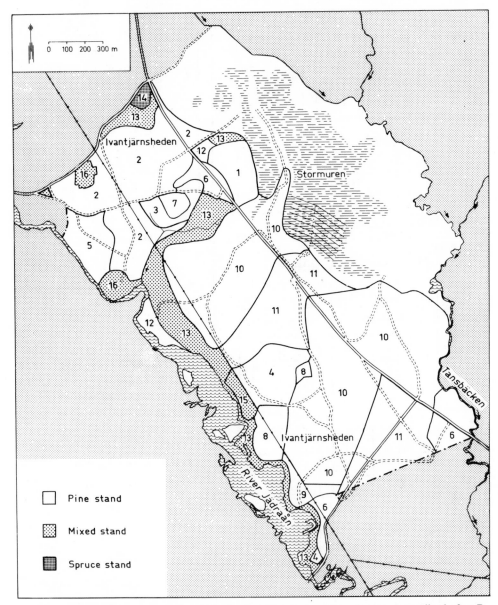

Figure 20. Map of the tree stands within the Ivantjärnsheden research area, generalized after B. Andersson (unpubl.). 1 = clear-cut (Ih 0); 2 = pine, ca. 10 yrs (Ih I); 3 = pine, 10–15 yrs; 4 = pine, 20 yrs (Ih II); 5 = pine, 23 yrs (Ih III); 6 = pine, 30 yrs; 7 = pine, 60 yrs (Ih IV); 8 = pine, 60–70 yrs; 9 = pine (admixture of spruce), 100 yrs; 10 = pine, 120 yrs (Ih V); 11 = pine with blanks, 160 yrs; 12 = pine, shelter or seed trees; 13 = mixed coniferous-deciduous, varying ages; 14 = spruce, planted, 23 yrs; 15 = spruce (admixture of pine, birch), 80 yrs; 16 = afforestation or mixed stands. – Permission for distribution approved by the Security Officer, the National Land Survey of Sweden, 1979-09-24.

45

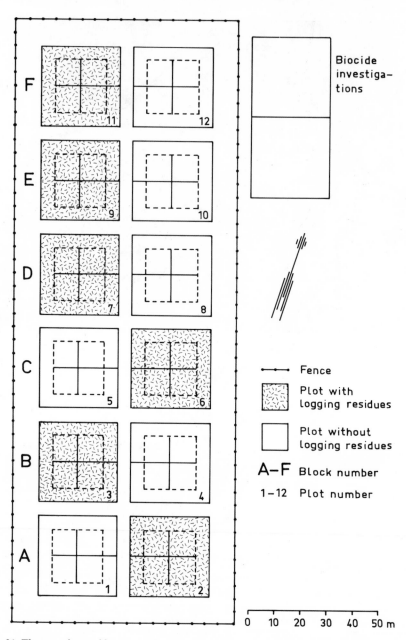

Figure 21. The experimental layout at plot Ih 0, where the area was clear-felled in March, 1976.

Figure 22. The pine stand at plot Ih 0 before clear-felling. (Photo B. Axelsson)

Figure 23. Plot Ih 0 from the west in May 1976. Quadrats with slash are light greyish, those without are darker. (Photo T. Persson)

Figure 24. Stand Ih I one year after planting with Scots pine (1972). (Photo S. Bråkenhielm)

Lund, 1973) or a lichen-dwarf-shrub forest type (Ebeling, 1978). The relatively frequent presence of *Vaccinium myrtillus* (bilberry) and the mosses *Dicranum majus, Hylocomium splendens* and *Ptilium crista-castrensis* and scarcity of lichens indicates greater availability of nutrients compared with Ih II and V. The pine stand was somewhat denser than at Ih V. Its previous history mainly agrees with that of the other stands on the heath. After the clear-felling, when the trunks had been removed and logging residues were left on half of the parcels (Fig. 23), the remaining vegetation was severely affected.

Ih I

The largely level plot is situated at the southeastern edge of a large clear-felled area. Fine-medium sand is dominant at 15 cm and fine sand at 70 cm. The ground-water table is at 1.5–3 m depth. The plant community is probably a *Cladonio-Pinetum (boreale)* or a lichen-dwarf-shrub type. It is in a state of regeneration after near extinction at the clear-felling (cf. Figs. 24 and 25). The area was clear-felled in 1967 after removal of suppressed and infected trees in 1960. In 1971–72 it was planted with Scots pine.

Ih II

The level plot is an opening in the surrounding old pine stand (Figs. 26 and 27). Dominant soil particles are medium sand at 15 cm and medium to coarse sand at 70 cm depth. The ground-water table is at 10 m depth at its upper level. The *Cladonio-Pinetum (boreale)* community or the lichen-dwarf-shrub type is re-

Figure 25. Stand Ih I on 20 September 1978. The pines are ca. 10 years old and the stand has many gaps, mainly because of summer-frosts (temperatures below −10°C). (Photo T. Persson)

generating after damage following tree-felling in 1957 and felling of seed-trees in 1962. The regeneration of the self-sown new pine stand was facilitated by soil scarification in patches. The young tree stand was cleared in 1972 and 1973. Later in 1973 the stand was made still more regular as to tree height before the onset of an irrigation and fertilization experiment.

Ih III

The plot (Fig. 28) is situated near the Jädraån river ravine. Its topography is somewhat irregular, the height differences being about 5 m at most. Dominant soil particles are medium sand at 15 cm and fine sand at 70 cm. The ground-water table is at 2–3.5 m depth. The plant communities are a *Cladonio-Pinetum (boreale)* or lichen-dwarf-shrub type in the elevated part and an *Eu-Piceetum* (Kielland-Lund, 1973) or dry to mesic dwarf-shrub type in the lower part. The earlier tree stand, which consisted of spruce and pine, was felled in 1953–54, except for seed-trees that were felled in 1959. The present stand is mainly pine with an admixture of spruce. Up to the early 1950s the area was grazed by cattle. By track-inventories B. Andersson & B. Axelsson (unpubl.) found fairly high population levels of moose (*Alces alces*), roe-deer (*Capreolus capreolus*) and hare (*Lepus timidus*) in this part of the research area (Fig. 29). Thus browsing most likely regulates the plant species composition in the stand.

Ih IV

The plot (Fig. 30) is just north of a branch of the ravine, sloping somewhat towards the north. Dominant soil particles are fine and medium sand at 15 and 70

49

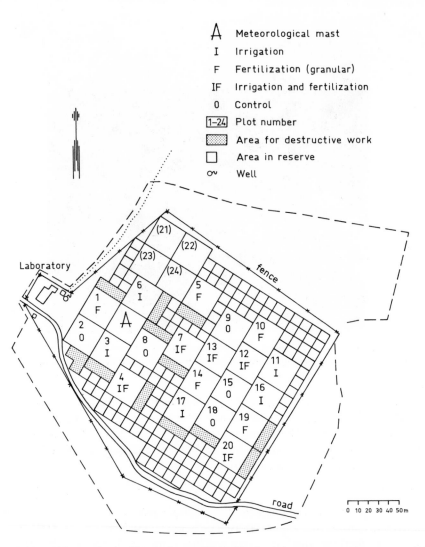

Figure 26. Map of the randomized blocks in stand Ih II. The fence is necessary to keep moose (*Alces alces*) outside the experimental area.

cm. The ground-water table is at 1.5–3 m depth. The plant community is a *Cladonio-Pinetum (boreale)* or a lichen-dwarf-shrub type, although with little *Calluna* and lichens and with indicators of better site quality. The tree stand, which was probably self-sown in the 1910s after previous clear-felling, was lightly thinned in about 1960 but is still comparatively dense.

Ih V

The topography of the plot is level (Fig. 31). It lies in the centre of the dominant tree stand of the heath and is probably the most representative of the plots. Dominant soil particles are fine, medium and coarse sand at 15 cm and medium

50

Figure 27. Control plot no. 2 within stand Ih II. The ground vegetation is mainly composed of heather, cowberry and lichens. (Photo S. Oscarsson)

Figure 28. The fairly uneven stand Ih III is situated in a part of the research area showing clear influence of cattle grazing. (Photo B. Axelsson)

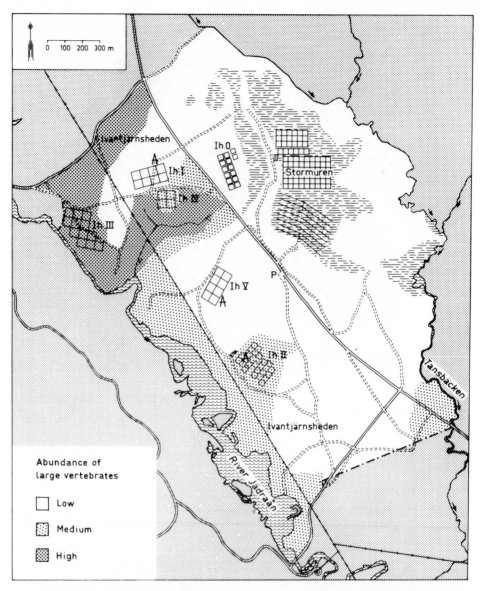

Figure 29. Generalized map indicating the relative distribution of large vertebrates in the Ivantjärnshe-den research area. The relative abundances are based on track-inventories made by B. Andersson and B. Axelsson during the winter 1976. The study included moose (*Alces alces*), roe-deer (*Capreolus capreolus*), hare (*Lepus timidus*), red squirrel (*Sciurus vulgaris*), capercaillie (*Tetrao urogallus*) and black grouse (*Tetrao tetrix*). The moose population has increased considerably during the last ten years and was estimated at 20–30 ind. per 1000 ha in the Jädraås region in 1976. – Permission for distribution approved by the Security Officer, the National Land Survey of Sweden, 1979-09-24.

52

Figure 30. Stand Ih IV, comparatively dense and with an understorey of spruce. The ground vegetation has indicators of better site quality, e.g., bilberry (*Vaccinium myrtillus*) and mosses. (Photo C-O. Tamm)

Figure 31. The fairly thin pine stand Ih V with a few suppressed spruces. (Photo S. Oscarsson)

53

Figure 32. Typical ground vegetation in stand Ih V with heather (*Calluna vulgaris*), cowberry (*Vaccinium vitis-idaea*), mosses (mainly *Pleurozium schreberi*) and "reindeer" lichens (*Cladonia rangiferina* and *C. silvatica*). (Photo T. Persson)

and coarse sand at 70 cm. The ground-water table is at 10 m depth at its upper level. The vegetation belongs to the *Cladonio-Pinetum (boreale)* association or the lichen to lichen-dwarf-shrub type. The ground vegetation is fairly stabilized from the successional view-point (cf. Fig. 32). Biomass estimates indicate somewhat smaller amounts of field layer (*Calluna vulgaris* and *Vaccinium vitis-idaea*) than of bottom layer (*Pleurozium schreberi, Cladonia rangiferina* and *C. silvatica*), 200 and 260 g dw m^{-2}, respectively (H. Persson, 1980). The tree stand, a fairly thin, regular pine stand with suppressed spruce underneath, originated in the 1850s. It was lightly thinned by removal of weak trees in about 1962.

Siljansfors

Geography and geomorphology

Siljansfors Experimental Forest, covering about 1475 ha, is situated within an area between latitude 60°52' and 60°55' N and longitude 14°20' and 14°24' E. The altitude varies between 210 m in the lower parts of the River Ryssån valley and 424 m on the top of the Leksberget hill. Two large valleys run through the forest, one containing Lake Jugen and River Jugån, the other containing River Ryssån with Lake Äjsjön and Lavasdammen.

In the northeastern part of the forest, a mixed mature stand of pine and spruce at an altitude ranging from 300 to 340 m and a northwestern aspect on the Nickobacken hill was chosen as research area (Figs. 33 and 34). In the western part of the forest, the Gusseltjärn drainage area is used for hydrological investigations.

Geology and soil

The experimental forest is situated in a strongly undulating till area above the highest sea shore limit which reached ca. 210 m within the area. On the other hand, "dead ice" remnants dammed up melting water to 220–270 m above sea level at many places in the district, resulting in terraced sedimentations (Lannerbro, 1953).

The bedrock throughout the entire area is Dala porphyry. Just outside the forest, granites and sandstones are parts of the bedrock. The Quaternary deposits are mainly till, but muddy peat soils form a conspicuous element. Sediments of alluvial sand, silt and clay are found adjacent to the peat soils and along the rivers. The most fertile soils, containing 2–3% of dolerite and schist, are in the eastern part of the area (Lundblad, 1927).

The soil in the area is an ordinary iron podzol with a thickness of the humus layer varying between 2 and 14 cm. The bleached layer varies as much as 1–40 cm, but is mostly within 9–17 cm. In parts of the slopes of Leksberget, the humus layer is of the mull type and the soil profile is a brown soil (Lundblad, 1927).

Within the research site at Nickobacken (cf. Fig. 33), the soil layer is 50–70 cm deep with the ground water table near the soil surface during periods with melting water or high precipitation. Thus the site is a typical affluence area with the humus layer (A_0) of about 9 cm, the bleached layer (A_2) of ca. 9–24 cm and the illuvial horizon (B) found from ca. 24–50 cm. The physical root zone is estimated at ca. 50 cm (L. Lundin, pers. comm.). According to preliminary analyses the upper part of the mineral soil (9–40 cm) contains 17% (by volume) of boulders (>20 cm) and 17% gravel (2–20 cm) while the subsoil (40–65 cm) holds the same percentage of gravel but only 3% of boulders. About 40% belong to finer fractions than gravel (Fig. 35), and the porosity is also around 40% in the subsoil.

Climate

The global radiation in Central Sweden is not subject to large fluctuations and therefore the data for Siljansfors are comparable with the figures for Jädraås (see Fig. 36). Siljansfors is situated in the part of Sweden where the climate is of the

55

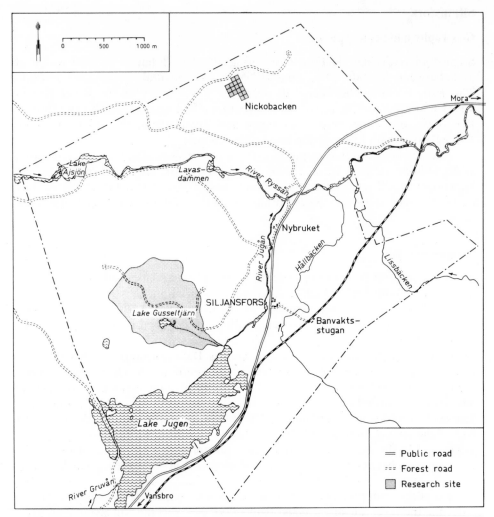

Figure 33. Map of Siljansfors Experimental Forest with the SWECON research sites Nickobacken and Gusseltjärn drainage area. Meteorological observations are made close to Banvaktsstugan. – Permission for distribution approved by the Security Officer, the National Land Survey of Sweden, 1979-09-24.

"local continental" type (Ångström, 1938), which has slightly warmer summers and distinctly colder winters than other places in Sweden at comparable latitudes (Table 4). However, the summer temperature and duration of growing season at Siljansfors do not differ from those at Jädraås (Åmotsbruk) and the winter is only slightly colder (Table 5 and Fig. 37). It appears that in 1975 the spring and summer minima were generally higher but most winter values slightly lower at Gusseltjärn, probably just features of the local climate. Considering the higher elevation of Nickobacken, the actual summer temperature here is probably even lower than at Ivantjärnsheden. July and August are the months with the largest amounts of

56

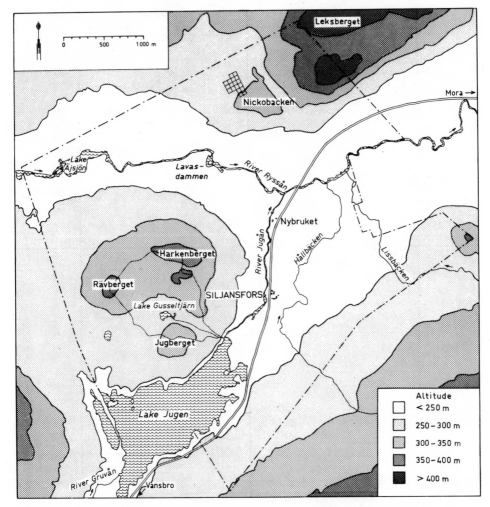

Figure 34. Topography of Siljansfors Experimental Forest. Two large valleys run through the forest, one containing River Jugån, the other River Ryssån with Lake Äjsjön. – Permission for distribution approved by the Security Officer, the National Land Survey of Sweden, 1979-09-24.

precipitation, while March has the smallest with only 26 mm (Table 6). The annual precipitation is about 700 mm, thus distinctly more than at Ivantjärnsheden. Wind speed is on average clearly lower at Siljansfors than at Jädraås (Table 7). The most frequent wind direction is NW in the district around Siljansfors, but SW in the Jädraås region.

Research plots and sampling layout at Siljansfors

The Gusseltjärn basin is surrounded by hills rising 350–370 m above sea level with Lake Gusseltjärn in a central position and with a water area of 9.2 ha (Figs. 33 and

57

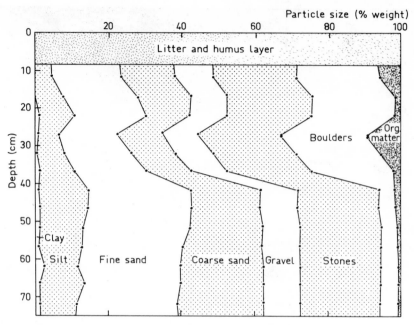

Figure 35. Particle size and organic matter distribution beneath the litter and humus in a soil profile at Nickobacken. (From L. Lundin, P-E. Jansson & H. Grip, unpubl.)

Table 7. Mean wind speed (m s^{-1}) for 10-day-periods during 1975 at Jädraås and Siljansfors. Mean values based on hourly observations. (Data from A. Lindroth, unpubl.)

Period	Jädraås	Siljansfors	Period	Jädraås	Siljansfors
Jan. 1–10	3.8	2.5	July 10–19	1.9	1.0
Jan. 11–20	3.2	no data	July 20–29	2.2	1.4
Jan. 21–30	2.7	1.3	July 30–Aug. 8	2.0	1.0
Jan. 31–Febr. 9	1.6	0.7	Aug. 9–18	2.4	1.0
Febr. 10–19	2.3	1.0	Aug. 19–28	1.6	0.9
Febr. 20–March 1	2.6	1.4	Aug. 29–Sept. 7	1.8	0.9
March 2–11	2.1	1.1	Sept. 8–17	3.0	1.8
March 12–21	1.7	1.2	Sept. 18–27	4.1	2.8
March 22–31	2.0	1.2	Sept. 28–Oct. 7	2.7	1.7
April 1–10	1.6	0.9	Oct. 8–17	1.5	1.0
April 11–20	1.8	1.0	Oct. 18–27	1.9	1.1
April 21–30	3.0	1.9	Oct. 28–Nov. 6	1.9	1.0
May 1–10	2.2	1.6	Nov. 7–16	1.5	0.4
May 11–20	1.8	1.1	Nov. 17–26	2.5	1.6
May 21–30	2.5	2.0	Nov. 27–Dec. 6	4.6	1.3
May 31–June 9	1.7	1.1	Dec. 7–16	3.4	1.9
June 10–19	2.6	1.6	Dec. 17–26	3.1	1.5
June 20–29	2.8	1.9	Dec. 27–Jan. 5	no data	no data
June 30–July 9	2.1	1.6			

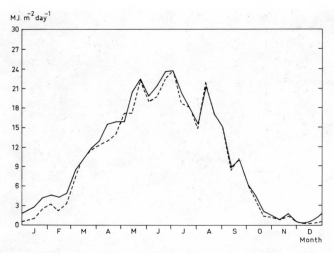

Figure 36. Incoming shortwave radiation at Siljansfors (Banvaktsstugan) (broken line) and Jädraås (plot Ih I) (solid line), January–December, 1976 (A. Lindroth, unpubl.).

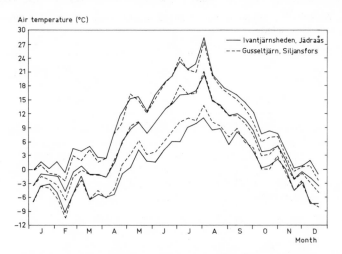

Figure 37. Mean monthly (normal, minimum and maximum) temperatures at Gusseltjärn (305 m above M.S.L.) and Ivantjärnsheden (185 m above M.S.L.), January–December, 1975 (A. Lindroth, unpubl.).

34). The brook Gusselbäcken drains the basin into Lake Jugen, a distance of about 700 m. A discharge gauging station is situated about 200 m above the discharge of the stream into the lake. The whole drainage area is estimated to have an area of 87 ha (Bergqvist & Grip, 1976).

The research plot at Nickobacken (Figs. 38 and 39) is a 4.5 ha area within a mixed mature stand of pine and spruce. The slopes adjacent to Nickobacken were partly burn-beaten land until the middle of the 19th century. The stand at Nickobacken originated in 1820–40 by natural regeneration. In about 1889 a dimension felling was carried out in the stand leaving mainly slowly growing pines. Thus

59

Figure 38. The Nickobacken research plot, a mixed mature stand of pine and spruce on sloping ground. (Photo S. Bråkenhielm)

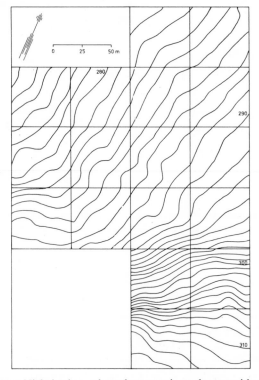

Figure 39. Contour lines at Nickobacken, where the aspect is north-west with altitudes between 274 m and 313 m above M.S.L. The excluded parts of the 6 ha area were either dry with the bedrock near the surface or swampy.

60

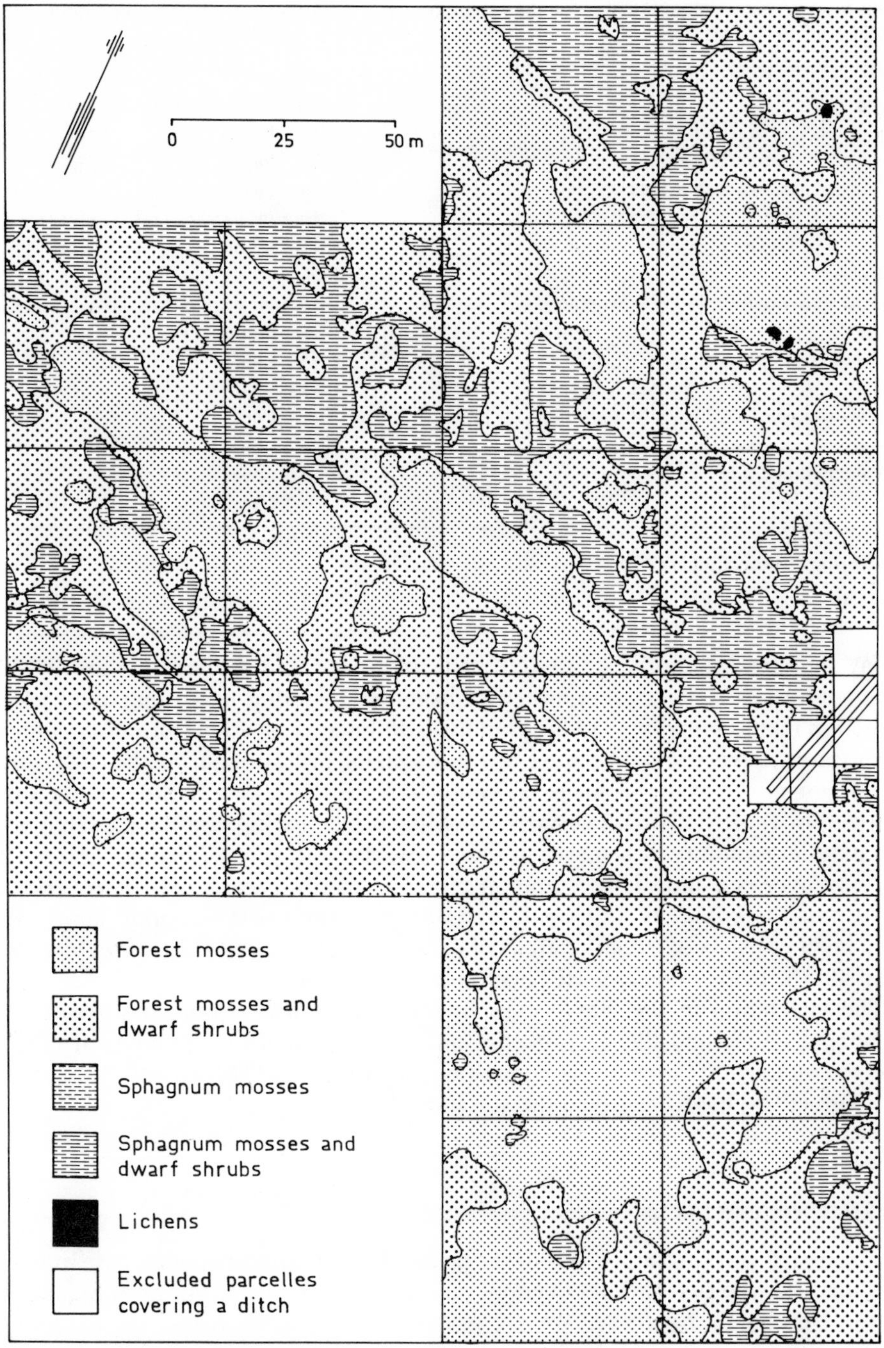

0
25
50 m
Forest mosses
Forest mosses and dwarf shrubs
Sphagnum mosses
Sphagnum mosses and dwarf shrubs
Lichens
Excluded parcelles covering a ditch

Figure 40. Generalized distribution of the ground vegetation at Nickobacken. The area can be stratified into: forest mosses and dwarf shrubs 44.5%, forest mosses 38.4%, peat mosses and dwarf shrubs 14.8%, peat mosses 1.2%, and lichens <1%. (After S. Bråkenhielm & H. Persson, unpubl.)

Table 8. Tree stand characteristics for the research plot at Nickobacken. (Data from Albrektson & Andersson, 1978)

Stand age	160	yrs
No. of trees, pine (*Pinus sylvestris*)	215	ha^{-1}
spruce (*Picea abies*)	1 222	ha^{-1}
broad-leaved trees	20	ha^{-1}
Basal area, pine	16.5	m^2 ha^{-1}
spruce	17.2	m^2 ha^{-1}
Site class*	G 24	
Annual stem production 1973–77, pine	2.9	m^3 ha^{-1} yr^{-1}
spruce	3.7	m^3 ha^{-1} yr^{-1}
Biomass above ground, pine	83.5	t ha^{-1}
spruce	83.8	t ha^{-1}
Stumps and coarse roots ($\geqslant$ 10 mm), pine	20.5	t ha^{-1}
spruce	23.5	t ha^{-1}
Needle biomass, pine	2.0	t ha^{-1}
spruce	6.5	t ha^{-1}

* According to Hägglund (1977).

today the stand comprises 140–160 years old pines and the spruces are 90–100 years old. In 1930 the regeneration was promoted by felling according to the group selection method and in 1938 the stand was thinned. The admixture of deciduous trees (birch) is very small because of cattle grazing pressure during the early stand development (O. Andersson, pers. comm.). Tree stand characteristics are summarized in Table 8. The till surface is bouldery and sloping. On the research area the plant community is a mesic to moist dwarf-shrub type (Ebeling, 1978). The bottom layer is a mosaic of common mosses, mainly *Pleurozium schreberi* and *Hylocomium splendens* and small areas of peat mosses (*Sphagnum* spp.). The field layer consists of irregular areas of dwarf-shrubs, mainly *Vaccinium myrtillus* (Fig. 40) (S. Bråkenhielm & H. Persson, unpubl. data).

The vegetation in the whole experimental forest was extensively treated by Lundblad (1927) and the bark beetle fauna was studied by Spessivtseff (1925). Studies on the soil fauna are presented in Axelsson *et al.* (1974), and Söderström & Bååth (1978) have described the soil microfungi.

Acknowledgements

The regional physiography and description of the Ivantjärnsheden research site was made by the two authors in cooperation, while the descriptions of Siljansfors were made by B. Axelsson. We are grateful to all people within the SWECON project for putting unpublished data at our disposal. Especially we thank Mr. P-E. Jansson, Mr. L. Lundin and Dr. H. Staaf for data on soil water, soil physics and soil chemistry, and Dr. Å. Lindgren, Mr. A. Lindroth and Dr. K. Perttu for meteorological data. We are also grateful to Dr. T. Persson for his extensive work with the illustrations and constructive criticism of the text.

References

Ahlner, S. 1950. Drag i Gästriklands flora. – In: Persson, E. & Curry-Lindahl, K. (eds.) Natur i Gästrikland, pp. 44–59. Göteborg: Bokförlaget Svensk Natur. (In Swedish)

Albrektson, A. 1976. The amount and the distribution of tree biomass in some pine stands (*Pinus silvestris*) in northern Gästrikland. – Swed. Conif. For. Proj. Int. Rep. 38, 27 pp. (In Swedish, English abstract)

Albrektson, A. & Andersson, B. 1978. Biomass in an old mixed coniferous forest in Dalarna. – Swed. Conif. For. Proj. Int. Rep. 79, 40 pp. (In Swedish, English abstract)

Ångström, A. 1938. Lufttemperatur och temperaturanomalier i Sverige 1901–1930. – Medd. Statens Meteorologiska och Hydrologiska Institut 7(2). (In Swedish)

Axelsson, B, Holmberg, O., Johansson, A., Larsson, S., Lohm, U., Lundkvist, H., Persson, T., Sohlenius, B., Tenow, O. & Wirén, A. 1974. Qualitative and quantitative survey of the fauna at Ivantjärnsheden – a pine forest in Gästrikland – and some other coniferous forest sites in Central Sweden. – Swed. Conif. For. Proj. Int. Rep. 6, 44 pp. (In Swedish, English abstract).

Bååth, E. & Söderström, B. 1977a. Mycelial lengths and fungal biomasses in some Swedish coniferous forest soils with special reference to a pine forest in central Sweden. – Swed. Conif. For. Proj. Tech. Rep. 13, 45 pp.

Bååth, E. & Söderström, B. 1977b. An estimation of annual production of basidiomycete fruitbodies in a 120-year-old pine forest in central Sweden. – Swed. Conif. For. Proj. Int. Rep. 67, 11 pp.

Bergqvist, E. & Grip, H. 1976. The Gusselbäck station – construction of a gauging station for accurate and continuous discharge measurement. – Swed. Conif. For. Proj. Int. Rep. 33, 23 pp. (In Swedish, English summary)

Bråkenhielm, S. 1974. The vegetation of Ivantjärnsheden. – Swed. Conif. For. Proj. Int. Rep. 18, 51 pp. (In Swedish, English abstract)

Brammanis, L. 1975. Die Kiefernrindenwanze, *Aradus cinnamomeus* Panz. (Hemiptera – Heteroptera). Ein beitrag zur Kenntnis der Lebensweise und der forstlichen Bedeutung. – Stud. for. suec. 123, 81 pp.

Bringmark, L. 1977. A bioelement budget of an old Scots pine forest in Central Sweden. – Silva fenn. 11: 201–209.

Bringmark, L. & Petersson, G. 1975. Some chemical soil variables in a 120-year-old Scots pine forest growing on glacifluvial sand (Jädraås, Central Sweden). (In Swedish, English abstract)

Clarholm, M. 1977. Monthly estimations of soil bacteria at Jädraås and a comparison between a young and a mature pine forest on a sandy soil. – Swed. Conif. For. Proj. Tech. Rep. 12, 17 pp.

Curry-Lindahl, K. 1950. Djur och fåglar i Gästrikland – ett landskap där nordliga och sydliga arter mötas. – In: Persson, E. & Curry-Lindahl, K. (eds.) Natur i Gästrikland, pp. 67–76. Göteborg: Bokförlaget Svensk Natur. (In Swedish)

Ebeling, F. 1978. Nordsvenska skogstyper. – Sv. Skogsvårdsförbunds Tidskr. 4: 339–381. (In Swedish)

Flower-Ellis, J. G. K., Albrektson, A. & Olsson, L. 1976. Structure and growth of some young Scots pine stands: (1) Dimensional and numerical relationships. – Swed. Conif. For. Proj. Tech. Rep. 3, 98 pp.

Flower-Ellis, J. G. K. & Olsson, L. 1978. Litterfall in an age series of Scots pine stands and its variation by components during the years 1973–1976. – Swed. Conif. For. Proj. Tech. Rep. 15, 62 pp.

Fries, M. 1948. Limes Norrlandicus-studier. – Sv. Bot. Tidskr. 42: 51–69. (In Swedish)

Hägglund, B. 1977. Site index curves – the back-bone of the site quality evaluation system. – Sv. Skogsvårdsförbunds Tidskr. 5: 417–427. (In Swedish, English summary)

Jansson, P-E. 1977. Soil properties at Ivantjärnsheden. – Swed. Conif. For. Proj. Int. Rep. 54, 66 pp. (In Swedish, English abstract)

Kielland-Lund, J. 1973. A classification of Scandinavian forest vegetation for mapping purposes. – IBP i Norden 11: 173–206.

Lannerbro, R. 1953. Mora. Del I. Morabygdens Geologi, pp. 9–32. Mora: AB Wasatryckeriet. (In Swedish)

Larsson, S. & Tenow, O. 1980. Needle-eating insects and grazing dynamics in a mature Scots pine forest in Central Sweden. – In: Persson, T (ed.) Structure and Function of Northern Coniferous Forests – An Ecosystem Study, Ecol. Bull. (Stockholm) 32:269–306.

Lundblad, K. 1927. Geologi, jordmån och vegetation inom Siljansfors Försökspark i Dalarna. – Skogsförsöksanstaltens Exkursionsledare 12, 112 pp. (In Swedish)

63

Lundqvist, G. 1963. Beskrivning till jordartskarta över Gävleborgs län. SGU Ser. Ca: 42, 181 pp. (In Atlas över Sverige, pp. 23–24. Stockholm: Generalstabens Litografiska Anstalt. (In Swedish)

Magnusson, N. H. 1967. Berggrunden . – In: Atlas över Sverige, pp. 7–8. Stockholm: Generalstabens Litografiska Anstalt. (In Swedish)

Magnusson, N. H. & Lundqvist, M. 1957. Landytans brutenhet. – In: Atlas över Sverige, pp. 3–4. Stockholm: Generalstabens Litografiska Anstalt. (In Swedish)

Magnusson, N. H., Lundqvist, G. & Regnell, G. 1963. Sveriges Geologi. Stockholm: Sv. Bokförlaget/ Nordstedts. (In Swedish)

Pershagen, H. 1969. Snötäcket i Sverige 1931–60. – SMHI Medd. Ser. A:5, 54 pp. (In Swedish)

Persson, E. 1950. Skogslandet. – In: Persson, E. & Curry-Lindahl, K. (eds.). Natur i Gästrikland, pp. 107–131. Göteborg: Bokförlaget Svensk Natur. (In Swedish)

Persson, H. 1980. Structural properties of the field and bottom layers at Ivantjärnsheden. – In: Persson, T. (ed.) Structure and Function of Northern Coniferous Forests – An Ecosystem Study, Ecol. Bull. (Stockholm) 32: 153–163.

Persson, T. 1975. Abundance, biomass and respiration of the soil arthropod community in an old Scots pine heath stand on Ivantjärnsheden, Gästrikland (Central Sweden) – a preliminary investigation. – Swed. Conif. For. Proj. Int. Rep. 31, 35 pp. (In Swedish, English abstract)

Perttu, K. & Huszár, A. 1976. Growing seasons, day-degrees and frost frequencies calculated from SMHI-data. – Dept. of Reforestation, Royal College of Forestry, Stockholm, Research Notes 72, 101 pp. (In Swedish, English abstract)

Perttu, K., Grip, H., Halldin, S., Jansson, P-E., Lindgren, Å., Lindroth, A. & Norén, B. 1979. Abiotic research in the Swedish Coniferous Forest Project. I. Activities during the latest years. – Swed. Conif. For. Proj. Int. Rep. 84, 46 pp. (In Swedish, English abstract)

Popović, B. 1976. Nitrogen mineralisation in an old pine stand. – Swed. Conif. For. Proj. Int. Rep. 35, 16 pp. (In Swedish, English abstract)

Popović, B. 1977. Nitrogen mineralisation in an old and a young Scots pine stand. – Swed. Conif. For. Proj. Int. Rep. 60, 15 pp. (In Swedish, English abstract)

Rudberg, S. 1970. Geomorfologi. – In: Atlas över Sverige, p. 6. Stockholm: Generalstabens Litografiska Anstalt. (In Swedish)

Sjörs, H. 1965. Forest regions. – In: The Plant Cover of Sweden, Acta Phytogeogr. Suec. 50: 48–63.

SMHI referensnormaler 1931–60. Swedish Meteorological and Hydrological Institute, Norrköping. (In Swedish)

Söderström, B. & Bååth, E. 1978. Soil microfungi in three Swedish coniferous forests. – Holarctic Ecology 1: 62–72.

Sohlenius, B. 1977. Number, biomass and respiration of Nematoda, Rotatoria and Tardigrada in a 120-year-old Scots pine forest at Ivantjärnsheden, Central Sweden. – Swed. Conif. For. Proj. Tech. Rep. 9, 40 pp.

Spessivtseff, P. 1925. The barkbeetle-fauna of Siljansfors experimental park in Dalecarlia. – Skogsförsöksanstaltens Exkursionsledare 10, 52 pp. (In Swedish, English summary)

Staaf, H. & Berg, B. 1977. A structural and chemical description of litter and humus in a mature Scots pine stand. – Swed. Conif. For. Proj. Int. Rep. 65, 31 pp.

Tamm, O. 1959. Studien über die Humidität des Klimas in Schweden. – Kungl. Skogshögskolans Skrifter 32, 48 pp. (In Swedish, German summary)

Tenow, O. 1974. Development of forested landscape and forest use in Fennoscandia up to the 20th century – an outline. – Swed. Conif. For. Proj. Int. Rep 2, 60 pp. (In Swedish, English abstract)

Walter, H. & Lieth, H. 1960–67. Klimadiagramm-Weltatlas. Jena: VEB Fischer.

Wirén, A. 1975. Quantitative data on Collembola at Ivantjärnsheden, Gästrikland (Central Sweden), and some other Scots pine stands. – Swed. Conif. For. Proj. Int. Rep. 25, 13 pp. (In Swedish, English abstract)

Persson, T. (ed) 1980
Structure and Function of Northern
Coniferous Forests – An Ecosystem Study
Ecol. Bull. (Stockholm) 32: 65–71.

DATA HANDLING AND SIMULATION TECHNIQUE USED IN THE SWEDISH CONIFEROUS FOREST PROJECT

B. Engelbrecht[1], T. Lohammar[2], I. Pettersson[3], K-B. Sundström[2] and J. Svensson[2]

Abstract

Within the Swedish Coniferous Forest Project the software development has been concentrated upon (1) automatic data collection, (2) storage, retrieval and analysis of data, and (3) simulation. A minicomputer controls and reads several hundreds of measurement instruments in the field station at Jädraås. Storage, retrieval and analysis of data are made at the computer centre in Uppsala. Simulation models can easily use automatically collected data as an input. The programs are often interactive and commonly use graphic display.

Introduction

In fulfilling the aims of the Swedish Coniferous Forest Project (SWECON), data processing and simulation are important tools, and an ambitious programme of measurements was planned at the research site Ivantjärnsheden, Jädraås, from the beginning of the project. To handle these measurements and to give the scientists an opportunity to analyze their data at Jädraås, a computerized data collection system was required. When working up these and other measurement data it was necessary to have, for example, a data retrieval system, a statistical package and display routines as well as a powerful computer for the modelling work. Most of the analysis of data and simulations was planned to be done in Uppsala. We had to decide between using the university computer centre or getting one of our own. The accessibility decided the choice and we obtained our own minicomputer system. The purchase was made during the summer of 1974 and the computer systems at Jädraås and Uppsala were delivered the next winter. The data system in its present set-up is shown in Fig. 1.

The computer group was established at the same time as the purchase was made. This group is responsible for the data systems. Program development has been concentrated upon (1) automatic data collection, (2) storage, retrieval and analysis of data, and (3) simulation. The computer group has tried to make

---

[1] Section of Reforestation, Swedish University of Agricultural Sciences, S-770 73 Garpenberg, Sweden

[2] Dept. of Ecology and Environmental Research, Swedish University of Agricultural Sciences, S-750 07 Uppsala, Sweden

[3] Uppsala University Computing Centre, Box 2103, S-750 02 Uppsala, Sweden

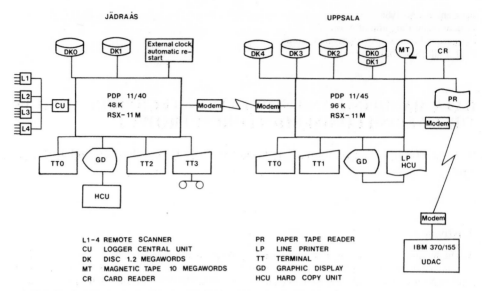

L1–4 REMOTE SCANNER
CU LOGGER CENTRAL UNIT
DK DISC 1.2 MEGAWORDS
MT MAGNETIC TAPE 10 MEGAWORDS
CR CARD READER

PR PAPER TAPE READER
LP LINE PRINTER
TT TERMINAL
GD GRAPHIC DISPLAY
HCU HARD COPY UNIT

Figure 1. The computer systems in Jädraås and Uppsala in its present set-up.

systems which are easy for the scientists to use. The programs are often interactive and commonly use graphic display.

Automatic data collection

The program system is called ECODAC and was developed for data collection
with a computer and a data logger. It also contains data retrieval programs.
ECODAC can handle a limited number of measurements. At the moment about
350 measurements are made whereby temperatures, radiation, activity of photosynthesis and many other variables are recorded. A disc is used as storage
medium and storage is made every ten minutes. Most values are then either a
ten-minute value or a mean value from one-minute measurements.

The outcoming signal from the logger is stored and conversions to physical
values are made at retrieval time. Necessary scale functions and other information about the measurements, such as responsibility for the measurement, and
measurement variable and measurement place, are stored in a special data description file. Measurement status can be changed dynamically, which enables
measurements to be started, stopped or given new parameters while data collection is in progress. The system also includes special routines for one-minute
measurements of evapotranspiration. These measurements are not running continuously and have their own storage file. The system features easy-to-use retrieval programs which create work files of the same structure as those from
the data base system, ECODATA. This enables the same list, graph, plot and
statistical programs to be used in both systems.

Checking of measurements is carried out in two different ways:

- the system will report errors when values exceed maximum and minimum limits or when the logger reports inconsistent signals, and
- each workday most measurements are checked visually by plotting values on the graphic screen.

Programs are written in FORTRAN IV except for the driver routines for the logger which are written in assembly language.

Storage, retrieval and analysis of data

For the storage, retrieval and analysis of measurement data there are two data base systems, ECODATA (see Svensson, 1979) and FYKE. ECODATA is used for analysis of continuous measurement series with fixed instruments and handles all automatically collected data. FYKE is used for manually collected data. FYKE handles more complex measurement structuring since, for instance, more background information is required for each sample than is usually the case for automatic measurements. ECODATA includes the following facilities:

(1) Insertion of data into a data base
Different programs are available to read data from different measurement systems. The program INSBAN reads data from ECODAC. Data are separated in different data bases for different research areas. Another program system, ECOLOG, reads measurement data from automatic, non-computerized measurements, e.g., data from the laboratory, test sites and mobile equipment. The program system ECOIN reads data punched on cards or magnetic tape cassettes and can be used for data evaluated from recorders.

(2) Storage of data
When analyzing data the work is done against a disc where the data base is stored. The long-term storage is on a magnetic tape which is copied to a disc when the data is needed. The physical value is often stored in the data base but the measurement signal can also be stored in millivolts, in which case the scale function is stored in a special file. The conversion to a physical value is done at retrieval time. The advantage of this procedure is that it is easier to correct the data if the scale function has to be changed, and also that it enables complex scale functions to be handled.

(3) Correction of data
The scientist may want to correct his data by, for instance, deleting erroneous data by testing them against maxi and mini limits. He may also discover that an instrument has been incorrectly calibrated and that its scale function must be changed. Several routines are available.

(4) Retrieval of data
This is done with the program GETU, which is interactive, the scientist giving the desired measurement numbers and time period. The selected data is

delivered on a work file and these data may be used in statistical calculations or in graphic display, etc.

(5) Statistics

A statistical package, ECOSTAT, includes elementary statistic routines like mean value, standard deviation and linear regression. A program for spline-approximation is also used in abiotic flow calculations. A very useful program is CALC, which enables the scientist to create new variables from old ones according to a formula, or to select data depending on certain conditions given, etc. CALC may be used for data from ECODATA and FYKE or from a terminal or card reader. The general statistical package BMDP is also available.

(6) Display program

A graphical package ECOGRAPH is also connected to the data base system ECODATA. As output media the programs use either a terminal in the Tektronix 4010 series or for hardcopy a Versatec printer/plotter. The plotting facilities are curve plotting, point plotting and bar charts. The programs give the user a high flexibility to tailor the size, shape and format of the graph by changing parameters such as scale values and time periods. They also allow the user to plot multiple curves with different scales on the same graph and multiple graphs on the same page. Programs are also available for tabulating data on the printer.

FYKE is a data base system developed by IVL (Swedish Water and Air Pollution Research Laboratory) and complemented with new routines for insertion and processing. The primary processing that can be done is sort/merge and statistics. Conversion of workfiles from FYKE to ECODATA can also be done which enables the statistical and displays programs under ECODATA to be used. FYKE includes:

(1) Insertion of data into a data base

FYKE was originally designed to have magnetic tapes of a certain format as input. A transformation program was written, with cards or sequential, formatted disc files as input. Data can be listed, tested and corrected on insertion.

(2) Retrieval and correction of data

Retrieval and correction of data is done with the program FKUPD. Retrieval of data is done by putting conditions on data. The data that fulfil the conditions are written on a workfile. Correction or deletion can be made on individual data or all data fulfilling certain conditions.

(3) Processing of retrieved data

Data can be processed in the following ways:

– Sort/merge.
– Conversion of workfiles to ECODATA-format.

- Creation of new variables from old ones according to a formula, to change data values depending on certain conditions.
- Statistics. Programs are available for elementary statistics (mean, standard error, etc.), t-test, correlation, linear regression and calculation of trends. Data can be grouped by putting conditions on the data.

Simulation

The program system SIMP (Lohammar, 1979) is intended for simulation of ordinary first order differential or difference equations. Some of the design objectives and requirements are:

- User coding should be minimized and performed in a standard high-level programming language (FORTRAN), i.e., no precompiler or translator is to be used.
- The user should not necessarily have to code complete differential equations, but only flow expressions, according to the frequently used box-and-flow idiom. Thus the responsibility for maintaining material balance in a system of boxes interconnected by flows rests with SIMP rather than with the user code.
- Simulation results should be easily and flexibly presented, the main output medium being a graphic display.
- Programs should be available, or easily written, that enable a series of complete model runs to be made automatically (e.g., for sensitivity analysis or parameter estimation).
- Input time series data should be easily read from, and output written to fit the file format used in the ECODATA program system.

A brief survey of the essential functions of the major programs in the SIMP package is given below (Fig 2):

- The PRP program reads from a terminal and stores on a disc file (1) initial state variable default values, (2) parameter names and default values, (3) flow names, indicating the box-and-flow structure of the model. The above values are default values in the sense that they will be used in subsequent simulations, unless explicitly changed for a particular simulation. The PRP program also edits the user FORTRAN file to establish the necessary communication of variables.
- The DRV program reads from a terminal and stores tabular data, time series or other data on a disc file, to be used for interpolation during simulations.
- The SIM program, before a simulation, reads in default values for all input quantities from disc files (except ECODATA time series), and modifications to these, from a terminal. It then passes control to
- the LOOP program, which performs the simulation, increases time, calls the user model subroutine, integrates state variables and outputs results to a disc file at specified intervals.
- the PLM program, after a simulation, reads selected data from the simulation

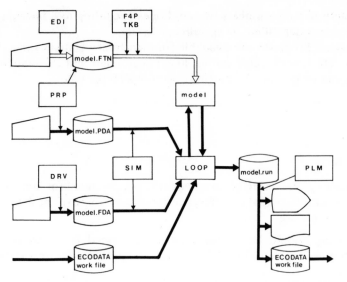

Figure 2. Interactions of major programs and disc data files used by the SIMP simulation program package. Symbols as in Fig. 1.

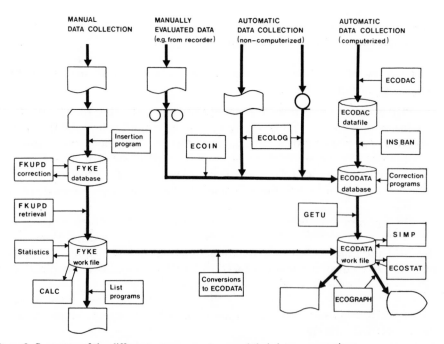

Figure 3. Summary of the different program systems and their inter-connections.

70

result file and plots on a graphic display, tabulates on the printer or converts the data to the ECODATA file format for subsequent processing or input to other models.

Inter-connection of the program systems

The different program systems are summarized in Fig. 3 which shows how the different program systems are inter-connected. The integration of the program systems for automatic data collection, storage, retrieval and analysis of data and simulation is valuable. The scientist may, for instance, read data from an experiment on the terminal and immediately have access to all the statistical and display programs. He can also use his data as input to the model which is a very valuable factor in the research environment.

References

Lohammar, T. 1979. SIMP – interactive mini-computer package for simulating dynamic and static models. – In: Halldin, S. (ed.) Comparison of Forest Water and Energy Exchange Models, pp. 35–43. Copenhagen: International Society for Ecological Modelling.

Svensson, J. 1979. Storage, retrieval and analysis of continuously recorded ecosystem data. – In: Halldin, S. (ed.) Comparison of Forest Water and Energy Exchange Models, pp. 27–33. Copenhagen: International Society for Ecological Modelling.

THE FOREST ECOSYSTEM

Persson, T. (ed) 1980
Structure and Function of Northern
Coniferous Forests – An Ecosystem Study
Ecol. Bull. (Stockholm) 32: 75–121.

MICROMETEOROLOGY AND HYDROLOGY OF PINE FOREST ECOSYSTEMS. I. FIELD STUDIES

K. Perttu[1], W. Bischof[2], H. Grip[1], P-E. Jansson[1], Å. Lindgren[1], A. Lindroth[3] and B. Norén[3] *

Abstract

The abiotic research programme within the Swedish Coniferous Forest Project involves measurements of local climate, bio- and micrometerology, CO_2, interception of rain, snow, frost in the soil, and soil water. A method was developed for estimation of global radiation from observed cloudiness at a nearby network station to be used when measurements were lacking. Fish-eye photos together with global radiation values were used for calculations of shortwave radiation below canopy. The Ångström equation seems to overestimate the longwave radiation loss for clear days. The energy balance-Bowen ratio method was used for evaluation of hourly latent and sensible heat fluxes. The equipment used is a specially designed movable trolley which permits gradient measurements every minute above a sparse Scots pine forest (Ih V) with one and the same set of sensors to minimize uncertainties. Calculations of evapotranspiration based on neutron probe and tensiometer measurements showed the best agreement with empirical functions when a 300 s m^{-1} surface resistance value was used. CO_2-measurements showed the wellknown seasonal variations. Diurnal changes in the assimilation and respiration activity were clearly reflected in the vertical CO_2 distribution. Interception losses measured by troughs were about 20% of the summer precipitation in Ih V. Crown density did not affect snow accumulation but had a marked effect on melting. Measurements of unsaturated conductivity in situ indicated that Mualem's form factor varied with depth in a layered soil. Soil heat flux calculations with a calorimetric method demanded good estimates of the lower boundary condition. Modelling aspects on the processes studied are presented in a second part of this investigation.

Additional keywords: Biometeorology, CO_2-gradients, energy exchange, evapotranspiration, fish-eye photos, instrumentation, interception, local climate, snow, soil water.

Introduction

The integrated Swedish Coniferous Forest Project (SWECON) was started in 1972. Abiotic research included local climate, biometeorological, micrometeorological (energy exchange), and hydrological investigations. The main field station was established at Jädraås (lat. 60°49′ N, long. 16°30′ E, alt. 185 m). The growing season

[1] Dept. of Ecology and Environmental Research, Swedish University of Agricultural Sciences, S-750 07 Uppsala, Sweden
[2] Dept. of Meteorology, University of Stockholm, S-104 05 Stockholm, Sweden
[3] Jädraås Ecological Research Station, Swedish University of Agricultural Sciences, S-816 00 Ockelbo, Sweden
* Author responsibilities given in Acknowledgements.

Table 1. Short description of the sites at Ivantjärnsheden (Ih) and Siljansfors (Sf) used for abiotic studies in the SWECON project. Additional data given by Axelsson & Bråkenhielm (1980). *Data not available.

	Ih 0	Ih I	Ih II	Ih III	Ih IV	Ih V	Sf
Stand:							
Age (years)[a]	Clear-felled	10	20	23	60	125	140–160
Trees (no. ha^{-1})	–	~2000	1100	2900	1200	400	1460
Mean height (m)	–	*	2.1	2.8	12.6	15.6	18.9
Max. height (m)	–	*	4.5	7.1	19.6	19.0	26.0
Crown diameter (m)	–	*	1.1	*	*	*	*
Basal area (m^2 ha^{-1})	–	*	2.15	5.04	19.98	15.04	33.7[b]
Crown length (m)	–	*	2.0	2.3	6.8	7.9	*
LAI (m^2 m^{-2})	–	*	*	*	*	1.4[c]	*
Stem volume (m^3 ha^{-1})	–	*	*	*	*	128.8	339
Ground vegetation	Dry dwarf-shrub	Dry dwarf-shrub	Very dry dwarf-shrub	Dry dwarf-shrub	Dry dwarf-shrub	Very dry dwarf-shrub	Moist dwarf-shrub
Soil:							
Profile	Iron-podsol	Iron-podsol	Iron-podsol	Iron-podsol	Iron-podsol	Iron-podsol	Iron-podsol
Texture	Homogeneous fine-medium sand	Fine-medium sand	Layered fine-coarse sand	Fine-medium sand	Fine-medium sand	Layered fine-coarse sand	Moraine
Ground water table (m)	1–3	1.5–3	10	2–3.5	1.5–3	10	d
Main usage of site	Climate Soil biol. Prim. prod.	Climate Hydrology Soil biol. Prim. prod.	Prim. prod. Climate	Prim. prod. Hydrology Climate	Prim. prod. Hydrology Climate	Micromet. Hydrology Soil biol. Soil chem. Prim. prod.	Hydrology Soil chem. Prim. prod.

[a] Stand age in 1979. Other quantitative data concern 1973.
[b] *Pinus sylvestris*: 16.5 m^2 ha^{-1}. *Picea abies*: 17.2 m^2 ha^{-1}
[c] Projected area.
[d] Intermittent rising of ground water table causing rapid lateral flow.

in the Jädraås area, defined as daily mean air temperature exceeding 6°C, lasts for 161 days on average (May 4–October 12). The average heat sum with the threshold temperature of 6°C is 950 day-degrees for the whole growing season. The corresponding heat sum at the timber line in northern Sweden is about 450 day degrees during the growing season, which is much shorter than at Jädraås. The average annual precipitation is 607 mm of which 326 mm fall during the growing season.

The main research within the abiotic group concerned energy and water balance studies of the different sites at Jädraås. Another area, Siljansfors Experimental Forest (Sf) (lat. 60°52′–60°55′ N, long. 14°20′–14°24′ E, alt. 210–424 m) was used for some complementary water balance studies and also for hydrologic research in a special catchment area.

The Jädraås field station is situated on sandy glacifluvial deposits at Ivantjärnsheden (Ih). The sites used for abiotic studies are numbered Ih 0–Ih V and Sf. The criteria used for description of the sites are: area, different stand parameters, ground vegetation, soil properties, ground water table, and site usage (Table 1). All research sites within SWECON are extensively presented by Bråkenhielm (1978) and Axelsson & Bråkenhielm (1980).

The equipment for the abiotic measurements is both comprehensive and expensive (Perttu et al., 1977). Full scale measurements, thus, could not start from the beginning of the SWECON project. The successive start of the different types of measurement was as follows:

February 1973 Local climate at two sites
October 1973 Depth and density of snow
May 1974 Biometeorology including soil temperature
June 1974 Interception of rain
May 1975 Soil temperature and moisture
June 1976 Energy exchange above canopy
August 1976 Energy exchange below canopy
June 1977 Evapotranspiration measured with a lysimeter

From the start the biometeorological measurements were connected to a datalogger. In the summer of 1975 a computer controlled system was built up and a major part of the abiotic measurements were incorporated to that system, which is thoroughly described by Engelbrecht & Svensson (1978).

The main purpose of the abiotic research within SWECON was to develop suitable models for the energy exchange components (especially evapotranspiration) above any forest stand in Sweden (Halldin et al., 1980). In order to develop such models, comprehensive micrometeorological and hydrological measurements were performed at Jädraås. Models will later be used to calculate evapotranspiration from different forest stands in different parts of Sweden.

The research was divided into three subprogrammes, namely:

(1) Water budget of forest stands on different sites
(2) Influence of stand and site on climate
(3) Regional evapotranspiration

Among the more specific purposes of the abiotic research within SWECON were the needs to:

Table 2. Programme for local climate measurements.

Measurement variable	Time resolution	Number of measurements in different stands								Approximate date for start of measurement	
		Jädraås				Siljansfors				Jädraås	Siljansfors
		Ih I	Ih II	Ih III	Ih V	Ni 0	Ni 1	Ni II	Bv		
Air temperature	hour	1			1	1	1	1*		730217	730216
Air humidity	hour	1			1	1	1	1*		730217	730216
Min. temp. near ground	day	5	3		5					740720	
Precipitation 1	day	1								730913	
Precipitation 2	10 minutes	1							1	740524	741015
Snow depth	day	4	3	4		2	3			741121	741125
Frost in ground	day	4	3	4		2	3			741121	741125
Irradiance	day	1							1	731124	731218
Wind speed	hour	1							1	740429	740503
Wind direction	hour	1							1	740429	740503

* Moved from Ni II to Gusseltjärn on 10 June 1974.

78

- Serve the biotic models with climate data
- Develop and test different methods and technics for special measurements.

The variables consist of both local climate and biometeorological elements.

This paper consists of two parts which both cover a wide range of abiotic research. The first part, Instrumentation and measurement programme, and the second part, Calculations and results, can be read independent of each other without losing the context.

Instrumentation and measurement programme

Measurement of local climate

Basic climate measurements were started in February 1973 to describe the local climate of the Jädraås and Siljansfors areas. During the first months only air temperature and humidity measurements in thermometer screens were made. The programme was successively increased to cover measurements of minimum temperatures near ground, precipitation, solar radiation, and wind speed and direction (Table 2). Measurements of snow depth and frost in the soil were added during the winter months. Since equipment and instrumentation are of standard type these measurements are comparable to measurements performed by the Swedish Meteorological and Hydrological Institute. By using a correlation method, the data from nearby stations can be used in obtaining extended time series for Jädraås and Siljansfors during the past. A description of the local meteorological measurements has been given by Lindroth & Perttu (1975).

Measurements of air temperature and humidity were performed partly with recording instruments, partly with mercury and alcoholic thermometers. The thermometer screen contains a thermohygrograph (Lambrecht 252 P), and normal, minimum and maximum thermometers. Thermometers of the same type as in the screens were used to measure minimum temperatures near the ground. The thermohygrograph gave a continuous record of air temperature and humidity and was evaluated for hourly readings. The thermometers are normally read off once a day and the thermohygrograph is calibrated every fortnight by means of an Assman aspiration psychrometer.

The precipitation was measured in the 5–10 years old Scots pine stand (Ih I) with a standard gauge and a recording gauge (Feuss 95 C), both with their openings at 1.8 m height. Daily amounts of precipitation were received from the standard gauge, while the recording instrument gave the time and intensity at 10-minute intervals.

Incident solar radiation was measured with a solarimeter (Kipp & Zonen CM 5), spectral range 300–3000 nm, connected to an integrator (Kipp & Zonen CC1). The integrator contains two counters controlled by a timer, one of which reports the value of insolation for the previous day. During the winter the solarimeter was equipped with a heating ring to keep the instrument free of snow and rime.

The duration of bright sunshine was measured with a Campbell-Stoke sunshine recorder. It consists of a glass ball which focuses the sunbeams onto a graded recording chart. With enough bright sunshine a mark is burned on the chart and a burnt trail is left as the sun moves across the sky. The length of the trail is proportional

79

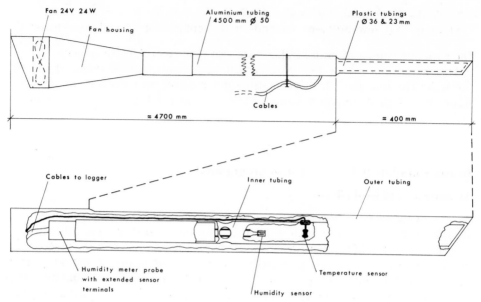

Figure 1. Assembly drawing of the ventilated radiation shield and mounting of the temperature and humidity sensors.

to the duration of sunshine. The number of minutes of bright sunshine per hour were evaluated from the recordings.

The wind speed and direction instrument (Lambrecht 1482) consists of a unit which measures both wind run and direction. The instrument was placed 3 m above the ground at Ih I and the evaluation gave the sum of the wind run and the mean direction per hour.

Biometeorological measurements

The term biometeorological measurements refers to measurements made by the computerized logger. These measurements were only intended to provide the scientists in the SWECON project with necessary meteorological data. They took place in three different stands (Ih I, Ih II, Ih V) at the research site at Jädraås.

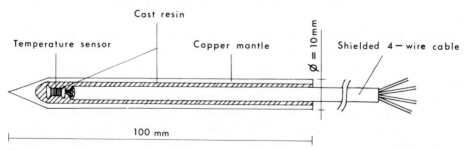

Figure 2. Assembly drawing of the soil temperature transducer.

80

Table 3. Location of the soil temperature transducers in the different stands. Each "x" denotes one transducer. Soil surface defined here as where irradiation ceases. H = heather, L = lichens, M = mosses.

Depth below soil surface (cm)	Ih I		Ih II (Reference plot)		Ih II (Irrigated plot)		Ih II (Irrigated/fertilized plot)		Ih V		
	H	L	H	L	H	L	H	L	H	L	M
1	×	×	×	×	×	×	×	×	×	×	×
2			×	×	×	×	×	− ×			
3	×	×							×	×	×
5	×	×	×	×	×	×	×	×	×	×	
7									×	×	
10	×	×		×		×		×	×	×	
15									×		
18									×		
20				×		×		×	×		
50				×		×			×		
100				×					×		
200									×		

The computerized logger to which the different instruments were connected is capable of making voltage and resistance measurements and thus the instruments used had a DC voltage or a resistance output. The logger system has been described by Perttu et al. (1977, App. B).

To enable measurements at different heights in and above the stands, three masts were erected within the research area. A 9 m mast was placed in each of the stands Ih I and Ih II and a 51 m mast in stand Ih V. The locations of these masts within the research area are shown in Axelsson & Bråkenhielm (1980). The instrumentation for the biometeorological measurements has been thoroughly discussed by Perttu et al. (1977).

The sensors for air temperature and air humidity measurements were placed in ventilated radiation shields (Fig. 1). The temperature sensor is of resistance type (Cuproswem K4 652, Swema, Sweden). The humidity transducer (Humicap HMP-11, Vaisala OY, Finland) consists of a sensor, the capacitance of which changes with the relative air humidity, and a capacitance-to-voltage converter. A sintered metal filter (not shown in Fig. 1) was found necessary to protect the humidity sensor against damage due to condensation. The accuracy of the temperature measurement is $\pm 0.2°C$ and of the humidity measurement $\pm 3\%$ RH. For calibration purposes a modified version of the radiation shield was used for humidity measurements with the psychrometer method. In this case the Humicap was replaced by a second Cuproswem temperature sensor with a wet cotton wick.

For soil temperature measurements (Table 3) similar sensors as for air temperature were used. The sensors were cast in copper casings (Fig. 2), and the accuracy of the measurement was $\pm 0.2°C$ if the long-term drift was disregarded. The long-term stability cannot be verified until the measurements have been concluded and the transducers can be dug up for recalibration.

81

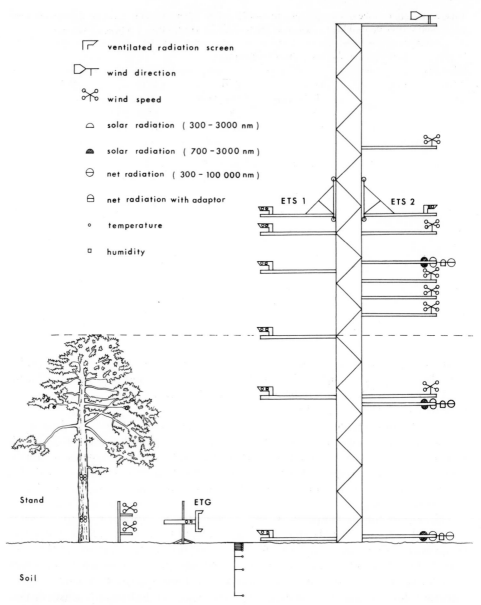

Figure 3. Instrumentation for bio- and micrometeorological measurements in the 51 m mast and for soil temperature measurements down to 2 m depth (other scale) in the mature stand Ih V. ETS = equipment for measurement of evapotranspiration from the stand. ETG = equipment for measurement of evapotranspiration from the ground (cf. Fig. 5).

Vegetation temperature in the trunks, branches and twigs of the trees were measured by thermocouples (type T copper/constantan). The electrically insulated hot junctions were 3 mm long and 2 mm in diameter. The cold junctions were held at about 0°C by means of an electronically regulated reference bath. The temperature of the bath was measured by a high accuracy temperature sensor of the same type as

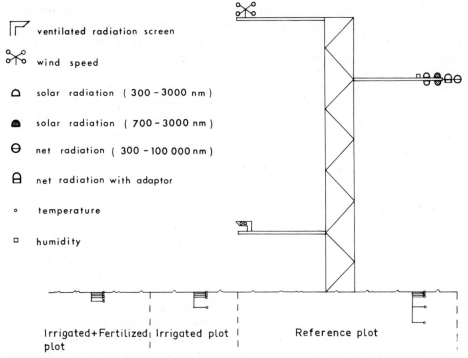

Figure 4. Instrumentation for biometeorological measurements in the 9 m mast and for soil temperature measurements down to 1 m depth in the 20-year-old stand Ih II.

used for air temperature measurement. The accuracy of the vegetation temperature measurements was $\pm 0.5°C$. Temperature changes were, however, measured with an accuracy better than 0.2°C for a 10°C range.

Two types of transducers were used for measurement of global radiation, a Kipp & Zonen Solarimeter CM 5 and a Spectrolab Inc. Pyranometer SR-75. The spectral range for both types of sensors is 300–3000 nm when using their original filters. The IR part of the radiation was measured by fitting a filter made by Eppley Co. on both types of sensors.

The net radiation was measured with a sensor (Siemen Ersking, Denmark), which can be used together with a black body adapter to enable separation of the incoming and the outgoing components of the net radiation. The spectral range for the net radiation sensor is 300–80 000 nm.

The short wave radiation sensors were calibrated against an Ångström Compensation Pyrheliometer. The net radiation sensors were calibrated using melting snow as a reference. A detailed description of the calibration procedure is given by Lindroth (1978).

Wind speed was measured with two types of transducers, Aanderaa 2219, which gives the wind run, and Teledyne 1564B with a Staggered Six Cup Set, which gives the momentary wind speed. The sensors have been calibrated in a wind tunnel at Chalmers Institute of Technology, Gothenburg. The temperature dependence of the sensors is unknown. The calibration accuracy is about ± 0.2 m s^{-1} for both types of sensors, the temperature dependence being disregarded. The deviation between different sensors of the same type is much smaller. At calibration the Teledyne sensors were within 0.03 m s^{-1} of each other and this was in the same order of magnitude as the repeatability of the wind tunnel setting. Wind direction was measured with a Anderaa 2053 wind vane.

The biometeorological measuring programme (Figs. 3 and 4) was prepared in consultation with the scientists concerned and was regularly revised. Some of the measurements started already in May 1974, and by October 1975 most of the measurements were running. All of the biometeorological measurements were stored as 10-minute values, either as a 10-minute mean value of 1-minute measurements or as a single value measured every 10th minute.

Micrometeorological measurements

The energy exchange measurements were performed in and above the 120-year-old Scots pine stand, Ih V. The aim of these measurements was to calculate the fluxes of water vapour and heat for the entire stand. This could be done in many ways with a number of different methods. The micrometeorological methods usually demand fairly accurate determinations of temperature and humidity gradients in the constant flux layer of the atmosphere. A brief description of the instruments used for measuring these gradients is given in this section. The other sensors used for energy exchange measurements were the same as those described earlier (Fig. 3). A detailed description of all the instruments used in biometeorological and micrometeorological measurements is given by Perttu *et al.* (1977).

The measurements of temperature and humidity profiles above the stand took place in the 51 m high mast at Ih V. A special equipment was developed in order to measure the profiles with sufficient accuracy (Perttu *et al.*, 1977). The equipment named ETS, EvapoTranspiration from Stand, was hoisted up and down the mast (cf. Fig. 17). On two sides of the triangular mast, guide rails were mounted from ground level up to a height of 40 m. Two trolleys of tubular steel were attached to the guide rails on the two sides. On each trolley an aluminium profile was mounted to support a ventilated radiation shield with temperature and humidity transducers. The movement up and down was made by means of a motorized hoist for each trolley. Each hoist was controlled automatically by the computerized logger via a programmer. Information on the trolley's height was obtained from switches placed at 2 m intervals up the mast.

The advantage of having movable transducers is that the same set of transducers can be used to measure temperature and humidity at different heights, which radically limits the accuracy requirements for the sensors since only short-term stability is required to get accurate differences between the levels. The reason for having two complete systems of trolleys, hoists, programmers and transducers was to enable measurements in all wind directions without disturbance from the mast, and also to enable comparative measurements with different types of transducers. The ventilated radiation shields used are of the same type as those already described above. The sintered metal filter for the humidity sensor would in this case increase the inertia of the sensor too much and was not used. Instead, the radiation shields were fitted with a heater which was activated at humidities approaching 100% RH and in this way condensation was prevented from forming on the sensor. During

84

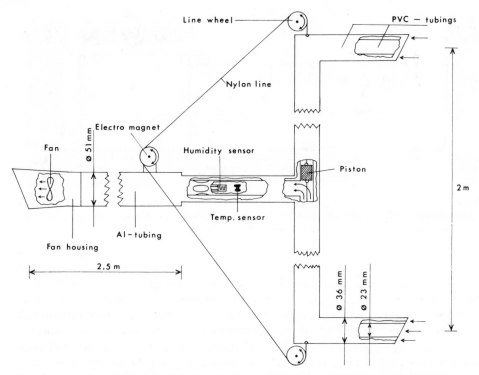

Figure 5. Assembly drawing of the equipment for measurement of evapotranspiration from ground, ETG.

the heating periods, no measurements were made with the equipment.

Similar equipment was developed for measuring the energy balance above ground (Fig. 5). In this system, named ETG, EvapoTranspiration from Ground, as in the ETS, only one set of temperature and humidity sensors was used. The sensors in the ETG were not movable as in the ETS. Instead, the air samples were taken separately from two different levels. The sample level was selected by a piston connected to a rotary magnet operated by the logger's computer via a controller. The two branches of the radiation shield were made of two concentrically oriented plastic tubes. The sample air was sucked through the inner tubing. To maintain the inner tubing at the ambient temperature, the air also always passed through the space between the outer and the inner tubing. The protective heating of the radiation shield at high humidities, as described above for the ETS, was also applied to the ETG.

A direct method for measuring evapotranspiration from a vegetated surface is to place a sample on a balance and measure the decrease in weight resulting from evapotranspiration. A balance for this kind of measurement, called a weighing lysimeter, was installed at Jädraås in May 1977 (Fig. 6). A sample of $1 \times 1 \times 0.7$ m was placed in the lysimeter. The stepping motor and the optocoupler were connected to an electronic controller. The heavy counterweight was used for a coarse adjustment of the balance. The balance was always kept in oscillation by the stepping motor moving the light counterweight in one direction or the other depending on the position of the balance arm, as indicated by the arrows in the figure. The position of the

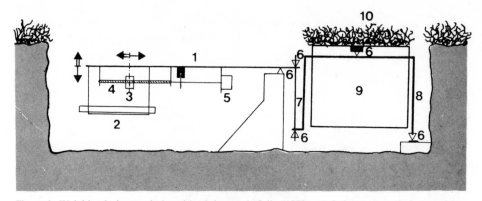

Figure 6. Weighing lysimeter designed by Johnson & Odin (1978). (1) Balance arm, (2) heavy counter-weight, (3) light counterweight, (4) screw, (5) stepping motor, (6) balance edges, (7) link arm, (8) frame, (9) stainless steel container, and (10) vegetation sample.

balance arm was detected by a sensor on the arm and an optocoupler (not shown in the figure). The displacement of the mean position of the light counterweight corresponded to the weight changes of the vegetation sample. This displacement was detected by the controller which was equipped with an analogue output connected to the data logging system. A more detailed description of the lysimeter has been given by Johnson & Odin (1978). The resolution of the balance was better than 10 g h^{-1}, corresponding to an evapotranspiration amount of 0.01 mm h^{-1}.

Continuous recording of accurate temperature and humidity gradients is very difficult to achieve and, consequently, the intention has been to measure as much as possible from Tuesday p.m. until Friday a.m. during every week throughout the whole summer. The rest of the time was reserved for calibration and maintenance of the instruments. All variables were sampled every minute and most of them were stored as 10-minute mean values.

The individual one-minute values from the measurements of temperature and humidity gradients were stored on a separate file to be handled in a special way (see section Evapotranspiration calculated with the energy balance method).

Measurements of CO_2

The installation and working pattern of an air sampling system for measurements of CO_2-profiles within and above the stand at Ih V was outlined by Bischof & Odh (1976). The instrumentation (Fig. 7) included a standard programme for periodical measurements in an one-hour cycle from 8 air inlets on the 51 m mast (at 0, 2, 5, 10, 20, 30, 40 and 50 m above ground). Extended measurements could be made by means of movable tubes and a second analyzer. The infrared gas analysis needed careful calibration of both analyzer and standard gases, a procedure incorporated in the calibration system at the CO_2 laboratory, Institute of Meteorology at Stockholm University.

Most of the humidity in sampling air was removed by a water collector placed in a gas cooler. Although this type of gas analyzer (UNOR) was relatively insensitive to water vapour, a freeze-out trap was installed and used during periods of measure-

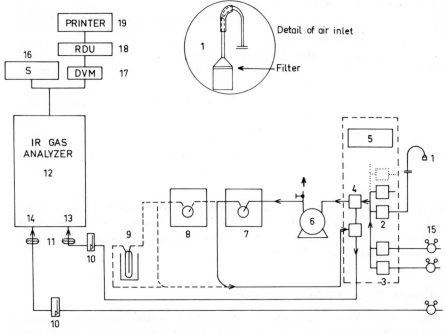

Figure 7. Instrumentation for measurement of CO_2-profiles at the mature stand Ih V. (1) Air inlet with filter, (2) solenoid valves (a number of 8) for sampling air, (3) solenoid valves for standard gas, (4) solenoid valves for changing the airflow, (5) timer, (6) pump with flow regulator and by-pass, (7) gas cooler, (8) refrigerator, (9) freeze-out trap, (10) flow meter, (11) filter, (12) gas analyzer, (13) sample cell, (14) reference cell, (15) standard gas tanks with pressure regulators, (16) paper strip recorder, (17) digital voltmeter, (18) recorder drive unit, and (19) tape punch.

ments with high accuracy. The analyzer, having a total span of 200 ppm, is operated within a range of about 250–450 ppm, depending on the gas concentration in the comparison cell. The accuracy of the measurement is about 0.1 ppm for the range 300–350 ppm. The measurements from each air inlet were continually recorded on a strip chart recorder for operation checking and also stored on tape. The system was connected to the computerized logger at Jädraås in 1977.

Measurement of interception

Precipitation collected by the tree crowns as interception is lost as drip or evaporation. The part lost by evaporation is called interception loss. The interception loss in the canopy was measured as the difference between precipitation in the open and throughfall below the canopy. The amount of stem-flow is of minor importance in the mature pine stand investigated. The intention with the throughfall measurements was to collect data for development and validation of a model covering different degrees of canopy cover and different age-classes of Scots pine.

The throughfall was collected in troughs, 10 m long, 0.1 m wide and placed 0.6 m above ground, sloping 1:10 towards the centre, where the troughs were connected to shafts in which the water levels were recorded by water stage recorders (A. Ott X).

Table 4. Number of spots used in each snow survey.

Year	Stand				
	Ih 0	Ih I	Ih II	Ih III	Ih V
1973–74	–	15	15	15	15
1974–75	–	15	15	15	15
1975–76	18	21	18	–	21
1976–77	18	21	18	–	21
1977–78	18	21	18	–	21

Identical equipment was operated at Ih I to obtain precipitation in the open. Two troughs were operated in each of the Ih III, Ih IV and Ih V stands. A total of 60 to 160 storms were recorded for each trough. Data were evaluated at 5 min. intervals and the resolution was better than ± 0.03 mm.

Measurement of snow and frost in the soil

Snow is of interest both as an insulator protecting the ground from frost penetration and as a temporary storage of water. To cover these two aspects snow was measured in several ways. Snow was collected in rain gauges and in each stand snow depth was read off at fixed measuring rods. Those placed near the thermometer screens were read of daily and the others (up to five per stand) twice a week.

In Ih V snow depth and snow density were measured at eight spots every day preceded by snowfall or melt. Snow surveys (Table 4) were made every fortnight and during the melting season weekly. At all spots snow depth and density were measured. The sampler consisted of a PVC plastic tube equipped with a smooth sharp iron edge with 40 mm inner diameter. The snow samples were poured into plastic bags and weighed with a dynamometer. From the measurement programmes it was possible to calculate continuous time series of snow stored in each stand as well as melt released from the snow packs. At every point in the snow survey a vertical fish-eye photo was taken to document the canopy.

The equipment for measuring frost in the soil consists of a graded plastic tube containing methylene-blue solved in distilled water. The blue colour disappears when the solution reaches freezing point thus enabling the upper and lower limit of the zero degree isotherm in the soil to be read. The tubes were placed near the snow rods and were read together with the snow depth.

Measurement of soil water

The main objective of soil water measurements at Ivantjärnsheden was to study the water dynamics in the unsaturated zone with special regard to the root zone. The collected data were used to validate a soil water model developed for the different stands and soils at the glacifluvial research area at Jädraås. The objective of the model (Jansson & Halldin, 1979) was to describe the soil water status and fluxes during the whole year with a time resolution of one day.

Table 5. Network for soil moisture measurements with the neutron probe in the different stands. The numbers denote number of tubes/resolution in days. I = irrigated, F = fertilized, IF = irrigated and fertilized, 0 = reference plots.

Area	10 April–30 Sept. 1975	30 Sept.–22 Dec. 1975	25 Dec.–29 March 1975–76	24 March–30 Sept. 1976	30 Sept.–1 May 1976–77	1 May–15 Oct. 1977	15 Oct.–15 May 1977–78
Ih 0	–	12/30	6/30	12/30, 6/14, 2/7	6/30, 2/14, 1/7	12/30, 6/14, 2/7	2/14
Ih I	2/14	2/30	1/30	2/30, 1/14	1/30	2/30, 1/14	1/30
Ih II: I, IF	4/14	4/30	2/30	3/30, 2/7	2/30	4/30, 2/14	2/30
Ih II: 0, F	4/14	4/30	2/30	4/30, 2/7	2/30, 1/7	4/30, 2/7	2/14
Ih III	4/14	4/30	2/30	2/30, 2/14	2/30	4/30, 2/14	2/30
Ih IV	2/14	2/30	1/30	2/30, 1/14	1/30	2/30, 1/14	1/30
Ih V	4/14	2/30	2/30	4/30, 2/7	2/14, 1/7	4/30, 2/7	2/14

Neutron probes were used for measurements of water content in the soil profile. During the first season (1975) a BASC-probe was used but in the late autumn it was replaced by a Wallingford probe. This new probe was intercalibrated with the old BASC one in order to get continuous time-series of water content.

The initial measurement programme with a low time resolution (Table 5) was changed to one with higher time resolution towards the end of the period. The number of tubes was reduced due to the correlation obtained between different tubes. For practical reasons the measuring programme was reduced during the winter. The maximum depth of the different tubes was 4 m except for the tubes at Ih 0 where the depth varied from 1.2 to 3 m. Measurements were performed from 10 to 120 cm depth with intervals of 10 cm, from 120 to 200 cm with intervals of 20 cm and below 200 cm with intervals of 40 cm. From 1 May 1977 measurements were only made in the upper 2 m.

Due to the inaccuracy of neutron probe measurements, especially near the surface, other methods were used in the upper soil layers. Measurements were performed by gravimetric methods and by an instrument equipped with capacitive sensors.

The gravimetric determination of water content was performed during the growing seasons of 1975 and 1976. Samples were taken at Ih 0, Ih II and Ih V in the S-, F/H- and mineral layers three times a week at about 12 spots within each of the different stands. Capacitance measurements were made during the growing seasons of 1976 and 1977 three times a week in soil profiles from the S-layer down to 30 cm depth. The measurements were considered representative for the plots mentioned. During 1977 measurements were also made at Siljansfors in six profiles.

Conventional tensiometers were used for measurements of soil water potential. All except one of the manometers were of mercury-type for manual readings. Due to the limited measurement range of tensiometers, gypsum blocks were used to some extent during dry periods. One tensiometer, equipped with a pressure transducer, was connected to the computerized logger for automatic registration. The tensiometers were arranged in profiles from 15 to 150 cm depth, at intervals of 15 cm down to 90 cm depth and below that at intervals of 30 cm. At upper levels, where greater variations could be expected, duplicates of tensiometers were installed.

Profile measurements with tensiometers were made at Ih 0, Ih II and Ih V. Areas with and without slash were represented at Ih 0 and areas with different treatments at Ih II. The tensiometers were read in the mornings five times a week during 1975 and 1976 and three times a week during 1977. In 1975 the measurements did not start until the beginning of August but during the other years they were started in early June. The tensiometers were insulated with white painted tubes of insulating material to protect them from high insolation during the day and from frost during the night. Due to the frost, all tensiometer measurements were stopped during late September each year. Measurements with gypsum blocks were made at Ih V and at a special stress tree plot at Ih II during the growing seasons of 1976 and 1977. The blocks were installed in profiles from ground level down to 30 cm depth. Recording of the resistance of the blocks was made with the computerized logger every 10th minute.

Calculations and results

Estimated global radiation

Comparison between the cloudiness estimated at the Swedish Meteorological and Hydrological Institute (SMHI) network station at Åmotsbruk (20 km N Jädraås) for 1965–75 and the Jädraås global radiation measurements for 1974–75 enabled a longer radiation record to be calculated for the Jädraås site. A formula of the type:

$$R_{is}/R_{is}^* = (a_0 - a_1 c - a_2 c^2) \tag{1}$$

was used for the daily values, where R_{is} is the global radiation (300–3000 nm), c the cloudiness and R_{is}^* a crude estimate of the maximum radiation possible on a clear day, chosen as:

$$R_{is}^* = R_1 + R_2 \sin[(t - D) 2\pi/365] \tag{2}$$

where $R_1 = 15.588$, $R_2 = 14.688$ and $D = 78$ if R_{is}^* is given in MJ m^{-2}day^{-1}. t is the day number, i.e., $1 \leq t \leq 365$. The coefficient a_i, where $i = 0, 1, 2$ is a function of t according to:

$$a_i = b_i + e_i \sin[(t - d_i) 2\pi/365] \tag{3}$$

The constants in this expression, b_i, e_i and d_i, were estimated from the data records by multiple linear regression analysis.

Thus R_{is}/R_{is}^* was given as a function of t and c with nine parameters:

$b_0 = 0.82633$	$e_0 = -0.413$	$d_0 = -78.7$
$b_1 = 0.01334$	$e_1 = 0.2134$	$d_1 = 49.7$
$b_2 = 0.00759$	$e_2 = -0.00324$	$d_2 = 25.5$

Cloudiness c should be given as eighths, i.e., $0 \leq c \leq 8$. The correlation coefficient was 0.86, and mean and standard error was 0.52 and 0.13, respectively. Thus, the deviation of the daily values was, on average, 25%. If the formula for R_{is}/R_{is}^* was correct for every t and c, the deviation of the monthly means would be in the order of $25/\sqrt{30} \approx 5\%$. However, it should not be expected to be equally valid regardless of the time of the year. Of the 21 months of data used, 16 monthly means were within 10%, the mean deviation being 12%. It must be noted that there is no independent period for comparing the results of the formula. When both cloudiness and radiation

90

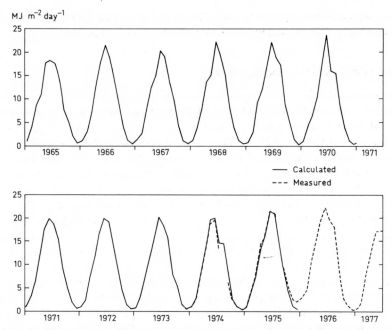

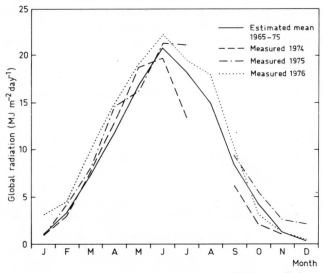

Figure 8. Calculated and measured monthly mean values of global radiation at Jädraås.

were available in the records they were used to estimate the parameters. Thus even greater deviations should be expected besides the 21 months of overlapping data.

Some of the measured values from the winter 1975–76 are clearly erroneous (Fig. 8) and were omitted in the regression analysis but not in the figure. A common annual time axis (Fig. 9) enables comparison of the different years. This kind of

Figure 9. Calculated and measured monthly mean values of global radiation at Jädraås.

radiation data has been used to run simulation models. Although the input data were crude they were quite sufficient for some of the modeling purposes.

Potential global radiation and daylength

The maximum amount of solar radiation reaching the earth's surface on a clear day primarily depends on the latitude, time of the year and influence of the atmosphere. Direct radiation from the sun is partially absorbed, reflected and scattered by different substances in the air. Some of the reflected and the scattered radiation together with the transmitted direct beam radiation reaches the earth. The amount of reflection, scattering and absorption normally varies throughout the year on account of cloudiness, air pollution, different air masses, etc.

A good estimation of the maximum possible global radiation, e.g., the potential global radiation, and the daylength at a certain location requires knowledge of how the horizon is affected by the topography and the vegetation. This was determined by a compass and an elevation meter with an accuracy of $\pm 0.5°$ sited at the same place as the radiation meter and the sunshine recorder. Taking into consideration the data received from the horizon estimation (Fig. 10), the daily totals of incoming direct radiation outside the atmosphere (a solar constant of 1360 W m^{-2} was used) and the maximum possible duration of sunshine, e.g., daylength, were calculated for the 1st and the 15th day of every month during one year. These values, when using daynumber as an independent variable, were fitted to each set of data (Fig. 11). The highest of the recorded values represent days which are clear or almost clear. Some of these values should in fact reach as far as the curve representing daylength. However, the sunshine recorder has the disadvantage of not detecting the very low radiation intensities just after sunrise and just before sunset and thus the recorded values are slightly too low.

A transmissivity of 70% (see below) was used to calculate the potential global radiation at Ih I. Some of the measured values exceeded the calculated ones (Fig. 12), but this was to be expected when considering the variation of the atmosphere's influence (cf. Fig. 13). Nevertheless, the calculated curve was considered to give a rather good estimate of the potential global radiation at Ih I.

For the calculated daily totals of direct radiation outside the atmosphere, the

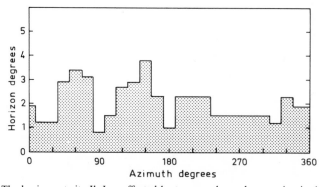

Figure 10. The horizon at site Ih I as affected by topography and vegetation in August 1977.

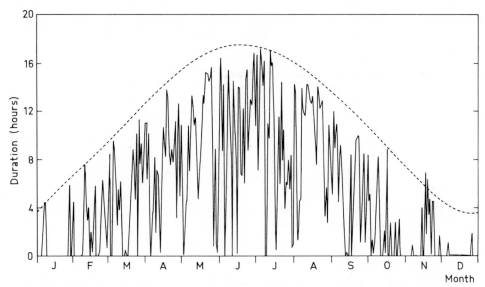

Figure 11. Duration of sunshine (solid line) and daylength (broken line) at Ih I during 1976.

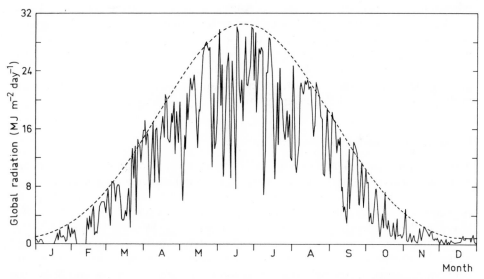

Figure 12. Measured daily totals of global radiation at Ih I during 1976 (solid line), and the corresponding maximum amounts for perfectly clear days calculated with a transmissivity of 70% (broken line).

influence of the topography and vegetation has already been considered.

The quotient between measured solar radiation on clear days at the earth's surface and the calculated values of direct radiation outside the atmosphere (Fig. 13) shows the influence of the air. The average transmissivity was 0.70, i.e., 70% of the radiation from the sun reached the earth's surface. However, the accuracy of the measured

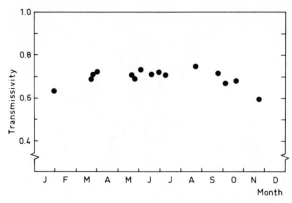

Figure 13. Quotient between measured global radiation at ground level and calculated beam radiation outside the atmosphere for 15 clear days during 1976.

global radiation was about 5–8% and that of the calculated radiation outside the atmosphere about 2–3%. This gives an average transmissivity of $70\pm5\%$. The lower values in winter are probably caused by the lower solar elevations and, hence, the rays have a longer path through the air, which causes increased reflection, scattering and absorption. Ångström (1956) gives a value of 74% at Stockholm (about 200 km SSE Jädraås). The uncertainties in the measurements of solar radiation are of such a magnitude that it is impossible to say whether the difference between the values reported here (70%) and by Ångström (74%) is significant. Support for the lower value is found in the fact that increasing air pollution throughout the world causes less transmission and consequently a decrease in the amount of global radiation reaching the earth's surface.

Global radiation above and below the canopy

The radiation below the canopy in Ih V was measured continuously only at one single spot. This is not fully satisfactory since it was not immediately known how typical this spot was for the entire stand. Consequently, this aspect required special investigations. As regards the measurements made at this single spot, it was possible to reduce the influence of the temporary conditions there by calculating mean values over a time interval sufficiently long for the sun to pass both covered and uncovered parts of the canopy. Two-hour mean values seemed to be satisfactory. The ratio between measured incoming global radiation (300–3000 nm) below and above the canopy (R_{isb}/R_{isa}) has been calculated from a function of the form:

$$R_{isb}/R_{isa} = a(1 - e^{-bh}) \tag{4}$$

where h denotes sun elevation angle in degrees above horizon, and the constants $a=0.45$ and $b=0.076$. The calculation of R_{isb}/R_{isa} from this curve (Fig. 14) for $0°\leq h\leq55°$, the latter being the maximum sun elevation at Jädraås, shows that on average 34% of the global radiation above the canopy reaches the ground.

During two clear days, 19 and 20 August 1976, a special investigation was made of the radiation conditions below the canopy of Ih V (Gemmel & Perttu, 1978). A

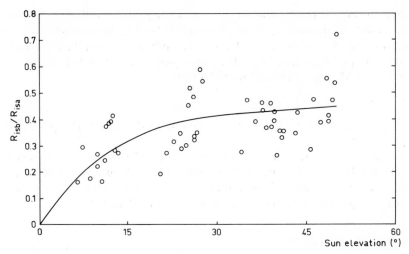

Figure 14. Quotient between incoming global radiation below (R_{isb}) and above (R_{isa}) the canopy as a function of the sun elevation. The solid line represents a fitted exponential function.

starting point was randomly chosen from a map. From that point a straight line southwards was laid out on which 14 solarimeters (Kipp & Zonen, CM5) were placed at 10-meter intervals. A reference solarimeter was placed above the canopy. Readings were made regularly between 08.00 and 16.00 during the two days. The canopy was photographed at the 14 measurement spots, using a camera with a fish-eye lens.

During the days concerned, the diffuse radiation was not measured separately. Gemmel & Perttu (1978) gave the formula:

$$R_{ida}/R_{isa} = 0.6020 - 0.1319 \ln \delta \tag{5}$$

where R_{ida}/R_{isa} was the quotient between the diffuse radiation and the global radiation above the canopy and δ was the angle with $0°$ at horizon and $90°$ at zenith. The equation was developed from data given by Lunelund (1940). Direct beam radiation above canopy (R_{iba}) could then be expressed as:

$$R_{iba} = R_{isa} - R_{ida} \tag{6}$$

From the fish-eye photographs it was found that, on average, the part of the sky covered by trees (d_c) could be approximated by:

$$d_c = 1.0062 \cdot \exp(-0.0138\delta) \tag{7}$$

The diffuse radiation from a clear sky (R_{id}^*) can be described by a model for a "standard overcast sky" (SOC), adopted in 1955 by the Commission Internationale de l'Eclairage, as:

$$R_{id}^* = 6.60 \cdot 10^{-3} + 9.89 \cdot 10^{-4}\delta + 2.10 \cdot 10^{-4}\delta^2 - 4.04 \cdot 10^{-6}\delta^3 + 1.75 \cdot 10^{-8}\delta^4 \tag{8}$$

This equation is a modification given by Anderson (1964). Hence the amount of diffuse radiation reaching the ground below the canopy is:

$$R_{idb} = (1 - d_c) R_{id}^* \tag{9}$$

95

According to these formulas the mean value of the diffuse radiation beneath the canopy was 46% of that above. By multiplying (5) by 0.46 the amount of R_{idb} of the total R_{isa} was found to be about 5%. The corresponding figure for the beam radiation below the canopy (R_{ibb}) was 26%. The mean global radiation below the canopy, R_{isb} for $0° \leq h \leq 55°$ was calculated with the formula:

$$R_{isb} = R_{iba}(1 - d_c) + 0.46 \cdot R_{ida} \tag{10}$$

to be 35% of R_{isa}, which is close to the value obtained at the single spot calculated with equation (4).

The techniques used to calculate the mean value of the global radiation below the canopy can be applied to an arbitrary stand. For Ih V further calculations must be made because of the limited amount of fish-eye data available. Diffuse radiation above the canopy must also be measured instead of calculated.

Albedo above the canopy

The albedo (reflectivity) measurements were made at the 27 m level from the mast at Ih V, i.e., about 9 m above the tree top level. The results (Fig. 15) are summarized in the following formula, valid for $5° \leq h \leq 55°$:

$$\alpha = 10.96 - 0.074h \tag{11}$$

where α is the albedo and h the sun elevation.

Albedo calculations for solar elevations lower than 5° are very inaccurate because of uncertainties in the measurements. The coefficients in equation (11) are estimated from one-hour mean values obtained on the following clear days: 13 July, 16 August, 20–22 August 1976, 18 May and 9 July 1977. The average albedo from the range of sun elevations mentioned above was 7.5%. The global radiation below the canopy was found to be about 35% of the corresponding radiation above the stand (see above). The short-wave radiation budget for the canopy of Ih V (Fig. 16) includes the assumption that the albedo of the ground vegetation was 13%. Consequently, on clear days 62% of the incoming global radiation, R_{isa}, was utilized in the canopy for energy exchange processes, photosynthesis, etc.

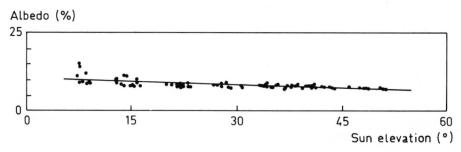

Albedo (%)

Sun elevation (°)

Figure 15. Albedo above the canopy as a function of the sun elevation between 5 and 55 degrees.

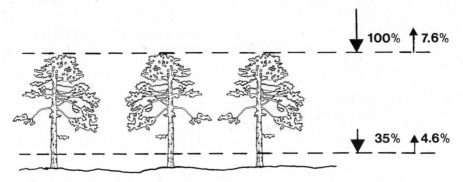

Figure 16. Short-wave radiation budget for the canopy at Ih V.

In- and out-going long-wave radiation

In most methods used to calculate the evapotranspiration from an area it is necessary to estimate the radiation balance. The radiation balance, or the net radiation, R_{nt}, can be written as:

$$R_{nt} = R_{is}(1 - \alpha/100) + R_{nl} \tag{12}$$

where R_{is} = global radiation (300–3000 nm), α = albedo and R_{nl} = net long-wave radiation (3000–80 000 nm). All bodies emit radiation at intensities proportional to the fourth power of their absolute temperature (Stefans' law). The net long-wave radiation consists of the difference between the radiation emitted from the different substances in the atmosphere and that from the surface of the earth and can be written as:

$$R_{nl} = R_{il} - R_{ol} \tag{13}$$

where R_{il} = incoming long-wave radiation from the atmosphere and R_{ol} = outgoing long-wave radiation from the earth's surface.

Global radiation, R_{is}, is nowadays measured at many of the meteorological network stations and the albedo is a well-known property for many types of vegetation. R_{nl} is rarely measured and usually must be estimated in one way or another.

Consider again the radiation (R) from a body following Stefans' law:

$$R = \varepsilon \sigma T^4 \tag{14}$$

where ε = emissivity, σ = Stefan-Boltzmann constant and T = absolute surface temperature. Hence, the long-wave radiation from the earth's surface can be written as:

$$R_{ol} = \varepsilon_e \sigma T_e^4 \tag{15}$$

where ε_e = emissivity of the earth's surface. The emissivity, ε, of a body is a parameter that characterizes how well a body emits radiation of a specific wave length compared to a perfect black body, for which ε is unity. Values of the earth's emissivity, ε_e, given in the literature, vary from 0.85 to 1.00. The surface temperature, T_e, can usually be approximated either with the 24-hour average of the air temperatures or with an arithmetic mean value of the daily maximum and minimum temperatures.

Following the same discussion as for R_{ol}, the incoming long-wave radiation from the atmosphere, R_{il}, can (for clear skies) be written as:

$$R_{il} = \varepsilon_a \sigma T_a^4 \, f(e) \tag{16}$$

where ε_a is the emissivity of the atmosphere, T_a is the mean air temperature and $f(e)$ is a function of the humidity in the air. This function is introduced to compensate for the dependence of the long-wave radiation on the water vapour content in the atmosphere (de Jong, 1973). Hence, R_{nl} for clear skies can be written as:

$$R_{nl} = \varepsilon_a \sigma T_a^4 \, f(e) - \varepsilon_s \sigma T_a^4 \tag{17}$$

Empirical formulas for R_{nl} are given, e.g., by Brunt (1944) and Ångström. The Ångström equation (see Liljequist, 1970) reads:

$$R_{nl} = -\sigma T_a^4 \, (a + b \cdot 10^{-ce}) \tag{18}$$

where a, b and c are constants and e is the water vapour pressure in mm Hg. The formula given by Brunt is:

$$R_{nl} = -\sigma T_a^4 \, (a - b\sqrt{e}) \tag{19}$$

where a and b are constants. Divergent values of these constants are reported, probably caused by uncertainties in the measurements. For the Jädraås site both formulas gave almost the same result for a suitable set of coefficients. For the Ångström equation, Geiger (1961) recommended the coefficient values given by Boltz & Falkenberg, i.e., $a = 0.180$, $b = 0.250$ and $c = 0.126$.

Applying equation (18) with the coefficients given above, values of R_{nl} were calculated for six clear days (Table 6). The necessary values of T_a and e were derived from the meteorological standard measurements in stand Ih V. Values of R_{ol} according to equation (15), using an emissivity of 0.97 (Rosenberg, 1974), were also calculated (Table 6).

So far, theoretical and empirical formulas for calculating R_{il} and R_{ol} have been discussed, but it is also possible to measure these elements by using suitable combinations of instruments. In fact, no single instrument actually measures R_{il} or R_{ol} but a computed value can be obtained by correct combination of the values from the different sensors. A description of this procedure is given in Perttu et al. (1977).

When considering the data presented in Table 6 it is necessary to emphasize that there were very few clear days to enable definite conclusions. The plausibility of the measured values of R_{ol} is verified by the fairly good agreement with the calculated values. Since the uncertainty in the measured values is about 8–12% it is difficult to say whether the calculated values are more reliable than the measured. The values of R_{nl} showed an almost constant negative difference except for two days, 20 August 1976 and 18 May 1977. This can be explained by the fact that the first of these two days had a slightly overcast sky during the night decreasing the radiation loss. The second day had a very low soil surface temperature compared with the air temperature, because the soil was frozen until May 10. Under such conditions air temperature appears to overestimate the temperature of the radiative surface and, hence, causes the value of R_{nl} to be too low (cf. Eq. 18).

The conclusion is that the Ångström formula, with the constants used above, seems to overestimate the radiation loss, at least above sparse pine stands.

Table 6. Measured and calculated daily mean values of long-wave radiation.

Date	Net long-wave radiation (R_{nl})			Outgoing long-wave radiation (R_{ol})		
	Calcul-ated (W m^{-2})	Meas-ured (W m^{-2})	Diff-erence (W m^{-2})	Calcul-ated (W m^{-2})	Meas-ured (W m^{-2})	Diff-erence (W m^{-2})
13 July 1976	−85.6	−61.5	−24.1	366.5	361.0	5.5
16 Aug. 1976	−80.9	−59.7	−21.2	379.0	357.6	21.4
20 Aug. 1976	−82.6	−70.4	−12.2	354.3	339.1	15.2
21 Aug. 1976	−83.8	−60.2	−23.6	359.6	336.3	23.3
18 May 1977	−90.9	−55.6	−35.3	338.3	322.7	15.6
9 July 1977	−86.7	−61.2	−26.5	380.5	384.8	−4.3

Estimation of evapotranspiration

The watershed technique of estimating evapotranspiration cannot be used at Jädraås since the experimental site is located on sedimentary deposits. Four other methods can be used, namely, micrometeorological, lysimetric and physiological methods and the water balance method of the unsaturated zone (see review by, e.g., Federer, 1970). The physiological methods are left out of the discussion here. In an attempt to reduce the errors, it was decided to estimate evapotranspiration with two independent methods, the energy balance-Bowen ratio method and the water balance method. A comparison between these methods is presented by Grip et al. (1979) for Ih V during the growing season of 1977.

The main three resistances against vapour fluxes are surface resistance, which is the stomatal resistances of all needles and leaves, the sum of the resistances within the tree crowns and ground vegetation, and the aerodynamical resistance between vegetation and atmosphere.

The stand at Ih V is a sparse pine forest with about 400 trees ha^{-1} with a mean height of 16 m. The surface roughness is therefore comparatively high, which gives a low aerodynamical resistance. As a consequence the gradients above the canopy are extremely small. Recognizing this fact, the measuring system has been designed to allow measurements of small differences in air temperature and humidity. The total accuracy is of such an order that the gradient measurements give statistically satis-factory results. For technical reasons wind profile measurements have not been used. The only micrometeorological method suitable for calculations of evapotranspira-tion was the energy balance-Bowen ratio method.

The only hydrological method for estimation of the evapotranspiration from the stand Ih V was to calculate the water balance of the unsaturated zone of the soil, whereby the evapotranspiration was given by the change in water content above the zero flux plane at two different times. The drawback with the water budget method was that the calculation involved a small difference between two large numbers if the period was chosen too short. The fluctuating conditions, with rapid infiltration and percolation at depths below root zone, made it also difficult to use the method during certain situations.

Evapotranspiration calculated with the energy balance method

The calculation of evapotranspiration is based on the simplified energy balance equation:

$$R_n = LE + H + S \tag{20}$$

where the energy used for photosynthesis is neglected. R_n is the net radiation and S is the energy being stored in air, trees and ground. The latent heat flux or evapotranspiration (LE) and the sensible heat flux (H) are related to the gradients of potential temperature θ and specific humidity q according to:

$$LE = -L\varrho \, K_E \, \frac{dq}{dh} \tag{21}$$

and

$$H = -C_p\varrho \, K_H \, \frac{d\theta}{dh} \tag{22}$$

where L is the heat of vapourization of water, ϱ the density of air, C_p the specific heat of air and K_E and K_H the exchange coefficients for latent and sensible heat fluxes, respectively. It is generally assumed that K_E and K_H are equal or approximately equal under neutral and near-neutral conditions. Evaluation of dq/dh and $d\theta/dh$ enables division of $R_n - S$ into its two components (LE and H). To achieve this, the Bowen ratio:

$$\beta = H/LE = \frac{Cp}{L} \cdot \frac{d\theta}{dh} \Big/ \frac{dq}{dh} \tag{23}$$

is calculated. LE and H are then given by:

$$LE = \frac{R_n - S}{1 + \beta} \tag{24}$$

and:

$$H = \beta \cdot LE \tag{25}$$

The gradients, $d\theta/dh$ and dq/dh, have been calculated from temperature and humidity measurements performed with the ETS equipment (see section Micrometeorological measurements).

Evaluation of temperature and humidity profiles from the measured values requires a number of corrections and calculations to be made. The method is described for evaluation of the temperature profile but is also applicable for the relative humidity profile.

(1) Correction for inertia of transducers

Let the first measurement received be T_1. The transducer is then moved to an elevation with the temperature T_2. Because of the inertia it will not completely adapt

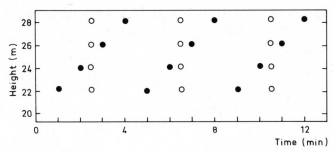

Figure 17. Procedure for interpolation of the temperature and humidity measurements above the mature stand Ih V. Locations in time and space of measured (●) and interpolated values (○).

to the new situation in a finite time but will report the temperature T. Suppose that the adaptation is exponential, i.e.:

$$T_2 - T = e^{-t/\alpha}(T_2 - T_1) \tag{26}$$

where t is the time between the measurements and α is the known time constant. The correct temperature T_2 can then be calculated.

(2) Elimination of variations in the background temperature

Temperature T_i from the movable instrument is replaced by $T_i - T$, where T is the background temperature measured simultaneously. Like T_i, T has been corrected according to step 1 before reaching step 2. In some cases background measurements were not performed and, then, this step was excluded.

(3) Interpolation of values to get temperatures representing the same time for each level of the vertical profile

A comparison between the temperatures at different levels is meaningful only if they refer to the same time. Suppose that at time t_1 the temperature is T_1 on a certain level and that the next measurement at the same level at time t_2 gives the temperature T_2. A value T for time t (where $t_1 \le t \le t_2$) is then given as a weighted mean of T_1 and T_2 (Fig. 17) by:

$$T = [T_1(t_2 - t) + T_2(t - t_1)]/(t_2 - t_1) \tag{27}$$

(4) Subtraction of the mean from each individual value

The values T_1, T_2, ..., T_m from m levels at time t are now available. Since only the temperature differences between the levels are of interest, T_i is replaced by $T_i' = T_i - T$ where $T = \dfrac{1}{m}\sum_1^m T_i$. Then:

$$\sum T_i' = 0 \tag{28}$$

(5) Evaluation of a regression line

A value of the temperature gradient is then the result of a least-squares fit of the temperature difference with the level as the independent variable. The calculations are carried out with the values from a suitable period, e.g., one hour. Suppose there

101

are n pairs of values (T_i, h_i) $i = 1, \ldots, n$, where T_i is the temperature difference at the level h_i. Then the slope b of the regression line is accepted as the gradient dT/dh, and b is given by:

$$b = \Sigma \, T_i h_i / [\Sigma \, h_i{}^2 - \frac{1}{n}(\Sigma \, h_i)^2] \tag{29}$$

In this way the gradient of the temperature T and of the relative humdity RH are calculated. The potential temperature gradient $d\theta/dh$ and the specific humidity gradient dq/dh needed to determine β, the Bowen ratio, can be related to dT/dh and dRH/dh. θ is approximately given by:

$$\theta = T + 0.01 \, h$$

where h is the measurement height. Hence, the potential temperature profile:

$$\frac{d\theta}{dh} = \frac{dT}{dh} + 0.01 \tag{30}$$

The specific humidity (q) is given by:

$$q = 0.622 \, \text{RH} \cdot e_s(T) / [P_a - \varrho g h - 0.378 \, \text{RH} \cdot e_s(T)] \tag{32}$$

where $e_s(T)$ is the saturated vapour pressure, P_a the air pressure and g the acceleration of gravity. Differentiation gives the profile:

$$\frac{dq}{dh} = \frac{0.622 \, P_a}{[P_a - 0.378 \, \text{RH} \cdot e_s(T)]^2} \left(\frac{\varrho q}{P_a} \text{RH} \cdot e_s(T) + \frac{d\text{RH}}{dh} e_s(T) + \text{RH} \cdot \Delta \cdot \frac{dT}{dh} \right) \tag{33}$$

where $\Delta = de_s(T)/dT$. Finally (31) and (32) give:

$$\beta = \frac{C_p}{L} \cdot \frac{P_a}{0.622} \cdot \frac{dT/dh + 0.01}{\varrho \cdot g \cdot \text{RH} \cdot e_s(T)/P_a + \dfrac{d\text{RH}}{dh} e_s(T) + \text{RH} \cdot \Delta \cdot \dfrac{dT}{dh}} \tag{34}$$

When measurements were made with the ETG equipment the relations will be slightly different since the measured temperature T was in fact θ:

$$\frac{d\theta}{dh} = \frac{dT}{dh} \tag{31'}$$

$$q = \frac{0.622 \, \text{RH} \cdot e_s(T)}{P_a - 0.378 \, \text{RH} \cdot e_s(T)} \tag{32'}$$

$$\frac{dq}{dh} = \frac{0.622 \, P_a}{[P_a - 0.378 \, \text{RH} \cdot e_s(T)]^2} \left[\frac{d\text{RH}}{dh} e_s(T) + \text{RH} \cdot \Delta \cdot \frac{dT}{dh} \right] \tag{33'}$$

and

$$\beta = \frac{C_p}{L} \cdot \frac{P_a}{0.622} \cdot \frac{dT}{dh} \bigg/ \left[\frac{d\text{RH}}{dh} e_s(T) + \text{RH} \cdot \Delta \cdot \frac{dT}{dh} \right] \tag{34'}$$

The period from June 1 to July 8, 1977, covered 252 hours of measurement, of which 171 hours yielded values of latent heat fluxes with an uncertainty less than 100 W m^{-2} (Fig. 18). Hourly means of net radiation for 29 days of the measurement period were

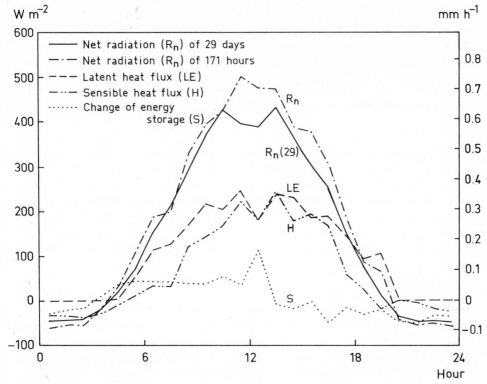

Figure 18. Mean diurnal variations of the different fluxes calculated with the energy balance method for 171 hours during the period June 1–July 8, 1977. Net radiation for 29 days during the same period given for comparison.

slightly higher than for the 171 hour period. The average daily sum of evapotranspiration during the period was calculated to be 3.7 mm (Fig. 18).

Evapotranspiration calculated with the water balance method

Water losses from the soil caused by evapotranspiration were calculated during periods with controlled boundary conditions at a fixed level in the soil profile. If water content from the soil moisture characteristic curve and the corresponding water tensions from tensiometers were used, a time resolution of one to three days was obtained in the calculations. With water content values obtained from neutron probe measurements, the time resolution decreases to a week or more.

The method is limited to situations when a fixed lower boundary exists in the soil profile. This is a common situation during the growing season in the Ivantjärnsheden area (Ih I–Ih V). The water balance method has often been used in hydrology to determine evapotranspiration. The traditional way of calculating evapotranspiration is to solve the familiar water-balance equation, which can be written as:

$$E = P - F_{surf} - F_{stream} - \Delta S \tag{35}$$

103

where E is evapotranspiration, P is precipitation, F_{surf} is surface runoff, F_{stream} is streamflow and ΔS is change of storage. When the equation is applied to a watershed, the change of storage is usually the most critical term of an accurate determination of evapotranspiration. It is unusual to have a better time resolution than one month when equation (35) is used for watersheds.

If the water balance method is applied to a horizontal area where no streamflow or surface runoff occurs, the water balance equation can be written as:

$$E = P - F_{perc} - \Delta S \qquad (36)$$

where F_{perc} is deep percolation. This equation was used to calculate deep percolation and evapotranspiration for the Jädraås area.

A special programme was developed to calculate the different terms of equation (36) by the instantaneous profile method (IPM). The programme requires measured values of precipitation, water content and water potential in a soil profile. Between two consecutive water content measurements a calculation was made of precipitated, evapotranspired and percolated water. The water contents were fitted to a cubic spline polynomial with the soil depth as independent variable. The same procedure was also applied to the total water potential (pressure head), but with a different purpose. The water content was integrated over arbitrary depth intervals. The total water potential was derived, and if a change in sign of the derivative was found in the profile, a zero flux plane was assigned to the level where the derivative was equal to zero. If a zero flux plane was found during the period between two measured water contents, an average level of zero flux plane was calculated. The change in water content, above and below that level, gave transpiration and percolation during the time period. Any amount of water precipitated during the period was added to the calculated evapotranspiration. Thus, evapotranspiration and percolation rates were obtained with a zero flux plane used as a boundary condition to the flux calculations.

In situations when no zero flux plane was found in the profile, calculation of transpiration could not be done accurately. If the time period was short and no zero flux plane existed, i.e., during an infiltration period with a wetting front penetrating the profile, calculations of percolation could be performed with the infiltration rate as an upper boundary condition. The transpiration was then assumed to be small compared to percolation and could be neglected or estimated in the calculation.

Sometimes the zero flux plane varied widely during a measurement period. This was a typical situation when sudden changes had occurred in the precipitation-transpiration pattern. A drying period could be followed by heavy rain which penetrated deep into the profile. If the measured water contents then represented a time many days earlier and some days after the rain, no reasonable calculation was possible. In such complex situations a soil water model had to be used to obtain water flows. Since the IPM method requires a pattern in the soil profile which is relatively constant between two occasions, a high time resolution was necessary for water content measurements. Water contents were measured with a neutron probe once a week but water potentials have been calculated from tensiometer measurements for five occasions every week.

Tensions at 15 cm depth for Ih 0, Ih II and Ih V indicated different degrees of drought during 1976 (Fig. 19). Since it was difficult to evaluate a zero flux plane at Ih 0, calculations have only been made for Ih II and Ih V. Evapotranspiration at Ih 0 was instead obtained from a soil water model (see Halldin *et al.*, 1980).

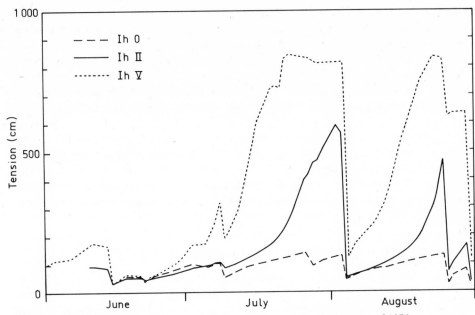

Figure 19. Tension at 15 cm depth in three different stands during the summer of 1976.

Table 7. Evapotranspiration calculated with the water balance method accumulated over two periods during the growing season 1976. Values within parentheses are daily means. All values are in mm. Precipitation was 25 mm during the first and 35 mm during the second period.

Calculations based on:		June 23–August 3 1976 41 days		August 3–24 1976 21 days	
		Ih II	Ih V	Ih II	Ih V
Neutron probe	Evapotranspiration	60	65	30	32
		(1.5)	(1.6)	(1.4)	(1.5)
	Percolation at 90 cm depth	10	10	10	4
		(0.2)	(0.2)	(0.5)	(0.2)
Tensiometers	Evapotranspiration	61	86	33	50
		(1.5)	(2.1)	(1.6)	(2.4)
	Percolation at 90 cm depth	10	10	10	4
		(0.2)	(0.2)	(0.5)	(0.2)
Penman evapotranspiration		270		118	
		(6.5)		(5.6)	
Penman-Monteith evapotranspiration					
for $r_s = 100$ s m^{-1}		200		88	
		(4.5)		(2.1)	
for $r_s = 200$ s m^{-1}		131		60	
		(3.2)		(2.9)	
for $r_s = 300$ s m^{-1}		97		46	
		(2.4)		(2.2)	

The mature pine stand, Ih V, showed higher evapotranspiration than the 20-year-old stand Ih II (Table 7). The clear-cut area, Ih 0, had a much lower evapotranspiration than the other two stands.

Penman's formula has no direct applicability to forests like those at Ivantjärnsheden (Table 7) but the obtained values serve as references. The best agreement between calculated and measured evapotranspiration was obtained when the Penman–Monteith formula (Monteith, 1965) was used. The choice of $r_s = 300$ s m^{-1} gave values of the same order as those measured. Since r_s in this case was considered to be constant with time, the evapotranspiration should be considered as potential, i.e., soil moisture was not a limiting factor. It is, however, evident from measured tensions (Fig. 19) that soil moisture could have been a considerable limiting factor for evapotranspiration at Ih V, especially during the first drought period. Consequently, calculated evapotranspiration should be considered as a rough estimate which only gives an idea of the magnitude.

Atmospheric CO_2-measurements above and within stands

Measurements of atmospheric CO_2 made at the Institute of Meteorology in Stockholm are mainly done to study the seasonal variations and the general trend for CO_2 to increase in the free atmosphere (Bischof, 1970, 1975). Samples collected from commercial aircraft on a global scale give background values. Some results shown in Fig. 20 demonstrate the rapid and accelerating increase which occurred from 1963

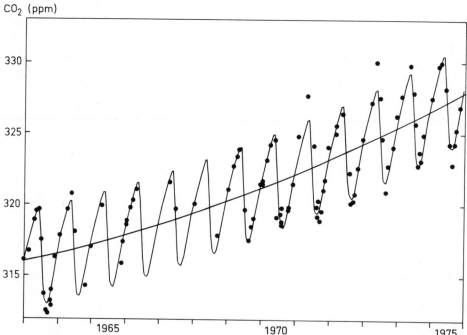

Figure 20. Seasonal variation and trend for CO_2 to increase in the upper troposphere (Northern hemisphere). From Bischof (1977).

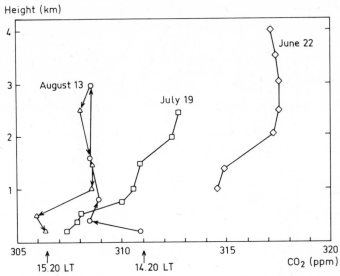

Figure 21. Vertical CO_2-profiles in eastern Central Sweden (Skå) during the summer of 1963.

to 1975 and the seasonal variations which can still be measured far away from sources and sinks located on the earth's surface (Bischof, 1977). The increase rate, which is in fair agreement with data obtained from the Mauna Loa and South Pole stations, is of special interest for considerations concerning the atmospheric radiation balance. However, in predicting a possible climate change with regard to an increasing CO_2 content and as a result of combustion of fossil fuels, the role of the oceans and the biosphere is of fundamental importance. There is reason to believe that the interaction between the atmosphere and these two reservoirs is not fully comprehended. Measurements within and above areas for sources and sinks should be made in order to obtain vertical gradients and to study exchange and transport processes in the atmosphere.

The study of vertical CO_2 fluxes within and above a forest stand from the meteorological mast at Ih V was included in the SWECON project. It was hoped to extend the measurements with samples from a light aircraft in order to obtain profiles from the forest ground to the free atmosphere, since earlier measurements made from light aircraft (Fig. 21) functioned satisfactorily.

The data collection at Ih V was connected to the computer system. The results (Fig. 22) represent the well-known diurnal variation during the summer season and are of about the same order as those reported, for example, by Baumgartner (1969). Similar results have been obtained in the Velen project, some 250 km south of Jädra-ås. However, the Jädraås data clearly show smaller gradients in daytime during the summer season, whereas larger gradients exist in the Velen data throughout the whole vegetation period, which is probably due to differences between the two investigated areas.

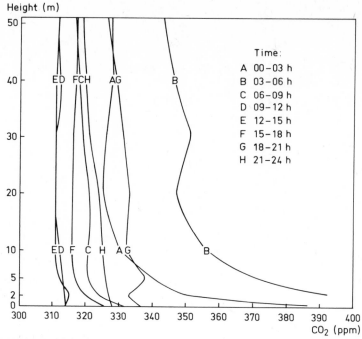

Figure 22. Vertical distribution of CO_2 in and above the mature stand Ih V on 28 August 1975.

Interception

Interception loss in the canopy was calculated as the difference between precipitation in the open and throughfall in the stand. The forest canopy above the troughs was documented by fish-eye photos evaluated for the degree of canopy cover in different zenith angles and in different directions (Fig. 23). Together with wind velocity measurements it should be possible to distinguish between throughfall emanating from parts of the canopy with different degrees of cover. Storms with different wind directions caught in the two troughs resulted in a sample of precipitation/thoughfall relations related to the documented distribution of canopy cover. Parameters deduced from these relations will probably enable generalization to other pine stands.

The first step in the analysis was to plot cumulated precipitation *versus* cumulated throughfall (Leyton *et al.*, 1967; Rutter *et al.*, 1971). The lines for saturated and unsaturated interception storage were fitted graphically (Fig. 24). It is obvious that the fit cannot be absolute, as errors like different rain intensity over the forest and the open, evaporation from interception storage, etc., are involved. Degrees of canopy cover obtained from fish-eye photographs (Table 8) were, however, fairly similar to the estimated ones.

The instantaneous release from a stand is related to canopy structure. Rutter *et al.* (1971) suggested the drainage rate to be described by:

$$D = D_s \exp[b(C - S)] \tag{37}$$

108

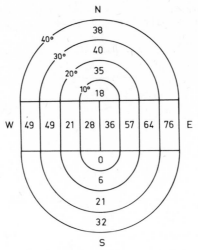

Figure 23. Degree of canopy cover (%) in different zenith angles as evaluated from fish-eye photos from trough no. 1 in the mature stand Ih V.

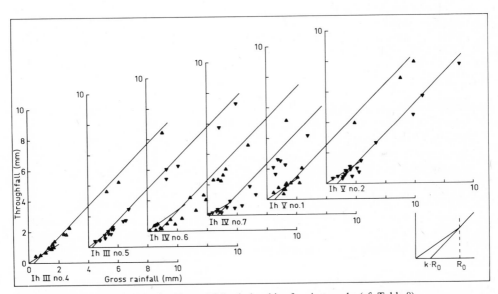

Figure 24. Cumulated precipitation/throughfall relationships for six troughs (cf. Table 8).

where D is drip, D_s is drip when $C = S$, where C is actual storage in canopy and S is canopy storage capacity. Rutter *et al.* argue that it is possible to estimate D_s and b only during periods when the canopy is draining after a storm, since the change in storage, C, during a time unit (in their case 5 min) may otherwise be considerable. On the other hand, they determined the storage at the end of a storm by running water balance calculations, involving estimation of evaporation. The systematic

Table 8. Storage capacities for canopy ($k \cdot R_0$) for covered part of canopy (R_0) and degree of canopy cover (k) estimated from data in Fig. 24. The degree of canopy cover obtained from fish-eye photographs (k').

Stand	Trough no.	$k \cdot R_o$	R_o	k	k'
Ih III	4	0.35	0.85	0.41	0.44
	5	0.25	0.95	0.26	0.29
Ih IV	6	0.72	2.20	0.33	–
	7	0.65	1.40	0.46	–
Ih V	1	0.50	1.50	0.30	0.32
	2	0.75	1.95	0.38	0.55

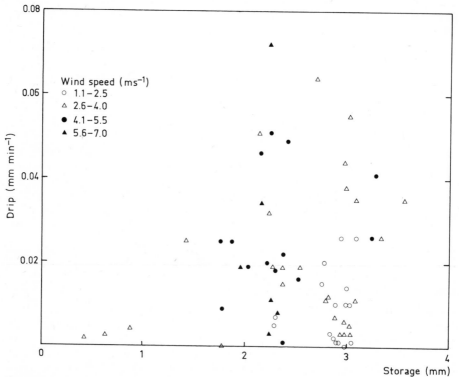

Figure 25. Relationship between storage and release of water for the storm from September 6, 18.30, to September 7, 05.30, 1977, as measured in trough no. 7 in Ih IV.

error in these calculations will give a maximal error in computed storage after a rain, so their choice of calculation period cannot be optimal.

To avoid the prediction of a finite drainage from a dry canopy inherent in the Rutter drainage function, Calder (1977) suggested a threshold formulation:

$$D = D_s \exp[b(C-S)] \qquad\qquad C > C_0 \qquad\qquad\qquad\qquad (38)$$

$$D = 0 \qquad\qquad\qquad\qquad C \leq C_0 \qquad\qquad\qquad\qquad (39)$$

where C_0 was the threshold value, but a more general expression would be:

$$D = a[\exp(b \cdot C) - 1] \qquad\qquad\qquad\qquad\qquad (40)$$

where a and b are parameters. Eq. (40) excludes the drainage when the canopy is dry but still accepts a finite drainage when the storage is small.

The relationship between storage and release was studied in detail for one storm with 18.6 mm precipitation (Fig. 25). The storage C was calculated by the running water balance method accounting for a mean evaporation rate of 0.002 mm min^{-1}. The total evaporation during the storm was calculated as the difference between total precipitation and total throughfall. Additional correction was made for stemflow (0.5% of precipitation) and canopy storage at the end of the storm (0.65 mm). The scatter is considerable and more data are needed for a relevant curve fitting. There is a weak dependence of drainage on wind speed, measured as 10 min means. If wind speed is to be included in equation (40), it will affect the parameter b.

At Ih V about 20% of the summer precipitation was lost by evaporation of intercepted water during 1974, so predictions of interception loss had a considerable influence on water balance calculations.

Snow accumulation and melt

The intention with the snow measurements was to give estimates of snow depth, density and water equivalent for each stand on a daily basis from which, for instance, daily infiltration could be calculated. The network and sampling programme was designed to achieve the intentions with reasonable costs.

The time series $U_{i,t}$, from Ih V, where measurements of snow depth and density were made on eight spots, each day preceded by snowfall or melt, were interpolated by disregarding ageing and other changes during periods without snowfall or melt. Between two measurements snow depth and snow density were left constant and equal to the former value.

The results from the snow surveys, $V_{i,t}$, every fortnight showed comparatively small sampling errors. The interpolation of these to daily values were made by forcing the continuous time series in Ih V through the mean values of the snow surveys (Fig. 26).

It was suggested that the ratio $V_{i,t}/U_{i,t}$ changed linearly between the snow surveys. The interpolation formula used to construct a continuous time series is:

$$V_{i,t_1+\tau} = \left(\frac{V_{i,t_1}}{U_{i,t_1}} \cdot \frac{\tau}{t_2-t_1} + \frac{V_{i,t_2}}{U_{i,t_2}} \cdot \frac{t_2-t_1-\tau}{t_2-t_1} \right) \cdot U_{i,t_1+\tau} \qquad\qquad (41)$$

where i denotes the type of measurement (e.g., snow depth or snow density), t_j is time for snow survey j ($j=1,2$), U and V are time series from the intensive plot at Ih V and the snow survey in any stand, respectively.

The total variance of the interpolated time series were derived using the theory outlined by Eriksson (1972).

If $V_{i,t_1+\tau}/U_{i,t_1+\tau}$ denotes the true value of the ratio at time $t_1+\tau$ and the expression within parentheses in Eq (41) the estimated value, the difference $\varepsilon_{i,t_1+\tau}$ is defined by:

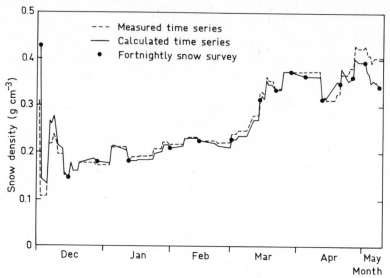

Figure 26. Snow density during the winter of 1976–77 in the mature stand Ih V.

$$\varepsilon_{t_1+\tau} = z_{t_1+\tau} - \left(z_{t_1} \cdot \frac{\tau}{t_2-t_1} + z_{t_2} \cdot \frac{t_2-t_1-\tau}{t_2-t_1} \right) \tag{42}$$

where $z = V/U$, $\varepsilon_{t_1+\tau}$ expresses the interpolation error. Using E[ ] for expectation:

$$E[\bar{\varepsilon}_{t_1}] = \frac{1}{t_2-t_1} - E\left[\sum_{\tau=0}^{t_2-t_1} \varepsilon_{t_1+\tau} \right] \tag{43}$$

which means that the expected value of the interpolation error is zero.

If stationarity is assumed the index t_1 can be chosen arbitrarily. The variance of $\bar{\varepsilon}_t$ can then be defined as:

$$\mathrm{Var}(\bar{\varepsilon}_t) = E[\bar{\varepsilon}_t^2] = E\left[\left\{ z_{t_1+\tau} - \left(z_{t_1} \cdot \frac{\tau}{t_2-t_1} + z_{t_2} \cdot \frac{t_2-t_1-\tau}{t_2-t_1} \right) \right\}^2 \right] \tag{44}$$

Let $a_1 = \dfrac{\tau}{t_2-t_1}$ and $a_2 = \dfrac{t_2-t_1-\tau}{t_2-t_1}$. Then (44) becomes:

$$\mathrm{Var}(\bar{\varepsilon}_t) = E[(z_{t_1+\lambda} - a_1 z_{t_1} - a_2 z_{t_2})^2] =$$

$$= E[z_{t_1+}^2 + a_1^2 z_{t_1}^2 + a_2^2 z_{t_2}^2 - 2a_1 z_{t_1+\tau} z_{t_1} - 2a_2 z_{t_1+\tau} z_{t_2} + 2a_1 a_2 z_{t_1} z_{t_2}] \tag{45}$$

The expectations can be estimated from the autocorrelation function, r_t:

$$\mathrm{Var}(\bar{\varepsilon}_t) = C_0(1 + a_1^2 + a_2^2 - 2a_1 r_{t_1+\tau,t_1} - 2a_2 r_{t_1+\tau,t_2} + 2a_1 a_2 r_{t_1,t_2}) \tag{46}$$

where C_0 is Var (z). Equation (46) was used to calculate the total variance of the interpolated time series $V_{i,t+\tau}$ as:

$$\mathrm{Var}(V_{i,t+\tau}) = \mathrm{Var}(V_{i,t}) + \mathrm{Var}(\bar{\varepsilon}_{i,t+\tau}) \tag{47}$$

112

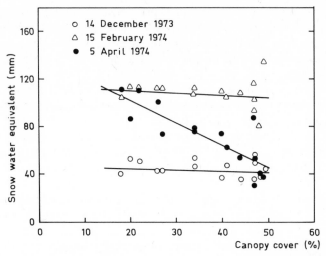

Figure 27. Snow water equivalent in relation to canopy cover in 0–40° zenith angle in the mature stand Ih V.

To get a preliminary insight into the causalities of within-stand variation and its development, water equivalent was plotted against mean degree of canopy cover in the interval 0–40 degrees zenith angle above the sampling spots (Fig. 27).

A suggested interpretation of Fig. 27 is that snow accumulation was unaffected by crown density in the relatively open stand of Ih V. Turbulence below canopy seemed to be strong enough to make the air mass within the stand homogeneous regarding snow flake content.

Later in the season there was a clear dependence of water equivalent on degree of canopy cover. This was accentuated as the season advanced and could be explained as horizontal variability in net long-wave radiation and/or back radiation from stems. Drip from melting snow in the canopy might also have been of importance.

Soil water flow and hydraulic conductivity

Most of the data from field soils have been computed with the instantaneous profile method (IPM) and with the crust test procedure. Many authors have used the instantaneous profile method described by Klute (1972) while others (Bouma *et al.*, 1971; Bouma & Denning, 1972; Bouma, 1973) have used the crust test procedure. This section deals with a field experiment where the IPM was used. The method was applied in a layered soil with an upper layer of fine-medium sand and a lower layer of coarse sand (Ih II and Ih V). In an earlier experiment at Jädraås in 1976 (Jansson, 1977) only measurements of soil water content were performed, whereas in the present experiment both water content and water potential were measured. The measured conductivities were compared with values calculated according to the Brooks & Corey (1964) method which is based on soil moisture characteristics and a measured value of saturated conductivity. A description of the Brooks & Corey method is given by Halldin *et al.* (1980).

Double metal cylinders with radius 0.75 and 2.5 m, respectively, were used for the

113

experiment on a special plot. The cylinders prevented lateral soil water flow down to a depth of about 45 cm. For neutron probe measurements tubes were installed with one in the inner area (1.5 m deep) and two in the outer area (0.75 m deep). In both areas sets of tensiometers were installed at 15 cm intervals from 15 cm down to 90 cm depth.

No data on texture or moisture characteristics were available for the conductivity plot. However, data from soil cores taken in pits around the plot showed a very clear pattern with a finely textured upper layer and a coarser lower layer (see Axelsson & Bråkenhielm, 1980, Fig. 8). Data on soil moisture characteristics were also available from the pits (Halldin et al., 1980, Fig. 9), which were taken 100–300 m from the plot. The saturated conductivity was measured on the undisturbed soil cores from these pits.

The experiment started by irrigating with 150–250 mm per day during three days after which the whole plot was covered with a plastic sheet to prevent evapotranspiration and precipitation infiltration. Measurements of water content and water potential were made during a period of 23 days with a small time interval (one hour) at the start of the period and an interval of about one week at the end. This procedure created conditions to which the instantaneous profile method could be applied. Using a cubic spline method all water content values were fitted to a suitable curve to get appropriate integrals between arbitrary depths in the profile. The applicability of spline functions for soil water calculations have been reported by Erh (1972). The pressure head gradient was obtained both with a spline function, with a polygon method (Flühler & Richard, 1977), and with the assumption of a unit gradient, i.e., the drainage was caused by gravitational forces and no gradients in matric potential occurred. Water content values were obtained directly from measurements with the neutron probe and indirectly from tensions and the corresponding soil moisture characteristics.

The unsaturated conductivity according to the Brooks & Corey method is given by:

$$K = K_{sat}(\psi_a/\psi)^{2 + (2 + n)\lambda} \tag{48}$$

where K_{sat} = saturated conductivity, ψ_a = air entry tension, ψ = water tension, n = parameter and λ = pore size distribution index. This expression was used with n chosen as 1.5 for the upper finely textured layer and 0.5 for the lower coarser layer. These values for n were chosen since they gave the best fit with measurements (Fig. 28). Conductivities obtained with the assumption of a unit gradient were not well correlated with the Brooks & Corey method (Fig. 28A). Better agreement was obtained by using measured pressure head gradients (Fig. 28B).

Proper calculation of conductivities from a heterogeneous soil profile must be based on measured gradients of pressure head since a unit gradient will not develop in heterogeneous soil profiles (Miller, 1973). The differences which remain (see Fig. 28B) between the Brooks & Corey method and the measured conductivities can be interpreted in several ways. The following sources of error can be found in the instantaneous profile method:

(1) Inaccuracy of measured changes in water content.
(2) Poor representativity of tensiometer measurements.
(3) Inexact calculations of pressure head gradients.

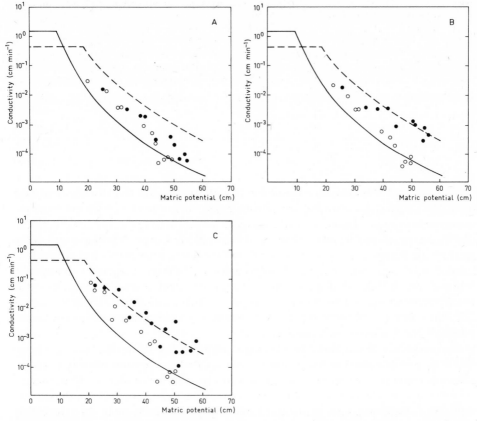

Figure 28. Conductivity at depths of 30 (●) and 60 cm (○), calculated with unit gradients (A), with measured pressure head gradients (B and C), with water contents obtained from neutron probe measurements (A and B) and from tensiometer measurements and soil moisture characteristics (C). Conductivity obtained by the Brooks & Corey method at 30 cm (broken line) and 60 cm (solid line).

(4) Difficulty in controlling boundary conditions.

(5) Omittance of lateral water flows.

Errors involved in the use of the Brooks & Corey theory will not be discussed here. The different representativity of the soil cores and the different levels in the conductivity plot, were enough to explain the difference between conductivities obtained with the two methods.

Using only tensiometer measurements the water content values were calculated from soil moisture characteristics and from the corresponding tensions (Fig. 28C). The measured pressure head gradients were used in the same manner as above. The patterns in Figs. 28B and 28C are similar. The tendency seems to be that calculations based on measurements with tensiometers overestimated the conductivities. Since a new source of error was introduced in the calculation of water content from measurements of tensions, the best way seemed to be to rely on calculations of water contents from the neutron probe measurements.

Table 9. Vertical and horizontal pressure head gradients in cm cm^{-1} at different depths beneath the layer where horizontal flows were stopped by metal sheets.

Depths	6 Sept. 1977		7 Sept. 1977		23 Sept. 1977	
	Vertical	Horizontal	Vertical	Horizontal	Vertical	Horizontal
45 cm	0.86	−0.01	0.44	0.06	0.52	0.09
60 cm	1.05	−0.03	1.34	−0.07	1.32	−0.09
90 cm	1.10	−0.03	0.87	0.06	0.52	0.09

Baker *et al.* (1974) have referred to errors with tensiometer measurements caused by water accumulation around the porous cups. Such a tendency should have influenced the calculated conductivities in Fig. 28C by increasing the difference between the instantaneous profile method and that of Brooks & Corey. A more serious error was the calculation of pressure head gradients from tensiometer measurements. In a layered soil the gradients commonly approach zero. In this experiment a gradient of 1:10 was found. If the gradient approaches zero the calculations of conductivity will be extremely sensitive. The instantaneous profile method could, thus, not be used to calculate accurate conductivities at all depths in a layered soil even if gradient measurements were made with tensiometers.

The problem of lateral water flow increases rapidly when the vertical pressure head gradient approaches zero. A small horizontal gradient in tension can cause a considerable amount of water in a lateral flow in this case. Since there is no barrier of avoiding lateral flow beneath 45 cm depth, it may have serious effects on the experiment. Measured horizontal gradients (Table 9) were, however, small compared with vertical gradients.

The requirement of controlled boundary conditions, i.e., no water flow at ground level, seemed to be a technical problem. With a watertight plastic sheet completely covering the plot, no flow could occur.

Brooks & Corey (1964) have the n value in the conductivity expression (Eq. 48) inherently equal to one. Mualem (1976) suggested an n value of 0.5 to be optimal. This experiment confirmed that n can differ from one and might also vary with depth in a layered soil profile. The n value of 0.5 for the lower layer, which gave the best fit with measured values, should be considered as more accurate than the $n = 1.5$ for the upper, since the latter included greater uncertainties in gradient estimates.

Soil heat flow

Different methods have been proposed and used to obtain soil heat flows under field conditions. Reviews are given by Tanner (1963) and Kimball & Jackson (1975). A calorimetric method combined with a calculated flow caused by a temperature gradient and an estimated conductivity at a fixed reference level in the soil is described here. A similar method for calculating surface heat flow has been used by Kimball *et al.* (1976b). They also showed (Kimball *et al.*, 1976a) that de Vries' (1963) theory overestimated conductivity in the soil compared to the null-alignment method developed by Kimball & Jackson (1975). With the null-alignment method conductivity at a reference level is calculated by using a zero flux plane developed above the reference level at some time during the day. The calculated conductivity is then used, together with temperature gradients, to get appropriate heat flows during the whole day at the reference level. Above this level a calorimetric method was used to obtain the heat flows. The calculations made in this paper are based on thermal conductivities obtained by a null-alignment method which ignores latent heat flow, since the temperatures at the reference level are generally too low to create latent heat flows. The reference level was chosen at a depth where the daily temperature variations were small, the surface flows then became rather insensitive to changes in conductivity at that level.

Since no soil water content measurements with acceptable resolutions in time and space were available for vapour flow calculations, no attempts were made to calculate thermal or isothermal vapour flows here. Soil water content measurements were used in the calculations of heat content. Small temporal changes in water content would not be explained by vapour flows since the soil profile was not prevented from water uptake by roots.

Other methods to calculate heat flows in soil make use of measurements with heat flux plates or involve simple calculations of temperature gradients in combination with a known conductivity. None of these methods are able to account for heat flows due to gradients in vapour pressure. The heat flux plates disturb the water movement and may also be inaccurate due to poor contact with the soil. The disadvantage with the temperature gradient method is the difficulty to measure temperature gradients accurately and also to know thermal conductivities which vary with temperature and water content. Probes for measuring thermal conductivity are described by Jackson & Taylor (1965) and Fritton et al. (1974).

The heat capacities are calculated as the weighed sum of the different soil constituents:

$$C_H = \sum_{i=1}^{n} X_i C_i \tag{49}$$

where C_H = heat capacity of the soil, X_i = volume fractions, and C_i = heat capacities, of the different constituents. The contributing constituents are organic material, inorganic material and water. The heat content is given by the product of temperature and heat capacity. Calculations were made with cubic spline polynomials to integrate heat contents in arbitrary soil layers.

The next step in the calorimetric method is to calculate changes in heat storage over time. The flow can then be calculated if a fixed boundary condition is given anywhere in the soil profile. Temperature gradients obtained with a cubic spline method give the direction of the heat flow. When the gradient changes sign anywhere in the profile, a zero flux plane is created and this plane can be used as a fixed boundary condition. If no zero flux plane is found, the calculation of heat flow uses the bottom of the profile as a fixed boundary condition. The calculation of the boundary heat flow is based on the temperature gradient and on the calculated conductivity.

Calculations of soil heat flow were made during six days in July 1976. Temperature variations during these days (Fig. 29) were measured with sensors situated at different depths in the soil profile within Ih V.

117

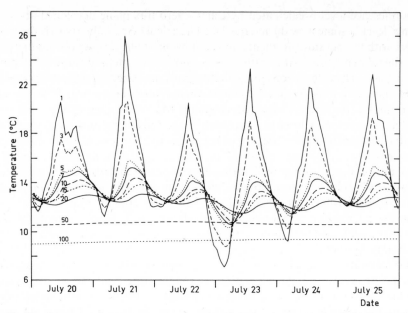

Figure 29. Hourly mean soil temperatures measured at Ih V for six days during 1976. Depth (in cm) below soil surface is defined from where irradiance ceases. The values at 1, 3 and 5 cm are means of three sensors and the values at 7 and 10 cm are means based on two sensors.

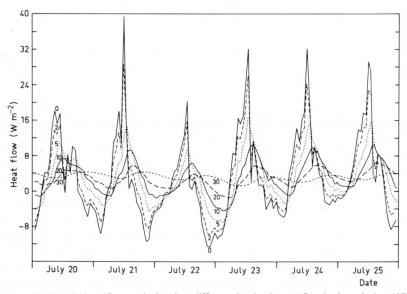

Figure 30. Hourly heat flows calculated at different depths (in cm) for six days during 1976.

118

Water contents were measured with the capacitance technique at the beginning and end of the period. Since no drastic changes occurred, a linear interpolation was used to get appropriate water contents during the whole period.

The method of calculating heat fluxes was first used with a zero flux plane as boundary condition when it occurred in the profile and with a calculated heat flow at the lower boundary when no zero flux plane occurred. The result showed a slight tendency of discontinuity when the method altered between the different boundary conditions. The most reliable results (Fig. 30) were obtained when a calculated heat flow at the bottom of the considered profile was used as boundary condition during the whole period. The calculation of thermal conductivity at the bottom of the profile was then obtained in a previous step, when a zero flux plane existed. An average of thermal conductivities obtained during the period was used to calculate the heat flow at the bottom of the profile.

Acknowledgements

The present study was mainly carried out as a teamwork. K. Perttu coordinated the research. The main responsibilities in the present paper were: K. Perttu: Global radiation above and below canopy, Albedo above the canopy, Estimation of evapotranspiration; W. Bischof: Measurements of CO_2, Atmospheric CO_2-measurements above and within stands; H. Grip: Measurement of interception, Measurement of snow and frost in the soil, Estimation of evapotranspiration, Interception, Snow accumulation and melt; P-E. Jansson: Measurement of soil water, Evapotranspiration calculated with the water balance method, Soil water flow and hydraulic conductivity, Soil heat flow; Å. Lindgren: Estimated global radiation, Evapotranspiration calculated with the energy balance method; A. Lindroth: Measurement of local climate, Biometeorological measurements, Micrometeorological measurements, Potential global radiation and daylength, Albedo above the canopy, In- and out-going long-wave radiation; B. Norén: Biometeorological measurements, Micrometeorological measurements. The authors are indebted to S. Halldin, who has been involved in the planning work and in the discussions of results from the modeller's viewpoint. The authors are also grateful to E. Henningsson, E. Lindquist, L. Löthman and S. Ramström for their work in doing different kinds of observations and measurements.

References

Anderson, M. C. 1964. Studies of the woodland light climate. I. The photographic computation of light conditions. – J. Ecol. 52: 27–41.

Ångström, A. 1956. On the computation of global radiation from records of sunshine. – Arkiv för Geofysik 22: 471–479.

Axelsson, B. & Bråkenhielm, S. 1980. Investigation sites of the Swedish Coniferous Forest Project – biological and physiographical features. – In: Persson, T. (ed.) Structure and Function of Northern Coniferous Forests – An Ecosystem Study, Ecol. Bull. (Stockholm) 32: 25–64.

Baker, F. G., Veneman, P. L. M. & Bouma, J. 1974. Limitations of the instantaneous profile method for field measurement of unsaturated hydraulic conductivity. – Soil. Sci. Soc. Amer. Proc. 38: 885–888.

Baumgartner, A. 1969. Meteorological approach to the exchange of CO_2 between the atmosphere and vegetation. – Photosynthetica 3(2): 127–149.

119

Bischof, W. 1970. CO_2 measurements from aircraft. – Tellus 22: 545–549.

Bischof, W. 1975. Measurements of atmospheric CO_2. – Swed. Conif. For. Proj., Tech. Rep. 1: 98–107.

Bischof, W. 1977. Comparability of CO_2 measurements. – Tellus 29: 435–444.

Bischof, W. & Odh, S-A. 1976. CO_2 measurements within and above a Scots pine stand. – Swed. Conif. For. Proj. Int. Rep. 45, 18 pp.

Bouma, J. 1973. Use of physical methods to expand soil survey interpretations of soil drainage conditions. – Soil Sci. Soc. Amer. Proc. 37: 413–421.

Bouma, J. & Denning, Y. L. 1972. Field measurement of unsaturated hydraulic conductivity by infiltration through gypsum crusts. – Soil Sci. Soc. Amer. Proc. 36: 846–847.

Bouma, J., Hillel, D. I., Hole, F. D. & Amerman, C. R. 1971. Field measurements of unsaturated hydraulic conductivity by infiltration through artificial crusts. – Soil Sci. Soc. Amer. Proc. 35: 362–364.

Bråkenhielm, S. 1978. Ivantjärnsheden, Jädraås, – regional physiography and description of the research area. – Swed. Conif. For. Proj. Tech. Rep. 16, 58 pp.

Brooks, R. H. & Corey, A. T. 1964. Hydraulic properties of porous media. – Colorado State University, Fort Collins, Hydrology Paper 3, 27 pp.

Brunt, D. 1944. Physical and Dynamical Meteorology. London: Cambridge University Press, 428 pp.

Calder, I. R. 1977. A model of transpiration and interception loss from a spruce forest in Plynlimon, central Wales. – J. Hydrol. 33: 247–265.

Engelbrecht, B. & Svensson, J. 1978. Data collection, storage, retrieval and analysis of continuous measurements. – Swed. Conif. For. Proj. Tech. Rep. 17, 47 pp.

Erh, K. T. 1972. Application of the spline function to soil science. – Soil Sci. 114: 333–338.

Eriksson, E. 1972. On design and operation of hydrologic networks. – In: Tollan, A. (ed.) Nordic Hydrological Conf. 1972, Sandefjord 6–8 Sept., Bind 1, pp. 285–302. Oslo.

Federer, C. A. 1970. Measuring forest evapotranspiration – theory and problems. – U.S.D.A. Forest Service Research Paper, NE-165, 25 pp.

Fritton, D. D., Busscher, W. Y. & Alpert, J. E. 1974. An inexpensive but durable thermal conductivity probe for field use. – Soil Sci. Soc. Amer. Proc. 38: 854–855.

Flühler, H. & Richard, F. 1977. Geometrische Interpolation von Saugspannungsverteilungen. – Z. Pflanzenern. Bodenk. 140: 571–578.

Geiger, R. 1961. Das Klima der Bodennahen Luftschicht. Ein Lehrbuch der Mikroklimatologie, 4. Auflage. Braunschweig: Friedr. Vieweg & Sohn, 646 pp.

Gemmel, P. & Perttu, K. 1978. Short wave radiation within a pine stand. Comparison between measured radiation and radiation calculated from fish-eye photographs. – Swed. Conif. For. Proj. Int. Rep. 76, 18 pp. (In Swedish, English abstract)

Grip, H., Halldin, S., Jansson, P-E., Lindroth, A., Norén, B. & Perttu, K. 1979. Discrepancy between energy and water balance estimates of evapotranspiration. – In: Halldin, S. (ed.) Comparison of Forest Water and Energy Exchange Models, pp. 237–255. Copenhagen: International Society for Ecological Modelling.

Halldin, S., Grip, H., Jansson, P-E. & Lindgren, Å. 1980. Micrometeorology and hydrology of pine forest ecosystems. II. Theories and models. – In: Persson T. (ed.) Structure and Function of Northern Coniferous Forests – An Ecosystem Study, Ecol. Bull. (Stockholm) 32: 463–503.

Jackson, R. D. & Taylor, S. A. 1965. Heat transfer. – In: Black, C. A. (ed.) Methods of Soil Analysis, Part 1, pp. 349–360. Agronomy 9, Madison, Wisconsin: American Society of Agronomy, Inc.

Jansson, P-E. 1977. Soil water studies within the Swedish Coniferous Forest Project. – Vannet i Norden 2: 18–27. (In Swedish)

Jansson, P-E. & Halldin, S. 1979. Model for annual water and energy flow in a layered soil. – In: Halldin, S. (ed.) Comparison of Forest Water and Energy Exchange Models, pp. 145–163. Copenhagen: International Society for Ecological Modelling.

Johnson, T. & Odin, H. Measurements of evapotranspiration using a dynamic lysimeter. – Stud. for. suec. 146, 29 pp.

de Jong, B. 1973. Net Radiation Received by a Horizontal Surface at the Earth. Delft University Press, 51 pp.

Kimball, B. A. & Jackson, R. D. 1975. Soil-heat flux determination: A null-alignment method. – Agric. Meteorol. 15: 1–9.

Kimball, B. A., Jackson, R. D., Reginato, R. Y., Nakayama, F. S. & Idso, S. B. 1976a. Comparison of field-measured and calculated soil-heat fluxes. – Soil Sci. Soc. Amer. J. 40: 18–25.

Kimball, B. A., Jackson, R. D., Nakayama, F. S., Idso, S. B. & Reginato, R. J. 1976b. Soil-heat flux determination: Temperature gradient method with computed thermal conductivities. – Soil Sci. Soc. Amer. J. 40: 25–28.

120

Klute, A. 1972. The determination of the unsaturated hydraulic conductivity and diffusivity of unsaturated soils. – Soil Sci. 113: 264–276.

Leyton, L., Reynolds, E. R. C. & Thompson, F. B. 1967. Rainfall interception in forests and moorland. – In: Sopper, W. E. & Lull, H. W. (eds.) Forest Hydrology, pp. 163–178. Oxford: Pergamon Press.

Liljequist, G. H. 1970. Klimatologi. Stockholm: Generalstabens Litografiska Anstalt, 427 pp.

Lindroth, A. 1978. Calibration of radiation meters. – Swed. Conif. For. Proj. Int. Rep. 81, 17 pp. (In Swedish, English abstract)

Lindroth, A. & Perttu, K. 1975. Routines for collecting, processing and reporting of standard climatic data. – Swed. Conif. For. Proj. Int. Rep. 26, 30 pp. (In Swedish, English abstract)

Lunelund, H. 1940. Bestrahlung verschieden orientierter Flächer in Finnland durch Sonne und Himmel. – Soc. Scient. Fenn., Comm. Phys. – Math. 10 (13), 28 pp.

Miller, D. E. 1973. Water relation and flow in layered soil profiles. – In: Bruce, R. R., Flach, K. W., Taylor, H. M., Stelly. M., Dinauer, R. C. & Hach, J. M. (eds.) Field Soil Water Regime, pp. 107–117. Madison, USA: Soil Sci. Soc. Amer., Inc.

Monteith, J. L. 1965. Evaporation and environment. – In: Fogg, G. E. (ed.) The State and Movement of Water in Living Organisms. – 19th Symp. Soc. exp. Biol., pp. 205–234. Cambridge: The Company of Biologists.

Mualem, Y. 1976. A new model for predicting the hydraulic conductivity of unsaturated porous media. – Water Resour. Res. 12: 513–522.

Penman, H. L. 1963. Vegetation and hydrology. – Tech. Comm. No 53. Commonwealth Agric. Bur., Farnham Royal, England.

Perttu, K., Lindgren, Å., Lindroth, A. & Norén, B. 1977. Micro- and biometeorological measurements at Jädraås. Instrumentation and measurement technics. – Swed. Conif. For. Proj. Tech. Rep. 7, 67 pp.

Rosenberg, N. J. 1974. Microclimate. The Biological Environment. New York–London–Sydney–Toronto: John Wiley & Sons, 315 pp.

Rutter, A. J., Kershaw, K. A., Robins, P. C. & Morton, A. J. 1971. A predictive model of rainfall interception in forest. 1. Derivation of the model from observations in a plantation of Corsican pine. – Agric. Meteorol. 9: 367–384.

Tanner, C. B. 1963. Basic instrumentation and measurements for plant environment and micrometeorology. – Soils Bull. 6, Dept. of Soil Sci., Univ. Wisconsin, Madison.

de Vries, D. A. 1963. Thermal properties of soils. – In: Van Wijk, W. R. (ed.) Physics of the Plant Environment, pp. 210–235. New York: John Wiley & Sons.

Persson, T. (ed) 1980
Structure and Function of Northern
Coniferous Forests – An Ecosystem Study
Ecol. Bull. (Stockholm) 32: 123–124.

STUDIES OF PLANT AND VEGETATION PROCESSES WITHIN THE SWEDISH CONIFEROUS FOREST PROJECT – AN INTRODUCTION

S. O. Falk[1]

Abstract

The main problems of plant and vegetation process studies within the Swedish Coniferous Project are presented as a general background to the papers presented in this volume.

Aims

The studies of plant and vegetation processes have been a central task of the Swedish Coniferous Forest Project (SWECON). A prime objective was to be able to understand and predict plant growth in a forest ecosystem context. The aims required an understanding of growth at three levels: the stand, the plant and the organ (shoot, needle, etc.) levels. One particular problem was that the time scales range from a stand rotation period of approximately 100 years down to minutes for studies of, for example, gaseous exchange. Therefore, simulation models of different time domains were to be developed.

Investigations

The investigations at Ivantjärnsheden, Central Sweden, were primarily carried out in an age series of Scots pine (*Pinus sylvestris* L.) stands. The structure and processes of these stands were studied under natural as well as under experimental conditions, mainly fertilization (complete nutrient solution) and irrigation. The latter experiment was intended to provide an opportunity to study plant processes under optimal conditions where water and mineral nutrients were not limiting factors.

The plant biomass with its seasonal dynamics provides an essential part of the ecosystem. The paper by Flower-Ellis & Persson supplies information on the distribution of various plant biomass fractions, which is a prerequisite for studies of gas exchange, growth and nutrient cycling. The contributions by Persson and that by

---

[1] Dept. of Plant Physiology, University of Göteborg, S-413 19 Göteborg, Sweden

Bråkenhielm & Persson give information on the biomass dynamics of trees and ground vegetation both above and below ground.

An understanding of primary production and plant growth also requires attention to physiological processes like photosynthesis, respiration and transpiration (Hellqvist, Hillerdal-Hagströmer & Mattson-Djos; Linder & Troeng) as well as assimilate dynamics (Ericsson & Persson), nutrient status (Aronsson & Elowson), nutrient uptake (Jensén & Pettersson), and water stress (Bengtson). The preliminary results concerning net primary production and carbohydrate metabolism imply that growth is more limited by other factors than carbohydrate production. This view was also supported by the fact that moderate consumption of roots and needles had very little influence on the annual growth (Larsson & Tenow; Magnusson & Sohlenius). However, the field studies of insect consumption and experiments simulating insect defoliation (Ericsson, Hellkvist, Hillerdal-Hagströmer, Larsson, Mattson-Djos & Tenow) have increased our knowledge of the mutual relationships between needle-eating insects and Scots pine.

The papers presented on plant processes illustrate approaches, methods and results mostly from individual investigations. Among the most unexpected results is the high production of fine roots, indicating rapid turnover. Using the information available for assimilate production, respiration and growth of various biomass fractions of a young Scots pine, Ågren, Axelsson, Flower-Ellis, Linder, Persson, Staaf & Troeng found that more than 50% of the assimilates formed was used for growth and maintenance of the root system.

Tree and stand growth was subjected to detailed analyses. In this volume Lohammar, Larsson, Linder & Falk present a model analysis of gas exchange in a short-term perspective, and Ågren & Axelsson report on a tree growth model with the time step of one day.

It is of interest to be able to generalize results from one site to a whole region. Therefore, the possibility of using traditional forest production data was investigated. A great number of production estimates with various treatments are available from the whole of Sweden, and as a first step Albrektson has tested the relationships between total tree production, estimated after separation into fractions, and conventional forestry production measures.

Plant and vegetation processes have been studied at many levels and on many time scales. Further work within the project will concentrate on synthesizing the data from the forests studied to obtain an integrated knowledge of these processes. The generalization of this knowledge will hopefully lead to possibilities to predict growth at the stand level, and also to predict the effects of forest fertilization and increased acid deposition in a long-term perspective.

Acknowledgements

I wish to thank my colleagues and friends in the project leading group, G. I. Ågren, F. Andersson, U. Lohm and K. Perttu for a very stimulating scientific co-operation in the project from the beginning to the end. S. Linder is especially thanked for all his help in the planning and organization of the plant process studies.

Persson, T. (ed.) 1980
Structure and Function of Northern
Coniferous Forests – An Ecosystem Study
Ecol. Bull. (Stockholm) 32: 125–138.

INVESTIGATION OF STRUCTURAL PROPERTIES AND DYNAMICS OF SCOTS PINE STANDS

J. G. K. Flower-Ellis[1] and H. Persson[2]

Abstract

An outline is given of the reasoning underlying the planning of studies of the structure and dynamics of the pine stands investigated within the Swedish Coniferous Forest Project. The progress of these studies is indicated and the extent to which the original aims have been fulfilled is evaluated. The studies have shown that an increase in the degree of detail in study of the dynamic relations within the ecosystem, as compared to normal practice hitherto, is essential to the understanding of the biology and ecology of the species composing it, hence to the understanding of ecosystem functioning.

Additional keywords: Fine-root biomass, fine-root production, forest ecosystem, litterfall, *Pinus sylvestris*, primary production.

Aims

The studies of biomass distribution and structure may be divided into two parts: those concerned with the structure of the stands at a given moment, i.e., a static description, and those concerned with the rate and direction of change within them. The second of these may be further subdivided into those studies describing the instantaneous rate of change, such as leading shoot and diameter growth, and those reconstructing the historical events of growth leading to the status of a stand at a given moment.

The structural description of a stand at a moment in time is a prerequisite to the description of most processes in the stand, e.g., mineral nutrient fluxes must be related to the total amounts present in the system. Such a description in itself, if related to stand age, provides information about the net rates of accretion of various stand components, although this information may be subject to serious shortcomings. The tree stand, as the dominating component of the forest ecosystem, may appear to be the natural unit for which changes are to be expressed, but many of the most important processes involved in the modelling of the functioning of the ecosystem can by no means be studied at stand level. Examples must suffice to illustrate this: studies of photosynthesis are primarily concerned with individual shoots of defined age and position within the crown; studies of the effects of consumption by insects (rather than the amount consumed) are similarly specific. Hence the degree of resolution in the structural description must be commensurate with these.

[1]Dept. of Forest Site Research, Swedish University of Agricultural Sciences, S–901 83 Umeå, Sweden
[2]Institute of Ecological Botany, Uppsala University, Box 559, S–751 22 Uppsala, Sweden

125

At the same time, the unity of the stand must not be forgotten. Highly detailed descriptions of growth and mortality, however clearly they may be related to a given order and age-class of shoot (Fig. 1), are valueless unless they can be extended to tree and finally to stand level. The studies of structure and growth in the Swedish Coniferous Forest Project (SWECON) were therefore designed to be applicable at three levels: (1) organ, i.e., needle, shoot, etc., (2) tree and (3) stand level, all within the context of an age sequence of stands. Those processes, such as litterfall, which by their nature must be studied at stand level, were to be connected nonetheless to processes at organ level, as will be illustrated below.

Similar reasoning was applied to the study of the field-layer vegetation, here mainly ericacaeous dwarf shrubs (Persson, 1979a). Modification of the approach was necessary, because of the number of species involved and because of their growth habit. For fractioning the shoots of the dwarf shrubs, the suggestions made by Mork (1946) and further developed by Mohamed & Gimingham (1970) and Chapman *et al.* (1975) were adopted. In short, the aim of the studies was to relate the biomass and production above and below ground of these shrubs to the age of tillers and rhizomes in the system, to derive figures for litterfall from observation of the number, dimensions and mortality rate of their organs, and finally, to demonstrate how all of these features were related to the time scale associated with the age sequence of stands.

For the fine roots, the problems of an approach at other than ecosystem level at first appeared almost insurmountable. In order to study the temporal and spatial distribution of such roots, it was necessary to extract soil cores of known area and volume at regular intervals during the growing season (Fig. 2). At the same time, it was considered so important to describe and quantify the temporal variation in fine-root biomass in relation to events above ground, preferably in relation to individual trees, that two experimental methods were adopted in addition to the programme of sampling from the stand at large. These were (a) root isolation of individual trees, (b) ingrowth experiments – the insertion of cores of sifted sand of local origin, enclosed in net cylinders, into holes made by the withdrawal of a soil core (cf. Fig. 3). Both of these involve more or less serious disturbance of the root systems of several trees, and as estimators of the amounts of biomass developed subsequently are open to objection. However, it was considered that they should be capable of revealing (a) the temporal variations in fine-root amount and unit weight, (b) the rate at which new fine roots were produced and died, or by diameter increment entered another class.

Implementing the aims

The methods adopted for study of the distribution of biomass were initially those familiar from the IBP projects, i.e., destructive sampling of trees and other plants, followed by their separation into fractions (cf. Newbould, 1967). The information thus obtained was used to construct estimative regressions (Fig. 4), which were applied, e.g,. to a stand diameter distribution, to obtain estimates per hectare of the amounts of various components. The same material was further processed to provide information about the number, distribution and dimensions of organs by

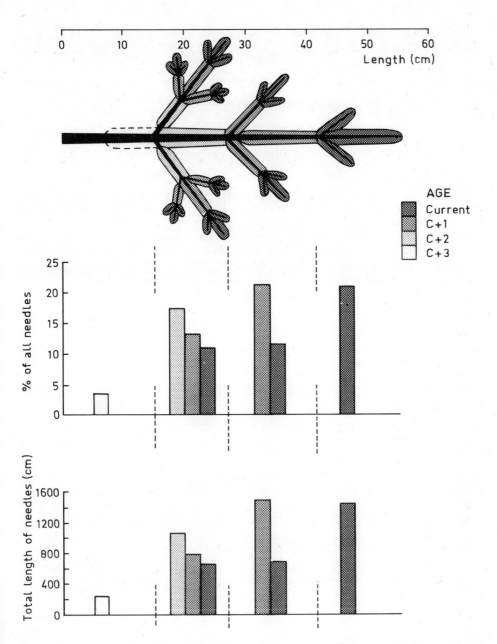

Figure 1. Example of distribution of needles along the first-order axis of a branch in the fourth whorl of a ca. 15-year-old Scots pine. Top: schematic representation of branch, showing distribution of needle age-classes. Middle: distribution of needles by zones from the tip of the first-order axis (delimited by dashed lines), per cent of all needles on mean branch by classes of age. Bottom: distribution of total length of needles by zones as above, by classes of age.

Figure 2. Root samples were extracted by means of a steel corer with an internal diameter of 6.7 cm at the hardened steel cutting edge. The diameter of the upper part of the tube was 2 mm larger, thus allowing the cores to be transferred into a plastic gutter by inversion of the corer.

Figure 3. Example of a root ingrowth container removed from the soil about a year after the establishment of the experiment. Surrounding roots and soil removed. The container consists of a net cylinder filled with sifted sand and having peat at the surface instead of raw humus. Such containers were placed in holes made by the withdrawal of soil cores (cf. Fig. 2).

128

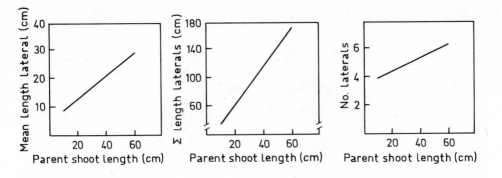

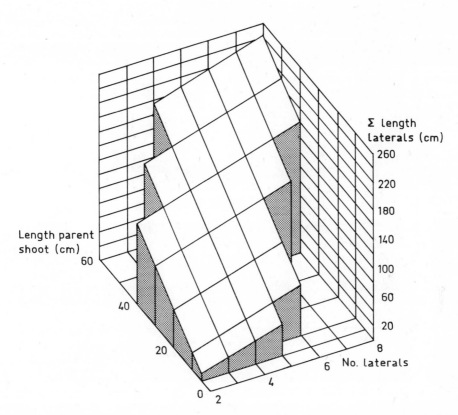

Figure 4. Some relationships illustrating the development of the crown of a young Scots pine. Above: examples of the interplay between the length and number of first-order laterals in the topmost whorl, and the length of the parent shoot (previous year's leader). Below: summary diagram of the above relationships. The gaps in the block diagram indicate that short parent shoots bore few, relatively short laterals, while long parent shoots usually bore a larger number of laterals of greater mean length.

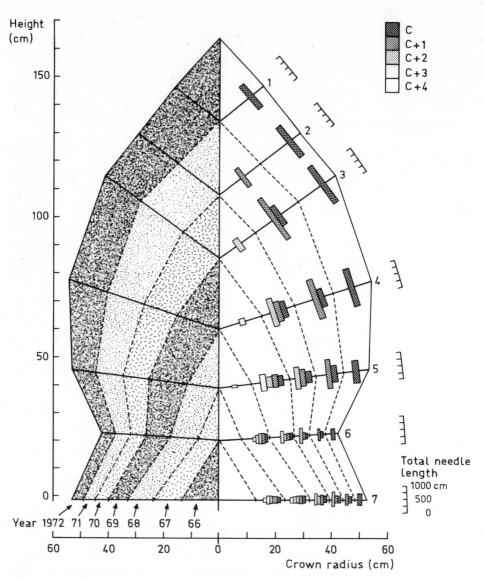

Figure 5. Development of crown form and distribution of needle length by age-classes in a ca. 15-year-old Scots pine. Left: development of successive "shells" of the crown by growth of leading shoot and first-order axes. Note the increasing length of both, and the paraboloid form of the crown. Right: distribution of needle length, by age-classes, within the "shells". Total needle length on any branch reaches a maximum in whorl 4, cf. Fig. 1. The structure shown here forms the starting-point for calculation of a carbon budget for the tree.

strata or classes of age. This latter information was intended to be applied both to the refinement of the stand description, and to estimation of the rates of change in organs, e.g., current shoot production, diameter and weight increment, needle weight change and mortality rate (Flower-Ellis *et al.*, 1976).

From description of the stands at a single point in time, as outlined above,

130

Proportions of needles
(% weight)

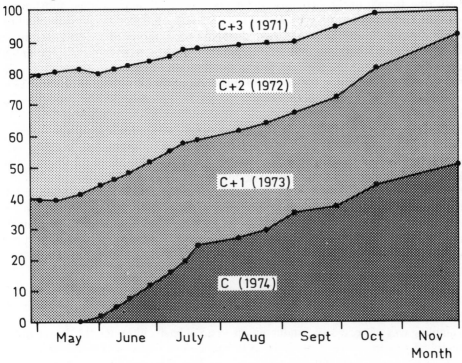

Figure 6. Changes in the relative proportions of needles of different age in whorl 4 during the growing season, expressed as the weight of a single needle of each age-class multiplied by the number of needles present in that age-class. Needle mortality taken into account. This is a further constituent in the carbon budget.

sampling was continued to discover rates of change during a single year, in this case for defined organs, sampled in such a way as to be representative for individual trees. This destructive sampling was complemented with non-destructive measurement of shoot growth and diameter growth, the aim being to establish time-specific relationships between non-destructive measurements of some readily accessible character, e.g., shoot length, and less readily accessible characters, such as shoot weight, needle number, needle area. With the application of these relationships in mind, tree structure was expressed in terms of numbers and dimensions of components, as well as in more conventional weight terms (Fig. 5).

One of the most striking features of conifers, and indeed of many evergreen plants, including the dwarf shrubs of the field-layer, is the extent to which the needles or leaves are utilised as storage organs for carbohydrates (cf. Ericsson, 1978). This function gives rise to substantial (16–28% of dry weight) variation in the unit weight of a needle during the year, and, to a lesser extent, that of shoots too (Fig. 6). It is evident that this variation may have several consequences, among which only a few need be mentioned: (a) that biomass estimates made at different times in the year will be affected, (b) consequently, that other estimates using dry weight as a base must be adjusted, (c) that growth in the sense adopted here (the formation of structural elements, i.e., excluding storage substances) must be corrected for the presence of the reserves. Thus the weight increment of, e.g., a shoot during the year, was conceived of in terms of the increase in its weight per unit length per unit time, separated into xylem and "bark", excluding reserves. Given the number and length distribution of such shoots on a tree, the total structural accretion for shoots of this class might be estimated. Estimates at this level of resolution were considered to be essential to the modelling of structural carbon allocation.

This type of study, in varying degrees of detail, was applied to all age stages of stand and to the dwarf shrubs. Similarly, roots of different size classes were processed in such a way that not only dry weight (Figs. 5 and 7–9), but also length, weight per unit length and volume would be available. This, in combination with studies of reserve substances, would indicate how the tree allocated its fixed carbon, both above and below ground. It is clear that the problems of estimating the amount and distribution of root biomass are far more formidable than those of making similar estimates above ground; nevertheless, the effort had to be made to provide material of a similar degree of detail to that available from the aerial parts of the system.

Study of other processes in the stand, such as litterfall (Fig. 10), was planned as an integral part of the biomass studies. Here again, estimates were expressed, as far as possible, in terms of the numbers and unit weights of organs per unit time. Sampling was of necessity conducted on an areal basis, although the design of the sampling system made it possible to introduce estimates of the contribution of individual trees. Litterfall studies integrated in this way made it possible to regard, e.g., needle litter not solely as an input into a decomposer or mineralisation cycle, but also as the expression for an observed needle mortality (withdrawal of photosynthesising area), the theoretical rate of which had already been calculated from needle number depletion curves on living shoots.

In short, the structure-growth-mortality-litterfall studies were designed within the limitations imposed by sampling problems, as an integrated whole, the degree of detail in which was tailored to the requirements of those other studies which were bound to specific and well defined organs. That the approach involved detail in excess of that considered necessary by those concerned perforce with studies at ecosystem level, was not considered a valid reason for abandoning the original level of ambition. Knowledge of the details of structure may be dispensed with at the stage of synthesis to ecosystem level, but is a prerequisite to understanding of processes below that level, and to intelligent simplification. For, as is pointed out by Jeffers (1978), when working within the framework of the scientific method, it is necessary to address carefully bounded problems.

Realisation of the aims

At this stage in the development of SWECON, it is necessary to examine the extent to which the biomass studies outlined above have fulfilled their stated aims. In common with other investigations carried out under field conditions,

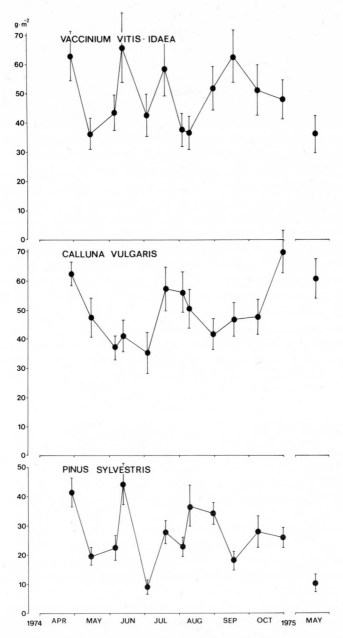

Figure 7. Variation in the fine-root biomass (<2 mm in diameter) of the most important species in terms of weight in a young Scots pine stand (Ih II) during the 1974 and 1975 samplings. The estimates are means $\pm$ standard error from 16 samples in each of the two strata (I =*Calluna*, II = non-*Calluna*) at each sampling. Stratum I and II accounted for 47.9 and 52.1%, respectively, of the total area (Persson, 1975).

133

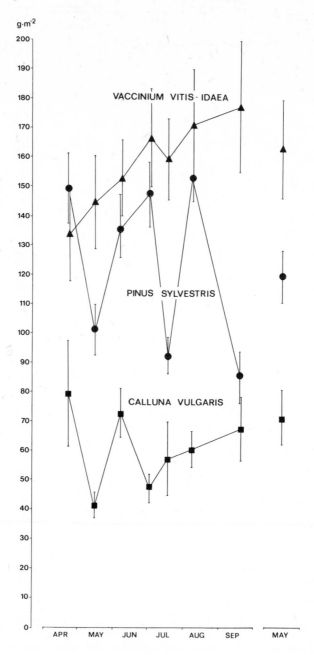

Figure 8. Variation in the fine-root biomass (<2 mm in diameter) of the most important species in a mature Scots pine stand (Ih V) during the 1974 and 1975 samplings. The estimates are means ± standard error from 20–30 samples on each sampling occasion.

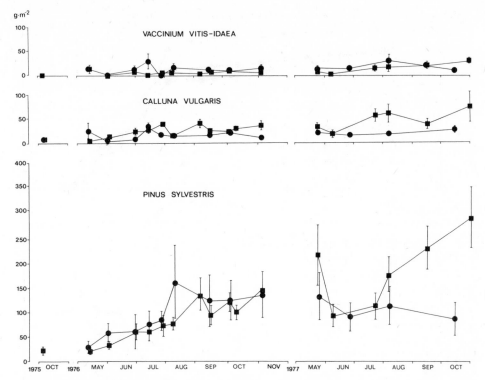

Figure 9. The amount of root biomass in ingrowth cores (containers) in a young (Ih II; circles) and a mature Scots pine stand (Ih V; squares). The containers were inserted between August and mid-September 1974, and were removed at regular intervals, starting in Autumn 1975, and continuing during the 1976 and 1977 growing seasons. It may be concluded from the accumulation of new roots in the cores that a considerable fine-root accretion has taken place.

dealing with species having a high degree of predetermined growth, these studies required a minimum of three full years to produce estimates of value for use in describing the dynamics of the main biomass components. In addition, the more experimental studies (root isolation and ingrowth) needed a period of recovery after establishment, of at least one year.

Most of the studies were set up in the field in 1973 and 1974. Those requiring a long period of observation (litterfall, dendrometers, height increment, root sampling series, needle weight dynamics and mortality) have by now been in operation for four years. Some of them, e.g., litterfall (cf. Flower-Ellis & Olsson, 1978), have produced the information likely to be of use to the project during its lifetime. Others, amongst which are the highly labour-intensive biomass and growth-analytical studies above and below ground, have taken far longer to process, compile and report than was originally expected. The yardstick applied to early data from the International Biological Programme (IBP) cannot validly be applied to those from work started a decade later, especially in view of the growth in interest in the dynamic relations within the ecosystem, which has developed since the IBP started (cf. Whittaker & Marks, 1975). In particular, the need for better

135

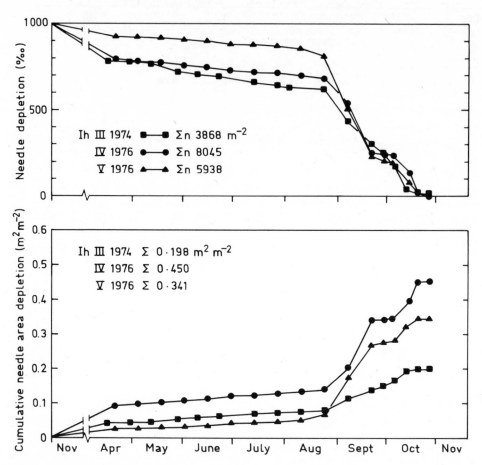

Figure 10. Needle depletion (‰ of all needles falling between 1 November and 31 October in the following year) above; and cumulative depletion of needle area corresponding to this, below, in an 18-year-old (Ih III), a 60-year-old (Ih IV) and a 120-year-old (Ih V) pine stand in 1973/74 and 1975/76. Note the similarity of rates and the difference in mortality.

estimates of the rate of change in belowground components, as opposed to a structural description of them, might be considered to justify fully the efforts devoted to root studies, and indeed to call for their redoubling (cf. Persson, 1978a, b, 1979b, 1980a, b).

In spite of the difficulties involved in the collection, and especially in the processing of the material, many results have been evaluated and made available to other workers within the project. But the investigations cannot be considered complete until the material has been thoroughly analysed statistically, and both primary data and digests of data have been stored in the SWECON data bank for future use.

As regards the approach to the problem of describing tree structure, it has resulted in data having a high degree of resolution, capable of providing an accurate description of the geometry of the tree, and its change with time. It is, however, subject to one serious shortcoming: *viz.*, that "reconstitution" of the tree from the sub-populations of shoots into which it was divided, proved less simple than might at first appear. This has considerably delayed efforts at modelling at a higher level of ecosystem organisation, although it is to be expected that this modelling will be founded on a firm base.

The fine-root sampling has produced results which, it may be said, have greatly changed our view of the relations between the various parts of the tree in respect of growth and rate of turnover (cf. Fig. 7). It is evident that caution must in future be observed when evaluating the results of single samplings, in view of the variation in the fine-root fraction. The conventional way of assessing the root production of forest trees, using the growth percentage of the aboveground parts, appears to have no relevance as regards small-diameter roots and may lead to serious underestimates. In future ecosystem studies, greater attention must be paid to the dynamics of the root system, since it is there that the main sink for photosynthate seems to lie (cf. Ågren *et al.*, 1980).

References

Ågren, G., Axelsson, B., Flower-Ellis, J. G. K., Linder, S., Persson, H., Staaf, H. & Troeng, E. 1980. Annual carbon budget for a young Scots pine. – In: Persson, T. (ed.) Structure and Function of Northern Coniferous Forests – An Ecosystem Study, Ecol. Bull. (Stockholm) 32: 307–313.

Chapman, S. B., Hibble, I. & Rafarel, C. R. 1975. Net aerial production by *Calluna vulgaris* on lowland heath in Britain. – J. Ecol. 63:233–258.

Ericsson, A. 1978. Seasonal changes in translocation of ^{14}C from different age-classes of needles on 20-year-old Scots pine trees (*Pinus silvestris*). – Physiol. Plant. 43:351–358.

Flower-Ellis, J. G. K. & Olsson, L. 1978. Litterfall in an age series of Scots pine stands and its variation by components during the years 1973–1976. – Swed. Conif. For. Proj. Tech. Rep. 15, 62 pp.

Flower-Ellis, J. G. K., Albrektson, A. & Olsson, L. 1976. Structure and growth of some young Scots pine stands: (1) Dimensional and numerical relationships. – Swed. Conif. For. Proj. Tech. Rep. 3, 98 pp.

Jeffers, J. N. R. 1978. General principles for ecosystem definition and modelling. – In: Holdgate, M. W. & Woodman, M. I. (eds.) The Breakdown and Restoration of Ecosystems, Nato Conference Series 1(3):85–103. New York: Plenum Publ. Corp.

Mohamed, B. F. & Gimingham, C. H. 1970. The morphology of vegetative regeneration in *Calluna vulgaris*. – New Phytol. 69:743–750.

Mork, E. 1946. On the dwarf shrub vegetation on forest ground. – Medd. Norske Skogforsøksv. 33:269–356.

Newbould, P. J. 1967. Methods for Estimating the Primary Production of Forests, IBP Handbook 2. Oxford–Edinburgh: Blackwell Scientific Publications, 62 pp.

Persson, H. 1975. Dry matter production of dwarf shrubs, mosses and lichens in some Scots pine stands at Ivantjärnsheden, Central Sweden. – Swed. Conif. For. Proj. Tech. Rep. 2, 25 pp.

Persson, H. 1978a. Root dynamics in a young Scots pine stand in Central Sweden. – Oikos 30:508–519.

Persson, H. 1978b. Data on root dynamics in a young Scots pine stand in Central Sweden. – Swed. Conif. For. Proj. Int. Rep. 72, 13 pp.

Persson, H. 1979a. The possible outcomes and limitation of measuring quantitative changes in plant cover on permanent plots. – In: Hytteborn, H. (ed.) The Use of Ecological Variables in Environmental Monitoring. Swedish National Environment Protection Board, Rep. PM 1151:81–87.

Persson, H. 1979b. Fine-root production, mortality and decomposition in forest ecosystems. – Vegetatio 41:101–109.

Persson, H. 1980a. Spatial distribution of fine-root growth, mortality and decomposition in a young Scots pine stand in Central Sweden. – Oikos 34:77–87.

Persson, H. 1980b. Death and replacement of fine roots in a mature Scots pine stand. – In: Persson, T. (ed.) Structure and Function of Northern Coniferous Forests – An Ecosystem Study, Ecol. Bull. (Stockholm) 32: 251–260.

Whittaker, R. H. & Marks, P. L. 1975. Methods of assessing terrestrial productivity. – In: Lieth, H. & Whittaker, R. H. (eds.) Primary Productivity of the Biosphere, Ecol. Stud. 14:55–118. Berlin–Heidelberg–New York: Springer–Verlag.

Persson, T. (ed.) 1980
Structure and Function of Northern
Coniferous Forests – An Ecosystem Study
Ecol. Bull. (Stockholm) 32: 139–152.

VEGETATION DYNAMICS IN DEVELOPING SCOTS PINE STANDS IN CENTRAL SWEDEN

S. Bråkenhielm[1] and H. Persson[2]

Abstract

The dynamics of the field and bottom layers were studied by non-destructive sampling of cover percentage in an age series of Scots pine (*Pinus sylvestris*) stands. Four developmental stages were distinguished,*viz.*, the stage of retrogression, the stage of recolonization, the unthinned mature stage and the thinned mature stage. It was demonstrated that the apparent stability in a forest community is disturbed by silvicultural measures, e.g., thinning and clear-cutting causing successions resembling those which follow from death of single trees, storm-felling, fires, etc. in the "primeval" forest.

Additional keywords: Bottom layer, *Calluna vulgaris*, cover percentage, field layer, forest ecosystem, permanent quadrats, *Pinus sylvestris*, succession, *Vaccinium vitis-idaea*.

Introduction

Change is an inherent quality of all living systems. One of the main objectives for the plant ecologist working within the plant community is, therefore, to identify, quantify and ultimately explain the changes in definable quantitative units (cf. Sjörs, 1979). For measurements of the long-term changes in a plant community, the disadvantage of a destructive sampling programme via cropping is obvious, since the plant individuals on the sample quadrats are removed, necessitating new quadrats to be laid out on each sampling occasion.

Cover percentages of the plant species are readily estimated in a set of sample quadrats, and the arithmetical mean (mean cover $\bar{C}$) (Persson, 1975a; Bråkenhielm, 1977) of the species and of collective species groups may be calculated (see text below). Cover estimates may also be used as a substitute for dry weight estimates since it is possible to establish weight-to-cover regression relationships (Persson, 1975a, 1979a).

This paper reports results from repeated sampling of, among others, cover percentage on permanent sample quadrats in an age series of Scots pine (*Pinus sylvestris*) stands at Ivantjärnsheden, Jädraås, Central Sweden. A description of the research area is found in Axelsson & Bråkenhielm (1980). A less extensive destructive sampling programme was also carried out parallel to the non-destructive one (Persson, 1980b). Aims and strategies of these studies are outlined in Flower-Ellis & Persson (1980).

[1] Swedish National Environment Protection Board, Box 1302, S-171 25 Solna, Sweden
[2] Institute of Ecological Botany, Uppsala University, Box 559, S-751 22 Uppsala, Sweden

Table 1. Stand characteristics of the investigated research plots (Ih 0–Ih V) at Ivantjärnsheden (Data sources: Albrektson, 1976; Flower-Ellis *et al.*, 1976; Flower-Ellis & Olsson, 1978; Axelsson & Bråkenhielm, 1980). The cover analyses were carried out each year during August–October on randomly distributed 0.5×0.5 m quadrats. The sampling scheme in Ih II and Ih III was based on two broad divisions, *Calluna* and non-*Calluna* (strata I and II) (Persson, 1975b, 1980b). The number of quadrats in each stand and in stratum I is given. Stratum I occupied in Ih II 49.8% (1973), 47.5% (1974), 47.1% (1975), 37.5% (1976), 38.1% (1977), 45.3% (1978), 49.8% (1979) and in Ih III 12.0% (1973). n.e. = not estimated, u.s. = unstratified, d.s. = deviating stratification.

| | Research plots | | | | | |
	Ih 0	Ih I	Ih II	Ih III	Ih IV	Ih V
Year of clear-cutting	1976	1967	1957	1953–54	ca. 1900	ca. 1850
Number of trees ha^{-1} (1973)	453	2000	1095	2933	1176	393
Mean tree height (m) (1973)	19	<1	2.1	2.8	12.6	15.8
Basal area (m^2 ha^{-1}) (1973)	19.70	n.e.	2.15	5.04	19.98	15.05
Number of quadrats	48	24	14	79	36	66
Quadrats in stratum I	u.s.	d.s.	7	14	u.s.	u.s.

The chief aims of the non-destructive sampling programme were:

(1) to describe long-term changes in the field and bottom layers during the rotation period of Scots pine stands;
(2) to quantify population dynamics in terms of cover percentage of the most important species and species groups;
(3) to distinguish short-term fluctuations, e.g., due to climatical changes between years from long-term successional trends.

In the long run, an increased knowledge of changes in the components of the ecosystem is essential for the basic understanding of its processes and for the prediction of future conditions (Sjörs, 1979).

One drawback today for the plant ecologist, who seeks to understand how terrestrial vegetation functions in order to predict changes in structure and species composition, is that it is extremely expensive to obtain sufficient data at an ecosystem level. Non-destructive sampling of cover percentage may, from many aspects, be a useful complement to and even a substitute for destructive sampling. It may be carried out more extensively because of its less time-consuming nature. Non-destructive vegetational variables may be of considerable importance for monitoring the long-term effect on the ecosystem by environmental changes due to the integrating character of the plant community (Bråkenhielm, 1979; Persson, 1979a).

Material and methods

The dynamics of the field and bottom layers were studied in a number of Scots pine stands of similar environmental conditions. The vegetation in these stands was of a lichen-dwarf-shrub to lichen-type (Ebeling, 1978). The stands covered a rotation period of more than one hundred years (cf. Table 1). The research plots included in the study were Ih 0, I, II, III, IV, V (Ih = Ivantjärnsheden). The data of the different research plots were treated as if representing different stages of the same succession. Thereby it was assumed that the plots had equal site quality and historical background, which, however, is not quite true (cf. Bråkenhielm, 1974, 1978; Axelsson & Bråkenhielm, 1980). It should be noted that Ih III, in some respects, was treated differently from the others, due to a better site quality and, consequently, deviating vegetation (cf. Table 2).

The permanent 0.5×0.5 m quadrats used for the cover analyses were distributed randomly in each research plot inside larger 10×10 m quadrats. The number of sample quadrats in each research plot is given in Table 1. Sampling in Ih 0 was undertaken in two strata, where one stratum (50% of the total area) was cleaned of felling litter and the other stratum had all felling litter from the total area. For the purpose of the present paper, means of the two strata were calculated.

Research plots Ih II and Ih III were divided into two broad vegetation categories, viz., the *Calluna* clones (stratum I) and the areas between them, viz., non-*Calluna* (stratum II). Sampling was considered to occur in stratum I if more than 75% of the 0.5×0.5 m sample quadrat was covered by *Calluna* clones. Otherwise it was referred to stratum II. New sample quadrats were added until an appropriate number had been placed in each stratum. The areas covered by the two strata were estimated by transect inventory (cf. Persson, 1980b). Results from the repeated transect inventories are given in the text of Table 1.

The above-ground cover (i.e., the proportion of the ground area covered vertically by foliage), of all species and separate layers (litter, bottom and field layers) in the quadrats was directly estimated as percentages, using methods described in Persson (1975a) and Bråkenhielm (1977). On the basis of the non-destructive cover estimates, furthermore, apparent cover ($\bar{C}_a$) and the shading percentage ($\overline{Sh}$) could easily be calculated (see Persson, 1975a). Other related concepts, readily calculated from the data are, for instance, characteristic cover ($\bar{C}_c$) and frequency. For a more complete description of the vegetation structure on the research plots and its variation, these concepts are very profitable.

The cover estimation method has the advantage of being quick and causing relatively little disturbance to the vegetation, as compared with the measurement method (e.g., the "point quadrat method" *sensu* Heslehurst, 1971). However, variations in the estimate from one person to another and from time to time with the same person are likely to occur. In order to reduce this variation the authors together made their estimates uniform, shortly before the start of this study.

The most extensive analyses were carried out in Ih 0 (which was of similar age to Ih V before clear-cutting) and in Ih II (cf. Figs. 1, 2 and 3). The data from Ih II are from untreated plots, leaving aside data from experimental plots for future interpretation. In Ih III, Ih IV and Ih V less extensive samples were taken. The reason is the deviating nature of Ih III and the apparent slow rate of change in Ih IV and V.

The species nomenclature follows Lid (1974) for vascular plants, Nyholm (1954-69) and Arnell (1956) for bryophytes, Dahl & Krog (1973) for lichens, except for *Lecidea granulosa*, and the collective group *Cladonia silvatica*, where Magnusson (1929, 1952) was followed.

In this study so-called "pioneer lichens" were defined as those lichens which tend to colonize the bare, disturbed soil surface, among others, species with cup- or needle-like podetia such as *Cladonia cornuta*, *C. deformis*, *C. fimbriata*, *C. pyxidata*. Included in this group were also *Cetraria islandica* and *Lecidea granulosa*. "Reindeer lichens" were defined as those species which successfully competed in more stable vegetation, such as *Cladonia rangiferina*, *C. silvatica* and *C. alpestris*.

Results

Stage of retrogression

The most rapid changes in the field and bottom layers took place during the first two years following the clear-cutting (cf. data in Table 2 from Ih 0). From 1975 to 1977 the cover of the dominant dwarf shrubs *Calluna vulgaris* and *Vaccinium vitis-idaea* decreased from about 50% in the mature Scots pine stand to 5% and the bottom layer from about 90% to 30% (Fig. 4).

After the clear-cutting in March–April 1976 the shoots of *Calluna* turned red

Figure 1. Research plot Ih 0 in May 1976, shortly after the clear-cutting in March–April. (Photo: H. Persson)

Figure 2. Research plot Ih II in November 1973. In the foreground are typical young *Calluna*-clones with an interspacing mat of pioneer lichens etc. (strata I and II). (Photo: S. Bråkenhielm)

Figure 3. Research plot Ih V in May 1976. No clear clones of *Calluna* could be distinguished in this area and, therefore, an unstratified sampling was applied. The white sticks mark permanent 0.5×0.5 m sample quadrats. (Photo: H. Persson)

and subsequently died during the growing season. At the time of the quadrat analysis in September most of the leaf and shoot parts of *C. vulgaris*, *V. vitis-idaea*, *V. myrtillus* and *Empetrum nigrum* had withered and were in very bad condition. Mosses were very affected and their apical shoot parts turned yellow and whitish and lost their turgor, but the shoots were apparently still alive. Lichens appeared to be little affected.

In general, the most rapid effects in the vegetation of the field and bottom layers were observed on the plots without felling litter. On the plots with twice the ordinary amount of felling litter the bulk of dwarf shrubs and mosses did not die until the needles and small twigs had fallen off the remaining tree branches (cf. Figs. 5 and 6).

It was clear that under the felling litter, more vascular plants and mosses had survived the first three years after clear-cutting and these were later to become the centres for recolonization. On the other hand, lichens were markedly disfavoured by the felling litter.

On the plots without felling litter practically all plants except lichens died during the first three years after clear-cutting. Of the two main reindeer lichens, viz., *Cladonia rangiferina* and *C. silvatica*, the former appeared to be more affected by the clear-cutting, being dark, greyish and losing turgor, while the latter species was seemingly in good condition. However, both species had a net increase in cover during the period of observation, probably favoured by the death of dwarf-shrubs and mosses (Fig. 6).

143

Table 2. Mean cover (%) ± s.e. for the field and bottom layer species in different Scots pine stands at Ivantjärnsheden (Ih). The analyses were carried out on permanent 0.5 × 0.5 m quadrats, the numbers of which are given in Table 1. The samplings in Ih 0 and Ih II were based on stratified sampling (see text). Stand age (years) refers to the number of years after clear-cutting. Cover of litter (twigs, leaf and needle remnants) is also indicated. – denotes absence and 0 (<0.5) denotes presence.

	Ih 0					Ih I	Ih II							Ih III		Ih IV	Ih V	
	1975	1976	1977	1978	1979	1978	1973	1974	1975	1976	1977	1978	1979	1974	1977	1976	1974	1976
Stand age (years)	150	0	1	2	3	11	16	17	18	19	20	21	22	21	24	65	120–130	120–130
LITTER	29±1	74±2	82±2	86±2	70±3	82±4	18±6	28±7	28±5	33±12	21±4	31±4	33±3	49±3	53±3	36±4	23±1	21±1
TOTAL FIELD LAYER	50±3	37±2	4±1	2±1	2±1	4±1	45±3	47±6	49±2	32±5	40±4	52±3	67±6	21±2	21±2	33±3	52±2	47±2
TOTAL BOTTOM LAYER	93±1	91±1	31±2	26±2	41±3	27±4	64±7	58±7	61±6	72±6	71±6	71±6	71±5	50±3	54±3	69±4	90±2	88±1
Trees and shrubs < 1 m																		
Betula pubescens	–	–	–	–	–	–	1±1	1±1	0±0	0±0	0±0	0±0	0±0	0±0	–	–	–	–
Juniperus communis	–	–	–	–	–	–	–	–	–	–	–	–	–	0±0	0±0	–	–	–
Malus sylvestris	1±1	–	–	–	–	–	–	–	–	–	–	–	–	0±0	–	–	–	–
Picea abies	0±0	–	–	–	–	–	–	–	–	–	–	–	–	0±0	3±2	8±2	1±1	2±2
Pinus sylvestris	–	–	–	0±0	0±0	1±1	3±3	1±1	1±1	1±1	2±1	2±1	4±2	0±0	3±1	–	0±0	0±0
Populus tremula	–	–	–	–	–	–	–	–	–	–	–	–	–	0±0	0±0	–	–	–
Dwarf shrubs																		
Calluna vulgaris	28±2	23±1	1±1	1±1	1±1	1±1	41±3	42±2	39±2	25±4	25±4	34±4	39±5	10±1	7±1	10±2	26±2	21±1
Empetrum nigrum	1±1	2±1	–	–	–	–	–	–	–	–	–	–	–	–	–	0±0	2±1	2±1
Linnaea borealis	–	–	–	–	–	–	–	–	–	–	–	–	–	0±0	0±0	–	–	–
Vaccinium myrtillus	1±1	0±0	0±0	0±0	0±0	–	–	–	–	0±0	0±0	–	0±0	0±0	0±0	4±1	0±0	0±0
V. uliginosum	0±0	–	–	–	–	–	–	–	–	–	–	–	–	–	–	–	–	–
V. vitis-idaea	21±2	16±1	3±1	1±1	1±1	2±1	6±1	6±1	11±2	15±2	16±2	22±2	24±2	0±0	2±1	15±2	27±1	26±1
Herbaceous species																		
Chamaenerion angustifolium	–	–	–	–	–	–	–	–	–	–	–	–	–	0±0	0±0	–	–	–
Convallaria majalis	–	–	–	–	–	–	–	–	–	–	–	–	–	0±0	0±0	–	–	–
Lycopodium annotinum	–	–	–	–	–	–	–	–	–	–	–	–	–	0±0	0±0	–	–	–
L. complanatum	–	–	–	–	–	–	–	–	–	–	–	–	–	1±1	1±1	–	–	–
Maianthemum bifolium	–	–	–	–	–	–	–	–	–	–	–	–	–	0±0	0±0	–	–	–
Melampyrum pratense	–	–	–	–	–	–	–	–	–	–	–	–	–	0±0	0±0	–	–	–
Solidago virgaurea	–	–	–	–	–	–	–	–	–	–	–	–	–	0±0	0±0	–	–	–
Trientalis europaea	–	–	–	–	–	–	–	–	–	–	–	–	–	0±0	0±0	–	–	–
Graminaceous species																		
Agrostis tenuis	–	–	–	–	–	–	–	–	–	–	–	–	–	0±0	0±0	–	–	–
Calamagrostis arundinacea	–	–	–	–	–	–	–	–	–	–	–	–	–	–	–	–	–	–
Deschampsia flexuosa	–	–	–	–	–	–	–	–	–	–	–	–	–	1±1	0±0	0±0	–	–
Luzula pilosa	–	–	–	–	–	–	–	–	–	–	–	–	–	6±1	6±1	0±0	–	–

Table with plant cover data (mean ± standard error) for bottom-layer species across sample plots Ih 0 – Ih V and years.

	Ih 0					Ih I	Ih II							Ih III			Ih IV	Ih V	
	1975	1976	1977	1978	1979	1978	1973	1974	1975	1976	1977	1978	1979	1974	1977	1976	1976	1974	1976
Bryophytes																			
Dicranum fuscescens	9±2	–	0±0	–	1±1	–	–	–	0±0	0±0	1±1	1±1	1±1	0±0	1±1	0±0	0±0	0±0	0±0
D. polysetum	12±1	7±1	7±1	7±1	9±1	1±1	1±1	1±1	0±0	0±0	1±1	1±1	1±1	3±1	5±1	15±3	15±3	6±1	7±1
Hepaticae sp.	–	0±0	0±0	–	0±0	–	–	–	–	–	–	–	–	0±0	0±0	0±0	0±0	0±0	–
Hylocomium splendens	0±0	0±0	–	–	0±0	–	–	–	–	–	–	–	–	1±1	1±1	–	–	0±0	–
Plagiothecium sp.	–	–	–	0±0	–	–	–	–	–	–	–	–	–	–	0±0	–	–	–	–
Pleurozium schreberi	78±2	73±2	15±2	12±1	16±2	0±0	21±6	18±5	14±4	13±8	13±3	15±4	17±5	6±1	9±2	48±5	66±3	72±3	59±3
Pohlia nutans	0±0	–	–	–	–	0±0	0±0	0±0	0±0	0±0	1±1	0±0	1±1	0±0	0±0	–	–	–	–
Polytrichum commune	0±0	–	0±0	0±0	0±0	0±0	0±0	0±0	–	0±0	0±0	0±0	0±0	–	–	–	–	–	–
P. juniperinum	–	–	0±0	0±0	0±0	1±1	–	0±0	–	–	–	0±0	0±0	0±0	1±1	1±1	1±1	–	–
Ptilidium ciliare	–	–	–	–	–	–	–	–	–	–	–	–	–	–	1±1	–	–	–	–
P. pulcherrimum	–	–	0±0	–	–	0±0	–	–	–	–	–	–	–	–	–	–	–	–	–
Ptilium crista-castrensis	0±0	–	–	–	–	–	–	–	–	–	–	–	–	0±0	0±0	–	–	–	–
Bryophytes, total	87±2	85±2	22±2	19±2	24±2	1±1	22±5	19±5	15±5	14±3	15±3	18±5	20±5	12±2	14±2	64±5	72±3	72±3	66±4
Lichens																			
Cetraria islandica	–	–	–	–	–	–	–	–	0±0	0±0	–	0±0	0±0	1±1	1±1	1±1	1±1	–	–
Cladonia alpestris	0±0	–	–	–	–	0±0	–	1±1	0±0	0±0	0±0	0±0	0±0	0±0	1±1	0±0	0±0	–	0±0
C. botrytes	0±0	–	0±0	0±0	0±0	0±0	0±0	1±1	0±0	0±0	0±0	0±0	0±0	1±1	1±1	0±0	0±0	0±0	0±0
C. cenotea	0±0	0±0	0±0	0±0	–	0±0	1±1	1±1	0±0	1±1	0±0	0±0	0±0	1±1	1±1	0±0	0±0	0±0	0±0
C. cornuta	0±0	–	–	0±0	–	0±0	2±1	2±1	3±1	3±1	3±1	2±1	2±1	2±1	2±1	0±0	0±0	0±0	0±0
C. crispata	0±0	–	–	0±0	0±0	0±0	0±0	0±0	1±1	0±0	0±0	0±0	0±0	0±0	1±1	0±0	0±0	0±0	0±0
C. deformis	0±0	–	–	0±0	0±0	1±1	2±2	2±1	2±1	4±1	5±1	6±2	6±2	5±1	2±1	0±0	0±0	0±0	0±0
C. fimbriata	–	–	–	0±0	0±0	0±0	2±1	2±1	2±1	4±1	3±1	2±1	3±1	6±1	7±1	0±0	0±0	0±0	0±0
C. floerkeana	0±0	0±0	0±0	0±0	0±0	0±0	2±1	1±1	0±0	1±1	2±1	2±1	1±1	1±1	1±1	0±0	0±0	0±0	0±0
C. gracilis	0±0	–	–	0±0	0±0	0±0	0±0	0±0	1±1	1±1	1±1	1±1	1±1	0±0	0±0	0±0	0±0	0±0	0±0
C. macilenta	0±0	–	0±0	1±1	0±0	1±1	2±1	3±1	3±1	1±1	1±1	1±1	1±1	5±1	5±1	5±1	3±1	16±2	19±3
C. pyxidata	5±1	4±1	8±1	7±1	13±2	10±2	15±5	14±4	23±4	26±5	26±5	21±4	20±3	4±1	5±1	3±1	3±1	8±2	19±3
C. rangiferina	3±1	2±1	4±1	4±1	6±1	3±1	13±6	13±5	12±5	18±6	19±16	16±5	16±5	2±1	3±1	3±1	3±1	8±2	7±1
C. silvatica coll.	3±1	2±1	4±1	4±1	6±1	3±1	13±6	13±5	12±5	18±6	19±16	16±5	16±5	2±1	3±1	3±1	3±1	8±2	7±1
C. squamosa	–	–	–	–	–	–	–	–	–	–	–	–	–	0±0	0±0	–	–	–	–
Lecidea granulosa	–	–	–	–	2±1	2±1	1±1	3±1	3±1	3±1	4±2	2±1	2±1	1±1	1±1	3±1	–	–	–
L. uliginosa	–	–	–	–	1±1	1±1	–	–	–	–	–	–	–	1±1	1±1	–	–	–	–
Parmelia sp.	–	–	–	–	–	–	–	–	–	–	–	–	–	–	–	0±0	–	–	–
Peltigera aphthosa	–	–	–	–	–	–	–	–	–	–	–	–	–	1±1	0±0	–	–	–	–
Unidentified squamules	–	–	0±0	–	0±0	8±2	–	–	–	–	–	–	–	11±4	11±2	–	–	0±0	0±0
Lichens, total	8±1	7±0	12±2	11±2	20±3	28±4	40±7	39±6	49±5	62±6	63±5	53±3	52±4	41±3	41±3	64±5	8±3	24±3	27±4
"Pioneer" lichens, total	0±0	0±0	0±0	0±0	1±1	15±3	12±2	12±2	14±2	18±4	19±4	17±4	17±4	35±3	33±3	2±1	2±1	0±0	0±0
BOTTOM LAYER, TOTAL	96±2	92±2	34±2	29±2	44±3	30±4	63±8	58±8	64±6	76±6	78±5	71±4	72±4	50±3	57±3	72±4	96±2	96±2	93±1

145

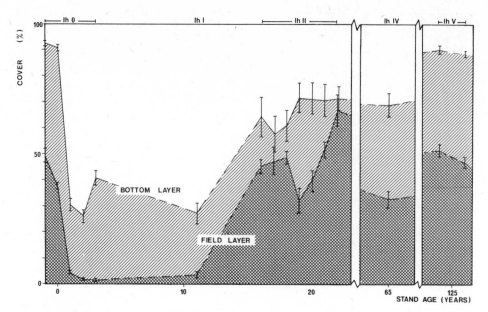

Figure 4. Mean cover ± one standard error of the total field and bottom layers in an age series of five Scots pine stands at Ivantjärnsheden (Ih 0, I, II, IV and V). Ih III was omitted due to its deviating site quality. Stand ages refer to the number of years after clear-cutting (cf. Table 1). See Table 2 for related data.

Surviving, suppressed dwarf individuals of *Pinus sylvestris* were also sparsely occurring in the field layer. In Ih 0 pioneer lichens had just begun to colonize three years after clear-cutting.

Stage of recolonization

The recolonization stage, which may last up to 50–60 years after clear-cutting in this forest type, is represented in the present study by research plots Ih I, Ih II and Ih III (Table 2). The early stage of recolonization was characterized by the establishment and vegetative spread of *Calluna vulgaris* and *Vaccinium vitis-idaea*. Much of the surviving *Calluna* and most of the *V. vitis-idaea*, as well as other related dwarf shrubs, regenerated from stem-bases or below-ground rhizomes, which survived sporadically sheltered by slash or stumps. Individuals of *Calluna* regenerated from seeds were also frequently found.

Characteristic for this stage was the regular appearance of pioneer lichens in places free of dwarf shrubs and mosses. The pioneer lichens, as a rule, first appeared as squamules, which were initially difficult to connect with proper podetia. Interspaced with the pioneer lichens were frequently occurring *Polytrichum juniperinum* and *P. piliferum*. The former species also preferably colonized disturbed places such as the trampled pathways in Ih 0. The reindeer lichens continued their growth in areas free of the shading canopy of *Calluna*. Soredia and fragmentation were apparently the most important means of reproduction, since apothecia and spores were seldom produced.

146

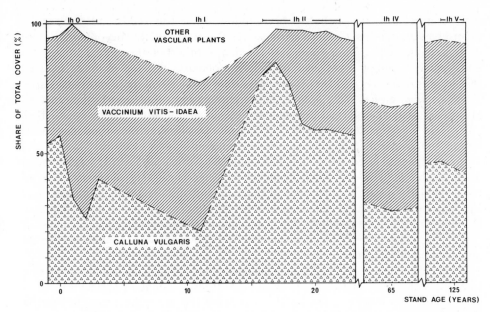

Figure 5. Percentage share of the total field-layer cover of *Calluna vulgaris, Vaccinium vitis-idaea* and other vascular plants in an age series of Scots pine stands at Ivantjärnsheden (Ih 0, I, II, IV and V). For additional information see text of Fig. 4.

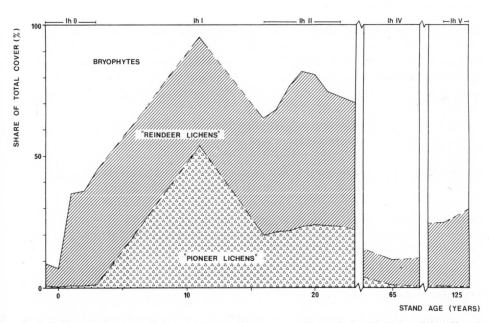

Figure 6. Percentage share of the total bottom layer cover of bryophytes, "reindeer lichens" and "pioneer lichens" in an age series of Scots pine stands at Ivantjärnsheden (Ih 0, I, II, IV and V). For additional information see text of Fig. 4.

147

In contrast to the lichens, bryophytes often survived and propagated themselves under the *Calluna* canopy. The pioneer of the bryophytes in the *Calluna* clones was *Pohlia nutans*. In the dense thickets it developed a long, thin and sparsely leafed form. As the clones became thinner in their centres, *Pleurozium schreberi* and *Dicranum polysetum* established there more regularly.

The *Calluna* clones were initially dense enough to exclude most other species. However, as they enlarged peripherally by means of adventitious roots, their older, less vigorous shoots continuously died off, allowing pine seedlings, bryophytes and, in the final degenerate phase, reindeer lichens to settle.

An unexpected effect of the mechanical soil-scarification in Ih II (cf. Axelsson & Bråkenhielm, 1980) was that *Calluna* seedlings preferably regenerated in the fairly regularly distributed patches of bare mineral soil. The tree individuals as a rule grew between these patches, which were approximately 1 m in diameter. During the stage of recolonization, the pine stand grew vigorously. Surviving suppressed dwarf trees from the stand before clear-cutting also took part in the process of recolonization.

During the stage of recolonization the Scots pines grew from suppressed dwarf trees, or from seeds or two-year-old nursery trees to about 13 m height in Ih IV (Table 1). In Ih 0 only a few small trees were left after the clear-cutting (the number of trees were 453 ha^{-1} in 1973). In Ih I there were around 2000 trees ha^{-1} in 1973 with an uneven height and spread. The self-sown stand Ih II was cleaned at about the normal time in 1972, but more trees than normal were cut off (cf. data for Ih II and Ih III in Table 1).

The unthinned mature stage

The succession into the mature stage involved the continued centrifugal expansion and central degeneration of the *Calluna* clones. At the same time the clones met and merged with each other. The bryophytes, mainly *Pleurozium schreberi* and *Dicranum polysetum* expanded with the *Calluna* clones, at the expense of the pioneer lichens. At the end, the latter had disappeared almost completely. An example of this stage is Ih IV (Table 2).

The resulting structural composition of the vegetation depended on the density of the tree canopy. In the dense stand Ih IV, with 1176 trees ha^{-1} (Table 1) *Calluna* was set back and developed sparsely. Even *V. vitis-idaea* was somewhat impeded in growth and flowering. The reindeer lichens were also disfavoured and occurred as isolated groups or individuals. On the other hand, the bryophytes and also *Vaccinium myrtillus* grew vigorously – the latter species if site quality permitted. During this stage also more sparsely occurring species such as *Empetrum nigrum, Lycopodium complanatum, Dicranum spurium* and *D. drummondii* were established in the area.

The thinned mature stage

The thinned mature stage may be exemplified by Ih V and Ih 0 before clear-cutting (cf. Table 1). The completely merging, sparsely developed *Calluna* clones and extensive cover of mosses interspersed with reindeer lichens were characteristic of this stage (Table 2). *Vaccinium vitis-idaea* was frequent and often flowering, particularly at the tree bases and stumps.

One characteristic feature in Ih V was circular, fairly regular carpets up to 20 m in diameter of reindeer lichens, in which *Calluna*, *V. vitis-idaea* and mosses were almost absent. In some of them there were, however, thin concentric rings of *Calluna*.

Sparsely occurring species in the thinned mature stage were *Empetrum nigrum*, *Vaccinium myrtillus*, *V. uliginosum*, *Monotropa hypopitys*, *Lycopodium complanatum*, *Hylocomium splendens*, *Dicranum spurium*, *D. drummondii* and pioneer lichens. Of these, *Empetrum nigrum* could locally be fairly abundant.

Discussion

The vegetation structure in the age series of Scots pine stands was demonstrated to vary considerably. Certain developmental stages were recognized, although certainly there were exceptions and irregularities due to varying site conditions. The stages probably represent the following general time series in development:

(1) The stage of retrogression, when the former indigenous forest species die, i.e., *Calluna vulgaris*, *Vaccinium vitis-idaea*, *Dicranum polysetum* and *Pleurozium schreberi*. This stage may last about three years.
(2) The stage of recolonization, which in the early phase is characterized by the invasion of pioneer lichens and development of small *Calluna* plants. Later on, the field and bottom layers expand vigorously and in the final phase the *Calluna* clones merge and grow into each other without distinct boundaries. This stage, which also involves development of the tree stand may last up to 40–50 years after clear-cutting.
(3) The unthinned mature stage, in which the field and bottom layers are completed as regards presence of indigenous forest species. However, the quantitative composition may still be rather variable, due to the density of the tree stand and its canopy (cf. Jonsson, 1957). In a dense Scots pine stand *Calluna* predominates where there are gaps in the canopy. Mosses and *Vaccinium* spp. are then often fairly vigorously developed.
(4) The thinned mature stage, in which dwarf shrubs and to some extent suppressed dwarf trees and reindeer lichens temporarily undergo an upsurge in growth (cf. Persson, 1980b) due to reduced competition and a better light climate.

Primeval or primitive forests (e.g., *sensu* Sernander, 1936) are rarely found nowadays in Sweden due to human influence. Regeneration in the primeval forests almost exclusively depended on catastrophes such as storm-felling, fires, etc. (Wretlind, 1934; Sernander, 1936; Arnborg, 1942, 1943) which were followed by long-term successions such as those described above.

Sernander (1936) and Arnborg (1942, 1943) stressed, in particular, the importance of storm-gaps in the tree canopy from overthrow of single trees for the successive regeneration of forests. They concluded that the suppressed, often 40–50 years old, dwarf trees, in the shade of the closed tree canopy, played an important role in the regeneration process of the forest stand, since they had already established root systems and photosynthetic apparatus.

Oosting & Kramer (1946) found that light intensity was probably more important than soil moisture for the survival and seedling establishment in a mature *Pinus echinata* stand. Seedlings preferably were established at the margins of the stand, since they received several times as much light there. Experimental evidence by Björkman (1945) of the regeneration difficulties in Scots pine stands of similar types as at Ivantjärnsheden, suggested that the main obstacle to survival was the first few years.

A conspicuous feature of the flora of the investigated Scots pine stands is the preponderance of evergreen species (cf. Persson, 1975b; 1980b). The advantage of the evergreen habit is that food resources need not be spent on wholly new photosynthetic apparatus each year (cf. Billings & Mooney, 1968), which is of considerable importance for the competitive ability of the species on this poor habitat type. Most of the dwarf shrubs are long-lived woody perennials characterized by vigorous vegetative reproduction. Most of them have the bulk of their biomass in the below-ground organs (Persson, 1978, 1979b, 1980a). Reproduction by seeds is less frequent depending on suitable habitats for seed germination and seedling establishment (cf. Miles, 1979).

The apparent stability in a mature forest community is disturbed by events such as thinning, clear-cutting, fertilization or by hazards such as death of single trees, local windthrow, storm-felling or fire (Tamm, 1947; Arnborg, 1949; Malmström, 1949; Zachrisson, 1977). Disturbance in this connection may be understood in the sense of a sudden upset, but in practice this is often the case in many ecosystems. Zachrisson (1977) demonstrated that forest fires occurred about each 100 years in different North Swedish boreal forest ecosystems, before the efficient fire suppression movement during the 19th century. New species, e.g., pioneer lichens, may come in temporarily when empty space is left. Even in a primeval forest, many of the "early" species would undoubtedly be part of the succession after some unforeseen local catastrophe. However, directly or indirectly, man is nowadays the principal agent in many of the sudden disturbances.

For many reasons, it may indeed be a paradox to speak of stability in a forest ecosystem, since it is constantly in a state of flux (e.g., death and replacement take place simultaneously). Even seasonal fluctuations which are not included in the long-term successional trends, since they are operating on a closer time-scale (Persson 1975a; 1979a), may be superimposed upon the long-term changes. So far few studies have been made in forest ecosystems to determine either the environmental fluctuations or the structural variation of the vegetation. It is obvious that such studies would require detailed data over a long period of time.

Year-to-year changes are the main concern of the present study (Table 2), mainly from Ih 0 and Ih II. Some of them may be caused by environmental changes and others by the development of the tree stand. It may be concluded from this study that even if the environment in the mature stand is fairly stable, the species populations of the field and bottom layers will never remain static. The plant community is indeed a mosaic of individuals growing more or less dispersed with an irregular density and a clustered (contagious) distribution. Although there is change in time at a given place, the whole community as recorded from the quadrat analyses will remain apparently the same.

Acknowledgements

This study was performed as a part of the Swedish Coniferous Forest Project. The planning of the study was carried out in cooperation with J. G. K. Flower-Ellis. B. Andersson and E. Lindquist are thanked for help and practical assistance during the field work.

References

Albrektson, A. 1976. The amount and the distribution of tree biomass in some pine stands (*Pinus silvestris*) in Northern Gästrikland. – Swed. Conif. For. Proj. Int. Rep. 18, 51 pp. (In Swedish, English abstract)

Arnborg, T. 1942. Lågaföryngringen i en sydlappländsk granurskog. –Sv. Skogsv.fören. Tidskr. 1942:47–78. (In Swedish)

Arnborg, T. 1943. Granberget. Eine pflanzenbiologische Untersuchung eines südlappländischen Fichtenwaldgebiets unter besonderer Berücksichtigung von Waldtypen und Verjüngung. – Norrländskt Handbibliotek 14, 298 pp. (In Swedish, German summary)

Arnborg, T. 1949. Aspects of vegetational analysis in studying coniferous forests in northern districts. – Sv. Bot. Tidskr. 43: 195–214. (In Swedish, English summary)

Arnell, S. 1956. Illustrated Moss Flora of Fennoscandia. 1. Hepaticae. Lund: Gleerup, 315 pp.

Axelsson, B. & Bråkenhielm, S. 1980. Investigation sites of the Swedish Coniferous Forest Project – biological and physiographical features. – In: Persson, T. (ed.) Structure and Function of Northern Coniferous Forests – An Ecosystem Study, Ecol. Bull. (Stockholm) 32: 25–64.

Billings, W.D. & Mooney, H. A. 1968. The ecology of arctic and alpine plants. – Biol. Rev. 43: 481–529.

Björkman, E. 1945. On the influence of light on the height-growth of pine plants on pine-heaths in Norrland. – Medd. Statens Skogsförs. Anst. 34: 497–542. (In Swedish, English summary)

Bråkenhielm, S. 1974. The vegetation of Ivantjärnsheden. – Swed. Conif. For. Proj. Int. Rep. 18, 51 pp. (In Swedish, English summary)

Bråkenhielm, S. 1977. Vegetation dynamics of afforested farmland in a district of South-eastern Sweden. – Acta Phytogeogr. Suec. 63, 106 pp.

Bråkenhielm, S. 1978. Ivantjärnsheden, Jädraås. – Regional physiography and description of the research area. – Swed. Conif. For. Proj. Tech. Rep. 16, 58 pp.

Bråkenhielm, S. 1979. Plant community changes as criteria of environmental change. – In: Hytteborn, H. (ed.) The Use of Ecological Variables in Environmental Monitoring, Swedish National Environment Protection Board, Rep. PM 1151: 73–80.

Dahl, E. & Krog, H. 1973. Macrolichens. Oslo–Bergen–Tromsø: Universitetsforlaget, 185 pp.

Ebeling, F. 1978. Nordsvenska skogstyper. – Sv. Skogsv. Fören. Tidskr. 4: 339–381. (In Swedish)

Flower-Ellis, J. G. K., Albrektson, A. & Olsson, L. 1976. Structure and growth of some young Scots pine stands: (1) Dimensional and numerical relationships. – Swed. Conif. For. Proj. Tech. Rep. 3, 98 pp.

Flower-Ellis, J. G. K. & Olsson, L. 1978. Litterfall in an age series of Scots pine stands and its variation by components during the years 1973–1976. – Swed. Conif. For. Proj. Tech. Rep. 15, 62 pp.

Flower-Ellis, J. G. K., & Persson, H. 1980. Investigation of structural properties and dynamics of Scots pine stands. – In: Persson, T. (ed.) Structure and Function of Northern Coniferous Forests – An Ecosystem Study, Ecol. Bull. (Stockholm) 32: 125–138.

Heslehurst, M. R. 1971. The point quadrat method of vegetation analysis; a review. – Univ. Reading. Dept. Agric., Study 10, 18 pp.

Jonsson, B. 1957. Heidekrautsstudien auf Kiefernsand in Södertörn. – Sv. Skogsv. Fören. Tidskr. 55: 413–451. (In Swedish, German summary)

Lid, J. 1974. Norsk og Svensk Flora, Andre Utgåva. Oslo: Det Norske Samlaget, 808 pp. (In Norwegian)

Magnusson, A. H. 1929. Flora över Skandinaviens Busk- och Bladlavar. Stockholm: P. A. Nordstedt & Söner, 127 pp. (In Swedish)

151

Magnusson, A. H. 1952. Key to the species of *Lecidea* in Scandinavia and Finland. 2. Non-saxicolous species. – Sv. Bot. Tidskr. 46: 313–323.

Malmström, C. 1949. The forest type and its importance in silviculture. – Kungl. Lantbruksakademiens Tidskr. 88: 226–242. (In Swedish, English summary)

Miles, J. 1979. Vegetation Dynamics. London: Chapman & Hall, 80 pp.

Nyholm, E. 1954, 1956, 1958, 1960, 1965, 1969. Illustrated Moss Flora of Fennoscandia. 2. Musci. Lund: Gleerup, 799 pp.

Oosting, H. J. & Kramer, P. J. 1946. Water and light in relation to pine reproduction. – Ecology 27: 47–53.

Persson, H. 1975a. Deciduous woodland at Andersby, Eastern Sweden: Field-layer and belowground production. – Acta Phytogeogr. Suec. 62, 72 pp.

Persson, H. 1975b. Dry matter production of dwarf shrubs, mosses and lichens in some Scots pine stands at Ivantjärnsheden, Central Sweden. – Swed. Conif. For. Proj. Tech. Rep. 2, 25 p.

Persson, H. 1978. Root dynamics in a young Scots pine stand in Central Sweden. – Oikos 30: 508–519.

Persson, H. 1979a. The possible outcomes and limitations of measuring quantitative changes in plant cover on permanent plots. – In: Hytteborn, H. (ed.) The Use of Ecological Variables in Environmental Monitoring. Swedish National Environment Protection Board, Rep. PM 1151: 81–87.

Persson, H. 1979b. Fine-root production, mortality and decomposition in forest ecosystems. – Vegetatio 41: 101–109.

Persson, H. 1980a. Spatial distribution of fine-root growth, mortality and decomposition in a young Scots pine stand in Central Sweden. – Oikos 34: 77–87.

Persson, H. 1980b. Structural properties of the field and bottom layers at Ivantjärnsheden. – In: Persson, T. (ed.) Structure and Function of Northern Coniferous Forests – An Ecosystem Study, Ecol. Bull. (Stockholm) 32: 153–163.

Sernander, R. 1936. The primitive forests of Granskär and Fiby. A study of the part played by storm-gaps and dwarf trees in the regeneration of the Swedish spruce forest. – Acta Phytogeogr. Suec. 8, 232 pp. (In Swedish, English summary)

Sjörs, H. 1979. What are the criteria of an environmental change – natural or man-made? – In: Hytteborn, H. (ed.) The Use of Ecological Variables in Environmental Monitoring. Swedish National Environment Protection Board, Rep. PM 1151: 25–36.

Tamm, C. O. 1947. Soil-improving measures on a poor site. – Medd. Statens Skogsf. Inst. 36: 1–115. (In Swedish, English summary)

Wretlind, I. E. 1934. Die Naturbedingungen für die Entstehung der Kiefernheiden und *Hylocomium*-reichen Waldgesellschaften der nordschwedischen eisenpodsolierten Moränenböden. – Sv. Skogsv. Fören. Tidskr. 1934: 329–396. (In Swedish, German summary)

Zachrisson, O. 1977. Influence of forest fires on the North Swedish boreal forest. – Oikos 29: 22–32.

Persson, T. (ed) 1980
Structure and Function of Northern
Coniferous Forests – An Ecosystem Study
Ecol. Bull. (Stockholm) 32: 153–163.

STRUCTURAL PROPERTIES OF THE FIELD AND BOTTOM LAYERS AT IVANTJÄRNSHEDEN

H. Persson[1]

Abstract

Estimates are given of the standing crop in the field and bottom layers of two young *Pinus sylvestris* stands with *Calluna vulgaris* in different phases, and one mature *P. sylvestris* stand with *Calluna* in a mature-to-degenerate phase. The shoot production of dwarf shrubs was estimated by classifying them into different annual categories, *viz.* current-year shoots (C), and previous shoot generations (C + 1, C + 2 ...), after cropping. Attached dead plant material, fruits, etc., were sorted separately into categories. Samples in the young stands were stratified into *Calluna* (stratum I) and non-*Calluna* (stratum II), the distribution of which was estimated along diagonals in randomly chosen 100 m^2 quadrats. The shoot + leaf production of dwarf shrub totals in the C fraction was estimated at 89 ± 6 and 13 ± 1 g dw m^{-2} in the young stands and 61 ± 3 g m^{-2} in the old stand (estimates $\pm$ s.e.). The related biomass of dwarf shrub totals was estimated at 310 ± 23, 56 ± 5 and 197 ± 14 g m^{-2}. The biomass of mosses was estimated at 29 ± 6, 28 ± 11 and 139 ± 20 g m^{-2} and of lichens at 130 ± 26, 59 ± 14 and 118 ± 28 g m^{-2}. The percentage share of the field-layer biomass accounted for by *C. vulgaris* was fairly high in the stands, *viz.* 92, 96 and 70% respectively. In the old stand *Vaccinium vitis-idaea* is co-dominant with *C. vulgaris*, where it accounted for 30% of the total dwarf-shrub biomass.

Additional keywords: Biomass, *Calluna vulgaris*, dwarf shrubs, forest ecosystem, lichens, *Pinus sylvestris*, mosses, primary production, *Vaccinium vitis-idaea*.

Introduction

This paper reports results from investigations in three different Scots pine, *Pinus sylvestris*, stands at Ivantjärnsheden (Ih), Jädraås, Central Sweden (site description see Axelsson & Bråkenhielm, 1980, Bråkenhielm & Persson, 1980), with *Calluna vulgaris* in various phases of development. An outline of the aims and the reasoning underlying the planning of these studies is given in Flower-Ellis & Persson (1980). The growth forms of *Calluna* in a forest stand diverge considerably from those to be found on open heathlands (cf. Jonsson, 1957). Distribution patterns in forest stands are almost certainly related to variations in, for example, light intensity and competition from the tree and bottom layers (cf. Björkman, 1945; Jonsson, 1957). The relatively closed, 120-year-old stand, Ih V, has many examples of *Calluna* with elongated, often etiolated shoots, which readily become prostrate. In the young more open stands, Ih II (aged 15–20 years) and Ih III (aged 20–25 years), *Calluna* develops stronger upward-growing branches.

---

[1] Institute of Ecological Botany, Uppsala University, Box 559, S-751 22 Uppsala, Sweden

The balance which the forest stand might be expected to attain under natural conditions of development, is disturbed every time the tree stand is thinned, as in the case of the old stand, which was thinned in 1962. Light conditions become more favourable for the shrub-, field- and bottom-layer species, which compete with the tree roots for water and mineral nutrients.

Material and methods

Harvesting was carried out on randomly stratified quadrats in early October, 1973. Quadrats for field-layer sampling measured 0.5×0.5 m, while those used for sampling of the bottom layer were 0.25×0.25 m. Included by definition in the field layer were dwarf shrubs, herbaceous and graminaceous species and tree and shrub individuals less than 1 m in height. The bottom layer was composed of mosses and lichens. The nomenclature used follows Lid (1974) for vascular plants, Nyholm (1954–69) for mosses and Krok-Almquist (1962) for lichens except for *Cladonia silvatica* which was determined collectively.

All individuals rooted with the 0.5×0.5 m and 0.25×0.25 m frames were harvested. The plants were clipped at ground level, *viz.* immediately above the highest adventitious roots so that no aboveground parts remained, and were then placed in polythene bags, before being transported to the laboratory at Jädraås. With regard to the fractioning of shoot generations of dwarf shrubs, the suggestions and methods outlined by Mork (1946) and further defined and elaborated by Mohamed & Gimingham (1970) and Chapman *et al.* (1975a), were adopted. All species were sorted individually and dried to constant weight at 85°C for a minimum of 48 hours. They were then weighed to the nearest 0.01 g.

Dead plant material still attached to living parts (attached dead) was sorted into a special category. Floral parts and fruits were separated and weighed individually. At least two, in some cases three, shoot generations of dwarf shrubs were differentiated, the current year (C) and earlier (C + 1, C + 2 ...) shoot generations. Mosses were sorted into two fractions, one comprising living plant material (biomass) and one containing attached-dead material. The former fractions was defined at that part of the moss which still was green. As regards lichens, no attached-dead fraction was distinguished (see text to Table 1).

In order to reduce the variance in the samples the sampling scheme in Ih II and III was based on two broad divisions into *Calluna* (stratum I) and non-*Calluna* (stratum II), in which quadrats were distributed at random. In Ih V no obvious clones of *Calluna* could be distinguished. The field layer, mainly consisting of *C. vulgaris* and *V. vitis-idaea*, was distributed in a micro-pattern throughout its entire extent. Mosses and reindeer lichens were abundant in the bottom layer. Since no straightforward strata could be distinguished, sampling was carried out on small randomised 0.5×0.5 m and 0.25×0.25 m quadrats in the larger 10×10 m quadrats.

The number of 10×10 m quadrats reserved for the sampling programme was 40 in Ih II, 30 in Ih III and 24 in Ih V. Approximately 30 small quadrats (0.5×0.5 m and 0.25×0.25 m) were distributed throughout each stratum and stand. The 0.25×0.25 m quadrats from which the bottom layer was harvested were placed in the middle of the 0.5×0.5 m field-layer quadrats.

The distribution of strata I and II in Ih II and Ih III were measured by making an inventory of the length occupied by the two strata along transects drawn diagonally across each of the 10×10 m sampling quadrats. A total of 34 10×10 m quadrats were analysed in Ih II and 30 in Ih III. A special programme for the statistical evaluation of the latter data was drawn up by G. I. Ågren (see Appendix), from which it was possible to estimate the area occupied by *Calluna* strata in stands Ih II and Ih III at $48 \pm 3\%$ and $12 \pm 4\%$ (95% confidence interval), respectively.

Results

Table 1 shows estimates of the standing crop (above-ground biomass and attached-dead separately) of field- and bottom-layer species, which were harvested by the quadrat harvesting method described above. Since harvesting took place so late in the growing season, many herbaceous and particularly graminaceous species, had withering or dead organs. *Vaccinium myrtillus* leaves had started to wither, but

154

Table 1. Standing-crop estimates (g dw m^{-2} at 85°C) fractioned into biomass and attached-dead, of field-layer and bottom-layer species in stands Ih II, Ih III and Ih V, Ivantjärnsheden. Harvesting took place in late September/early October 1973. Certain species, e.g., *Chamaenerion angustifolium, Convallaria majalis, Solidago virgaurea* and *Deschampsia flexuosa* were harvested within the main, either withered or dead, foliage. No special attached-dead fraction was determined in the case of lichens. The number of sample quadrats, 0.5 × 0.5 m and 0.25 × 0.25 m, for the field and bottom layers, respectively, were 30 in Ih II, stratum I and II, 28 and 29 in Ih III, stratum I and II, respectively, and 30 in Ih V. The estimates in Ih II and Ih III were calculated by using the percentage ratio between the two strata in each of the stands. These accounted for 47.9% and 52.1% of the area in Ih II and 12.0% and 88.0% in Ih III, respectively. The estimates are given ± one standard error. − denotes absence, 0 denotes a value smaller than 0.5.

	Ih II		Ih III		Ih V	
	Biomass	Attached dead	Biomass	Attached dead	Biomass	Attached dead
Dwarf shrubs						
Calluna vulgaris	287 ± 23	63 ± 6	54 ± 5	17 ± 2	137 ± 13	8 ± 1
Vaccinium myrtillus	1 ± 1	0	0	0	0	0
V. vitis-idaea	22 ± 2	2 ± 1	2 ± 1	0	60 ± 4	1 ± 1
Herbaceous species						
Chamaenerion angustifolium	−	−	−	0	−	−
Convallaria majalis	−	−	−	0	−	−
Lycopodium complanatum	−	−	0	2 ± 2	−	−
Solidago virgaurea	−	−	0	0	−	−
Graminaceous species						
Deschampsia flexuosa	−	−	6 ± 3	15 ± 6	−	−
Mosses						
Dicranum polysetum	6 ± 2	0	3 ± 2	0	17 ± 5	5 ± 2
D. fuscescens	2 ± 1	7 ± 5	−	−	−	−
Hylocomium splendens	−	−	0	0	0	−
Pleurozium schreberi	20 ± 4	3 ± 1	25 ± 10	4 ± 1	122 ± 18	20 ± 6
Pohlia nutans	0	−	−	−	−	−
Polytricum juniperinum	1 ± 1	1 ± 1	−	−	−	−
P. piliferum	0	−	−	−	−	−
Ptilium crista-castrensis	1 ± 1	−	−	−	−	−
Lichens						
Cetraria islandica	0	−	1 ± 1	−	1 ± 1	−
Cladonia alpestris	0	−	−	−	0	−
C. botrytes	0	−	1 ± 1	−	0	−
C. cenotea	2 ± 1	−	3 ± 1	−	−	−
C. cornuta	9 ± 4	−	4 ± 2	−	0	−
C. crispata	2 ± 1	−	0	−	−	−
C. deformis	4 ± 1	−	4 ± 1	−	−	−
C. fimbriata	4 ± 2	−	7 ± 3	−	0	−
C. gracilis	1 ± 1	−	1 ± 1	−	0	−
C. pyxidata	1 ± 1	−	8 ± 4	−	0	−
C. rangiferina	78 ± 24	−	16 ± 8	−	37 ± 14	−
C. silvatica	28 ± 9	−	13 ± 8	−	80 ± 28	−
Peltigera aphthosa	−	−	0	−	−	−

Table 2. Biomass estimates (g dw m^{-2} at 85°C) of the major plant categories in the field and bottom layers of stands Ih II and Ih III (strata I and II) and Ih V at Ivantjärnsheden. Estimates are given ± standard error. – denotes absence, 0 denotes a value smaller than 0.5. As regards other data see Table 1.

	Ih II		Ih III		Ih II	Ih III	Ih V
	I	II	I	II	Overall estimates	Overall estimates	Overall estimates
Tree species	10 ± 5	0	0	1 ± 1	5 ± 2	1 ± 1	0
Dwarf shrubs	627 ± 48	18 ± 4	459 ± 38	1 ± 1	310 ± 23	56 ± 5	197 ± 14
Herbaceous plants	–	–	0	0	–	0	–
Graminaceous plants	–	–	0	7 ± 3	–	6 ± 3	–
Field layer, total	637 ± 49	18 ± 4	459 ± 38	10 ± 3	314 ± 23	64 ± 5	197 ± 14
Mosses	54 ± 11	7 ± 4	38 ± 7	27 ± 12	29 ± 6	28 ± 11	139 ± 20
Lichens	62 ± 19	194 ± 46	21 ± 13	65 ± 16	130 ± 26	59 ± 14	118 ± 28
Bottom layer, total	116 ± 21	201 ± 46	59 ± 13	92 ± 18	161 ± 26	88 ± 16	257 ± 24

had not yet fallen to any appreciable extent. This species, herbs and grasses (cf. Table 1) were fairly uncommon in all stands except Ih III, with the result that losses due to withering and leaf-fall in the investigated stands were, in general, comparatively small. In stand Ih III, the most important secondary species was *Deschampsia flexuosa,* which occurred in the field layer among and between *Calluna vulgaris* clones.

The highest total standing crop of *C. vulgaris* was in Ih II (calculations as in Table 2), where an overall biomass of 287 ± 23 g m^{-2} was recorded for the stand total (the mean in stratum I was 600 ± 48 g m^{-2}). The overall biomass amounted to only 54 ± 5 g m^{-2} in stand Ih III (mean within stratum I was 450 ± 38 g m^{-2}) and to 137 ± 13 g m^{-2} in Ih V. Thus, the biomass per unit area within the *Calluna* stratum in the stands Ih II and Ih III was fairly high, but was counterbalanced to some extent by the low biomass in the non-*Calluna* stratum.

The percentage share of the total biomass of dwarf shrubs accounted for by *C. vulgaris* in stands Ih II, Ih III and Ih V was 92, 96 and 70% respectively. From this, it may be deduced that *Calluna* clones had a more compact growing habit in stands Ih II and Ih III than in stand Ih V, where they were rather sparsely distributed (see above), leaving space for other field- and bottom-layer species.

Vaccinium vitis-idaea was co-dominant with *C. vulgaris* in stand Ih V, where it accounted for 30% of the total biomass of dwarf shrubs. This species was fairly unimportant in Ih II and Ih III in terms of weight, although it was in a stage of re-growth, especially in Ih II (cf. Persson, 1979). The percentage share of *V. vitis-idaea* in the total dwarf shrub biomass in stratum I and II in Ih II was 4 and 94%, respectively. In stand Ih III, where *V. vitis-idaea* represented a diminutive fraction of the total field-layer biomass, competition from herbaceous and graminaceous species was strong (cf. Tables 1, 2 and 3). The other dwarf shrub found in the

Table 3. Structural composition of the standing crop of dominant dwarf shrubs (g dw m^{-2} at 85°C) in stands Ih II and Ih III (strata I and II) and Ih V at Ivantjärnsheden. Current year's shoots (C) are distinguished as well as older shoot generations (C + 1, C + 2 ...). Fruits (undehisced capsules of *Calluna vulgaris*) and attached-dead fractions are also categorized. Only two shoot generations of *C. vulgaris* are distinguished, *viz.*, C and C + 1. Estimates are given ± one standard error. – denotes absence, 0 denotes a value smaller than 0.5. As regards the date of sampling, number of sample quadrats, etc., see Table 1.

	Ih II		Ih III		Ih V
	I	II	I	II	
Calluna vulgaris					
C	177 ± 13	0	106 ± 10	–	41 ± 4
C + 1	122 ± 10	0	112 ± 10	–	38 ± 3
Fruits	6 ± 1	–	2 ± 1	–	1 ± 1
Attached dead	132 ± 13	–	142 ± 17	–	8 ± 1
Biomass	600 ± 48	0	450 ± 38	–	137 ± 12
Vaccinium vitis-idaea					
C	4 ± 1	4 ± 1	1 ± 1	1 ± 1	3 ± 1
C + 1	12 ± 2	8 ± 2	2 ± 1	1 ± 1	22 ± 2
C + 2	6 ± 1	3 ± 1	1 ± 1	0	0
Fruits	–	0	–	–	0
Attached dead	2 ± 1	1 ± 1	1 ± 1	0	1 ± 1
Biomass	26 ± 3	17 ± 4	6 ± 1	1 ± 1	60 ± 4
Vaccinium myrtillus					
C	0	0	0	0	0
C + 1	0	0	0	0	0
C + 2	0	0	0	0	0
Fruits	–	–	–	–	0
Attached dead	0	0	0	0	0
Biomass	1 ± 1	0	0	0	0
Dwarf shrub totals					
C	181 ± 13	4 ± 1	107 ± 10	1 ± 1	43 ± 4
C + 1	135 ± 10	8 ± 2	114 ± 10	0	61 ± 3
Fruits	6 ± 1	0	2 ± 1	–	1 ± 1
Attached dead	134 ± 13	2 ± 1	142 ± 17	0	9 ± 1
Biomass	627 ± 48	18 ± 4	459 ± 38	1 ± 1	197 ± 14

stands investigated, *viz.*, *Vaccinium myrtillus*, was usually insignificant in terms of weight.

Mosses and lichens represented an important weight fraction of the total biomass in Ih II (stratum II), Ih III (stratum II) and Ih V. Only in the *Calluna* stratum in Ih II and Ih III, with young *Calluna* clones in stages of vigorous regrowth, was the share of the bottom layer in biomass low. Mosses, mainly *Pleurozium schreberi* and *Dicranum polysetum*, accounted for major weight fractions in Ih V, while lichens, *inter alia, Cladonia rangiferina* and *C. silvatica,* were important in terms of weight in Ih II and Ih III. Cup-lichens, original colonisers in Ih II and Ih III after clear-felling, accounted for a small and rather variable weight fraction (Table 1).

Production figures for dwarf shrubs (i.e., shoot + leaf production) were derived from estimates obtained by the method outlined above (Table 3). Material harvested from 0.5×0.5 m quadrats was classified into current shoots C and earlier shoot generations (C + 1, C + 2 ...). The C + 2 shoot generation was distinguished only in the case of *Vaccinium* spp. This procedure does not include radial increments in older stem sections, probably insignificant in the case of *Vaccinium myrtillus* and *V. vitis-idaea* (cf. Flower-Ellis, 1971; Teär, 1972), but probably not so in *C. vulgaris,* where a large part of the biomass totals is to be found in older stems (J. G. K. Flower-Ellis & H. Persson, in prep.).

The two shoot generations distinguished in *C. vulgaris,* i.e., C and C + 1, correspond fairly well with the green sections of the plant during autumnal conditions. These fractions accounted together for 50, 48 and 58% of the total biomass (cf. Table 3) in Ih II, Ih III and Ih V. The leaves of older shoot generations were probably lost when harvesting took place. On the shoots below the C shoots (i.e., C + 1) bare regions could be observed, resulting from the loss of flowering laterals. Among the latter, mainly capsules, the losses on C shoots should also be considered as being high owing to unavoidable damage during harvesting. The capsules (undehisced fruits still covered by a persistent calyx), were easily broken off, for example, when transferring the sample into polythene bags.

Fruit loss in the case of *Vaccinium vitis-idaea* probably also appeared in the estimates but, in this case, this was due to natural fruit dispersal before harvesting took place. *V. vitis-idaea* fruit was abundant only in the old stand, Ih V (cf. Table 3). The low estimates might have been a result of a poor fruiting year.

The amount of attached-dead material in *C. vulgaris* in Ih II (stratum I) and Ih III (stratum I) was proportionately higher than in Ih V. In the former two stands, the *Calluna* clones grew more compactly, with the result that there was little space between the individual plants for wind and air movements, which would break off dead material or cause it to fall.

Discussion and conclusions

Plant cover in a coniferous forest stand can be divided into four competing layers: (1) tree layer, (2) shrub layer, (3) field layer and (4) bottom layer. Of these four vegetation categories, the shrub layer in a dry pine-heath community of the same type as at Ivantjärnsheden is of minimal significance with regard to the development of the other layers, since it is mainly composed of isolated and often suppressed individuals.

The growth of the field layer is limited by the degree of closure in the tree canopy. A negative correlation exists between the canopy cover of trees and the development of the field layer (cf. Persson & Hytteborn, 1975). At ground level, the field layer, composed mainly of *Calluna vulgaris* and *Vaccinium vitis-idaea,* competes with the bottom layer, i.e., the mosses and lichens. Lichens grow most abundantly in patches between the heather, whereas mosses, mainly *Pleurozium schreberi,* are to be found growing among heather individuals, at times attaining considerable density (cf. Table 1). In the bottom layer lichens are more important in terms of weight in Ih II and Ih III than in Ih V, where a comparatively large part of the living matter is accounted for by mosses. The biomass of the bottom layer is, on the whole, greater in Ih V than in Ih II and Ih III. The number of lichen species is greater in Ih II and Ih III than in Ih V, since a number of the colonisers from the clear-felled stages of the former stands, e.g., cup lichens, still remain.

A clear trend may therefore be observed in the development of ground cover, from heterogeneity (dynamics) in the building phase towards homogeneity and a comparatively small number of species in the final phases of the stand's development (stability). Simultaneously, distinctly developed *Calluna* clones disappear, giving rise to a more uniform vegetation, where *Calluna* clones grow into each other without distinct boundaries. At the same time, the small-scale pattern of vegetation becomes more varied and real stratified units, corresponding to strata I and II, are no longer distinguishable. Furthermore, the bottom layer increases in weight and expands in size (Tables 1 and 2).

The above-ground biomass of *Calluna* in all the stands investigated is considerably lower than that reported from other ecosystem studies (cf. Forrest, 1971; Tyler *et al.,* 1973; Chapman *et al.,* 1975a; Smith & Forrest, 1978). These studies are, however, from non-wooded areas, such as heaths and moors. Nevertheless, Mork (1946) reported a fairly high figure for the total above-ground biomass (1440 g m^{-2}) from a sub-alpine forest area in Norway. However, Mork's sites were more humid than the investigated stands at Ivantjärnsheden.

Mälkönen (1974) has reported fairly low estimates, *viz.,* 107, 166, and 56 g m^{-2}, for the dwarf shrub biomass of three Scots pine stands (28, 47, and 45 years of age, respectively) in southern Finland. These stands were all in intermediate stages of development with high annual increments in the fairly closed tree layer. In the dwarf shrub totals from these stands the proportions of *Calluna vulgaris,* which is usually the most abundant species weightwise, were fairly low, i.e., 44, 78, and 26%, if one compares the latter figures with those obtained from Ivantjärnsheden. The diversity of species was greater in the Finnish stands, which were sparsely developed with both low cover and frequency.

The *Calluna* biomass is highest in the *Calluna* strata of Ih II and Ih III, which are almost exclusively composed of *Calluna,* 600 and 450 g m^{-2}, respectively. The fairly low overall estimates could be explained by the fact that *Calluna* in a forest stand often develops very sparsely owing to competition from other species with regard to space, light, moisture and nutrients.

In the Scots pine stand studied by Mälkönen (1974), mosses were the main producers in the field and bottom layers, apart from dwarf shrubs. Mälkönen assumed the annual production of the mosses to be a third of their total biomass since their shoots are usually composed of three living annual segments (cf. Romell, 1939; Tamm, 1953). If this assumption is applied to Ivantjärnsheden, the annual moss production in stands Ih II, Ih III and Ih V would be in the region of 10, 9, and 46 g m^{-2}, respectively.

As regards shoot production, estimates from Ih II and Ih III are considerably higher than those from Ih V, all taken from *Calluna* strata (Table 3). However, annual increments in older stem sections were not included in these estimates. Determination of age structure, together with morphological studies, could be of help in the calculation of the total net primary production (J. G. K. Flower-Ellis & H. Persson, in prep.).

The age of all the *Calluna* stems is being determined by means of basal ring counts. Preliminary results from Ih V point to a mean age in older stems of between 20–25 years (J.G.K. Flower-Ellis, pers. comm.). Stems from Ih II and Ih III are considerably younger. Since older basal stem sections are successively embedded into the litter, most older stems are found below ground. The age of the tillers increases from the distal to the middle sections of the stem.

The net production of *Calluna* C-shoots compared with the total biomass of the field-layer species in the young building phase in Ih II and Ih III was 30 and 24% respectively. The corresponding figure for Ih V was 21%. These figures can be compared with those of Barclay-Estrup (1970) who, reporting from a heath in N.E. Scotland, estimated the net production of *Calluna* through its different phases to 29% of the total biomass in the building phase, 19% in the mature and 14% in the degenerate phase.

The high production of *Calluna* in Ih V could be explained by the fact that this particular stand was thinned in 1962 and that, consequently, the *Calluna* was temporarily undergoing an upsurge in growth. However, the trees had just (1971–72) entered the downward part of the growth development after thinning (J.G.K. Flower-Ellis, pers. comm.), indicating that the same would be the case of the field layer and *Calluna* in particular.

The presence of *Calluna* tends to lower the soil temperature, thus retarding the process of decomposition in the humus layer and the activity of the tree roots (cf. Mork, 1946). The shallow-rooted dwarf shrubs also prevent an important part of the precipitation from reaching and benefitting the tree roots, simultaneously depriving the latter of substantial quantities of nutrients (cf. Persson, 1980). Dense *Calluna* in forest stands thus affects the production of merchantable timber to an appreciable extent. *Calluna* also acidifies the soil by producing litter with large quantities of polyphenols (Handley, 1954). Another negative influence on the growth of the trees is that of reindeer lichens, which inhibit the growth of mycorrhiza on the tree roots (cf. Brown & Mikola, 1974).

Calluna litter comprises woody stems, long shoots and short shoots. Leaves are seldom shed separately but remain attached to the shoots. Flowers, in the form of undehisced capsules, still covered by calyx, often remain attached to the plant until the next flowering period occurs.

There are two maxima in the annual cycle of *Calluna* litter fall (cf. Cormack & Gimingham, 1964; Chapman *et al.*, 1975b) – one late in autumn (October–November) and the other in winter (February). This seasonal pattern, observed by the above-mentioned authors in different habitats of the British Isles, is probably also the case elsewhere in the Northern temperate zone.

Since harvesting at Ivantjärnsheden took place in early October, probably prior to the first of the above-mentioned peaks, one might expect the amount of attached dead material to be fairly high. In Ih II and Ih III, the attached-dead fractions were of the same order as the current shoot production. Since most of the attached-dead fraction had been produced during the newly terminated growth period, one might also expect equivalence between annual decay and replacement of organic matter per unit area in the building phase of *Calluna*. Consequently, the increase in biomass which occurs during the building-to-mature phase must to a greater or lesser extent be the result of the vegetative spread of the species to other sections of the habitat. Clone growth and spread (Watt, 1955) is primarily centrifugal, i.e., at its most intense in the expanding, outer parts.

The high proportion of current biomass (C) in stratum II in Ih II indicates a low mean age in this stratum (e.g., *Calluna* in a pioneer-to-building phase). However, this was not the case in Ih III, since the *Calluna* clones had developed more distinctly in this stand, with the result that newly formed parts of the clones were rarely encountered in the sample quadrats.

A fairly low estimate of attached-dead material was obtained from Ih V. Besides the fact that the plants were extensively spread and thus more susceptible to damage from wind, etc., the low estimate could also be an effect of the stimulus that the growth had received from the thinning of the stand.

Capsule shedding follows a seasonal pattern similar to that for the main litter fractions (cf. Cormack & Gimingham, 1964). However, a large number of capsules were broken off during the harvest and during transportation to the laboratory. As regards the fruits of *Vaccinium vitis-idaea,* the crop was most probably underestimated, since most of the fruit had been shed or eaten before harvesting took place. According to Teär (1972), who gives a very detailed description of the fructificative development of cowberry, a normal Scots pine forest produces 162 g m^{-2}, approximately twice the amount estimated for Ih V (cf. Table 3).

Acknowledgements

This study was performed as a part of the Swedish Coniferous Forest Project. The study was carried out with the cooperation of J.G.K. Flower-Ellis, who also afforded me a great deal of critical advice, based on an extensive knowledge of dwarf shrubs. G. I. Ågren wrote up a statistical evaluation programme for the transect inventory. I am also indebted to M. Dahlgren, K-B. Sundström, B. Andersson and I. Asplund, who assisted in the final stage of the data processing. The siting of sampling quadrats and sampling was carried out with the help of G. Juhlin and H. Letocha. Most of the material was sorted at Jädraås by L. Ramström and G. Nilsson. B. Andersson, site manager, contributed with practical advice.

References

Axelsson, B. & Bråkenhielm, S. 1980. Investigation sites of the Swedish Coniferous Forest Project – biological and physiographical features. – In: Persson, T. (ed.) Structure and Function of Northern Coniferous Forests – An Ecosystem Study, Ecol. Bull. (Stockholm) 32: 25–64.
Barclay-Estrup, P. 1970. The description and interpretation of cyclical processes in a heath community. 2. Changes in biomass and shoot production during the *Calluna* cycle. – J. Ecol. 58: 243–249.
Björkman, E. 1945. On the influence of light on the height-growth of pine plants on pine-heaths in Norrland. – Medd. Statens Skogsförs. Anst. 34: 497–542. (In Swedish, English summary)
Bråkenhielm, S. & Persson, H. 1980. Vegetation dynamics in developing Scots pine stands in Central Sweden. – In: Persson, T. (ed.) Structure and Function of Northern Coniferous Forests – An Ecosystem Study, Ecol. Bull. (Stockholm) 32: 139–152.

Brown, R. T. & Mikola, P. 1974. The influence of fructicose soil lichens upon the mycorrhizae and seedling growth of forest trees. – Acta Forest. Fenn. 141, 23 pp.

Chapman, S. B., Hibble, J. & Rafarel, C. R. 1975a. Net aerial production by *Calluna vulgaris* on lowland heath in Britain. – J. Ecol. 63: 233–258.

Chapman, S. B., Hibble, J. & Rafarel, C. R. 1975b. Litter accumulation under *Calluna vulgaris* on a lowland heath in Britain. – J. Ecol. 63: 259–271.

Cormack, E. & Gimingham, C. H. 1964. Litter production by *Calluna vulgaris* (L.) Hull. – J. Ecol. 52: 285–297.

Flower-Ellis, J. G. K. 1971. Age structure and dynamics in stands of bilberry (*Vaccinium myrtillus* L.). – Dept. of Forest Ecology and Forest Soils, Royal College of Forestry, Stockholm, Research Notes 9, 108 pp.

Flower-Ellis, J. G. K. & Persson, H. 1980. Investigation of structural properties and dynamics of Scots pine stands. – In: Persson, T. (ed) Structure and Function of Northern Coniferous Forests – An Ecosystem Study, Ecol. Bull. (Stockholm) 32: 125–138.

Forrest, G. I. 1971. Structure and production of North Pennine blanket bog vegetation. – J. Ecol. 59: 453–479.

Handley, W. R. C. 1954. Mull and mor formation in relation to forest soils. – Bull. For. Commun., Lond. 23, 115 pp.

Jonsson, B. 1957. Heidekrautstudien auf Kiefernsand in Södertörn. – Sv. Skogsv. Fören. Tidskr. 55: 413–451. (In Swedish, German summary)

Krok, T. O. B. N. & Almquist, S. 1961. Svensk Flora för Skolor. 2. Kryptogamer utom Ormbunks-växter. Stockholm: Sv. Bokförlaget, 390 pp. (In Swedish)

Lid, J. 1974. Norsk og Svensk Flora, Andre Utgåva. Oslo: Det Norske Samlaget, 808 pp. (In Norwegian)

Mälkönen, E. 1974. Annual primary production and nutrient cycle in some Scots pine stands. – Commun. Inst. For. Fenn. 84(5), 87 pp.

Mohamed, B. F. & Gimingham, C. H. 1970. The morphology of vegetative regeneration in *Calluna vulgaris*. – New Phytol. 69: 743–750.

Mork, E. 1946. On the dwarf shrub vegetation on forest ground. – Medd. Norske Skogforsøksv. 33: 269–356. (In Norwegian, English summary)

Nyholm, E. 1954, 1956, 1958, 1960, 1965, 1969. Illustrated Moss Flora of Fennoscandia. 2. Musci. Lund: Gleerup, 799 pp.

Persson, H. 1979. The possible outcomes and limitations of measuring quantitative changes in plant cover on permanent plots. – In: Hytteborn, H. (ed.), The Use of Ecological Variables in Environmental Monitoring, Swedish National Environment Protection Board, Rep. PM 1151: 81–87.

Persson, H. 1980. Spatial distribution of fine-root growth, mortality and decomposition in a young Scots pine stand in Central Sweden. – Oikos 34: 77–87.

Persson, H. & Hytteborn, H. 1975. Studies of the productivity of changeable deciduous forest and shrubland ecosystems. – Mimeographed paper presented at the 12th Int. Bot. Congr., Leningrad 1975, 11 pp.

Romell, L-G. 1939. Litter production and annual growth of blueberry bushes and mosses in Northern spruce woods. – Sv. Bot. Tidskr. 33: 366–382. (In Swedish, English summary)

Smith, R. A. H. & Forrest, G. I. 1978. Field estimates of primary production. – In: Heal, O. W. & Perkins, D. F. (eds.). Production of British Moors and Montane Grasslands, Ecological Studies 27: 17–37. Berlin-Heidelberg-New York: Springer-Verlag.

Tamm, C. O. 1953. Growth, yield and nutrition in carpets of a forest moss (*Hylocomium splendens*). – Medd. Stat. Skogsforskn. Inst. 43(1), 140 pp.

Teär, J. 1972. Vegetativ och fruktifikativ utveckling av vildväxande och odlade lingon. – Available at the library of the Swedish University of Agricultural Sciences, Uppsala, mimeographed, 107 pp. (In Swedish)

Tyler, G., Gullstrand, C., Holmquist, K-Å. & Kjellstrand, A-M. 1973. Primary production and distribution of organic matter and metal elements in two heath ecosystems. – J. Ecol. 61: 251–268.

Watt, A. S. 1955. Bracken versus heather, a study in plant sociology. – J. Ecol. 43: 490–506.

Appendix

STATISTICAL ANALYSIS OF COVER OF CALLUNA

G. I. Ågren[1]

In order to estimate the distribution of *Calluna* and non-*Calluna* strata, the lengths along the diagonal transects occupied by these strata were measured in a number of quadrats, N. One may consider one of these quadrats as hypothetically subdivided into n^2 smaller quadrats. n should be chosen so that, within each of the smaller quadrats, only one stratum exists, being so small in size that two adjacent quadrats can be assumed to grow independently. These two stipulations can, in all probability, be only approximately satisfied, but despite this drawback the following derivation is based upon them. Instead of measuring the actual length, one can count the number of small quadrats along a diagonal, m_i, in which *Calluna* grows in each, i, of the larger quadrats. Under the assumptions made, m_i is binomially distributed (n, p), p is the probability that *Calluna* grows in a small quadrat, and $n^2 p$ is the average number of small quadrats in which *Calluna* grows. p is therefore the relative cover of *Calluna*.

Since n is a large number, one may take m_i as approximately normally distributed $(np, \sqrt{np(1-p)}$ and the relative length of *Calluna* along a diagonal is then approximately normally distributed $(p, \frac{\sqrt{p(1-p)}}{n})$. One has thus established that the relative cover of *Calluna* is normally distributed and that the relative length of *Calluna* along a diagonal is equal to the relative cover. One can then proceed by applying the well known theories of normally distributed variables to area measurements.

[1] Dept. of Ecology and Environmental Research, Swedish University of Agricultural Sciences, S-750 07 Uppsala, Sweden.

Persson, T. (ed) 1980
Structure and Function of Northern
Coniferous Forests – An Ecosystem Study
Ecol. Bull. (Stockholm) 32: 165–181.

PHOTOSYNTHESIS AND TRANSPIRATION OF 20-YEAR-OLD SCOTS PINE

S. Linder[1] and E. Troeng[1]

Abstract

A system of air-cooled assimilation chambers was developed for continuous measurement of gas exchange in a 20-year-old stand of Scots pine. The period of net photosynthetic activity was approximately eight months a year, starting in April as soon as the soil was no longer frozen. Photosynthesis stopped in December largely because of low irradiance and air temperature. Calculation of the mesophyll conductance for carbon dioxide showed that it took more than two months of the growing season to repair winter damage to the photosynthetic apparatus. Needle age had a much more pronounced effect on photosynthetic efficiency and performance than had the position of needles within the crown. The variation between trees was small, and smaller for photosynthesis than for transpiration.

Stem and branch respiration measured *in situ* exhibited large seasonal variation. The pronouncedly increased rate of respiration during the growth period was probably caused by "growth respiration" plus an adaptation to temperature of the maintenance respiration. In light, stem and branch respiration decreased as a result of the refixation of carbon dioxide in the chlorophyll-containing tissue immediately beneath the thin periderm.

Additional keywords: Fertilization, irrigation, mesophyll conductance, respiration, stomatal conductance.

Background

One of the main aims of the Swedish Coniferous Forest Project (SWECON) was the construction of simulation models for prediction of the primary production of a forest dominated by Scots pine (*Pinus sylvestris* L.). To achieve this a better understanding of the processes and factors regulating growth was needed. Photosynthesis and respiration are key processes for the understanding and description of the dynamics of primary production in an ecosystem and, consequently, a study of the gas exchange of Scots pine was carried out as an integrated part of the project.

[1] Section of Forest Ecophysiology, Swedish University of Agricultural Sciences, S-750 07 Uppsala, Sweden

165

Introduction

In spite of the fact that Scots pine has been the most popular species for the study of CO_2-exchange of forest trees, very little is known about its physiological capacity and performance under field conditions. Of the more than one hundred papers concerning CO_2-exchange of Scots pine, only nine deal with *in situ* measurements on trees for periods longer than a few days. Two of these reports concern stem respiration (Johansson, 1933; Linder & Troeng, 1977), the others deal with net photosynthesis (Polster & Fuchs, 1963; Ungersson & Scherdin, 1965, 1968; Neuwirth, 1974; Künstle & Mitscherlich, 1975; Linder & Ingestad, 1977; Troeng & Linder, 1977). Three of these investigations were carried out with titration methods (Johansson, 1933; Ungersson & Scherdin, 1965, 1968) which made continuous measurements impossible. The lack of information about the gas exchange of Scots pine under natural conditions is not unique; the situation is approximately the same for all conifers (cf. Linder, 1979). The only exception is *Pinus cembra* L., on which Tranquillini (1955, 1959a, b, 1963a, b) carried out pioneer studies of gas exchange in a severe climate.

It is well-known that there is a pronounced seasonal variation in the net photosynthetic rate of conifers (cf. Larcher, 1969; Jarvis *et al.*, 1976), partly because of seasonal variation in the weather and partly because certain biological processes are dependent upon the season. The start of net photosynthesis in spring depends on the temperature (Ludlow & Jarvis, 1971), and seems to be independent of day-length (Bamberg *et al.*, 1967). During early spring there is a dehardening process in conifers and a simultaneous reconstruction of the photosynthetic apparatus which has been partly destroyed by low winter temperatures. Hardened plant material has a lower photosynthetic capacity than dehardened material. This can be seen both in the net photosynthetic rate (Turner & Jarvis, 1975) and in the electron transport capacity (Öquist & Hellgren, 1976). Even when part of the photosynthetic capacity has been restored in the needles, positive net photosynthesis will not occur until the water in the soil is no longer frozen. Conifers can maintain a high rate of water uptake at soil temperatures 2–3°C above the freezing point (Havranek, 1972; Linder, 1972; Turner & Jarvis, 1975).

During summer, the rate of net photosynthesis is mainly controlled by irradiance, air-temperature and access to water. However, adaptation of the physiological processes to the prevailing temperature must also be taken into account (Rook, 1969; Neilson *et al.*, 1972; Strain *et al.*, 1976).

In the autumn, day-length and irradiance are the main factors limiting photosynthesis. In a mild climate, this reduction in photosynthesis can take place without a reduction in photosynthetic capacity (Fry & Phillips, 1977). Conifers are capable of photosynthesis at temperatures below 0°C (cf. Larcher, 1969), and the lower limit is set by the temperature at which the water in the needles freezes (Pisek *et al.*, 1967; Neilson *et al.*, 1972). This critical temperature varies with season and depends on the degree of hardening (Tranquillini & Holzer, 1958; Neilson *et al.* 1972).

The photosynthetic production of the current shoots increases rapidly during shoot elongation, and reaches peak values in late summer, when needle growth has ceased and the needles are mature (Troeng & Linder, 1977). In Sitka spruce the increase in net photosynthetic rates is mainly the result of a decrease in mesophyll resistance, while stomatal resistance and respiration are relatively constant (Ludlow & Jarvis, 1971). After the needles have attained maturity, the photosynthetic efficiency decreases with age (Freeland, 1952; Künstle & Mitscherlich, 1975), one of the reasons being an increasing stomatal resistance with age (Jeffree et al., 1971).

Before the "gross production" of a tree or a stand can be calculated or the dynamics of primary production understood, the amounts of carbon fixed in photosynthesis together with the amounts lost in respiration must be known. Despite this requirement, most of the literature available is concerned with CO_2-balance of the assimilating part of the biomass (cf. Larcher, 1969; Linder, 1979), and little is known about respiration losses from non-green parts of the tree.

Respiration can be considered as consisting of two components; maintenance respiration and growth respiration. Maintenance respiration supplies the energy for a number of processes, i.e., active transport, rebuilding of organic structures and maintenance of certain ion concentrations within the cells (cf. Penning de Vries, 1975). "Growth" or "constructive" respiration supplies the additional energy needed for growth. This is seen as a large increase in respiration rate (Kinerson, 1975; Linder & Troeng, 1977).

The magnitude of these two components of respiration and their responses to abiotic and biotic factors need to be known when modelling primary production and growth.

Most of the respiration in stems and branches takes place in the tissues outside the cambium, where the major part of the living cells is found. However, respiration also occurs in the ray cells and the epithelial cells of the resin ducts in the xylem, and has been reported to be approximately 10% of that taking place outside the xylem cylinder (Shain & Mackay, 1973).

A number of problems arise when attempts are made to correlate "growth respiration" with stem growth. Normally, stem growth is monitored by measuring the radial increase of the stem and the first problem encountered is the difference between earlywood and latewood. The former contains less carbon per unit of radial increase than latewood and therefore needs less carbon and energy per millimeter radial change. The second problem is the diurnal swelling and shrinkage of the stem. This makes attempts to find correlations between "growth respiration" and short-term increases of stem radius very difficult (Linder & Troeng, 1977). A third problem is that volume and density do not increase in parallel (Žumer, 1969a, b), and that the energy demand for the formation of secondary and tertiary wall structures probably is higher per unit volume than for the initial increase in volume.

The present report describes briefly the investigations carried out in SWECON on the gas exchange of pine. The primary purpose has been to provide relevant information for the project's models on growth and primary production (cf. Lohammar et al., 1980).

Materials and methods

The study was carried out at the Jädraås research site of SWECON in central Sweden (60°48′N, 16°30′E, alt. 185 m above M. S. L.). Most of the physiological sub-projects were conducted in a

167

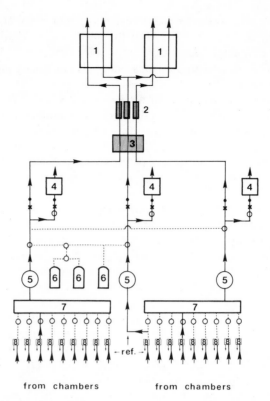

Figure 1. Diagramme showing the analysing system. (1) IRGA, (2) drying agent, (3) water vapour trap, (4) dew-point meter, (5) pump, (6) calibration gas, (7) manifold, (8) over-flow, (○) magnetic valve, (●) flow-meter, and (x) needle valve.

20-year-old stand of Scots pine (*Pinus sylvestris* L.). Since 1974 the stand has been subjected to an irrigation/fertilization experiment. The experimental stand is a natural stand regenerated under seed-trees and thinned before the treatment started in 1974. A detailed description of the stand structure can be found in Flower-Ellis *et al*. (1976) and the experiment is described in Aronsson *et al*. (1977). The biological and physiographical features of the Jädraås site can be found in Axelsson & Bråkenhielm (1980).

The initial task was to develop a system for continuous measurements of gas exchange in the 20-year-old pine stand.

The following criteria were set when designing the system:

– continuous measurement of carbon dioxide and water vapour exchange throughout the year;
– the system should consist of more than 10 chambers;
– chamber-temperature to track ambient temperature with a deviation of less than 2 °C without the use of water as cooling agent;
– the chambers should be capable of being attached to any branch or age-class of needles without changing the normal position of the branch;
– control of the system and collection and storage of data should be computerized.

Measuring system

A detailed description of the system can be found in Linder *et al*. (1980) and, therefore, only a brief description is given here.

168

The system consists of 16 temperature-controlled chambers divided between two analysing systems running in parallel (Fig. 1) in order to speed up the sampling rate and to ensure that some measurements could be carried out even when parts of the system are being repaired.

Each system is open and semi-continuous so that only two chambers can be analysed at a time. Carbon dioxide concentration is measured using an infra-red gas analyser (UNOR, Maihak, FRG) and water vapour pressure with a dew-point meter (Heinz Walz, Mess- und Regeltechnik, FRG). Air from any chamber passes through a mass flow-meter (Brooks Model 5811) with an automatic flow-control and the analysers for five minutes before the values are recorded. The normal flow rate used is 0.42 $m^3 h^{-1}$. The air pumped to the chambers is taken from a height of 10 m and afterwards distributed to the different chambers and to a reference line (Fig. 2). The reference air is sampled at the end of every sampling cycle.

Since the winter of 1976/77, one of the sampling lines has been connected to a chamber in the laboratory to enable measurement of the response of gas exchange to irradiance and temperature under constant conditions.

Assimilation chambers

The cylindrical chambers are made from thin perspex (1 mm) and have a diameter of 12 cm. The chamber is attached to a base-plate where a fan, an air-intake and air-outlet are situated. The chamber is enclosed in a wider perspex tube which is also attached to the base-plate.

The base-plate is fixed in a bifurcated holder, which enables the chamber to be mounted in the natural position of the branch. Each chamber is provided with thermocouples (copper/constantan) for measurement of needle- and air-temperatures and a quantum sensor (Lambda).

The temperature in the chamber is regulated by a draught of cool air flowing in the space between the chamber and the outer tube (Fig. 3). The cool air is supplied by a strong fan which blows air over a heat-exchanger with a temperature that is always kept 8 °C below ambient temperature. The flow of air is controlled by a damper placed in the air-stream. The damper opens to increase the flow as soon as the temperature in the chamber is more than 0.5 °C above ambient temperature and closes again when the chamber temperature returns to the ambient level.

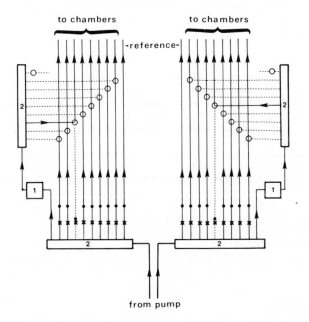

Figure 2. Diagramme of the air-supply to the chambers. (1) mass flow-meter with automatic flow control, (2) manifold, (O) magnetic valve (three-way), (●) flow-meter, and (x) needle valve. When a chamber is sampled, the air to the chamber flows through the mass flow-meter (cf. Fig. 1).

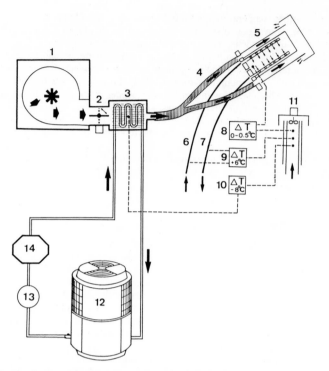

Figure 3. Schematic diagramme of the chamber system. (1) fan, (2) damper, (3) heat exchanger, (4) tubes for cooling air, (5) assimilation chamber, (6) air intake (from tower), (7) air outlet (to laboratory), (8) temperature controller for chamber, (9) temperature controller for tubes, (10) temperature controller for heat exchanger, (11) ventilated radiation shield, (12) cooler, (13) pump, and (14) electrical heater.

The cooling system has operated satisfactorily and has kept the chamber temperature within 1°C of ambient temperature in all weather conditions and at any time of the year.

The main problem during the first year was to avoid condensation of water in the chambers and in the tubing during periods of rain and high air humidity. The first attempt to avoid the problem was the installation of a heat-exchanger at the main air intake in the tower. The heat exchanger is connected to the cooling system of the chambers, which means that the dew point of the air going out to the chambers can never come closer to ambient temperature than 8°C below ambient. Initially this was sufficient to avoid problems of condensation but during the winter of 1976/77 there was a deep snow-cover (> 100 cm) and the tubes to the chambers were permanently covered with snow. Therefore, during mild days, ice could form in the tubes and this would hinder or even stop the air supply to the chambers. In the following spring the tubes to the chambers were furnished with heating foil and insulated. Since then there have been no problems of condensation in the chambers or in the tubes, and the records of transpiration have been uninterrupted since April 1977.

The chambers used for stem- and branch respiration are split PVC-tubes with top- and base-plates. The two halves are screwed together around the stem or branch with seals made of foam-rubber to avoid strangulation. The whole chamber is surrounded by a radiation-shield made of white-painted aluminium.

Design of experiments

The system has run continuously since July 1975 with only minor interruptions, generally as a result of damage to the data-loggers by lightning. During the growing seasons all chambers have been used, but during winter the number has been reduced to five or six.

170

Most measurements were carried out on current and one-year-old shoots in the third whorl on trees from the untreated plot. However, to enable calculation of the total annual production of a tree, simultaneous measurements on all age-classes of needles were carried out at different times of the year. Similarly, the same age-class of needles was measured in different positions on one tree, or in the same position on a number of trees.

Throughout the investigated period, 1975–79, four chambers have been used for "reference measurements". One-year-old shoots on the third whorl on trees from untreated, irrigated, and irrigated/fertilized plots have been measured continuously as well as one stem respiration chamber on an untreated tree. The other chambers available have been used for different kinds of experiments and replications.

During the first two years most of the chambers were used to get a good description of the seasonal variation in net photosynthesis (Troeng & Linder, 1977) and respiration (Linder & Troeng, 1977) within the stand. In the summer of 1977 the variation between and within trees was investigated (Linder & Troeng, 1978; Troeng & Linder, 1978) together with an experiment with water stress (cf. Bengtson, 1980). In the following year the effect of insects (Troeng *et al.*, 1979) and air-born pollutants (Hällgren *et al.*, in prep.) upon the gas exchange was studied.

All data gathered are stored and processed by a computer (PDP 11/40) capable of making most calculations directly at the site. A detailed description of the data acquisition system (ECODAC) is given by Engelbrecht *et al.* (1980).

Calculations

Carbon dioxide flux density (net photosynthesis) is calculated according to Catsky *et al.* (1971). Stomatal conductance, for water, is the ratio of water vapour (mass) flux density and the difference in water vapour concentration (mass/volume) between intercellular air and air in the chamber. In the calculations needle temperature is assumed to equal air temperature in the chamber. Boundary layer conductance is included in the calculated stomatal conductance.

Mesophyll conductance is calculated as the ratio of carbon flux density and intercellular CO_2 concentration thus neglecting the small but finite value of the CO_2 compensation point (cf. Jarvis, 1971).

All the entities are calculated on a projected needle area basis. The projected needle area is measured by a "leaf area meter" (Lambda model LI-300).

Results and discussion

Most of the information gathered still remains to be analysed and compiled, but a few examples are given here to illustrate the kind of results obtained.

Seasonal variation in net photosynthesis

In spite of quite different weather in the four years (1976–79), photosynthesis started in early April every year. The performance in spring 1977 is shown in Fig. 4. The main limiting factor was access to water. As soon as the soil temperature increased above 0 °C, the supply of water was sufficient for the tree to maintain a low but positive rate of net photosynthesis for more than 12 hours a day. However, the low rate of photosynthesis was not solely the result of limited water supply, but was largely caused by a very low mesophyll conductance (Fig. 5). It took more than two months to re-establish full photosynthetic capacity after the damage to the photosynthetic apparatus caused by low temperatures in winter.

In the autumn the rate of photosynthesis decreased rather rapidly, as a result of decreasing day-length and low irradiance (Fig. 6). However, during mild and clear

171

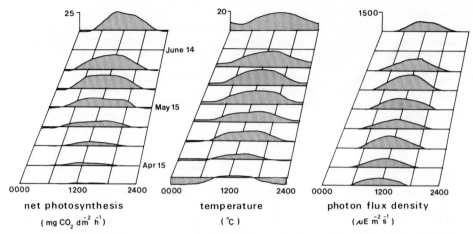

Figure 4. Average diurnal patterns of net photosynthesis, temperature, and photon flux density for a one-year-old shoot of Scots pine April–June 1977. Each curve represents an average of ten days. The missing data in June are the result of logger failure.

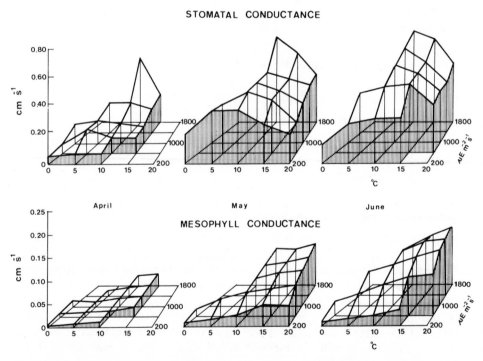

Figure 5. Average response of stomatal conductance (g_s) and mesophyll conductance (g_m) to temperature (°C) and photon flux density (μE m^{-2} s^{-1}) during April, May and June 1977 for a one-year-old shoot of Scots pine.

172

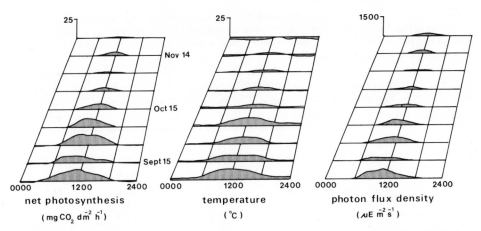

| 25⌐ | 25⌐ | 1500⌐ |

Nov 14

Oct 15

Sept 15

| 0000 | 1200 | 2400 | 0000 | 1200 | 2400 | 0000 | 1200 | 2400 |

net photosynthesis   temperature   photon flux density

$(mg\,CO_2\ dm^{-2}\ h^{-1})$ $(°C)$ $(\mu E\ m^{-2}\ s^{-1})$

Figure 6. Average diurnal patterns of net photosynthesis, temperature and photon flux density for a current shoot of Scots pine September–November 1976. Each curve represents an average of ten days.

days the photosynthetic rate could come close to summer values even in October. In mid-November the daily carbon balance for a shoot was close to zero and in early December the balance became negative (cf. Troeng & Linder, 1977). During days with favourable weather – mild and clear – positive net photosynthesis was found for a couple of hours even during the period December–March.

Photosynthesis was recorded at temperatures down to $-7°C$, which is in agreement with earlier findings (Pisek *et al.*, 1967; Neilson *et al.*, 1972).

Variation in net photosynthesis between trees

Extrapolation of the results obtained on one branch to the whole tree, and from the tree to a whole stand requires knowledge not only of the variation within the tree but also of that between trees. During three weeks in July 1977 the performances of gas exchange of one-year-old shoots on the third whorl on eight different trees were compared (cf. Linder & Troeng, 1978). The differences found were small in spite of rather large variation in the appearance of the trees (Table 1). The most important factor for the between-tree variation was the light climate for each tree.

Effect of needle age and position within the crown upon gas exchange

Throughout the summer, the one-year-old shoots had the highest photosynthetic capacity as well as performance, but in mid-August the current shoots had reached approximately the same photosynthetic rates as the one-year-old ones (Fig. 7, Table 2). At this time the rate of photosynthesis by the two-year-old shoots, at light saturation, was 30% less and that by the three-year-old shoots 55% less, compared with that of the one-year-old shoots (Table 2). When comparing the performance of the different age-classes the differences were even more

Table 1. Comparison of the average diurnal photosynthetic production (mg dm^{-2} day^{-1}) and diurnal water loss (g dm^{-2} day^{-1}) between eight different trees during 12–27 July 1977. The measurements were carried out on one-year-old shoots. Transpiration is overestimated as an effect of the design of the system (cf. Linder & Troeng, 1978).

Tree no.	Photosynthesis (mg dm^{-2} day^{-1})	Deviation from mean (%)	Transpiration (g dm^{-2} day^{-1})	Deviation from mean (%)	$\dfrac{\text{mg } CO_2}{\text{g } H_2O}$
1	195.3	+5.3	11.9	±0	16.4
2	198.2	+6.9	11.9	±0	16.6
3	178.9	−3.9	10.5	−11.8	17.0
4	182.9	−1.4	9.7	−18.5	18.9
5	169.5	−8.6	12.3	+3.4	13.8
6	182.8	−1.5	12.1	+1.7	12.1
7	193.3	+4.2	11.7	−1.7	16.5
8	185.3	−0.1	14.7	+23.5	12.6
$\bar{x}\pm$ s.d.	185.8±9.5		11.9±1.5		15.6

Table 2. Net photosynthetic rate at light saturation for four different age-classes of shoots, based on field data from August 10–13 (C = current shoot, C + 1 = one-year-old shoot, etc.). Values are selected within the temperature range 15–25°C and photon flux densities above 800 μE m^{-2} s^{-1}.

Shoot age	F_{CO_2} (mg dm^{-2} h^{-1})	s.e.	Irradiance (μE m^{-2} s^{-1})	s.e.
Current	21.3	0.61	1182	84
C + 1	22.9	0.71	1203	100
C + 2	15.9	0.62	938	72
C + 3	10.1	0.90	1101	69

pronounced as an effect of lower photon flux densities for the inner parts of the crowns.

In the open stand where the studies were made, there did not seem to be any major influence of needle position in the crown upon the photosynthetic capacity, measured as quantum yield or mesophyll conductance (cf. Troeng & Linder, 1978). However, because of shading the photosynthetic rate in the lower and north-facing parts of the crown was lower than in the south-facing or upper parts of the crown.

Effect of irrigation and fertilization upon gas exchange

The irrigation/fertilization experiment was designed to eliminate water and mineral nutrition as limiting factors for growth (cf. Aronsson et al., 1977). The measurements of gas exchange were not as intensive in the treated plots as in the

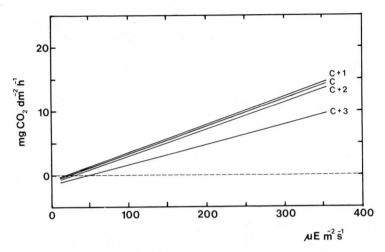

Figure 7. The response of net photosynthesis to photon flux density for four different age-classes of shoots based on field data from August 10–13 (C = current shoot, C + 1 = one-year-old shoot, etc.). The regression lines are based upon data within the temperature range 10–15°C. Regression coefficients (r^2): C = 0.89; C + 1 = 0.98; C + 2 = 0.92; C + 3 = 0.85. Number of samples per line 40–50.

untreated, but simultaneous measurements with at least one chamber per treatment were carried out throughout the whole investigated period. The effects of irrigation were most pronounced during 1976, which had a rather dry summer. Irrigation eliminated or decreased the "midday-depression" in gas exchange during days with a high evaporative demand. However, the effect of irrigation was so small that a special experiment was designed to study the effect of water-stress upon gas exchange and growth (cf. Bengtson, 1980).

In the plots which were both irrigated and fertilized with a complete nutrient solution, the main effect was a great increase in needle biomass. The photosynthetic rate per unit needle area increased by approximately 20% on irrigated and fertilized plots, compared with plots only irrigated (Fig. 8). The apparently low temperature optimum of net photosynthesis seen in Fig. 8 is an effect of water-stress caused by the warm and dry conditions in August 1975. This caused partial stomatal closure on most days and illustrates why it is important to measure the exchange of both carbon dioxide and water vapour if the aim is to analyse the responses to the variables, and not record the performance only. This can be illustrated by measurements from the laboratory chamber, in which the light response curves of two detached branches, one from an untreated and one from an irrigated and fertilized plot were determined (Table 3).

During the opening of the stomata both the rate of net photosynthesis and the stomatal conductance increased, but the mesophyll conductance remained constant. The difference in photosynthetic rate between the two treatments was approximately the same as that seen from field data. The mesophyll conductance was 50% lower for a shoot from an untreated plot than from the irrigated and fertilized plot, but this was to some extent counterbalanced by a higher stomatal conductance, so that the difference in photosynthesis was only 26%.

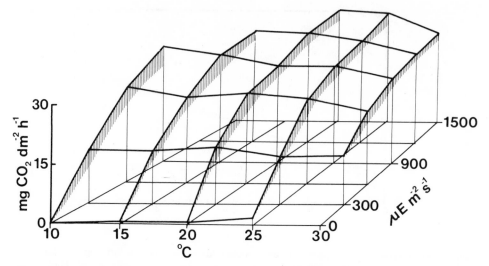

Figure 8. Light and temperature response of net photosynthesis for a current shoot of Scots pine on irrigated and irrigated/fertilized plots. The shaded area shows the difference in photosynthetic rate per unit area of needles where the irrigated/fertilized plot always had the higher rates. The diagramme is based on measurements from August 1975. (After Linder & Ingestad, 1977)

Table 3. Net photosynthetic rate (F_{CO_2}), stomatal conductance (g_s) and mesophyll conductance (g_m) at saturating irradiance during the opening of stomata and at steady state for a detached shoot from an irrigated and fertilized plot (IF). For comparison, steady state values are given for a shoot from an untreated plot (0). The values are instant readings from an experiment. Date 15 September 1977, temperature 15 °C, water vapour deficit 4 g m^{-3}.

Plot	Irradiance (μE m^{-2} s^{-1})	g_s (cm s^{-1})	g_m (cm s^{-1})	F_{CO_2} (mg dm^{-2} h^{-1})	Stomatal condition
IF	1700	0.18	0.17	18.9	opening
IF	1700	0.22	0.17	20.8	opening
IF	1700	0.24	0.18	21.7	steady state
0	1700	0.34	0.09	16.1	steady state

Stem respiration

A pronounced seasonal variation was found in stem respiration (Fig. 9). From late autumn until the start of the growing season, the respiration rate was low, but as soon as stem growth started the rate of respiration increased greatly with a maximum in late June. Comparison of stem growth and the pattern of respiration showed that the maximum rate of diameter increase occurred one month earlier than the peak in respiration (cf. Linder & Troeng, 1977). The reason for this is probably that the secondary and tertiary wall-thickening takes place after the increase in volume. This creates a problem of separating growth respiration from maintenance respiration without knowing the pattern of wall thickening.

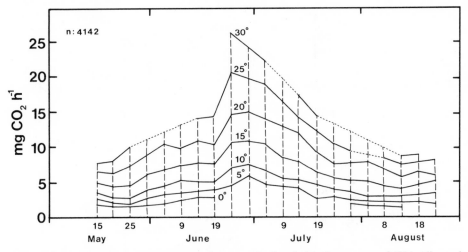

Figure 9. Change in temperature response of stem respiration during the summer of 1976. All samples have been divided into five-day periods and thereafter assorted into temperature classes. The values presented are the average in each class. Broken curves indicate that the temperatures in question were not represented during that period. The enclosed stem area increased during the measured period from 3.0 dm² to 3.6 dm².

To study the relationship between the age of the stem and its respiration, a tree was cut down and stem sections were taken from different levels. The cut ends of the sections were sealed with paraffin wax (Paraplast) and the respiration rates were determined at constant temperature in the laboratory chamber (Fig. 10). Each of the stem sections was tested for its capacity to refix carbon dioxide in light, by measuring respiration in darkness and at different levels of irradiance. All the stem sections refixed carbon dioxide released by respiration but with a decreasing capacity with increasing age (Fig. 10). A similar refixation of respiratory carbon dioxide was found in green cones and conelets. The refixation was of such a magnitude that when making a carbon budget for a pine tree it is necessary to take this process into consideration (cf. Ågren *et al.*, 1980).

Conclusions

Measurements over four years indicate that the photosynthetically active period of Scots pine in central Sweden is approximately eight months (April–November), but that the length of the period can probably vary by one month during a specific year as an effect of the weather.

The photosynthetic rates are rather low during late spring and early summer as an effect of winter damage to the photosynthetic apparatus. One-year-old needles have the highest photosynthetic efficiency during the summer, but after maturation the current needles are as effective. Considerable amounts of carbon are fixed in photosynthesis during the autumn after stem growth has ceased. This carbon is not stored above ground but translocated to the roots (cf. Ågren *et al.*, 1980).

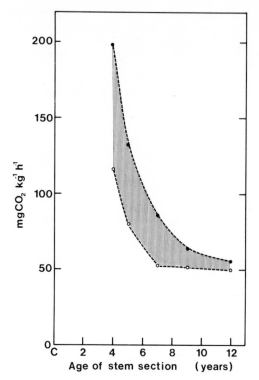

Figure 10. Respiration rates of cut stem sections per unit dry weight from different parts of a 15-year-old pine tree. Measurements were carried out both in darkness (filled circles) and light (open circles) at 15 °C. The results shown are from late June 1977.

Stem respiration is not in phase with increase of stem radius, but reaches its maximum approximately one month after the peak in stem growth. The amounts of carbon lost in branch and stem respiration are low in a young tree but will increase with increasing age. The ability to refix carbon dioxide in "non-green" parts of the above ground biomass is a feature that will have a significant effect upon the carbon balance of older trees.

Acknowledgements

We want to express our sincere thanks to Mr. J. Parsby for his skilful work in developing and building the equipment. Thanks are also due to Mr. T. Lohammar for his invaluable help with processing and analysing the data.

References

Ågren, G. I., Axelsson, B., Flower-Ellis, J. G. K., Linder, S., Persson, H., Staaf, H. & Troeng, E. 1980. Annual carbon budget for a young Scots pine. – In: Persson, T. (ed.) Structure and Function of Northern Coniferous Forests – An Ecosystem Study, Ecol. Bull. (Stockholm) 32: 307–313.

Aronsson, A., Elowson, S, & Ingestad, T. 1977. Elimination of water and mineral nutrition as limiting factors in a young Scots pine stand. I.Experimental design and some preliminary results. – Swed. Conif. For. Proj. Tech. Rep. 10, 38 pp.

Axelsson, B. & Bråkenhielm, S. 1980. Investigation sites of the Swedish Coniferous Forest Project – biological and physiographical features. – In: Persson, T. (ed.) Structure and Function of Northern Coniferous Forests – An Ecosystem Study, Ecol. Bull. (Stockholm) 32: 25–64.

Bamberg, S., Schwarz, W. & Tranquillini, W. 1967. Influence of daylength on the photosynthetic capacity of Stone pine (*Pinus cembra* L.). – Ecology 48: 264–269.

Bengtson, C. 1980. Effects of water stress on Scots pine. – In: Persson, T. (ed.) Structure and Function of Northern Coniferous Forests – An Ecosystem Study, Ecol. Bull. (Stockholm) 32: 205–213.

Catsky, J., Janac, J. & Jarvis, P. G. 1971. General principles of using IRGA for measuring CO_2 exchange rates. – In: Sestak, Z., Catsky, J. & Jarvis, P. G. (eds.) Plant Photosynthetic Production – Manual of Methods, pp. 161–166. The Hague: Dr. W. Junk N. V. Publishers.

Engelbrecht, B., Lohammar, T., Pettersson, I., Sundström, K-B. & Svensson, J. 1980. Data handling and simulation technique used in the Swedish Coniferous Forest Project. – In: Persson, T. (ed.) Structure and Function of Northern Coniferous Forests – An Ecosystem Study, Ecol. Bull. (Stockholm) 32: 65–71.

Flower-Ellis, J. G. K., Albrektson, A. & Olsson, L. 1976. Structure and growth of some young Scots pine stands: (1) Dimensional and numerical relationships. – Swed. Conif. For. Proj. Tech. Rep. 3, 98 pp.

Freeland, R. O. 1952. Effect of age of leaves upon rate of photosynthesis in some conifers. – Plant Physiol. 27: 685–690.

Fry, D. J. & Phillips, I. D. J. 1977. Photosynthesis of some conifers in relation to annual growth cycles and dry matter production. II. Seasonal photosynthetic capacity and mesophyll ultrastructure in *Abies grandis*, *Picea sitchensis*, *Tsuga heterophylla* and *Larix leptolepis* growing in S. W. England. – Physiol. Plant. 40: 300–306.

Havranek, W. 1972. Über die Bedeutung der Bodentemperatur für die Photosynthese und Transpiration junger Forstpflanzen und für die Stoffproduktion an der Waldgrenze. – Angew. Bot. 46: 101–106.

Jarvis, P. G. 1971. The estimation of resistances to carbon dioxide exchange transfer. – In: Sestak, Z., Catsky, J. & Jarvis, P. G. (eds.) Plant Photosynthetic Production – Manual of Methods, pp. 566–631. The Hague: Dr W. Junk N. V. Publishers.

Jarvis, P. G., James, G. B. & Landsberg, J. J. 1976. Coniferous Forest. – In: Monteith, J. L. (ed.) Vegetation and Atmosphere, pp. 171–240. London–New York: Academic Press.

Jeffree, C. E., Johnson, R. P. C. & Jarvis, P. G. 1971. Epicuticular wax in the stomatal antechamber of Sitka spruce and its effect on the diffusion of water vapour and carbon dioxide. – Planta 98: 1–10.

Johansson, N. 1933. The relation between the tree-stem's respiration and its growth. – Svenska Skogs-vårdsför. Tidskr. 10:53–134. (In Swedish, English summary)

Kinerson, R. S. 1975. Relationship between plant surface area and respiration in Loblolly pine. –J. appl. Ecol. 12:965–971.

Künstle, E. & Mitscherlich, G. 1975. Photosynthese, Transpiration und Atmung in einem Misch-bestand im Schwarzwald. I Teil: Photosynthese. – Allg. Forst- u. JagdZtg 146:46–63.

Larcher, W. 1969. The effect of environmental and physiological variables in the carbon dioxide exchange of trees. – Photosynthetica 3: 167–198.

Linder, S. 1972. The influence of soil temperature upon net photosynthesis and transpiration in seedlings of Scots pine and Norway spruce. – Dissertation,University of Umeå, 26 pp.

Linder, S. 1979. Photosynthesis and respiration of conifers. A classified reference list, 1891–1977. – Stud. for. suec. 149, 71 pp.

Linder, S & Ingestad, T. 1977. Ecophysiological experiments under limiting and non-limiting conditions of mineral nutrition in field and laboratory. – In: Bicentenary Celebration of C. P. Thunberg's Visit to Japan, pp. 69–76. Tokyo: The Royal Swedish Embassy – The Botanical Society of Japan.

Linder, S. & Troeng, E. 1977. Gas exchange in a 20-year-old stand of Scots pine. II. The variation in stem respiration during the growing season. – Swed. Conif. For. Proj. Int. Rep. 57, 14 pp. (In Swedish, English abstract)

Linder, S. & Troeng, E. 1978. Gas exchange in a 20-year-old stand of Scots pine. III. A comparison of

179

net photosynthesis and transpiration of eight different pine trees. – Swed. Conif. For. Proj. Int. Rep. 82, 19 pp. (In Swedish, English abstract)

Linder, S., Nordström, B., Parsby, J., Sundbom, E. & Troeng, E., 1980. A gas exchange system for field measurements of photosynthesis and transpiration in a 20-year-old stand of Scots pine. – Swed. Conif. For. Proj. Tech. Rep. 23, 34 pp.

Lohammar, T., Larsson, S., Linder, S. & Falk, S. O. 1980. FAST – simulation models of gaseous exchange in Scots pine. – In: Persson, T. (ed.) Structure and Function of Northern Coniferous Forests – An Ecosystem Study, Ecol. Bull. (Stockholm) 32: 505–523.

Ludlow, M. M. & Jarvis, P. G. 1971. Photosynthesis in Sitka spruce (*Picea sitchensis* (Bong.) Carr.). I: General characteristics. – J. appl. Ecol. 8:925–953.

Neilson, R. E., Ludlow, M. M. & Jarvis, P. G. 1972. Photosynthesis in Sitka spruce (*Picea sitchensis* (Bong.) Carr.). II: Response to temperature. – J. appl. Ecol. 9:721–745.

Neuwirth, G. 1974. Wald und Wasser aus der Sicht neuer Durchforstungsverfahren in Kiefern-Jung-beständen. – Arch. Naturschutz. u. Landschaftsforsch. 14:263–272.

Öquist, G. & Hellgren, N. O. 1976. The photosynthetic electron transport capacity of chloroplasts prepared from needles of unhardened and hardened seedlings of *Pinus silvestris*. – Plant Sci. Letters 7:359–369.

Penning de Vries, F. W. T. 1975. The cost of maintenance processes in plant cells. – Ann. Bot. 39:77–92.

Pisek, A., Larcher, W. & Unterholzner, R. 1967. Kardinale Temperaturbereiche der Photosynthese und Grenztemperatur des Lebens der Blätter verschiedener Spermatophyten. I. Temperaturminimum der Nettoassimilation. – Flora 157:239–264.

Polster, H. & Fuchs, S. 1963. Winterassimilation und -atmung der Kiefer (*Pinus silvestris*) im mitteldeutschen Binnenlandklima. – Arch. Forstwesen 12:1013–1023.

Rook, D. A. 1969. The influence of growing temperature on photosynthesis and respiration of *Pinus radiata* seedlings. – N. Z. J. Bot. 7: 43–55.

Shain, L. & Mackay, J. F. G. 1973. Seasonal fluctuation in respiration of aging xylem in relation to heartwood formation in *Pinus radiata*. – Can. J. Bot. 51: 737–741.

Strain, B. R., Higginbotham, K. O. & Mulroy, J. C. 1976. Temperature preconditioning and photo-synthetic capacity of *Pinus taeda* L. – Photosynthetica 10:47–53.

Tranquillini, W. 1955. Die Bedeutung des Lichts und Temperatur für die CO_2-Assimilation von *Pinus cembra* – Jungwuchs an einem hochalpinen Standort. – Planta 46:154–178.

Tranquillini, W. 1959a. Die Stoffproduktion der Zirbe an der Waldgrenze während eines Jahres. I. Standortsklima und CO_2-Assimilation. – Planta 54:107–129.

Tranquillini, W. 1959b. Die Stoffproduktion der Zirbe an der Waldgrenze während eines Jahres. II. Zuwachs und CO_2-Bilanz. – Planta 54: 130–151.

Tranquillini, W. 1963a. Die CO_2-Jahresbilanz und die Stoffproduktion der Zirbe. – Mitt. Forst. Bundes-Versuchsanst. Mariabrunn 60: 535–546.

Tranquillini, W. 1963b. Der Jahresgang der CO_2-Assimilation junger Zirben. – Mitt. Forst. Bundes-Versuchsanst. Mariabrunn 60: 501–534.

Tranquillini, W. & Holzer, K. 1958. – Über das Gefrieren und Auftauen von Koniferennadeln. – Ber. dtsch. bot. Ges. 71:143–156.

Troeng, E. & Linder, S. 1977. Gas exchange in a 20-year-old stand of Scots pine. I. The seasonal change of net photosynthesis in current and one-year-old needles. – Swed. Conif. For. Proj. Int. Rep. 56, 14 pp. (In Swedish, English abstract)

Troeng, E. & Linder, S. 1978. Gas exchange in a 20-year-old stand of Scots pine. IV. Photosynthesis and transpiration within the crown of one tree. – Swed. Conif. For. Proj. Int. Rep. 83, 20 pp. (In Swedish, English abstract)

Troeng, E., Linder, S. & Långström, B. 1979. Gas exchange in a 20-year-old stand of Scots pine. V. Pilot study on the effects on gas exchange during the attack of pine shoot beetle (*Tomicus piniperda*). – Swed. Conif. For. Proj. Int. Rep. 91, 16 pp. (In Swedish, English abstract)

Turner, N. C. & Jarvis, P. G. 1975. Photosynthesis in Sitka spruce (*Picea sitchensis* (Bong.) Carr.). IV. Response to soil temperature. – J. appl. Ecol. 12:561–576.

Ungersson, J. & Scherdin, G. 1965. Untersuchung über Photosynthese und Atmung unter natürlichen Bedingungen während des Winterhalbjahres bei *Pinus silvestris* L., *Picea abies* Link., und *Juniperus communis* L. – Planta 67: 136–167.

Ungersson, J. & Scherdin, G. 1968. Jahresgang von Photosynthese und Atmung unter natürlichen Bedingungen bei *Pinus silvestris* L. an ihrer Nordgrenze in der Subarktis. – Flora 157: 391–434.

180

Žumer, M. 1969a. Growth rhythm of some forest trees at different altitudes. – Meld. Nor. Lantbrukshøgsk. 48, 31 pp. (In Norwegian, English abstract)

Žumer, M. 1969b. Annual ring formation on Norway spruce in mountain forest. – Medd. norske SkogsforsVes. 97: 165–184. (In Norwegian, English summary)

Persson, T. (ed) 1980
Structure and Function of Northern
Coniferous Forests – An Ecosystem Study
Ecol. Bull. (Stockholm) 32: 183–204.

FIELD STUDIES OF WATER RELATIONS AND PHOTO-SYNTHESIS IN SCOTS PINE USING MANUAL TECHNIQUES

J. Hellkvist[1, 2], K. Hillerdal-Hagströmer[1] and E. Mattson-Djos[1]

Abstract

Water potential, stomatal conductance, rate of photosynthesis and stem radial changes in Scots pine (*Pinus sylvestris* L.) were measured in a 120-year-old and a 20-year-old stand, the latter stand submitted to differing nutrient and water regimes. Water potential was measured on fascicles with a pressure chamber, stomatal conductance on shoots with a null balance diffusion porometer and rate of photosynthesis as incorporation of $^{14}CO_2$ into separate needles. Stem radius changes were measured with strain gauge transducers connected to a computer system. Interrelations between the variables as well as their relations to abiotic and biotic variables were studied. Calculations were made of the transpiration rate and the apparent total liquid pathway conductance from bulk soil to needle. A high sensitivity of total liquid pathway conductance to varying soil water potential was found. About 60% of the total liquid resistance from bulk soil to needle was found in the soil-root part of the system in a 20-year-old Scots pine, while the resistance at about the same flow rate in the soil-root part of the system in 120-year-old trees was calculated to about 30% of the total liquid resistance, in spite of low soil water potential.

A stem height gradient of 0.2–0.8 bar m^{-1}, depending on prevailing water flow through the soil-plant-atmosphere continuum was found. Fertilization and irrigation were both found to affect water potential in the stand, causing smaller amplitude in the diurnal variation of water potential. Reasons for this and the influence of differing water status and nutrient regimes on radial stem increment rate are discussed.

Additional keywords: $^{14}CO_2$-technique, fertilization, irrigation, liquid pathway conductance, stand height gradient, stem radial change, stomatal conductance, water potential.

Background

Within the Swedish Coniferous Forest Project (SWECON) the main object has been a better understanding of the processes controlling and limiting the primary production of Scots pine (*Pinus sylvestris* L.). Studies on the water relations of Scots pine were carried out as an integrated part of the research programme.

Water deficit in trees can reduce growth directly through turgor effects on cambial activity and cell elongation and indirectly through effect on physiological processes like photosynthesis, respiration, ion uptake and translocation, and nitrogen metabolism (cf. Kramer, 1962; Hsiao, 1973).

The water status of a tree is dependent upon abiotic variables such as humidity,

---

[1] Institute of Physiological Botany, Uppsala University, Box 540, S-751 21 Uppsala, Sweden
[2] Present address: National Swedish Food Administration, Box 622, S-751 26 Uppsala, Sweden

soil water, irradiance and wind as well as on biotic factors such as distribution and density of roots, resistances against water transport in different parts of the tree, water reserves in trunk, roots and branches, and to a large extent upon the ability to reduce water losses by means of effective stomatal control.

Within the SWECON project studies of photosynthesis and water relations of Scots pine have been carried out in a young stand using (1) intensive measurements with cuvette technique (Linder & Troeng, 1980) and (2) extensive measurements with manual methods and instruments. The manual equipment was designed to be mobile and easy to handle under field conditions and enable measurements to be made in adjacent stands and special experiments (e.g., Ericsson *et al.*, 1980).

This paper presents preliminary results from the manual studies on water relations and photosynthesis from a young (20-year-old) stand, subjected to an irrigation and a fertilization experiment and an old (120 years) stand at Jädraås in central Sweden.

Abbreviations

Ψ_n	Needle water potential ($=$ xylem pressure potential)
Ψ_{max}	Highest value of Ψ_n during the day ($\approx \Psi_{predawn}$)
Ψ_{min}	Lowest value of Ψ_n during the day ($\approx \Psi_{noon}$)
Ψ_{grad}	Height gradient in Ψ_n
Ψ_{soil} .	Soil water potential
g_s	Stomatal conductance for water vapour
k_r/A	Total liquid pathway conductance for water from soil to needle (k_r) per needle area (A)
D	Vapour concentration deficit

Introduction

Needle water potential, Ψ_n, is a sensitive variable reflecting effects of abiotic and biotic conditions on water relations of plants. The decrease in Ψ_n as a result of loss of water by transpiration, and the resulting gradients in Ψ_n in the tree, are the driving forces for the movement of water in the plant (cf. Jarvis, 1975).

The diurnal variation of Ψ_n is normally characterized by a high value early in the morning, $\Psi_{predawn}$ (Slatyer, 1967) or Ψ_{max}, and by a low value Ψ_{noon} or Ψ_{min}, usually found about noon. The magnitude of Ψ_{min} is a complex result of plant reactions, balancing available water reserves outside and within the plant with water transport in the plant and loss of water in transpiration. The predawn value has been used as a measure of Ψ_{soil} (Slatyer & Gardner, 1965; Slatyer, 1967).

Because of the influence of gravity, under static conditions of no water flow, there is a water potential gradient of 0.1 bar m^{-1} between the soil and the needles. When there is a flow of water through the soil-plant-atmosphere continuum the water potential is further reduced as a result of the series of frictional resistances to flow through the plant. A gradient of 0.3–0.8 bar m^{-1} was earlier found for Scots pine (cf. Hellkvist *et al.*, 1974).

As a response to the change in water saturation of the trunk there is a diurnal swelling and shrinkage in stem diameters of trees (cf. Kozlowski, 1965, 1976).

Changes in the stem diameter lag behind the changes of Ψ_n by some hours because of water transfer between the water conducting tissues and the living tissues of the phloem and cambium, a thicker layer of living tissue giving a longer lag period (Klepper *et al.*, 1971).

Stomatal conductance (g_s) depends on the stomatal aperture which varies depending on changes in both external energy and internal water balance. For trees in the field the relation between g_s and Ψ_n is complicated and depends also on other determining variables (Watts *et al.*, 1976). Usually, under field conditions, g_s in Scots pine is large enough not to be the main rate-limiting factor for photosynthesis, other variables like irradiance, resistance to CO_2-transport from the intercellular spaces to the chloroplast and fixation in the chloroplast being more limiting (cf. Linder & Troeng, 1978). However, during pronounced stress periods, midday-depressions in photosynthesis caused by stomatal closure have regularly been observed (Linder & Troeng, 1980). If water stress induced closure of stomata frequently occurs in large parts of the needle biomass for long periods, the daily uptake of CO_2 could be reduced. Furthermore, during long-term exposure of a tree to stress many different physiological changes are induced, and these also change stomatal behaviour and affect the photosynthetic capacity of the chloroplast (Bunce, 1977). Water stress also results in reduced turgor potential in the cambial cells, which disturbs or prevents cell division and enlargement (cf. Hsiao, 1973).

Transpiration rate can be calculated from g_s using the Penman-Monteith equation (Monteith, 1965) or, in conifers, the isothermal simplification that $E_T = g_s \cdot D$ (Jarvis & Stewart, 1979).

The apparent total liquid pathway resistance, or conductance, can be calculated at steady state from the simplified formula (van den Honert, 1948):

$$E_T = k_r/A \ (\Psi_{soil} - \Psi_n) \tag{1}$$

where k_r is total liquid pathway conductance from soil to needle, A is needle area and Ψ_n and Ψ_{soil} are water potentials in needles and soil, respectively. This equation applies to the steady state situation when the water flow from soil to needle is equal to the water flow from needle to air. Thus the different flow patterns in the tree, as a result of the movement of water in and out of storage in stem and branches, are not taken into account. Furthermore, the total liquid pathway resistance to water transport in a plant is composed of many different resistances in the different parts of the plant (Richter, 1973). Some of these resistances change with flow rate (Weatherley, 1970; Stoker & Weatherley, 1971; Feddes & Ritjema, 1972, Fiscus, 1975). In most plants the root resistance to liquid flow is higher than stem or leaf resistance (for review, see Jarvis, 1975). In Scots pine, Roberts (1977) found the root resistance to be of the same magnitude as the stem and branch resistance together.

Materials and methods

Water potential in needles

Needle water potential (Ψ_n) was measured with a pressure chamber based on the design of Waring & Cleary (1967) (Hellkvist *et al.*, 1977) (Fig. 1). The fascicle was placed inside a shielding brass tube

185

Figure 1. Equipment used in manual measurements of gas exchange of Scots pine. Above left: Pressure chamber. Right: Null balance diffusion porometer, cuvette mounted on the shoot to be investigated. Below left: Equipment for measuring photosynthesis as incorporation of $^{14}CO_2$.

which was then forced through a rubber disc in the lid of the chamber, the brass tube being removed when the fascicle was suitably positioned. When pressure was applied, the rubber disc was pressed against the chamber lid, sealing the chamber. A pressure transducer on the bottom of the chamber transmitted the pressure to a digital microvoltmeter, where the pressure was displayed in bar. The pressure at the first appearance of xylem sap on the cut surface of the fascicle, as seen with a stereomicroscope ($\times$ 10–40), was taken as Ψ_n.

Stomatal conductance

Stomatal conductance (g_s) was measured with a null balance diffusion porometer (Fig. 1) modified after Beardsell *et al.* (1972). The shoot to be investigated was enclosed in the porometer chamber, where the transpiration from the shoot, proportional to the stomatal conductance of the needles, was determined at different defined levels of relative humidity in the air (Mattson-Djos & Hellkvist, 1977). The humidity level of the air in the chamber was balanced by inflow of dry air. The projected needle area was measured with a leaf area meter (Lambda Li 3000) after the shoot had been harvested.

Rate of photosynthesis

Rate of photosynthesis was measured as incorporation of $^{14}CO_2$ using an apparatus (Fig. 1) modified from Shimshi (1969) (Karlsson *et al.*, 1977). Sampled needles were exposed to $^{14}CO_2$ for 20 seconds

186

and immediately frozen in liquid nitrogen. Combustion of the sample was accomplished with a Packard Tri Carb Sample Oxidizer (model 306) and the radioactivity was measured in a liquid scintillation counter (Intertechnique SL 30). The $^{14}CO_2$-technique was calibrated against infra-red gas analyser (IRGA) equipment (Linder & Troeng, 1980) at Jädraås.

Changes of stem diameter

Changes in stem radius were measured with strain gauge transducers, mounted on the stem of the investigated trees (Hellkvist et al., 1975) and connected to the computer-controlled data acquisition system at the site. Transducers were mounted at two different levels, 30–50 cm and 150–200 cm above ground level, in the middle of the crown (cf. Dobbs & Scott, 1971). Usually the transducers were mounted against the periderm, so that water movement and growth of the living tissues were included in the measurement. However, during the last season transducers were also mounted directly against the xylem (phloem and cambium layers removed), thereby restricting the measurements to changes in the xylem cylinder.

Climatic variables

Simultaneous measurements of photon flux density (400–700 nm) were made in close proximity to the sampled shoots or needles. Measurements of irradiance (300–3000 nm), air temperature and air humidity at the time of sampling (± 2.5 minutes) were obtained from ECODAC (Perttu et al., 1977).

Sampling and experimental design

Measurements were made in a 20-year-old stand and in a 120-year-old stand. In the 20-year-old stand the influence of different irrigation and fertilization treatments on the water relations of Scots pine was investigated. The diurnal variations in Ψ_n, g_s, rate of photosynthesis and stem radius in trees from the different treatments were compared and analyzed in relation to corresponding data on climate and soil water.

Needles were usually collected from similarly exposed branches on the south-facing side of the tree, except when the variation within the crown was investigated. As a rule all the measurements were made in the stand, but when many samples were collected at the same time or when darkness or low temperatures restricted the use of the pressure chamber in the field, the water potential samples were stored in a refrigerator for later measurement in the laboratory (Hellkvist et al., 1977). All measurements of water potential and rate of photosynthesis were made on five replicates and the mean values and standard errors were calculated.

To investigate the effects on water relations and rate of photosynthesis of removing the soil-root resistance, whole trees were cut off at ground level under water in some experiments (cf. Roberts, 1977). Before and after the cut Ψ_n, g_s and rate of photosynthesis were measured. During and after cutting precautions were taken to avoid exposing the cut surface to air. The cut bole end was placed in a bucket of water and maize oil was poured on the water surface to avoid evaporation, this enabling water uptake to be measured. On each occasion two trees were cut at about noon at a time of high transpiration rate, when the trees had started to close their stomata.

In June 1976, to create soil water stress, the rooting area of a pine tree, isolated from the near-by soil to a depth of 0.4 m by vertical aluminium plates, was covered with polythene film to prevent rainfall from entering (cf. Bengtson, 1980). The water status of the tree was compared with an unstressed tree. In September 1976 the tree was irrigated and Ψ_n and stem increment were measured during recovery.

In the 120-year-old stand Ψ_n of needles was measured at different levels in the crown, at a distance of one meter from the trunk (cf. Richter, 1972) using a Sky-lift (Fig. 2) so that the approximate magnitude of the vertical gradient in water potential could be estimated. The gradient was measured on several different occasions in different trees.

Figure 2. Sky-lift equipment, used in manual measurements of gas exchange in the tree crowns of 120-year-old Scots pine.

Results and discussion

Variation in needle water potential

The needle water potential varied diurnally (Fig. 3). During dry weather the minimal value of Ψ_n occurred earlier in the morning because of reduced transpiration, which in turn was a result of stomatal closure in response to the high evaporative demand (Figs. 3 and 4). Fig. 3 shows the diurnal variations in Ψ_n, g_s and photosynthetic rate in two 20-year-old pine trees for a day during a dry weather period. Minimum Ψ_n in the unirrigated control tree (0-tree) was established before noon, while in the irrigated and fertilized tree (IF-tree) it occurred at about 13.00–14.00. The predawn values were –1.8 bar (0-tree) and –0.7 bar (IF-tree), in comparison with Ψ_{soil}-values of –814 and –271 mbar, respectively. Fig. 4 shows the variations in Ψ_n, g_s and photosynthetic rate during a dry and hot day

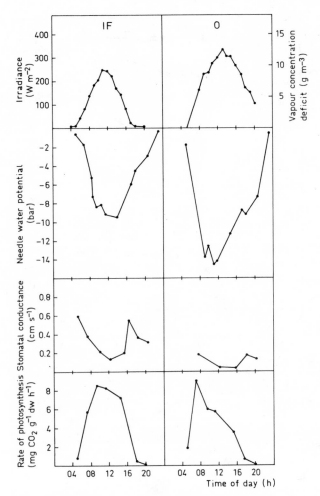

Figure 3. Diurnal variation in needle water potential, stomatal conductance and photosynthetic rate of current needles of two 20-year-old Scots pine trees on 25 August 1976. Irradiance and vapour concentration deficit are included. Ψ_{soil} (15 cm below ground level) -271 mbar in the irrigated and fertilized plot and -814 mbar in the control plot.

at five different heights in the crown of a 120 year old pine tree. The minimum value of Ψ_n occurred before noon in the highest levels of the tree crown because of decreasing g_s, while in the lower levels, where the evaporative demand was lower, the lowest values of Ψ_n occurred around noon. Noon values of Ψ_n were lower at low soil water potential (Table 1). The use of the predawn value as a measure of Ψ_{soil} (Slatyer, 1967) was of limited value as the short summer nights did not give the trees sufficient time to recover and reach a dynamic equilibrium with Ψ_{soil} (Table 1).

The water potential of needles at the same height in the crown was lower in older needles (Fig. 5). This could result from plugging of the conducting tissues to the older needles by waste material, air bubbles, resin, etc. Decreased cell wall

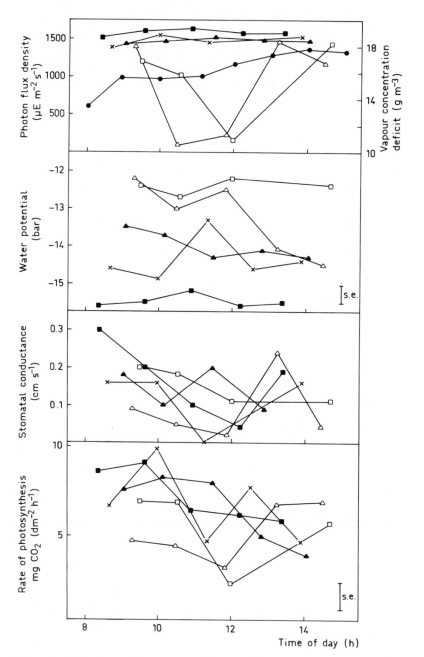

Figure 4. Diurnal variation in needle water potential, stomatal conductance and photosynthetic rate of current needles at five different height levels in the crown of a 120-year-old Scots pine tree on 10 July 1975. Photon flux density of the five levels and vapour concentration deficit (bulk value for the stand, ●) are included. Height levels: ■ = 17 m, × = 15 m, ▲ = 13 m, △ = 10 m and □ = 8 m above ground. Maximum standard errors in Ψ_n and photosynthetic rate are given. Bars represent one standard error.

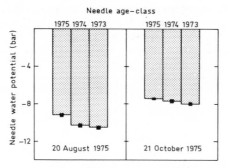

Figure 5. Needle water potential at noon of needles of different age-classes in 20-year-old Scots pine, sampled from the fifth branch whorl from the top, on two sampling occasions in 1975 representing different stress conditions. Mean values from eight trees (August 20) and four trees (October 21). Black bars indicate two standard errors.

elasticity as a result of dry matter increase, as well as a larger amount of storage and waste products in the older needles, thus decreasing the osmotic potential in the cells, could also affect the resistance to water transport into the needles. Stomatal regulation is also known to be affected with age, the stomata opening less and responding more slowly to microclimatic changes, thereby changing the resistance to water transport from needle to air (cf. Jeffree *et al.*, 1974).

The height gradient in Ψ_n in the stem of 120-year-old pine trees was usually about 0.2–0.3 bar m^{-1} (Fig. 4 and Table 2). The steepest gradient found in these trees was 0.4 bar m^{-1}. However, on none of the days investigated was there a very high evaporative demand. The transpiration rate per needle area at sampling time on the day pertaining to Table 2 was about 5 mg m^{-2} s^{-1}. Measurements of Ψ_{grad} in stems of Scots pine in another part of Sweden (Brunsberg, central Sweden) at transpiration rates of about 20 mg m^{-2} s^{-1} gave a gradient of 0.6–0.8 bar m^{-1}. The different sizes of the gradient reported (cf. Hellkvist *et al.*, 1974) are most likely to result from differing flow rates during the measurements. This makes direct comparison between the gradient in different species difficult without knowledge of the prevailing transpiration rate.

Table 1. Needle water potential values (Ψ_n) in a 20-year-old Scots pine before dawn ($\Psi_{predawn}$) and at noon (Ψ_{noon}) and soil water potential values (Ψ_{soil}) at 15 cm depth on six days during the long-term stress period 23 June–26 July 1976. Note the discrepancy between corresponding $\Psi_{predawn}$ and Ψ_{soil} values. The Ψ_{noon}-values are strongly affected by the weather. By sorting Ψ_n-values from the different Ψ_{soil}-conditions into irradiance and air temperature classes a normalized $\Psi_n (\Psi_{norm})$ is obtained, being the mean of Ψ_n-values at an irradiance of 600–800 W m^{-2} and an air temperature of 20–25°C.

Date	Ψ_{soil} (bar)	$\Psi_{predawn}$ (bar)	Ψ_{noon} (bar)	Ψ_{norm} (bar)
June 23	−0.05	−3.2	− 6.8	− 7.4
June 29	−0.08	−2.9	− 7.6	− 7.5
June 30	−0.10	−3.2	− 6.0	− 7.6
July 13	−0.26	−3.2	− 7.9	− 8.7
July 15	−0.35	−2.8	− 9.0	− 9.0
July 24	−0.83	−4.0	−11.5	−11.3

Table 2. Needle water potential at different heights in the crown of a 120-year-old Scots pine tree on 6 September 1974. The mean height gradient of Ψ_n was 0.2 bar m^{-2}. Weather conditions: Variable cloudiness in the morning, sun when the samples were collected at about 12.30.

Height above ground (m)	$\Psi_n \pm$ s.e. (bar)
17.5	-10.2 ± 0.1
15.5	$-\ 9.6 \pm 0.1$
13.5	$-\ 9.4 \pm 0.1$
11.5	$-\ 8.9 \pm 0.1$
9.5	$-\ 8.3 \pm 0.1$
7.5	$-\ 8.1 \pm 0.1$

Diurnal variation in stomatal conductance

The highest stomatal conductances occurred early in the morning in the illuminated parts of the crown (Fig. 6). The variable illumination conditions within the crown result in a wide variation in stomatal conductance in the same tree. During pronounced stress conditions the variation in the crown became more complex as a result of stomatal closure in response to water stress. For example, in the middle of the day, when the evaporative demand was high, stomatal conductance was lower at the top of the crown than at the lower levels (Fig. 4). Stomatal

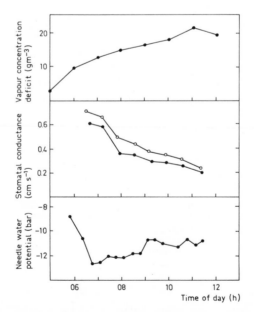

Figure 6. Variation in stomatal conductance and needle water potential (mean of five needles) in a 20-year-old Scots pine from morning until noon on 11 July 1976 (mean of two trees). Values of stomatal conductance given for illuminated (○) and shaded (●) shoots, the latter with an irradiance of about 30% of the illuminated shoots.

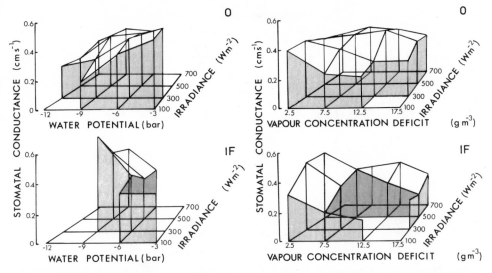

Figure 7. Stomatal conductance as a function of needle water potential and irradiance and vapour concentration deficit and irradiance. Values collected during the long-term stress period 23 June–26 July 1976 are given for two 20-year-old pine trees, growing on an irrigated and fertilized (IF) plot and on a control (0) plot.

conductance was lower in the old stand than in the young stand in the same climatic conditions (cf. Figs. 4 and 6).

Relation between needle water potential and stomatal conductance

The influence of Ψ_n and irradiance on g_s is illustrated in Fig. 7 which has been constructed by sorting Ψ_n- and g_s-values into different irradiance classes. Fig. 7 shows that trees in different nutrient and water regimes have different response surfaces, indicating that g_s is also responding to other variables. A three-dimensional plot of g_s-values against irradiance and vapour concentration deficit (Fig. 7) shows more similar response surfaces for trees from the two different nutrient and water regimes, suggesting that D is a better variable to use than Ψ_n for describing or predicting g_s. The different response of g_s to Ψ_n in different trees is probably a result of differences in the coupling between the "bulk" Ψ_n measured and the turgor potential in the guard cells (Beadle *et al.*, 1978). Such differences could result either from different nutrient and osmotic status in the needles or from acclimation to water stress.

Relation between water stress and rate of photosynthesis

During extremely dry periods of weather stomatal closure induced decreases in photosynthetic production in the young stand during days of high evaporative demand (Fig. 3) (cf. Linder & Troeng, 1980). In 120-year-old pine trees such a decrease in photosynthetic production rate during part of the day was frequently found during the growing season in parts of the crown (Fig. 4). In the absence of

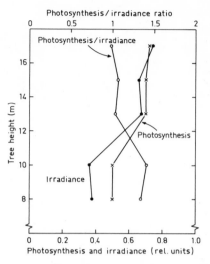

Figure 8. Irradiance and photosynthetic production (per cm needle length) in the crown of a 120-year-old pine on 10 July 1975 (cf. Fig. 4), integrated over the sampling period (09.00–14.00).

stress the highest rates of photosynthesis were found at the highest levels in the crown, where the highest irradiance occurred. However rapid stomatal closure at the higher levels, because of a high evaporative demand, often strongly limited the rate of photosynthesis at these levels in the middle of the day. In the afternoons the highest rates of photosynthesis were often found in the lower levels of the crown.

Comparison of the photosynthetic production at the different heights in Fig. 4 (measured as the integrated areas under the photosynthetic curves, between 09.00–14.00, representing about 40% of the photosynthetic production of the day, cf. Linder & Troeng, 1980), shows about the same total production at the different levels, the two lowest levels having a slightly lower production. On the other hand, comparison of photosynthetic production per unit irradiance shows higher values at the lower levels, because of the reduced efficiency of CO_2-fixation at the higher levels (Fig. 8). Apart from the stomatal effects discussed above, the higher efficiency at the lower levels may also be an effect of a long-term acclimation to lower irradiances in the lower parts of the crown, affecting the light response of g_s as well as other conductances concerned in CO_2-fixation (cf. Jarvis et al., 1975; Koch, 1976; Troeng & Linder, 1978).

Diurnal variations in stem radius

The diurnal variation in shoot water potential and the diurnal variation in stem radius in Scots pine trees are strongly correlated, although changes in the stem radius lag behind the changes in shoot water potential by some hours (Figs. 9 and 10) (cf. Hellkvist & Hillerdal, 1977). When the strain gauge transducers were mounted directly on the xylem tissue (phloem and cambium layers removed) a close correlation with no lag phase was found between changes in needle water

194

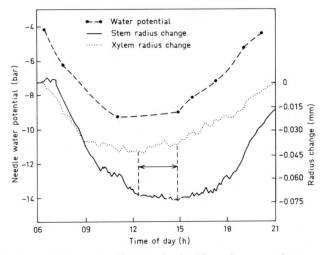

Figure 9. Needle water potential at the fifth branch whorl from the top, and stem and xylem radius changes in an irrigated and fertilized 20-year-old Scots pine on 21 August 1978. Note the time lag, indicated by arrows, of about three hours between xylem and intact stem radius change, and the lack of lag phase between change in needle water potential and xylem radius change. The xylem registration includes newly formed tracheids, still able to change considerably in dimension, but not the cambial initials, known to be the main barrier to radial water movements (cf. Jarvis, 1975).

potential and changes in stem radius (Fig. 9). Thus transducers mounted directly on xylem tissue provide a means of obtaining detailed information about diurnal changes in Ψ_n, at least for short time intervals. However, care must be taken to avoid wound callus tissue which interferes with such measurements.

Prolonged water stress affects the relation between Ψ_n and stem radius. This was demonstrated in the artificial water stress experiment in 1976. The experimental tree, having been water stressed since the beginning of June, was irrigated in September, and diurnal changes in Ψ_n and stem radius were measured during recovery (Fig. 10). About six hours after irrigation, Ψ_n of the experimental tree was about the same as Ψ_n in a reference tree. The stem radius of the stressed tree (transducer mounted outside phloem tissue) showed an tendency to increase after irrigation, probably because the stomata remained closed (cf. Bengtson, 1980), while the stem radius of the reference tree decreased during the same period because of high transpiration rates.

Seasonal variations in stem radius

The seasonal variation in stem radius is dependent both upon cambial growth and seasonal variation in stem water balance. Thus, neither the start nor the end of the cambial stem growth can be identified from stem radius registrations as the stem swells heavily in spring before growth begins, because of considerable water uptake, and shrinks in the autumn because of stem dehydration (cf. Kozlowski, 1965; Waring & Running, 1978). Different water regimes in different parts of the growing season also affect the stem radius, both directly through changes in the water reserves in the tree trunk, and possibly indirectly, since extremely dry

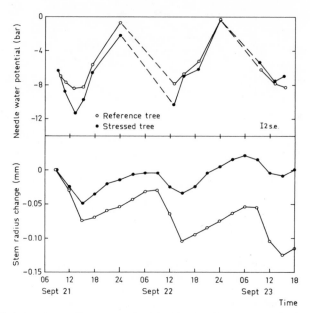

Figure 10. Diurnal change in needle water potential and stem radius in two root isolated 20-year-old pines on 21–23 September 1976. One of the trees had been artificially water stressed since the beginning of the summer by covering the ground area around the tree with a polyethene sheet. The tree was irrigated, starting at about 09.30 on 22 September. The reference tree was growing on an irrigated area, although the irrigation of the season had ended on September 18. Maximum value of 2 s.e. for Ψ_n is indicated.

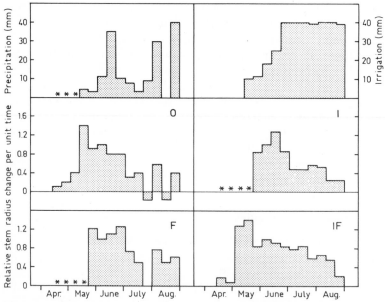

Figure 11. Relative stem radius changes per ten-day-periods during the growing season 1976 for four 20-year-old pines subjected to different water and nutrient regimes. 0 = control, I = irrigated, F = fertilized with dry nutrients, and IF = irrigated with nutrient solution. Precipitation and irrigation volumes for the same ten-day-periods are included. * = missing value.

196

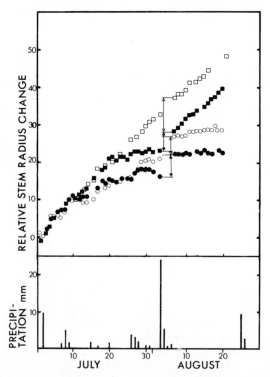

Figure 12. Relative stem radius changes of the four trees in Fig. 11 on 1 July–25 August 1976. □ = irrigated and fertilized, ■ = fertilized, ○ = irrigated and ● = control tree. Filled arrows represent the quick stem radius increment after the rain that broke a long drought period for the 0- and F-trees, while open arrows represent the relative stem radius increment that was lost during the dry period for the 0- and F-trees, compared with the I- and IF-trees.

weather periods affect both cell enlargement and cell division in the cambial region in different manners (cf. Hsiao, 1973). Fig. 11 shows the stem radial changes per ten days (transducers mounted outside phloem tissue) of four trees with different water and nutrient regimes during the growing season of 1976 and illustrates the rather complicated picture found when "growth" and "water balance" effects interact on stem radial changes. The radial increment rates of trees in unirrigated areas (0 and F) were obviously affected by the two dry weather periods in July and August. The changes from day to day before, during and after one of these dry periods are given in Fig. 12. During the dry period the radial increment of unirrigated trees (0 and F) was retarded and in some cases the stems even seemed to shrink from day to day, but after rain a larger stem radius was quickly reestablished, indicating that parts of the increment retardation were effects of depletion of water reserves in the trunk. However, the swelling was not large enough to give a relative stem radius of the same order as in irrigated trees (I and IF).

197

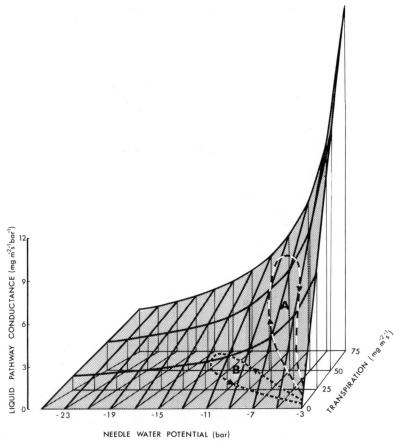

Figure 13. Calculated liquid pathway conductance (k_r/A) at $\Psi_{soil} = 0$ as a function of needle water potential and transpiration. The broken lines on the surface represent examples of the diurnal curves with hysteresis at unstressed (A) and stressed (B) state.

Apparent total liquid pathway conductance from soil to needle

Values of k_r/A (Equation 1) changed diurnally, the highest values being found at noon or earlier in the day, just before g_s started to limit the transpiration rate. Fig. 13 shows the dependence of k_r/A on E_T and Ψ_n, when $\Psi_{soil} = 0$, calculated from Equation (1).

The measured relation between k_r/A (calculated per unit needle area*) and Ψ_n for two 20-year-old pine trees, subjected to differing water and nutrient regimes, is shown in Fig. 14 for two periods in 1976. The data fall into two areas for a control tree and an irrigated and fertilized tree, one area representing diurnal variations in k_r/A and Ψ_n in a period in late June and early July 1976, and the other

---

* Note: The calculations should be made per unit tree rather than per unit leaf area. However, since a relation exists between sapwood area and leaf biomass (Grier & Waring, 1974), the calculations per unit needle area could be used as an approximation in this comparative study.

198

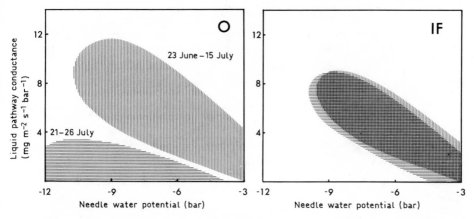

Figure 14. Response areas of k_r/A to diurnal changes in needle water potential of two 20-year-old pine trees growing on a control (0) and an irrigated and fertilized (IF) area, respectively, during two periods of the 1976 growing season with differing water regimes. 0-area: $\Psi_{soil} \geqslant -0.35$ and -0.80 bar for the first and second period, the transpiration varying within 0–50 and 0–25 mg m^{-2} s^{-1}, respectively. IF-area: $\Psi_{soil} \geqslant -0.08$ bar for both periods, the transpiration varying within 0–50 mg m^{-2} s^{-1} for both periods.

Table 3. Apparent total liquid pathway conductance from soil to needle (k_r/A) calculated per unit needle area, and needle water potential (Ψ_n) at a transpiration rate (E_T) per unit needle area around 8.4 mg m^{-2} s^{-1}. Values given for a 20-year-old and a 120-year-old Scots pine at wet and dry soil conditions.

	20-year-old		120-year-old	
	wet	dry	wet	dry
E_T (mg m^{-2} s^{-1})	8.6	8.6	8.2	8.3
Ψ_n (bar)	−5.2	−10.8	−10.9	−15.5
k_r/A (mg m^{-2} s^{-1} bar^{-1})	1.7	0.9	0.9	0.7

representing diurnal variations in a period in late July 1976, when the soil water reserves in the unirrigated plots were severely depleted. In late July the control tree had lower k_r/A-values than the IF-tree at all transpiration rates, showing that the resistance to water transfer from soil to needle was considerably larger in the unirrigated tree during this period. A comparison was made of k_r/A at a similar flow rate between a 20-year-old and a 120-year-old pine tree at a high and a low Ψ_{soil} (Table 3). The old tree showed lower k_r/A-values than the young tree indicating that the capacity to transfer water to the needles might be limiting in the old tree, in spite of the large water reserves which may be present in stem and branches of old conifers (cf. Jarvis, 1975; Waring & Running, 1978).

Soil-root resistance

More than half of the total liquid pathway flow resistance in a 20-year-old Scots pine was found to reside in the soil and root rather than the stem and shoot in an

199

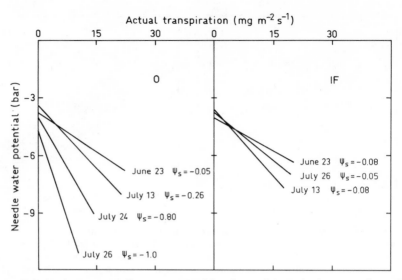

Figure 15. Relation between needle water potential and actual transpiration per unit needle area (calculated as $g_s \cdot D$) in two 20-year-old Scots pines during the long-term stress period June 23–July 26, 1976. Regression lines are based on values from measurements for various days during the morning reduction Ψ_n for a control tree (0) and an irrigated and fertilized tree (IF). Corresponding Ψ_{soil}-values are also given. The slope of the regression lines gives k_r/A.

experiment, in which the tree was cut off from the roots and placed in a bucket in early May 1977.

The conditions on the experimental day were extreme, with low soil temperature (about 0°C) and high air temperature (+28°C at noon). The stem cut under water made a quick recovery, as shown by a high rate of water uptake, a rise in Ψ_n and stomatal opening. The calculated k_r/A from the cut bole to the needle in the 3 m high tree was calculated to be 6.5 mg m^{-2} s^{-1} bar^{-1}, while k_r/A in the same tree before cutting off the stem was calculated to be 2.8 mg m^{-2} s^{-1} bar^{-1} at the same flow rate. The magnitude of the resistance found in the soil-root part of the system in relation to the total liquid pathway resistance is in agreement with earlier studies (cf. Roberts, 1977). This result is also confirmed by measurements in the same stand during the dry period in 1976, at which time a very high sensitivity in k_r/A to changes in Ψ_{soil} was found (Fig. 15).

To get an estimate of the importance of the soil-root resistance compared with the total liquid pathway resistance in a large 120-year-old pine tree, k_r/A from soil-root to needle was compared with k_r/A from the base of the stem at ground level to the needles, $(k_r/A)_{stem}$, calculated from:

$$(k_r/A)_{stem} = g_s \cdot D/\Psi_{grad} \cdot h \tag{2}$$

where Ψ_{grad} is the height gradient in Ψ_n and h is tree height. Calculations were made for a 17 m high tree, and gave only about one-third of the resistance in the soil-root part of the system, in spite of a low Ψ_{soil} on the day.

200

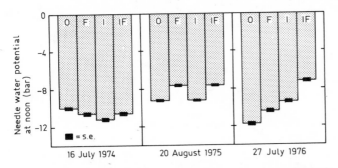

Figure 16. Needle water potential at noon in 20-year-old Scots pines, subjected to differing water and nutrient regimes, on three sampling occasions. The first date represents the start of the irrigation and fertilization experiment, the others represent one and two years of treatment (see Fig. 11). The Ψ_{soil} in the central area was −95 mbar on 20 August 1975 and −595 mbar on 27 July 1976. Means estimated from three trees per treatment. Black bars indicate two standard errors.

Effect of irrigation and fertilization on water balance

Fertilization affected Ψ_n of the trees, giving higher Ψ_{noon}, and smaller amplitude in the diurnal variation of Ψ_n (Hellkvist *et al.*, 1977). When the soil water was limiting, Ψ_{noon} of the unirrigated trees was lowered (Figs. 3 and 16).

A decreased amplitude in the diurnal variation of Ψ_n in a tree could be the result of either a lower water consumption per needle area, or of a change in the water balance in the needle, perhaps as a result of a higher k_r/A. The low Ψ_{noon} of unirrigated trees during dry weather periods was probably solely a result of a smaller conductance for water transport in the soil-root part of the system, while the increasing Ψ_{noon} caused by fertilization was a more complex result of many processes concerned. A decreasing transpiration per needle area was the result of more effective stomatal regulation, stomata becoming more sensitive to microclimatic changes, and thus being more able to control transpiration (cf. Glatzel, 1973, 1976; Mattson-Djos & Hellkvist, 1977). The increasing needle growth resulted in a decreased number of stomata per needle area, decreasing stomatal conductance per needle area but increasing conductance per tree. The enlarged, denser biomass also changed the microclimatic conditions in a direction that resulted in a lower transpiration rate per needle area, although the total transpiration from the trees of the fertilized plots was larger than from the unfertilized plots. The increasing growth in stem and branches resulted in increased stem diameter, which almost certainly means an increased conductance for water in stem and branches. Together with a lower osmotic potential of the cells an increasing stem diameter could also increase the water storage capacity of the tree. A lower osmotic potential in the root could result in more effective water uptake and possibly also a higher conductance in the xylem (cf. Fiscus, 1975). However, there were indications that the total liquid pathway conductance of water from soil-root to needle (k_r/A, see below) under non-stress conditions was of the same magnitude in fertilized and unfertilized trees (Fig. 17). During water stress the fertilized trees seemed to be able to maintain the

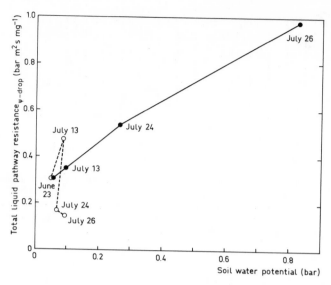

Figure 17. Total liquid pathway resistance, $1/(k_r/A)$, at the early morning Ψ_n-drop of four experimental days with differing soil water regimes during the long-term stress period June 23–July 26, 1976 in two 20-year-old pines, growing on an irrigated and fertilized area (open circles) and on a control area (filled circles), respectively.

same k_r/A-value or even to increase k_r/A, probably because of the ability for fast growth and water collection of fine roots (cf. Loomis *et al.*, 1971).

Concluding remarks

The present study of water relations and photosynthesis was part of an ecosystem study with the purpose of giving a better understanding of the growth dynamics in Scots pine. Growth and water relations are closely interrelated in the tree. Water conserving processes are very important contributors to the acclimation of the pine to its often very dry habitats. Closure of stomata in the early morning during dry periods causes lowered photosynthetic production but can be a necessary water conserving mechanism. In other words, investment for water conservation, although at the expense of growth maximisation, can be necessary for survival of the tree. The results reported here exemplify the complexity in the water regulating mechanisms.

Acknowledgements

The investigations were carried out at the Swedish Coniferous Forest Project experimental site, Ivantjärnsheden, Jädraås, in Central Sweden, during the growth periods of 1974 to 1977. We wish to thank Prof. Paul G. Jarvis for constructive criticism of the manuscript and for careful revision of the English text. We are also very grateful to Drs Stig Falk and Sune Linder for valuable criticism of the

202

manuscript and for stimulating discussions. It is a pleasure to acknowledge the skilful technical assistance of Miss Barbro Johansson and Mrs Lisbeth Mattson-Djos.

References

Beadle, C. L., Turner, N. C. & Jarvis, P. G. 1978. Critical water potential for stomatal closure in Sitka spruce. – Physiol. Plant. 43(2): 160–165.

Beardsell, M. F., Jarvis, P. G. & Davidson, B. 1972. A null-balance diffusion porometer suitable for use with leaves of many shapes. – J. appl. Ecol. 9: 677–690.

Bengtson, C. 1980. Effects of water stress in Scots pine. – In: Persson, T. (ed.) Structure and Function of Northern Coniferous Forests – An Ecosystem Study, Ecol. Bull. (Stockholm) 32: 205–213.

Bunce, J. A. 1977. Nonstomatal inhibition of photosynthesis at low water potentials in intact leaves of species from a variety of habitats. – Plant Physiol. 59: 348–350.

Dobbs, R. C. & Scott, D. R. M. 1971. Distribution of diurnal fluctations in stem circumference of Douglas-fir. – Can. J. For. Res. 1: 80–83.

Ericsson, A., Hellkvist, J., Hillerdal-Hagströmer, K., Larsson, S., Mattson-Djos, E. & Tenow, O. 1980. Consumption and pine growth. Hypotheses on effects on growth processes by needle-eating insects. – In: Persson, T. (ed.) Structure and Function of Northern Coniferous Forests – An Ecosystem Study, Ecol. Bull. (Stockholm) 32: 537–545.

Feddes, R. A. & Rijtema, P. E. 1972. Water withdrawal by plant roots. – J. Hydr. 17: 33–59.

Fiscus, E. L. 1975. The interaction between osmotic- and pressure- induced water flow in plant roots. – Plant Physiol. 55: 917–922.

Glatzel, G. 1973. Water use by spruce (*Picea abies* (L.) Karst.) in pot experiments as influenced by mineral fertilization. – FAO/IUFRO Symposium on Forests Fertilization, Paris, 7: 1–6.

Glatzel, G. 1976. Mineralstoffernährung und Wasserhaushalt von Fichtenpflanzen. Teoretische Überlegungen und Gefässversuche. Habilitationsschrift an der Universität für Bodenkultur in Wien in Selbstverlag des Verfassers, 84 pp.

Grier, C. C. & Waring, R. H. 1974. Estimating Douglas-fir and nobel-fir foliage mass from sap wood areas. – For. Sci. 20: 205–206.

Hellkvist, J. & Hillerdal, K. 1977. The relation between water potential and stem circumference change in 20 years old pine. – Swed. Conif. For. Proj. Int. Rep. 48, 19 pp. (In Swedish, English abstract).

Hellkvist, J., Hillerdal, K. & Parsby, J. 1975. Measurement of stem-diameter changes with a strain gage transducer. – Swed. Conif. For. Proj. Int. Rep. 29, 10 pp. (In Swedish, English abstract)

Hellkvist, J., Hillerdal, K. & Parsby, J. 1977. Influence of fertilization and irrigation on the water potential of young pine trees. – Swed. Conif. For. Proj. Int. Rep. 46, 23 pp. (In Swedish, English abstract)

Hellkvist, J., Richards, G. P. & Jarvis, P. G. 1974. Vertical gradients of water potential and tissue water relations in Sitka spruce trees measured with the pressure chamber. – J. appl. Ecol. 11: 637–668.

Honert, T. H. van den, 1948. Water transport in plants as a catenary process. – Disc. Faraday Soc. 3: 146–153.

Hsiao, T. C. 1973. Plant responses to water stress. – Ann. Rev. Plant Physiol. 24: 519–570.

Jarvis, P. G. 1975. Water transfer in plants. – In: de Vries, D. A. & Afgan, N. H. (eds.) Heat and Mass Transfer in the Biosphere. I. Transfer Processes in Plant Environment, pp. 370–394. Washington, D. C.: Scripta Book Co.

Jarvis, P. G. & Stewart, J. 1979. Evaporation of water from plantation forests. – In: Ford, E. D., Malcolm, D. C. & Atterson, J. (eds.) The Ecology of Even-Aged Forest Plantations, Proc. of the Meeting of Division I, IUFRO, pp. 327–349. Cambridge: Institute of Terrestrial Ecology.

Jarvis, P. G., James, G. B. & Landberg, J. J. 1975. Coniferous Forest. – In: Monteith, J. L. (ed.) Vegetation and Atmosphere, Vol. 2, pp. 171–240. London: Academic Press.

Jeffree, C. E., Johnson, R. P. C. & Jarvis, P. G. 1974. Epicuticular wax in the stomatal antechamber of Sitka spruce and its effects on the diffusion of water vapour and carbon dioxide. – Planta 98: 1–10.

Karlsson, G., Hellkvist, J. & Hillerdal, K. 1977. Field studies of photosynthesis and stomatal conductance in Scots pine. – Swed. Conif. For. Proj. Int. Rep. 47, 20 pp. (In Swedish, English abstract)

Klepper, B., Browning, D. & Taylor, H. M. 1971. Stem diameter in relation to plant water status. – Plant Physiol. 48: 683–685.

Koch, W. 1976. Blattfarbstoffe von Fichte (*Picea abies* (L.) Karst.) in Abhängigkeit vom Jahresgang, Blattalter und -typ. – Photosynthetica 10: 280–290.

Kozlowski, T. T. 1965. Expansion and contraction of plants. – Adv. Front Plant Sci. 10: 63–74.

Kozlowski, T. T. 1976. Diurnal variations in stem diameters of small trees. – Bot. Gaz. 28: 60–68.

Kramer, P. J. 1962. The role of water in tree growth. – In: Kozlowski, T. (ed.) Tree Growth, pp. 171–182. New York: Ronald Press Company.

Linder, S. & Troeng, E. 1978. Gas exchange in a 20-year-old stand of Scots pine. III. A comparison of net photosynthesis and transpiration of eight different pine trees. – Swed. Conif. For. Proj. Int. Rep. 82, 19 pp. (In Swedish, English abstract)

Linder, S. & Troeng, E. 1980. Photosynthesis and transpiration of 20-year-old Scots pine. – In: Persson, T. (ed.) Struction and Function of Northern Coniferous Forests – An Ecosystem Study, Ecol. Bull. (Stockholm) 32: 165–181.

Loomis, R. S., Williams, A. & Hall, A. E. 1971. Agricultural productivity. – Ann. Rev. Plant Physiol. 22: 431–468.

Mattson-Djos, E. & Hellkvist, J. 1977. Stomatal conductance and water potential of Scots pine. Introductory field studies. – Swed. Conif. For. Proj. Int. Rep. 68, 33 pp. (In Swedish, English abstract)

Monteith, J. L. 1965. Evaporation and environment. – Symp. Soc. exp. Biol. 19: 205–234.

Perttu, K., Lindgren, Å., Lindroth, A. & Norén, B. 1977. Micro- and biometeorological measurements at Jädraås. Instrumentation and measurement technics. – Swed. Conif. For. Proj. Tech. Rep. 7, 67 pp.

Richter, H. 1972. Wie entstehen Saugspannungsgradienten in Bäumen? – Ber. dtsch. Bot. Ges. 85: 341–351.

Richter, H. 1973. Frictional potential and total water potential in plants: a re-evaluation. – J. exp. Bot. 24: 983–994.

Roberts, J. 1977. The use of tree-cutting techniques in the study of the water relations of mature *Pinus sylvestris* L. I. The technique and survey of the results. – J. exp. Bot. 28: 751–767.

Shimshi, D. 1969. A rapid field method for measuring photosynthesis with labelled carbon dioxide. – J. exp. Bot. 20: 381–401.

Slatyer, R. O. 1967. Plant-Water Relationships. London – New York: Academic Press, 366 pp.

Slatyer, R. O. & Gardner, W. R. 1965. Overall aspects of water movement in plants and soils. – In: The State and Movement of Water in Living Organisms, 19th Symp. Soc. exp. Biol., pp. 113–129. Cambridge: Cambridge University Press.

Stoker, R. & Weatherley, E. 1971. The influence of the root system on the relationship between the rate of transpiration and depression of leaf water potential. – New Phytol. 70: 547–554.

Troeng, E. & Linder, S. 1978. Gas exchange in a 20-year-old stand of Scots pine. IV. Photosynthesis and transpiration within the crown of one tree. – Swed. Conif. For. Proj. Int. Rep. 83, 20 pp. (In Swedish, English abstract)

Waring, R. H. & Cleary, B. D. 1967. Plant moisture stress: Evaluation by pressure bomb. – Science 155: 1248–1254.

Waring, R. H. & Running, S. W. 1978. Sapwood water storage: Its contribution to transpiration and effect upon water conductance through the stems of old-growth Douglas-fir. – Plant Cell Environ. 1: 131–140.

Watts, W. R., Nielson, R. E. & Jarvis, P. G. 1976. Photosynthesis in Sitka spruce (*Picea sitchensis* (Bong.) Carr.). VII: Measurements of stomatal conductance and $^{14}CO_2$-uptake in a forest canopy. – J. appl. Ecol. 13: 623–638.

Weatherley, P. E. 1970. Some aspects of water relations. – Adv. Bot. Res. 3: 171–206.

Persson, T. (ed) 1980
Structure and Function of Northern
Coniferous Forests – An Ecosystem Study
Ecol. Bull. (Stockholm) 32: 205–213.

EFFECTS OF WATER STRESS ON SCOTS PINE

C. Bengtson

Abstract

The present investigation describes effects and after-effects of water stress on photosynthesis and transpiration of a 20-year-old tree of *Pinus sylvestris* L. The tree was exposed to water stress during 1977 by withholding water from May 23 to September 21, when it was rewatered. Photosynthesis, transpiration and soil water potential were continuously measured. Samples for determination of needle water potential were taken intermittently.

The pre-dawn needle water potential was reduced from –3.6 bar to –6.6 bar by the water stress treatment. On the day before rewatering the stomata of the stressed tree started to close at a needle water potential of –15 bar, reaching a minimum value of –17.3 bar while the needle water potential of the watered reference tree was never lower than –12 bar. On the first day after rewatering the changes in needle water potential of the stressed tree followed the trend of the reference tree closely, but photosynthesis and transpiration suffered from after-effects of the water stress for another five days.

Additional keywords: After-effects, needle water potential, photosynthesis, stomatal conductance, transpiration.

Introduction

Water stress can affect growth through two different types of processes: (1) formation of new tissue, and/or (2) "activity" of already formed tissue. Bud formation, formation of needle primordia, cell division and expansion of cells belong to the first type of processes, while photosynthesis and translocation are examples of the second type.

Effects and after-effects of water stress have been described for many species but information about conifers is still relatively scarce and most experiments concern young potted seedlings under controlled conditions (Rutter & Sands, 1958; Brix, 1962; Lister *et al.* 1967; Rutter, 1967; Kaufmann, 1968). However, there are a few investigations where relatively large trees have been studied (e.g., Lotan & Zahner, 1963; Garret & Zahner, 1973; Rook *et al.*, 1976). The work by Lotan & Zahner (1963) describes the effects of water shortage on shoot elongation, bud development and needle elongation using field measurements on 20-year-old trees of *Pinus resinosa* Ait., while Rook *et al.*(1976) used 5 m high (about 6-year-old) trees of *Pinus radiata* D. Don. raised in controlled environment

[1] Dept. of Plant Physiology, University of Göteborg, Carl Skottsbergs Gata 22, S-413 19 Göteborg, Sweden
Present address: Swedish Water and Air Pollution Research Institute, P. O. Box 5207, S-402 24 Göteborg, Sweden

rooms. The latter authors describe the effects of drought on such variables as plant water status, stomatal resistance, transpiration, photosynthesis and growth of shoots and roots.

To provide our growth models with the necessary data more information was needed on the effects of water stress on large coniferous trees in the field. The aim of the present investigation was to determine how water stress and after-effects of water stress affect the physiological state in a 20-year-old Scots pine tree, the ultimate goal being to describe in quantitative terms the effects and after-effects of water stress on growth.

Material and methods

A pilot experiment was planned during the early spring of 1976 and done during the summer as part of the Swedish Coniferous Forest Project. The results and experience obtained were used in planning an improved experiment for 1977–78.

Two trees of *Pinus sylvestris* about 20 years old, and with isolated roots, were exposed to water stress. One of these pines was used during 1976 while both were used during 1977. Because of low water-storing capacity of the soil and a ground-water level at about 10 m depth at the experimental site, the roots of a root-isolated tree do not get any water from the deep soil layers or from outside the metal plate (see Jansson, 1977), provided that no part of the root system gets under the metal plate. This arrangement should, thus, lead to a continuous drying of the isolated soil volume, the time needed to dry out the soil completely primarily depending on the evaporative demand created by the weather conditions and the resulting capability of the tree to absorb and transpire the water in the isolated volume of soil.

The tree introduced in 1977 was larger (5.0 m high as compared to 3.9 m) in order to increase the water stress. The following description refers to the larger tree. This tree was standing on a watered plot, i.e., it was watered regularly during the growth period (from about the end of May to mid-September) from mid-July 1974 until the start of the stress treatment in late May. For further information concerning the irrigation programme, see Aronsson et al. (1977).

The trees were exposed to water stress by withholding the irrigation water. For this purpose a roof of thin transparent plastic sheeting supported on a wooden frame was built over the root system. The frame was 1.5 m high at the centre and sloped down to 1.0 m at the outer edge which was about 1 m outside the metal plate used to isolate the roots. During 1977 the root system was covered with the plastic sheeting from May 23 to September 21. The tree was then rewatered.

The following measurements were carried out during 1977 on the water-stressed tree and on a reference tree. (1) Continuous measurements: Photosynthesis, transpiration (methods in Linder & Troeng, 1980), soil water content (θ) and soil moisture tension (Ψ_{soil}) (methods in Perttu et al., 1980). (2) Intermittent measurements: relative water content and water potential of the needles (Ψ_n), shoot length and needle length (methods in Larsson & Bengtson, 1980). When the tree was rewatered on September 19–22 simultaneous measurements of stomatal conductance, g_s, and Ψ_n were carried out.

Results

At the start of the stress period the water content of the soil was near field capacity. Thereafter the soil dried out with the strongest reduction in θ occurring from the beginning of June to the middle of July. However, the sharpest decrease in Ψ_{soil} occurred at the end of the drought period. Fig. 1 shows Ψ_{soil} as measured with gypsum blocks. The tensiometers are only usable down to a value of Ψ_{soil} of −1 bar. Down to this limit, however, they showed the same trend in Ψ_{soil} as the gypsum blocks. Towards the end of the stress period there was a steep gradient in Ψ_{soil} between the upper and the lower soil layers (Fig. 1).

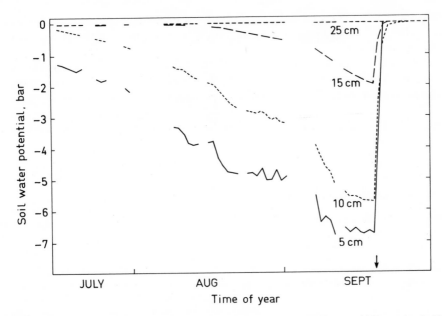

Figure 1. Soil water potential (Ψ_{soil}) of the soil close to a water-stressed 20-year-old Scots pine in 1977. The curves represent the mean values of Ψ_{soil} during 24 h at four different depths. The Ψ_{soil}-values were obtained from gypsum blocks which were placed in two separate profiles 0.5 m and 2.5 m from the tree, respectively. The arrow denotes the day of rewatering.

Table 1. Pre-dawn water potential (Ψ_n) of the needles of a water-stressed 20-year-old Scots pine and a watered control measured on four occasions during the summer 1977. The tree was rewatered during the night between September 20 and September 21. The Ψ_n-values from these two days represent the mean of two samples while the others represent the mean of 10 samples ± s.d.

Date	Ψ_n of stressed tree (bar)	Ψ_n of reference tree (bar)
May 23	-3.6 ± 0.2	-3.3 ± 0.2
June 21	-5.2 ± 0.3	-4.2 ± 0.4
August 11	-6.0 ± 0.4	-3.7 ± 0.3
September 20	-6.6	-2.6
September 21	-4.4	-3.2

Pre-dawn Ψ_n fell from -3.6 bar in late May to -6.6 bar in early August (Table 1). During the same period there was no significant reduction in the pre-dawn Ψ_n of the reference tree.

On September 20 the difference in pre-dawn Ψ_n between the stressed tree and the control was 4.0 bar. The parallel measurements of Ψ_n and g_s on the last day of water stress (September 20) showed that the stomata of the stressed tree were open to some extent before sunrise while those of the reference tree were almost totally closed (Fig. 2). In preliminary calculations of g_s from the cuvette data (not

207

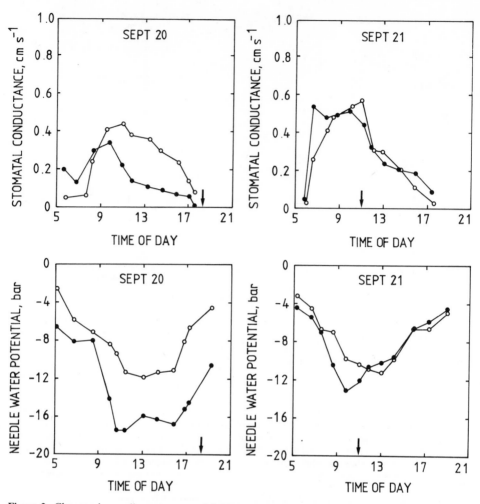

Figure 2. Changes in needle water potential (Ψ_n) and stomatal conductance (g_s) of a 20-year-old water-stressed Scots pine (●) and a watered reference tree (○). The Ψ_n-values were single samples; the g_s-values are means of three values (one per shoot of three different one-year-old shoots). The water-stressed tree was rewatered on September 20 by giving 250 mm of water between 18.00 h on September 20 to 05.00 h on September 21 and a further 50 mm between 11.00 h and 15.00 h on September 21.

shown here) the same tendency was shown during a period near the end of the stress treatment.

After sunrise there was first a slight reduction of the difference in Ψ_n but then Ψ_n of the water-stressed tree decreased faster than Ψ_n of the reference tree (Fig. 2). When Ψ_n of the stressed tree reached −15 bar the stomata were starting to close leading to simultaneous reduction in g_s. The stressed tree reached its minimum value of Ψ_n, −17.3 bar, at 10.50 a.m. and at that time the difference in Ψ_n between the two trees was 7.9 bar.

At noon g_s of the water-stressed tree was reduced to 40% of its maximum value

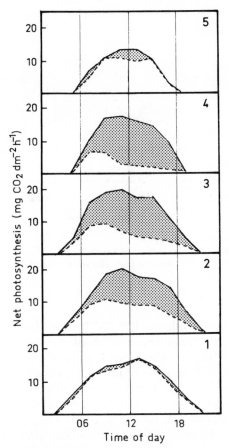

Figure 3. Changes in net photosynthesis (P_N) of an enclosed shoot (C + 1) of a water-stressed 20-year-old Scots pine (broken line) and a watered reference tree (solid line) during the water stress period (1–4) and during the recovery (5). The P_N-values are the mean values during (1) May 21 – June 20, (2) June 21 – July 20, (3) July 21 – August 20, (4) August 21 – September 20, and (5) September 21 – October 20 in 1977. The shaded area indicates the reduction in P_N.

during that day while at the same time g_s of the reference tree reached its maximum level.

After sunset g_s of both trees was reduced to about zero. At 19.00 h Ψ_n of the reference tree had almost returned to the pre-dawn level. However, at the same time Ψ_n of the stressed tree was about 3.5 bar below its pre-dawn level.

The change in rate of net photosynthesis, P_N, of the stressed tree during the stress period and during the recovery period, and the change in P_N of the watered reference tree during the same period, are shown in Fig. 3. P_N of the water-stressed tree was affected by the stress treatment and the impact of the treatment was stronger as the drought got more severe. This applied both to the maximum P_N reached during the day and to the total amount of assimilated carbon dioxide per day. Fig. 4 shows the mean P_N per day of the water-stressed tree in relation to the reference tree. On the first day after rewatering (September 21) the values of Ψ_n

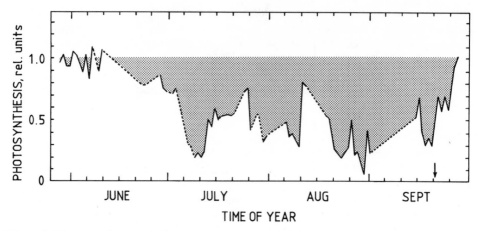

Figure 4. Mean net photosynthesis (P_N) of a water-stressed 20-year-old Scots pine in relation to a watered reference tree. The curve represents the mean daily P_N of an enclosed shoot (C + 1) of the water-stressed tree in relation to the reference tree. The shaded area indicates the reduction in P_N.

did not follow the same trends as they did the day before (cf. Fig. 2), i.e. on September 21 Ψ_n of the stressed tree followed Ψ_n of the reference tree rather closely, at least after 12.00 a.m. Consequently, these results seem to indicate that Ψ_n of the stressed tree had recovered fully on September 21. However, P_N of the stressed tree in relation to the reference tree (Fig. 4) did not return to the pre-stress level until September 27. Thus, the water-stressed tree suffered from an after-effect of water stress on P_N lasting for about 5 days. Corresponding data on transpiration rate (not shown here) point to an after-effect on transpiration of at least the same duration.

Discussion

Although the summer of 1976 was comparatively dry and hot the effects of water stress during the experiment were far less than expected. The pine used during 1976 was also exposed to water stress in 1977 (results not shown here) but showed no signs of being affected during the second year. One possible explanation was that roots could have grown under the metal plate used to isolate the root system so that the tree could have got access to extra sources of water. When this tree was felled in early October 1977 this suspicion was confirmed and it was also found that this pine had a developed taproot as well. Moreover, the metal plate had only been put in to a depth of 35 cm instead of 50 cm.

As indicated in Fig. 4, limited recovery in P_N took place from mid-July to mid-August. This recovery might partly have been attributable to local leakage of water through a hole in the plastic sheet. The θ-values obtained with a neutron probe (data not shown) showed a sudden increase in water content between July 20 and August 2 in the upper 20 cm at one of the measurement holes. However, the recovery might also have been caused by the weather conditions which gave rise to a very low evaporative demand during that period, i.e., a low transpiration rate as a result of the high humidity of the air and the partially closed stomata. It is also possible that the needles might have taken up water through the cuticle under certain conditions (see the review by Stone, 1957). Leyton & Juniper (1963) showed that the cuticle at the base of Scots pine needles differs from that of the exposed part and is capable of absorbing any water which runs down into the fascicle sheath. Water might also be absorbed through the lenticels of the twigs, thereby partially helping the tree to recover from a water deficit (Rutter, 1963).

The partial opening of the stomata on the stressed tree before sunrise (Fig. 2, September 20) might have been caused by osmotic adjustment which can occur during water stress of long duration (Hsiao et al., 1976a). A reduced osmotic potential may lead to an increase in turgor potential at the same Ψ_n and thus might maintain extension growth and stomatal opening during conditions of reduced water supply (Hsiao et al., 1976b).

The results demonstrate that water stress affects photosynthesis. The reduction in P_N probably depends mainly on the reduction in g_s but may also be affected by reduction in the mesophyll conductance (g_m) (Slavík, 1975; Boyer, 1976; Beadle & Jarvis, 1977). However, preliminary calculations of both g_s and g_m made from the gas exchange data (see Linder & Troeng, 1980) indicate that reduction in g_s was more important than reduction in g_m.

The data in Fig. 2 show no evident after-effect of stress on g_s but the cuvette data imply that both P_N and transpiration were affected by after-effects of water stress. One possible explanation for this discrepancy is that the gas exchange measurements were carried out on one-year-old needles while the measurements of g_s were made on current needles.

Using seedlings of Scots pine Jarvis & Jarvis (1963) found that stomatal closure occurred around a Ψ_n of -15 bar and similar results have also been reported for other pines (Rutter & Sands, 1958; Kaufmann, 1968; Lopushinsky, 1969; Dykstra, 1974). These values need not, of course, be regarded as universal but the stomata of pines are often thought of as being more sensitive to water stress than other conifers, i.e., pine stomata often close at comparatively high levels of Ψ_n. The stomata of the stressed tree started to close at a Ψ_n of about -15 bar (Fig. 2, September 20) but a Ψ_n of -12 bar reached by the reference tree on September 20 and by both trees on September 21 did not cause stomatal closure.

Closure of the stomata at -15 bar could mean a comparatively large reduction in P_N but as the transpiration is reduced as well it also means a saving of water which would be especially beneficial during longer periods of reduced precipitation and high evaporative demand. Hsiao (1973) and Hsiao et al. (1976a) present tables showing the difference in sensitivity to stress exhibited by different "processes or parameters" based only on the "reduction in leaf water potential required to affect the process". However, Bengtson et al. (1977) have shown the importance of also considering the duration of the stress (see also Bengtson, 1979). Although the sensitivity is not the same for different processes (or in different species), it is probably beneficial for maintenance of growth and for the prevention (or diminution) of damage as a result of water stress for the tree not to be exposed to extremely low water potentials for long periods.

A more thorough analysis of the data collected during 1977, together with analysis of data collected during 1978 (especially concerning elongation of shoots and amounts of current needles) should lead to a better description of the effects on growth of water stress during the growth period (see Larsson & Bengtson, 1980). Special attention will be paid to the combined adverse effect on growth of a reduction in total leaf area and the reduced photosynthetic production per unit leaf area resulting from the additional reduction in Ψ_n (affecting g_s and/or g_m) caused by the water stress.

Acknowledgements

The "stress experiment" was carried out in collaboration between researchers within the SWECON project. Photosynthesis and transpiration were measured by Sune Linder and Erik Troeng. Leaf water potential was measured by the author, stomatal conductance by Graham Russel and David Whitehead, and soil water potential by Per-Erik Jansson. The data handling was done mainly by Tomas Lohammar, Erik Troeng, and the author.

References

Aronsson, A., Elowson, S. & Ingestad, T. 1977. Elimination of water and nutrition as limiting factors in a young Scots pine stand. I. Experimental design and some preliminary results. – Swed. Conif. For. Proj. Tech. Rep. 10, 38 pp.

Beadle, C. L. & Jarvis, P. G. 1977. The effects of water status on some photosynthetic partial processes in Sitka spruce. – Physiol. Plant. 41: 7–13.

Bengtson, C. 1979. Effects and after-effects of water stress on transpiration rate (Ph. D. thesis at University of Göteborg, 1978). – Swed. Conif. For. Proj. Tech. Rep. 21, 50 pp.

Bengtson, C., Falk, S. & Larsson, S. 1977, The after-effect of water stress on transpiration and abscisic acid content in young wheat plants. – Physiol. Plant. 41: 149–154.

Boyer, J. S. 1976. Photosynthesis at low water potentials. – Phil. Trans. R. Soc. Lond. 273: 501–512.

Brix, H. 1962. The effect of water stress on the rates of photosynthesis and respiration in tomato plants and loblolly pine seedlings. – Physiol. Plant. 15: 10–20.

Dykstra, G. F. 1974. Photosynthesis and carbon dioxide transfer resistance of lodgepole pine seedlings in relation to irradiance, temperature, and water potential. – Can. J. For. Res. 4: 201–206.

Garret, P. W. & Zahner, R. 1973. Fascicle density and needle growth responses of red pine to water supply over two seasons. – Ecology 54: 1328–1334.

Hsiao, T. C. 1973. Plant responses to water stress. – Ann. Rev. Plant. Physiol. 24: 519–570.

Hsiao, T. C., Acevedo, E., Fereres, E. & Henderson, D. W. 1976a. Water stress, growth, and osmotic adjustment. – Phil. Trans. R. Soc. Lond. 273: 479–500.

Hsiao, T. C., Fereres, E., Acevedo, E. & Henderson, D. W. 1976b. Water stress and dynamics of growth and yield of crop plants. – In: Lange, O. L., Kappen, L. & Schulze, E-D. (eds.) Water and Plant Life. Problems and Modern Approaches, pp. 281–305. Berlin–Heidelberg: Springer-Verlag.

Jansson, P-E. 1977. Soil properties at Ivantjärnsheden. – Swed. Conif. For. Proj. Int. Rep. 54, 66 pp.

Jarvis, P. G. & Jarvis, M. S. 1963. The water relations of tree seedlings. IV. Some aspects of the tissue water relations and drought resistance – Physiol. Plant. 16: 501–516.

Kaufmann, M. R. 1968. Water relations of pine seedlings in relation to root and shoot growth. – Plant. Physiol. 43: 281–288.

Larsson, S. & Bengtson, C. 1980. Effects of water stress in growth in Scots pine. – Swed. Conif. For. Proj. Tech. Rep. 24, 21 pp.

Leyton, L. & Juniper, B. E. 1963. Cuticle structure and water relations of pine needles. – Nature, Lond. 198:770.

Linder, S. & Troeng, E. 1980. Photosynthesis and transpiration of 20-year-old Scots pine. – In: Persson, T. (ed.) Structure and Function of Northern Coniferous Forests – An Ecosystem Study, Ecol. Bull. (Stockholm) 32: 165–181.

Lister, G. R., Slankis, V., Krotkov, G. & Nelson, C. D. 1967. Physiology of *Pinus strobus* L. grown under high or low soil moisture conditions. – Ann. Bot. 31: 121–132.

Lopushinsky, W. 1969. Stomatal closure in conifer seedlings in response to leaf moisture stress. – Bot. Gaz. 130: 258–263.

Lotan, J. E. & Zahner, R. 1963. Shoot and needle responses of 20-year-old red pine to current soil moisture regimes. – For. Sci. 9: 497–506.

Perttu, K., Bischof, W., Grip, H., Jansson, P-E., Lindgren, Å., Lindroth, A. & Norén, B. 1980. Micrometeorology and hydrology of pine forest ecosystems. I. Field studies. – In: Persson, T. (ed.) Structure and Function of Northern Coniferous Forests – An Ecosystem Study, Ecol. Bull. (Stockholm) 32: 75–121.

Rook, D. A. , Swanson, R. H. & Cranswick, A. M. 1976. Reaction of radiata pine to drought. – N. Z. For. Ser. Rep. 1036: 55–68.

Rutter, A. J. 1963. Studies of the water relations of *Pinus sylvestris* in plantation conditions. I. Measurements of rainfall and interception. – J. Ecol. 51: 191–204.

Rutter, A. J. 1967. Studies of the water relations of *Pinus sylvestris* in plantation conditions. V. Responses to variation in soil water conditions. – J. appl. Ecol. 4: 73–81.

Rutter, A. J. & Sands, K. 1958. The relation of leaf water deficit to soil moisture tension in *Pinus sylvestris* L. I. The effect of soil moisture on diurnal changes in water balance. – New Phytol. 57: 50–65.

Slavík, B. 1975. Water stress, photosynthesis and the use of assimilates. – In: Cooper, J. P. (ed.) Photosynthesis and Productivity in Different Environments, pp. 511–536. Cambridge–London–New York–Melbourne: Cambridge University Press.

Stone, E. E. 1957. Dew as an ecological factor. I. A review of the literature. – Ecology 38: 407–413.

Persson, T. (ed) 1980
Structure and Function of Northern
Coniferous Forests – An Ecosystem Study
Ecol. Bull. (Stockholm) 32: 215–218.

WATER TRANSPORT IN HARDENED AND NON-HARDENED SEEDLINGS OF SCOTS PINE

L-Å. Andersson[1]

Abstract

The transpiration rates of 20-week-old seedlings of Scots pine preconditioned to short photoperiods and different temperature regimes, were measured. A short photoperiod reduced the transpiration rate in the light by about 10%, whereas a short photoperiod together with low temperature for 3 weeks decreased the rate by 50%. After 6 weeks the transpiration rate was reduced nearly to dark transpiration rate, indicating that the stomata were almost closed. The results are compared with similar effects caused by water stress and abscisic acid.

Additional keywords: Stress, transpiration.

Introduction

Ecophysiological studies have revealed that two important factors influencing the physiological state of trees in the temperate zones are daylength and temperature (e.g., Kramer, 1936; Heide, 1974). Short photoperiods and low temperature will, for example, induce winter rest and frost hardiness (Weiser, 1970; Christersson, 1978). Changes in water transport and photosynthesis during the year with a decline in the winter season have also been reported (Parker, 1963; Linder, 1977). This investigation was to study the changes of transpiration rate of pine seedlings preconditioned to short photoperiods and different temperatures, to find out which environmental factors are responsible for the decrease in the water transport during autumn and how they act.

Material and methods

The plant material consisted of 20-week-old seedlings of Scots pine (*Pinus sylvestris* L.) grown under conditions described by Andersson et al. (1977). The 20-week-old seedling had a 9 cm long shoot with a fresh weight of 3.5 g. The seedlings were divided into eight groups with five plants in each. The groups were exposed to different daylength and temperature regimes (Table 1). After these preconditions the transpiration rate of the seven groups of seedlings during dark and light periods were determined in the laboratory.

[1] Dept. of Plant Physiology, Botanical Institute, University of Göteborg, Carl Skottsbergs Gata 22, S-413 19 Göteborg, Sweden

215

Table 1. The photo- and thermoperiodic treatments of the seedlings.

Group	Day/night temperature (°C)	Period (weeks)
Daylength 8 h		
A1	25/15	3
A2	25/15 + 15/10	3 + 3
A3	25/15 + 15/10 + 2/2	3 + 3 + 3
B1	15/10	3
B2	15/10 + 2/2	3 + 2
C1	2/2	3
C2	2/2	6
Daylength 17 h		
D (Control)	25/15	0

The transpiration rates were measured in an open system with the plant enclosed in a plexiglass chamber. The relative humidities of the inlet and outlet air from the plexiglass chamber were measured using a humidity meter with a thin film capacitive sensor (HM 11, Vaisala). Temperature was measured by platinum resistance thermometers (100 ohm). During the measurements in light the irradiance in the chamber was 50 W m^{-2}, temperature 25.0 ± 0.5°C and water vapour pressure of the inlet and outlet air 1.6 ± 0.1 kPa and 3.2 ± 0.1 kPa, respectively.

Results and discussion

The measurements indicate that short photoperiods (8 h light per day) decrease the transpiration rate in light (Fig. 1, A1, A2, and B1, B2). A larger reduction of the transpiration rate takes place when the temperature is lowered to some degrees above zero after the seedlings have been placed in short day conditions (Fig. 1, C1 and C2). The transpiration rate of such plants is nearly that in darkness (Fig. 1, C2). The results show good agreement with the assumption that the stomata are almost closed during the winter (Christersson, 1972). There were no detectable effects on the transpiration rate in darkness.

The decreasing transpiration rate in light during a frost-hardening process resulting in closed stomata during the winter period is a result similar to the effect of water stress. If short photoperiod and low temperature induce water stress and accompanied strain, e.g., closed stomata, the results can be explained in two ways:

(1) The stress increases respiration and reduces photosynthesis. This will increase the CO_2-concentration in the leaf and cause the stomata to close (Fischer, 1970).

(2) The stress increases the abscisic acid content of the leaf (Bengtson *et al.*, 1977), which inhibits the opening of the stomata (Jones & Mansfield, 1970).

There may also be a photoperiodic inductive increase in abscisic acid with closed stomata as result.

Determinations of abscisic acid content in hardened and non-hardened seed-

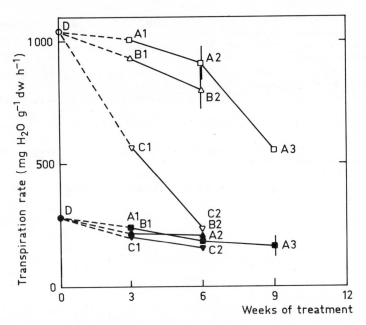

Figure 1. Transpiration rates in light (○, □, △, ▽) and darkness (●, ■, ▲, ▼) of pine seedlings preconditioned at short photoperiod and different temperatures. The transpiration is expressed as mg water per gram dry weight of needles per hour. The precondition treatments of the different groups of seedlings are given in Table 1. Bars indicate standard errors, $n = 5$

lings will provide further information on the hormonal regulation of water transport during the winter.

Conclusion

Short photoperiod and low temperature caused a decrease in the transpiration rates of pine seedlings, probably an effect of water deficit stress.

Acknowledgement

This study was performed within the Swedish Coniferous Forest Project.

References

Andersson, L-Å., Bengtson, C., Falk, S.O., & Larsson, S. 1977. Cultivation of pine and spruce seedlings in climate chambers. – Swed. Conif. For. Proj. Tech. Rep. 5, 17 pp.

Bengtson, C., Falk, S. O. & Larsson, S. 1977. The after-effect of water stress on transpiration and abscisic acid content in young wheat plants. – Physiol. Plant. 41: 149–154.

Christersson, L. 1972. The transpiration rate of unhardened, hardened and dehardened seedlings of spruce and pine. – Physiol. Plant. 26: 258–263.

Christersson, L. 1978. The influence of photoperiod and temperature on the development of frost hardiness in seedlings of *Pinus silvestris* and *Picea abies*. – Physiol. Plant. 44: 288–294.

Fischer, R. A. 1970. After-effect of water stress on stomatal opening potential. II. Possible causes. – J. Exp. Bot. 21: 384–404.

Heide, O. 1974. Growth and dormancy in Norway spruce ecotypes (*Picea abies*). I. Interaction of photoperiod and temperature. – Physiol. Plant. 30: 1–12.

Jones, R. J. & Mansfield, T. A. 1970. Suppression of stomatal opening in leaves treated with abscisic acid. – J. Exp. Bot. 21: 714–719.

Kramer, P. J. 1936. Effect of variation in length of day on growth and dormancy of trees. – Plant. Physiol. 11: 127–137.

Linder, S. 1977. The diurnal and seasonal changes in net photosynthesis of Scots pine. – Swed. Conif. For. Proj. Int. Rep. 55, 26 pp. (In Swedish, English abstract)

Parker, J. 1963. Cold resistance in woody plants. – Bot. Rev. 29: 123–205.

Weiser, C. J. 1970. Cold resistance and injury in woody plants. – Science 169: 1269–1278.

Persson, T. (ed) 1980
Structure and Function of Northern
Coniferous Forests – An Ecosystem Study
Ecol. Bull. (Stockholm) 32: 219–228.

EFFECTS OF IRRIGATION AND FERTILIZATION ON MINERAL NUTRIENTS IN SCOTS PINE NEEDLES

A. Aronsson[1] and S. Elowson[1]

Abstract

An attempt was made to maximize the biomass production of young pines in a field experiment by eliminating the main growth-limiting factors, i.e., water and mineral nutrients. There were three treatments in addition to the control: irrigation, fertilization and irrigation plus fertilization. The pine needles were analyzed for their contents of macronutrients and most nitrogen was found in needles from fertilized plots. In fertilized plus irrigated plots the N-content was lower and not within the range for maximum growth. The effects of the treatments on vegetation are also described.

Additional keywords: Boron deficiency, growth maximization.

Introduction

In Swedish forests growth on mineral soils is often limited by the supply of nutrients, especially nitrogen (cf. Tamm, 1968; Tamm et al., 1974; Holmen et al., 1976). During the growth period, or at least part of it, water will probably limit growth of most forests on mineral soils. When nitrogen availability is increased, as for example after fertilization, other nutrients and also water are likely to be the growth determining factors. Under such conditions, the efficiency of the applied nitrogen could be severely reduced, sometimes to an insignificant level. Laboratory experiments have demonstrated that a balance between the nutrients in the plants is essential for the physiological status and growth ability of various plant species (Ingestad, 1971, 1974). In conifers the connections between nutrient status, water balance, photosynthesis, and growth are further complicated and obscured by dynamic changes in the amounts and location in the tree crown of needles of various age. Furthermore, conifers seem to have mechanisms for redistribution of nutrients within the plant, which probably implies an economical utilization of nutrients once taken up, and adaptation of needles and root biomass to the site conditions. Such adaptation processes may occur slowly over several years and therefore all such studies are time-consuming.

The aim of the present investigation is to assess the productivity of the ecosystem and the dynamic turnover of the mineral nutrients under conditions of adequate

---

[1] Dept. of Ecology and Environmental Research, Swedish University of Agricultural Sciences, S-750 07 Uppsala, Sweden

water and mineral nutrient supply. To do this the ecosystem is gradually saturated with nutrients, the rate of supply being adjusted to match the rate of uptake. Thus, the supply of mineral nutrients must be increased in parallel with the increasing biomass. When the ecosystem is becoming saturated with mineral nutrients, the assumption is that a progressively increasing proportion of the total amount of nutrients is being circulated within the ecosystem. When the ecosystem is saturated with mineral nutrients, it is necessary to apply only small amounts of nutrients in order to maintain circulating nutrients at a level which is not growth-limiting.

Site description and allocation of experiments

The experimental plots are situated in a young Scots pine stand, Ih II, within the Swedish Coniferous Forest Project research area of Ivantjärnsheden (see Axelsson & Bråkenhielm, 1980). The trees were 15–20 years old at the start of the experiment in 1974. The soil consists of a deep layer of sand. The stand was cleaned and space-regulated during preparation for the experiment. Subsequently there were about 1100 trees taller than 1 m per ha with an average height of about 1.1 m (Flower-Ellis et al., 1976).

The experiment consists of control plots (0) and three treatments: irrigation (I), fertilization (F), and irrigation plus fertilization (IF). Each treatment has five replicates according to a randomized blocks design, the whole experiment thus consisting of 20 plots. The assessment plot is 20×20 m with a margin of 5 m. In cases where different treatments are imposed on neighbouring plots, they are isolated from each other by sheets of aluminium inserted to a depth of about 30 cm.

Treatments of the plots

The water for irrigation is taken from a drilled well and applied as small droplets from sprinklers placed at a height of about 50 cm above ground level. Irrigation normally takes place each day, except after heavy rains when the irrigation programme is modified. The amounts of water irrigated in different years are given in Table 1.

Fertilization of F-plots is done manually with solid fertilizer once a year at the beginning of the growth period. Nitrogen is applied annually, whereas potassium and phosphorus are applied once every three years (see Table 1).

The irrigation and fertilization (IF) treatment is done with a complete fertilizer consisting of both macro- and micronutrients in fixed proportions to nitrogen (see Table 2). The fertilizer is applied as a very dilute solution, using the same equipment as for irrigation. Fertilization takes place five days a week from mid-May to mid-August each year, apart from the first year (Table 1 and Fig. 1). The highest application so far has been 0.3 g N day^{-1} m^{-2} with all other mineral nutrients in proportion to nitrogen (Table 2). Fig. 1 illustrates how the applications have changed during the four years. At the start of the experiment it was calculated that 10 g N m^{-2} yr^{-1} were required for maximum production. The experiment started on 12 July 1974 in the middle of the growth period and, therefore, it was decided to fertilize only 7 g m^{-2} in order to get a smooth start to the experiment. In the following year, 1975, the treatments started at the beginning of the summer and the fertilization took the form of an

Table 1. Irrigation and fertilization regime during the summers from 1974 onwards and the total precipitation during the same period.

Year	Irrigation		Precipitation	Fertilization					
				Liquid fertilizer[1]		Solid fertilizer[2]			
								g element m^{-2}	
	Duration	mm	mm	Duration	g N m^{-2}	Date	N	P	K
1974	12/7–19/9	100	100	12/7–9/8	7	15–16/7	8	3	6
1975	23/5–12/9	300	180	23/5–22/8	10	6/6	8	–	–
1976	20/5–18/9	300	250	20/5–20/8	15	3–4/6	8	–	–
1977	16/5–30/8	250	240	16/5–19/8	15	16–17/5	8	3	6
1978	23/5–12/9	220	320	23/5–12/9	20	30/5	8	–	–

[1] Other essential elements than N given in fixed proportion to N.
[2] N as ammonium nitrate granulated with dolomite, P as triple superphosphate and K as potassium sulphate.

Table 2. Composition of liquid fertilizer. The N content is put to 100 units and the other elements expressed in proportion to N (Ingestad, 1967).

Element	Proportions		Element	Proportions	
	by weight	by molarity		by weight	by molarity
N	100	100	Fe	0.70	0.18
K	65	23	Mn	0.40	0.10
P	13	5.9	B	0.20	0.26
			Cu	0.030	0.0067
Ca	7	2.5	Zn	0.030	0.0064
Mg	8.5	4.9	Mo	0.007	0.0010
S	9	3.9	Na	0.0034	0.0020
			Cl	0.033	0.013

S-curve with the highest application around June 25 when the new shoots and needles were in the period of fastest growth. However, the analysis of needles for mineral nutrients (Fig. 2) showed that the N-content was at a minimum on this occasion. This is probably partly a "dilution effect" but there may also be a "time lag" between the time for fertilization and the time the nitrogen reached the needles. In order to stabilize the percentage content in the needles the plots were fertilized earlier in the following summers. As the concentration of nitrogen in the needles was rather low it was also decided to increase the fertilization from 10 to 15 g N m^{-2} yr^{-1}

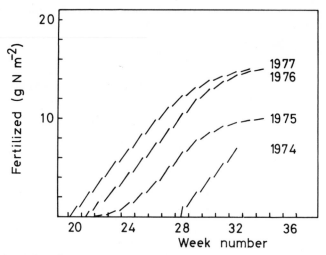

Figure 1. Fertilization regimes for IF-plots, 1974 onwards. All other elements are given in fixed proportion to N.

Visible effects of the treatments on the vegetation

On the IF-plots the ground vegetation growth increased during the first season (1974) after the treatment started in mid-July. That lichens increased their growth so much was most remarkable. Under normal fertilizer regime lichens usually do not increase growth and may sometimes suffer a negative effect. The results clearly demonstrate that application of a very dilute liquid fertilizer five days a week promoted the growth not only of pines and lesser vegetation as mosses, *Calluna* and *Vaccinium* but also of the lichens.

During the second year of treatment (1975) *Rubus idaeus* L. and *Chamaenerion angustifolium* (L.) Scop. entered the IF-plots and have since increased gradually. *Chamaenerion* in particular has grown vigorously and in some patches has almost completely suppressed all other ground vegetation.

Although the experimental area is on a sandy plain, the area is not quite homogeneous in all respects. Stand density and tree height were greatest in blocks 1 and 5 before treatment. The ground vegetation also showed the fastest response to treatment in these blocks. However, the pattern of response was the same in all blocks, with a delay of about one year. On plots which were only fertilized or irrigated there were very small, if any, effects on the ground vegetation.

The pine needles on the F and IF plots became greener a month or two after treatment commenced and at the same time an increase in the nitrogen percentage content of the needles occurred (Fig. 2). In the years after fertilization the pines have grown vigorously with longer and thicker needles and more and longer branches.

During the summer 1977 a growth disorder occurred in some pines on some of the F- and IF-plots. The disorder resembled those reported from different parts of Scandinavia (Albrektson *et al.*, 1977; Braekke, 1977; Huikari, 1977). It is always located at the top of the tree and seems to be caused by damage to the meristems in apical buds and shoots. Needles do not extend in the normal fashion but become bent

222

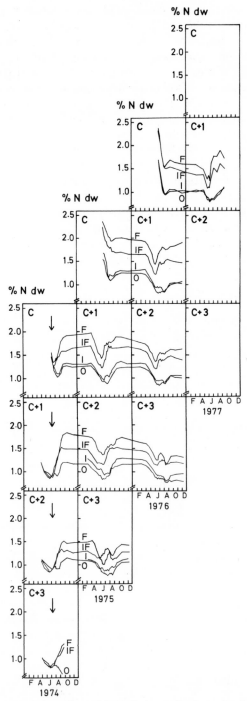

Figure 2. Nitrogen concentration on dry weight basis in needles from the third whorl, 1974 onwards. Moving average for three values except the initial and ending value for each line and for the year 1977, which are discrete values. C = current needles; C + 1, C + 2, and C + 3 = one, two, and three-year-old needles, respectively. 0 = control, I = irrigation, F = fertilization, and IF = irrigation plus fertilization. Arrows = start of the treatments.

or curled. The needles on the same shoot are of very different length. Apical dieback also occurs and sometimes the shoot does not elongate, giving it a brushlike appearance. From the few Scandinavian reports published, it seems that deficiency of one or more micronutrient elements cause the damage. Boron is considered the most likely. Up to the present the F plots have received only nitrogen, potassium and phosphorus and a deficiency of other elements might occur as a "dilution effect" caused by increased growth. The IF plots are fertilized with a complete fertilizer that includes both macro- and micronutrients (Table 2) and which has been shown to give an optimum effect on the growth of many species, including pine and spruce in solution culture (Ingestad, 1979). Nevertheless, a few of the pines on the IF-plots are also damaged. The mechanisms behind these growth disturbances are still unknown, but the demand for micronutrients (boron) during the period of most rapid growth may possibly be in excess of the availability of the element in the soil, and in this situation boron within older parts of the tree cannot be translocated sufficiently quickly to counteract the deficiency in the young shoots.

Macronutrient content in the needles

There is a cyclical variation of macronutrients in needles, with a clear minimum towards the end of June (Fig. 2). To a great extent this might be a "dilution" of the nutrients within the tree, caused by the rapid growth of shoots and new needles during this period. However, the dry weight of the needles also has a cyclical variation during the year, which is mainly caused by fluctuation of the starch content, which can vary from about 5 to 25% of dry weight (A. Ericsson, pers. comm.), with the highest contents during the first half of June. Thereafter the content decreases to a rather low level at the end of July. If the concentration of nutrients is expressed on the basis of dry weight minus starch content instead of on dry weight, the minimum in the nutrient concentration will be levelled out to some extent.

Four to five weeks after start of the treatments the concentration of macronutrients in the needles on F and IF plots began to increase (Figs. 2 and 3). This increase took place in current (C) as well as in older needles. Even most of the 3-year-old needles increased their concentration of nitrogen, although they were going to be dropped later in the autumn.

The highest nitrogen concentrations are in needles from the F-plots, while the IF-plots are at a lower level and with a clear difference between the two treatments. At the end of the vegetation period in 1975, the F- and IF-plots received about the same amount of nitrogen, 16 and 17 g m^{-2} respectively. At the end of 1977 the same plots received 32 and 47 g m^{-2}, respectively. Despite this difference in fertilization, these plots have maintained the inverse relationship in nitrogen concentration established during the first autumn of the experiment. The irrigation and control plots, where the nitrogen concentrations were approximately the same at the end of the first season, have also maintained the same pattern in succeeding years. The explanation of the difference in levels between F- and IF-plots may be partly attributed to the faster growth of the trees in the IF-plots, which a consequent "dilution effect", and partly to the apparently greater uptake of nutrients by the ground vegetation of these plots. Initially (1975), the irrigation treatment increased the

224

Table 3. Nitrogen contents as percentages of dry weight in exposed needles taken from the third whorl from the top of the tree 1974–1978. Each value ($\pm$s.d.) is an average of five plots. For explanation of needle age see Fig. 2.

Treatment	Needle age	Date for needle sampling				
		1974-09-26	1975-09-18	1976-09-16	1977-09-15	1978-09-14
IF	C	1.65 ± 0.06	1.73 ± 0.03	1.52 ± 0.05	1.59 ± 0.08	1.69 ± 0.05
	C+1	1.56 ± 0.04	1.64 ± 0.04	1.59 ± 0.03	1.56 ± 0.06	1.67 ± 0.05
	C+2	1.45 ± 0.02	1.55 ± 0.01	1.48 ± 0.04	1.40 ± 0.09	1.56 ± 0.02
	C+3	1.21 ± 0.03	1.31 ± 0.02	1.26 ± 0.04	1.36 ± 0.15	1.37 ± 0.14
F	C	1.96 ± 0.02	2.03 ± 0.03	1.66 ± 0.02	1.68 ± 0.07	1.59 ± 0.05
	C+1	1.91 ± 0.04	1.93 ± 0.03	1.80 ± 0.04	1.84 ± 0.11	1.67 ± 0.04
	C+2	1.61 ± 0.04	1.78 ± 0.05	1.65 ± 0.05	1.69 ± 0.08	1.62 ± 0.08
	C+3	1.40 ± 0.04	1.48 ± 0.03	1.38 ± 0.02	1.54 ± 0.20	1.45 ± 0.17
I	C	1.38 ± 0.02	1.31 ± 0.04	1.03 ± 0.01	1.08 ± 0.07	1.15 ± 0.05
	C+1	1.32 ± 0.02	1.37 ± 0.04	1.05 ± 0.03	1.11 ± 0.03	1.12 ± 0.04
	C+2	1.25 ± 0.01	1.27 ± 0.01	1.08 ± 0.03	1.03 ± 0.04	1.12 ± 0.05
	C+3	–	1.11 ± 0.03	0.98 ± 0.04	1.04 ± 0.02	1.08 ± 0.06
0	C	1.29 ± 0.03	1.23 ± 0.01	1.11 ± 0.03	1.12 ± 0.11	1.26 ± 0.03
	C+1	1.28 ± 0.08	1.21 ± 0.04	1.03 ± 0.02	1.13 ± 0.04	1.24 ± 0.03
	C+2	1.17 ± 0.04	1.18 ± 0.01	1.00 ± 0.01	1.04 ± 0.03	1.24 ± 0.03
	C+3	–	1.03 ± 0.02	0.95 ± 0.02	0.97 ± 0.10	1.09 ± 0.05

nitrogen concentration in the needles slightly above the control, but in 1976 the difference had almost disappeared.

Normally, samples are taken from only two blocks on each sampling occasion but once a year, in the autumn, they are taken from all five blocks. The highest concentrations of nitrogen are normally found in the current needles, with a decrease of about 5 to 15% to the next year-class of needles (Table 3). In autumn 1976 this applied only to the control plot. The treatments had lower nitrogen concentrations in current than in older needles.

For optimum growth, the nitrogen concentration in needles may be in the range 1.7–2.5% of dry weight (Ingestad, 1962; Tamm, 1977) if all other nutrients are in appropriate proportions to nitrogen. However, it is only the trees on the F-plots that have had a nitrogen concentration within or almost within this range. The trees on IF-plots only reached this level occasionally, and the trees on I and 0-plots never attained that level.

As mentioned above, dry weight is not a good basis on which to express nutrient concentration. An attempt to find a better expression is shown in Fig. 3, where the nitrogen content in the needles is set to 100 weight units and the other macronutrients analysed are expressed in relation to this base. This enables comparison of the contents with the composition of the liquid fertilizer used (Table 2). The clearest effect is the rather low percentage in the F-plots, which is probably caused by the fact that the F-plots were fertilized with nitrogen, potassium and phosphorus in 1974

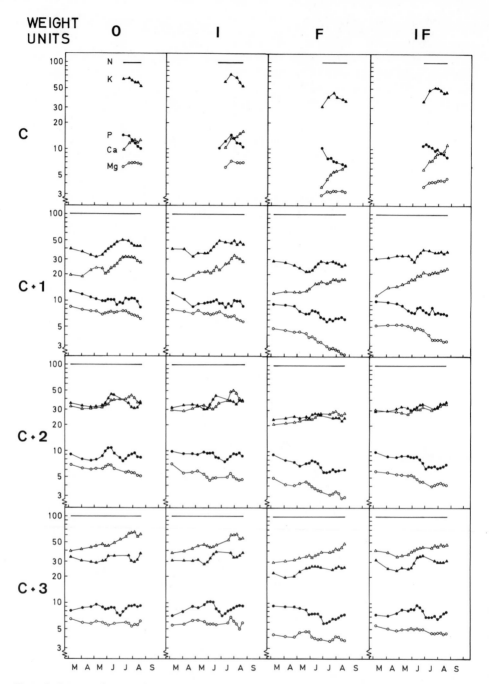

Figure 3. Content of some mineral nutrients in relation to nitrogen (100 weight units). Needles taken from the third whorl, 1975. Logarithmic scale.

and only nitrogen in 1975. The increased growth therefore caused a "dilution" of the other nutrients while the demand for nitrogen was more or less satisfied. For the current needles of the other three treatments the proportions are almost of the same orders as in Table 2. For older needles the levels of IF-, I- and 0-plots are also very much alike. This means that the lower growth rate of pines in I- and 0-plots compared with IF-plots is not, or only to a small extent, caused by unbalanced proportions of the macronutrient elements in the needles but generally by the low concentration. Calcium concentration increases with needle age while potassium decreases. In the one-year-old needles $(C+1)$ the concentrations of both calcium and potassium increase during the vegetation period, while phosphorus and magnesium decrease.

No balance table for the mineral budget has been prepared on account of the lack of relevant data for the increase in production resulting from the treatments. Moreover, the content of mineral nutrients in the needles necessary for maximum growth has not yet been reached. In order to achieve this optimum situation in the needles, the fertilizer prescription for the plots will be modified, both through an increase in the total quantity to be applied and through an extension of the treatment period. The consumption of nutrients by the very dense herb vegetation on the IF-plots must also be considered.

As a result of great increase in growth, the trees in the IF-plots are now approaching canopy closure with consequent self-pruning. When the canopy is completely closed there will be an almost constant volume of needles within the stand, situated in the upper part of the canopy. In the lower part, the needles will gradually die off and fall to ground. Through litter decomposition the major part of the nutrients needed for the trees will become available. Fertilization will then only be required at a relatively low level in order to compensate for nutrient immobilization.

Acknowledgement

This study was made as a part of the Swedish Coniferous Forest Project.

References

Albrektson, A., Aronsson, A. & Tamm, C. O. 1977. The effect of forest fertilisation on primary production and nutrient cycling in the forest ecosystem. – Silva fenn. 11 (3): 233–239.
Axelsson, B. & Bråkenhielm, S. 1980. Investigation sites of the Swedish Coniferous Forest Project – biological and physiographical features. – In: Persson, T. (ed.) Structure and Function of Northern Coniferous Forests – An Ecosystem Study, Ecol. Bull. (Stockholm) 32: 25–64.
Braekke, F. H. 1977. Fertilization for balanced mineral nutrition of forests on nutrient-poor peatland. – Suo 28: 53–61.
Flower-Ellis, J., Albrektson, A. & Olsson, L. 1976. Structure and growth of some young Scots pine stands: (1) Dimensional and numerical relationships. – Swed. Conif. For. Proj. Tech. Rep. 3, 98 pp.
Huikari, O. 1977. Micro-nutrient deficiencies cause growth-disturbances in trees. – Silva fenn. 11 (3): 251–254.
Holmen, H., Nilsson, Å., Popović, B. & Wiklander, G. 1976. The optimum nutrition experiment Norrliden. A brief description of an experiment in a young stand of Scots pine (*Pinus silvestris* L.) – Dept. of Forest Ecology and Forest Soils, Royal College of Forestry, Stockholm. Research Notes 26, 34 pp.
Ingestad, T. 1962. Macro element nutrition of pine, spruce, and birch seedlings in nutrient solutions. – Medd. Statens Skogsforskn. Inst. 51 (7): 1–150.

227

Ingestad, T. 1967. Methods for uniform optimum fertilization of forest tree plants. – In: Proc. 14th IUFRO Congress, Section 22, pp. 265–269.

Ingestad, T. 1971. A definition of optimum nutrient requirements in birch seedlings. II. – Physiol. Plant. 24: 118–125.

Ingestad, T. 1974. Towards optimum fertilization. – Ambio 3: 49–54.

Ingestad, T. 1979. Mineral nutrient requirements of *Pinus silvestris* L. and *Picea abies* Karst. seedlings. – Physiol. Plant. 45: 373–380.

Tamm, C. O. 1968. An attempt to assess the optimum nitrogen level in Norway spruce under field conditions. – Stud. for. suec. 61: 1–67.

Tamm, C. O. 1977. Skogsekosystemets reaktion på växtnäringstillförsel. Produktionseffekter och miljöförändringar. – Skogs- o. LantbrAkad. Tidskr. Suppl. 11: 7–15.

Tamm, C. O., Nilsson, Å. & Wiklander, G. 1974. The optimum nutrition experiment Lisselbo. A brief description of an experiment in a young stand of Scots pine (*Pinus silvestris* L.). – Dept. of Forest Ecology and Forest Soils, Royal College of Forestry, Stockholm. Research Notes, 18, 25 pp.

Persson, T. (ed) 1980
Structure and Function of Northern
Coniferous Forests – An Ecosystem Study
Ecol. Bull. (Stockholm) 32: 229–237.

NUTRIENT UPTAKE IN ROOTS OF SCOTS PINE

P. Jensén[1] and S. Pettersson[2]

Abstract

Effects of some internal and external factors on the efficiency of ion uptake in young Scots pine seedlings cultivated under laboratory conditions were studied. Tracer-techniques, including the ^{15}N-technique, were used to follow ion fluxes into roots of plants grown in nutrient solutions or in pot cultures. The intracellular ion content in root cells (potassium or nitrogen) regulates the efficiency of ion uptake in the roots. Only young parts of pine roots develop a high efficiency of uptake. The rate of ion uptake in winter-hardened plants is low, but rises gradually when temperature is increased. The rate of uptake in plants with a fully developed ion uptake efficiency is limited by temperature, the Q_{10} being approximately 2 in the temperature range 5–25°C. Water status of the soil greatly affects growth of pine, but apparently not via effects on the ion uptake mechanism. However, a close relationship exists between water and ion transport within the plants.

Additional keywords: Active root area, assimilate status, growth, nutrient status, tracer technique, water status, Q_{10}.

Introduction

Mineral nutrients, especially nitrogen, as well as water, are generally growth-limiting factors in Swedish forests (Tamm, 1974; Holmen et al. 1976). Uptake of inorganic nutrients from the soil depends on, among other factors, the availability of nutrients in the soil solution and on the ion uptake efficiency of the roots. Therefore the size and distribution of the root system as well as the different physiological ages of the individual root members, are of great importance in determining the magnitude of nutrient uptake.

In the present investigation, relationships between ion uptake efficiency of young pine roots and some external and internal factors were studied on a laboratory scale (Fig. 1). The aim was to provide data which might be interesting when constructing and testing soil-nutrient models, such as that proposed by Bosatta & Bringmark (1976) for simulating the transport and adsorption of nutrients in the soil and uptake of nutrients in Scots pine roots growing at Ivantjärnsheden (60°49'N, 16°30'E), the experimental site for the Swedish Coniferous Forest Project (SWECON) in central Sweden (see Axelsson & Bråkenhielm, 1980).

[1] Dept. of Plant Physiology, University of Lund, Box 7007, S-220 07 Lund 7, Sweden
[2] Dept. of Plant Physiology, Swedish University of Agricultural Sciences, S-750 07 Uppsala, Sweden

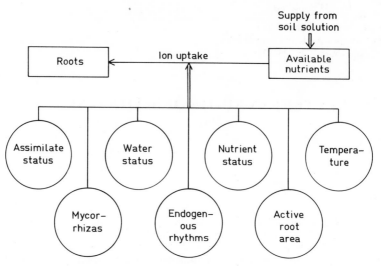

Figure 1. Factors regulating ion uptake efficiency of roots.

Table 1. Composition of nutrient solutions used in cultivations and experiments. Nutrient solution II = I/10 and III = I/100.

Element	Nutrient solution I (mM)	Nutrient solution IV (mM)	Element	Nutrient solution I (μM)	Nutrient solution IV (μM)
N	3.57	7.0	Fe	17.0	20.0
K	1.28	2.0	Mn	3.1	1.54
P	0.32	0.9	B	16.0	10.0
Ca	1.00	1.0	Zn	0.3	0.25
Mg	0.62	2.0	Cu	0.3	0.26
Na	–	1.4	Na	0.062	–
Cl	3.29	–	Mo	0.03	0.08
S	0.48	0.5	Cl	–	0.52

Material and methods

Scots pine seeds (*Pinus sylvestris* L., provenance: Södra Ydre, Sweden) were spread for germination in vermiculite at 20°C and 80 ± 5% RH. After 2–3 weeks, when the seedlings had emerged, the shoots were given a photoperiod of 16 h (Mercury lamps, Philips HPLR 400 W, 70–90 W m^{-2}).

The plants were placed in groups of five on discs of plastic foam which floated on nutrient solution in black-painted vessels, each containing 40 litres of solution (except in the experiment illustrated in Fig. 7). The compositions of the solutions are shown in Table 1. The nutrient solutions were continuously aerated and were changed twice a week. The temperature during cultivation was 20°C (except in the experiment illustrated in Fig. 4 and Table 2) and RH was ca. 65%. The light period was 16 h per day (Dysprosium lamps, HQI 400 W, 70–80 W m^{-2}).

The plants were transferred into a climate chamber with continuous illumination (except in the experiment shown in Fig. 5) from General Electric F 48 'power groove' 17-CVX 110 W fluorescent tubes (20–25 W m^{-2}) and with a temperature of 20°C, RH 50% (except in the experiment in Table 2), 24 h before an experiment. After a specified period in a labelled nutrient solution (for composition see Table 1), the roots were either washed for 10 minutes in a neutral nutrient solution (with the same

230

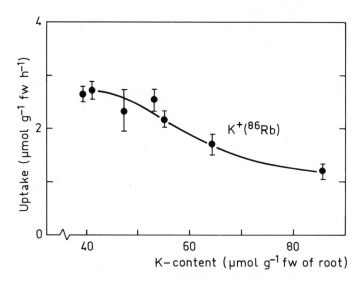

Figure 2. Uptake in pine of K^+ (^{86}Rb) as a function of K^+-content in the roots. Plants were cultivated in nutrient solution IV (see Table 1) and then starved for different times before the experiment (0, 6, 11, 14, 18, 22 and 28 days) in solution IV minus K^+ and with 5.0 mM NO_3^- to produce material with different K^+ status. Uptake was determined on day 48 in time interval 0–2 hours from a ^{86}Rb-labelled nutrient solution IV containing 2.0 mM of K^+ followed by a 10 min. rinse in neutral nutrient solution IV. Values are means ± s.e. of 6 replicates.

composition as the labelled solution) to remove labelled ions on the root surface and in the free space (experiments illustrated in Figs. 2, 5 and 6), or carefully blotted between filter papers (experiments illustrated in Figs. 3 and 4) and the plants were divided into roots and shoots. Fresh weight of the plant parts was determined.

The plant material labelled with radiosotopes (^{86}Rb, ^{35}S and ^{32}P) was wet combusted and radioactivity analyzed by liquid scintillation spectrometry. Potassium content was determined by atomic absorption spectrophotometry. After ^{15}N-uptake total nitrogen content was determined by a modified Kjeldahl method. ^{15}N was analyzed in a Straton (Packard) NOI-5 optical ^{15}N-analyzer according to Christersson & Lundborg (1975). Special conditions for the particular experiments are indicated below.

The chemical determination of a nutrient in a plant part is a measure of the net content or net uptake. In short term experiments with tracer-techniques, including ^{15}N, ^{86}Rb (for K), or ^{35}S, influx is isolated. As net uptake = influx – efflux, the distinction between net uptake and influx experiments must be kept in mind, since they show different aspects of the activity of the mechanisms of uptake and transport.

Results and discussion

Variations in ion uptake efficiency in relation to the nutrient status of pine roots follow a pattern well in accordance with that experienced in other plant species (Jensén & Pettersson, 1978; Lundborg, pers. comm.). On a potassium-rich substrate, a rapid uptake of potassium occurs at the same time as the potassium uptake efficiency gradually becomes lower. This is achieved by a negative feedback mechanism regulating the magnitude of the uptake (Jensén & Pettersson, 1978). The gradual decline of potassium influx at high potassium contents in the roots is shown in Fig. 2. Fine roots from pine grown at Ivantjärnsheden

231

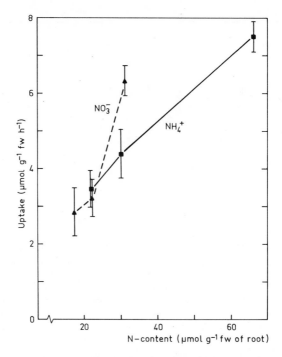

Figure 3. Uptake in pine of NO_3^- and NH_4^+ as a function of N-content in the roots. Plants were cultivated for 34 days in nutrient solution I (see Table 1), but with variation of the nitrogen factor in the interval N/100–10N (N = 3.57 mM N-ion = standard concentration) with ammonium or nitrate as nitrogen source. The counter ion for ammonium was chloride and, correspondingly, for nitrate it was sodium. Uptake in time interval 0–6 hours from ^{15}N-labelled solutions I containing 3.57 mM of ammonium and 3.57 mM of nitrate, respectively. Values are means ± s.e. of 6 replicates.

contain ca. 40 μmol K^+g^{-1}fw. Thus, according to Fig. 2, these roots work with full potassium uptake efficiency, but are not potassium deficient.

The relationship between the content of nitrogen in the roots and the uptake of nitrate or ammonium (Fig. 3) appears to reflect a close correlation between influx and content that does not exist for potassium (Fig. 2). There could be at least two explanations for this difference between potassium and nitrogen. Firstly, nitrogen probably limits growth and, secondly, the uptake of nitrate may be linked to the induction of nitrate reductase in the roots. However, in experiments with wheat we have found relationships between nitrate uptake efficiency and the concentration of nitrate in the ambient nutrient solution that are similar to the relationship for potassium, as illustrated in Fig. 2 (Lundborg, pers. comm.).

Pines growing on the unfertilized soils at Ivantjärnsheden have a low nitrogen supply around the roots (Bringmark & Petersson, 1975). Nitrogen limits the growth. If the supply of nitrogen is increased, there is also an increase in nitrogen uptake and growth is stimulated (Aronsson *et al.*, 1977).

Some of the experiments were performed to elucidate questions such as: When during the day or the year do pine roots absorb ions most rapidly and which parts of the root systems are then active?

Plants were winter-hardened by subjecting them to short-day conditions and to

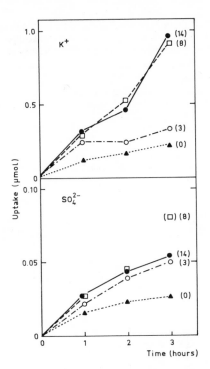

Figure 4. K^+ (^{86}Rb)- and SO_4^{2-}-uptake in pine dehardened for 0, 3, 8 and 14 days before the experiment. Plants (80 days old) were short-day treated (8 h illumination per day) at 3°C for 60 days. They were then moved to 20°C and continuous illumination. Cultivation and experiment in standard I solution (see Table 1). Uptake calculated per fresh weight of plant (mean values: 1.30 g of shoot, 0.80 g of root). Values are means of 6 replicates.

3°C for about two months. They were then moved to continuous illumination at 20°C. Both potassium and sulphate uptake were determined immediately after transfer and after 3, 8 and 14 days in dehardening conditions (Fig. 4). The ion uptake efficiency of winter-hardened roots was low but increased rapidly during the first 8 days of dehardening. Treating the plants for longer periods did not induce further increases of uptake.

In nature, the winter season is a period of rest. Plant metabolism is slow and has survival value only. Growth of roots and uptake of nutrients are low. As mean temperature rises in spring the metabolism also increases, but the activity of the plants lags behind the change in climate. Fig. 4 illustrates the lag period for the ion uptake when the external conditions are changed rapidly. A gradual increase of ion uptake efficiency for a month or longer, in pace with the slow rise of soil temperature, is the most probable situation in a natural soil.

Root temperature also exerted a direct effect on the rate of ion uptake in the roots (Table 2). The uptake of N, P and K was approximately doubled as the temperature was increased 10°C in the physiologically interesting interval 5–25°C. In nature, ion transport in the soil may be limiting for the ion uptake process, thus partly diminishing the stimulating effect on ion uptake efficiency by a rise in temperature.

Table 2. Net uptake of N, P and K in pine seedlings at different temperatures. Plants were cultivated 111 days in nutrient solution II (see Table 1). During the uptake period of 28 days, net uptake of N($^{15}NO_3$), P($^{32}PO_4$) and K was determined at 5, 15, and 25°C. Values are means ± s.e. of 5 replicates.

Element	Uptake (μg plant^{-1} day^{-1})			Q_{10}	
	5°C	15°C	25°C	5–15°C	15–25°C
N	38.6 ± 2.7	60.7 ± 2.9	–	1.57	–
P	4.3 ± 0.1	10.8 ± 0.4	22.8 ± 1.7	2.51	2.11
K	9.0 ± 0.8	18.7 ± 1.3	48.8 ± 2.9	2.08	2.61

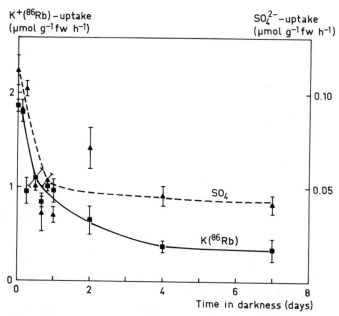

Figure 5. K$^+$ (^{86}Rb)- and SO$_4^{2-}$-uptake in pine pretreated for different times in darkness. Pretreatment times: 0, 6, 12, 16, 20, 24, 48, 96, 168 hours. Plants not treated in darkness were grown in continuous light. Plants were grown for 90 days in solution II (see Table 1). Uptake time was 2 h in double-labelled (^{86}Rb and ^{35}S-sulphate) nutrient solution I. The roots were washed for 10 min. in neutral solution I after the uptake period. Values are means ± s.e. of 5 replicates.

An experiment in which the ion uptake efficiency was determined after treating the plants for 0–7 days in darkness showed that after about 12 hours in darkness the uptake rate of both potassium and sulphate decreased to about half of the initial rate (Fig. 5), probably due to a decreasing organic nutrient status in the dark period. The ion uptake efficiency is normally maintained at a high level only if the supply of assimilates in the root is good.

Although principally the same in nature, variations in ion uptake efficiency at Ivantjärnsheden due to variations of the nutrient status of roots, may be much less than in the laboratory experiments. The bulk of a tree some years old is large enough to buffer temporary diurnal variations of assimilate production in the

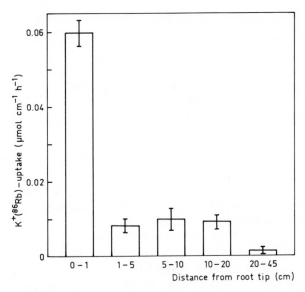

Figure 6. K$^+$ (^{86}Rb)-uptake in different zones of young pine roots. Plants were grown for 110 days in nutrient solution II. Root length was then about 50 cm and laterals were few. Different zones of the root were placed in small Petri dishes containing ^{86}Rb-labelled nutrient solution I. Uptake time was 1 h followed by a 10 min. rinse in neutral nutrient solution I. Values are means ± s.e. of 6 replicates.

leaves. Moreover, the nights, at least in the north of Sweden, are short and light in summer. However, in late autumn with short light periods the average organic nutrient level in the trees may be low enough to have an effect on ion uptake. At that time other factors are also critical, such as slow root growth rate, partly due to lowered soil temperature.

In long-term models for nutrient uptake, growth of the roots is an important variable. However, the uptake of nutrients does not necessarily increase proportionally to the increase in root biomass. Often only a small part of the total biomass is effective in absorbing nutrients. This active part is continuously renewed (Persson, 1978) at the same time as the rate of uptake in older parts of the roots decreases (Jensén, 1978).

In one of the experiments uptake of potassium was studied in different zones of the pine root (Fig. 6). The potassium uptake was high only in the proximal 20 cm of the young actively growing root at 20°C. In nature, with soil temperatures often below 20°C, the absorbing zone may be even narrower due to slow growth of the root system. Under all circumstances, knowledge of growth and spatial distribution of the fine roots in the soil is of the greatest importance for estimating the average ion uptake efficiency of a given root system. Moreover, the average ion uptake efficiency of a root is certainly linked more closely to the number of growing root tips than to the weight of the biomass.

In a pot experiment, pines were cultivated for 90 days in a fertilized sand-peat-mould mixture. The soil in the pots was kept at different water contents by different irrigation: (a) 10 ml, (b) 30 ml and (c) 60 ml distilled water were added to each of the pots per day. Limited water supply hampered plant growth severely,

Table 3. Fresh weight of pine grown at three different water levels in the substrate. Values are means ± s.e. of 5 replicates.

Water supply (ml day⁻¹)	Root	Shoot	Plant
10	0.09 ± 0.01	0.12 ± 0.01	0.21 ± 0.01
30	0.23 ± 0.02	0.16 ± 0.02	0.39 ± 0.02
60	0.17 ± 0.02	0.12 ± 0.01	0.29 ± 0.02

especially that of the roots (Table 3). Ion transport from root to shoot, which is linked to the transpiration stream, was significantly increased at high water supply (Fig. 7). This observation illustrates the close relationship that exists between the mineral and water relations of plants and may be of interest when interpreting results from irrigation experiments.

In conclusion, ion supply in the soil solution normally limits plant growth in nature. The ion uptake efficiency of the root system determines how effectively the roots can exploit the nutrient pool of the soil solution. In pine, only young growing root tips have a high ion uptake efficiency. This efficiency increases gradually in spring and is regulated mainly by temperature in summer and autumn. An adequate water supply in the soil is important for an effective transport of mineral nutrients from roots to shoots.

Acknowledgements

We thank Mrs. Lena Lundh for skilful technical assistance. The work was supported by grants from the Swedish Coniferous Forest Project.

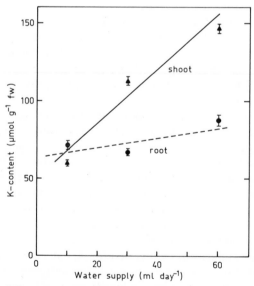

Figure 7. K⁺-contents of pine roots and shoots grown at three different water levels. Values are means ± s.e. of 5 replicates.

References

Aronsson, A., Elowson, S. & Ingestad, T. 1977. Elimination of water and mineral nutrition as limiting factors in a young pine stand. I. Experimental design and some preliminary results. – Swed. Conif. For. Proj. Tech. Rep. 10, 38 pp.

Axelsson, B. & Bråkenhielm, S. 1980. Investigation sites of the Swedish Coniferous Forest Project – biological and physiographical features. – In: Persson, T. (ed.) Structure and Function of Northern Coniferous Forests – An Ecosystem Study, Ecol. Bull. (Stockholm) 32: 25–64.

Bosatta, E. & Bringmark, L. 1976. A model for transport and adsorption of inorganic ions in a pine forest soil ecosystem – a development paper. – Swed. Conif. For. Proj. Int. Rep. 43, 42 pp.

Bringmark, L. & Petersson, G. 1975. Some chemical soil variables in a 120-year-old Scots pine forest growing on glacifluvial sand (Jädraås, Central Sweden). – Swed. Conif. For. Proj. Int. Rep. 27, 40 pp. (In Swedish, English abstract)

Christersson, L. & Lundborg, T. 1975. Optisk emissionsanalys av kväve-15. Teoretisk och praktisk metodbeskrivning. Upplaga 1, Växtfysiologiska institutionen, Lunds Universitet, Lund, 16 pp. (Mimeographed, in Swedish)

Holmen, H., Nilsson, Å., Popović, B. & Wiklander, G. 1976. The optimum nutrition experiment Norrliden. A brief description of an experiment in a young stand of Scots pine (*Pinus silvestris* L.) – Dept. of Forest Ecology and Forest Soils, Royal College of Forestry, Stockholm. Research Notes 26, 34 pp.

Jensén, P. 1978. Changes in ion transport in spring wheat during ontogenesis. – Physiol. Plant. 43: 129–135.

Jensén, P. & Pettersson, S. 1978. Allosteric regulation of potassium uptake efficiency in plant roots. – Physiol. Plant. 42: 207–213.

Persson, H. 1978. Data on root dynamics in a young Scots pine stand in Central Sweden – Swed. Conif. For. Proj. Int. Rep. 72, 13 pp.

Tamm, C. O. 1974. Experiments to analyse the behaviour of young spruce forest at different nutrient levels. – In: Cavé, A. J. (ed.) Structure, Functioning and Management of Ecosystems, Proc. 1st Int. Congr. Ecol., pp. 266–272. Wageningen: Pudoc.

237

Persson, T. (ed) 1980
Structure and Function of Northern
Coniferous Forests – An Ecosystem Study
Ecol. Bull. (Stockholm) 32: 239–250.

SEASONAL CHANGES IN STARCH RESERVES AND GROWTH OF FINE ROOTS OF 20-YEAR-OLD SCOTS PINES

A. Ericsson[1] and H. Persson[2]*

Abstract

The seasonal changes in growth and starch content in fine roots of young Scots pines (*Pinus sylvestris* L.) were studied. The investigation was carried out both on irrigated and fertilized (IF) plots as well as on control (0) plots. The temporal variation in the fine-root amounts was estimated in ingrowth cores removed at regular intervals during the growing season. Starch analyses were carried out on the different diameter fractions of the tree roots.

The fine-root fraction < 1 mm was significantly longer and thinner in IF-plots than in 0-plots, while there was no significant difference in weight. Both the length and weight of the diameter fraction 1–2 mm was significantly larger in the IF-plots. The number of root tips was, furthermore, larger per unit area in IF-plots than in 0-plots, although the number of root tips per unit length was larger in the 0-plots.

The starch content of the fine roots increased during spring and early summer. The starch reserves were mobilized at the time of shoot elongation. The decrease in starch content tended to be more rapid in roots from the IF-plots. The starch content of the roots increased during autumn to approximately the same level as that observed in early spring. The results are discussed in relation to the growth and the carbohydrate dynamics of the whole tree.

Additional keywords: Fine-root biomass, fine-root length, long roots, root dynamics, short roots, starch dynamics.

Introduction

Because of the difficulties involved in studying the tree root system, few researchers have investigated the dynamic aspects of death and replacement in the fine roots *in situ*, in spite of the fact that such studies are prerequisite to an understanding of most processes in the forest stand, e.g., mineral nutrient fluxes and carbon dynamics. This information is also of prime significance in assessing the total carbon flow (cf. Ågren *et al.*, 1980; Flower-Ellis & Persson, 1980).

The usual method adopted for studying temporal variations in the fine roots (cf. Persson, 1978, 1979, 1980a, 1980b) is to use data obtained by sequential core

[1] Dept. of Plant Physiology, University of Umeå, S-901 87 Umeå, Sweden
  Present address: Dept. of Forest Genetics and Plant Physiology, Swedish University of Agricultural Sciences, S-901 83 Umeå, Sweden
[2] Institute of Ecological Botany, Uppsala University, Box 559, S-751 22 Uppsala, Sweden
* Authors given alphabetically. See also Acknowledgements.

sampling during the growing season. The root fragments are then separated into living (biomass) and dead (necromass) fractions, which are subsequently confirmed and estimated. One obvious disadvantage is then the fact that the necromass fraction is extremely large and variable, partly since the life span and activity of the fine roots is short and may extend over a few days only (Persson, 1978). In the present study an entirely new method was applied for studying fine-root growth, the results of which are planned to be more completely reported in future publications. The ingrowth of new roots was measured in root-free containers (ingrowth cores) by removing the containers at regular intervals using the same sorting technique as for the sequential core samples. Further brief information about the ingrowth experiment may be found in Persson (1979) and in Flower-Ellis & Persson (1980).

Many publications report starch accumulation in conifer needles, stem bark and roots during the spring, before bud-break. How rapidly the starch is hydrolysed and utilized in the growth processes depends on the production of newly assimilated carbon and the growth rate. Thus, if the intention is to obtain a correct description of the carbon flow in a tree, it is necessary to know the balance between production and consumption of carbohydrates and the amount of reserves in the tree.

Previous studies within the Swedish Coniferous Forest Project have demonstrated that the above-ground parts of Scots pines (*Pinus sylvestris* L.) contain high levels of starch reserves during the growing season (Ericsson, 1979, 1980), which indicates that availability of carbohydrates is not limiting for growth. The present paper shows the seasonal changes of starch content in different root diameter-classes, and these changes are discussed in relation to growth and carbohydrate availability on a whole-tree basis.

Material and methods

The area studied is situated at the field station of the Swedish Coniferous Forest Project at Jädraås, 30 kilometers northwest of Gävle (60°49′N, 16°30′E, 185 m above M.S.L.). The forest type is of lichen to lichen-dwarf-shrub type (cf. Ebeling, 1978), with 15–20 year-old Scots pines (*Pinus sylvestris* L.). The stand is self-sown from seed trees, after clear-cutting in 1957, and with an average height of about 2.1 m in the spring of 1974. Parts of the stand were cleaned in August 1972, i.e., before investigation started. A less extensive cleaning was undertaken late in the winter 1972–1973, in an attempt to create the same density throughout the area. The area has been described by Axelsson & Bråkenhielm (1980) and the stand by Flower-Ellis *et al.* (1976).

The soil is a podsol, with an F/H layer thickness of approximately 2.5 cm and an Ahh/Ahu layer (Babel, 1970) of about 2.5 cm in 1974, i.e., before the investigation had started (Persson, 1980a). The mineral soil consists of sand sediment of glacifluvial origin (coarse sand with fractions of medium sand). The soil surface had been treated with a tractor scarifier after the 1957 clear-felling, resulting in fairly regular patches (approximately 1 m in diameter) of exposed mineral soil.

The experimental area is divided into plots treated differently with respect to water and mineral nutrient supply. Details of the irrigation and fertilization programme are given by Aronsson *et al.* (1977). The present work was limited to the control (0) and the irrigated and fertilized (IF) plots. The irrigation and fertilization started in 1974. Periods of irrigation and fertilization during 1974–77 are shown in Table 1. The water supplied by irrigation was about 3 l m^{-2} day^{-1} and the total amounts of nitrogen supplied to the IF-plots were 7, 10, 15 and 15 g m^{-2} during the years 1974–77, respectively. All other essential elements were given in proportion to nitrogen according to Ingestad (1967). The fertilizer was distributed to the IF-plots dissolved in the irrigation water.

The temporal variation in the fine-root amounts was estimated in ingrowth cores (containers) removed on successive occasions regularly during the growing season. The containers were placed in the holes left by the withdrawal of the soil cores (diameter 6.7 cm) with the help of a long steel corer. They consisted of

Table 1. Periods of irrigation and fertilization of the fertilized and irrigated plots (IF) during 1974–77. Data supplied by Aronsson *et al.* (1977, pers. comm.).

Year	Period of irrigation	Period of liquid fertilization
1974	July 12–Sept. 19	July 12–Aug. 9
1975	May 23–Sept. 12	May 23–Aug. 22
1976	May 20–Sept. 18	May 20–Aug. 20
1977	May 16–Aug. 30	May 16–Aug. 19

cylindrical net "stockings" filled with sand of local origin and peat instead of raw humus at the F/H layer. The mesh size of the "stockings" was 7.5 mm, thus allowing the roots to penetrate freely. In all, 300 containers were installed in the 0 and IF-plots from August to the middle of September 1974, equally distributed between the two different experimental plots. Random samples of 9 cores were taken from each treatment, beginning in autumn 1975, and continuing throughout the growing seasons of 1976 and 1977 (cf. Persson, 1979). The data in the present paper are, however, restricted to the growing season of 1976, when the most intensive root sampling was carried out. The surrounding roots and soil were removed, and sand sifted away and the samples were then stored in a deep-freeze at $-20°C$ until the final root sorting could be carried out; cf. Persson (1978, 1980a, 1980b) with regard to the sample treatment.

The excavated root fragments were separated into different diameter classes (<1, $1-2$, $2-5$ mm in diameter; very few fragments were >2 mm) following diameter measurements made in the middle of each fragment with a pair of vernier callipers. The total lengths in each diameter-class were estimated with a "line intersect method" similar to that used by Newman (1966) and further elaborated by Tennant (1975). The root tips were separated into long and short roots and counted; for definition see Hatch & Doak (1933) and Hatch (1937). The long-root tips are readily distinguished from short-root tips by their white, often swollen terminal parts, which are often more than 10 mm in length, depending on the size of the root. The short roots are often converted into complex mycorrhizal structures, either irregularly or racemously branched, and form coralloid types of mycorrhiza. They may also dichotomize repeatedly and thus form branches in successions of higher order towards the apex of the long roots.

Tests were made of the magnitude of the root variables (i.e., root length and weight in varying diameter fractions and the number of short- and long-root tips) in the 0-plots compared with IF-plots. In the test the number of negative outcomes (k) in the total number of samplings (m) (*viz.* a higher estimate of the root variable in one of the samplings from the 0-plots) was compared with the binomial distribution (cf. Snedecor & Cochran, 1968: 204). Thus, the probability of obtaining at the most k negative outcomes is given by the formula:

$$P = \frac{\sum_{n=0}^{k} \binom{m}{n}}{2^m}$$

where P is the significance level and:

$$\binom{m}{n} = \frac{m!}{n!\,(m-n)!} = \frac{m(m-1)(m-2)\ldots(m-n+1)}{n(n-1)(n-2)\ldots 3 \cdot 2 \cdot 1}$$

The null hypothesis (i.e., that root variables did not differ between the 0 and the IF-plots) was rejected at $P=0.1$. However, the specific significance levels are given separately in the text (see Results).

Starch analysis was carried out on the fine root fraction of the samples. All living roots of the same diameter class (<1 and $1-2$ mm) from the nine cores were combined for each sampling occasion. After sorting, the roots were dried at 85°C for 24 hours and analysed according to the description below.

During 1977 two or more root pieces with a length of about 30 cm and with a diameter of $2-5$ mm were sampled at random from each of the two treatments on each sampling occasion. The roots were always collected from the uppermost 10 cm of the soil profile. The samples were stored in a deep-freeze at $-20°C$ for further treatment. The sampling was undertaken at intervals of one to two weeks; starting in late May, continuing during June, July and August, and less frequently during September and October. The bark (i.e., the living part of the bark) and the wood of roots were analysed separately for the starch content. The samples were dried at 85°C for 24 hours and thereafter analysed.

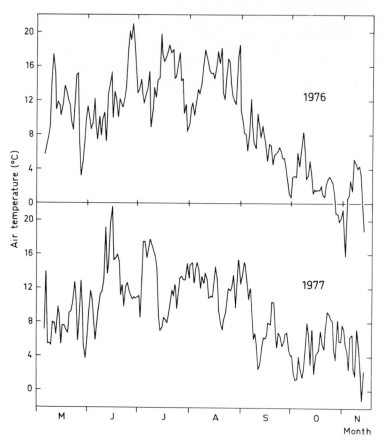

Figure 1. Daily mean temperature 1.5 m above soil surface during the growing seasons of 1976 and 1977.

The extraction and analysis procedures for the starch determination where those described by Hansen & Møller (1975) as modified by Ericsson (1979). Two parallel determinations were made for each sample to check the reproducibility of the analysis procedure.

Data shown in Fig. 1 have been provided by other groups within the Swedish Coniferous Forest Project. Instrumentation and measurement techniques for the temperature data are described by Lindroth & Perttu (1975).

Results

It may be concluded from the accumulation of new roots in the ingrowth cores, that a considerable fine-root accretion had taken place, both in the 0 and in the IF-plots (Fig. 2). As regards the increments in fine-root length of the <1 mm fraction, the ingrowth of new roots evidently proceeded more rapidly in the IF-plots, since the mean length throughout all 9 samplings during 1976 (Fig. 2A) fluctuated constantly at a higher level. This is also confirmed by the test discussed above at $P = 0.002$. If all samplings are included (*viz.*, one sampling in 1975, nine samplings in 1976 and four in 1977), the same test gives $P = 0.001$.

As regards the fine-root weight of the same diameter fraction (Fig. 2B), no

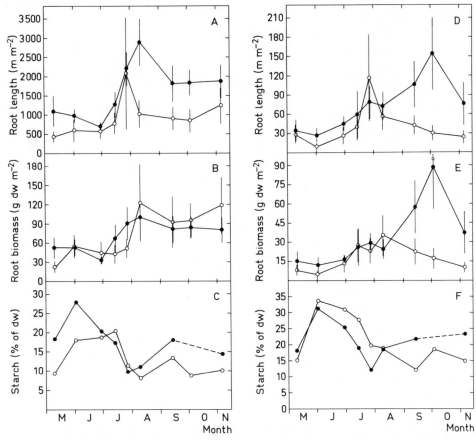

Figure 2. Changes in length, dry weight and starch content of the root fraction <1 mm in diameter (left) and 1–2 mm (right) during the growing season of 1976. ○ = control plots (0), ● = irrigated and fertilized plots (IF). Standard errors ($n=9$) are indicated. Each point on the starch curves represents the mean of two determinations. The difference between the mean of two determinations seldom exceeded 1 % of dry weight.

significant difference was found when using the same test. It is therefore reasonable to conclude that the fine roots in the IF-plots were considerably longer and thinner than those in the 0-plots. This agrees with unpublished data on the diameter of excavated root fragments (Persson, in prep.).

The length of the fine roots in the diameter fraction 1–2 mm was also larger in the cores from IF-plots than 0-plots (Fig. 2D). The significance level, as calculated for the 9 samplings in 1976 was at $P=0.020$, and for all 14 samplings at $P=0.001$. The related probability of a larger difference for the root weight (Fig. 2E) in the IF-plots was $P=0.090$ and $P=0.007$, respectively. Thus, the test shows that the root lengths and weights in the samples were significantly larger in IF-plots than in 0-plots.

The seasonal pattern of the fluctuations in fine-root length and weight was similar in the number of root tips; short-root tips were the most numerous (Fig. 3). The average number of long-root tips during the whole period of study was only 2.3 and 3.0 % of the total number of root tips in the 0-plots and IF-plots, respectively.

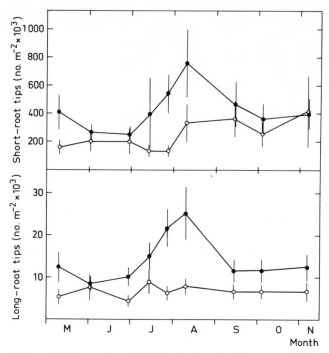

Figure 3. Seasonal changes in the number of short-root (above) and long-root (below) tips per square meter during the growing season of 1976. $\bigcirc$ = control plots (0), $\bullet$ = irrigated and fertilized plots (IF). Standard errors (n = 9) are indicated.

The number of long-root and short-root tips per m^2 fluctuated at a higher level in the cores from IF-plots than from 0-plots. The significance levels for the 9 samplings in 1976 was at P = 0.002 and at P = 0.020 for the long-root and short-root tips respectively, and for all 14 samplings at P = 0.001 and 0.007, respectively. The test thus confirms that both the numbers of long-root and short-root tips were larger in IF-plots than in 0-plots. It should, however, be noted that these estimates are given per unit area. If the number of long-root and short-root tips are calculated per unit length of fine roots, larger estimates should be expected in the 0-plots.

The accretion of fine-root length and weight in the above diameter fractions (<1 mm, 1–2 mm) was at its greatest in the IF-plots, and was followed by a successive increase in fine-root length and weight in the diameter fraction >2 mm in diameter, the increase being substantial at the end of the growing season of 1976 and during 1977 (Persson, in prep.). The irregular occurrence of the fragments >2 mm in diameter in the samples, however, made it impossible to obtain enough material for the starch analyses throughout the period of study; they were, therefore, excluded from the analysis programme. Root material from the samplings in 1975 and in 1977 was also excluded from the starch analyses, as too few samplings were carried out.

In 1976, the starch content of the roots increased during May and reached its maximum level in June (Figs. 2C, 2F). This was found for both types of plots. The highest levels were nearly always found in the diameter-class 1–2 mm. The lowest levels were found on the sampling occasions in late July and in August. A comparison

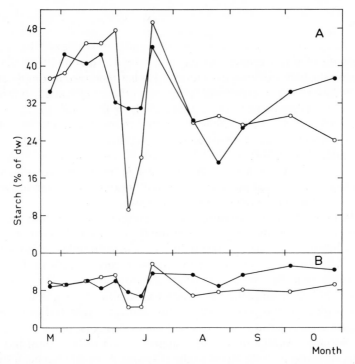

Figure 4. Seasonal changes in starch content in the living part of the bark (A) and in the wood (B) of the root diameter-class 2–5 mm during 1977. ○ = control plots (0), ● = irrigated and fertilized plots (IF). Each point on the curves represents the mean of two determinations. The difference seldom exceeded 1% of dry weight.

between the two treatments shows that roots of the IF-trees lose starch more rapidly from July to August than those of the 0-trees. There was also a tendency for roots of the IF-trees to contain more starch during the autumn than roots of the 0-trees.

The seasonal variation of starch content in bark from the root fraction 2–5 mm during 1977 is shown in Fig. 4A. The amount increased during May and June, thereafter a distinct decrease took place during the first weeks of July. The amount increased in late July and again reached the same level as in late June. The same general pattern was found for both IF-trees and 0-trees. After this second maximum, the starch content decreased to a low level in August. The lowest level during this period was found for the IF-trees. The starch content in the root bark from the 0-plots was approximately constant from August and during the autumn, while the content in roots of the IF-trees increased during this time.

The seasonal variation of starch in the wood of the roots during 1977 (Fig. 4B followed the same general pattern as for the corresponding bark samples. However, the amount never reached the same maximum levels as found for the bark. The highest values for the bark were about 40–50% of dry weight, while the wood never contained more than 15% of dry weight. The difference in content between the two treatments was never more than about 4% of dry weight.

245

Discussion

In spite of the growing interest during recent decades in studies of the productivity and functioning of forest ecosystems (cf. review in Hermann, 1977), the effect of fertilization on the fine-root growth of forest trees has remained incompletely investigated. According to *in situ* experiments, although these are limited to fairly young planted seedlings (Paavilainen, 1967, 1968, 1974; White *e al.*, 1971), fertilization causes an increase in the total weight of the fine roots. Tamm (1979), referring to unpublished data of Flower-Ellis concerning investigations in a Scots pine stand established after wind-felling in 1954 and fertilized annually from 1969 onwards, showed that while there was a significant increase in the biomass of almost all fractions of the trees on fertilized plots, there was remarkably little difference in the fine-root biomass (<2 mm in diameter) between treatments.

One of the more striking observations in the present study was that the fine roots (<1 mm in diameter) in the IF-plots were significantly longer and thinner than in the 0-plots, while there was no significant difference in the weight of this root fraction. In a teleological sense, it is reasonable to expect, in agreement with the conclusion of Tamm (1979), that the trees do not need as many roots, if they are well supplied with nutrients. However, since the root length was significantly greater in the IF-plots than in the 0-plots in the present study, this indicates that fertilization induced changes in the growth strategy of the small diameter roots, other than changes in the total root weight. As regards the larger diameter fractions (1–2 mm and >2 mm), both lengths and weights were larger in the IF-plots. Another change in the growth strategy was shown by the number of root tips, which was larger in the IF-plots than in the 0-plots, probably due to the fact that the total length was greater in the former. However, on almost all sampling occasions, the number of root tips per unit root length was larger in the 0-plots. These observations are in agreement with Björkman's (1941, 1942, 1944) classical works, in which he showed that the number of short-root ramifications (*sensu* mycorrhizal frequency) drastically decreased with application of fertilizers.

Several investigators have demonstrated accumulation of starch in the roots of conifer species before bud-break (Wight, 1933; Hepting, 1945; Parker, 1959; Kreuger & Trappe, 1967; Kimura, 1969). The present results show one really pronounced peak in the starch content of the roots for each of the investigated years, i.e., at the beginning of the growth season (Figs. 2C, 2F and 4). At the same time, according to results obtained in the same stand (Ericsson, 1979, 1980), the starch level in the needles and in the living part of the stem bark, fluctuated in essentially the same way. The roots differed, however, from the above-ground parts of the tree in that they contained considerable amounts of starch even during the late autumn. This was most evident for coarser diameter-classes of the roots. High values for the root-system of other conifer species during autumn and winter have been reported by, e.g., Wight (1933), Hepting (1945) and Parker (1959).

Seasonal variation in the translocation of current photosynthates to the roots of conifer seedlings has been demonstrated by several investigators (Shiroya *et al.*, 1966; Gordon & Larsson, 1968, 1970; Ziemer, 1971; Loach & Little, 1973). The general opinion seems to be that there are two periods, one before and one after shoot elongation, when translocation of carbohydrates is strongly directed toward the root-system.

Thus, Loach & Little (1973) concluded that the accumulation of starch in the roots during spring is the result of pre-budbreak export of current photosynthate from the previous season's shoots. This conclusion was supported by Ford & Deans (1977), who found a considerable amount of carbohydrates accumulated in the fine roots of *Picea sitchensis* (Bong.) Carr. before the start of shoot elongation. The results of the present investigation also support this conclusion, since an accumulation of carbohydrates occurred at the same time for both the above- and the below-ground parts of the tree, and since the increase in the reserves coincides with the onset of photosynthesis (cf. Ericsson, 1979). In previous studies in the same stand, it was demonstrated, using ^{14}C-technique, that current photosynthate was translocated from the needles when the growth activities were still limited (Ericsson, 1978).

In June and July, the starch content of the fine roots decreased parallel to the increase in root biomass (Fig. 2), which indicates that the reserves are utilized for root growth (cf. Ford & Deans, 1977). The decrease was found to be more rapid for the trees on IF-plots than for those on 0-plots. Thus, an increased sink activity brought about by fertilization affects the starch pool of the roots and of the needles similarly (cf. Ericsson, 1979). The more rapid decline of carbohydrates in the IF-trees should probably be explained by a higher degree of utilization in the above-ground parts of the tree, resulting in a limited amount of current photosynthates available for translocation to the roots. However, since at least the length growth of the fine roots is more intense for the IF-trees, the sink demand should also be expected to increase for the roots.

The fluctuations in the starch content of the needles have been shown to be fairly well correlated with the variation in air temperature during the period of most intense growth (Ericsson, 1979). This may be explained by changes in the sink activities of the tree in relation to the photosynthetic production of carbohydrates. Such a relationship was not possible to detect for the fine roots in 1976, since root sampling was not undertaken frequently enough during the period of study. However, in 1977 changes in the temperature conditions may explain the sudden fall and increase in starch concentration of the 2–5 mm roots found in July for both the IF-trees and the 0-trees (Fig. 4). The mean daily air-temperature (Fig. 1) during the first two weeks of July was rather high, about 14°C, and coincided with the period when low levels of starch were observed. From July 14 to July 20 the mean temperature fell abruptly, to ca. 8.5°C, and a rapid increase in the starch level was observed simultaneously. Thus, the conclusion by Ericsson (1979) as regards the influence of temperature on growth rate and utilization of the carbohydrate reserves of the needles, may also be applied to the roots. The starch reserves are obviously important for the tree in avoiding shortage of carbohydrates for growth, when favourable environmental conditions induce a greater carbohydrate consumption than can be replaced by production of current photosynthates. This also implies that translocation to the roots continues throughout the growing season (cf. Ursino *et al.*, 1968), but the amount translocated is dependent on the sink demand of the above-ground parts of the tree. However, it should be emphasized that the number of root fragments excavated and analysed on each sampling occasion was small, and thus it is difficult to decide whether these results are really representative of the whole root system.

A comparison between the two smallest root diameter-classes shows that the starch concentration increases with increased diameter (Fig. 2), a result also obtained by Ford & Deans (1977) for *P. sitchensis*. However, the highest level found in the present

247

investigation was in the living part of the root bark of the diameter fraction 2–5 mm, which indicates that these roots are important storage organs for satisfying the demand of the expanding fine root system when carbohydrates are limiting.

It might be concluded from the results of the present investigation that the food supply is not limiting for root growth, since carbohydrate reserves were present in large amounts throughout the growing season. This conclusion is also supported by results obtained for *Abies procera* by Wilcox (1954). Wilcox emphasized that the hormonal balance or accumulated toxic material are more important as regulating factors for the growth of the roots than is carbohydrate availability. Thus, the availability of carbohydrates seems generally to be good for the whole tree during the growing season, since high levels of starch reserves are also present in the aboveground structures (Ericsson, 1979, 1980). It is therefore reasonable to conclude that growth is more regulated by the rate of conversion of carbohydrates into new tissues than by carbohydrate limitation (Kozlowski & Keller, 1966).

Acknowledgements

The planning of the study was carried out in cooperation with J. G. K. Flower-Ellis. B. Andersson, I. Asplund, M. Dahlgren, and B.-I. Magnusson assisted in the field and in the laboratory. Å. Lindgren assisted with statistical advice and G. I. Ågren and K.-B. Sundström with computer programming. H. Risberg typed the manuscript. We are sincerely grateful to all these persons. H. Persson was responsible for the growth measurements and for reporting of incident results and A. Ericsson for the starch analyses and subsequent reporting. The work was carried out within the Swedish Coniferous Forest Project.

References

Ågren, G. I., Axelsson, B., Flower-Ellis, J. G. K., Linder, S., Persson, H., Staaf, H. & Troeng, E. 1980. Annual carbon budget for a young Scots pine. – In: Persson, T. (ed.) Structure and Function of Northern Coniferous Forests – An Ecosystem Study, Ecol. Bull. (Stockholm) 32: 307–313.

Aronsson, A., Elowsson, S. & Ingestad, T. 1977. Elimination of water and mineral nutrition as limiting factors in a young Scots pine stand. 1. Experimental designs and some preliminary results. – Swed. Conif. For. Proj. Tech. Rep. 10, 38 pp.

Axelsson, B. & Bråkenhielm, S. 1980. Investigation sites of the Swedish Coniferous Forest Project – biological and physiographical features. – In: Persson, T. (ed.) Structure and Function of Northern Coniferous Forests – An Ecosystem Study, Ecol. Bull. (Stockholm) 32: 25–64.

Babel, U. 1970. Gliederung und Beschreibung des Humusprofils in mitteleuropäischen Wäldern. – Mitt. Dtsch. Bodenkundl. Ges. 10: 289–293.

Björkman, E. 1941. Die Ausbildung und Frequenz der Mykorrhiza in mit Asche gedüngten und ungedüngten Teilen von entwässertem Moor. – Medd. Stat. Skogsförsöksanst. 32: 255–296. (In Swedish, German summary)

Björkman, E. 1942. Über die Bedingungen der Mykorrhizabildung bei Kiefer und Fichte. – Symb. Bot. Ups. 6(2), 190 pp.

Björkman, E. 1944. Forest planting and soil biology. – Sv. Skogsvårdsfören. Tidskr. 5: 334–335. (In Swedish, English summary)

Ebeling, F. E. 1978. Nordsvenska skogstyper. – Sv. Skogsvårdsförb. Tidskr 4: 340–381. (In Swedish)

Ericsson, A. 1978. Seasonal changes in translocation of ^{14}C from different age-classes of needles on 20-year-old Scots pine trees (*Pinus silvestris*). – Physiol. Plant. 43: 351–358.

Ericsson, A. 1979. Effects of fertilization and irrigation on the seasonal changes of carbohydrate reserves in different age-classes of needle on 20-year-old Scots pine trees (*Pinus silvestris*). – Physiol. Plant. 45: 270–280.

Ericsson, A. 1980. Some Aspects of Carbohydrate Dynamics in Scots Pine Trees (*Pinus sylvestris* L.). Thesis, University of Umeå, 21 pp.

Flower-Ellis, J. G. K., Albrektson, A. & Olsson, L. 1976. Structure and growth of some young Scots pine stands: (1) Dimensional and numerical relationships. – Swed. Conif. For. Proj. Tech. Rep. 3, 98 pp.

Flower-Ellis, J. G. K. & Persson, H. 1980. Investigations of structural properties and dynamics of Scots pine stands. – In: Persson, T. (ed.) Structure and Function of Northern Coniferous Forests – An Ecosystem Study, Ecol. Bull. (Stockholm) 32: 125–138.

Ford, E. D. & Deans, J. D. 1977. Growth of a Sitka spruce plantation: spatial distribution and seasonal fluctuations of lengths, weights and carbohydrate concentrations of fine roots. – Plant & Soil 47: 463–485.

Gordon, J. C. & Larsson, P. R. 1968. Seasonal course of photosynthesis, respiration, and distribution of ^{14}C in young *Pinus resinosa* trees as related to wood formation. – Plant Physiol. 43: 1617–1624.

Gordon, J. C. & Larsson, P. R. 1970. Redistribution of ^{14}C-labelled reserve food in young red pines during shoot elongation. – For. Sci. 16: 14–20.

Hansen, J. & Møller, I. 1975. Percolation of starch and soluble carbohydrates from plant tissue for for quantitative determination with anthrone. – Anal. Biochem. 68: 87–94.

Hatch, A. B. 1937. The physical basis of mycotrophy in *Pinus*. – Black Rock Forest Bull. 6, 168 pp.

Hatch, A. B. & Doak, K. D. 1933. Mycorrhizal and other features of the root system of *Pinus*. – J. Arnold Arb. 14: 85–99.

Hepting, G. M. 1945. Reserve food storage in shortleaf pine in relation to little-leaf disease. – Phytopatol. 35: 106–119.

Hermann, R. K. 1977. Growth and production of the roots: a review. – In: Marshall, J. K. (ed.) The Belowground Ecosystem: A Synthesis of Plant-Associated Processes, pp. 4–28. Fort Collins: Range Science Dept. Sci. Ser. 26, Colorado State Univ.

Ingestad, T. 1967. Methods for uniform optimum fertilization of forest tree plants. – 14th IUFRO-Congress, München Section 22: 265–269.

Kimura, M. 1969. Ecological and physiological studies on the vegetation of Mt. Shimagare. VII. Analysis of production processes of young *Abies* stand based on the carbohydrate economy. – Bot. Mag. Tokyo 82: 6–19.

Kozlowski, T. T. & Keller, T. 1966. Food relations of woody plants. – Bot. Rev. 32: 293–382.

Krueger, K. W. & Trappe, J. M. 1967. Food reserves and seasonal growth of Douglas-fir seedlings. – For. Sci. 13: 192–202.

Lindroth, A. & Perttu, K. 1975. Routines for collecting, processing and reporting of standard climate data. – Swed. Conif. For. Proj. Int. Rep. 26, 30 pp. (In Swedish, English abstract)

Loach, K. & Little, C. H. A. 1973. Production, storage, and use of photosynthate during shoot elongation in balsam fir (*Abies balsamea*). – Can. J. Bot. 51: 1161–1168.

Newman, E. I. 1966. A method of estimating the total length of root in a sample. – J. appl. Ecol. 3: 139–145.

Paavilainen, E. 1967. The effect of fertilization on the root systems of swamp pine stands. – Folia Forestalia 31: 1–9.

Paavilainen, E. 1968. Root studies at the Kivisuo forest fertilization area. – Commun. Inst. Forestal. Fenn. 66(1): 1–31. (In Finnish, English summary)

Paavilainen, E. 1974. Die Einwirkung der Düngung auf die Wurzelverhältnisse der Kiefer auf Moorböden. – In: Hoffman, G. (ed.) Ecology and Physiology of Root Growth, II. International Symposium, pp. 255–261. Berlin: Akademie-Verlag.

Parker, J. 1959. Seasonal variations in sugars of conifers with some observations on cold resistance. – For. Sci. 5: 56–63.

Persson, H. 1978. Root dynamics in a young Scots pine stand in Central Sweden. – Oikos 30: 508–519.

Persson, H. 1979. Fine-root production, mortality and decomposition in forest ecosystems. – Vegetatio 41: 101–109.

Persson, H. 1980a. Spatial distribution of fine-root growth, mortality and decomposition in a young Scots pine stand in Central Sweden. – Oikos 34: 77–87.

Persson, H. 1980b. Death and replacement of fine-roots of a mature Scots pine stand. – In: Persson, T. (ed.) Structure and Function of Northern Coniferous Forests – An Ecosystem Study, Ecol. Bull. (Stockholm) 32: 251–260.

Shiroya, T., Lister, G. R., Slankis, V., Krotkow, G. & Nelson, C. D. 1966. Seasonal changes in respiration, photosynthesis, and translocation of ^{14}C labelled products of photosynthesis in young *Pinus strobus* L. plants. – Ann. Bot. 30: 81–91.

249

Snedecor, G. W. & Cochran, W. G. 1968. Statistical Methods, 6th edn. Ames: Iowa State University Press, 593 pp.

Tamm, C. O. 1979. Nutrient cycling and productivity of forest ecosystems. – In: Leaf, A. L. (ed.) Impact of Intensive Harvesting of Forest Nutrient Cycling, pp. 2–21. State Univ. of New York, College Environmental Science and Forestry, Syracuse, N.Y.

Tennant, D. 1975. A test of a modified line intersect method of estimating root length. – J. Ecol. 63: 995–1001.

Ursino, D. J., Nelson, C. D. & Krotkov, G. 1968. Seasonal changes in the distribution of photo-assimilated ^{14}C in young pine plants. – Plant Physiol. 43: 845–852.

White, E. H., Prichett, W. L. & Robertson, K. 1971. Slash pine biomass and nutrient conditions. – In: Young, H. E. (ed.) Forest Biomass Studies, pp. 165–176. Univ. of Maine at Orono.

Wight, W. 1933. Radial growth of the xylem and the starch reserves of *Pinus sylvestris*: a preliminary survey. – New Phytol. 32: 77–96.

Wilcox, H. 1954. Primary organization of active and dormant roots of noble fir, *Abies procera*. – Amer. J. Bot. 41: 812–821.

Ziemer, R. R. 1971. Translocation of ^{14}C in ponderosa pine seedlings. – Can. J. Bot. 49: 167–171.

Persson, T. (ed) 1980
Structure and Function of Northern
Coniferous Forests – An Ecosystem Study
Ecol. Bull. (Stockholm) 32:251–260.

DEATH AND REPLACEMENT OF FINE ROOTS IN A MATURE SCOTS PINE STAND

H. Persson[1]

Abstract

Death and replacement of fine roots were investigated by core sampling throughout the growing season in a 120-year-old Scots pine (*Pinus sylvestris*) stand at Ivantjärnsheden in Central Sweden. Both the fine-root biomass and necromass (diameter < 2 mm) of the most important species, *P. sylvestris*, *Calluna vulgaris* and *Vaccinium vitis-idaea*, varied considerably during the season. Pooled averages of 123, 62 and 158 g dw m^{-2} and 64, 15 and 32 g dw m^{-2}, respectively, were calculated for the period of study. The corresponding root biomass and necromass totals (diameter < 10 mm) were 313, 158 and 158 g dw m^{-2} and 117, 58 and 32 g dw m^{-2}, respectively. The annual turnover of fine roots of *P. sylvestris* was estimated to be 73, 149 and 188 g dw m^{-2} in the F/H layer, in the mineral soil and in the total soil profile, respectively. The largest annual turnover and supply of dead fine roots of *P. sylvestris* were observed in the mineral soil, whereas the superficially distributed fine roots of the dwarf shrubs showed larger annual turnover and supply of dead fine roots in the F/H layer. These observations agreed largely with results from an investigation carried out during the same period in an adjacent 15–20 years old Scots pine stand.

Additional keywords: *Calluna vulgaris*, fine-root biomass, fine-root necromass, fine-root production, *Pinus sylvestris*, *Vaccinium vitis-idaea*.

Introduction

Death and replacement in root systems of perennial plants have largely eluded exploration because of the technical difficulties involved in their study. Many workers have demonstrated that considerable changes take place in the below-ground fine-root components during the growing season (Heikurainen, 1955; Kalela, 1955; Göttsche, 1972; Kohman, 1972; Roberts, 1976; Ford & Deans, 1977; Deans, 1979). However, surprisingly few papers have so far been published of fine-root production *sensu stricto* (cf. review in Hermann, 1977).

In many previous studies at an ecosystem level, rough estimates have been used in preference to no estimate at all (cf. Lieth, 1968; Newbould, 1968; Head, 1970). Many such data have been obtained under the assumption that the ratio of production to biomass (or standing crop) above ground must be similar to that below ground. Since the ratio of above-ground to below-ground production may differ considerably (even in the same species) in different communities (Persson,

---

[1] Institute of Ecological Botany, Uppsala University, Box 559, S-751 22 Uppsala, Sweden.

1975, 1979a), there is no evidence to support this assumption and serious under-estimates may result from it.

Information on the contribution of fine roots to the total productivity of an ecosystem is scarce. Nevertheless, a lot of recent papers (e.g., Harris *et al.*, 1973; Caldwell & Camp, 1974; Kummerow *et al.*, 1978; Persson, 1978a, b, 1979b, 1980a; Santantonio, 1979), some of these published as results of the research pro-gramme of the present investigation, indicate considerable turnover rates in small diameter roots. It is apparent that the fine roots play quite an important role in the total dynamics of carbon (cf. the carbon budget in Ågren *et al.*, 1980).

Two methods were adopted in the present study in order to investigate the temporal variation of fine-root death and renewal (cf. Persson, 1979b), (1) using data obtained by sequential core sampling and (2) measuring the ingrowth of new roots into root-free containers removed regularly. The data in the present paper is devoted to those obtained from the sequential sampling of soil cores in a mature Scots pine stand at Ivantjärnsheden (Ih V). The nomenclature used for vascular plants follows Lid (1974). Aims and strategies of these studies are broadly outlined by Flower-Ellis & Persson (1980).

Material and methods

The investigation was conducted in the 120-year-old Scots pine stand Ih V (cf. site description in Axelsson & Bråkenhielm, 1980) located on sandy sediments of glacifluvial origin at Ivantjärnsheden in Central Sweden (60°49'N, 16°30'E, 185 m above M.S.L.). The soil is a podzol, with an F/H (humus) layer thickness of 26 ± 1 mm ($x \pm$ s.e.; $n = 188$).

The samples were removed with a long steel corer with an internal diameter at the hardened steel cutting edge of 6.7 cm (area 36.26 cm²). Random samples of 30 cores were made on each sampling occasion giving a total number of 240 cores. However, due to lack of funds for the extensive work of sorting the samples, the latter work had to be reduced and a total of 210 cores were finally sorted. The cores were sliced into three 10 cm sections starting at the litter (L) horizon, the uppermost section being divided into F/H and mineral soil horizons. The cores were stored in a deep-freeze before root sorting took place.

The living and dead root fragments (biomass and necromass, respectively) were sorted into different diameter fractions (Persson, 1978a, 1980a). Dead root fragments < 1 mm in diameter were ascribed to necromass in cases where they were longer than 2 cm; otherwise they were included in the soil organic matter. Dead root fragments > 1 mm in diameter were ascribed to necromass when they were longer than 1 cm. However, the bulk of the necromass < 1 or > 1 mm in diameter consisted of root fragments considerably longer than 2 cm and 1 cm, respectively.

Fine-root biomass production (P_s) and necromass production (N_s) were calculated according to methods described in Persson (1978a, 1980a). P_s was derived either from increments (the positive difference) in biomass + necromass ($b + n$) or biomass (b) and N_s from increments in necromass (n) according to:

$$(P_s)_1 = \Sigma(b + n)_j^+ - OE; \qquad (P_s)_2 = \Sigma b_j^+ - OE; \qquad \text{and } N_s = \Sigma n_j^+ - OE$$

respectively, where OE is the correction for overestimation according to Lindgren in Persson (1978a) and j the total number of samplings (cf. text to Table 2). OE was estimated as the average difference at 5000 separate simulations of the sampling procedure between the expected value of the sum of the observed increments and the correct sum of these increments.

The estimate of P_s, depending on which method of calculation gave the highest numerical value, was used in order to calculate the fine-root "turnover" (T). Turnover, in this context, means the annual replacement of fine root material plus losses due to ageing and decay. It was calculated as:

$$T = P_s - (b_j - b_1)$$

252

Table 1. The distribution of fine-root biomass (FRB), fine root necromass (FRN), total root biomass (TRB) and total root necromass (TRN) in the F/H layer, mineral soil layer and total sampling depth at Ih V (FRB and FRN < 2 mm in diameter; TRB and TRN < 10 mm in diameter). Estimates (g dw m^{-2}) are pooled averages from 8 samplings taken during 1974–75 ± standard errors. 0.0 denotes a value smaller than 0.05 g m^{-2}. The estimates of *Vaccinium myrtillus* (not given below) were smaller than this value. The total number of samples was 210.

		F/H layer (0–2.6 cm depth)	Mineral soil (2.6–30 cm depth)	Total (0–30 cm depth)
Pinus sylvestris	FRB	58.5 ± 2.4	64.0 ± 2.8	122.5 ± 3.7
	FRN	8.5 ± 0.9	55.7 ± 2.8	64.2 ± 3.7
	TRB	78.8 ± 5.3	234.3 ± 13.6	313.1 ± 14.8
	TRN	10.3 ± 1.0	106.3 ± 5.7	116.6 ± 5.8
Empetrum nigrum	FRB	1.4 ± 0.7	0.4 ± 0.2	1.8 ± 0.8
	FRN	0.4 ± 0.3	0.0 ± 0.0	0.4 ± 0.3
	TRB	2.0 ± 1.1	0.7 ± 0.4	2.8 ± 1.2
	TRN	0.4 ± 0.3	0.0 ± 0.0	0.4 ± 0.3
Calluna vulgaris	FRB	36.0 ± 3.3	25.8 ± 1.3	61.8 ± 3.7
	FRN	9.3 ± 1.5	5.8 ± 0.8	15.0 ± 1.7
	TRB	117.8 ± 10.5	40.2 ± 3.3	158.0 ± 11.1
	TRN	41.3 ± 5.3	16.8 ± 3.0	58.1 ± 6.1
Vaccinium vitis-idaea	FRB	117.8 ± 5.3	40.1 ± 3.0	157.9 ± 5.8
	FRN	25.0 ± 2.3	7.0 ± 0.9	32.0 ± 2.5
	TRB	117.8 ± 5.3	40.1 ± 3.0	157.9 ± 5.8
	TRN	25.0 ± 2.3	7.0 ± 0.7	32.0 ± 2.5

where $(b_j - b_1)$ is the estimate of fine-root biomass at the last sampling (b_j) minus that on the first sampling (b_1). The last correction was done to ensure that only material included in the annual cycling of organic matter was counted (cf. Persson, 1980a).

Results

Distribution of root weight

The estimates of the average fine-root biomass (FRB) and total root necromass (TRN) should be regarded as average scores during the 1974–75 season (Table 1), especially as regards FRB and fine root necromass (FRN), and should not be interpreted as static.

The most important species in terms of weight, i.e., *Pinus sylvestris, Calluna vulgaris* and *Vaccinium vitis-idaea* had quite different vertical distributions (Fig. 1). The dwarf shrubs were fairly superficially distributed with a major part of their root weight in the F/H layer, whereas the roots of *P. sylvestris* were concentrated immediately below the upper part of the mineral soil. The FRB for *P. sylvestris, C. vulgaris* and *V. vitis-idaea* of the F/H layer in relation to that for the whole core

253

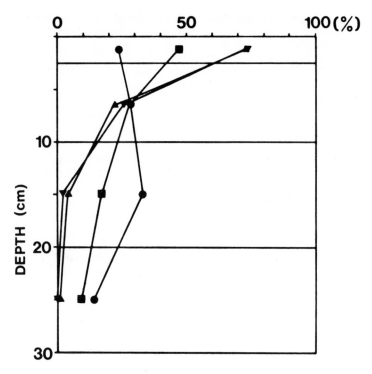

Figure 1. Vertical distribution of root biomass (< 10 mm in diameter) of *Pinus sylvestris* (■ = fine roots <2 mm; ● = < 10 mm in diameter), *Calluna vulgaris* (▲) and *Vaccinium vitis-idaea* (▼) in the mature stand at Ivantjärnsheden. The weight determinations in the different soil layers (F/H and the mineral soil to depths of 2.6–10, 10–20 and 20–30 cm) are given as percentages of the total root amount in the whole profile.

were 48, 58 and 75%, respectively. The corresponding figures for FRN were 13, 62 and 78%. These estimates indicate in the case of *P. sylvestris* an accumulation of FRN in the mineral soil compared with that in the F/H layer, since the ratio of FRN to FRB was 0.87 compared with 0.15 (Table 1). The same ratios in a young (15–20 years old) Scots pine stand (Ih II) were 3.24 compared with 1.08 (Persson 1980a), indicating that an even larger accumulation of FRN had taken place during the early stage of stand development in the mineral soil.

The average total root biomass (TRB) for *P. sylvestris* increased largely with stand age. The TRB in the mature stand Ih V was 6.29 times that in the young stand Ih II (cf. Persson, 1980a). However, the TRN was only 0.71 times that in Ih II. In Ih V the average FRB was 4.69 and FRN 0.95 times as much as the corresponding averages in Ih II, in agreement with the ratios for both TRB and TRN. As a consequence of the fact that the average FRN reached nearly the same level in both Ih II and Ih V and since the average FRB was considerably larger in Ih V, the relative annual supply of dead fine roots to the soil in Ih II must be fairly large. A large proportion of the TRB consisted of FRB in both Ih II and Ih V, *viz.* 52 and 39%, respectively.

As regards *C. vulgaris* and *V. vitis-idaea* the TRB in Ih V was 1.54 and 3.23

times the corresponding amounts in Ih II, respectively. The corresponding estimates of the TRN were 1.07 and 0.80. The fairly large average of TRB for *V.
vitis-idaea* in Ih V was probably a result of an upsurge in growth following the
thinning in 1962 (cf. Persson, 1980b; Bråkenhielm & Persson, 1980).

Death and replacement of fine roots

The significance of the below-ground production, as estimated from the sum of
increments in the FRB or FRB + FRN (i.e., the standing crop of the fine roots)
during the period of sampling, 1974–75, and "production" of the FRN (i.e., the
cumulative necromass totals) was tested by employing a two-tailed test of the
F-distribution (cf. Table 2). The test confirmed in the case of *P. sylvestris* that a
considerable production of fine roots had taken place in both horizons, with
figures of 77 ± 16 g m^{-2} ($\pm$ s.e.) in the F/H layer and 115 ± 17 g m^{-2} in the mineral
soil (5% level of significance). The estimates are the largest figures derived from
either of the two calculation methods (see Material and methods). The corresponding figures calculated for the cumulative annual totals of FRN were 37 ± 5
g m^{-2} and 145 ± 15 g m^{-2} for the F/H layer and the mineral soil, respectively.
Obviously, these results suggest for *P. sylvestris* a larger production and supply of
FRN to the mineral soil than to the F/H layer.

As regards *C. vulgaris* and *V. vitis-idaea* no significant annual increments of the
below-ground production and cumulative necromass totals were arrived at (Table
2), allowing a comparison between the two soil horizons. However, significant
increments were arrived at for *C. vulgaris* in the mineral soil for all calculation
methods, *viz.* either from the sum of increments in FRB or in FRB + FRN or in
FRN. In the whole soil core (from the soil surface down to 30 cm), significant
increments were arrived at only for the cumulative annual totals in FRN. The
non-significant estimates given within parentheses (cf. Table 2) should be regarded as guesses of their real magnitude. The non-significant increments of *C.
vulgaris* and *V. vitis-idaea* in Ih V were generally considerably lower than those in
Ih II (cf. Persson, 1978a, b, 1979b, 1980a).

The production estimates (cf. Table 2) for *P. sylvestris* given above, suggest an
annual turnover (see Material and methods) of fine roots in the F/H layer of
73 ± 19 g m^{-2} and in the mineral soil of 149 ± 21 g m^{-2}. The data related to the
whole core (from the soil surface to a depth of 30 cm) suggest an annual turnover
of 188 ± 31 g m^{-2}, which is slightly lower than if the same figure is calculated from
the sums of the separate figures for the two horizons, which was 222 ± 28 g m^{-2}.
However, some discrepancies were expected due to the variation in depth of the
F/H layer. These discrepancies were considered not to influence the figures
calculated for the whole core, but certainly those derived from the sums of the
separate estimates. As regards the dwarf shrubs, the annual turnover of fine roots
could be calculated only for *C. vulgaris* in the mineral soil to 30 ± 11 g m^{-2} (cf.
Table 2).

These estimates strengthen the general impression from the parallel sampling in
Ih II as regards the vertical distribution of mortality and replacement in the fine
roots (Persson, 1978a, b, 1979b, 1980a). The largest annual turnover as well as
supply of dead fine roots of *P. sylvestris* obviously went to the mineral soil,

255

Table 2. Below-ground production and cumulative necromass totals (mean ± standard error) of fine roots (<2 mm in diameter) during the 1974–75 samplings in Ih V. The number of replicates in each of the 8 samplings were, in progressive order, 25, 30, 25, 25, 30, 25, 20 and 30. The estimates in parentheses did not consist of significant (5 % level of significance) increments. The test of significance was a two-tailed test of the distribution of F (cf. Sokal & Rohlf, 1969; 181–203), in this case used to test whether the variance of the changes of positive sign (cf. Lindgren in Persson, 1978a) differed from the variances of the samples.

	Sum of increments (g dw m^{-2} yr^{-1}) for:		
	Pinus sylvestris	*Calluna vulgaris*	*Vaccinium vitis-idaea*
F/H layer			
b_j	77 ± 16	(33 ± 19)	(47 ± 30)
$(b+n)_j$	65 ± 18	(21 ± 20)	(28 ± 36)
n_j	37 ± 5	(7 ± 10)	(21 ± 13)
Mineral soil			
b_j	68 ± 16	29 ± 9	(0 ± 18)
$(b+n)_j$	115 ± 17	18 ± 11	(15 ± 16)
n_j	145 ± 15	20 ± 5	(9 ± 6)
Total			
b_j	139 ± 21	(43 ± 14)	(14 ± 35)
$(b+n)_j$	159 ± 27	(44 ± 23)	(0 ± 40)
n_j	179 ± 16	24 ± 11	(28 ± 15)

whereas the superficially distributed fine roots of the dwarf shrubs had both the largest annual turnover and supply of dead fine roots in the F/H layer. The dead fine-root material evidently constitutes a very important source of organic input to the soil environment. As regards *P. sylvestris,* no significantly different estimates were arrived at in Ih V as compared with Ih II. As regards the dwarf shrubs, no general conclusions can be made due to the non-significant annual increments in Ih V.

Discussion

Extensive observations in literature make it clear that tree-root biomass in a forest stand increases with stand age, as does the biomass of its above-ground parts (cf. review of literature in Santantonio *et al.,* 1977; Hermann, 1977). Lateral roots of Scots pine frequently attain maximal length during the early stand age (Wagenhoff, 1938; Röhrig, 1966). In old stands whole skeletal roots may die back. These are gradually replaced by new laterals which, however, contribute to an increased density rather than to the horizontal spread of the root systems (Hermann, 1977). Root-grafting is, furthermore, wide-spread; observations in the investigated stand (J.G.K. Flower-Ellis, pers. comm.) proved that many root systems of the trees cut down during the thinning in 1962 (cf. Axelsson &

Bråkenhielm, 1980) were taken over by the root systems of the remaining trees.

Quantitative changes in tree roots are still incompletely described, especially as regards the small-diameter components. The coarse tree roots evidently shed a considerable amount of fine ramifications as they extend outwards from the trees (Reynolds, 1970; Kolesnikov, 1968). Due to the intermingling nature of the tree roots, the growth pattern of these fine ramifications as regards distance to the surrounding trees is masked and the changes in discrete volumes of the forest soil may take place apparently independently (Persson, 1980a).

Reynolds (1974) proposed a model of root activity in a *Pseudotsuga menziesii* plantation, according to which the optimization by growth and death of rootlets took place in discrete cells adapted to local environmental conditions. The long lateral roots, which could initiate absorbing (and ephemeral) rootlets, then persisted in dry cells, in cases when their distal ends subtended fine ramifications in adjacent moist cells. Root growth is essentially compensatory, i.e., it is most intensive in areas with good water and nutrient supplies and is inhibited by deficiencies of the latter (cf. Russel, 1977:54–55). On the whole, fine-root ramifications seem to be fairly sensitive to desiccation. Substantial losses of fine root biomass occur whenever incident precipitation fails to maintain the soil moisture tension near zero (Deans, 1979). Zak (1964) reviewed the works of several investigators and concluded that the elongation of roots and mycorrhizal formation may cease during periods of drought and be resumed again when soil moisture and temperature are once again favourable.

These experiences agree with observations from the present study; root systems extend where and whenever the soil moisture and temperature conditions allow (cf. Persson, 1978a, 1979b). Large variations in the amount of fine roots (FRB and FRN) were found, in both the young stand (Ih II) dealt with in some earlier publications (Persson, op.cit.), and in the mature Scots pine stand (Ih V) discussed in the present paper. The fluctuations in FRB and FRN of *P. sylvestris*, differed considerably between Ih II and Ih V, suggesting microclimatical differences as the cause of variation. A substantial mortality of the fine roots during the winter in Ih V may, furthermore, be interpreted from the unusually large amount of FRN at the first sampling in spring 1975 (cf. Persson, 1979b).

Santantonio (1979) concluded from investigations of the seasonal patterns and live-to-dead ratios of fine roots in a wet, moderate and dry *Pseudotsuga menziesii* stand, that root dynamics from one forest stand to another differ along a moisture gradient. The wet stand then had more living than dead roots (average live/average dead = 1.78), the opposite (0.57) held for the dry stand and the moderate was intermediate (0.98). The average live/average dead fine roots ratio of *Pinus sylvestris* in Ih V was 6.88 in the F/H layer, 1.15 in the mineral soil and 1.91 in the total soil core (Table 1). The related ratios in Ih II were 0.93, 0.31 and 0.39 (Persson, 1980a).

One immediate expectation from these results, bearing Santantonio's hypothesis in mind, is that Ih II should be considerably dryer than Ih V, which however, was not the case at the time of study, since the stand was not closed (P-E. Jansson, pers. comm.). Consequently, the existence of differences in the average live/average dead ratio must either be related to changes in the growth strategy between the two stands for the root systems with increasing age of the forest stand, or to microclimatical differences much more decisive for death and replacement in fine roots than the soil water conditions. Nevertheless, Santantonio's hypothesis holds in both stands for the average live/average dead ratio in the F/H layer as compared with the mineral soil (cf. ratios above). This ratio was larger in the F/H layer, probably as a result of improved soil moisture and nutrient status.

As regards *C. vulgaris,* the average live/average dead ratios in Ih II were 2.54, 3.17 and 2.85 in the F/H layer, in the mineral soil horizon and in the total soil core, respectively, and 3.87, 4.45 and 4.12 in Ih V. The related estimates for *V. vitis-idaea* were 1.04, 1.79 and 1.22 in Ih II and 4.71, 5.73 and 4.93 in Ih V. The dwarf shrubs, as demonstrated above (see Results), in contrast to *P. sylvestris,* had the bulk of their root weight in the F/H layer. The thin and fibrous root systems of the dwarf shrubs in the mineral soil were to a great extent concentrated along old root channels of dead and decaying tree roots and were seemingly in good condition, probably as a result of profilic nutrients and soil moisture.

A surprisingly large amount of soil organic matter, which must to a great extent originate from the dead tree roots, was found in the mineral soil (Staaf & Berg, 1977). This may be explained by the fairly large annual turnover of the tree roots in the latter horizon (see Results). Evidently the whole soil profile is most efficiently exploited by the different root systems, growth is then promoted in the soil horizon where they experience the best water and nutrient conditions. The turnover estimates in the different soil environments are, therefore, probably closely related to the degree of exploitation.

Acknowledgements

This study was performed as a part of the Swedish Coniferous Forest Project. The planning of the study was carried out in cooperation with J.G.K. Flower-Ellis. M. Dahlgren, B. Andersson and I. Asplund gave valuable technical assistance, and G. I. Ågren, Å. Lindgren and K-B. Sundström are thanked for statistical advice and computer programming.

References

Ågren, G. I., Axelsson, B., Flower-Ellis, J. G. K., Linder, S., Persson, H., Staaf, H. & Troeng, E. 1980. Annual carbon budget for a young Scots pine. – In: Persson, T. (ed.) Structure and Function of Northern Coniferous Forests – An Ecosystem study, Ecol. Bull. (Stockholm) 32: 307–313.

Axelsson, B. & Bråkenhielm, S. 1980. Investigation sites of the Swedish Coniferous Forest Project – biological and physiographical features. – In: Persson, T. (ed.) Structure and Function of Northern Coniferous Forests – An Ecosystem Study, Ecol. Bull. (Stockholm) 32: 25–64.

Bråkenhielm, S. & Persson, H. 1980. Vegetation dynamics in developing Scots pine stands in Central Sweden. – In: Persson, T. (ed.) Structure and Function of Northern Coniferous Forests – An Ecosystem Study, Ecol. Bull. (Stockholm) 32: 139–152.

Caldwell, M. M. & Camp, L. B. 1974. Belowground productivity of two cool desert communities. – Oecologia (Berl.) 17: 123–130.

Deans, J. D. 1979. Fluctuations of the soil environment and fine root growth in a young Sitka spruce plantation. – Plant & Soil 52: 195–208.

Flower-Ellis, J. G. K. & Persson, H. 1980. Investigation of structural properties and dynamics of Scots pine stands. – In: Persson, T. (ed.) Structure and Function of Northern Coniferous Forests – An Ecosystem Study, Ecol. Bull. (Stockholm) 32: 125–138.

Ford, E. D. & Deans, J. D. 1977. Growth of Sitka spruce plantation: spatial distribution and seasonal fluctuations of lengths, weights and carbohydrate concentrations of fine roots. – Plant & Soil 47: 463–485.

Göttsche, D. 1972. Verteilung von Feinwurzeln und Mykorrhizen im Bodenprofil eines Buchen- und Fichtenbestandes im Solling. Hamburg: Kommissionsverlag, Buchhandlung Max Wiedebusch, 103 pp.

Harris, W. F., Goldstein, R. A. & Henderson, G. S. 1973. Analyses of forest biomass pools, annual primary production and turnover of biomass for a mixed deciduous forest watershed. – In: Young, H. E. (ed.), IUFRO Biomass Studies, Univ. Maine at Orono, pp. 43–64.

Head, G. C. 1970. Methods for the study of production in root systems. – In: Phillipson, J. (ed.) Methods of Study in Soil Ecology, Proc. Paris Symp., 1967, pp. 151–157. Paris: Unesco.

Heikurainen, L. 1955. Über Veränderungen in den Wurzelverhältnissen der Kiefernbestände auf Moorböden im Laufe des Jahres. – Acta Forest. Fenn. 65, 70 pp.

Hermann, R. K. 1977. Growth and production of tree roots. – In: Marshall, J. K. (ed.) The Below-ground Ecosystem: A Synthesis of Plant-Associated Processes, pp. 4–28. Fort Collins: Range Science Dept. Sci. Ser. 26. Colorado State Univ.

Kalela, E. K. 1955. Über Veränderungen in den Wurzelverhältnissen der Kiefernbestände im Laufe der Vegetationsperiode. – Acta Forest. Fenn. 65, 42 pp.

Kohman, K. 1972. Root-ecological investigations on pine (*Pinus silvestris*). I. Problems of methodology and general root relationships. – Det Norske Skogsforsøksvesen 30: 325–357. (In Norwegian, English summary)

Kummerow, J., Krause, D. & Jow, W. 1978. Seasonal changes of fine root density in Southern Californian chaparral. – Oecologia (Berl.) 37: 201–212.

Kolesnikov, V. A. 1968. Cyclic renewal of roots in fruit plants. – In: Ghilarov, M. S., Kovda, V. A., Novichova–Ivanova, L. N., Rodin, L. E. & Sveshnikova, V. M. (eds.) Methods of Productivity Studies in Root Systems and Rhizosphere Organisms, Int. Symp. USSR, pp. 102–106. USSR Academy of Sciences, Publ. House "Nauka".

Lid, J. 1974. Norsk og Svensk Flora, Andre Utgåva. Oslo: Det Norske Samlaget, 808 pp. (In Norwegian)

Lieth, H. 1968. The determination of plant dry-matter production with special emphasis on the underground parts. – In: Eckart, F. E. (ed.) Functioning of Terrestrial Ecosystems at the Primary Production Level, Proc. Copenhagen Symp, pp. 179–186. Unesco.

Newbould, P. J. 1967. Methods for Estimating the Primary Production of Forests. – IBP Handbook No. 2. Oxford: Blackwell Scientific Publications, 62 pp.

Newbould, P. J. 1968. Methods of estimating root production. – In: Eckart F. E. (ed.) Functioning of Terrestrial Ecosystems at the Primary Production Level, Proc. Copenhagen Symp. pp. 187–190. Unesco.

Persson, H. 1975. Deciduous woodland at Andersby, Eastern Sweden: Field-layer and below-ground production. – Acta Phytogeogr. Suec. 62, 72 pp.

Persson, H. 1978a. Root dynamics in a young Scots pine stand in Central Sweden. – Oikos 30: 508–519.

Persson, H. 1978b. Data on root dynamics in a young Scots pine stand in Central Sweden. – Swed. Conif. For. Proj. Int. Rep. 72. 13 pp.

Persson, H. 1979a. The possible outcomes and limitations of measuring quantitative changes in plant cover on permanent plots. – In: Hytteborn, H. (ed.) The Use of Ecological Variables in Environmental Monitoring, Swedish National Environment Protection Board, Rep. PM 1151: 81–87.

Persson, H. 1979b. Fine-root production, mortality and decomposition in forest ecosystems. – Vegetation 41: 101–109.

Persson, H. 1980a. Spatial distribution of fine-root growth, mortality and decomposition in a young Scots pine stand in Central Sweden. – Oikos 34: 77–87.

Persson, H. 1980b. Structural properties of the field and bottom layers at Ivantjärnsheden. – In: Persson, T. (ed.) Structure and Function of Northern Coniferous Forests – An Ecosystem Study, Ecol. Bull. (Stockholm) 32: 153–163.

Reynolds, E. R. C. 1970. Root distribution and the cause of its spatial variability in *Pseudotsuga taxifolia* (Poir.) Britt. – Plant & Soil 32: 501–517.

259

Reynolds, E. R. C. 1974. The distribution pattern of fine roots of trees. – In: Hoffmann, G. (ed.) Ecology and Physiology of Root Growth, II. Int. Symp., pp. 101–112. Berlin: Akademie-Verlag.

Roberts, J. 1976. A study of root distribution and growth in a *Pinus silvestris* L. (Scots pine) plantation in East Anglia. – Plant & Soil 44: 607–621.

Röhrig, E. 1966. Die Wurzelentwicklung der Waldbäume in Abhängigkeit von den oekologischen Verhältnissen. – Forstarchiv 37(10): 217–229, 37(11): 237–249.

Russel, S. R. 1977. Plant Root Systems: Their Function and Interaction with the Soil. London: McGraw-Hill Comp., 298 pp.

Santantonio, D. 1979. Seasonal dynamics of fine root in mature stands of Douglas-fir of different water regimes – a preliminary report. – In: Riedacker, A. & Gagnaire-Michard, J. (eds.) Physiologie des Racines et Symbioses, C. R. des Reunions du Groupe d'Etude des Racines, pp. 190–203. Nancy, France.

Santantonio, D., Hermann, R. K. & Overton, W. S. 1977. Root biomass studies in forest ecosystems. – Pedobiologia 17: 1–31.

Sokal, R. R. & Rohlf, F. J. 1969. Biometry. San Francisco: W. H. Freeman & Co., 776 pp.

Staaf, H. & Berg, B. 1977. A structural and chemical description of litter and humus in a mature Scots pine stand. – Swed. Conif. For. Proj. Int. Rep. 65, 31 pp.

Wagenhoff, A. 1938. Untersuchungen über die Entwicklung des Wurzelsystems der Kiefer auf diluvialen Sandböden. – Z. For. Jagdwes. 70: 449–494.

Zak, B. 1964. Role of mycorrhiza in root disease. – Ann. Rev. Phytopathology 2: 377–392.

Persson, T. (ed) 1980
Structure and Function of Northern
Coniferous Forests – An Ecosystem Study
Ecol. Bull. (Stockholm) 32: 261–268.

ROOT CONSUMPTION IN A 15–20 YEAR OLD SCOTS PINE STAND WITH SPECIAL REGARD TO PHYTOPHAGOUS NEMATODES

C. Magnusson[1] and B. Sohlenius[2]

Abstract

Nematodes associated with plant roots were studied in a 15–20 year old stand of Scots pine. Eight–nine genera of root/fungal feeding nematodes were found. A *Geocenamus*-species was considered as the only obligate root feeder, while fungal feeding was observed in some other species. The kind of field layer vegetation influenced the distribution of the nematodes. The root/fungal feeders amounted to $2.1 \cdot 10^6$ ind. m^{-2}, being equal to 0.1 g fw m^{-2}. The annual nematode root consumption was estimated to be 0.4 g carbon m^{-2}, equal to about 0.3% of the annual production of fine roots.

Introduction

The role of below-ground herbivores in connection with primary production and material flow has often been neglected in ecosystem studies. Studies on such interactions are fundamentally very difficult, and our knowledge of these aspects of the soil fauna is so poor that it might be inconvenient to include them in short-term ecosystem studies.

Two fundamental obstacles in evaluating the influence of root consumption on ecosystem processes are the poor knowledge of the feeding habits of soil animals and the difficulty in evaluating the impact of these animals on primary production and soil processes. Omnivorous and facultative feeding habits are widespread, and among nematodes it is difficult to distinguish between root consumers, fungal consumers and species that use both food sources. Although the amount of plant material consumed can be roughly estimated, this amount as such might not indicate the real effects involved. Interactions with soil microflora might occur which would increase the effect of the consumption beyond that of the simple removal of plant tissue. Within one of the sites (a 15–20 year old Scots pine forest) of the Swedish Coniferous Forest Project, efforts were made to study the occurrence and importance of root consumption. It was considered that the nematodes could be of particular importance as consumers of fine roots and studies on phytophagous nematodes were coordinated with studies on root dynamics. Apart from nematodes other root

[1] Dept. of Plant and Forest Protection, Swedish University of Agriculture Sciences, Box 7044, S-750 07 Uppsala, Sweden
[2] Dept. of Zoology, University of Stockholm, Box 6801, S-113 86 Stockholm, Sweden

261

consumers at the site were certain elaterid larvae, aphids and symphylids (Persson, 1975).

Initially, nothing was known about the occurrence of phytophagous nematodes at the site. However, results from other ecosystem studies indicated that the nematodes could be an important group. The first goal was to investigate which root-feeding nematodes were present and to what degree they were associated with different roots and root fractions. The second goal was to estimate the amount of material consumed.

Research site

The investigation was undertaken in a 15–20 year old Scots pine stand at Ivantjärnsheden (Ih II) in central Sweden. The site was described in Sohlenius *et al.* (1977) and more thoroughly in Axelsson & Bråkenhielm (1980).

The field and bottom layer vegetation was composed of clones of heather, *Calluna vulgaris* (L.) Hull, which alternated with reindeer lichens, cup lichens, etc. Two strata were distinguished for sampling purposes, *viz. Calluna* and non-*Calluna*. These accounted for 47.9% and 52.1% of the total area, respectively. In another study the nematode fauna was investigated in an adjacent 120-year-old stand (Ih V) (Sohlenius, 1977).

Methods

The field populations in Ih II were studied according to a coordinated sampling programme where soil cores for nematode extraction were paired with cores for estimation of root biomass as described in Sohlenius *et al.* (1977). The animals were extracted according to a modified Baermann method (Sohlenius, 1977). The cores were taken down to a depth of 10 cm below the border between the S- and F/H-layers. A later sampling down to 40 cm including the S-layer indicated that the former samplings only included 51–66% of the nematode number.

The study also included laboratory experiments, where efforts were made to raise populations of root feeders both under controlled conditions in monoxenic agar cultures with pine seedlings and in pot experiments with soil material from the site.

Results and discussion

Species composition and feeding behaviour

At both Ih II and Ih V the genera *Tylenchus* (Bastian 1865) Golden 1971 (2–4 spp.), *Malenchus* (1 sp.), *Ditylenchus* (3 spp.), *Geocenamus* (Thorne & Malek 1963) (1 sp.), *Aphelenchoides* (2–3 spp.) and *Tylencholaimus* (2 spp.) occurred, while the genera *Diphtherophora* (1 sp.), *Deladenus* (1 sp.) and ?*Nothotylenchus* (1 sp.) were recovered in the younger stand, Ih II. The species of *Malenchus* is near to *M. tantulus* Siddiqi 1979. The species of *Geocenamus* comes close to, or is identical with *G. arcticus* (Mulvey) Tarjan. The two *Tylencholaimus* species are *T. mirabilis* (Bütschli) Loof & Jairajpuri and *T. stecki* Steiner.

All genera except *Geocenamus* have been previously reported from coniferous forests (Bassus, 1962; Boag, 1974; Massey, 1974). *Geocenamus* was also observed from a pine heath soil west of Lake Inari in Finnish Lapland, and could be extensively

Table 1. Number and biomass (with 95% confidence interval) of nematodes in a young Scots pine stand (Ih II) in *Calluna* and non-*Calluna* strata from five samplings (June–October 1974). Figures concern the uppermost 10 cm of the F/H and mineral layers.

Category	*Calluna*		Non-*Calluna*	
	Number (thousands m^{-2})	Biomass (mg fw m^{-2})	Number (thousands m^{-2})	Biomass (mg fw m^{-2})
Nematoda, total	3 226 ± 417	377	2 611 ± 333	337
Root/fungal feeders	1 366 ± 244	72	1 099 ± 189	58
Bacterial feeders	1 634 ± 299	132	1 294 ± 232	105
Miscellaneous feeders	232 ± 45	145	185 ± 33	116
Tylenchus	231 ± 60	4	256 ± 78	5
Ditylenchus	118 ± 49	5	83 ± 39	3
Geocenamus	13 ± 6	6	10 ± 4	5
Aphelenchoides	727 ± 13	13	384 ± 128	7
Tylenchida sp.	2 ± 4	0.1	0	0
Tylencholaimus mirabilis	256 ± 59	56	355 ± 83	77
Tylencholaimus stecki	37 ± 20	16	46 ± 23	19

distributed in Scandinavia. *Malenchus* has been observed from pine forests both in Sweden (Magnusson, 1977) and Finland (Sarakoski, pers. comm.). At Ih II 8–9 genera of root/fungal feeding nematodes were discovered, which agrees rather well with results from pine forests. In Germany Bassus (1962), in Poland Wasilewska (1970) and in Scotland Boag (1974) reported 6, 10 and 11 genera, respectively.

Judging from its morphology and the feeding behaviour in related genera *Geocenamus* must be regarded as an obligate root feeder. The feeding habits of other members of this group are not clear. Fungal feeding was demonstrated for an *Aphelenchoides*-species from Ih V (Sohlenius *et al.*, 1975) and for the two *Tylencholaimus*-species from Ih II (Sohlenius *et al.*, 1977). Probably also members in the genera *Tylenchus*, *Malenchus*, *Ditylenchus*, *Deladenus* and *Nothotylenchus* can feed on fungi. Efforts to establish cultures of potential root feeders on pine seedlings have so far only succeeded for a *Rotylenchus*-species from a pine forest near Säter in Dalarna (C. Magnusson, unpubl.).

Abundance

Table 1 shows the mean numbers and biomasses of nematodes in the upper 10 cm of the soil profile (S-layer excluded) from the sampling period June–October 1974. In both strata the root/fungal feeders and the bacterial feeders dominated while the miscellaneous feeders reached rather low numbers. On average, the root/fungal feeders made up 42% of the total number of nematodes, but maximal relative frequencies of 50–55% were observed in August and September. As pointed out by Sohlenius *et al.* (1977), this frequency is rather low and higher values were later observed in another pine forest in central Sweden (Magnusson, 1978). Regardless of strata, *Tylenchus*, *Ditylenchus*, *Aphelenchoides* and *Tylencholaimus mirabilis* accounted for the major part of the root/fungal feeders while *T. stecki* and *Geocena-*

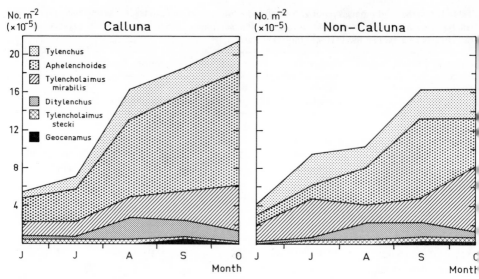

Figure 1. Population densities of root/fungal feeding nematodes in a young Scots pine stand (Ih II) in *Calluna* and non-*Calluna* strata during the period June–October 1974.

mus were of minor importance. *Malenchus, Diphtherophora, Deladenus* and *Nothotylenchus* were very rarely encountered and are not included in Table 1. *Tylenchus, Aphelenchoides* and *T. mirabilis* were, on average, obtained in numbers exceeding 200 000 ind. m^{-2} in both strata. *Aphelenchoides* clearly dominated in the *Calluna* stratum whereas both *Aphelenchoides* and *T. mirabilis* were dominant in the non-*Calluna* stratum. When the biomass is taken into consideration a completely different picture emerges. With regard to weight the miscellaneous and the bacterial feeders clearly dominated over the root/fungal feeders. Regardless of strata, the latter group is almost wholly dominated by *T. mirabilis* followed by the numerically insignificant *T. stecki*. For the period June–October 1974 the average total number of root/fungal feeders were comparable in Ih II and Ih V.

Seasonal dynamics and vertical distribution

In Ih II the root/fungal feeders increased under both *Calluna* and non-*Calluna*, but there was a considerable difference in the development of individual populations. Fig. 1 shows the seasonal change in the total group and in different genera and species. Under *Calluna* both *Aphelenchoides* and *T. mirabilis* increased in numbers towards October, but under non-*Calluna*, *T. mirabilis* had a population peak both in July and October, while *Aphelenchoides* had a single population maximum in September. The fauna was far more stable under *Calluna* while drastic rearrangements occurred under non-*Calluna*. Obviously, the kind of cover has a profound effect on the composition and the seasonal dynamics of the nematodes. Tendencies for horizontal stratification of root/fungal feeding nematodes were also observed in another pine forest (Magnusson, 1977).

Fig. 2 shows the vertical distribution of the root/fungal feeding nematodes and of

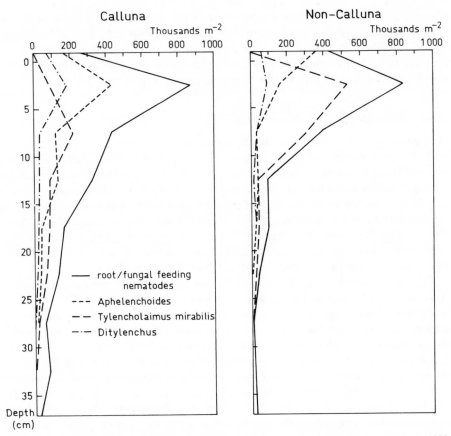

Figure 2. Vertical distribution of nematodes in Ih II in *Calluna* and non-*Calluna* strata in October 1977.

different genera and species. The nematodes occurred down to a depth of at least 35–40 cm, with a deeper distribution under *Calluna*, where 13% of the population was found below 20 cm compared to 3% under non-*Calluna*. Thus, the field layer vegetation clearly affects the vertical distribution of the nematodes, which probably reflects the differences in production of fine roots and the standing crop of total roots under *Calluna* and non-*Calluna* strata found by Persson (1978). In the 20–30 cm layer the average standing crop of total roots (roots having a diameter less than 10 mm) was estimated at 6.6 g dw m^{-2} under *Calluna* compared to 4.4 g dw m^{-2} under non-*Calluna*. The annual production of fine roots (diameter less than 2 mm) in *Calluna* mineral soil was estimated at 91 g dw m^{-2} compared to 68 g dw m^{-2} in non-*Calluna* mineral soil.

Apart from serving as a food source for the herbivorous nematodes, the root activity also stimulates the microflora with its accompanying consumers among the microbivorous nematodes. Thus, the deeper distribution of the nematodes under *Calluna* could reflect both the deeper distribution of the roots and the higher fine root production in *Calluna* mineral soil. There were some differences in the vertical distribution of the different genera and species: *T. stecki* was rather superficial;

265

T. mirabilis, *Geocenamus* and *Diphtherophora* were deeper, while *Tylenchus*, *Ditylenchus* and *Aphelenchoides* were distributed throughout the soil profile sampled. The distribution at Ivantjärnsheden differs drastically from the superficial types reported from Danish raw humus soils (Nielsen, 1949), but are more comparable to those reported from a Polish pine forest on sand (Wasilewska, 1974).

Association with roots and consumption

Only a few positive relationships between nematode numbers and root fractions have been detected, the reason being discussed elsewhere (Sohlenius *et al.*, 1977). In the younger stand a positive connection was observed in July between numbers of root/fungal feeding nematodes and the fine root fraction of *Pinus* and *Vaccinium vitis-idaea* L. and between these nematodes and the total root biomass in *Calluna* mineral soil. In contrast to the results by Ausmus *et al.* (1977), the temporal variation in the fine root fraction (Persson, 1978) had few connections with the variation in numbers of nematodes. However, population peaks of *Geocenamus* coincided with declines in *Pinus* fine root fraction during the period June–October 1974.

Extensive measurements for determination of nematode biomass according to Andrassy's (1956) method were undertaken at Ih V (Sohlenius, 1977). The annual individual mean biomass values obtained from Ih V were used in the present study assuming that the size distribution of the different genera and species was similar in the two stands. To calculate nematode respiration and consumption m^{-2} the abundance values in Table 1 were corrected for the fauna in the S-layer and for the fauna occurring below a depth of 10 cm. Considering the percentage cover of the two strata, a mean value for the site of $2.1 \cdot 10^6$ root/fungal feeding nematodes m^{-2} with a fresh weight of about 0.1 g was obtained. Assuming that the size distribution and the field temperatures were similar to those at Ih V, the population at Ih II emitted about 0.2 g carbon m^{-2} yr^{-1} by respiration. Using the carbon or energy budgets proposed by Heal & MacLean (1975) for fungal feeders and herbivores and assuming that half the respiration originated from each group, it was estimated that the root/fungal feeders consumed about 0.8 g carbon m^{-2} yr^{-1}. As more than half of this amount probably originates from fungi the annual amount removed from plant roots was estimated at 0.4 g carbon m^{-2} in Ih II. This is only about 0.3% of the annual fine root production of 348 g dw m^{-2} estimated by Persson (1978).

Influence on primary production

It is generally considered that the influence of a herbivore on the primary production is widely different from the amount consumed. For root feeders it is known that invasions by pathogenic microorganisms might occur as a result of the damage caused to the roots. Some root feeders might also induce drastic changes in the plants. In other cases no obvious influence is observed in spite of extensive consumption. It is very difficult to evaluate the effects of root consumers on forest trees, but the study of effects on juvenile plants in pot experiments was considered to be a possible approach. Unfortunately, these experiments have been unsuccessful so far.

However, some interesting results have been obtained in another study on the mineralisation processes in microcosm experiments (Bååth, *et al.*, 1978). When pine seedlings in humus from Ih V were supplied with glucose there was a pronounced increase in the numbers of *Aphelenchoides* and *Ditylenchus*, which was found to be connected with an increase in fungal activity and a decrease in the growth of the pine seedlings. Although mycophagous nematodes probably dominated among the root/ fungal feeders in Ih II the effects on primary production should not be ignored. Reproduction and negative effects of fungal feeding nematodes on mycorrhiza-forming fungi have been reported (Riffle, 1967; Sutherland & Fortin, 1968) as well as their interference with mycorrhizal synthesis in pine (Sutherland & Fortin, 1968; Riffle, 1975). Although the impact on primary production via the mycorrhizal component is difficult to quantify, Gubina (1971), by inoculating Norway spruce seedlings with nematode suspensions rather rich in mycophages, demonstrated a reduction of root- and above-ground parts by 22 and 13%, respectively.

Acknowledgements

The sampling programme was organized by Drs. J. G. K. Flower-Ellis and H. Persson. Mrs. I. Sohlenius processed and counted the samples. Valuable comments on the manuscript were kindly made by Prof. B. Eriksson and Drs. H. Persson and T. Persson.

References

Andrassy, I. 1956. Die Rauminhalts- und Gewichtbestimmung der Fadenwürmer (Nematoden). – Acta Zool. Acad. Sci. Hung. 2: 1–15.

Ausmus, B. S., Ferris, J. M., Reichle, D. E. & Williams, E. C. 1977. The role of primary consumers in forest root dynamics. – In: Marshall, J. (ed.) The Belowground Ecosystem: A Synthesis of Plant Associated Processes, Range Science Department Series No. 26, pp. 261–265. Colorado State University, Fort Collins.

Axelsson, B. & Bråkenhielm, S. 1980. Investigation sites of the Swedish Coniferous Forest Project – biological and physiographical features. – In: Persson, T. (ed.) Structure and Function of Northern Coniferous Forests – An Ecosystem Study, Ecol. Bull. (Stockholm) 32: 25–64.

Bååth, E., Lohm, U., Lundgren, B., Rosswall, T., Söderström, B., Sohlenius, B. & Wirén, A. 1978. The effect of nitrogen and carbon supply on the development of soil organism populations and pine seedlings: a microcosm experiment. – Oikos 31: 153–163.

Bassus, W. 1962. Untersuchungen über die Nematodenfauna mittel-deutscher Waldböden. – Wiss. Z. Humboldt-Univers. Berlin, Math. Nat. R. 11: 145–177.

Boag, B. 1974. Nematodes associated with forest and woodland trees in Scotland. – Ann. appl. Biol. 77: 41–50.

Gubina, V. G. 1971. Effect of plant nematodes on dry matter content of Norway spruce seedlings. – Trud. Gel'mint. Lab. 21: 176–178. (In Russian)

Heal, O. W. & MacLean, S. F. 1975. Comparative productivity in ecosystems–secondary productivity. – In: Van Dobben, W. H. & Lowe-McConnell, R. H. (eds.) Unifying Concepts in Ecology, pp. 89–108. The Hague: Dr. W. Junk and Wageningen: Pudoc.

Magnusson, C. 1977. Investigation of Nematodes in a Swedish Pine Forest. – Master of Science Thesis, Imperial College, London Field Station, 79 pp. (Mimeographed)

Magnusson, C. 1978. Plant-parasitic nematodes in pine forests in Central Sweden. – In: Laux, W. (ed.) Abstracts of Papers, 3rd Int. Congr. of Plant Pathology: München, Federal Republic of Germany, 16–23 August 1978, pp. 158.

Massey, C. L. 1974. Biology and Taxonomy of Nematode Parasites and Associates of Bark Beetles in the United States. Agriculture Handbook No. 446. Forest Service, U.S. Dept. of Agriculture, 233 pp.

Nielsen, C. O. 1949. Studies on the soil microfauna. II. The soil inhabiting nematodes. – Natura jutl. 2: 1–132.

Persson, H. 1978. Root dynamics in a young Scots pine stand in central Sweden. – Oikos 31: 508–519.
Persson, T. 1975. Abundance, biomass and respiration of the soil arthropod community in an old Scots pine heath stand at Ivantjärnsheden, Gästrikland (Central Sweden) – a preliminary investigation. – Swed. Conif. For. Proj. Int. Rep. 31, 35 pp. (In Swedish, English abstract)
Riffle, J. W. 1967. Effect of an *Apelenchoides* species on the growth of a mycorrhizal and a pseudomycorrhizal fungus. – Phytopathology 57: 541–544.
Riffle, J. W. 1975. Two *Aphelenchoides* species supress formation of *Suillus granulatus* ectomycorrhizae with *Pinus ponderosa* seedlings. – Plant Dis. Reptr. 59: 951–955.
Sohlenius, B. 1977. Numbers, biomass and respiration of Nematoda, Rotatoria and Tardigrada in a 120-year-old Scots pine forest at Ivantjärnsheden, central Sweden. – Swed. Conif. For. Proj. Tech. Rep. 9, 40 pp.
Sohlenius, B., Lagerlöf, J. & Magnusson, C. 1975. Studies on feeding ecology of nematodes from a pine heath soil. – Swed. Conif. For. Proj. Int. Rep. 24, 23 pp. (In Swedish, English abstract)
Sohlenius, B., Persson, H. & Magnusson, C. 1977. Root-weight and nematode numbers in a young Scots pine stand at Ivantjärnsheden, Central Sweden. – Swed. Conif. For. Proj. Tech. Rep. 4, 22 pp.
Sutherland, J. R. & Fortin, J. A. 1968. Effect of the nematode *Aphelenchus avenae* on some ectotrophic mycorrhizal fungi and on a red pine mycorrhizal relationship. – Phytopathology 58: 519–523.
Wasilewska, L. 1970. Nematodes of the sand dunes in the Kampinos Forest. I. Species structure. – Ekol. pol. 18: 429–442.
Wasilewska, L. 1974. Vertical distribution of nematodes in the soil of dunes in the Kampinos Forest. – Zesz. probl. Post. Nauk roln. 154: 203–212.

268

Persson, T. (ed) 1980
Structure and Function of Northern
Coniferous Forests – An Ecosystem Study
Ecol. Bull. (Stockholm) 32: 269–306.

NEEDLE-EATING INSECTS AND GRAZING DYNAMICS IN A MATURE SCOTS PINE FOREST IN CENTRAL SWEDEN

S. Larsson[1] and O. Tenow[1] *

Abstract

Abundance, faeces production, green litter production and grazing of different groups of needle-eating insects were repeatedly estimated and compared with available needle biomass in a mature *Pinus sylvestris* L. stand at Ivantjärnsheden, Central Sweden, in 1974. Abundance, grazing and needle biomass were determined from samples of foliage taken by means of a skylift, while faeces and green litter production were estimated by means of litter-traps placed on the ground. From known bioelement concentrations, bioelement fluxes with faeces and green litter were calculated. The insect populations were in endemic numbers; for the groups "Microlepidoptera", Geometridae, Noctuidae, Lasiocampidae/Sphingidae and Diprionidae maximal figures were 33 100, 18 100, 4 100, 1 300 and 19 200 specimens ha^{-1}, respectively. The total amount of faeces production was estimated at 11.0 kg dw ha^{-1} and green litter production at 1.5 kg dw ha^{-1}. Input to soil of N, P, K with faeces and green litter was 92, 10 and 48 g ha^{-1}, respectively, nitrogen making up 8.0% of the total N-input of foliar origin during summer. From faeces data and specific assimilation efficiencies, an indirect estimate of consumption from all needle-eating insects was calculated to be 14.0 kg dw ha^{-1}. The grazing study indicated that one-year-old needles were preferred by the insects; grazing on this age-class was estimated at 8.6 kg dw ha^{-1}, and that on current-year and older needles at 1.7 and 5.2 kg dw ha^{-1}, respectively. Total grazing (15.5 kg dw ha^{-1}) corresponds to 0.7% of total needle biomass or 2.5% of the needle production in 1974. Adaptive relations between the insects and the host tree are discussed.

Additional keywords: Abundance, adaptation, bioelement fluxes, Diprionidae, Lepidoptera, needle biomass, needle consumption, production of faeces and green litter, species composition.

Introduction

During the last two decades, estimates of consumption of leaf-eating insects in forest canopies, mostly deciduous, have been obtained in connection with energy flow and/or nutrient cycling studies (e.g. Bray, 1964; Carlisle *et al.*, 1966; Rafes, 1971; Smith, 1972; Gosz *et al.*, 1972; Grimm, 1973; Axelsson *et al.*, 1974, 1975; Kaczmarek & Wasilewski, 1977; Nielsen, 1978). Some of the studies concern grazing by single-species outbreak populations during only part of the season while others give figures on consumption on an annual basis without any further time dimension. Reichle & Crossley (1967) and Reichle *et al.* (1973) used a different approach by estimating directly from feeding damage on leaves both consumption rates and total consumption for a complete season, estimating feeding on different age-classes of leaves and

---

[1] Dept. of Entomology, Uppsala University, Box 561, S-751 22 Uppsala, Sweden
* Authors given alphabetically. See also Acknowledgements.

relating grazing to different consumer groups. Lately, Schroeder (1978) has reported on consumption rates as well as on totals for a whole season, estimated from faeces production.

Some of the studies comprise estimates on bioelement inputs to the soil, transferred by the consumption processes (Carlisle et al., 1966; Rafes, 1971; Gosz et al., 1972; Reichle et al., 1973; Nilsson, 1978; Schroeder, 1978).

Most ecological studies on needle-eating insects have centered on population dynamics of economically important species. Thus, corresponding information on coniferous forests is scarce, and of the above studies only Gosz et al. (1972) gives data on total consumption and nutrient transfer by canopy insects in a mixed deciduous-coniferous forest stand. In addition, Kaczmarek (1967) reports preliminary data on energy transfer of insects in a Scots pine forest.

From studies on faeces production some additional information can be obtained. Frass-drop as an index of larval number and feeding activities of needle-eating insects was early utilized as a tracer of rising populations (Schwerdtfeger, 1931; Gösswald, 1934; Eckstein, 1938; Mors, 1942; Morris, 1949) and as an evaluation of chemical control applications (Rhumbler, 1929; Schwerdtfeger, 1930). However, like other investigations on coniferous forest insects these studies only concern outbreak species; analyses of general consumption patterns thus are still lacking.

A few studies follow up the species succession and abundance changes of pine canopy insects throughout the growing season or the major part of it (Engel, 1941; Höregott, 1960; Klomp & Teerink, 1973).

The aim of the present study was to describe the process of consumption by needle-eating insects in a coniferous canopy throughout the season, in relation to available needle biomass, different age-classes of needles, different insect groups and insect numbers, and to estimate the transfer of some bioelements from the canopy to the soil caused by grazing. The investigation is part of the Swedish Coniferous Forest Project (SWECON). The fieldwork was done in 1974 in a mature Scots pine (*Pinus sylvestris* L.) forest at Ivantjärnsheden (Ih), Jädraås in Central Sweden, the main field site of the project.

Materials and methods

Study plot

The regional physiography of the research area and the layout of research plots of the SWECON project are described by Axelsson & Bråkenhielm (1980). Descriptions of the vegetation are given by Axelsson & Bråkenhielm (1980) and Persson (1980). Bringmark (1977), Flower-Ellis & Olsson (1978) and Albrektson (1980) inform on biomass structure, bioelement budget and litterfall, respectively. Main statistics on the climate in 1974 are found in Axelsson & Bråkenhielm (1980).

The research plot of the present study, Ih V (S), covers an area of a little more than one hectare and is situated in a pure, about 120 years old (1974), stand of Scots pine growing on a level heath about 185 meters above sea level, underlain with mainly glacifluvial sand. The ground vegetation is characterized by a rich occurrence of heather (*Calluna vulgaris* L.) and abundant mosses and lichens.

The characteristics of the trees and the position and form of the plot are given in Table 1 and Fig. 1, respectively. Ivantjärnsheden is situated in a region with an intermediate climate although, as a result of the topography, the local climate sometimes gets a continental trait. The averages of annual temperature and precipitation are $+3.8°C$ and 570 mm, respectively, and the growing season (daily temperatures $> +6°C$) lasts about 160 days (Axelsson & Bråkenhielm, 1980). The temperature and precipitation climate of Ivantjärnsheden in 1974 is illustrated in Fig. 2. In Fig. 3 the phenology of needle growth and needle litterfall in 1974 are shown, together with dates for different sampling campaigns.

Table 1. Characteristics of the Scots pine (*Pinus sylvestris*) trees on Ih V(S) in 1974. Stand age 120 years, density 380 trees ha^{-1}.

Character	Mean	s.e.	n
Tree height (m)	16.0	0.4	34
Basal area o.b. (m^2 ha^{-1})	15.7[a]	0.5	30
DBH (mm)	230.3[a]	7.4	30
Crown projection (m^2)	6.9[b]	0.6	27
Live crown length (m)	8.3	0.4	34
Branches per crown (no.)	97.3	4.5	30
Upper half	74.7	3.7	30
Lower half	22.6	1.7	30

[a] From a randomized sample of trees, used for branch sampling in the larval abundance study.
[b] Canopy cover 26%.

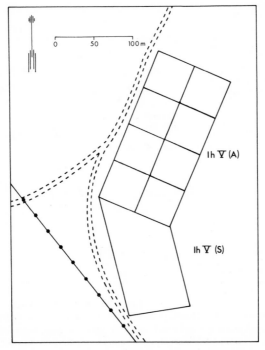

Figure 1. Layout of the investigation plot, Ih V(S).

Larval abundance

Larval abundance was studied on May 20, June 11–12, June 26, July 15, July 30, August 14–15, September 5–6 and October 2, 1974, i.e., on eight occasions with a mean interval of about 20 days. The abundances of all investigated insect groups were estimated with the same sampling method. The branch was the unit of collection, and was randomly selected in two stages; first by the drawing of ten trees (out of a population of 388 trees) and then of five branches per tree.

In order to spread the units of collection each crown was stratified in an upper and a lower half. Three of the branches were taken from the upper half and two from the lower half. The selection was done by randomizing one height and one direction within the stratum for each branch to be sampled and then by

271

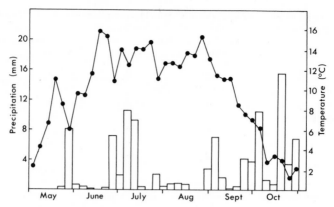

Figure 2. Climatical data, Ivantjärnsheden 1974. Curve = five-day averages of air temperature. Columns =
= amount of precipitation over five-day periods.

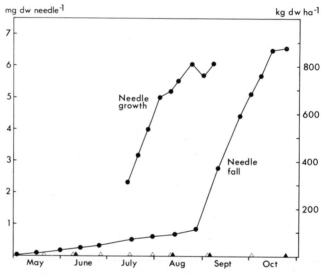

Figure 3. Pine needle (*Pinus sylvestris*) phenology at Ivantjärnsheden in 1974 according to data provided
by J. G. K. Flower-Ellis (pers. comm.). Needle growth = mean weight of current-year needles of 15-year-old
trees, Ih II. Needle fall = cumulative needle fall, Ih V(A). Dates of sampling of larval abundances are
indicated by open triangles on the time axis (May 20, June 11–12, June 26, July 15, July 30, Aug. 14–15,
Sept. 5–6, Oct. 2), dates for sampling of needle biomass and grazing by filled triangles (June 11–12,
Aug. 14–15, Sept. 5–6, Oct. 24–25).

collecting the nearest one. Each tree was sampled on three successive occasions and after the third sampling
a new set of ten trees was selected from the remaining population.

The low tree density of the plot made it possible to use a mobile skylift for the sampling of branches.
The skylift had a maximal operative height of 23 m. It was operated from the skylift platform, from which
the branches were reached. The selected branches were carefully cut off with a pruner and sectioned into a
transparent plastic bag. The bags were transported to the laboratory for further treatment within ten hours.
The fifty branches were collected within one day, or, when additional sampling of needle biomass was done
(see below), within two consecutive days.

In the laboratory, all needle-bearing shoots were cut off. The remaining parts of the branches were examined for insects and then discarded. The shoots were spread out in a thin layer within the bags, which were stored for about three days, during which time the larvae present on the foliage, fed and defecated. Even small larvae were then easily discovered from the heaps of faeces accumulated below the feeding places.

With a staff of 2–4 persons, the examination of each sample required about three days. Before the examined foliage was discarded, each bag was again checked for any remaining larvae and microlepidopterous moths that had hatched from pupae attached to the foliage.

As far as possible, the larvae were identified as to species and age (instar). When this was not possible they were coded according to preliminary descriptions and reared to imagines for determinations. The rearing was made in transparent plastic jars in the laboratory. The cocoons or pupae were transferred to plastic cylinders, the tops and bottoms of which were covered with netting, and then placed on the ground at the study plot. In the following spring, the cylinders were inspected at appropriate intervals and hatched imagines were collected and subsequently determined to species (see Acknowledgements).

The distance between the whorls in the pine crown increases and the number of branches per whorl decreases down the stem, and, in the same direction, the needle biomass per branch increases. The number of branches in different directions of the compass may also be different. Further, when sampled, the crowns of the trees were increasingly stunted by the removal of branches. With the method of selection used, this meant that the different branches in a stratum had unequal chances of being selected.

An analysis of the crown structure based on data provided by J. G. K. Flower-Ellis (pers. comm.) indicates that the number of live branches per length unit of stem within the upper half of the crown is fairly constant. In the lower stratum, however, branch frequency and vertical distribution change significantly. Nevertheless, the biomass of needles per branch in this half of the crown does not change drastically, which should indicate that the number of larvae on each branch is about equal. Thus, by sampling from the two crown halves separately, biases due to vertical differences of the branch distribution should be substantially reduced. In addition, the data obtained do not indicate any systematic differences during the season in the number of larvae per branch in the four main directions of the compass.

With reference to the discussion above, statistical standard formulas for a two-stage sampling procedure were applied when calculating means and variances of larval abundance:

$$N \cdot \mu_A = N \cdot \frac{1}{n} \cdot \sum_{i=1}^{n} \frac{M_{iJ}}{m_J} \sum y_{iJk} = N \cdot \frac{1}{n} \cdot \sum_{i=1}^{n} z_i \tag{1}$$

$$\widehat{\mathrm{Var}}(N \cdot \hat{\mu}_A) = \frac{N^2}{n} \cdot \frac{1}{n-1} \cdot \sum_{i=1}^{n} (z_i - \hat{\mu}_A)^2; \quad \mathrm{d.f.} = n-1 \tag{2}$$

where N = number of trees per ha, $\hat{\mu}_A$ = the mean number of insects per tree, n = the number of sampled trees, M_{iJ} = the number of branches in the crown half J (= upper or lower) of sampled tree i, m_J = the number of sampled branches in the crown half J, and y_{iJk} = the number of larvae on sampled branch k in crown half J of tree i.

At the end of the sampling program a large proportion of the trees on the plot and the branches of the selected trees had been sampled. However, the trees are looked upon as representative for the trees of the surrounding forest and no corrections for finite populations have been applied (cf. Cochran, 1963: 286).

Needle biomass and grazing

The biomass of different needle age-classes and the amount of grazed needles were estimated by sampling vertical columns of foliage from the forest canopy on three of the eight occasions of branch sampling in 1974; June 11–12, August 14–15, September 5–6, and on an additional occasion on October 24–25. As with branches, the columns were sampled from the skylift. They were selected in two stages. In a first step, 6, 10, 9 and 9 trees, respectively, were selected on the four sampling occasions. This was done by choosing the tree growing closest to each of the branch sampling trees (see above), so that both trees could be reached from the same positioning of the skylift. The crown projections of the trees to be sampled were then mapped on the ground surface by means of a mirror. In a second step, two columns per tree were selected. This was done as a desk work by transforming each crown projection to a coordinate system and determining randomly two points within each projection, the point representing a defined corner of the quadratic cross-section of each column (Fig. 4).

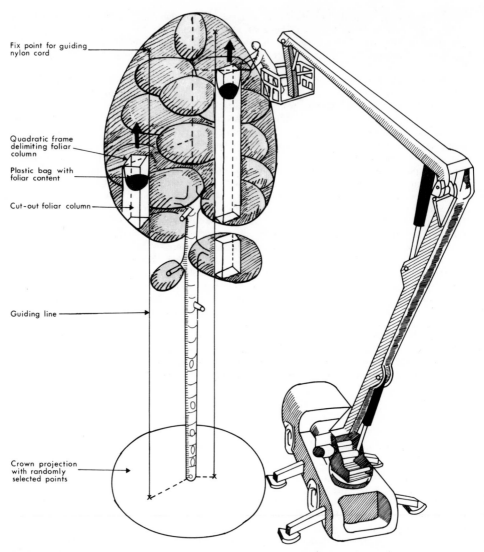

Figure 4. Principle of sampling foliar columns for estimation of needle biomass and amount of grazing by needle-eating insect larvae in pine crowns. For further explanation, see text.

The direction and distance of the selected points from the stem were measured and the points identified in the field. By means of a lead-weight, a fine nylon cord was then dropped from the skylift through the crown down to the ground over each point. The cord was stretched and tied to the uppermost branch which was strong enough to support it. The perpendicular cord marked the inner rim (facing the stem) of the column and served as a guiding line when the foliage within the column was cut. This was done by moving a quadratic frame, delining the cross-section of the column (20 × 20 cm), along the cord and cutting with a pruner all shoots within the column. The cut shoots fell into a plastic bag attached below the frame (Fig. 4).

The bags were transported to the laboratory and stored at −18°C. When sorted, the needles of each column were separated according to the age-classes 1974 (current-year needles), 1973 and "older than 1973". A fourth class was introduced for needles that fell off in the bags or during subsequent handling. Grazed needles were searched, partly eaten needles picked off and pooled in a pile (*a*) for each age-class.

274

Their intact twin needles or nearest intact needle pair (in cases where both needles in a pair were eaten) were pooled in another pile (*b*) and remaining intact needles in a third (*c*). After counting the needle pairs of each pile and age-class, the piles were dried (+85°C, 48 hours) and weighed to the nearest 0.001 g. The difference $b-a$ approximated the grazed amount of needle biomass and the sum $a+b+c+(b-a)= =2b+c$ equalled the total needle biomass of each needle age-class.

On October 24–25, a separate study was made on the older age-classes of needles. From complete twigs of the age-class "older than 1973" a random subsample of six twigs per column was taken to estimate the age distribution and the relative proportion of needles of different ages.

The needle biomass or amount of grazed needles and its variance was calculated according to:

$$N \cdot \hat{\mu}_B = N \cdot \frac{1}{2n} \cdot \sum_{ij} \frac{A_i}{a} \cdot y_{ij} = N \cdot \frac{1}{2n} \cdot \sum_{ij} z_{ij} = N \cdot z.. \tag{3}$$

$$\widehat{\text{Var}}(N \cdot \hat{\mu}_B) = \frac{N^2}{n} \cdot \frac{1}{n-1} \cdot \sum_i (z_i. - z..)^2; \text{d.f.} = n-1 \tag{4}$$

where $N=$ the number of trees per ha, $\hat{\mu}_B=$ the mean biomass per tree, $n=$ the number of sampled trees, $A_i=$ the area of the crown projection of sampled tree i, $a=$ the cross area of the column (400 cm^2) and $y_{ij}=$ the needle biomass, total or grazed, of column j of tree i.

Faeces and green litter

The amount of faeces and "green litter" (needle litter cut off by the insects) produced by canopy-living larvae was studied parallel to the abundance and grazing of larvae. The study was made on the same plot as the skylift sampling. Faeces pellets and green litter were collected in aluminium traps, consisting of an upper part functioning as a wind shelter and a bottom tray for collection. The trap measured 52 × 32 cm in horizontal area and 26 cm in height, the rim being well above the field layer vegetation. The construction of the traps is described and the reliability of the method discussed in Larsson & Tenow (1975). The traps were assumed to catch representative samples of the frass-drop, thus giving essentially unbiased estimates of faeces production, except for weight losses due to leaching (see below).

When the traps were visited, the bottom tray was exchanged for a new one. The trays with their contents were transported to the laboratory for examination. The trays were emptied on sixteen occasions during the period from 28 May to 5 November, 1974, i.e., about every tenth day. In the laboratory the contents of the trays were air-dried. Faeces and green litter were sorted out, put into glass tubes and stored at −18°C. The faeces were classified according to identification keys (e.g. Nolte, 1939) and a reference collection of faeces obtained from rearings. Faeces from the following families or family groups were discerned: (1) Geometridae, (2) Noctuidae, (3) Lasiocampidae/Sphingidae and (4) Diprionidae. Faeces and needle fragments from each trap and sampling occasion were dried (+85°C, 48 hours) and weighed to the nearest 0.01 mg.

Between the emptying occasions, the collected faeces pellets were exposed to a varying amount of precipitation. The weights of faeces thus were corrected for leaching. When determining the percentage loss of weight as a function of precipitation, faeces from *Bupalus piniarius* L., *Dendrolimus pini* L. and *Neodiprion sertifer* Geoffr. were used in leaching experiments as representative for the family groups Geometridae, Lasiocampidae/Sphingidae and Diprionidae, respectively. For the fourth group, Noctuidae, a sufficient amount of faeces was not available and weight loss values were approximated from data for the other species. The leaching experiments will be more comprehensively reported in another context (Larsson & Tenow, to be publ.).

The pine stand studied is fairly open with a canopy cover of 26%. Hence, the horizontal distributions of both consumption and frass-drop are aggregated (cf. Nilsson, 1978; Flower-Ellis & Olsson, 1978). The average fall height of litter from the canopy is about 12 m (Table 1). Due to wind dispersal during the falling, the distribution at ground level of tiny items of consumption litter like faeces pellets, however, should be less clumped than consumption itself. Consequently, a stratification of the ground area when sampling the litter was assumed unnecessary, and 16 traps were randomly distributed over the plot area without considering canopy and non-canopy sub-areas. The estimates of faeces and green litter production and their variances were calculated according to standard formulas (e.g., Snedecor & Cochran, 1967: 44).

Table 2. Concentrations of various bioelements (% of dw) used to calculate bioelement transfers due to normal litterfall, production of insect faeces and green litter, and bioelement content of needle biomass in a mature Scots pine (*Pinus sylvestris*) stand, Ih V(S), in 1974.

	C	N	P	K	Ca	Mg	S	Na
Live needles, green litter	50.7	(1.35)[a]	0.12	0.50	0.30	0.09	0.13	0.002
Shed needles[b]	no data	0.41	0.03	0.08	0.36	0.04	0.04	0.01
Faeces	52.1	0.68	0.07	0.36	0.36	0.06	0.10	0.01

[a] Autumn value, probably not representative. A value of 1.10% was used as an average for the whole feeding season (cf. Aronsson *et al.*, 1977).
[b] Calculated from Bringmark (1977).

Consumption derived from data on faeces production

The method of quantifying insect consumption from faeces production requires a correlation between consumption (C) and defecation (F) and the knowledge of specific consumption/defecation ratios ($a = C/F$). In laboratory experiments the correlation has been shown to be very strong for a variety of lepidopterous species (Mukerji & Guppy, 1973; Mathavan & Pandian, 1974; cf. also Southwood, 1978). These strong correlations have been exploited here. Starting from the known faeces production at the study plot (corrected for weight losses from leaching) the consumption of each of the four insect groups is approximated according to the relationship: $C = a \cdot F$.

C/F ratios of some important species were used as representatives for whole family groups. From own laboratory studies, data were available for *Neodiprion sertifer* (Diprionidae) and *Dendrolimus pini* (Lasiocampidae). The rearing and analysis methods are described and the reliability of laboratory estimates of C/F ratios is discussed in Larsson & Tenow (1979). The C/F ratios used for *Bupalus piniarius* and *Panolis flammea* Schiff., taken from literature (see below), were used as representatives for Geometridae and Noctuidae, respectively. These ratios are derived from dry weight data obtained in laboratory or semi-laboratory experiments with essentially the same rearing methods as used in our experiment.

The following C/F values were used when consumption was calculated from our data on faeces production: 1.5 for both early and late season Geometridae (Oldiges, 1959; Schwenke, 1952), 1.3 for Noctuidae (Oldiges, 1959), 1.2 and 1.4 for early season Lasiocampidae and late season Lasiocampidae/Sphingidae, respectively (Larsson & Tenow, unpubl. data) and finally, 1.2 for Diprionidae (Fogal & Kwain, 1972; Larsson & Tenow, 1979).

Bioelement transfers

An estimate of the flow of bioelements due to insect feeding and normal needle litterfall was derived by combining data on consumption, frass-drop, green litter production and needle litterfall, with data on bioelement content of faeces, green needles and brown shed needles. Figures on concentrations in brown needles were calculated from Bringmark (1977), contents of the other two constituents were analysed within the present study. The concentration figures used are given in Table 2.

Total-N and total-C were determined with the method of semi-micro-Kjeldahl and by means of the Leco induction furnace, respectively. The residual elements were determined on extracts obtained by oxidation in $HNO_3 + HClO_4$, P colorimetrically by the vanadate method (Kitson & Mellon, 1944), S by a turbidometric analysis as $BaSO_4$-precipitate, K and Na by flame emission spectrophotometry, and Ca and Mg by atomic absorption spectrophotometry. The determinations of total-C were performed at the National Swedish Laboratory for Agricultural Chemistry, Uppsala, Sweden, those of the other elements at the Department of Plant Ecology, University of Lund, Sweden.

Faeces for analyses were obtained by rearing larvae of *Bupalus piniarius*, *Panolis flammea*, *Hyloicus pinastri* L., *Diprion pini* L., *Macrodiprion nemoralis* Ensl. and *Gilpinia* spp. as representatives for the four insect groups studied. The larvae were reared in transparent plastic jars, and fed weekly with food taken from branches which were sampled on Ih V(S) during the abundance study in 1974. Tests of the needles fed and faeces obtained indicated that significant changes in studied bioelement contents of food and faeces due to rearing conditions, e.g. respiratory losses in the needles, did not occur. Differences in contents between the faeces of the six species were not large enough to call for specific consideration and, conse-

Table 3. Biomass (kg dw ha^{-1}) of different age-classes of needles in a mature Scots pine (*Pinus sylvestris*) stand, Ih V(S), in 1974. Standard error within parentheses.

Date of sampling	n	Needle age-class			Total biomass
		1974	1973	"Older than 1973"	
June 11	6	No data*	996 (203)	1751 (208)	2747 (358)
Aug. 14	10	488 (110)	713 (133)	1565 (235)	2766 (429)
Sept. 5	9	451 (66)	640 (92)	1238 (194)	2330 (313)
Oct. 24	9	626 (135)	771 (172)	804 (168)	2201 (446)

* Needles too young to be sampled.

quently, the various determinations of each bioelement were averaged.

Figures on the bioelement content of needle biomass and of the transfer with green litter and consumption were all calculated from concentrations in live needles. A point estimate is here accepted as being representative for the whole feeding period, and one-year-old needles, sampled in autumn 1974 during the ordinary sampling programme on Ih V(S), were chosen for analyses. Finally, the bioelement content of fallen needles was analysed on needles shed on Ih V(A) in autumn 1974 (Bringmark, 1977). The analysis methods were the same as those used in the present study.

Results and discussion

Needle biomass

Estimates of the total needle biomass and the biomasses of the three needle age-classes 1974, 1973 and "older than 1973" are given in Table 3 for four occasions during 1974: (1) before the new shoots were fully extended and while the current-year needles still were small and hidden by bud scales (June 11); (2) after the shoot elongation was completed and when the full weight of current-year needles was approached, but before the annual main drop of old needles had started at the end of August (August 14); (3) when the main drop of needles had just begun (September 5); (4) after the main drop of needle litter had ceased (October 24) (cf. needle phenology, Fig. 3).

The mean value of total needle biomass varied between 2 200 and 2 800 kg dw ha^{-1}; the differences, however, are not statistically significant. Of the totals, current-year needles made up about one-third, i.e., 626 kg in 1974 and, approximately, 996 kg in 1973.

In Table 4 these figures are put together with results of studies on stand biomass and structure, performed independently at Ivantjärnsheden. In order to allow a comparison, all data are normalized to a base of 380 trees ha^{-1}, i.e., the stand density of Ih V(S). This operation was possible since there were no basic differences in forest type. Reference to an areal standard (e.g., basal area o.b.) gives a similar result. As seen, the figures from the different studies agree rather well, discrepancies being explainable from random and annual variation as well as slight differences in stand characteristics and time of the year when the samples were taken. Thus, stand Ih O, now clear-cut, had a somewhat higher productivity than Ih V. Further, the high values of 2 396 kg (C+) and 3 628 kg (total), obtained by J. G. K. Flower-Ellis, are probably explained by the fact that the annual needle litterfall was not yet completed when the sampling was performed in contrast to the two other studies.

Table 4. Biomass of needles of 120-year-old Scots pine (*Pinus sylvestris*) stands at Ivantjärnsheden. Comparison between estimates of the present study and of independent investigations in adjacent stands. Biomasses normalized to the stand density of Ih V(S), 380 trees ha^{-1}. C=current-year needles, C+ = =needles older than current. Estimates of variation within parentheses.

Site	Basal area (m^2 ha^{-1})	Tree density (no. ha^{-1})	Date of sampling	Biomass (kg dw ha^{-1})			Reference
				C	C+	Total	
Ih V(A)	15.0	393	21 Sept.– 5 Oct. 1973	1232 (21)	2396 (76)	3628 (100)	J. G. K. Flower-Ellis (pers. comm.)[a]
Ih V(S)	15.7	380	11 June– 12 June 1974	996 (203)[b]	1751 (208)	2747 (358)	Present study[c]
Ih V(S)	15.7	380	24 Oct.– 25 Oct. 1974	626 (135)	1576 (320)	2201 (446)	Present study[c]
Ih O	19.7	453	9 Oct.– 5 Nov. 1975	679 (44)	2220 (192)	2899 (236)	Albrektson (1980)[d]

[a] Variation expressed as confidence interval from regression analysis.
[b] Needles of the 1973 age-class.
[c] Variation expressed as standard error, n cf. Table 2.
[d] Variation expressed as standard deviation from regression analysis.

The dynamics of the needle biomass (Table 3) may be commented upon as follows. The needle age-classes of 1974 and 1973 did not exhibit any significant biomass changes, except for the new foliation occurring between June 11 and August 14. Needles "older than 1973", on the other hand, decreased significantly ($p < 0.005$), reflecting the annual needle litterfall (cf. Fig. 3).

On the four sampling occasions, and during the handling of the samples thereafter, a certain amount of needles loosened from their shoots' axes, corresponding to 30(s.e. = 13), 475(103), 298(46) and 42(8) kg dw ha^{-1}, respectively. It can be assumed that these fractions would have fallen in 1974 regardless of our sampling, and thus, most parts of them can be placed in the needle age-class "older than 1973". Therefore, in Table 3, they are included in the mean weights 1751, 1565, 1238 and 804 kg dw ha^{-1} of this age-class. Consequently, this weight series reveals a cumulative reduction of the needle biomass amounting to 186, 513 and 947 kg dw ha^{-1} until the end of the season (October 24) due to needle litterfall. During the same time periods, on an adjacent litter sampling plot, Ih V(A), a cumulative amount of shed needles, corresponding to 59, 340 and 842 kg dw ha^{-1} was caught in litter-traps (Flower-Ellis & Olsson, 1978; see also Fig. 3). These figures should correspond to 80, 461 and 1 142 kg dw of green needles when normalized to 380 trees ha^{-1} (see above) and corrected for weight losses due to translocation prior to abscission (a weight loss of 28.8% found by Stachurski & Zimka (1975) was used as an approximation of conditions prevailing at Ivantjärnsheden).

After the main fall of old needles in 1974 was completed, the needle biomasses of the age-classes 1974, 1973 and "older than 1973" were about equally sized. The number of needle pairs on October 24 for each of the reported age-classes, as well as for the different year-classes within the age-class "older than 1973", are presented in Table 5. As is seen, the age-classes 1974, 1973 and "older than 1973"

Table 5. Age distribution of needles in a mature Scots pine (*Pinus sylvestris*) stand, Ih V(S), on 24 October 1974. Standard error within parentheses, $n=9$. Age-classes 1974, 1973 and 1972–67 were estimated from a direct count of sampled needles, and the separate age-classes 1972–67 from a direct count of sampled shoots multiplied by the corresponding number of needle pairs per shoot, the latter estimated from subsamples.

Age-class	Needle pairs	
	Millions ha^{-1}	Percentage
1974	53.5 (10.5)	33.0
1973	54.8 (12.9)	34.0
1972–67	53.9 (12.0)	33.0
1972	34.5	21.3
1971	16.0	9.9
1970	2.8	1.7
1969	0.1	0.1
1968	0.01	<0.1
1967	0	0
Total 1974–67	162.2 (30.7)	100.0

make up one-third each of the total number of needle pairs, in accordance with the weight figures. Further, age-class 1972 is about one-fifth of the total needle biomass and two-thirds of the needles "older than 1973". The proportions of older age-classes then rapidly decrease until there are no needles left of the 1967 age-class.

The needle population of the investigated stand is here looked upon as having reached a stable age distribution. The production of new needles approximately balances the drop of old needles, deviations being the effect of random variations and systematic reductions of needle formation due to flowering and cone production (cf. Flower-Ellis & Olsson, 1978). In the present study (Table 3), an estimate on new needle biomass in 1974 of 626 (s.e. = 135) kg dw ha^{-1} is to be compared with a drop of needles, predominantly those older than 1973, calculated to be 947 (s.e. = 267) kg dw ha^{-1}. Thus, if a steady state can be assumed, the distribution of needle biomass on different needle age-classes on October 1973 should have been approximately that as found in October 1974 (Table 5). Furthermore, if it can be assumed that only an insignificant fall of needle litter occurs during winter (cf. Flower-Ellis & Olsson, 1978), this distribution should have persisted up to the formation of current-year needles in early summer 1974.

In conclusion, the amount of needles available to herbivores changes both in quantity and quality throughout the year due to the specific dynamics of Scots pine needles. During spring and early summer in 1974, the foliage was mainly composed of the 1973, 1972 and 1971 age-classes, the two first classes making up about one-third each of the total needle biomass, the third class about one-fifth. The new generation of needles, still protected inside the bud scales were at that time available only to mining insects such as young larvae of *Panolis flammea* (see below). Gradually the new needles developed, being fullgrown at the end of August, before the main shedding of needles (Fig. 3). For a short period, then, a maximum of four age-classes of needles should have been available, i.e., the 1974, 1973, 1972 and 1971 needles.

Finally, after the main fall of needle litter, the 1971 needle age-class became thinned to only one-tenth of the total needle biomass, which then was dominated by the needles of 1974, 1973 and 1972, making up 33, 34 and 21 %, respectively, of the total (Table 5).

It may finally be concluded that the good agreement between needle biomass estimates of this and independent studies justifies the use of the present needle biomass data as a basis for estimates of larval abundance and grazing, as well as bioelement transfers due to insect feeding.

Insect species and abundance

Species of needle-eating larvae collected from foliage of Scots pine within the Ivantjärnsheden area are listed in Table 6. All species, except where otherwise denoted, were found during the ordinary sampling programme of the abundance study. They were either moths (Lepidoptera) or sawflies (Hymenoptera Symphyta). The list is not complete. Some rearings of less frequent species failed (e.g., one noctuid and two geometrid species), and a few mining species may have been over-looked.

The most representative group of the needle-eating species is the sawfly family Diprionidae, all being typical pine insects except for *Gilpinia polytoma*. According to Escherich (1942) and Lorenz & Kraus (1957), this species feeds on spruce needles. However, there are also early reports on occurrence on Scots pine (Eckstein, 1937, 1939).

Needle-eating beetles (Coleoptera) were also found on the foliage, e.g., imagines of *Strophosomus* sp., *Brachyderes incanus* L. and *Brachonyx pineti* Payk. They were less numerous on the plot and were omitted from the present investigation.

When reporting the abundance estimates below, the insects are grouped as follows: "Microlepidoptera", Geometridae, Noctuidae, Lasiocampidae/Sphingidae and Diprionidae (Table 7, Fig. 5).

In spring a large number of microlepidopterous specimens of the family Yponomeutidae was recorded, the maximal abundance possibly occurring before the sampling programme started. Larvae of *Cedestis* spp. and *O. piniariellum* mine the needles early in the season and only leave the mines to pupate between needles spun together (Trägårdh, 1911, 1915). The first estimate of 33 000 individuals ha^{-1} (May 20) was founded mainly on larval finds after the very tiny larvae had left their mines, and is probably rather conservative. Most of the successfully reared moths were determined as *Cedestis* spp. In addition, the gelechiid species *E. dodecella* mines several needles during summer and autumn. The larva hibernates in the needle and in the following spring it mines the young buds until pupation (Trägårdh, 1915). When penetrating the buds, the larva spins a light-coloured tube at the entrance hole (cf. Trägårdh, 1915), which is thus easily recognised. Several neighbouring buds may be mined by the larva. At the sampling on August 14, when the imagines had left, these feeding places were counted; their number corresponding to 11 870 (s.e. = = 3 130) larvae ha^{-1}. This number is not included in the estimates of Table 7 and Fig. 5.

E. dodecella and *Cedestis* spp. seem to have one generation a year, *O. piniariellum* two, the second generation of larvae occurring in late summer (Trägårdh, 1911, 1915; Schwenke, 1978). No microlepidopterous specimens were found in that part of the

Table 6. Species list of the needle-eating insect larvae collected from Scots pine (*Pinus sylvestris*) foliage at Ivantjärnsheden.

Order and family	Species
Lepidoptera	
Gelechiidae	*Exoteleia dodecella* L.
Yponomeutidae	*Cedestis gysselinella* Dup.
"	*C. farinatella* Dup.
"	*Ocnerostoma piniariellum* Z.
Geometridae	*Cidaria obeliscata* Hb.
"	*C. firmata* Hb.
"	*Ellopia fasciaria* L.
"	*Semiothisa liturata* Cl.
"	*Bupalus piniarius* L.
Noctuidae	*Panolis flammea* Schiff.
Lasiocampidae	*Dendrolimus pini* L.
Sphingidae	*Hyloicus pinastri* L.
Hymenoptera Symphyta	
Diprionidae	*Diprion pini* L.*
"	*D. simile* Hart.
"	*Neodiprion sertifer* Geoffr.*
"	*Microdiprion pallipes* Fall.
"	*Macrodiprion nemoralis* Ensl.
"	*Gilpinia frutetorum* Bens.
"	*G. virens* Klg.
"	*G. variegata* Hart.
"	*G. socia* Klg.*
"	*G. pallida* Klg.
"	*G. polytoma* Hart.

* Found outside the sampling programme.

summer, indicating that the two-generation *O. piniariellum* occurred infrequently compared to *Cedestis* spp.

Like the microlepidopterous species, the first and second instar larvae of *P. flammea* mine when feeding, hollowing buds and young needles of the new shoots, but change to an external feeding in later instars (Sachtleben, 1929). On May 20, newly hatched larvae of this species were found to be 4 100 individuals ha^{-1}. Once again an underestimation of the number might have occurred due to the mining habit of the species. This should apply especially to the sampling occasion on June 11, when no larvae were found. Later on, older instars of *P. flammea* larvae were found anew on the foliage until pupation in the second half of July.

The following species are external feeders during the whole of their larval stage. The geometrid occurrence displayed two clearly distinguishable maxima, the first (June 11) consisting of early season species, mainly larvae of *C. firmata* and *C. obeliscata*, and the second (August 14) of the late summer and autumn species *S. liturata* and *B. piniarius*, of which the latter constituted the main species until the end of the season. Fullgrown larvae of *B. piniarius* may be found as late as in early November.

The larval population of *B. piniarius* rapidly increased from July 15 to August 14

Table 7. Abundance (no. ha^{-1}) of needle-eating insect larvae in a mature Scots pine (*Pinus sylvestris*) stand, Ih V(S), in 1974. Standard error within parentheses, $n = 10$[a].

Date of sampling	"Microlepidoptera"	Geometridae	Noctuidae	Lasiocampidae/ Sphingidae	Diprionidae	Total
May 20	33 140 (12 970)	2 570 (1 730)	4 070 (4 060)	0	0	39 710 (13 180)[d]
June 11	5 740 (2 310)	10 300 (3 640)[b]	0	0	19 150 (13 650)	35 040 (15 100)
June 26	1 940 (1 510)	2 090 (1 500)	2 850 (1 430)	0	12 920 (5 400)	19 800 (5 530)
July 15	0	680 (680)[b,c]	2 170 (1 160)	360 (360)	8 050 (1 760)	11 260 (2 550)[d,e]
July 30	0	8 060 (2 950)	0	230 (230)	14 290 (4 060)	22 580 (6 450)
Aug. 14	0	18 100 (4 080)[c]	0	1 280 (1 280)	12 000 (3 470)	31 380 (7 080)[e]
					28 640 (19 670)[f]	48 020 (23 120)[f]
Sept. 5	0	10 430 (3 420)	0	550 (550)	6 160 (3 630)	17 140 (6 110)
Oct. 2	0	6 840 (2 280)	0	0	0	6 840 (2 280)

[a] Temporal differences tested according to standard t-test (e.g., Snedecor & Cochran 1967: 100).
[b] June 11–July 15, $p < 0.02$.
[c] July 15–Aug. 14, $p < 0.001$.
[d] May 20–July 15, $p < 0.05$.
[e] July 15–Aug. 14, $p < 0.02$.
[f] Including *G. pallida* (see text).

282

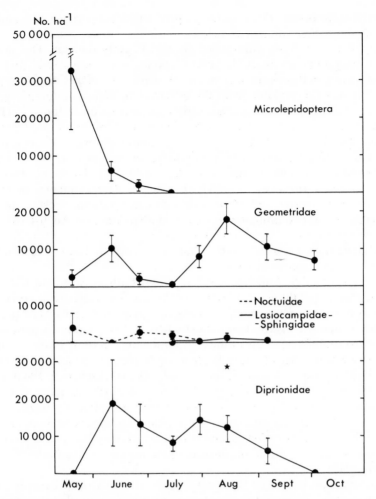

Figure 5. Abundance of needle-eating insect larvae in a mature Scots pine (*Pinus sylvestris*) stand, Ih V(S), in 1974. Vertical bars = s.e., * = abundance if a single find of a larval colony of *G. pallida* was included in the estimate.

when all eggs were hatched and a maxium of early instar larvae occurred on the foliage. From then onwards the population decreased almost equally rapidly to October 2 when the larvae had reached the last instar. The form of the abundance curve is very similar to that of a crashing population, depressed by starvation and enemies (cf. Subklew, 1939: 31), and a large proportion of the *B. piniarius* larvae collected on the two last sampling occasions of the present study (September 5 and October 2) succumbed from an unknown disease which may have contributed to the decrease of the population at Ivantjärnsheden. In a more "healthy" population the larvae suffer from high mortality when very young but in medium instars the number of larvae may remain rather constant until during the last instar, when mortality again increases (Subklew, 1939: 28, 49; Klomp, 1966: 221).

Only few larvae of the lasiocampid/sphingid group (*D. pini* and *H. pinastri*, respectively) were found. Data on faeces production support the low abundance figures found for these species (see below).

Young larvae of solitary diprionids appeared in early summer. The abundance reached a maximum on June 11. Several species were successfully reared from collections taken on this occasion, namely, *D. simile, M. pallipes, G. frutetorum* and *G. virens*. It was not possible from the estimates to demonstrate any significant changes in the sawfly abundance until the final decline on October 2. However, a considerable alteration of the species composition probably occurred during the season. This is supported by the rather different outcome of the rearings from the sampling on July 30, namely, *M. nemoralis, G. frutetorum, G. virens, G. variegata, G. pallida* and *G. polytoma*, compared to that on June 11. Thus, only two species, *G. frutetorum* and *G. virens*, were found both in early and late summer within the area. Numerically, *Gilpinia* spp. and *M. nemoralis* dominated during most of the season.

The higher of the two estimates of diprionid abundance on August 14 (Table 7, Fig. 5) originates from a single finding of a colony of *G. pallida*. This was the only record of gregarious species within the abundance study, indicating an insignificant occurrence of those species in 1974.

The occurrence of *G. frutetorum* and *G. virens* both in early and late summer evokes the question of the generation time of the sawflies. Most sawfly species found in this study have one or two generations a year, varying with climate and position of the locality within the distribution area (Escherich, 1942; Lorenz & Kraus, 1957). Fennoscandia is in the outskirts of the distribution area of some species, as revealed by the absence or scarcity of outbreaks (e.g., of *D. pini, D. simile*) and the existence of only one generation per year in, for example, *D. pini* (Escherich, 1942). Further, Hsin (1935) found that *G. frutetorum* and *G. virens* in northern Germany succeeded in producing two larval generations only during exceptionally warm years. In addition, in some species a prolonged eonymphal diapause is common, i.e., part of the population has an extended cocoon period, which may last one or several years before the emergence of the adults, instead of the normal 8–10 months of inactivity (Escherich, 1942).

Thus, it seems probable that the sawfly species at Ivantjärnsheden only have one generation a year, although this question must remain unsettled for the present. The long-lasting occurrence of diprionids may then be explained as being a protracted emergence of adults and egg-laying of some species (e.g., *G. frutetorum* and *G. virens*, cf. Hsin, 1935; Sturm, 1942), combined with the separate occurrence of early and late season species. The occurrence of members of one and the same generation may also be bi-modal, due to the existence of two strains of the species, e.g., by a prolonged eonymphal stage in one of the subpopulations (Escherich, 1942: 71–72).

If, finally, numbers are summarized over all groups (Table 7) two well defined abundance maxima can be discerned, one during spring and early summer, and one during late summer, the two being separated by a marked minimum in mid-season.

Consumption and faeces production

Data on faeces production and specific C/F ratios are the original information from which estimates on consumption are derived. Consumption, in turn, is used as a reference when grazing is evaluated (see below). The underlying assumption is that the use of faeces production as an index is a reliable method of estimating

Table 8. Temporal distribution of faeces production (upper figure) and consumption (lower figure) (kg dw ha^{-1}) for different groups of needle-eating insect larvae in a mature Scots pine (*Pinus sylvestris*) stand, Ih V(S), in 1974. Standard error within parentheses, $n=16$.

Time period	Geometridae	Noctuidae	Lasiocampidae/ Sphingidae	Diprionidae
May 28–June 5	0.040 (0.017)	0	0.066 (0.036)	0
	0.060 (0.026)	0	0.079 (0.044)	0
June 5–June 13	0.012 (0.005)	0	0.051 (0.028)	0
	0.018 (0.008)	0	0.061 (0.033)	0
June 13–June 25	0.040 (0.012)	0.026 (0.024)	0.013 (0.013)	0.005 (0.002)
	0.060 (0.018)	0.034 (0.031)	0.015 (0.015)	0.006 (0.003)
June 25–July 4	0.034 (0.012)	0.107 (0.022)	0.035 (0.021)	0.097 (0.017)
	0.051 (0.018)	0.140 (0.028)	0.045 (0.027)	0.116 (0.018)
July 4–July 10	0.054 (0.022)	0.064 (0.023)	0	0.135 (0.045)
	0.080 (0.034)	0.083 (0.029)	0	0.162 (0.055)
July 10–July 24	0.039 (0.014)	0.808 (0.213)	0.086 (0.079)	1.280 (0.165)
	0.059 (0.021)	1.050 (0.277)	0.120 (0.111)	1.536 (0.198)
July 24–Aug. 2	0.014 (0.004)	0.135 (0.037)	0.015 (0.011)	0.967 (0.120)
	0.022 (0.006)	0.175 (0.052)	0.020 (0.015)	1.160 (0.144)
Aug. 2–Aug. 12	0.032 (0.010)	0.052 (0.034)	0.037 (0.028)	1.186 (0.177)
	0.048 (0.015)	0.067 (0.044)	0.052 (0.040)	1.424 (0.213)
Aug. 12–Aug. 22	0.120 (0.011)	0.006 (0.006)	0.272 (0.122)	1.355 (0.188)
	0.180 (0.016)	0.007 (0.007)	0.381 (0.171)	1.626 (0.225)
Aug. 22–Sept. 2	0.258 (0.055)	0.006 (0.006)	0.130 (0.086)	1.221 (0.138)
	0.386 (0.082)	0.008 (0.008)	0.182 (0.120)	1.466 (0.165)
Sept. 2–Sept. 13	0.228 (0.062)	0.014 (0.014)	0.094 (0.071)	0.609 (0.082)
	0.342 (0.093)	0.018 (0.018)	0.131 (0.099)	0.730 (0.098)
Sept. 13–Sept. 23	0.447 (0.097)	0	0.040 (0.040)	0.137 (0.036)
	0.670 (0.146)	0	0.056 (0.056)	0.165 (0.043)
Sept. 23–Oct. 3	0.382 (0.099)	0	0	0.051 (0.016)
	0.573 (0.149)	0	0	0.061 (0.020)
Oct. 3–Oct. 14	0.126 (0.024)	0	0	0.020 (0.005)
	0.188 (0.035)	0	0	0.024 (0.006)
Oct. 14–Oct. 25	0.045 (0.013)	0	0	0.014 (0.007)
	0.068 (0.020)	0	0	0.017 (0.008)
Oct. 25–Nov. 5	0.004 (0.002)	0	0	0.005 (0.002)
	0.007 (0.003)	0	0	0.006 (0.002)
Total for all	1.872 (0.267)	1.216 (0.222)	0.837 (0.263)	7.081 (0.705)
periods	2.808 (0.400)	1.580 (0.288)	1.142 (0.368)	8.497 (0.846)

consumption. Thus, estimates on faeces production are of fundamental importance and the first step to be taken in the study of consumption dynamics. However, since consumption is of primary interest in this study it is treated first, and most of the feeding activities are presented and discussed in terms of consumption.

Data on consumption and faeces production, for each insect group and in total, are presented in Table 8 and Table 9, respectively. The faeces production will be discussed below in terms of transfer of bioelements.

Larvae of early geometrid species and of the lasiocampid/sphingid group started

Table 9. Temporal distribution of faeces production, consumption and green litter production (kg dw ha^{-1}), summarized for all groups of needle-eating insects, in a mature Scots pine (*Pinus sylvestris*) stand, Ih V(S), in 1974. Standard error within parentheses, $n = 16$.

Time period	Faeces production	Consumption	Green litter
May 28–June 5	0.106 (0.037)	0.139 (0.069)	no data
June 5–June 13	0.061 (0.027)	0.079 (0.041)	0.104 (0.068)[a]
June 13–June 25	0.083 (0.027)	0.115 (0.067)	0.156 (0.109)[a]
June 25–July 4	0.274 (0.035)	0.351 (0.091)	0.083 (0.055)
July 4–July 10	0.252 (0.057)	0.325 (0.117)	0.005 (0.003)
July 10–July 24	2.213 (0.317)	2.766 (0.607)	0.032 (0.022)
July 24–Aug. 2	1.131 (0.144)	1.377 (0.217)	0.400 (0.094)
Aug. 2–Aug. 12	1.307 (0.207)	1.590 (0.311)	0.192 (0.077)
Aug. 12–Aug. 22	1.752 (0.223)	2.193 (0.420)	0.248 (0.126)
Aug. 22–Sept. 2	1.615 (0.180)	2.042 (0.374)	0.014 (0.014)
Sept. 2–Sept. 13	0.944 (0.165)	1.222 (0.308)	0.017 (0.011)
Sept. 13–Sept. 23	0.624 (0.105)	0.891 (0.245)	0.018 (0.014)
Sept. 23–Oct. 3	0.433 (0.107)	0.635 (0.169)	0.149 (0.078)
Oct. 3–Oct. 14	0.145 (0.025)	0.212 (0.042)	0.032 (0.026)
Oct. 14–Oct. 25	0.059 (0.017)	0.085 (0.027)	0.012 (0.010)
Oct. 25–Nov. 5	0.009 (0.004)	0.012 (0.006)	0
Total for all periods	11.005 (1.169)	14.030 (1.517)	1.461 (0.237)

[a] Data from a nearby part of the stand, Ih V(A).

the feeding activity (Fig. 6) together with the mining microlepidopterous species (*Cedestis* spp., *O. piniariellum*) and young *P. flammea* larvae. The faeces of the mining species, however, are retained within the needles. Consumption of the lasiocampid/ sphingid group continued at a low rate until August when a maximum was reached, followed by a successive decline of the feeding, which stopped in the later half of September.

The feeding period of geometrids extended over five months. Consumption in early summer was caused by *Cidaria* spp., and later in the season mainly by *B. piniarius*, the consumption of which culminated in mid and late September. For *B. piniarius*, Schwerdtfeger (1930) demonstrated the large difference between "normal" feeding activity and the feeding activity of a succumbing larval population as indicated by frass-drop curves. In the former case, the feeding steadily accelerates until a sharp peak is reached at the end of the larval period when the larvae are full-grown. In the crashing population, the culmination of the feeding activity occurs earlier during the larval stage, thus explaining why the feeding curve becomes almost bell-shaped.

Accordingly, the early and smooth culmination of the late maximum found in the present study, points at a high mortality of medium instar *B. piniarius* larvae. Thus, both the abundance curve and the consumption curve strongly indicate a regressive phase in the population cycle of *B. piniarius* in 1974.

Consumption by noctuid larvae showed only one maximum, the result of feeding mainly by *P. flammea*. The recognizable feeding started late but may have commenced earlier than was possible to detect because of the frass-drop being trapped in the buds mined by the young larvae. The consumption culminated and fell

286

kg dw ha^{-1}day^{-1}

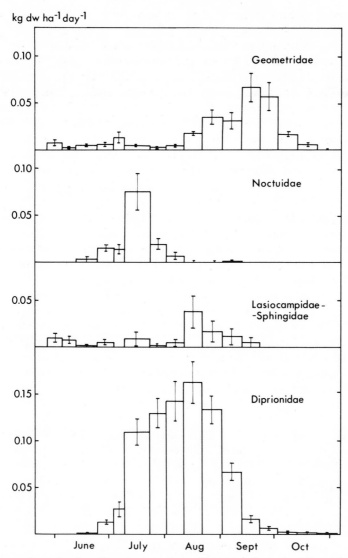

Figure 6. Consumption rates of needle-eating insect larvae in a mature Scots pine (*Pinus sylvestris*) stand, Ih V(S), in 1974. Width of columns = time period over which the rate is averaged. Vertical bars = s.e.

off rapidly in the second decade of July. However, still in September small amounts of faecal pellets similar to those of *P. flammea* were caught in the litter-traps.

The diprionid larvae started to feed rather late in the season, in late June and early July. The consumption rate rose rapidly but in contrast to the other groups the period of maximal feeding was protracted, lasting about two months, from early July to early September. As was suggested in the previous section, the long-lasting occurrence of sawfly larvae mainly is the result of several species replacing each other during the season.

The reliability of the consumption estimates of the four insect groups can to some

287

extent be tested against literature data on individual consumption of important representatives of each group.

According to consumption rates and larval numbers found in the present study, the average late instar larva of *B. piniarius* consumed 8 mg dw day^{-1} during the period from September 23 to October 3, i.e., a weight corresponding to one needle per day (cf. Albrektson & Andersson, 1978). For the same species, Oldiges (1959) found a consumption rate of 5.3 and 16.0 mg dw day^{-1} for a fourth and a fifth instar larva, respectively, at a temperature of $+14°C$, which is higher than the mean air temperature prevailing at Ivantjärnsheden in late September, 1974 (Fig. 2). In the same laboratory experiment, Oldiges (1959) demonstrated a positive relation between consumption rate and temperature. Thus, the lower value obtained in the present field study compared to that in Oldiges' experiment, may be explained by the lower temperature in the field than in the laboratory in these two studies.

From our field data the consumption rate of a late instar larva of *P. flammea* may be approximated at 35 mg dw day^{-1} during the period July 10–July 24. Oldiges (1959) gives the values of 17.4 and 47.0 mg dw day^{-1} for a fourth and a fifth instar larva, respectively, at a temperature of $+12°C$, which should be representative for the average temperature climate at Ivantjärnsheden in July 1974.

With regard to the *D. pini/H. pinastri* group, field data point at a maximal consumption rate of 25–35 mg dw day^{-1} larva^{-1}. This average "larva" is, however, rather complex. Of the two species of this group, *H. pinastri* has one generation per year, the larvae feeding during the second half of the summer until fullgrown in early autumn. The young *D. pini* larvae start to feed in the second half of the summer. In eastern Central Sweden, in the province of Uppland, the generation time may be one year; the larvae hibernate halfgrown (instar III and IV) and resume their feeding in the following spring. In western Central Sweden, in the province of Värmland, Grönberg (1903) found the generation time to be two years, the larvae hibernating twice and becoming fullgrown in early summer. During July to September, thus, mixed populations of young and older *D. pini* larvae may occur on the foliage together with *H. pinastri* larvae. In May and June hibernated *D. pini* larvae, possibly of different developmental stages, are alone responsible for the consumption.

According to Otto (1970), a third and fourth instar larva of *D. pini* may consume 14 and 27 mg dw day^{-1}, respectively. Data are lacking on consumption rates for *H. pinastri*. However, assuming a consumption capacity equal to that of *D. pini*, a fullgrown *H. pinastri* larva should consume about 122 mg dw day^{-1} (cf. Otto, 1970).

The consumption rate of a late instar diprionid larva was about 11 mg dw day^{-1} during September 2–September 13, which may be compared to 23.9 mg dw day^{-1} for an average *N. sertifer* larva during the last week of its actively feeding larval period (laboratory studies at a mean air temperature of $+17°C$; Larsson & Tenow, 1979).

Thus, for all four insect groups, the individual consumption rate, as calculated from the field data, was somewhat lower than that of an ultimate instar larva or was intermediary to those of larvae of different species as found in laboratory studies. This is what could be anticipated from the mixed age or species composition of the larval populations in the field, and sometimes much lower air temperature in the field than in the laboratory.

In Fig. 7, the consumption rates are pooled over all insect groups. Maximal rates averaged about 0.20 kg dw ha^{-1} day^{-1} in the second decade of July and the second decade of August.

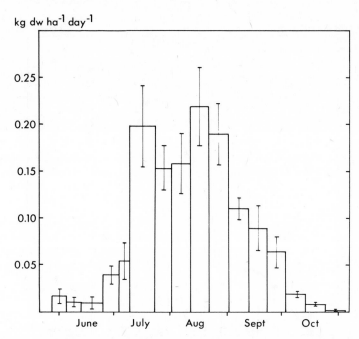

Figure 7. Overall consumption rate of needle-eating insect larvae in a mature Scots pine (*Pinus sylvestris*) stand, Ih V(S), in 1974. Width of columns = time period over which the rate is averaged. Vertical bars = s.e.

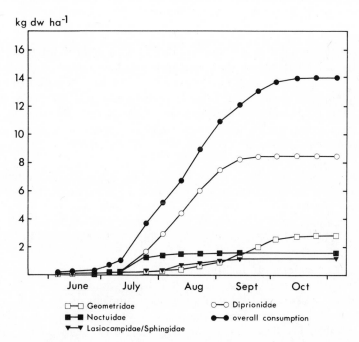

□—□ Geometridae   ○—○ Diprionidae
■—■ Noctuidae   ●—● overall consumption
▼—▼ Lasiocampidae/Sphingidae

Figure 8. Cumulative consumption of needle-eating insect larvae in a mature Scots pine (*Pinus sylvestris*) stand, Ih V(S), in 1974.

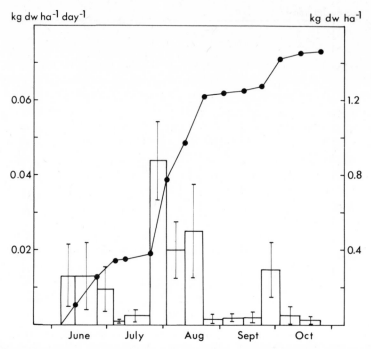

Figure 9. Green litter production, due to grazing of needle-eating insect larvae in a mature Scots pine (*Pinus sylvestris*) stand, Ih V(S), in 1974. Columns = rate of green litter production. Width of columns = time period over which the rate is averaged. Vertical bars = s.e. Curve = cumulative production of green litter.

Fig. 8 shows the cumulative consumption, both totally and for different consumer groups. At the end of the season the consumption had amounted to 14.0 (s.e. = 1.5) kg dw ha^{-1}. To this may be added 0.3 (s.e. = 0.1) kg dw ha^{-1} contributed by 33 000 microlepidopterous larvae ha^{-1} (cf. Table 7), each mining and consuming one needle (Trägårdh, 1911, 1915), weighing approximately 8 mg dw (cf. Albrektson & Andersson, 1978). As a group, the diprionids were the most important consumers in 1974, their consumption making up about 60% of the total consumption of needles (Tables 8 and 9).

Due to the close parallelity of the two feeding activities, consumption and defecation, most of the discussion on the dynamics of consumption is applicable to that of faeces production. Maximal faeces production occurred in the second decades of July and August, respectively, when rates of 0.16–0.17 kg dw ha^{-1} day^{-1} were reached. The total faeces production during the season was 11.0 (s.e. = 1.1) kg dw ha^{-1}.

Basic data on green litter production are given in Table 9, and Fig. 9 gives the drop rate and cumulative production of green litter during the feeding season. Prior to June 25, data are lacking and the series has been supplemented with data from a similar study made in a nearby part of the stand, Ih V(A). Three maxima in the drop rate are discernible. The first appeared in early June when *Dendrolimus pini* larvae and larvae of early geometrids are feeding, the second occurred in August, concurrent with the peak consumption of diprionid and sphingid larvae. The third maximum,

290

in late September, was caused by the peak feeding of *B. piniarius* larvae. The total green litter production for the whole feeding period was 1.5 (s.e. $= 0.2$) kg dw ha^{-1}.

To our knowledge only one study has been made on green litter production from grazing of Scots pine insects. Schwenke (1952), studying the assimilation efficiency of *B. piniarius* under semi-laboratory conditions, discriminated between consumption performed (*Frass*) and production of green litter (*Abbiss*), needle parts drying due to injury (*Trockniss*) and faeces (*Kot*), caused by the grazing activities during the whole feeding period. He found a green litter production of 5.9% of total grazing (*Frass* + *Abbiss*). If green litter is defined as *Abbiss* + *Trockniss*, the production was 17.2%. In our study the green litter production during the main feeding period of *B. piniarius* (September 13–November 5) amounted to 10.3% of the total grazing (consumption + green litter). Inevitably, some blown down *Trockniss* would have contributed to our green litter estimates.

For the main feeding period of diprionids (July 10–September 13), the corresponding value is 7.5%. This period also includes the main grazing of *P. flammea* (Noctuidae) and *D. pini* / *H. pinastri* (Lasiocampidae/Sphingidae) (see Fig. 6). The largest relative production of green litter (Table 9) occurred early in the season during the feeding of larvae of *Dendrolimus pini* and early season geometrids.

Bioelement transfers to the soil

The concentration of bioelements in faeces and green litter produced by insect larvae during grazing is given in Table 2. Applying these constants, the total input to the soil of C, N, P, K, Ca, Mg, S and Na in faeces is estimated at 5731, 75, 8, 40, 40, 7, 11 and 1 g ha^{-1}, respectively. Of the same elements 741, 17, 2, 8, 5, 1, 2 and 0.03 g ha^{-1} was transferred with green litter. Both transfers culminated during July and August (cf. Figs. 7 and 9).

The relative magnitude of this influx may be evaluated from a comparison with the average annual total litterfall from the stand, as estimated on Ih V(A) in 1973–76 (Bringmark, 1977). Thus, in 1974, faeces and green litter taken together transferred about 1% of the carbon, calcium and sodium, 2% of the nitrogen, phosphorus, magnesium and sulphur and 4% of the potassium, carried annually to the forest floor by total pine litter. This means a transference of the same order of magnitude as, for instance, the mean annual nutrient drop with pine cones (cf. Bringmark, 1977).

In addition, increased leaching losses of certain elements should be expected to occur from the damaged needles. Kimmins (1972) demonstrated this after a heavy defoliation of *N. sertifer*; experimentally inoculated cesium-134, used as a chemical analogue of potassium, was found to be more easily leached from the foliage of partly defoliated *Pinus resinosa* Ait. trees than from control trees. However, the magnitude of leaching varies according to, among other things, the amount of damaged needles, the element which is studied, and precipitation. To the total influx of bioelements, induced by grazing, may also be added the transfer with dried, damaged needles and defoliated needle sheaths which are abscissed with varying lengths of delay after the grazing injury. Normally, this transfer should be negligible, and neither it nor that occurring with leaching has been considered in the present study.

For further discussion concerning bioelement transfers, see below.

Table 10. Apparent grazing (kg dw ha^{-1}) on different age-classes of needles in a mature Scots pine (*Pinus sylvestris*) stand, Ih V(S), in 1974. Standard error within parentheses.

Date	*n*	Needle age-class			Total grazing
		1974	1973	"Older than 1973"	
June 11	6	no data*	4.1 (0.6)	17.4 (3.2)	21.5 (2.6)
Aug. 14	10	0.7 (0.1)	3.2 (0.5)	10.8 (1.9)	14.7 (2.3)
Sept. 5	9	0.4 (0.1)	2.6 (0.4)	7.6 (0.7)	10.6 (1.0)
Oct. 24	9	0.6 (0.2)	2.7 (0.8)	3.4 (0.5)	6.8 (1.3)

* Needles too young to be sampled.

Grazing dynamics

Grazing is here defined as the removal of leaf material (*MR*) from the foliage by leaf-eating insect larvae. It includes both leaf tissue actually consumed (*C*) and green leaf material not used (*NU*), so that $MR = C + NU$ (cf. Petrusewicz & Macfadyen, 1970). Thus, given $C = 14.0$ kg and $NU = 1.5$ kg, according to Table 9, *MR* for the whole feeding period in 1974 amounted to 15.5 kg dw ha^{-1}. The cumulative development of grazing should be the sum of the two curves for total consumption (Fig. 8) and green litter production (Fig. 9), respectively.

The cumulative grazing should also be possible to follow by sampling the foliage repeatedly during the season and estimating directly the *MR* on each sampling occasion. In Table 10 estimates of grazing in 1974 on different occasions and for different needle age-classes are given as obtained from the amount of damaged needles found in foliar columns taken with the skylift (Fig. 4). The season started with an *MR* of 21.5 kg dw ha^{-1} in all (June 11), which is larger than the total $C + NU$ for the whole season of 1974, 15.5 (see above). Then, paradoxically as it may seem, total *MR* gradually diminished to 6.8 kg dw ha^{-1} on October 24, in spite of the consumption process going on continuously during 1974.

A separation of *MR* over different needle age-classes shows that this decrease was mainly due to a large reduction in *MR* of the age category "older than 1973", the *MR* on younger needle age-classes being approximately constant throughout (Table 10).

When some of the needles "older than 1973" loosened from their shoot axes during handling some of the damaged needles also loosened, the amounts corresponding to *MR* of 0.4 (s.e. = 0.4), 3.5(0.7), 1.8(0.3) and 0.2(0.1) kg dw ha^{-1} on June 11, August 14, September 5 and October 24, respectively. Then, after adding these weights, the *MR* of needle age category "older than 1973" attains the constantly falling weights of 17.4, 10.8, 7.6 and 3.4 kg dw ha^{-1}, respectively, for the four successive sampling occasions.

According to data on faeces production, which is assumed to offer a reliable measure of consumption (see above), only 0.2 kg of needle tissue was consumed between May 28 and June 13. Besides, about 0.1 kg *NU* was produced (Table 9). Thus, a total of only about 0.3 kg dw ha^{-1} of needles was removed in 1974 between these two dates. In addition, some negligible grazing should have occurred early in the season, before trapping of litter started.

Accordingly, the high initial *MR* value of 17.4 kg is only explainable from a large

292

preservation of feeding marks on older needles, probably caused by a temporarily raised feeding activity during the preceding year(s) of one or a few species of the plot.

The above discussion on the initial MR value of needles "older than 1973" also applies to the MR of the 1973 needles. Needles of this age-class started the season with an MR of 4.1 kg of which maximally about 0.3 kg may have been caused in 1974, prior to June 11 (see above). Hence, the major part of this early MR was carried over from 1973.

The final MR of the needle age-classes "older than 1973" and 1973 was 3.4 and 2.7 kg dw ha^{-1}, respectively, on October 24. Then, the potential MR to be carried over to 1975, comparable with the 17.4 kg at the start of the 1974 season, was 6.1 kg dw ha^{-1}.

Why does MR remain constant (on the 1974 and 1973 needles) or diminish (on needles "older than 1973") in 1974, rather than accumulate during the season? During the larval stage of a leaf-eating insect more than 90% of its total consumption is performed during the last two instars (e.g., Axelsson et al., 1975). When doing their late instar feeding, most needle-eating insect larvae consume all of the grazed needle, leaving only a short stump closest to the sheath of the fascicle (e.g., Grönberg, 1903; Escherich, 1931, 1942; Monro, 1935; Nunberg, 1939). Further, it is well-known that severely damaged needles, inclusive of their sheaths, dry up and drop to the ground rather soon after the injury (e.g., Escherich, 1931, 1942) which, then, cannot be distinguished from normal shedding of needles. Thus, the answer to the question above is that grazed needles normally do not accumulate but are rapidly abscissed, and that the "pool" of MR in the foliage will remain constant when the production of MR equals the abscission and will decrease when abscission overtops production; the recognizable amount of grazing is only "apparent" grazing.

The extensive preservation of feeding marks, observed at Ivantjärnsheden at the start of the season in 1974, indicates a special situation where at least part of the grazing in previous year(s) was not severe enough to shorten the life of the needles very much. Some circumstances point at B. piniarius as the cause of this grazing. The young larvae feed only on one-year-old needles which they furrow longitudinally. From the fourth instar on, they eat both one-year-old and current-year needles which now become more severely damaged. The needles are gnawed laterally in their outer parts, from one or both sides so that an irregular, jagged edge of varying length is formed. Only when nearly fullgrown, may the larvae consume almost the whole needle, leaving a stump at the base (Holmgren, 1867; Escherich, 1931; Engel, 1939; Gruys, 1970). Thus, compared to many other species, B. piniarius devours its food less thoroughly (Trägårdh, 1939), leaving many needles only slightly damaged. As a consequence, the damaged needles remain attached to the foliage longer than usual (cf. Escherich, 1931).

Furthermore, in 1973, moths and larvae of B. piniarius were observed in considerable numbers in parts of Ivantjärnsheden and, being a late season species, it should have been the main attacker in autumn 1973 on the current-year needles of 1973. Finally, in 1974 the larval population of B. piniarius displayed characteristics of a crashing population (see above) which indicated an abundance peak prior to 1974. It is known that a population maximum of B. piniarius often lasts for 2–3 years (Eidmann & Klingström, 1976; cf. also Klomp, 1966).

Judging from these indications, it is concluded that the frequent grazing marks preserved to 1974, emanated from an earlier population maximum of B. piniarius.

At the beginning of the feeding period and during most of the summer in 1974, the needle age-class "older than 1973" was composed of needles mainly from 1972, 1971 and 1970, making up about 33, 20 and 10%, respectively, of the total needle biomass. Maximally, the needles may have carried feeding marks inflicted as early as 1970. Due to the different food preferences of different instars of *B. piniarius*, light, medium and severe injuries should be inflicted on one-year-old needles, and medium and severe injuries on current-year needles (cf. Escherich, 1931). Accordingly, at the start of the 1974 season extensive light and medium injuries may have been preserved on the 1972, 1971 and 1970 needle age-classes, and medium and severe injuries on the 1973 needles. The different degrees of damage, then, affected the longevity of the needles differently in 1974 so that the lightly and moderately damaged needles "older than 1973" should have been abscissed only slightly earlier than normally shed needles, while the severely injured needles of the 1973 age-class were dropped fairly early in 1974.

If total grazing and grazing dynamics are to be described, the abscission dynamics of damaged needles must be considered. It is reasonable to assume that the individual needles in a "cohort" of damaged needles are abscissed over a period of time, with the cumulative fall summing up sigmoidally until a hundred percent drop has occurred. Further, we know that such cohorts are continuously formed and abscissed during the season. Thus, a single observation of MR at the end of the season would seriously underestimate the total grazing. However, if the foliage is sampled several times at short enough intervals, underestimates of MR due to abscission during the sampling interval will be compensated for by MR "surviving" from previous sampling interval(s). If the length of the sampling interval equals the time taken for 50% of a single cohort of damaged needles to be abscissed (AT_{50}), this compensation will balance the underestimate, provided that the abscission time is short compared to the grazing season. Each estimate of MR, then, is an approximation of the grazing between two consecutive samplings and a measure of the total grazing is obtained by adding successive estimates.

Although very little precise information is available on the abscission rate, some data useful for the present study are available. In an investigation in 1976 by the present authors on the effect of consumption by *N. sertifer* larvae on the growth of 18-year-old Scots pine trees, observations were made on the drop of grazed needles. First instar larvae consume only the outer, parenchymous tissue of one-year-old needles, leaving the vascular bundle to wilt. This feeding behaviour continues for 10–12 days, thereafter the larvae consume the entire needle, leaving only short stumps near the sheath at the base of the fascicle. Both needles in a needle pair are grazed. The skeletonized needles soon dry up and are later abscissed together with their sheaths. Later the same happens to the needle stumps left by the older larvae. Fallen needles, eaten by first instar larvae are thus easily distinguished from those eaten by older larvae, and if collected beneath the tree, may indicate the abscission time. In our experiment, the time taken from the onset of feeding by newly hatched larvae to the first appearance of fallen, skeletonized needles, and from the onset of devouring of entire needles to the first appearance of fallen needle stumps, was in both cases about one month.

In a similar experiment with the same herbivore and host species, Wilson (1966) found the time interval between the cessation of feeding and the fall of the last needle stumps to be about two months. According to Trägårdh (1939), needles eaten by late

Table 11. Tentative model on insect grazing (kg dw ha^{-1}) on different needle age-classes of a mature Scots pine (*Pinus sylvestris*) stand, Ih V(S), in 1974. Standard error within parentheses. *n* according to Tables 9 and 10.

Time period	Needle age-class				Overall grazing according to litter-trap data[b]
	1974	1973	1974 + 1973	"Older than 1973"[a]	
–June 11	0	0.1[c]	0.1[c]	0.2[c]	0.3 (0.1)[d]
June 11–Aug. 14	0.7 (0.1)	3.2 (0.5)	3.9 (0.5)	3.5 (0.9)	7.4 (0.8)
Aug. 14–Sept. 5	0.4 (0.1)	2.6 (0.4)	3.0 (0.4)	1.5 (0.6)	4.5 (0.5)
Sept. 5–Oct. 24	0.6 (0.2)	2.7 (0.8)	3.3 (1.0)	0	3.3 (0.4)
June 11–Oct. 24	1.7 (0.2)[d]	8.5 (1.0)[d]	10.2 (1.2)[d]	5.0 (1.1)	15.2 (1.6)
Whole feeding season	1.7	8.6	10.3	5.2	15.5 (1.6)[d]

[a] Grazing according to litter-trap data minus grazing on needle age-classes 1974 + 1973. Standard error calculated according to Hansen *et al.* (1953: 513–514).
[b] Consumption plus green litter, cf. Table 9.
[c] Assumed grazing, derived from litter-trap data.
[d] Standard error calculated according to Hansen *et al.* (1953: 513–514).

instar larvae of *B. piniarius* dry up in their grazed outer part while the undamaged basal part remains green, at least until late autumn, but fall off during winter or the following spring.

The abscission time may thus depend on the time of the year and the type of grazer. The age of the needles and of the tree, as well as the weather, may also modify the abscission process.

According to referred observations, AT_{50} during summer can be set at around 1.5 months. Because the mean sampling interval used in this study was 45 days and as a retarded abscission in late autumn 1974 should not influence our estimate much, we believe it is possible to obtain an approximation on grazing dynamics and annual MR for needle age-classes 1974 and 1973 by adding the apparent MR values for the different sampling occasions.

However, this method is not applicable to the found MR of needle age-class "older than 1973". As stated earlier, needles of this age-class carried a considerable MR from previous year(s), most probably caused by an increased grazing of *B. piniarius* at that time. Although decreasing, part of this MR was preserved throughout the season, concealing the MR originated during 1974. Instead, the MR of needle age-class "older than 1973", on each sampling occasion and totally, can be approximated by subtracting the found MR of needle age-classes 1974 and 1973 from the total grazing ($MR = C + NU$), established from litter-trap data.

Thus, referring to the discussion above, the following assumptions and simplifications are made when constructing the tentative model for MR dynamics in 1974, presented in Table 11:

(1) AT_{50} for all damaged needles was 1.5 months during the whole feeding period. If a sampling interval of 45 days is used, the successive MRs of needle age-classes 1974 and 1973, respectively, are then additive.
(2) Separate values of MR are somewhat underestimated (August 14 and October 24)

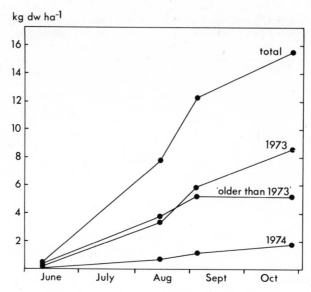

kg dw ha⁻¹

Figure 10. Cumulative grazing of insect larvae, totally and on different needle age-classes, in a mature Scots pine (*Pinus sylvestris*) stand, Ih V(S), in 1974.

or overestimated (September 5) due to sampling intervals deviating from AT_{50}. However, over- and underestimates approximately balance each other on an annual basis.

(3) The indirect method of estimating grazing from data on faeces and green litter production ($MR = C + NU$) is valid and sufficiently reliable to serve as a reference when evaluating direct estimates of MR and deducing grazing in 1974 on the needle age-class "older than 1973".

(4) Due to severe damage (caused by late instar larvae of *B. piniarius*) most MR of needle age-class 1973, carried over from 1973 to 11 June 1974, was dropped prior to the next sampling occasion (August 14).

(5) With the small endemic grazer populations prevailing in 1974, only insignificant amounts of MR on needle age-classes 1974 and 1973 were carried forward in a "permanent pool" of damage during the season, thus causing little or no overestimation of MR.

(6) Of the initial MR of needle age-class 1973 (4.1 kg), 0.1 kg is set as the result of grazing during spring and early summer up to June 11. Similarly, 0.2 kg is assumed to have been removed from age-class "older than 1973".

The grazing model for 1974 (Table 11) shows that 1.7, 8.6 and 5.2 kg dw ha⁻¹ were removed from the needle age-classes 1974, 1973 and "older than 1973", respectively. The cumulative grazing on each age-class as well as totally, is indicated in Fig. 10. As seen, grazing on current-year needles accumulated rather slowly compared to grazing on the 1973 needles. Further, while grazing on the two younger needle age-classes accumulated at a fairly constant rate during the whole season, grazing on needles "older than 1973" first increased constantly, with a rate as for grazing on the 1973 needles, then ceased to increase from early September when the grazing rate

296

reached zero. It is interesting to note that when this occurred, consumption of the most important consumer group, the diprionids, ceased and was succeeded by the accelerating consumption of *B. piniarius* (Fig. 6) which feeds mainly on current-year and one-year-old needles.

Some of the assumptions underlying this model are uncertain, e.g., that on abscission time. Here, the assumption of too high an abscission rate will lead to an overestimation of grazing on needle age-classes 1974 and 1973 and, consequently, to an underestimation of that on needles "older than 1973". Thus, with an AT_{50} of 2 months instead of 1.5, grazing on needle age-classes 1974, 1973 and "older than 1973" should have been 1.3, 6.0 and 8.2 kg dw ha^{-1}, respectively, according to our data (excluding the estimate of September 5 to simulate a two-month sampling interval).

Significance of grazing

Fig. 11 is a schematic representation of the needle biomass, annual grazing and needle litterfall, as estimated in the present study. Related to the October needle biomasses, 0.3, 1.1 and 0.7% were grazed of the needle age-classes 1974, 1973 and "older than 1973", respectively. Total grazing, 15.5 kg dw ha^{-1} (exclusive of consumption by mining insects), corresponds to 0.7% of the total October needle biomass (2201 kg dw ha^{-1}) or 2.5% of the 1974 production of new foliage (626 kg dw ha^{-1}). Of the total amount of grazed needles, 10% dropped to the ground as green litter and of the amount actually consumed by non-mining insects (14.0 kg dw ha^{-1}), 79% was, by definition, released to the soil as faeces.

The total amount of grazing, corresponding to 2.5% of annual needle production, is in accordance with the degree of consumption estimated by Reichle *et al.* (1973) and Nielsen (1978), 2.6% and 3%, respectively, in deciduous forests. A grazing of the same order of intensity was also observed by Schroeder (1978) on *Prunus serotina* Ehrh. in a mixed deciduous forest. Higher values (5.0–7.7%) recorded in some other studies during endemic grazing conditions (e.g., Bray, 1964; Reichle & Crossley, 1967) might have been overestimates due to leaf-hole expansion after insect feeding (Reichle *et al.*, 1973). Using faeces production as an index of consumption, Gosz *et al.* (1972) found a 1.8% consumption of annual leaf production in a mixed deciduous – coniferous forest and, with similar methods, Kaczmarek (1967) estimated a preliminary consumption figure of 9.2% in a Scots pine forest, based on energetical data.

Thus, whether it be a deciduous or a coniferous forest, and despite large differences in annual production of leaf biomass between and within these forest types, chronic consumption seems to vary within remarkably restricted limits, removing photosynthetic tissue corresponding to less than 10% of the new foliage.

Artificial defoliation experiments with Scots pine trees have shown that aboveground growth losses first occur at high defoliation degrees (Ericsson *et al.*, 1980). Further, the results indicate that this "tolerance" may be due to the existence of compensating mechanisms in the tree, which efficiently reduce the effects of defoliation. The compensation was shown to be more effective when the trees were deprived of their older needles (early in the season) than when the current-year needles were defoliated.

Accordingly, the low degree of grazing on Ivantjärnsheden in 1974, with the largest impact probably on one-year-old needles, could reasonably be considered to have

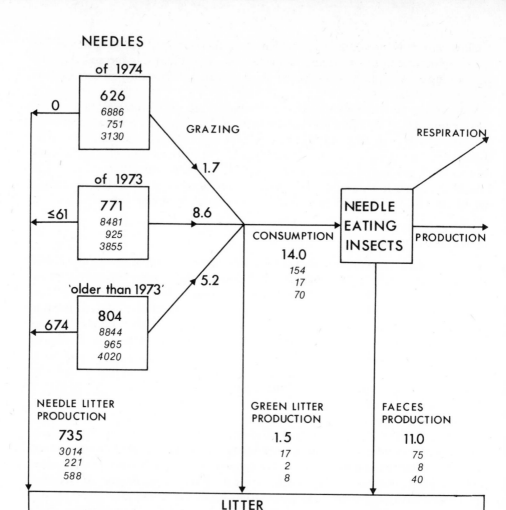

NEEDLES

Figure 11. Schematic representation of needle biomasses and transfers of dry matter and some bio-elements, due to grazing of needle-eating insects and normal needle litterfall in a mature Scots pine (*Pinus sylvestris*) stand, Ih V(S), in 1974. Needle biomass weights are for October, 1974, and transfers are on an annual basis. For the biomasses of the 1974 and 1973 needles, weight reductions of 0% and 10% (at the most), due to normal litterfall, are assumed. The weight reduction of needle biomass "older than 1973" is calculated according to Table 3. Figures on needle litterfall are corrected for a 28.8% weight reduction, due to withdrawal of nutrients (according to Stachurski & Zimka, 1975). Bold figures; kg dw ha^{-1}; italics: g ha^{-1} of nitrogen, phosphorus and potassium (read top-down).

had no significant, direct effects on total photosynthetic production and subsequent growth of the trees. The low grazing degrees commonly met with demonstrate that this is probably the normal situation.

Embedded in the grazed needles, a part of the bioelement content of the ecosystem is circulated through the consumer chain (Fig. 11). Totally the trees lost 170 g ha^{-1} of nitrogen, of which 154 g was consumed and the rest fell to the ground with green litter. Following ingestion a further 75 g was defecated and the remaining 79 g should

Table 12. Approximate weights of needle-eating insect larvae on Scots pine (*Pinus sylvestris*), used when calculating larval standing crop.

Date of sampling	Species (instar)	Weight (g dw ind^{-1})	Reference
July 15	*P. flammea* (V)	0.057[a]	Oldiges (1959)
	Dendrolimus pini (III)	0.153 (0.020)[b]	Present study
	Cidaria spp. (ultimate)	0.015 (0.002)[b]	Present study
	Gilpinia spp. (IV, V)	0.025 (0.004)[b]	Present study
Sept. 5	*H. pinastri* (V)	0.598[a]	Schwerdtfeger (1952)
	B. piniarius (III, IV)	0.006[c]	Gruys (1970)
	Gilpinia spp. (IV, V)	0.025 (0.004)[b]	Present study
Oct. 2	*B. piniarius* (IV, V)	0.020[c]	Gruys (1970)

[a] Calculated from pupal live weight, assuming a dry weight/live weight ratio of 0.286 (cf. Hågvar & Østbye, 1974).

[b] Oven-dried, 48 hours at 85°C. Standard error within parentheses, $n=6$.

[c] Calculated from larval live weight, assuming a dry weight/live weight ratio of 0.208 (cf. Smith, 1972; Haukioja & Niemelä, 1974; Hågvar & Østbye, 1974), a sex ratio of 1:1 and an instar ratio of 1:1.

be dispersed with secondary consumers, carcasses and surviving specimens.

Of the amount of fallen needles, green litter and faeces (748 kg dw ha^{-1}), the two latter fractions together constituted 1.7% of the total dry weight. However, as the concentration of nitrogen in green litter and faeces is higher than in shed needles (Table 2), the transfer of nitrogen to the soil with green litter and faeces will be higher, making up 2.9% of the nitrogen content of the total litter that originated annually from the needle biomass.

Most of this transfer occurred during summer when needle litterfall was minimal. Concerning this period (July 10–September 2), nitrogen transfer with green litter and faeces constituted as much as 8.0% of the total nitrogen of foliar origin. Further, the material is distributed over the ground as small pellets and fragments which are minute in comparison with fallen needle pairs.

The effect of this transfer of nitrogen and of other bioelements on soil processes is unknown. Further, other constituents may be of importance, e.g., cellulose and soluble carbohydrates may constitute about one-third and 2–5%, respectively, of the total weight of faeces (Otto, 1970; Otto & Geyer, 1970). However, the amount of nitrogen, phosphorus, potassium and other bioelements in grazing litter is large enough to warrant attention when soil processes are studied (cf. Owen & Wiegert, 1976).

The occasional outbreaks of needle-eating insects will radically reduce the needle biomass of the pine forest. Thus, applying the consumption/defecation ratio used in this study to the figures on faeces production by *B. piniarius* in an outbreak situation as reported by Schwerdtfeger (1930: Fig. 8, p. 88), gives a consumption estimate of 2 100 kg dw ha^{-1}, which indicates a severe defoliation of the forest. In addition, the transfer of grazing litter to the soil should imply an impact on the soil processes. In this case, still assuming that our data are valid (cf. Table 2), the frass-drop alone would add to the soil 14.3, 1.5 and 7.6 kg ha^{-1} of nitrogen, phosphorus and potassium, respectively, during the 85 days period of *B. piniarius* consumption.

There are no direct estimates of mean standing crop or annual production of larvae on Ih V(S). However, the standing crop may be approximated from our field data

Table 13. Food preferences of some insect larvae feeding on needles of Scots pine (*Pinus sylvestris*). C=current-year needles; C+ =needles older than current; C+1 and C+2=one-year-old and two-year-old needles, respectively; − =no information available.

	Needle age-class				Reference
	C	C+	C+1	C+2	
Cedestis spp.	−	×	−	−	Trägårdh (1911, 1915)
C. firmata	−	×	×	×	Larsson & Tenow (present study)
E. fasciaria	−	×	−	−	Escherich (1931)
S. liturata	−	×	−	−	Schwenke (1978)
B. piniarius	×	×	×	−	Escherich (1931), Engel (1939)
P. flammea	×	×	×	−	Escherich (1931), Schwerdtfeger (1970)
Dendr. pini	×	×	×	−	Grönberg (1903)
H. pinastri	−	×	−	−	Nunberg (1939)
Diprion pini	×	×	×	−	Escherich (1942)
D. simile	−	×	−	−	Monro (1935)
N. sertifer	−	×	×	×	Escherich (1942)
M. pallipes	×	×	×	×	Eidmann & Klingström (1976)
G. frutetorum	−	×	×	−	Escherich (1942)

on abundance (Table 7), combined with data on individual weights of important species (Table 12). With few exceptions, available weight data are on fullgrown specimens. Therefore, calculations must be restricted to sampling occasions when most larvae of current populations were nearly fullgrown or else determined to instars, *viz.*, 15 July, 5 September and 2 October 1974.

Accordingly, the standing crop was 0.4, 0.5 and 0.1 kg dw ha^{-1}, respectively, on the three sampling occasions.

On pine/insect relationships

In both coniferous and deciduous forests the phenology of the foliage may be divided into three parts: (1) the juvenile phase of developing leaves; (2) the mature phase of medium-aged leaves with a high level of photosynthesis; (3) the senescent phase of old leaves with diminishing photosynthesis, ended by withdrawal of important nutrients and abscission.

In a pine forest, the generation time of needles is prolonged over several years in contrast to that of the annual leaves of deciduous forests. Thus, in the Scots pine forest at Ivantjärnsheden the juvenile period can be considered to be terminated in early autumn when current-year needles are full-grown (cf. Fig. 3) and succeeded by the mature phase, which at least lasts for the following year. The senescent phase, then, makes up the remaining time until the needles fall (cf. Linder & Troeng, 1980).

In a deciduous forest a seasonal grouping of insects coincides with a grouping according to host tree phenology, i.e., spring species always feed on young leaves and summer species most often on mature leaves. In a pine forest, due to the contemporary occurrence of needles of different age-classes, insects occurring in the same season may feed on needles of different age, while on the other hand insects occurring in different seasons may feed on needles of the same year-class. Therefore, along with a seasonal grouping of needle-eating insects, a different grouping in relation to the phenological stage of their food may be applied.

Accordingly, young larvae of, for example, *P. flammea* occurring in spring and *B. piniarius* larvae in autumn both feed on current-year needles and, similarly, the early summer and late summer waves of diprionids both feed on one-year-old needles (Table 13). Further, one and the same species, like larvae of *P. flammea* and *Dendrolimus pini*, change their food preference when growing and, thus, should belong first to one phenological group and later to another.

Feeny (1970) attributes the successive occurrence of insect groups in oak forests to the adaptations of the insects to seasonal changes of the chemical composition of the foliage, e.g., its content of tannins and available nitrogen. According to current theory (Feeny, 1976; Rhoades & Cates, 1976), compounds like tannins and other phenolic compounds are chemical defences, evolved in the plant as a reaction to the feeding pressure of insects. Moreover, in the oak leaves the content of tannins increases as the season progresses (Feeny, 1970). Consequently, counter-adaptation of the insect should lead either to the timing of feeding with the leafing out of the foliage or to the coping with the defence mechanisms of the host. Of these alternatives, the first one seems to have been most successful. Thus, of oak insects the spring group is the most abundant and species-rich (Feeny, 1970), and normally in deciduous forests the abundance of larvae and the consumption rate seem to be highest during the first half of the summer (e.g., Rothacker *et al.*, 1954; Feeny, 1970; Patočka & Čapek, 1971; Reichle *et al.*, 1973; Rafes & Sokolov, 1976; Kaczmarek & Wasilewski, 1977). One exception is feeders on leaves of black cherry (*Prunus serotina* Ehrh.), the consumption of which culminates in late July, as demonstrated by Schroeder (1978). Cyanide may be a deterrent to feeding by larvae on black cherry leaves but, unlike tannins in oak leaves, its potential is high early in the season and declines as the cherry leaves mature. Accordingly, the feeding of larvae on black cherry would be low early in the season and would increase as the cyanide concentration declines (Schroeder, 1978).

In the same way, many needle-eating insects may have evolved feeding adaptations according to the phenology of the host tree. However, information on the preference of the larvae for different needle age-classes of food is only scarce and subordinate. In Table 13 a survey is given of food preferences for species found in this study, according to existing literature data. For some of the species, no information exists; however, of these the early occurring *C. obeliscata* and *Gilpinia* spp. larvae most probably feed on older needles, as also their relatives *C. firmata* and *G. frutetorum*. All of the listed species feed on older needles, preferably one-year-olds. A minor part also feed on needles of the current season. Most of the latter species either do so late in the season when the new needles are becoming fully grown (*B. piniarius*, *Diprion pini*, *M. pallipes*) or they have the special habit of mining needles and buds (*P. flammea*). This information reveals little about the quantitative distribution of grazing on different needle age-classes and, instead, the grazing distribution may be considered from a general point of view.

Pine needles contain several kinds of acidic resins, which generally are considered as defensive against insects. In this respect, there are obvious differences between the new needles and the older ones. The flow of resin from damaged current-year needles may be twice as intense as that from one-year-old needles (Otto & Geyer, 1970). There are probably also qualitative differences. In experiments with two sawfly species which feed on mature needles of Jack pine (*Pinus banksiana* Lambert),

301

it was demonstrated that the concentration of the most effective deterrent compound of the resin was much higher in juvenile needles than in mature ones and efficiently prevented feeding. Feeding did not commence until late in the season when the concentration within the maturing needle gradually had sunk to a tolerable level, which was characteristically different for the two species (Ikeda et al., 1977). If forced to feed on juvenile needles, the larvae suffered from an extended larval period, reduced body size and higher mortality (All & Benjamin, 1975).

On the other hand, the content of water (Beckwith, 1976), soluble carbohydrates (Ericsson, 1979) and vital nutrients as nitrogen, phosphorus and potassium (Tamm, 1955; Aronsson et al., 1977) are lower in older conifer needles than in younger ones, while lignification has an opposite trend (Fogal, 1974). Beckwith (1976) could demonstrate that larvae of the Douglas-fir tussock moth (Orgyia pseudotsugata McDunnough) which is adapted to feed on the new needles of Douglas fir (Pseudotsuga menziesii Franco) and some other fir species (Abies spp.), experienced increases in development time, frass production and number of instars, and a decreased head capsule size and egg production when forced to feed on old-growth foliage. Larvae, stressed in this way, should consequently suffer from a higher mortality than normally fed ones.

The needle-eating insects are thus affected by two main quality changes of the needles: the content of noxious compounds which decreases with the age of the needles and which forces the insects to feed on older needles, and the continuous nutritive deterioration of the needles with age, which forces the insects to feed on younger needles. Hypothetically, then, feeding should be directed to the medium-aged needles where, consequently, a more intense grazing should most often be encountered.

These conclusions are consistent with the observed distribution of grazing on different needle age-classes put forward in Table 11 and Fig. 10. According to these data, 11% of the total grazing in 1974 was performed on the current-year needles, 55% on one-year-old needles and 34% on two-year-old and older needles. The distribution of grazing over needle age-classes will vary from year to year. However, a dominant grazing on current-year needles implies high abundance of, e.g., B. piniarius larvae which feed on current and one-year-old needles (Table 13) and should occur only infrequently.

Thus, literature data on food preferences, information on nutritive qualities of needles, and field data of the present study, indicate that grazing here, as in most deciduous forests, mainly is directed towards foliage of a certain phenological phase. The preferred foliage, however, appears to be different for the two types of forests, mostly being the lush, early season leaves in the deciduous forest and the medium-aged needles in the pine forest, as probably in most coniferous forests.

Acknowledgements

Messrs. B. Cederberg, C. Swensson, A. Wirén, Uppsala and members of the staff of the Jädraås Ecological Station assisted in the field and in the laboratory. Miss B. Henriksson, Stockholm, made the final laboratory studies, tabular calculations and the drawings. Prof. P. Seeger and Fil. mag. B. Vegerfors-Persson, Dept. of Economics and Statistics, Swedish University of Agricultural Sciences, Uppsala, formulated the statistical instruments and assisted in the evaluation of data, respectively.

Forest Officer I. Svensson, Kristianstad, determined the microlepidopterous specimens, Dr. S. Jonsson, Dept. of Entomology, Uppsala University, and Dr. M. Viitasaari, Dept. of Agricultural and Forest Zoology, University of Helsinki, determined the sawflies. Dr. J. G. K. Flower-Ellis, Dept. of Forest Site Research, Swedish University of Agricultural Sciences, Umeå, put at our disposal data on the pine stand at Ivantjärnsheden. Dr. B. Långström, Dept. of Forest Entomology, Swedish University of Agricultural Sciences, Garpenberg, and several colleagues within the Swedish Coniferous Forest Project read the manuscript and suggested improvements. We are sincerely grateful to all of them. The two authors contributed equally to each phase of the study: the planning, performance, analysis and reporting.

References

Albrektson, A. 1980. Total tree production as compared to conventional forestry production. – In: Persson, T. (ed.) Structure and Function of Northern Coniferous Forests – An Ecosystem Study, Ecol. Bull. (Stockholm) 32: 315–327.

Albrektson, A. & Andersson, B. 1978. Biomass in an old mixed coniferous forest in Dalarna. – Swed. Conif. For. Proj. Int. Rep. 79, 40 pp. (In Swedish, English abstract)

All, J. N. & Benjamin, D. M. 1975. Influence of needle maturity on larval feeding preference and survival of *Neodiprion swainei* and *N. rugifrons* on Jack pine, *Pinus banksiana*. – Ann. Entomol. Soc. Am. 68: 579–584.

Aronsson, A., Elowson, S. & Ingestad, T. 1977. Elimination of water and mineral nutrition as limiting factors in a young Scots pine stand. I. Experimental design and some preliminary results. – Swed. Conif. For. Proj. Tech. Rep. 10, 38 pp.

Axelsson, B. & Bråkenhielm, S. 1980. Investigation sites of the Swedish Coniferous Forest Project – biological and physiographical features. – In: Persson, T. (ed.) Structure and Function of Northern Coniferous Forests – An Ecosystem Study, Ecol. Bull. (Stockholm) 32: 25–64.

Axelsson, B., Lohm, U., Persson, T. & Tenow, O. 1974. Energy flow through a larval population of *Phytodecta pallidus* L. (Col., Chrysomelidae) on *Corylus avellana* L. II. Population energy budget. – Zoon 2: 153–160.

Axelsson, B., Lohm, U., Nilsson, A., Persson, T. & Tenow, O. 1975. Energetics of a larval population of *Operophthera* spp. (Lep., Geometridae) in Central Sweden during a fluctuation low. – Zoon 3: 71–84.

Beckwith, R. C. 1976. Influence of host foliage on the Douglas-fir tussock moth. – Environ. Entomol. 5: 73–77.

Bray, J. R. 1964. Primary consumption in three forest canopies. – Ecology 45: 165–167.

Bringmark, L. 1977. A bioelement budget of an old Scots pine forest in Central Sweden. – Silva fenn. 11: 201–209.

Carlisle, A., Brown, A. H. F. & White, E. J. 1966. Litter fall, leaf production and the effects of defoliation by *Tortrix viridana* in a sessile oak (*Quercus petraea*) woodland. – J. Ecol. 54: 65–85.

Cochran, W. G. 1963. Sampling Techniques, 2nd ed. New York–London–Sydney: Wiley & Sons, 391 pp.

Eckstein, K. 1937. Zoologische Beobachtungen. *Lophyrus-* (*Diprion-*) Frass an Kiefer und Fichte. – Forst. Wschr. Silva 25: 29–32.

Eckstein, K. 1938. Die Bewertung des Kotes der Nonnenraupe *Psilura monacha* Z., als Grundlage für die Feststellung ihres Auftretens und der zu ergreifenden Massregeln. – Allg. Forst Jagdztg 114: 132–148.

Eckstein, K. 1939. Exkremente und Bohrmehl forstschädlicher Insekten. – In: Jordan, K. & Hering, E. M. (eds.) Verh. VII. Intern. Kongr. Ent., Bd III, pp. 1930–1940. Weimar: G. Uschmann.

Eidmann, H. H. & Klingström, A. 1976. Skadegörare i skogen. Borås: LTs Förlag, 288 pp. (In Swedish)

Engel, H. 1939. Beiträge zur Biologie des Kiefernspanners (*Bupalus piniarius* L.). – Mitt. Forstw. Forstwiss. 10: 51–64.

Engel, H. 1941. Beiträge zur Faunistik der Kiefernkronen in verschiedenen Bestandstypen. – Mitt. Forstw. Forstwiss. 12: 334–361.

Ericsson, A. 1979. Effects of fertilization and irrigation on the seasonal changes of carbohydrate reserves in different age-classes of needles on 20-year-old Scots pine trees (*Pinus silvestris*). – Physiol. Plant. 45: 270–280.

Ericsson, A., Hellkvist, J., Hillerdal-Hagströmer, K., Larsson, S., Mattson-Djos, E. & Tenow, O. 1980. Consumption and pine growth. Hypotheses on effects on growth processes by needle-eating insects. – In: Persson, T. (ed.) Structure and Function of Northern Coniferous Forests – An Ecosystem Study, Ecol. Bull. (Stockholm) 32: 537–545.

Escherich, K. 1931. Die Forstinsekten Mitteleuropas, 3. Bd. Berlin: Verlag Paul Parey, 825 pp.

Escherich, K. 1942. Die Forstinsekten Mitteleuropas, 5. Bd. Berlin: Verlag Paul Parey, 746 pp.

Feeny, P. 1970. Seasonal changes in oak leaf tannins and nutrients as a cause of spring feeding by Winter moth caterpillars. – Ecology 51: 565–581.

Feeny, P. 1976. Plant apparency and chemical defense. – In: Wallace, J. W. & Mansell, R. L. (eds.) Biochemical Interaction between Plants and Insects, Rec. Adv. Phytochem., Vol. 10, pp. 1–40. New York–London: Plenum Press.

Flower-Ellis, J. G. K. & Olsson, L. 1978. Litterfall in an age series of Scots pine stands and its variation by components during the years 1973–1976. – Swed. Conif. For. Proj. Tech. Rep. 15, 62 pp.

Fogal, W. H. 1974. Nutritive value of pine foliage for some diprionid sawflies. – Proc. Entomol. Soc. Ont. 105: 101–118.

Fogal, W. H. & Kwain, M.-J. 1972. Host plant nutritive value and variable number of instars in a sawfly, *Diprion similis*. – Isr. J. Ent. 7: 63–72.

Gösswald, K. 1934. Über die Frasstätigkeit von Forstschädlingen unter dem Einfluss von Altersunterschieden und der Einwirkung verschiedener Temperatur und Luftfeuchtigkeit und ihre praktische und physiologische Bedeutung. 1. Untersuchung an *Dendrolimus pini* L. – Z. Angew. Entomol. 21: 183–207.

Gosz, J. R., Likens, G. E. & Bormann, F. H. 1972. Nutrient content of litter fall on the Hubbard Brook experimental forest, New Hampshire. – Ecology 53: 769–784.

Grimm, R. 1973. Zum Energieumsatz phytophager Insekten im Buchenwald. I. Untersuchungen an Populationen der Rüsselkäfer (Curculionidae) *Rhynchaenus fagi* L., *Strophosomus* (Schönherr) und *Otiorrhynchus singularis* L. – Oecologia (Berl.) 11: 187–262.

Grönberg, G. 1903. Tallspinnaren, *Lasiocampa pini* (L.), dess naturhistoria och fiender, samt medel mot densamma. – Tidskr. Skogshushålln. 31: 195–214. (In Swedish)

Gruys, P. 1970. Growth in *Bupalus piniarius* (Lepidoptera: Geometridae) in relation to larval population density. – Rijksinst. Natuurbeheer, Verh. 1, 127 pp.

Hågvar, S. & Østbye, E. 1974. Oxygen consumption, caloric values, water and ash content of some dominant terrestrial arthropods from alpine habitats at Finse, south Norway. – Nor. Entomol. Tidsskr. 21: 117–126.

Hansen, M. H., Hurwitz, W. N. & Madow, W. G. 1953. Sample survey methods and theory. I. Methods and applications. New York–London–Sydney: Wiley & Sons, 638 pp.

Haukioja, E. & Niemelä, P. 1974. Growth and energy requirements of the larvae of *Dineura virididorsata* (Retz.) (Hym., Tenthredinidae) and *Oporinia autumnata* (Bkh.) (Lep., Geometridae) feeding on birch. – Ann. Zool. Fennici 11: 207–211.

Holmgren, A. E. 1867. De för träd och buskar nyttiga och skadliga insekterna jemte utrotningsmedel för de sednare. Stockholm: Bonnier, 362 pp. (In Swedish)

Höregott, H. 1960. Untersuchungen über die qualitative und quantitative Zusammensetzung der Arthropodenfauna in den Kiefernkronen. – Beitr. Entomol. 10: 891–916.

Hsin, C. S. 1935. Beiträge zur Naturgeschichte der Blattwespen. – Z. Angew. Entomol. 22: 253–294.

Ikeda, T., Matsumura, F. & Benjamin, D. M. 1977. Mechanism of feeding discrimination between matured and juvenile foliage by two species of pine sawflies. – J. Chem. Ecol. 3: 677–694.

Kaczmarek, W. 1967. Elements of organization in the energy flow of forest ecosystems (preliminary notes). – In: Petrusewicz, K. (ed.) Secondary Productivity of Terrestrial Ecosystems, Principles and Methods, Vol. 2., pp. 663–678. Warszawa–Kraków: Państwowe Wydawnictwo Naukowe.

Kaczmarek, M. & Wasilewski, A. 1977. Dynamics of numbers of the leaf-eating insects and its effect on foliage production in the "Grabowy" reserve in the Kampinos national park. – Ekol. pol. 25: 653–673.

Kimmins, J. P. 1972. Relative contributions of leaching, litter-fall and defoliation by *Neodiprion sertifer* (Hymenoptera) to the removal of cesium-134 from red pine. – Oikos 23: 226–234.

Kitson, R. E. & Mellon, M. G. 1944. Further studies of the molybdenum blue reaction. – Ind. Eng. Chem., Anal. Ed. 16: 466–469.

Klomp, H. 1966. The dynamics of a field population of the Pine looper, *Bupalus piniarius* L. (Lep., Geom.). – Adv. Ecol. Res. 3: 207–305.

Klomp, H. & Teerink, B. J. 1973. The density of the invertebrate summer fauna on the crowns of pine trees, *Pinus sylvestris*, in the central part of the Netherlands. – Beitr. Entomol. 23: 325–340.

Larsson, S. & Tenow, O. 1975. Frass-drop from needle-eating insect larvae in a Scots pine forest in Central Sweden. – Swed. Conif. For. Proj. Int. Rep. 32, 23 pp. (In Swedish, English abstract)

Larsson, S. & Tenow, O. 1979. Utilization of dry matter and bioelements in larvae of *Neodiprion sertifer* Geoffr. (Hym., Diprionidae) feeding on Scots pine (*Pinus sylvestris* L.). – Oecologia (Berl.) 43: 157–172.

Linder, S. & Troeng, E. 1980. Photosynthesis and transpiration of 20-year-old Scots pine. – In: Persson, T. (ed.) Structure and Function of Northern Coniferous Forests – An Ecosystem Study, Ecol. Bull. (Stockholm) 32: 165–181.

Lorenz, H. & Kraus, M. 1957. Die Larvalsystematik der Blattwespen (Tenthredinoidea und Megalodonto-idea). – Abh. Larvalsyst. Insekten 1, 339 pp.

Mathavan, S. & Pandian, T. J. 1974. Use of faecal weights as an indicator of food consumption in some lepidopterans. – Oecologia (Berl.) 15: 177–185.

Monro, H. A. U. 1935. The ecology of the pine sawfly *Diprion simile* Htg. Unpublished thesis, McGill University, 73 pp.

Morris, R. F. 1949. Frass-drop measurement in studies of the European spruce sawfly. – Univ. of Michigan, School of Forestry and Conservation, Bulletin no. 12, 58 pp.

Mors, H. 1942. Aktivität und Frass der Nonnenraupe in den verschiedenen Jahren ihrer Massenvermehr-ung. – Monogr. Angew. Entomol. 15: 126–175.

Mukerji, M. K. & Guppy, J. C. 1973. Quantitative relationship between consumption and excretion by larvae of *Pseudaletia unipuncta* (Lepidoptera: Noctuidae). – Can. Entomol. 105: 491–492.

Nielsen, B. O. 1978. Above ground food resources and herbivory in a beech forest ecosystem. – Oikos 31: 273–279.

Nilsson, I. 1978. The influence of *Dasychira pudibunda* (Lepidoptera) on plant nutrient transports and tree growth in a beech *Fagus sylvatica* forest in southern Sweden. – Oikos 30: 133–148.

Nolte, H.-W. 1939. Über den Kot von Fichten- und Kieferninsekten. – Tharandter Forstl. Jahrb. 90: 740–761.

Nunberg, M. 1939. Das massenhafte Vorkommen des Kiefernschwärmers *Sphinx pinastri* L. in Polen. – Verh. VII. Intern. Kongr. f. Ent., Bd. 3: 2033–2051.

Oldiges, H. 1959. Der Einfluss der Temperatur auf Stoffwechsel und Eiproduktion von Lepidopteren. – Z. Angew. Entomol. 44: 115–166.

Otto, D. 1970. Zur Bedeutung des Zuckergehaltes der Nahrung für die Entwicklung nadelfressender Kieferninsekten. – Arch. Forstwes. 19: 135–150.

Otto, D. & Geyer, W. 1970. Zur Bedeutung des Kiefernnadelharzes und des Kiefernnadelöles für die Entwicklung nadelfressender Insekten. – Arch. Forstwes. 19: 151–167.

Owen, D. F. & Wiegert, R. G. 1976. Do consumers maximize plant fitness? – Oikos 27: 488–492.

Patočka, J. & Čapek, M. 1971. Population changes of certain oak defoliators (Lepidoptera) in Slovakia. – Acta Inst. For. Zvolenensis 1971: 461–485.

Persson, H. 1980. Structural properties of the field and bottom layers at Ivantjärnsheden. – In: Persson, T. (ed.) Structure and Function of Northern Coniferous Forests – An Ecosystem Study, Ecol. Bull. (Stockholm) 32: 153–163.

Petrusewicz, K. & Macfadyen, A. 1970. Productivity of Terrestrial Animals. Principles and Methods. IBP Handbook No. 13. Oxford–Edinburgh: Blackwell Scientific Publications, 190 pp.

Rafes, P. M. 1971. Pests and the damage which they cause to forests. – In: Duvigneaud, P. (ed.) Produc-tivity of Forest Ecosystems, Ecology and Conservation 4, Proc. Brussels Symp. 1969, pp. 357–367. Paris: Unesco.

Rafes, P. M. & Sokolov, V. K. 1976. Interaction between primary consumers of the foliage and the host trees. – Dokl. Akad. Nauk SSSR 228: 246–247. (In Russian)

Reichle, D. E. & Crossley, D. A. Jr. 1967. Investigation on heterotrophic productivity in forest insect communities. – In: Petrusewicz, K. (ed.) Secondary Productivity of Terrestrial Ecosystems, Principles and Methods, Vol. 2, pp. 563–587. Warszawa–Kraków: Państwowe Wydawnictwo Naukowe.

Reichle, D. E., Goldstein, R. A., Van Hook, R. I. Jr. & Dodson, G. J. 1973. Analysis of insect consumption in a forest canopy. – Ecology 54: 1076–1084.

Rhoades, D. F. & Cates, R. G. 1976. Toward a general theory of plant antiherbivore chemistry. – In: Wallace, J. W. & Mansell, R. L. (eds.) Biochemical Interaction between Plants and Insects, Rec. Adv. Phytochem., Vol. 10, pp. 168–213. New York–London: Plenum Press.

Rhumbler, L. 1929. Zur Begiftung des Kiefernspanners (*Bupalus piniarius* L.) in der Oberförsterei Hersfeld–Ost 1926. – Z. Angew. Entomol. 15: 137–158.

Rothacher, J. S., Blow, F. E. & Potts, S. M. 1954. Estimating the quantity of tree foliage in oak stands in the Tennessee Valley. – J. For. 52: 169–173.

Sachtleben, W. 1929. Die Forleule, *Panolis flammea* Schiff. – Monogr. PflSch. 3, 160 pp.

Schroeder, L. A. 1978. Consumption on black cherry leaves by phytophagous insects. – Am. Midl. Nat. 100: 294–306.

Schwenke, W. 1952. Unsicherheitsfaktoren bei der Kiefernspannerprognose und Mögligkeiten ihrer Überwindung. – Beitr. Entomol. 2: 189–243.

Schwenke, W. 1978. Die Forstschädlinge Europas, 3. Bd, Schmetterlinge. Hamburg–Berlin: Verlag Paul Parey, 467 pp.

Schwerdtfeger, F. 1930. Beobachtungen und Untersuchungen zur Biologie und Bekämpfung des Kiefernspanners während des Frassjahres 1929 in der Letzlinger Heide. – Z. Forst. Jagdwes. 62: 65–93, 133–166.

Schwerdtfeger, F. 1931. Die Ermittlung der Mortalität von Raupen während einer Insektenepidemie. – Anz. Schädlingskd. 12: 85–90.

Schwerdtfeger, F. 1952. Untersuchungen über den "Eisernen Bestand" von Kiefernspanner (*Bupalus piniarius* L.), Forleule (*Panolis flammea* Schiff.) und Kiefernschwärmer (*Hyloicus pinastri* L.). – Z. Angew. Entomol. 34: 216–283.

Schwerdtfeger, F. 1970. Waldkrankheiten, 3 Aufl. Hamburg–Berlin: Verlag Paul Parey, 509 pp.

Smith, P. H. 1972. The energy relations of defoliating insects in a hazel coppice. – J. Anim. Ecol. 41: 567–587.

Snedecor, G. W. & Cochran, W. G. 1967. Statistical Methods, 6th ed. Ames, Iowa: The Iowa State University Press, 593 pp.

Southwood, T. R. E. 1978. Ecological Methods, 2nd ed. London: Chapman and Hall, 524 pp.

Stachurski, A. & Zimka, J. R. 1975. Methods of studying forest ecosystems: Leaf area, leaf production and withdrawal of nutrients from leaves of trees. – Ekol. pol. 23: 637–648.

Sturm, H. 1942. Untersuchungen über Buschhornblattwespen (*Diprion*). – Z. Angew. Entomol. 29: 412–442, 601–635.

Subklew, W. 1939. Untersuchungen über die Bevölkerungsbewegung des Kiefernspanners (*Bupalus piniarius* L.) – Mitt. Forstw. Forstwiss. 10: 10–51.

Tamm, C. O. 1955. Studies on forest nutrition. I. Seasonal variation in the nutrient content of conifer needles. – Medd. Statens Skogsforskningsinst. (Swed.) 45, 34 pp.

Trägårdh, I. 1911. Om biologin och utvecklingshistorien hos *Cedestis gysselinella* Dup., en barrminerare. – Medd. CentAnst. Försöksv. Jordbr., Stockh. 53, 23 pp. (In Swedish, English summary)

Trägårdh, I. 1915. Bidrag till kännedommen om tallens och granens fiender bland småfjärilarna. – Medd. Statens Skogsförsöksanstalt 12: 71–132. (In Swedish)

Trägårdh, I. 1939. Sveriges Skogsinsekter, 2nd ed. Stockholm: Gebers förlag, 508 pp. (In Swedish)

Wilson, L. F. 1966. Effects of different population levels of the European pine sawfly on young Scotch pine trees. – J. Econ. Entomol. 59: 1043–1049.

Persson, T. (ed) 1980
Structure and Function of Northern
Coniferous Forests – An Ecosystem Study
Ecol. Bull. (Stockholm) 32: 307–313.

ANNUAL CARBON BUDGET FOR A YOUNG SCOTS PINE

G. I. Ågren[1], B. Axelsson[1], J. G. K. Flower-Ellis[2], S. Linder[1], H. Persson[3], H. Staaf[4]
and E. Troeng[1]

Abstract

An annual carbon budget was calculated for a 14-year-old Scots pine. Net photosynthetic production
was estimated to be 1723 g C. The utilization of carbon was distributed between respiration 173 g C (10%),
stem growth 145 g C (9%), branch growth 132 g C (8%), current needle growth 286 g C (17%), and fine
root growth 960 g C (57%). All the values reported were estimated from independent measurements.

Introduction

To our knowledge, an annual carbon budget for a tree or a forest in which all inflows
and outflows have been estimated from independent measurements has not yet been
constructed. Important contributions have been made by Tranquillini (1963, 1979)
who, by pioneer work using the gas-exchange method, established a carbon balance
for *Pinus cembra*. He had, however, to rely upon production tables, the accuracy of
which is doubtful, for the estimate of root production, and his budget is not balanced.
Other budgets (e.g., Kinerson *et al.*, 1977) balance because some inflows or outflows
were not measured. Especially detailed studies of the photosynthesis component of
the budget were made by Schulze *et al.* (1977). An annual carbon budget for a tree,
incorporating independent, but rather crude, estimates of all the major inflows and
outflows, *viz.*, net photosynthesis, respiration, growth, and mortality, is reported
here. To obtain a complete budget it was necessary to combine data from different
years of the period 1974–76; i.e., the budget does not represent one particular year.
All measurements were made in the predominantly 15–20 years old Scots pine (*Pinus
sylvestris* L.) stand at the main research site, Ivantjärnsheden, of the Swedish Coniferous Forest Project. This site is described in detail by Axelsson & Bråkenhielm
(1980).

[1] Dept. of Ecology and Environmental Research, Swedish University of Agricultural Sciences,
S-750 07 Uppsala, Sweden
[2] Dept. of Forest Site Research, Swedish University of Agricultural Sciences, S-901 83 Umeå, Sweden
[3] Institute of Ecological Botany, Uppsala University, Box 559, S-751 22 Uppsala, Sweden
[4] Dept. of Plant Ecology, University of Lund, S-223 62 Lund, Sweden

Table 1. Characteristics of the mean tree.

Age	14 years
Height	278 cm
Diameter at 10 cm above base	6.2 cm
Number of live whorls	8
Dry weight, stem	628 g C
Dry weight, branch-axes	312 g C
Dry weight, needles	615 g C

Table 2. Needle biomass distribution for whorls and age-classes.

| | Biomass (g C) of needles for whorl 1–8 | | | | | | | | | |
	1	2	3	4	5	6	7	8	All whorls	%
C	10.4	33.6	53.8	65.7	48.3	23.4	29.9	21.0	286.1	47
C+1	–	9.4	24.6	45.9	38.2	20.6	27.2	23.0	188.9	31
C+2	–	–	5.5	17.0	19.2	13.9	16.7	18.4	90.7	15
C+3 and older	–	–	–	3.2	10.5	9.2	16.5	10.1	49.5	8
All age-classes	10.4	43.0	83.9	131.8	116.1	67.0	90.2	72.5	615.2	100
%	2	7	14	21	19	11	15	12	100	

Tree structure

The tree used for the budget was an average tree for the stand. Some characteristics of the tree are given in Tables 1 and 2. Structural properties of the stand are extensively reported by Flower-Ellis et al. (1976).

A major difficulty in establishing the carbon budget depended on the fact that all measurements of below-ground properties were expressed per square metre, and were therefore not directly attributable to a specific tree. The area exploited by the tree used in the carbon budget must be estimated. To this end it was assumed that the fine-root biomass of a tree is proportional to its basal area at 10 cm above ground. The basal area for the stand (excluding trees smaller than 1 m) was 2.15 cm^2 m^{-2} (Flower-Ellis et al., 1976). There were, however, approximately twice as many small trees (height < 1 m) as large. With an average height of 50 cm, the basal area of these smaller trees was estimated at 3.58 cm^2 per tree or 0.79 cm^2 m^{-2} giving a total basal area of 2.94 cm^2 m^{-2}. The basal diameter of the tree used in the carbon budget was 6.16 cm, giving an area of 29.8 cm^2; thus the effective area at the disposal of the budget tree was 29.8/2.94 = 10 m^2. With this result, transformations between tree and stand could be done very easily and g C per tree is simply replaced by kg C per hectare.

Net photosynthesis

The net photosynthetic production was estimated from continuous field measurement of CO_2-exchange (cf. Linder & Troeng, 1980). Results from two assimilation

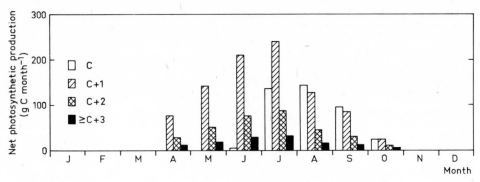

Figure 1. The annual course (1976) of net photosynthetic production in a young Scots pine, assorted by different age-classes of needle.

chambers were used for the calculations. Both chambers were placed in the third whorl on current (C) and one-year-old (C + 1) shoots, respectively. The photosynthetic production of the whole tree was obtained by scaling the data from these chambers with respect to the total needle length of the tree. The photosynthetic production of two-year-old (C + 2) and three-year-old (C + 3) shoots was calculated from the C + 1 shoot, by assuming the efficiencies of the C + 2 and C + 3 shoots to be 75% and 50%, respectively, of the efficiency of the C + 1 shoot (Linder & Troeng, 1980).

The annual course of photosynthetic production for different age-classes of needle is shown in Fig. 1. In these estimates of the amount of carbon fixed, no correction was made for the decrease in photon flux density in the lower parts of the crown or for the fact that the lowest whorls have a lower photosynthetic efficiency than the rest of the crown (Troeng & Linder, 1978). Estimates of the effect of these two factors indicate that they may decrease net photosynthetic production by 5–10%. However, since at present detailed information on this problem is lacking, it was preferred not to try to include any corrections. The results from the estimates of the annual photosynthetic production in different parts in the crown are summarized in Table 3.

The annual course of photosynthetic production in the two years 1976 and 1977 varied considerably (Fig. 2), as a result of pronounced differences in the weather

Table 3. Net photosynthesis during a year for all whorls and age-classes of needle.

Age-class	Net photosynthesis (g C yr^{-1}) for whorl 1–8									
	1	2	3	4	5	6	7	8	All whorls	%
C	14.2	47.2	75.7	92.3	67.8	33.1	42.2	29.6	388.1	22
C + 1	–	44.5	116.7	217.3	180.8	97.3	129.1	109.1	894.8	52
C + 2	–	–	19.8	60.8	68.7	49.5	59.4	65.5	323.7	19
C + 3 and older	–	–	–	7.6	23.3	22.4	38.7	24.0	116.0	7
All age-classes	14.2	91.7	212.2	378.0	342.6	202.3	269.4	228.2	1 722.6	100
%	1	5	12	22	20	12	15	13	100	

309

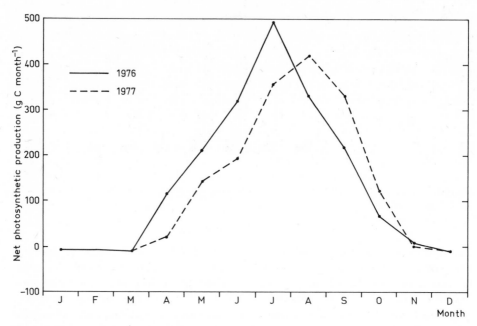

Figure 2. The annual course of net photosynthetic production of the entire tree for two different years (1976 and 1977), but based on the same structural data.

of the two years (Axelsson & Bråkenhielm, 1980). The large discrepancy in April was probably caused by favourable chamber temperatures in 1976, owing to problems with the chamber cooling system (cf. Linder *et al.*, 1980). The differences found in August were the result of an extremely dry spell in August 1976, which caused pronounced water stress during more than two weeks. It should be noted that the comparison between the photosynthetic production during the two years used the same structural data, but the CO_2-exchange measurements were from 1976 and 1977, respectively. Despite the differences found in the seasonal patterns, the estimated annual photosynthetic production differed by less than 10%.

Respiration

The respiration of the stem and branches refers to the non-needle-bearing parts only. The respiration of the needle-bearing parts is included in the net photosynthetic production.

Stem respiration values were obtained from continuous chamber measurements (Linder & Troeng, 1980). These measurements gave an annual respiration of 6.84 g C from a stem segment (C+6) of 3.36 dm^2 at the beginning of the year, and 3.65 dm^2 at the end of the year. Using the mean value of these two areas to obtain respiration per unit area, the respiration of the entire non-needle-bearing stem (25.11 dm^2) was calculated as 49.0 g C.

A few measurements only of branch respiration were available. From these it

310

could be seen that the branches respired about half as much per unit area as the stem. A respiration per unit area half that of the stem was therefore assumed. After scaling with respect to the area of the non-needle-bearing branches (15.8 dm^2), branch respiration was calculated from stem respiration, as 15.4 g C.

Root respiration was measured by Gilson respirometry on detached samples. The respiration rate (as measured in June) can be described by the function $a \cdot e^{0.092\,T}$, where T is temperature (°C) and a (μg C g^{-1} dw h^{-1}) is a parameter depending on the diameter of the root ($a = 19.7$ for 0–1 mm; $a = 20.3$ for 1–2 mm; $a = 13.8$ for 2–3 mm; $a = 10.9$ for 3–10 mm). The annual course of temperature was approximated by the cosine function $T(t) = 4.89 - 7.5 \cos [2\pi(t - 50)/365]$, where t is time in days from 1 January. The variations in root biomass were taken from Persson (1978), with linear interpolations between the measurements. The root respiration calculated in this way was 10.9 g C m^{-2}. Distributed between the different diameter classes, it was 4.5 g C m^{-2} for 0–1 mm, 2.3 g C m^{-2} for 1–2 mm, 1.2 g C m^{-2} for 2–3 mm, and 2.9 g C m^{-2} for 3–10 mm, respectively.

Growth

The growth of the stem was calculated by multiplying the surface area of the stem (2820 cm^2) by an estimated increment in stem radius (0.28 cm), and adding the volume of the current shoot (37 cm^3). This volume was converted to increase in carbon content by utilizing a density of 0.35 g dw cm^{-3} and a 50% carbon content of the dry weight, giving a stem growth of 145 g C. The estimates of branch growth were based on quadratic regressions of shoot dry weight on shoot length for different ages of shoot. The growth of a given shoot was thus estimated as the difference in weight of a shoot of that age and that of a shoot one year younger of the same length. With the aid of structural data giving the average length and number of shoots in all positions, branch growth could then be obtained by summing over the tree, giving 132 g C.

From the same structural data, the amount of current needles was found to be 572 g dw; again assuming a 50% carbon content, needle growth (possible growth of older needles being neglected) was estimated at 286 g C. Root growth is given by Persson (1978) as 183 g dw m^{-2} yr^{-1} for the fine roots (diameter <2 mm) and 9 g dw m^{-2} yr^{-1} for the coarser roots and the stump, giving a total growth of 96 g C m^{-2} yr^{-1}.

Discussion

The annual carbon budget is summarized in Table 4. The accuracy of the estimates of the different components of the carbon budget differs considerably. Some estimates – stem respiration, stem growth, and current needle growth – are believed to have been estimated accurately. It is of especial value that the estimate of net photosynthesis can be relied upon. The estimates of the respiration and growth of branches are, however, much less certain. Since they are of minor importance in the total budget, even fairly large errors will not upset the budget. In absolute terms, the most uncertain parts of the budget are the estimates of the growth and respiration of the roots. Errors may have been introduced in two ways: (1) the estimate of root biomass and root production per square metre is in itself subject to an uncertainty of

Table 4. Carbon budget for the mean tree. The carbon budget for the stand is obtained by replacing $g \ C \ yr^{-1}$ with $kg \ C \ ha^{-1} \ yr^{-1}$.

	Carbon uptake ($g \ C \ yr^{-1}$)	Carbon utilization ($g \ C \ yr^{-1}$)	(%)
Net photosynthetic production	1 723		
Respiration		173	10
– stem, non-needle-bearing part		49	2.9
– branch-axes, non-needle-bearing part		15	0.9
– roots		109	6.4
Growth		1 523	90
– stem		145	8.5
– branch-axes		132	7.8
– current needles		286	16.9
– roots		960	56.6
Total utilization		1 696	100

about 15%, and (2) the translation from terms of per square metre to a given tree is associated with an unknown uncertainty. The uncertainty in the latter estimate is not reduced by expressing the data on an areal basis rather than relating it to a mean tree, because the production of the mean tree is certainly not equal to the average production of a tree in the stand.

Although considerable errors may exist in some of the components of the carbon budget, it seems to balance well. However, the proportion of root respiration to root production can be questioned from a theoretical point of view. The respiration, on a carbon basis, associated with growth has been estimated to 28% of the growth for Scots pine (cf. Penning de Vries, 1974; Axelsson & Ågren, 1976), i.e., a root growth of 960 g C should imply a growth respiration of 270 g C which, together with the maintenance respiration of at most 100 g C is far greater than that estimated from the respiration measurements. A probable reason for this discrepancy is that the respiration measurements do not truly represent the respiration of the roots. Other studies of root respiration (Eidmann, 1943, 1950; Keller & Wehrmann, 1963) also show much higher respiration rates than those reported here. In particular, it is reasonable to believe that the rapidly growing long root tips, as well as short root tips converting into large mycorrhizal clusters (Persson, 1980) are not adequately accounted for in the respiration measurements. A considerable part of the total short root weight consists of mycorrhizal mycelia (Harley, 1959, 1978) in immediate contact with the root surface. Because no attempt was made before weighing to remove the fungal sheath of the mycorrhiza (Persson, 1978), it was included in the calculation of root growth. If the theoretical estimate of the root respiration is correct, this should give a deficit of about 300 g C in the budget. However, a reduction of about 30% in the area available to the tree would again make the budget balance. Such a reduction could easily be justified by changing the fairly arbitrary assumptions about the relation between fine root production and basal area.

Although the budget was established by combining data from different years, its overall behaviour should be valid for any year, in spite of quite large variations in, for example, needle growth or the annual course of net photosynthesis (cf. Fig. 2).

Acknowledgements

G. I. Ågren and B. Axelsson were responsible for the compilation of this work in collaboration with the other authors. Structural data for the trees were provided by J. G. K. Flower-Ellis (above-ground) and H. Persson (below-ground). Measurements of above-ground gas exchange were made by S. Linder and E. Troeng. Measurements of root respiration were made by H. Staaf. This work was carried out within the Swedish Coniferous Forest Project.

References

Axelsson, B. & Bråkenhielm, S. 1980. Investigation sites of the Swedish Coniferous Forest Project – biological and physiographical features. – In: Persson, T. (ed.) Structure and Function of Northern Coniferous Forests – An Ecosystem Study, Ecol. Bull. (Stockholm) 32: 25–64.

Axelsson, B. & Ågren, G. I. 1976. Tree growth model (PT 1) – A development paper. – Swed. Conif. For. Proj. Int. Rep. 41, 79 pp.

Eidmann, F. E. 1943. Untersuchungen über die Wurzelatmung und Transpiration unserer Hauptholzarten. – Schriftenr. der Hermann-Göring – Akad. Deutsch. Forstwiss. 5: 1–144.

Eidmann, F. E. 1950. Investigations on root respiration of 15 European tree species characterizing their pioneer quality in virgin soils. – In: Proc. World Forest Congr. 3, pp. 22–25.

Flower-Ellis, J., Albrektson, A. & Olsson, L. 1976. Structure and growth of some young Scots pine stands: (1) Dimensional and numerical relationships. – Swed. Conif. For. Proj. Tech. Rep. 3, 98 pp.

Harley, J. L. 1959. The Biology of Mycorrhiza. London: Leonard Hill, 233 pp.

Harley, J. L. 1978. Ectomycorrhizas as nutrient absorbing organs. – Proc. R. Soc. Lond. B. 203: 1–21.

Keller, T. & Wehrmann, J. 1963. CO_2 Assimilation, Wurzelatmung und Ertrag von Fichten- und Kiefersämlingen bei unterschiedlicher Mineralstofferernährung. – Mitt. Schweiz. Anst. Forst. Versuchsw. 39: 215–242.

Kinerson, R. S., Ralson, C. W. & Wells, C. G. 1977. Carbon cycling in a Loblolly pine plantation. – Oecologia (Berl.) 29: 1–10.

Linder, S. & Troeng, E. 1980. Photosynthesis and transpiration of 20-year-old Scots pine. – In: Persson, T. (ed.) Structure and Function of Northern Coniferous Forests – An Ecosystem Study, Ecol. Bull. (Stockholm) 32: 165–181.

Linder, S., Nordström, B., Parsby, J., Sundbom, E. & Troeng, E. 1980. A gas exchange system for field measurements of photosynthesis and transpiration in a 20-year-old stand of Scots pine. – Swed. Conif. For. Proj. Tech. Rep. 23, 34 pp.

Penning de Vries, F. W. T. 1974. Substrate utilization and respiration in relation to growth and maintenance in higher plants. – Neth. J. agric. Sci. 22: 40–44.

Persson, H. 1978. Root dynamics in a young Scots pine stand in Central Sweden. – Oikos 30: 508–519.

Persson, H. 1980. Spatial distribution of fine root growth, mortality and decomposition in a young Scots pine stand in Central Sweden. – Oikos 34: 77–87.

Schulze, E.-D., Fuchs, M. & Fuchs, M. I. 1977. Spatial distribution of photosynthetic capacity and performance in a mountain spruce forest of northern Germany. – Oecologia (Berl.) 30: 239–248.

Tranquillini, W. 1963. Die CO_2-Jahresbilanz und die Stoffproduktion der Zirbe. – Mitt. Forstl. Bundes-Versuchsanstalt Mariabrunn 60: 535–546.

Tranquillini, W. 1979. Physiological ecology of the alpine timberline. – Ecological Studies 31, 137 pp. Berlin–Heidelberg–New York: Springer-Verlag.

Troeng, E. & Linder, S. 1978. Gas exchange in a 20-year-old stand of Scots pine. IV. Photosynthesis and transpiration within the crown of one tree. – Swed. Conif. For. Proj. Int. Rep. 83, 20 pp. (In Swedish, English abstract)

Persson, T. (ed) 1980
Structure and Function of Northern
Coniferous Forests – An Ecosystem Study
Ecol. Bull. (Stockholm) 32: 315–327.

RELATIONS BETWEEN TREE BIOMASS FRACTIONS AND CONVENTIONAL SILVICULTURAL MEASUREMENTS

A. Albrektson[1]

Abstract

Tree biomass fractions were investigated in several Scots pine stands of different age-classes. Biomass and development of biomass are analyzed, and methods of calculating the amount of biomass by non-destructive methods are discussed. An attempt is made to describe changes in tree biomass fractions during stand development.

Additional keywords: Coarse root, needle biomass, needle production, sapwood area, Scots pine, stand development, stemwood production, stump.

Introduction

The research efforts of the Swedish Coniferous Forest Project have been concentrated to a very limited number of sites. The need for obtaining more generality in the results is therefore obvious. One approach has been to use the detailed information obtained in the project on total tree biomass and production and try to find relationships between this material and conventional forestry data in terms of stem production and stem volume. The latter type of data is available for different regions and over a great range of sites in Sweden. The present paper contains preliminary results from a study dealing with this problem, where the specific aims are:

(1) to estimate biomass by fractions in different types of stands,
(2) to find a satisfactory way to describe tree biomass and biomass production with non-destructive variables suitable for comparison with conventional forestry measurements,
(3) to control the applicability of the relationships established, and
(4) to construct theoretical stand development models.

Description of biomass in some pine stands

Material and methods

Stands suitable for biomass description were selected with the following restrictions: (1) The age of the trees in each stand should be even. (2) Scots pine should dominate (more than 90% of basal area). (3) Site quality should not be extreme. (4) Soil material should be sandy sediment or sandy till. (5) The stands should be located in Central Sweden. (6) The stands should represent different age-classes.

---

[1] Dept. of Silviculture, Swedish University of Agricultural Sciences, S-901 83 Umeå, Sweden

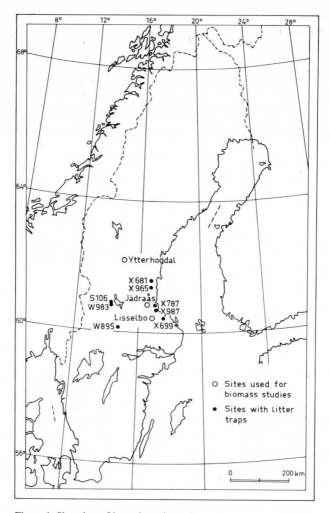

Figure 1. Situation of investigated stands.

These restrictions could not be followed consistently, but formed the basis in the selection of stands. Investigated stands (Fig. 1) are described in Tables 1 and 2. The stands are spaced and thinned in different ways and site quality varies. Stands 10 and 11 (Lisselbo) are parts of an optimum nutrition experiment carried out by the Department of Forest Ecology and Forest Soils (Tamm *et al.*, 1974). Stand 4 is another fertilizer experiment (fertilized 1968) (see Falck, 1973), while the remaining stands were examined especially for this investigation.

Sample trees were used for description of biomass. Stems of mean basal area in basal area classes were selected. In this way, sample trees were evenly spread over the diameter distributions. Sample trees were weighed and cut into fractions in the field. Subsamples were taken to the laboratory where the distributions of subfractions in each fraction and their dry weights were determined.

A total of 66 sample trees were examined in the Lisselbo experiment (15 trees from control plots and 51 from fertilized plots), six trees were examined from each of stands 1–9 and 10 trees from each of stands 12–15; i.e., a total of 160 sample trees. Stands 1–9 were examined in summer–autumn 1974, 10 and 11 in spring 1975 and 12–15 in autumn 1975 (Albrektson, 1976, 1978).

Biomass dry weight per ha for each stand was calculated in two ways, along the lines described by, for example, Ovington *et al.* (1967) and Madgwick (1976):

316

Table 1. General data of the investigated sites. Sites 1–3, 5–9 and 12–15 are at Jädraås, 4 at Ytterhogdal and 10–11 at Lisselbo.

	Site no.														
	1	2	3	4[3]	5	6	7	8	9	10	11	12	13	14	15
Geographical data															
Latitude	60°50'	60°51'	60°51'	62°10'	60°51'	60°52'	60°51'	60°51'	60°48'	60°28'	60°28'	60°51'	60°51'	60°52'	60°50'
Longitude	16°28'	16°27'	16°27'	14°50'	16°27'	16°25'	16°29'	16°27'	16°31'	16°57'	16°57'	16°27'	16°27'	16°35'	16°30'
Altitude (m above M.S.L.)	195	200	200	295	200	205	190	200	170	10	10	200	200	185	185
Climatic data															
Growing season[1]															
Mean temp. (°C)	12.0	12.0	12.0	11.5	12.0	12.0	12.0	12.0	12.0	12.3	12.3	12.0	12.0	12.0	12.0
Precipitation (mm)	326	326	326	330	326	326	326	326	326	320	320	326	326	326	326
Annual[2]															
Mean temp. (°C)	3.8	3.8	3.8	2.1	3.8	3.8	3.8	3.8	3.8	4.8	4.8	3.8	3.8	3.8	3.8
Precipitation (mm)	607	607	607	558	607	607	607	607	607	593	593	607	607	607	607
Soil															
Texture	sand	sand	sand	sandy till	fine sand	sand	fine sand	sand	sand[4]	coarse sand	coarse sand	fine sand	sand	coarse sand	sand
Soil profile	iron podsol	iron podsol	iron podsol	iron podsol	iron podsol	iron podsol	iron podsol	iron podsol	mull[4]	iron podsol	iron podsol	iron podsol	iron podsol	iron podsol	iron podsol
Vegetation															
Dwarf-shrub type	dry–mesic dry	dry–very dry	dry	dry	dry	dry	dry–mesic dry	dry–very dry	[4]	dry	dry	dry	dry–very dry	dry–very dry	dry–very dry

[1] Perttu & Huszár (1976). Åmotsbruk (60°58'N, 16°27'E) and Ytterhogdal (62°11'N, 14°57'E).
[2] SMHI (1973a, b). Åmotsbruk and Sveg (62°02'N, 14°20'E).
[3] Fertilized.
[4] Old field, basic sand with a top-layer of mull. Ground vegetation characterized by grass and herbs.

317

Table 2. Properties of the investigated stands.

	Stand no.														
	1	2	3	4	5	6	7	8	9	10	11	12	13	14	15
Age at bh (year)	34	27	14	84	29	7	26	12	9	13	13	28	14	50	100
Dominant height[1] (m)	15.1	13.3	7.2	20.4	14.8	17.1	13.7	6.6	5.7	6.8	7.0	13.4	7.7	14.8	19.2
Trees per ha															
Pine (*Pinus sylvestris*)	1 038	2 904	2 502	825	1 250	866	3 393	1 783	1 371	1 131	1 219	2 828	2 538	1 775	453
Spruce (*Picea abies*)	67	264	25	0	87	10	66	18	25	0	0	264	0	0	0
Broad-leaved trees	11	0	0	0	0	0	0	0	25	0	0	0	0	0	0
Total	1 116	3 168	2 527	825	1 337	876	3 459	1 801	1 421	1 131	1 219	3 102	2 538	1 775	453
Basal area at bh (m²ha⁻¹)															
Pine	21.04	27.25	12.04	25.31	22.15	21.09	28.75	6.41	8.71	9.95	14.35	29.60	15.10	22.90	19.70
Spruce	0.56	0.16	0.01	0.00	0.38	0.02	0.76	0.00	0.07	0.00	0.00	0.20	0.00	0.00	0.00
Broad-leaved trees	0.06	0.00	0.00	0.00	0.00	0.00	0.00	0.00	0.01	0.00	0.00	0.00	0.00	0.00	0.00
Total	21.76	27.41	12.05	25.31	22.43	21.73	29.51	6.41	8.79	9.95	14.35	29.80	15.10	22.90	19.70

[1] Mean height of the 100 largest pines per ha (Hägglund, 1974).

(1) The regression method. The trees examined were used to form regression equations where the biomass of a subfraction of a tree was described by the diameter of the tree. Regression equations were of the type log (weight) = $a + b$ log (diameter). Biomass per ha was calculated as the sum of calculated tree weights.

(2) The basal area method. The dry weight of a subfraction was assumed to be correlated to the basal area (at bh) of a tree. Biomass per ha was calculated as the product of basal area per ha and the mean value of biomass per unit basal area.

Method 1 was used for biomass calculations in stands 12–15 and at Lisselbo (except for cone biomass) and method 2 was used in all other cases. Method 1 is not suitable when sample trees are few or the variance is very large (Beauchamp & Olsen, 1973).

It should be noted that the investigations in 1974 were partly carried out during the summer when the trees were still growing. Trees investigated during the summer (three trees from each of stands 1–9) were considered unusable for calculations of branch and needle biomass but not for stem-, stump- and coarse root biomass. The precision of branch and needle biomass calculations in these stands might therefore be low but, nevertheless, the results may be of interest when reported in connection with data from other stands in the age-series.

Result and discussion

The biomass fractions in the various stands are given in Table 3. The youngest stands (nos. 3, 8, 9, 10, 11 and 13), aged 9–14 years, had a large proportion of their biomass bound to living branches, where axes and needles were of equal importance. Of these stands, stand 11 and, in particular, stand 9 differed by having larger biomass in the branches than in the boles. The divergence in biomass distribution is probably caused by higher nutrient status, since stand 11 was fertilized and stand 9 was situated on an abandoned field. These two stands, together with stand 4 that was also fertilized, were excluded from Fig. 2 which shows the development of biomass fractions when the stands are grouped according to age.

Fig. 2 shows that stem, stump and coarse root biomass increase when the stand is young. The increment continues throughout a very long period but slows down when the stand reaches maturity. In relation to stem biomass, the biomasses of the coarse roots and stumps are almost proportional. Production of stem, stump and coarse root biomass correspond to the biomass increase since all production is accumulated.

Branch and needle biomass and needle production seem to increase very rapidly in young stands and culminate at a stand age of about 30 years. After this there is a slight reduction in branch and needle biomass and needle production. There also seems to be a great variation in the number of age-classes of needles, although part of this variation may be an artefact, caused by a variation in sampling dates.

The influence of site quality on biomass could be analysed by comparing unfertilized and fertilized trees in the optimum nutrition experiment at Lisselbo. Table 4 shows that the biomass of all above-ground fractions develops faster on sites with a richer supply of nutrients. However, fine root biomass is reported to be unaffected by fertilization in that experiment (Tamm, 1979). The increase in branch and needle biomass is also explained by this table. The number of branches, shoots and needles are higher, and branch and needle size increase on fertilized in relation to unfertilized plots. An increment in stem-wood production could be related to an increment in needle biomass (Fig. 3). However, this is only an indication of the character of differences between rich and poor sites, judged from one fertilization experiment.

319

Table 3. Tree biomass (kg dw ha^{-1}) in investigated stands.

	Stand no.														
	1	2	3	4	5	6	7	8	9	10	11	12	13	14	15
Roots > 30 mm															
Bark	981	723	241	1 309	803	744	813	101	210	–	–	970	319	1 163	1 805
Wood	7 703	5 430	1 396	8 704	4 891	5 825	5 791	543	1 058	–	–	6 525	1 881	6 458	10 675
Total	8 684	6 153	1 637	10 013	5 694	6 569	6 604	644	1 268	–	–	7 495	2 200	7 621	12 480
Stumps															
Bark	504	381	186	785	408	624	489	116	143	105	204	705	208	659	816
Wood	4 490	3 552	973	6 137	3 045	4 191	3 758	635	1 082	821	1 586	3 961	1 120	3 798	5 725
Total	4 994	3 933	1 159	6 922	3 453	4 815	4 247	751	1 225	926	1 790	4 665	1 328	4 457	6 542
Boles															
Bark	5 308	7 197	2 916	6 999	5 746	5 730	7 820	1 423	1 790	1 613	2 215	7 158	2 954	6 598	4 902
Wood	61 406	66 946	12 627	101 609	57 489	61 235	76 526	5 910	7 783	8 034	12 153	68 672	18 784	57 968	76 408
Total	66 714	74 141	15 543	108 608	63 235	66 965	84 346	7 330	9 573	9 647	14 368	75 829	21 738	64 566	81 309
Living branches															
Axes[1]	7 432	7 067	3 454	8 550	10 003	5 514	5 397	2 218	3 074	2 868	5 215	7 737	3 391	4 784	8 199
Axes[2]	1 027	1 595	2 268	1 837	1 985	1 087	4 698	1 162	4 770	1 617	2 715	2 309	2 266	1 146	851
Axes[3]	411	474	709	346	440	252	581	269	1 063	365	769	556	350	182	255
Needles (C+)	4 043	3 317	3 720	6 707	4 282	4 438	8 392	2 435	5 871	2 407	4 405	4 796	3 117	3 537	2 646
Needles (C+)	4 043	3 317	3 720	6 707	4 282	4 438	8 392	2 435	5 871	2 407	4 405	4 796	3 117	3 537	2 646
Needles (C)	1 358	1 569	2 358	1 125	1 458	1 010	1 922	897	3 186	1 174	2 414	1 836	1 170	907	810
Cones (C+1)	121	0	0	393	214	141	23	0	21	25	159	0	0	0	219
Cones (C)	2	0	0	39	5	7	0	0	0	1	10	3	1	2	21
Attached dead	889	1 281	179	778	772	1 711	305	272	52	172	336	460	285	464	1 372
Total	15 283	15 303	12 688	19 775	19 159	14 160	21 318	7 253	18 037	8 629	16 023	17 697	10 580	11 024	14 373
Dead branches	2 779	5 167	1 328	1 450	2 784	2 408	4 504	559	94	420	764	6 887	2 373	3 107	2 329
GRAND TOTAL	98 454	104 697	32 355	146 768	94 325	94 917	121 019	16 537	30 197	–	–	112 633	38 282	90 802	117 038

[1] Axes which have not carried needles.
[2] Axes which have carried needles (C +).

320

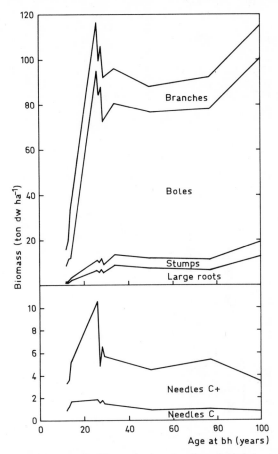

Figure 2. "Empirical stand development" of Scots pine based on investigated sites except nos. 4, 9 and 11 (cf. Table 3). Root biomass in site no. 10 is calculated. C = current-year needles, C+ = older age-classes of needles. Cumulative curves.

Estimations by using conventional forestry measurements

The value of being able to calculate biomass production by using conventional forestry measurements is obvious as it enables transformation of a great number of stand characteristics of boles into biomass figures.

This part of the investigation is now in progress and it is still too early to present final results. The aim is to find regression equations on biological-functional characteristics. The material in this investigation consists of the trees used in describing biomass in different stands (Table 3). Some examples of ways in which the material is analysed are shown in Figs. 3–6.

At present it appears that estimates of root and stump biomass and production, branch production, and production of flowers and cones will be less accurate than stem and foliage data. As regards root and stump biomass a difficulty arises since it is hard to define stump and roots and because their biomasses are assumed to be affected by different types of soil (Köstler *et al.*, 1968). Branch production is

Table 4. Responses to fertilization. Experiment E40 Lisselbo, fertilized yearly from 1969 onwards. All figures in percentages of controls (Albrektson *et al.*, 1977).

Branch whorl	Arithmetic means from lateral branches							Biomass and production 1974
	Number[1]	Diameter	Length	Number of needles		Single needle weight		
				C	C+1	C	C+1	
0	107	–	–					Boles
1	111	104	99	95		124		Bark and wood biomass 149
2	114	96	92					Production 165
3	113	100	94					Branches
4	105	135	104	158	139	135	141	Bark and wood biomass 179
5	103	119	113					Needle biomass 190
6	84	150	127					Needle production 206
7	100	116	114	127	132	133	143	
8	98	130	114					
9	95	112	109					
10	93	101	102					
11	107	100	106	138	151	128	154	

[1] Living + dead branches for whorl "0", lateral buds. Whorl 0 corresponds to the year 1975 and whorl 5 is the first whorl which could have been affected by the treatment already from bud setting.

322

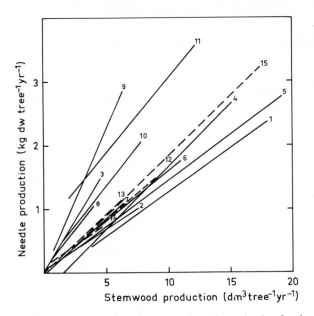

Figure 3. Relationships between stemwood production and needle production for the stands described in Table 1.

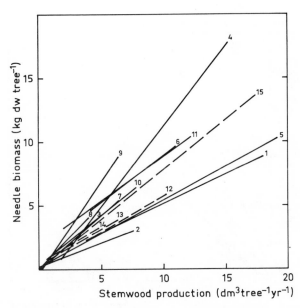

Figure 4. Relationships between stemwood production and needle biomass for the stands described in Table 1.

323

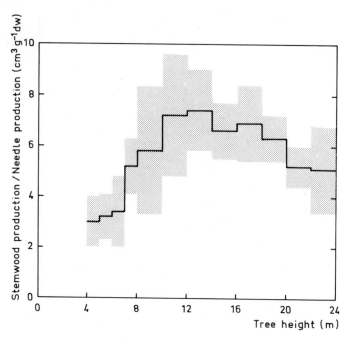

Figure 5. Relationships between tree height and stemwood production/needle production ratio. Shaded area indicates mean ± standard deviation.

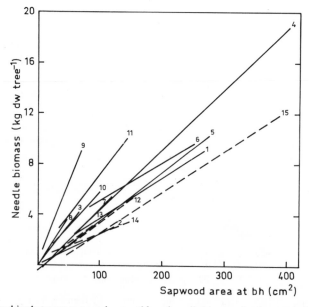

Figure 6. Relationships between sapwood area at bh and needle biomass for the stands described in Table 1.

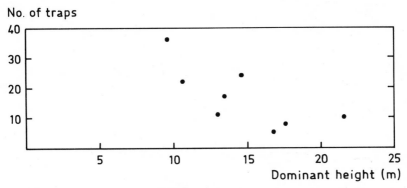

No. of traps

Figure 7. Relationships between dominant height and number of litter traps (0.25 m²) required to get a standard error less than 5% of the mean value.

difficult to measure directly. Regression equations have to be made from data calculated indirectly and there is an obvious risk of systematical errors. Branch production should be divided into diameter growth and development of new shoots, but diameter growth is particularly difficult to calculate. Flower and cone production is irregular and might affect the production of other biomass fractions, thus increasing the scattering around the relationships established.

Testing of suggested methods to calculate biomass

The material used to form regression equations is very limited in many ways and there is a need of material with a wider geographical range representing different age-classes and site qualities. There is also a need of material from other species. Literature data and litterfall studies will be used in generalizing and testing.

Large amounts of data are available from biomass studies of Scots pine and Norway spruce (*Picea abies* L.) in Sweden, Norway and Finland as a result of the increased interest in complete tree utilization. However, this material is not enough. A pilot study in litterfall (Albrektson & Andersson, 1978) shows that needle production and needle biomass can be measured indirectly on an area basis (Fig. 7). The litter method is cheap and the precision is good and this method will be expanded in order to complement literature data. The litter study is being carried out on permanent plots belonging to the Department of Forest Yield Research, Swedish University of Agricultural Sciences (Fig. 1).

Biomass changes during stand development

If conventional forestry measurements can be used to describe total biomass in a stand it is also possible to describe biomass development. Models describing stem volume development already exist in most countries with sustained yield forest management. For spruce and pine in Sweden yield tables have been published by Andersson (1963) and Eriksson (1976), and attempts to convert the data into biomass

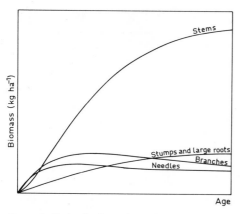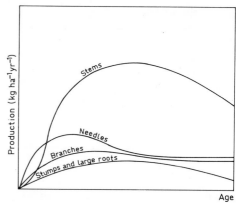

Figure 8. Generalized stand development of Scots pine.

figures could be based upon these models. There are also many empirical measurements of stem volume development at the Department of Forest Yield Research (Anonymous, 1974).

At this point it is not possible to make accurate biomass conversions from conventional yield tables, but qualified guesses of the change in biomass and production during the stand development could be made from the discussion above. The generalized development pattern is indicated in Fig. 8. This pattern correlates to the biomass development suggested by Amilon (1925), Tirén (1927), Burger (1953) and Kira & Schidei (1967).

It seems as if many scientists have the same idea of biomass development and production in forest stands but in all investigations there is a lack of data to verify the validity of the models. These circumstances justify continued collection of data and work along the lines suggested here.

References

Albrektson, A. 1976. The amount and the distribution of tree biomass in some pine stands (*Pinus silvestris*) in northern Gästrikland. – Swed. Conif. For. Proj. Int. Rep. 38, 26 pp. (In Swedish, English abstract)

Albrektson, A. 1978. Tree biomass in some Scots pine stands (*Pinus silvestris* L.). – Swed. Conif. For. Proj. Int. Rep. 73, 19 pp. (In Swedish, English abstract)

Albrektson, A. & Andersson, B. 1978. Estimates of litterfall in pine stands (*Pinus silvestris* L.). A pilot survey of a method. – Swed. Conif. For. Proj. Int. Rep. 74, 17 pp. (In Swedish, English abstract)

Albrektson, A., Aronsson, A. & Tamm, C. O. 1977. The effect of forest fertilisation on primary production and nutrient cycling in forest ecosystems. – Silva fenn. 11 (3): 233–239.

Amilon, J. A. 1925. Barrmassan och Stamtillväxten hos Mellansvensk Tall. Stockholm. (In Swedish)

Andersson, S. O. 1963. Yield tables for plantations of Scots pine in northern Sweden. – Medd. Skogsforsknlnst. Stockh. 51(3), 337 pp.

Anonymous, 1974. Redovisning av fasta försöksytor. – Dept. of Forest Yield Research, Royal College of Forestry, Stockholm. Research Notes 32.

Beauchamp, J. J. & Olsen, J. S. 1973. Corrections for bias in regression estimates after logarithmic transformation. – Ecology 54: 1403–1407.

Burger, H. 1953. Holz, Blattmenge und Zuwachs. Fichten im gleichalterigen Hochwald. – Mitt. Schweiz. Anst. forstl. Versuchsw. 29: 38–130.

Eriksson, H. 1976. Yield of Norway spruce in Sweden. – Dept. of Forest Yield Research, Royal College of Forestry, Stockholm. Research Notes 41, 291 pp.

Falck, J. 1973. A sampling method for quantitative determinations of plant nutrient content of forest floor. – Dept. of Silviculture, Royal College of Forestry, Stockholm. Research Notes 1, 129 pp.

Hägglund, B. 1974. Site index curves for Scots pine in Sweden. – Dept. of Forest Yield Research, Royal College of Forestry, Stockholm. Research Notes 31, 54 pp.

Kira, T. & Schidei, T. 1967. Primary production and turnover of organic matter in different forest ecosystems of the western Pacific. – Jap. J. Ecol. 17 (2): 70–87.

Köstler, J. N., Bruckner, E. & Bibelriether, H. 1968. Die Wurzeln der Waldbäume. Untersuchungen zur Morphologie der Waldbäume in Mitteleuropa. Hamburg–Berlin: Parey Hamburg, 284 pp.

Madgwick, H. A. I. 1976. Mensuration of forest biomass. – In: Oslo Biomass Studies, pp. 11–27. 16th Int. Congr. of IUFRO. Orono, Maine: College of Life Sciences and Agriculture, Univ. of Maine.

Ovington, J. D., Forrest, W. G. & Armstrong, J. E. 1967. Tree biomass estimation. – In: Young, H. (ed.) Symposium on Primary Productivity and Mineral Cycling in Natural Ecosystems, AAAS 13th Annual Meeting, pp. 4–32. Maine: University of Maine Press.

Perttu, K. & Huszár, A. 1976. Vegetationsperioder, temperatursummor och frostfrekvenser beräknade ur SMHI-data. – Dept. of Reforestation, Royal College of Forestry, Stockholm. Research Notes 72, 101 pp. (In Swedish, English abstract)

SMHI 1973a. Sveriges Meteorologiska och Hydrologiska institut Referensnormaler. Medeltemperaturer 1931–60. Reviderad upplaga maj 1973, 16 pp. (In Swedish)

SMHI 1973b. Sveriges Meteorologiska och Hydrologiska Institut Referensnormaler. Normalnederbörd, Utgåva 3, maj 1973, 22 pp. (In Swedish)

Tamm, C. O. 1979. Nutrient cycling and productivity of forest ecosystems. – In: Leaf, A. L. (ed.) Impact of Intensive Harvesting on Forest Nutrient Cycling, pp. 2–21. State Univ. of New York, College of Environmental Science and Forestry, Syracuse, N. Y.

Tamm, C. O., Nilsson, Å. & Wiklander, G. 1974. The optimum nutrition experiment Lisselbo. A brief description of an experiment in a young stand of Scots pine (*Pinus silvestris* L.). – Dept. of Forest Ecology and Forest Soils, Royal College of Forestry, Stockholm. Research Notes 18, 25 pp.

Tirén, L. 1927. Om barrytans storlek hos tallbestånd. – Swedish Institute of Experimental Forestry, Report no. 23, pp. 295–336. (In Swedish, German abstract)

327

Persson, T. (ed) 1980
Structure and Function of Northern
Coniferous Forests – An Ecosystem Study
Ecol. Bull. (Stockholm) 32: 329–332.

SOIL PROCESS STUDIES WITHIN THE SWEDISH CONIFEROUS FOREST PROJECT – AN INTRODUCTION

U. Lohm[1]

Abstract

Main questions of soil process studies within the Swedish Coniferous Forest Project are presented as a background to the papers in this volume. A description of the research organization is made and the development lines are indicated.

Introduction

Fluxes of materials and nutrients are essential for the continuity and stability of any living system. In terrestrial ecosystems the soil processes are of major importance in this respect. Heal (1979) describes the decomposition sub-system as a complex interacting set of organisms and processes, whose activities are central to the availability of nutrients to plants and to the maintenance of the nutrient capital of the ecosystem.

During the establishment phase of the Swedish Coniferous Forest Project this was recognized and the research efforts were started along three main lines. Two focused on the organisms and were divided into decomposition processes, including microbial ecology and soil animal populations. The third line emphasized the biogeochemical cycle and mineral nutrient turnover. However, it soon became obvious that a research organization based on these three lines did not favour interdisciplinary work and consequently the project was replanned.

General aims

Since the ability of plant growth was chosen as a prime objective of the project's research (cf. Andersson, 1980), the problem area "soil processes" emphasized the availability of plant nutrients (in particular nitrogen) and the processes regulating this availability.

[1] Dept of Ecology and Environmental Research, Swedish University of Agricultural Sciences, S-750 07 Uppsala, Sweden
Present address: Dept. of Water in Nature and Society, University of Linköping, S-581 83 Linköping, Sweden

In the beginning of the investigation phase of the project the following questions to be analyzed were set up:

(1) How do abiotic and biotic factors regulate leaching of carbon, nitrogen, phosphorus and potassium (CNPK) between litter, humus and mineral layers and out of the system?
(2) How do abiotic and biotic factors regulate decomposition of different types of substrates (litter fractions) and how long does it take?
(3) How do abiotic factors regulate the mineralization of CNP from different kinds of substrates in the soil horizons?
(4) How great are the inputs to and outputs from the ecosystem of easily available nitrogen by means of nitrogen fixation and losses by denitrification and NH_3-evaporation, and which abiotic and biotic factors regulate these processes?
(5) What quantities of CNPK are immobilized in soil organisms and how long is the retention time?
(6) How does the interaction between soil organisms affect mineralization, and which are the nutrient relationships and flow rates in the main chains?
(7) How does mineralization affect the ion uptake by plant roots?

The research was organized in process groups based on the above-mentioned questions. However, the cooperation patterns of these groups gradually changed during the investigation phase of the project (Fig. 1).

The ideal research method with the loop: theoretical analysis – experimental research, was hoped to be achieved by integrating the knowledge into simulation models. The general aim of the modelling work was: "To describe the decomposition of soil organic matter within the year and between years with different climatic conditions; to describe the release of nutrients, their transport within and between horizons as well as the uptake by plants (mainly nitrogen). The models shall include inputs and outputs to and from the soil. The main output to other models is the uptake of nutrients, mainly nitrogen, by plants."

During the initial period the modelling work tended to combine broad areas such as decomposition of organic material and ion transport together with population dynamics of soil organisms. This approach led to dead ends, and it was realized that if the models were to reveal any new way of analyzing the major pathways of plant nutrient circulation, they had to be concentrated on processes and based on some general hypotheses. The development of this work and the general hypotheses are presented by Bosatta (1980). One consequence of this strengthening of the aim was that the model analysis of the dynamics and interactions of soil organism populations was left aside for the time being.

The field research was concentrated in the mature Scots pine stand at Ivantjärnsheden (Ih V). Several reasons for this could be given, but the main reason was that this stand was thought to be in a relatively steady state situation with regard to plant litter input and decomposition of organic material. Another reason for concentrating the field work to this site, with smaller surveys made in the stands of different ages, was that the different soil layers had not been disturbed by forest management practices for quite a long period of time (Axelsson & Bråkenhielm, 1980).

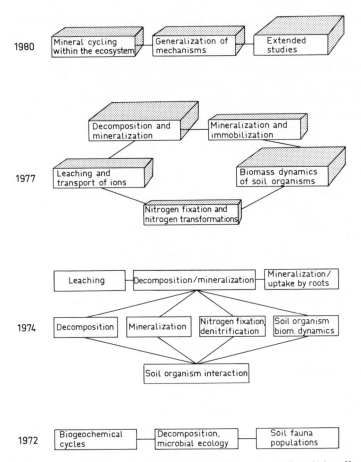

1980 Mineral cycling within the ecosystem — Generalization of mechanisms — Extended studies

Decomposition and mineralization — Mineralization and immobilization

1977 Leaching and transport of ions — Nitrogen fixation and nitrogen transformations — Biomass dynamics of soil organisms

1974 Leaching — Decomposition/mineralization — Mineralization/uptake by roots

Decomposition | Mineralization | Nitrogen fixation, denitrification | Soil organism biom. dynamics

Soil organism interaction

1972 Biogeochemical cycles — Decomposition, microbial ecology — Soil fauna populations

Figure 1. Soil process research groups during different stages of the project. The relative efforts allocated during the second stage of the project are indicated.

Final stage of the project

At present the field studies and experimental work within the investigation phase of the project have come to an end. The interest is now focused on synthesis work and generalization of knowledge gained from all research areas within the project. The papers following this introduction are either summaries of papers published earlier or original publications, and are primarily based on field investigations made in the Ivantjärnsheden area. The model analyses are presented in the next section of the volume. One common aspect of the following presentations is the seasonal dynamics of different soil processes. The contributions cover the influx of nutrients through precipitation and nitrogen fixation together with nutrient transport between different soil horizons. The nature of decomposition and release of nitrogen is analyzed in different respects. The biomass dynamics of soil organism populations are described and evaluated especially in relation to carbon retention and release. The model analysis synthesizes these processes and the interest is primarily focused on the cli-

331

matic influence on carbon and nitrogen transformations in coniferous forest soils with special emphasis on the balance between nitrogen leaching and uptake in plant roots.

The contributions in the present volume do not intend to present all studies made within the "soil processes areas" but should be regarded as a first step in the analysis of the questions (see above) listed in the beginning of the investigation phase. Several investigations, for example different soil respiration studies, are in preparation for publication while other research areas such as laboratory work on interaction of soil organisms already have been published (e.g., Bååth et al., 1978; Clarholm et al., in press).

Extended studies have been made in parallel with the studies presented in this volume. They involve more applied questions such as ecological effects of clear-cutting, forest fertilization and increasing acid deposition.

Today the interest is focused on generalizations of soil processes and the long-term perspective is of major concern. Basic research work is also continuing within research fields where large lacunas in knowledge are present, such as effects of soil heterogeneity on ion-exchange processes and interactions between soil organism populations. Hopefully, the research effort within the Swedish Coniferous Forest Project will be an important base for future research aiming at integrating understanding of the soil system in coniferous forests.

Acknowledgements

I wish to thank my colleagues in the project leading group, G. I. Ågren, F. Andersson, S. O. Falk and K. Perttu for a very stimulating scientific collaboration during all phases in the project. I also wish to thank U. Granhall for planning and organization of soil process studies.

References

Andersson, F. 1980. Ecosystem research within the Swedish Coniferous Forest Project. – In: Persson, T. (ed.) Structure and Function of Northern Coniferous Forests – An Ecosystem Study, Ecol. Bull. (Stockholm) 32: 11–23.
Axelsson, B. & Bråkenhielm, S. 1980. Investigation sites of the Swedish Coniferous Forest Project – biological and physiographical features. – In: Persson, T. (ed.) Structure and Function of Northern Coniferous Forests – An Ecosystem Study, Ecol. Bull. (Stockholm) 32: 25–64.
Bååth, E., Lohm, U., Lundgren, B., Rosswall, T., Söderström, B., Sohlenius, B. & Wirén, A. 1978. The effect of nitrogen and carbon supply on the development of soil organism populations and pine seedlings: a microcosm experiment. – Oikos 31: 153–163.
Bosatta, E. 1980. Modelling of soil processes – an introduction. – In: Persson, T. (ed.) Structure and Function of Northern Coniferous Forests – An Ecosystem Study, Ecol. Bull. (Stockholm) 32: 553–564.
Clarholm, M., Popović, B., Rosswall, T., Söderström, B., Sohlenius, B., Staaf, H. & Wirén, A. in press. Biological aspects of nitrogen mineralization in humus from a pine forest podsol incubated under different moisture and temperature conditions. – Oikos.
Heal, O. W. 1979. Decomposition and nutrient release in even-aged plantations. – In: Ford, E. D. & Malcolm, D. C. (eds.) The Ecology of Even-Aged Forest Plantations, pp. 257–291. Institute of Terrestrial Ecology, Natural Environment Research Council, United Kingdom.

Persson, T. (ed) 1980
Structure and Function of Northern
Coniferous Forests – An Ecosystem Study
Ecol. Bull. (Stockholm) 32: 333–340.

NITROGEN INPUT THROUGH BIOLOGICAL NITROGEN FIXATION

U. Granhall[1] and T. Lindberg[1]

Abstract

Nitrogen (C_2H_2) fixation studies in stands of varying ages of Scots pine (*Pinus sylvestris* L.) on glacifluvial sand and in an old stand of mixed Scots pine and Norway spruce (*Picea abies* (L.) Karst.) on sandy moraine in central Sweden show that there are major differences in the rate, origin, and localization of N_2-fixation between different coniferous forest ecosystems. Nitrogen fixation was mainly of asymbiotic origin at investigated sites. Depending mainly on the vegetation cover in field and bottom layers, the nitrogen input from N_2-fixation in different strata varied between 0.027 and 3.84 g N m^{-2} yr^{-1}. Overall mean annual N_2-fixation in a young and an old pine stand was calculated to be 0.27 and 0.31 kg N ha^{-1} yr^{-1}, respectively. A much higher rate, corresponding to 3.8 kg N ha^{-1} yr^{-1}, was found in the mixed pine and spruce stand.

Introduction

The total nitrogen input through biological N_2-fixation, its localization in time and space, and the fate of the fixed nitrogen is of great interest in natural forest ecosystems, as easily available combined nitrogen is generally the main limiting nutrient factor for the actual plant growth. Even small contributions from N_2-fixation may therefore be of importance to these ecosystems. Very few thorough investigations on total nitrogen fixation have so far been made in forest ecosystems, but within a range of fixation rates of 0.3–12 kg N ha^{-1} yr^{-1}, nitrogen fixation represents approximately 5–10% of the amount of nitrogen cycled annually by the vegetation and is often greater than the input by precipitation (Paul, 1978).

The present paper is a summary of results from the N_2-fixation studies carried out within the Swedish Coniferous Forest Project, 1972–77, much of which has been published elsewhere (Granhall & Nilsson, 1974; Lindberg 1974; Bringmark *et al.*, 1975; Granhall & Lindberg, 1977, 1978). All results discussed in this paper which are not explicitly shown refer to these earlier reports.

Materials and methods

Sites and sampling design

Pine stands of varying ages, 15–20 (Ih II), 60 (Ih IV) and 120 (Ih V) years old at Ivantjärnsheden were investigated. Randomized sampling sites (1 × 1 m) within 5–20 randomly chosen quadrats (10 × 10 m) were used for consecutive samplings.

---

[1] Dept. of Microbiology, Swedish University of Agricultural Sciences, S-750 07 Uppsala, Sweden

In the old mixed stand of pine and spruce at Siljansfors (Sf), quadrats and sampling sites were randomly chosen according to the cover of dominant field and bottom layer components (Stratum I: feather mosses; stratum II: feather mosses and dwarf shrubs; stratum III: *Sphagnum* mosses and dwarf shrubs; and stratum IV: spots with only *Sphagnum*).

Further site characteristics regarding vegetation cover and climatic data are given in Axelsson & Bråkenhielm (1980). For description of sampling procedures and numbers of various samples (phyllosphere, litter, soil and rhizosphere) see Granhall & Lindberg (1977, 1978).

Determination of nitrogenase activities

The acetylene reduction technique was used for determination of nitrogenase activities (Stewart *et al.*, 1967; Granhall & Lindberg, 1978). Incubations at constant temperature (22°C) were performed in the laboratory with 0.1 atm of acetylene under otherwise undisturbed (ambient) gas conditions or sometimes anaerobically (under N_2). Incubations under ambient gas conditions were initially shown to give considerably higher values than anaerobic incubation and ambient conditions were therefore used subsequently. Samples normally exposed to light were incubated under controlled light conditions. Parallel samples without acetylene and gas blanks were always included as controls for background ethylene (Lindberg *et al.* 1979).

Gas chromatographical determinations were performed according to Granhall & Lundgren (1971). Acetylene reduction rates given refer to maximum (linear) rates during 24 to 100 h incubations with subtracted controls.

Basic data on acetylene reduction rates, moisture conditions and pH-ranges of different components and soil horizons from all investigated ecosystems are given in Granhall & Lindberg (1977, 1978), where also further details about methods and recalculations of initial nitrogenase activities and components for estimation of total amounts of nitrogen fixed per site and season are described.

Identification and enumeration of N_2-fixing organisms

Identification and enumeration of N_2-fixing procaryots (blue-green algae and bacteria) were made microscopically, by plate or dilution counts as described in Granhall & Lindberg (1977, 1978) and Reynaud & Roger (1977).

Results and discussion

Acetylene reduction of different components

In the field- and S-layer at Ivantjärnsheden algal crusts, twigs and stumps showed relatively higher activities than other components. If the rather active algal crusts in the young pine stand are omitted, the overall acetylene reduction rates were found to be related to soil moisture levels in the field-, S- and A_0-layers and decreased in the order Ih IV > Ih V > Ih II. Specific activities in the subsoil (A_1, A_2 and B horizon) were higher in the rhizosphere of pine, spruce and dwarf shrubs than in non-rhizosphere (Table 1).

In the mixed pine and spruce stand at Siljansfors (Table 1) spruce shoots and spruce needle litter showed low activities compared with that of decaying woody litter. These results are in agreement with those for pine at Ivantjärnsheden. Decaying spruce bark and spruce logs, however, showed higher values than those from pine.

The S- and A_0-layer of all vegetational strata at Siljansfors showed relatively

334

higher acetylene reduction rates, moisture and pH levels than those at Ivantjärns-heden. Acetylene reduction and moisture in the S-layer of the four strata at Siljans-fors increased in the order I < II < III < IV, with about a tenfold increase in nitrogenase activity in strata dominated by *Sphagnum* (Table 1).

Nitrogenase activity of isolated *Sphagnum* patches responded dramatically to light, and light microscopic examination revealed the presence of intracellular blue-green algae (*Nostoc* sp.) within hyaline cells of the living part of moss plants. No epiphytic algae were observed. The occurrence of intracellular blue-green algae in certain *Sphagnum* mosses has previously been observed in a subarctic mire in northern Sweden (Granhall & Selander, 1973; Granhall & v. Hofsten, 1976).

Apart from rhizosphere fixation in the lower soil horizons, acetylene reduction rates were generally low in both A_0, A_2 and B horizons, declined rapidly with depth and were of the same order as those in the pine stands (Table 1).

Seasonal variations and correlation with environmental factors

Seasonal variations in acetylene reduction of various soil horizons were followed in 1974 at Ivantjärnsheden in the young and old pine stand and partly at Siljansfors in 1974–75. Temperature conditions in the field were very similar between sites, whereas differences in moisture conditions were pronounced between sites in general, but also within sites in relation to vegetation cover and depth.

Low soil moisture contents in the surface layers (field- and S-layer) during the summer influenced N_2-fixation negatively in the pine stands, whereas low soil temperatures were important for N_2-fixation in organogenic layers (S, A_0) in the pine stands and the mixed conifer stand during the early spring and autumn. Apart from this, light conditions influence seasonal changes of acetylene reduction in the S-layer, especially in *Sphagnum* strata at Siljansfors due to photosynthetic N_2-fixation by moss-associated blue-green algae. The season for N_2-fixation (at Ivantjärnsheden) closely coincided with the period with mean soil temperatures above $0°C$ in the field, i.e., approximately 7 months.

The effects of moisture and temperature were also studied separately in root-free humus from the old pine stand. Temperature and moisture optima for N_2-fixation were $28°C$ and 180% H_2O_{dw}, respectively and Q_{10} was close to 3.

N_2-fixation in the old pine stand was further positively correlated with soil respiration, certain soil animals, bacterial (aerobic) counts on N-free media and organic matter, but not with total C, N, P or K contents or with inorganic nitrogen (< 15 µg N g^{-1} dw; Popović, 1976).

Organisms

Aerobic potentially N_2-fixing bacteria, approximately 0.5% of the total bacterial population, were much more numerous than strict anaerobic N_2-fixers. N_2-fixing bacteria decreased in number with depth in relation to the distribution of organic matter. Blue-green algae occurred only in algal crusts in the young pine stand and in *Sphagnum* strata at Siljansfors. N_2-fixing lichens were rare or absent at all sites. Other symbiotic N_2-fixers were represented only by a few *Alnus incana* trees at Siljansfors.

Table 1. Comparison of nitrogen fixation in three different coniferous forest ecosystems considering activity of major components. Values within parentheses based on data from other sites of similar character. Revised from Granhall & Lindberg (1978).

Compartment	Ih II (15–20)	Ih V (120)	Sf (160)	Component	Weight (g dw m⁻²)	Mean nitrogenase activity (ng N g⁻¹ dw h⁻¹) at 10°C Q_{10}(12–22°C)~3	Estimated annual nitrogen fixation (mg N m⁻² yr⁻¹)
Phyllosphere	x			Pine, shoots	73[1]	0.04	<0.1
		x		,,	475[1]	(0.04)	0.1
			x	,,	272[7]	(0.04)	0.1
			x	Spruce, shoots	997[7]	0.06	0.2
	x			Pine, bark	–	0.00	0.0
		x		,,	305[1]	1.4	2.1
			x	,,	457[7]	(1.4)	3.2
			x	Spruce, bark	748[7]	(1.4)	5.3
Soil: Field & S layer	x	x		Crusts, blue-green algae	(5% cover)[3,8]	6.7 (μg N m⁻² h⁻¹)	17.0
		x		Pine, bark	45[2]	0.03	<0.1
			x	,,	61[2]	0.03	<0.1
			x	,,	(63)[3,7]	0.03	<0.1
	x			Spruce, bark	(107)[3]	30	16.1
		x		Pine, twigs & branches	(462)[2]	0.12	0.3
	x			,,	55[2]	0.45	0.1
			x	,,	(192)[3,7]	0.40	0.2
			x	Spruce, twigs & branches	(72)[3,7]	(0.40)	0.1
		x		Pine, logs	(312)[2]	(0.20)	0.6
	x			,,	(20)[3]	0.20	<0.1
	x			Pine & spruce, logs	(60)[3,9]	9.9	3.0
			x	Old stumps, total[12]	(1 650)[3]	0.63	5.2
		x		,,	(990)[3,8]	1.9	9.5
			x	,,	(70)[3,9]	0.54	0.2
	x			Field & S layer, dwarf shrubs, mosses & non-woody litter	1 150[2,4]	0.001	<0.1
Stratum I:			x		998[2,4]	0.06	0.3
Stratum II:			x	S layer, mosses & non-woody litter	7 200[3]	1.1	39.9
Stratum III:			x	,,	9 700[3]	2.1	102.7
				,,	10 400[3]	14.3	749.5

Component	Stratum / horizon			Amount	(g N tree^{-1} yr^{-1})[11]	
	Stratum I:		×	1 690[2]	0.09	0.8
	Stratum II:	×		1 900[3]	0.16	1.5
	Stratum III:	×	×	4 100[3]	0.29	6.0
	Stratum IV:	×	×	2 600[3]	0.19	2.5
	,,	×	×	(3 200)[3]	0.29	4.7
Pine root litter below ground	All horizons	×		(304)[3,4]	(1.0)	1.5
,,	,,	×	×	226[4]	2.0	2.3
Spruce root litter below ground	,,		×	(248)[3,7]	(4.6)	2.5
,,	,,	×	×	(355)[3,6]	(16.3)	16.3
Pine, stumps & large roots >0.2 cm below ground	,,	×		268[1]	(0.22)	0.3
	,,		×	1 905[1]	0.43	4.1
,,	,,		×	(2 088)[3,7]	(0.98)	10.0
Spruce, stumps & large roots >0.2 cm below ground	,,		×	(2 986)[3,6]	(3.5)	52.0
Alnus incana, root nodules	Stratum II:		×	(10 trees ha^{-1})[3,9]	(18)	18.0
Dwarf shrub roots, live & dead	A_1, A_2 & B horizons	×		83[4]	(1.3)	0.6
,,	,,		×	105[4]	(1.3)	0.7
,,	(0–30 cm		×	(178)[3,4,9]	(1.3)	1.2
Pine, fine roots <0.2 cm	below A_0)	×		18[4]	0.20	<0.1
,,	,,		×	64[4]	0.39	0.1
,,	,,		×	(70)[3,7]	(0.89)	0.3
Spruce, fine roots <0.2 cm	,,		×	(minor)	2.5	0.1
,,	,,		×	(100)[3,6]	(3.8)	1.9
Non-rhizosphere	,,	×		338 000[2]	0.001	1.7
,,	,,			350 000[5]	0.006	10.6
,,	Stratum I, II, IV:	×		(480 000)[3,10]	0.009	21.8
,,	Stratum III:	×		(480 000)[3,10]	0.017	41.1

[1] From J. G. K. Flower-Ellis (unpubl.).
[2] From H. Staaf & B. Berg (1977, unpubl.).
[3] Present study.
[4] From Persson (1980a, b).
[5] From Popović (1974).
[6] From B. Andersson (unpubl.).
[7] From Albrektson & Andersson (1978).
[8] From Bråkenhielm (1974).
[9] From S. Bråkenhielm, H. Persson & B. Andersson (unpubl.).
[10] From Troedsson & Nykvist (1973).
[11] Recalculated from Akkermans (1971).
[12] Assumption of 15 kg dw stump^{-1} and heartwood/sapwood ratio of 3:1.

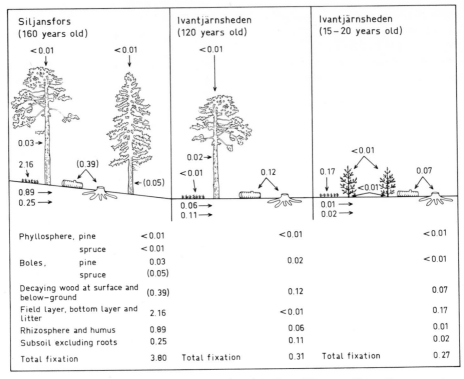

	Siljansfors	Ivantjärnsheden	Ivantjärnsheden
	(160 years old)	(120 years old)	(15–20 years old)

	Siljansfors	Ivantjärnsheden	Ivantjärnsheden
Phyllosphere, pine	<0.01	<0.01	<0.01
spruce	<0.01		
Boles, pine	0.03	0.02	<0.01
spruce	(0.05)		
Decaying wood at surface and below-ground	(0.39)	0.12	0.07
Field layer, bottom layer and litter	2.16	<0.01	0.17
Rhizosphere and humus	0.89	0.06	0.01
Subsoil excluding roots	0.25	0.11	0.02
Total fixation	3.80	Total fixation 0.31	Total fixation 0.27

Figure 1. Annual nitrogen fixation rates (kg N ha^{-1} yr^{-1}) in three different coniferous forest ecosystems. Values within parentheses are uncertain.

Annual nitrogen fixation

Annual N_2-fixation rates in three different ecosystems – young and old pine stands at Ivantjärnsheden and the old, mixed pine and spruce stand at Siljansfors – are summarized in Fig. 1. The phyllosphere of pine and spruce was found to be a rather insignificant source of fixed nitrogen in contrast to the findings of Jones (1970, 1978), Denison (1973) and Jones et al. (1973) for the phyllosphere of Douglas fir and larch. The S-layer in general is very important for N_2-fixation at Siljansfors but not at Ivantjärnsheden, except for algal crusts on bare soil in the young pine stand. The major N_2-fixing component in mature pine stands on sand seems to be decaying wood at surface and below ground, especially stumps. Further investigations on the role and distribution of N_2-fixation in pine stumps are reported in Granhall et al. (1978).

The most important N_2-fixing component at the mixed conifer site (Fig. 1) is the S-layer, followed by the rhizosphere, decaying wood and the subsoil. Major differences between vegetational strata were mainly due to the presence or absence of *Sphagnum* mosses. High fixation rates in *Sphagnum* communities have also been reported from minerotrophic mires (Granhall & Selander, 1973; Granhall & Lid-Torsvik, 1975; Basilier et al., 1978).

N_2-fixation in the A_0-horizon (Table 1) was also generally more important at Siljansfors than at Ivantjärnsheden, due to thicker layer, higher nutrient status,

338

higher moisture content and possibly also due to higher pH-values. In spite of low specific activities the mineral soil is not unimportant, due to the bulk of material present (Table 1 and Fig. 1). N_2-fixation in the lower soil horizons seems, however, (apart from alder) to be mainly associated with living and dead roots of spruce, pine and dwarf shrubs (in that order).

Total annual N_2-fixation 1974 in the young and old pine stand was about 0.027 and 0.031 g N m^{-2} yr^{-1}, respectively, which closely corresponds to an estimated deficit of 0.04 g m^{-2} yr^{-1} in the nitrogen budget for such ecosystems (P. Sollins, unpubl.). As leaching losses (Bringmark, 1980) and denitrification rates (Lindberg & Klemedtsson, unpubl.) seem very low in the pine stands at Ivantjärnsheden most of the fixed nitrogen will be kept within these ecosystems and sooner or later become available for plant growth as NH_4^+, since nitrification rates are also low (Popović, pers. comm.).

The total N_2-fixation of different strata (I–IV) at Siljansfors varied from 0.18–3.84 g N m^{-2} yr^{-1} with a mean overall value of 0.38 g N m^{-2} yr^{-1} (Fig. 1), taking the cover of the various strata into account. During a presumptive total forest rotation of 160 years at Siljansfors, and assuming similar annual inputs, this would correspond to a total input of over half a ton N ha^{-1} of slowly released but easily available nitrogen. This clearly demonstrates that asymbiotic N_2-fixation can be highly significant also in northern coniferous forests. Together with the input from wet deposition of 1–3 kg N ha^{-1} yr^{-1} in Central Sweden (Bringmark, 1980) and dry deposition of about the same magnitude (B. Nihlgård, pers. comm.), this should reduce the need for forest fertilizations considerably, especially in mesic coniferous forest ecosystems.

Acknowledgements

This work was carried out within the Swedish Coniferous Forest Project. We thank several members of the project for valuable contributions to this study.

References

Akkermans, A. D. L. 1971. Nitrogen Fixation and Nodulation of *Alnus* and *Hippophaë* Under Natural Conditions. – Ph D thesis. DSW, Dordrecht, The Netherlands, 85 pp.

Albrektson, A. & Andersson, B. 1978. Biomass in an old mixed coniferous forest in Dalarna. – Swed. Conif. For. Proj. Int. Rep. 79, 40 pp. (In Swedish, English abstract)

Axelsson, B. & Bråkenhielm, S. 1980. Investigation sites of the Swedish Coniferous Forest Project – biological and physiographical features. – In: Persson, T. (ed.) Structure and Function of Northern Coniferous Forests – An Ecosystem Study, Ecol, Bull. (Stockholm) 32: 25–64.

Basilier, K., Granhall, U. & Stenström, T. A. 1978. Nitrogen fixation in wet minerotrophic moss communities of a subarctic mire. – Oikos 31: 236–246.

Bringmark, L. 1980. Ion leaching through a podsol in a Scots pine stand. – In: Persson, T. (ed.) Structure and Function of Northern Coniferous Forests – An Ecosystem Study, Ecol. Bull. (Stockholm) 32: 341–361.

Bringmark, L., Bååth, E., Clarholm, M., Granhall, U., Lindberg, T., Lohm, U., Magnusson, C., Persson, T., Petersson, G., Rosswall, T., Sohlenius, B., Söderström, B. & Vegerfors-Persson, B. 1975. Simultaneous analysis of activity and biomass of soil organisms and soil chemistry in a 120-year-old pine forest at Jädraås, Gästrikland (Central Sweden). – Swed. Conif. For. Proj. Int. Rep. 21, 14 pp. (In Swedish, English abstract)

Bråkenhielm, S. 1974. The vegetation of Ivantjärnsheden. – Swed. Conif. For. Proj. Int. Rep. 18, 51 pp. (In Swedish, English abstract)

Denison, W. C. 1973. Life in tall trees. – Sci. Am. 228(6): 74–80.

Granhall, U. & v. Hofsten, A. 1976. Nitrogenase activity in relation to intracellular organisms in *Sphagnum* mosses. – Physiol. Plant. 36: 88–94.

Granhall, U. & Lid-Torsvik, V. 1975. Nitrogen fixation by bacteria and free-living blue-green algae in tundra areas. – In: Wielgolaski, F. E. (ed.) Fennoscandian Tundra Ecosystems, Part I, pp. 305–315. Berlin–Heidelberg–New York: Springer-Verlag.

Granhall, U. & Lindberg, T. 1977. Nitrogen fixation at coniferous forest sites within the SWECON project. – Swed. Conif. For. Proj. Tech. Rep. 11, 39 pp.

Granhall, U. & Lindberg, T. 1978. Nitrogen fixation in some coniferous forest ecosystems. – In: Granhall, U. (ed.) Environmental Role of Nitrogen-fixing Blue-green Algae and Asymbiotic Bacteria, Ecol. Bull. (Stockholm) 26: 178–192.

Granhall, U. & Lundgren, A. 1971. Nitrogen fixation in Lake Erken. – Limnol. Oceanogr. 16: 711–719.

Granhall, U. & Nilsson, B. 1974. A pilot study of nitrogen fixation at Ivantjärnsheden. – In: Granhall, U. (ed.) Research Notes on Soil Processes, Swed. Conif. For. Proj. Int. Rep. 13: 13–18.

Granhall, U. & Selander, H. 1973. Nitrogen fixation in a subarctic mire. – Oikos 24: 8–15.

Granhall, U., Lindberg, T. & Odö, E. 1978. Decay of woody material – influence of xylophages and nitrogen-fixing bacteria. – In: Granhall, U. (ed.) Nutrient Turnover in the Early Phase after Clear-cutting. Results from Introductory Investigations, Swed. Conif. For. Proj. Int. Rep. 70: 26–38. (In Swedish, English abstract)

Jones, K. 1970. Nitrogen fixation in the phyllosphere of the Douglas fir *Pseudotsuga douglasii*. – Ann. Bot. 34: 239–244.

Jones, K. 1978. The fate of nitrogen fixed by free-living bacteria in temperate coniferous forests. – In: Granhall, U. (ed.) Environmental Role of Nitrogen-fixing Blue-green Algae and Asymbiotic Bacteria, Ecol. Bull. (Stockholm) 26: 199–205.

Jones, K., King, E. & Eastlick, M. 1973. Nitrogen fixation by free-living bacteria in the soil and in the canopy of Douglas fir. – Ann. Bot. 38: 765–772.

Lindberg, T. 1974. Preinvestigation of nitrogen fixation in a coniferous forest ecosystem. – Swed. Conif. For. Proj. Int. Rep. 12, 28 pp. (In Swedish, English abstract)

Lindberg, T., Granhall, U. & Berg, B. 1979. Ethylene formation in some coniferous forest soils. – Soil Biol. Biochem. 11: 637–643.

Paul, E. A. 1978. Contribution of nitrogen fixation to ecosystem functioning and nitrogen fluxes on a global basis. – In: Granhall, U. (ed.) Environmental Role of Nitrogen-fixing Blue-green Algae and Asymbiotic Bacteria, Ecol. Bull. (Stockholm) 26: 282–293.

Persson, H. 1980a. Spatial distribution of fine-root growth, mortality and decomposition in a young Scots pine stand in Central Sweden. – Oikos 34: 77–87.

Persson, H. 1980b. Death and replacement of fine roots in a mature Scots pine stand. – In: Persson, T. (ed.) Structure and Function of Northern Coniferous Forests – An Ecosystem Study, Ecol. Bull. (Stockholm) 32: 251–260.

Popović, B. 1974. Nitrogen mineralization – a comparison between incubation experiments in the field and in the laboratory. – Swed. Conif. For. Proj. Int. Rep. 11, 17 pp. (In Swedish, English abstract)

Popović, B. 1976. Nitrogen mineralization in an old pine stand. – Swed. Conif. For. Proj. Int. Rep. 35, 16 pp. (In Swedish, English abstract)

Reynaud, P. A. & Roger, P. A. 1977. Mileux sélectifs pour la numeration des algues eucaryotes, procaryotes et fixatrices d'azote. – Rev. Ecol. Biol. Sol 14: 421–428.

Staaf, H. & Berg, B. 1977. A structural and chemical description of litter and humus in a mature Scots pine stand. – Swed. Conif. For. Proj. Int. Rep. 65, 31 pp.

Stewart, W. D. P., Fitzgerald, G. P. & Burris, R. H. 1967. *In situ* studies on N_2 fixation using the acetylene reduction technique. – Proc. Nat. Acad. Sci. 58: 2071–2978.

Troedsson, T. & Nykvist, N. 1973. Marklära och Markvård. Stockholm: Almqvist & Wiksell Förlag AB, 402 pp. (In Swedish)

Persson, T. (ed) 1980
Structure and Function of Northern
Coniferous Forests – An Ecosystem Study
Ecol. Bull. (Stockholm) 32:341–361.

ION LEACHING THROUGH A PODSOL IN A SCOTS PINE STAND

L. Bringmark[1]

Abstract

The major ions in rain and soil water were monitored during the growing seasons of 1975 and 1976 in a Scots pine stand in Central Sweden. Weekly sampling was conducted using funnel collectors for rainfall and litter layer leachate and tension lysimeters for mineral soil leachate. Estimates of water flow for calculation of ion flow in the soil were obtained from a hydrological model.

Large amounts of Na in the solution of the mineral soil were considered to be a long-term result of weathering. The solution was enriched with the internally circulating elements K, Ca and Mg in the litter layer. The input of K was especially large in spring and summer. NH_4 was released from surface litter during summer, but effectively immobilised in autumn. NO_3 in rainfall was intercepted in the litter layer during all seasons. The nitrogen flow from the litter layer was one of the few examples where the inflow was not completely controlled by water flow. The very small nitrogen flow through the mineral soil indicated a tight nitrogen cycle. The stand was accumulating nitrogen during the two years of investigation. Another notable observation was that H^+ concentrations in the mineral soil were high early in the year but decreased later.

Additional keywords: Cycling, immobilisation, lysimeters, nutrients, seasonal, weathering.

Introduction

The chemical composition of water undergoes significant changes on its passage through a forest stand. The canopy and the different soil layers all have their specific set of processes, which act in such a way that ions are added or withdrawn from the solution. The ionic composition of the solution closely reflects these processes.

The aim of the present investigation, conducted in a Scots pine forest, was to determine the flows of major ions in vertical profiles. Such profiles may be used for identification of the biological and chemical processes controlling the ion flows. Further qualitative analyses of these processes have been postulated by investigating the ion flows in terms of their temporal patterns and dependence on water flow.

Site and climate

The studies were made in a 120-year-old Scots pine stand at the Swedish Coniferous Forest Project site, Ivantjärnsheden, Central Sweden. This stand (Ih V)

---

[1] Dept. of Plant Ecology, University of Lund, S-223 62 Lund, Sweden

has a well-developed dwarf shrub ground vegetation. The soil is an iron-podsol developed in a layered glacifluvial material, which consists of fine-medium sand overlying coarse sand at 40 cm. The nutrient status is very poor. Some chemical soil properties are given in Table 1. The mean air temperature is 3.8°C, the average annual precipitation 570 mm and the average duration of the snow cover from November 9 to April 24 (Bråkenhielm, 1978; Axelsson & Bråkenhielm, 1980). The two main years of this investigation, 1975 and 1976, were drier than the average (Fig. 1). Further information on site and climate can be found in Jansson (1977) and Axelsson &Bråkenhielm (1980).

Methods

Water sampling devices

Precipitation samples were collected in plastic funnels of 16 cm diameter furnished with stainless metallic sieves on the pipe. Five collectors for incident rain were placed on a nearby clear-cut area and twenty collectors for throughfall were placed in a 100×200 m plot inside the 120-year-old stand according to a randomized design.

Percolates from the litter layer (S) were collected in 10 filled-in funnel lysimeters of 20 cm diameter (Mayer, 1971) in 1974 and 15 lysimeters in 1975 and 1976. The surface litter and the living mosses and lichens forming this layer were carefully cut out and placed on a plastic net in the funnels. The lysimeters were embedded in the undisturbed litter layer with the collection vessels situated in cavities dug out in the soil underneath the funnels. The lysimeter sites were subjectively chosen in a 20×30 m portion of the large plot mentioned above so that different distances from trees were represented.

Tension lysimeters (Cole, 1958; Mayer, 1971) were used at three levels in the mineral soil; 6, 27 and 80 cm below the lower limit of the humus layer. The number of replicates was ten in the upper layers and six at 80 cm during 1975 and 1976, while it was six at all levels in 1974. Lysimeters at different depths were placed in the vicinity of each other so that profiles were formed. The sites were subjectively selected within the same 20×30 m area as the funnel lysimeters.

The porous ceramics used in the lysimeters were circular plates of aluminum oxide with a pore size of 0.6 μm and a diameter of 24 cm. This material has a great resistance to air entry and a very high conductance for water. Thus, extraction of soil water is possible by means of suction to overcome the water tension in the soil. Tests performed by Mayer (1971) revealed that most cations pass unaffected, but P and to some extent S are retained and Al is given off by the plates. pH-buffering strives towards 5.5. An electric pump maintained a continuous pressure at about 0.1 atm below the atmospheric pressure. The leachate volumes in the lysimeters could not be used as flow estimates (see below). Instead, water flow data provided by the water and energy model SOIL (Jansson & Halldin, 1979; Halldin *et al.*, 1980) were used for the calculation of ion flows in the mineral soil. For this procedure the water flows were assumed to be equal for all lysimeters at a certain depth.

Prior to installation, the lysimeters were washed by letting weak HCl and later deionized water pass through until the eluate obtained an electrical conductivity of about 5μS. The plates were dug into the sides of soil pits and placed with their edges at least 10 cm from the pits. In this way the soil above the lysimeters was kept practically undisturbed and root systems were cut only on one side. The pits were refilled with soil.

Sampling and chemical analysis

The collectors were emptied once a week when volume and pH was measured. The samples were usually combined into a composite two-week sample for each category of collectors and were frozen awaiting further chemical analyses. One lysimeter with high water flows at 80 cm depth was treated separately from the composite samples.

The chemical analysis always started with NH_4 and NO_3, which were determined by fractionated distillation, using Devarda's alloy for NO_3, followed by indophenol colorimetry. Na and K were analysed by flame emission, other metals by atomic absorption in air-acetylene flame (Ca, Mg, Mn) or

Table 1. Dry weights and some chemical properties of the iron podsol on the lysimeter location (Ih V). The zero depth is at the upper limit of the mineral soil. * Living mosses, lichens and roots excluded.

	Dry weight (kg m⁻²)*	C (% dw)	N (% dw)	Extractable in 1M NH$_4$Cl (µeq g⁻¹)						pH of the extracts
				Na	K	Ca	Mg	Al	H	
Litter layer (S)	0.70	45	0.94	2	22	90	27	13	34	3.5
Humus layer (FH)	1.99	31	0.65	2	10	47	11	45	32	3.0
Mineral soil, 0–10 cm	109	1.79	0.045	0.16	0.59	0.70	0.25	22	0.42	4.4
Mineral soil, 10–20 cm	121	0.62	0.025	0.13	0.22	0.17	0.11	2.5	0.01	4.7
Mineral soil, 20–30 cm	133	0.12	0.009	0.13	0.14	0.11	0.13	0.8	0.00	4.8

Table 2. Coefficient of variation ($s/\bar{x}$) for spatial distribution of ion flows (rainfall and S-layer) and ion concentrations (mineral soil), as determined on some selected occasions. Weekly water flows measured in the sampling devices are indicated. * = not calculated.

Date of sampling	Water flow (mm)	n	H	Na	K	Ca	Mg	NH$_4$	NO$_3$	Cl	SO$_4$
Incoming rain (flows)											
27 Aug. 1975	10.0	5	0.09	0.14	0.38	0.16	0.19	0.13	0.18	0.05	*
Throughfall (flows)											
27 Aug. 1975	8.7	20	0.27	0.49	0.84	0.73	0.68	0.63	0.22	0.51	*
S-layer outflow (flows)											
17 July 1974	13.7	10	0.46	0.45	0.63	0.48	0.50	0.43	0.53	0.32	0.49
27 Aug. 1975	8.9	15	0.58	0.58	0.95	0.39	0.47	0.80	0.45	0.42	0.63
6 cm depth in mineral soil (conc.)											
23 Oct. 1974	13.4	6	0.48	0.48	0.73	0.84	0.58	0.74	0.33	1.54	0.48
5 Nov. 1975	7.8	10	0.90	0.52	0.56	0.50	0.79	0.46	0.64	0.58	0.44
27 cm depth in mineral soil (conc.)											
9 July 1974	6.2	6	1.19	0.58	0.43	0.58	0.52	0.68	0.64	0.75	0.38
5 Nov. 1975	7.0	10	1.31	0.55	0.67	0.87	0.87	1.77	1.05	0.52	0.63
80 cm depth in mineral soil (conc.)											
9 July 1974	1.4	5	0.44	0.33	0.58	0.58	0.48	*	0.83	*	*

in a carbon rod atomizer (Al). $LaCl_3$ was added to samples to counteract disturbances in the Ca analysis. PO_4 was determined by antimon-molybdate colorimetry. Cl was titrated with $Hg(NO_3)_2$ in a phototitrator, using diphenylcarbazon as indicator. SO_4 was determined by photometric titration with $Ba(ClO_4)_2$, using Thurin-indicator and samples pretreated in H^+-saturated cation exchangers.

Statistical methods

The spatial variability of concentrations was estimated on a few events of high rainfall (Table 2), when sufficiently large water volumes were available for chemical analysis of individual samples. The standard deviations of water and ion flows were calculated for precipitation and litter layer leachate, while the standard deviations of concentrations had to be calculated for the tension lysimeters since these lysimeters yielded unreliable flow estimates (see below).

Under the assumption of constancy in the sources of heterogeneity, spatial standard deviations were extrapolated to longer periods. If different coefficients of variations $(s/\bar{x})$ were found on different occasions (Table 2), the largest value was used. For the tension lysimeters in the mineral soil the standard deviations of concentrations were regarded as valid for ion flows.

A t-test was performed on the null hypothesis of equality of ion flows at different depths (Tables 3 and 5). As standard deviations as well as population sizes were unequal, the t' procedure described by Snedecor & Cochran (1973) was used for the 0.05 level of significance. The degrees of freedom of the smallest population was used for the 0.01 level of significance. The same procedure was used for testing differences between periods at a certain depth.

The influence of water flow on ion flows was analysed by considering two extreme conditions:

(1) Concentrations are independent of water flow and, consequently, ion flow depends on water flow.
(2) Ion flow is independent of water flow.

The degree of agreement with the two conditions was described by the regression equation:

$$\log I = \beta \cdot \log W + \alpha \tag{1}$$

where I is weekly ion flow and W is weekly water flow. The two conditions correspond to $\beta = 1$ and $\beta = 0$, respectively, which were used as null hypotheses in tests with the variable $t = (b - \beta)/s_b$ (Snedecor & Cochran, 1973) and where b is the estimate of β.

Results

Water flows

Most of the rainfall (>85% of the throughfall) was recovered in the litter lysimeters (Fig. 1), hence the conclusion that the funnel lysimeters in the litter layer did not underestimate the water flow. However, it was often observed that in dry periods the water contents of the lysimeters were higher than in the surrounding undisturbed S-layer. In early spring and late autumn, freezing in the litter lysimeters impeded the water flow (Fig. 1). This effect was not present in the computed water flows from lower soil depths.

When water flows recorded in tension lysimeters were compared to water flows computed by the water model SOIL (Jansson & Halldin, 1979), it became clear that peak flows were underestimated by the tension lysimeters and low flows sometimes overestimated, as can be seen at the 27 cm depth in Fig. 1. These aberrations were due to a lower water conductivity and a different suction in the lysimeters compared to the soil. The periods of capillary rise resulting from the simulations could not be observed in the lysimeters. All these imperfections of the tension lysimeters are arguments for the use of SOIL data as estimates of water flow in the mineral soil. SOIL computes energy and water variables at different

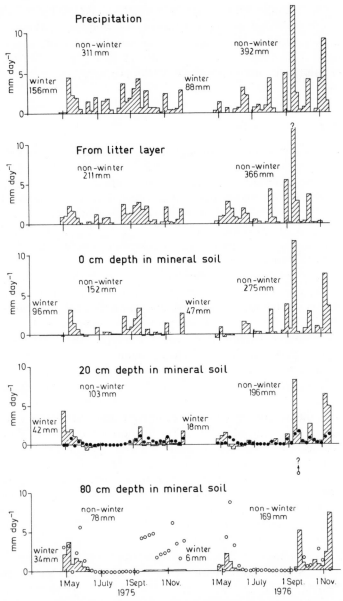

Figure 1. Weekly water flows (mm day^{-1}) in incoming precipitation above canopy and at different levels in the soil during the non-winter periods in 1975 and 1976. Total flows for these periods and the preceding winters are noted. Precipitation and litter layer outflow are measured, while percolation in the three levels of mineral soil is simulated (Halldin *et al.*, 1980). Measured flows in tension lysimeters at 27 cm (●) and in a single lysimeter with very large water flow at 80 cm (○) are shown for comparison. Underestimation due to overflow in collecting bottles is indicated by a question mark (?).

345

soil depths using climatic data as driving variables. The leachates sampled in the lysimeters were regarded as representative subsamples of the water passing through the soil, enabling the calculation of ion flows by the use of measured concentrations. This may not be fully correct in the early spring as tension lysimeters require some initial time to function properly.

Spatial heterogeneity of ion flows

When the incoming rain filtered through the canopy, there was an increase of the spatial variation of the ion fluxes (Table 2). A high level of spatial variability was also found in the different soil layers. The geometry of the tree crowns, the patchiness of the shrubs and bottom layer vegetation, the variable allocation of surface litter, and living and dead roots, all contributed to the spatial heterogeneity, and so did the dispersion of the water flows resulting from variations in pore velocities. The spatial variation is important in judging the statistical significance of differences between levels.

To allow the calculation of the variance in fluxes during longer periods using occasional determinations, the assumption of constancy in the coefficient of variation $(s/\bar{x})$ was necessary. An invariable geometry of the canopy and the soil pores supports this assumption. Each portion of water is subject to the same dispersion regardless of the flow rate (Day & Forsythe, 1957). On the other hand, wind speed, plant growth above and below ground, and seasonal developments in source-sink reactions in the soil, may alter the spatial variation. In the few cases where water flow is not limiting for the rate of soil reactions, the influence on each portion of water is different at different flow rates. Dry periods may also affect the ion distribution due to greater importance of diffusion and capillary rise.

The coefficient of variation $(s/\bar{x})$ of H^+ in the lysimeters was determined on several occasions. Of 15 weekly H^+ outflows from the S-layer, 10 had $s/\bar{x}$ in the range of 0.35 to 0.65. H^+ concentrations from the 6 cm level had $s/\bar{x}$ in the range of 0.65 to 0.95 in 17 cases out of 26. This reflects a rather unchangeable state of spatial H^+ distribution. At 27 cm the spatial heterogeneity was influenced by the seasonal development of the concentrations with an average $s/\bar{x}$ of 0.86 in periods of high concentrations (cf. Table 4) and 1.66 in periods of low concentration.

Other ion species showed spatial variations with small changes between two recordings of the S-layer output with the exception of K and NH_4 (Table 2), both having a seasonal trend in their flows. Two recordings at 27 cm made the assumption of constancy less justified, especially for nitrogen. However, the increased relative variability of nitrogen, as well as hydrogen ions, at 27 cm is associated with very small flows.

One tension lysimeter at 80 cm yielded very large water volumes, occasionally even exceeding rainfall (Fig. 1). The possible occurrence of narrow channels with high water flow is not easily discovered with lysimeter methods. The coincidence that one lysimeter was placed in such a passage revealed that concentrations were low, diminishing its importance as ion carrier. The water flow in this lysimeter was 4.6 times the simulated in 1975 and 2.0 times in the wetter 1976. In the autumn of 1975 large volumes of water penetrated through this passage

Table 3. Ion flows during April 25–December 1 in 1975 and 1976 at different levels in the forest. Depth figures refer to a zero level at the top of the mineral soil. Increase of fluxes after passage of a layer is marked (+) and (++) for the 5% and 1% levels of significance. Decreases of fluxes are marked correspondingly with (–). n.s. = not significant. * = not calculated.

	Ion flow (mmole m^{-2})								
	H	Na	K	Ca	Mg	NH$_4$	NO$_3$	Cl	SO$_4$
1975									
Incoming rain	12.2	3.4	1.3	3.2	1.2	6.4	6.6	3.5	*
	n.s.	+	+	+	+	−	n.s.	+	
Throughfall	11.1	5.7	5.5	5.9	2.6	4.2	6.3	6.0	*
	n.s.	n.s.	n.s.	++	+	n.s.	−−		
S-layer outflow	11.7	6.0	9.2	13.3	4.4	5.6	1.4	*	*
	n.s.	++	n.s.	−	n.s.	−−	−−		
6 cm depth	7.6	31.6	7.4	7.2	7.5	1.1	0.55	*	*
	−	−−	−	−−	−−	−−			
27 cm depth	*	13.9	0.96	2.2	0.88	0.15	0.16	*	*
	n.s.	−	−	n.s.	n.s.	n.s.			
80 cm depth	0.38	9.8	0.30	0.65	0.55	0.07	0.08	*	*
1976									
Incoming rain	14.1	2.5	1.3	1.9	0.60	12.2	11.6	3.9	*
	n.s.	++	++	++	++	−−	−	++	
Throughfall	12.1	4.4	4.9	4.0	1.7	7.2	9.0	7.3	*
	n.s.	+	+	++	++	n.s.	−−	++	
S-layer outflow	13.0	7.7	15.0	14.9	5.5	7.6	1.2	13.7	31.3
	−−	++	n.s.	−−	n.s.	−−	−−	n.s.	n.s.
6 cm depth	5.3	28.8	11.6	7.8	6.8	0.85	0.56	23.1	23.1
	n.s.	n.s.	−	n.s.	n.s.	n.s.	−	n.s.	−−
27 cm depth	2.7	24.9	3.2	5.0	2.9	0.69	0.26	13.8	9.6
	+	++	n.s.	n.s.	n.s.	n.s.	n.s.	*	*
80 cm depth	7.0	71.2	1.68	2.6	1.2	0.70	0.28	38.9	7.7

although simulated water flows were very small (Fig. 1). The ratio between the flow of individual ions in the lysimeter and the calculated average flow of ions at 80 cm in 1975 was in the range of 2.2 for Na to 6.4 for Ca and 5.0 and 3.0 for NH$_4$ and NO$_3$, respectively. In 1976 the same ratios were 0.2 (H, Na) to 1.8 (Mg), NH$_4$ and NO$_3$ having the values 1.3 and 1.0.

Ion flows at different levels

The ion flows on the individual occasions were summed for the non-winter periods in 1975 and 1976 (Table 3). When the sample volumes were insufficient, SO$_4$ and Cl had lowest priority for the chemical analysis, so that these ions in the soil lysimeters could not be summed for 1975. Another gap arose when the tension lysimeters at 6 cm were not started until May 28 in 1975. This gap was filled by using the average concentrations for that lysimeter level. The few occasions with very large water flows (Fig.1) are decisive for the sums. Likens *et al.* (1977) suggest longer observation periods than two years to get a sufficient number of flow events.

When the rain water came into contact with the tree canopy, the solution was enriched with metal cations and Cl (Table 3). The canopy absorbed nitrogen, especially NH_4, while it was indifferent to H^+. Despite the canopy processes, the most important ions in the throughfall remained those in the rain, namely, H^+, NH_4, and NO_3.

The layer of the ecosystem that is between the throughfall and the S-layer output contains shrubs, mosses, and surface litter.

In 1976, being wetter than 1975, the soil solution was enriched with Na, K, Ca, Mg, and Cl in the S-layer while in 1975, which was drier, Na and K differences could not be established with certainty. NO_3 was strongly absorbed in this layer, while the NH_4 flow calculated on an annual basis was not affected.

Between the S-layer output and the 6 cm depth lies a layer containing humified organic matter, dense root systems, root litter and an intensive weathering zone in the mineral soil. This layer absorbed Ca, NH_4 and NO_3. The flows of K, Mg, Cl and SO_4 were not changed significantly but the Na flow increased considerably. The Mg/Ca and the Cl/SO_4 ratios both increased in the humus layer.

In the mineral soil the fate of the ions depended on the water flow. During dry periods there was no deep percolation (Fig. 1), so the elements were prevented from leaching out of the root zone. This was very pronounced in 1975 (Table 3). In 1976 only K, NO_3 an SO_4 were absorbed above the 27 cm level.

At 80 cm depth the occasions with water flow were sparse (Fig. 1). Flushes of water occurred immediately after rainstorms, but this did not mean immediate penetration of water from the surface, as tension waves travel faster than the water itself through sand (Andersen & Sevel, 1974). The rather long residence time of the water made it very susceptible to local source-sink reactions. Na and Cl were the major ions at 80 cm and the annual leaching was very variable (Table 3).

There were other elements of importance besides those listed in Table 3, some of which were measured for shorter periods. In 1975 a rather substantial Mn flow of 1.4 mmoles m^{-2} was recorded in the S-layer, while the Mn flow was 0.6 at 6 cm and 0.04 at 27 cm. Recorded Al flows were of the same magnitude. During September–December 1976 there were 0.03 mmoles m^{-2} in incoming rain, 0.05 in throughfall, 2.6 in S-layer leachate, 0.7 at 6 cm and 0.6 at 27 cm.This means that only small amounts of Al were soluble in the sandy soil despite an occasionally low pH. A low level of soluble Al allows humus substances to be mobile in the soil profile (Petersen, 1976), a precondition for podsolisation.

PO_4 concentrations measured in the autumn of 1974 were always lower than 0.5 μM in the mineral soil and 3 μM in the S-layer output. However, it should be noted that the tension lysimeters are very unsuitable for PO_4 measurements.

Electric charge balance of soil solutions

The measured cations and anions should balance each other in acid rainwater (Ulrich *et al.*,1979a). This provides a check on the chemical analysis. This check

Table 4. Dependence of soil solution concentrations on water flow and season in the non-winter periods of 1974, 1975 and 1976. The slope (b) of the linear regressions log I (weekly ion flux in mmole m^{-2} day^{-1}) on log W (weekly water flow in mm day^{-1}) is noted, as well as rejections with level of significance of two null hypotheses concerning β. Dates are indicated where different seasons are treated separately.

Soil level	Number of observations	Mean conc. with (s.d.) (μM)		95% confidence interval of slope b	Rejections $\beta = 0$	$\beta = 1$
H						
S-layer outflow	58	66	(59)	0.82 ± 0.12	1%	1%
6 cm, April 25–Aug. 12	21	152	(198)	0.67 ± 0.26	1%	1%
6 cm, Aug. 12–Dec. 1	28	16	(27)	0.91 ± 0.23	1%	n.s.
27 cm, April 25–Aug. 12	26	169	(190)	1.15 ± 0.51	1%	n.s.
27 cm, Aug. 12–Dec. 1	27	10	(38)	1.01 ± 0.30	1%	n.s.
80 cm, April 25–Sept. 10	12	202	(112)	0.45 ± 0.50	n.s.	5%
80 cm, Sept. 10–Dec. 1	19	21	(30)	1.45 ± 0.50	1%	n.s.
Na						
6 cm	28	176	(102)	0.93 ± 0.26	1%	n.s.
K						
S-layer outflow, April 25–Sept. 10	27	75	(36)	0.80 ± 0.13	1%	1%
S-layer outflow, Sept. 10–Dec. 1	16	11	(16)	0.92 ± 0.15	1%	n.s.
6 cm	29	50	(18)	0.98 ± 0.10	1%	n.s.
27 cm	33	15	(12)	0.85 ± 0.15	1%	n.s.
Ca						
S-layer	43	60	(21)	0.92 ± 0.08	1%	5%
6 cm	26	45	(18)	1.03 ± 0.12	1%	n.s.
27 cm	31	30	(21)	0.94 ± 0.20	1%	n.s.
Mg						
S-layer outflow	41	22	(6.7)	0.85 ± 0.11	1%	1%
6 cm	31	41	(20)	0.99 ± 0.13	1%	n.s.
27 cm	32	15	(6.4)	0.82 ± 0.14	1%	5%
NH$_4$						
S-layer outflow, April 25–Sept. 1	20	89	(100)	0.34 ± 0.24	1%	1%
S-layer outflow, Sept. 1–Dec. 1	16	31	(42)	0.32 ± 0.38	n.s.	1%
6 cm	26	6.7	(7.1)	0.90 ± 0.19	1%	n.s.
NO$_3$						
S-layer outflow, April 25–Sept. 1	20	13	(12)	0.63 ± 0.16	1%	1%
S-layer outflow, Sept. 1–Dec. 1	13	5	(3)	0.68 ± 0.49	1%	n.s.
6 cm	24	2.1	(1.4)	0.90 ± 0.41	1%	n.s.
Cl						
S-layer outflow	32	73	(58)	0.53 ± 0.18	1%	1%
27 cm	25	167	(131)	0.83 ± 0.19	1%	n.s.
SO$_4$						
S-layer outflow	32	81	(34)	0.88 ± 0.14	1%	n.s.
27 cm	22	61	(32)	0.95 ± 0.11	1%	n.s.

Table 5. K, NH_4 and NO_3 flows at the topsoil layers during selected parts of non-winter periods. Increase and decrease marked as in Table 3.

	Ion flow (mmole m^{-2})					
	K		NH_4		NO_3	
	Before Sept. 10	After Sept. 10	Before Sept. 1	After Sept. 1	Before Sept. 1	After Sept.1
1975						
Throughfall	3.8	1.7	1.9	2.4	3.0	3.3
	n.s.	n.s.	+	n.s.	− −	− −
S-layer outflow	6.8	2.4	4.0	1.6	0.87	0.50
	n.s.	n.s.	− −	− −	− −	− −
6 cm depth	5.5	1.8	0.95	0.10	0.45	0.09
1976						
Throughfall	2.7	2.3	1.7	5.5	2.9	6.1
	+	n.s.	+ +	− −	− −	− −
S-layer outflow	10.0	5.0	6.4	1.2	0.82	0.38
	− −	n.s.	− −	− −	− −	n.s.
6 cm depth	3.8	7.8	0.35	0.50	0.15	0.39

revealed that the incoming rain and throughfall had an excess of anions. Some SO_4 determinations on occasions with high rainfall were obvious overestimates. For this reason SO_4 was omitted from the presentation of rainfall and throughfall data.

The soil solutions all showed an excess of cations. In the soil the existence of other anions besides the measured ones is plausible. Since the bicarbonate ion is unimportant in acid soil solutions, the excess is probably balanced by organic anions. The great importance of organic anions has been considered a characteristic feature of soils in cold climate (Johnson *et al.*, 1977).

Seasonal development of ion concentrations

The subjective inspection of leachate concentrations during the course of three years resulted in the identification of separate periods for K, NH_4, and NO_3 in the litter layer and H in the mineral soil (Table 4, Figs. 2, 3 and 4). Seasonal trends were not found for these ions at other soil levels or for other ion species.

The K, NH_4 and NO_3 concentrations from the S-layer were higher during the first half of the snow-free period than later. The level of significance for the difference was 1 % for K and 5 % for NH_4 and NO_3. The H$^+$-concentrations on the percolating solutions at the three mineral soil depths were also higher during the earlier parts of both years.

Due to the great spatial variability of K flows from the S-layer, an increasing flow during the S-layer passage could only be reliably recorded in 1976 (Table 5). However, the seasonal difference in the concentrations of K is an additional proof that leaching of this element from the litter layer takes place in the early part of

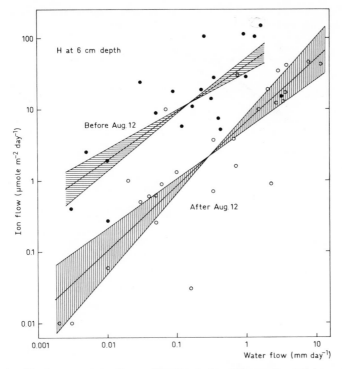

Figure 2. Relationships between water flow and H⁺ flow before (●) and after (○) August 12. The 95% confidence intervals of the slopes are indicated.

the year. NH_4 was also lost from the litter layer during the same periods, while a significant immobilisation occurred in the late part of 1976. NO_3 was always immobilised in the S-layer, although to a lesser extent in the early part of the year.

Influence of water flow on ion flow

In most cases the concentrations in soil percolates were independent of water flow, making the water flow decisive for the transported quantities. This is the condition were the slope (b) of the regression $\log I$ on $\log W$ is equal to 1 (Table 4). The concentrations may have a greater or smaller variation in time under this condition where the slope (b) of the regression $\log I$ on $\log W$ is equal to 1 (Table 4). while Na and H are not (Table 4,Figs. 2 and 3). However, some ion flows that pass a certain lysimeter level are diluted as the water flow increases. H, Ca and Mg concentrations in the S-layer are only slightly diluted, i.e., b is almost 1 (Table 4). Cl is intermediate, while the situation of ion flow being independent of water flow ($b = 0$) is very rare. Some of the latter cases have very scattered values, making it difficult to reject the hypothesis $b = 0$.

K in the S-layer and H⁺ in the mineral soil had a seasonal development with ion flows less dependent on water flow during spring and summer, when there was a greater supply from internal sources in the soil layers (Table 4). The NH_4 and NO_3

351

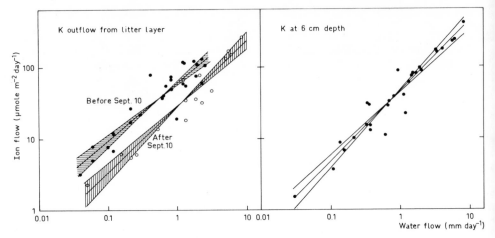

Figure 3. Relationships between water flow and K flow from the litter layer before (●) and after (○) September 10, and at 6 cm depth during the whole non-winter period. The 95% confidence intervals of the slopes are indicated.

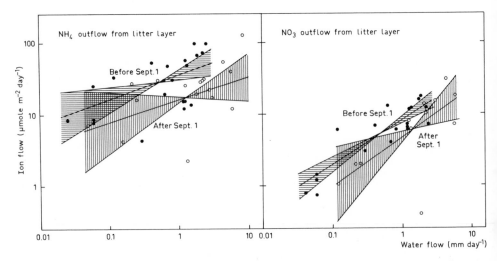

Figure 4. Relationships between water flow and ion flow for NH_4 and NO_3 before (●) and after (○) September 1. The 95% confidence intervals of the slopes are indicated.

flows in the S-layer output had a large scattering around the regression line in autumn, when immobilisation occurred intensively (Fig. 4). NH_4 had lower b values than NO_3, the latter not significantly different from $b = 1$ in autumn (Table 4). During periods of immobilisation, $b < 1$ means that immobilisation is diminished at low water flows, which occurred during autumn for NH_4 and before autumn for NO_3.

The winter period

The period from early December until late April was regarded as winter. The simulations with the SOIL model gave soil water flows which were substantial for the winter of 1974–75 (Fig. 1), indicating that the ion flows during that winter were of great importance for the estimate of the annual leaching in 1975. The following winter, 1975–76, had much smaller water flows.

Records of the soil water chemistry during the winters were restricted to a few occasions at the very end of the seasons in question. These determinations showed that the litter layer leachate concentrations of K, NH_4 and NO_3 in April were at least as in the first half of the non-winter period. The concentrations of these ions were low in the litter layer in November, which meant that an increase occurred during the winter, possibly as a result of frost action (Khonnolaynen & Reppo, 1975). However, the measurements are too few for reliable conclusions to be made. When concentrations are independent of water flow and well buffered (Table 4), the winter flows may be estimated from the average concentrations.

During the winter of 1974–75 the incoming snowfall was 156 mm (Fig. 1). The load of some of the ions in mmoles m^{-2} in this snow was: K 3.34, Ca 3.26, Mg 1.30, NH_4 2.52, NO_3 3.79, Cl 2.68. In these measurements dry deposition was probably included to a greater extent than in the rain recordings. Snow on the ground was analysed on 1 April 1976 and was found to contain much lower concentrations than incoming snow in the previous winter. The lower levels were more pronounced on a tree-less area than in the old pine stand, which probably reflects the degree of melting. A large part of the ionic content of snow is released into the melt-water already in the early phases of snow-melt (Johannesen et al., 1975).

Discussion

Water as ion-transport medium

Efflux-influx balances of ions in percolating water are the joint results of many processes in a soil layer, summarized by the equation:

$$\Delta = w + r - u - i - a \qquad (2)$$

where Δ is the vertical output minus input balance, w is weathering, r release from organic material, u root uptake, i immobilisation in litter and humus and a is change of the adsorbed amount. The different elements are more or less involved in these processes.

The ion flows become totally dependent on water flow (Table 4), a frequently occurring situation, when the quantitatively most important terms in the equation are dependent on the water flow or if the influx is large. Water flow might counteract the build-up of concentration gradients, which would otherwise retard processes for which diffusion through the soil pores are rate limiting.

The occurrence of locally very intensive water flows found at 80 cm indicates that water may pass the root zone unaffected. Some authors stress the very great importance of transport in large pores (Troedsson, 1955). Possible causes for such transport are the build-up of air-pressure, especially in small pores, at the entry of water (Dixon, 1971) and the seasonal occurrence of hydrophobic substances in the soil (Fridland, 1976).The most important reason, however, for irregular percolation in a layered soil is the vertical gradient of the hydraulic conductivity (Starr et al., 1978). When the soil solution enters a coarser layer with increased hydraulic conductivity, the broad-front percolation breaks up into so-called fingers of intensive flow.

Starr et al. (1978), investigating a soil similarly textured to that at Ivantjärnsheden, found that the fingers occupied 5% of the cross section. If this figure was applied to the lysimeter with abundant water flow, 10% to 30% of the individual ion flows at 80 cm passed through fingers in the dry year 1975, while corresponding values for the wetter 1976 were 1% to 9%. If the fingering in lower layers causes variable flow velocities in upper layers, this would affect the absorbing efficiency of the root system.

The large stochastic variation, the seasonal trends and the dilution of some ion concentrations in the soil profile reveal influences from factors other than the water flow. In contrast, the concentrations of all the major ions in streams of some forested watersheds are highly predictable from water flow, even if some may be diluted or increased with increased flow (Likens et al., 1977). The short-term fluctuations in the soil profile do not affect the stream chemistry, which is more dependent on the different origins of the water.

Weathering

Possible approaches to the quantification of weathering are an input/output analysis of the ecosystem combined with biomass increment or, alternatively, construction of a H^+ budget (Likens et al., 1977). A more direct approach is to set up element budgets in soil profiles (O. Tamm, 1920), but this cannot give the short-term dynamics. A weathering indicator in the soil solution would be desirable. Na has the advantage of being involved in biological cycles to a lesser degree than K, Ca and Mg. Furthermore, Na is entirely confined to feldspars in granitic rocks (Rueslåtten & Jørgensen, 1977) and may, thus, be related to mineralogical studies of the soil profile.

Rueslåtten & Jørgensen found that 50% of the feldspars had disappeared in the bleached horizon (A_2) of a Norwegian podsol as compared to the unaffected parent rock. This information makes possible a rough calculation of the weathering rates of different elements relative to Na. The C-horizon minerals of Ivantjärnsheden have the atomic ratios K/Na 0.71, Ca/Na 0.27 and Mg/Na 0.24 while the A_2 horizon has the ratios K/Na 1.02, Ca/Na 0.32 and Mg/Na 0.18 (Bringmark & Petersson, 1975). If the denominator (Na) is reduced by 50% in A_2 the corresponding losses of K are 28%, Ca 41% and Mg 62%, respectively. O. Tamm (1920) found similar figures for the loss of K, Ca and Mg from the A_2 horizons in seven podsols, while the Na losses were much lower. Assuming constant weathering ratios during the whole history of the soil profile each atom of Na was liberated with 0.40 atoms of K in the beginning and 0.57 atoms of K at the end due to the progressive change of the mineral composition.

354

Circulation of sodium and chloride

A considerable amount of the Na flow measured in the mineral soil at Ivantjärnsheden can be assigned to weathering. An alternative source of Na is deposition which, in this investigation, was underestimated due to the exclusion of the winter period. However, the winter deposition of Na at nearby meteorological stations is, according to the Meteorological Institute of Stockholm University (MISU), small in comparison with the total Na flows measured in the soil. Another factor that may influence the flow rates of Na in the soil is the internal storage and circulation of Na,which may delay the outflow. Successive analyses of annual budgets in forest ecosystems reveal great fluctuations of the Na storage (Ulrich et al., 1979b). The small Na flow recorded at 80 cm in 1975 followed by the large flow in 1976 indicated the same situation at Ivantjärnsheden (Table 3). A possible means to reduce the influence of internal circulation is, thus, to take a longer period into consideration. Since the winter deposition probably was small, the difference between Na in throughfall and the flow at 27 cm depth for the two-year investigation period can be regarded as an approximate estimate of the weathering.

Another non-essential nutrient that can be temporarily withheld is Cl (Ulrich et al., 1979b). The fact that Cl was only partly dependent on water flow in the S-layer (Table 4) indicates that Cl may circulate for electroneutrality reasons. As Cl is not adsorbed, it is more mobile than Na.

Release from organic material and immobilisation

Calcium, magnesium and potassium

There is a small input of fine litter during the whole growing season (Flower-Ellis & Olsson, 1978) but the bulk of the needle litter falls from the middle of August to the middle of October. According to Staaf & Berg (1977), K leaching starts immediately after litterfall, which would have implied increased outflow of K during the autumn. The lowered concentrations of K in litter layer leachates after September 10 (Table 4), thus, must depend on a delay mechanism in this layer. A probable explanation of the small losses of K may be the requirement of mosses, which have their predominant growth period in autumn (C. O. Tamm, 1953).

In determining the outflow of K, Ca and Mg from the litter layer, the leaching of litter as well as leaching of the canopy is important. The water flow is decisive to a great extent but a very small part of the flow is determined by some other source than mere leaching of the litter (Table 4). The ratio between the additions to the moisture stream in the canopies and in the litter layer is high for K and low for Ca, while Mg is intermediate. This reflects different degrees of binding to the organic material (Staaf & Berg, 1977).

In the soil layer between the litter layer and 6 cm depth, several terms in Eq. (2) are important, i.e., release from organic material, uptake in roots and weathering. The input/output balance in the lysimeters is the combined effect of these processes. The more or less continuous large root litter production in the layer (Persson, 1978), leads to a substantial liberation of K, Ca and Mg (Staaf & Berg, 1977). However, most of this is recycled for new root growth within the soil layer, Ca more efficiently than K and Mg.

In 1975 the small metal ion percolation measured at the 27 cm depth level probably favoured the diffusion to roots. In 1976 all metal ions had higher downward fluxes at 27 cm (Table 3). Metal ions stored in the mineral soil might, thus, have been released that year. The factors influencing uptake are root geometry, diffusion and adsorption properties of the ion in the soil pores, and transfers that increase the concentration (Bosatta et al., 1980). At the entry at 6 cm, K, Ca and Mg concentrations were approximately equal, but the Ca concentration was lowered less than the others at 27 cm (Table 4). This is in contrast to the humus layer, in which the Ca losses were the smallest. The buffering by soil adsorption obviously leads to other results with respect to the uptake/leaching ratios in the mineral soil.

Nitrogen

Nitrogen is of major interest in determining the primary production in boreal forests. The atmospheric deposition is the most important source of nitrogen for the nutrient deficient site of Ivantjärnsheden. Microbial fixation of N_2 is 2.5 mmoles m^{-2} (Granhall & Lindberg, 1977), which is only one-fifth to one-tenth of the deposition in 1975 and 1976. It should be noted that the atmospheric input of nitrogen in Central Sweden has increased considerably during recent decades (Odén, 1975). There may also be an additional input as deposition of particles which, like the nitrogen in rainwater, are intercepted in the canopy.

Newly formed needle litter accumulates nitrogen during the initial 1.5 years (Staaf & Berg, 1977) as a result of the microbial demand. There is always a balance between mineralisation and immobilisation in the litter layer, the latter being favoured by a low average age of the litter, high C/N-ratio and a high microbial activity. Before September 1 there was a net release of NH_4 from the S-layer as a whole, which turned into net immobilisation after this date (Table 5, Fig. 5). This may be explained by the concept of a critical C/N-ratio for the microorganisms (Parnas, 1975) but vigorous moss growth might also be an explanation. The populations of fungi and bacteria measured in the litter and humus layers were largest towards the autumn (Clarholm, 1977; Söderström, 1979). The litter layers in the lysimeters did not dry up as severely as the intact layer so conditions for microorganism growth were more favourable in the lysimeters during drought periods.

As the NH_4 outflow from the S-layer was only partly dependent on water flow (Table 4), other controlling factors have to be considered. These would be the ones important for the growth of the immobilising organisms. The climatic or biological factors may have an immediate influence, but part of the decomposer performance at a certain time is the result of the previous conditions during the year (Bosatta et al., 1980).

As NH_4 is the nitrogen form produced during mineralisation, immobilisation is the only process in Eq. (2) affecting NO_3 in the litter layer. There was no complete interruption in immobilisation of NO_3 at any time, but the concentrations in the S-layer outflow were higher in the beginning of the year than later, indicating a low initial effect of microorganisms and mosses (Tables 4 and 5). The water flow played a slightly greater role for the NO_3 flux out of the S-layer than for the NH_4 flux, but the amount coming through was very small at all times.

The leaching losses of both NH_4 and NO_3 from the humus layer were very small

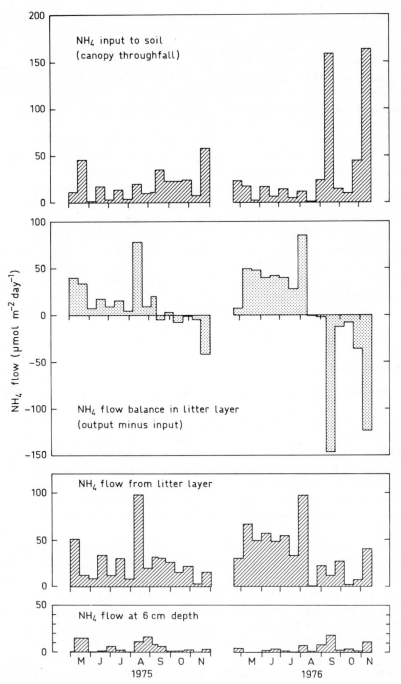

Figure 5. NH$_4$ flows at different levels in and adjacent to the mor layer during the snow-free periods of 1975 and 1976. The resulting flow balance in the litter layer is also shown.

357

(Table 3). The concentrations were independent of the water flow and very variable (Table 4). Although the stand at Ivantjärnsheden is extremely poor in nitrogen, there is still a large internal circulation in the humus layer (Staaf & Berg, 1977). One-third of this comes from humified surface litter originating from the above-ground part of the stand, the rest is an internal turnover of root litter in the humus layer. The amount transported in the water was found to be only 1/100 of the estimated release in the layer. Losses due to denitrification were considered small as formation of NO_3 was not found in incubation experiments (Sohlenius et al., 1976). The roots and mycorrhiza are very efficient in absorbing nitrogen in the humus layer. Mayer (1971), working in a beech forest on a richer locality, measured the input/output balance of a mor layer in which the living roots had been cut off. A substantial release of N was found in this case. The roots were less effective in intercepting NO_3 than NH_4, so the NO_3/NH_4 ratio changed from 0.2 to 0.6 in leachates passing the humus layer at Ivantjärnsheden.

The NH_4 and NO_3 flows remained small throughout the mineral soil (Table 3). The nitrogen involved in the root litter production of these soil layers seemed to be effectively incorporated in humus. The store of humus nitrogen in the mineral soil (Table 1) was 6500 mmoles m^{-2}. The recorded inflow at 6 cm of inorganic nitrogen would need several thousand years to reach this amount, so other transport mechanisms should be considered. Root growth is a probable alternative.

pH of soil solutions

The release of organic acids from litter (Jacquin & Bruckert, 1965) could be expected to have a pH-lowering effect. However, the H^+ quantities in the water flow were unchanged after percolation through the litter layer (Table 3). Typical equilibrium water extracts from this layer had pH values of about 3.6 (Bringmark & Petersson, 1975), while the average H^+ concentration in the lysimeters corresponded to pH 4.2. H^+-leaching from the litter layer was not fully dependent on the water flow ($b \neq 1$) (Table 4), which points at a larger effectivity of the local buffer system when the soil solution passes slowly. However, a tendency for increased concentrations of H^+ at small water flows was present already in the precipitation.

There was an accumulation of H^+ in the ecosystem as a whole during the snow-free periods of both 1975 and 1976 (Table 3). In 1975 no retention could be recorded with certainty in any single layer, but in 1976 an intensive retention occurred in the stratum containing the humus and bleached horizons. The interception occurred mainly on occasions with very large deposition of H^+, hence the difference between the years.

The high H^+ concentrations, 150 to 200 μM, corresponding to pH 3.8, at 6 and 27 cm before August and at 80 cm before September (Table 4) must have been influenced by organisms or organic matter. One possible hypothesis regarding the seasonally high acidity is that H^+ was released from roots to balance a higher rate of cation uptake. Another hypothesis is production of organic acid resulting from seasonally different decomposition processes. The increased H^+ concentrations encountered on occasions with low water flow (Table 4) indicate that the H^+ sources in the humus and upper mineral soil layers are internal. This was further

358

substantiated by observations of low pH during periods of capillary rise. Local sources are also indicated at 80 cm by $b < 1$ despite the large confidence interval (Table 4).

In the later part of the year the buffering of the soil by minerals seems to become more important leading to the increase in pH. The equilibrium pH of weathering derivates in a system with a CO_2 pressure typical for soils is pH 5 or higher (van Breemen & Wielemaker, 1974). The primary soil minerals have even higher pH values. The equilibrium pH of the bleached horizon at Ivantjärnsheden determined by water extraction (Bringmark & Petersson, 1975) is 4.3–4.6, which is a mixed effect of different minerals and humus. In the lower parts of the mineral soil, where the humus content is low, the equilibrium pH is in the range above pH 5. The pH values of tension lysimeter leachates are in the range of 4.0 to 6.8 at all mineral soil levels after August. A few days are required for near equilibrium between the soil solution and the minerals (van Breemen & Wielemaker, 1974), but the solution is not always resident that long.

Nutrient balance of the forest stand

Sources of elements leading to their circulation in the forest are atmospheric inputs or weathering products. The input/output balance of chloride, which is brought in by the former mechanism, can be observed in the downward moisture stream (Table 3). In 1976 Cl was emitted from the ecosystem. There had probably been an accumulation in the drier 1975. To confirm deviations from steady state conditions a longer observation period is needed as the annual outflow varies with the water flow. Furthermore, lack of dry deposition data and other systematic errors in the input data might lessen the usefulness of the analysis. There might also be neglected entities of the output data, for example, particulate and gaseous nitrogen. However, the dramatic decrease of the nitrogen flow in the mineral soil points to a large accumulation, i.e., conditions far from steady state.

It was previously concluded that the weathering rate of potassium at Ivantjärnsheden is roughly one-half of the sodium weathering. At 27 cm the sodium flow was many times higher than that of potassium (Table 3), which would indicate accumulation of weathered potassium in the ecosystem.

Forest ecosystems have a very large capacity to store nutrients in the biomass and soil organic matter. As long as these components are growing, leaching losses are low. But when the system reaches maturity the output should theoretically increase to match the input. This is actually the case in some old forests, while others continue to accumulate until they reach very old ages (Vitousek & Reiners, 1975). The accumulation appears to occur in cyclic patterns with long build-up periods followed by sudden degradations. In some forest types old stands may reach a state of small-scale tree death and regeneration. In boreal forests very long observation times are needed to record steady state conditions.

The long-term approach can be substituted for investigations on watersheds containing stands of different age. Even on this scale there is a substantial accumulation of N and S in the Swedish forest landscape (Andersson & Eriksson, 1978). The forest systems have probably not had sufficient time to adjust to the steadily increasing levels of these nutrients in the deposition.

The very small leaching losses of nitrogen encountered at Ivantjärnsheden

359

would result in drastic accumulations in the ecosystem at any level of deposition. Other pathways of export must be considered. The very long turn-over times for the organic matter in the mineral soil may warrant the view that this component is a sink for nitrogen. Even at the present high rate of deposition it would take 300 years to build up the store of 6500 mmoles m^{-2} of N in the mineral soil. It is open to discussion how this store is finally mobilized.

Acknowledgements

This work was conducted within the Swedish Coniferous Forest Project and is the result of many persons' efforts. Iréne Persson, Maj-Lis Gernersson, Gunnel Ersson and Bo Johansson deserve special gratitude.

References

Andersen, L. J. & Sevel, T. 1974. Six years environmental tritium profiles in the saturated and unsaturated zones, Grønhøj, Denmark. – In: Isotope Techniques in Groundwater Hydrology, IAEA Proc. Series, Vienna, pp. 3–20.

Andersson, U-M. & Eriksson, E. 1978. Hydrochemical investigations in three representative basins in Sweden. – Swed. Nat. Sci. Res. Council, Report 50, 71 pp.

Axelsson, B. & Bråkenhielm, S. 1980. Investigation sites of the Swedish Coniferous Forest Project – biological and physiographical features. – In: Persson, T. (ed.) Structure and Function of Northern Coniferous Forests – An Ecosystem Study, Ecol. Bull. (Stockholm) 32: 25–64.

Bosatta, E., Bringmark, L. & Staaf, H. 1980. Nitrogen transformations in a Scots pine forest mor – model analysis of mineralization, uptake by roots and leaching. – In: Persson, T. (ed.) Structure and Function of Northern Coniferous Forests – An Ecosystem Study, Ecol. Bull. (Stockholm) 32: 565–589.

Bråkenhielm, S. 1978. Ivantjärnsheden, Jädraås – regional physiography and description of the research area. – Swed. Conif. For. Proj. Tech. Rep. 16, 58 pp.

Breemen, N. van & Wielemaker, W. G. 1974. Buffer intensities and equilibrium pH of minerals and soils: II. Theoretical and actual pH of minerals and soils. – Soil Sci. Soc. Amer. Proc. 38: 61–66.

Bringmark, L. & Petersson, G. 1975. Some chemical soil variables in a 120-year-old Scots pine forest growing on glacifluvial sand (Jädraås, Central Sweden). – Swed. Conif. For. Proj. Int. Rep. 27, 44 p. (In Swedish, English abstract)

Clarholm, M. 1977. Monthly estimations of soil bacteria at Jädraås and a comparison between a young and a mature pine forest on a sandy soil. – Swed. Conif. For. Proj. Tech. Rep. 12, 17 pp.

Cole, D. W. 1958. Alundum tension lysimeter. – Soil Sci. 85: 293–296.

Day, P. R. & Forsythe, W. M. 1957. Hydrodynamic dispersion of solutes in the soil moisture stream. – Soil Sci. Soc. Amer. Proc. 21: 477–480.

Dixon, R. M. 1971. Infiltration role of large soil pores: a channel system concept. – In: Monke, E. J. (ed.) Biological Effects in the Hydrological Cycle, Proc. 3rd Int. Seminar for Hydrology Professors, pp. 136–147. Indiana, Lafayette, Pardue University: Ind. Dept. of Agricultural Engineering.

Flower-Ellis, J. G. K. & Olsson, G. 1978. Litterfall in an age series of Scots pine stands and its variation by components during the years 1973–1976. – Swed. Conif. For. Proj. Tech. Rep. 15, 62 pp.

Fridland, Y. V. 1976. Lipid (alcoholbenzene) fraction of organic matter in different soil groups. – Soviet Soil Sci. 8: 548–553.

Granhall, U. & Lindberg, T. 1977. Nitrogen fixation at coniferous forest sites within the SWECON project. – Swed. Conif. For. Proj. Tech. Rep. 11, 39 pp.

Halldin, S., Grip, H., Jansson, P-E. & Lindgren, Å. 1980. Micrometeorology and hydrology of pine forest ecosystems. II. Theory and models. – In: Persson, T. (ed.) Structure and Function of Northern Coniferous Forests – An Ecosystem Study, Ecol. Bull. (Stockholm) 32: 463–503.

Jacquin, F. & Bruckert, S. 1965. Identification et évolution des acides hydrosolubles des deux litières forestières. – C. R. Acad. Sci. Paris 260: 4556–4559.

Jansson, P-E. 1977. Soil properties at Ivantjärnsheden. – Swed. Conif. For. Proj. Int. Rep. 54, 66 pp. (In Swedish, English abstract)

Jansson, P-E. & Halldin, S. 1979. Model for annual water and energy flow in a layered soil. – In: Halldin, S. (ed.) Comparison of Forest Water and Energy Exchange Models, pp. 145–163. Copenhagen: International Society for Ecological Modelling.

Johannesen, M., Dale, T., Gjessing, E. T., Henriksen, A. & Wright, R. F. 1975. Acid precipitation in Norway: the regional distribution of contaminants in snow and the chemical concentration processes during snowmelt. – Isotopes and Impurities in Snow and Ice, Proc. of the Grenoble Symposium, IAHS Publ. no. 113: 116–120.

Johnson, D. W., Cole, D. W., Gessel, S. P., Singer, M. J. & Minden, R. V. 1977. Carbonic acid leaching in a tropical, temperate, subalpine and northern forest soil. – Arctic and Alpine Research 9: 329–343.

Khonnolaynen, G. I. & Reppo, E. A. 1975. Effect of freezing and thawing on the transformation of soil nitrogen. – Soviet Soil Sci. 7: 574–578.

Likens, G. E., Bormann, F. H., Pierce, R. S., Eaton, J. S. & Johnson, N. M. 1977. Biogeochemistry of a Forested Ecosystem. Heidelberg–London–New York: Springer-Verlag, 146 pp.

Mayer, R. 1971. Bioelement-Transport im Niederschlagswasser und in der Bodenlösung eines Wald-Ökosystems. – Göttinger Bodenkundliche Berichte 19: 1–119.

Odén, S. P. 1975. Acid precipitation: a world concern. – Proc. Conf. Emerging Environmental Problems – Acid Precipitation. EPA-902/9-75-001, Cornell University, pp. 5–44.

Parnas, H. 1975. Model for decomposition of organic materials by microorganisms. – Soil Biol. Biochem. 7: 161–169.

Persson, H. 1978. Root dynamics in a young Scots pine stand in Central Sweden. – Oikos 30: 508–519.

Petersen, L. 1976. Podzols and Podzolization. Copenhagen: DSR Forlag, 293 pp.

Rueslåtten, H. G. & Jørgensen, P. 1977. Mineralogical composition and changes due to podzol weathering in tills from southern Norway. – In: Paquet, H. & Tardy, Y. (eds.) Proc. 2nd Int. Symp. on Water-Rock Interaction 1, pp. 184–194. Strasbourg: CNRS, Inst. de Geologie.

Snedecor, G. W. & Cochran, W. G. 1973. Statistical Methods. Iowa State University Press, 593 pp.

Söderström, B. E. 1979. Seasonal fluctuations of active fungal biomass in horizons of a podzolized pine forest in Central Sweden. – Soil Biol. Biochem. 11: 149–154.

Sohlenius, B., Berg, B., Clarholm, M., Lundkvist, H., Popović, B., Rosswall, T., Staaf, H., Söderström, B. & Wirén, A. 1976. Mineralisation and soil organism activity in a coniferous humus – a model building experiment. – Swed. Conif. For. Proj. Int. Rep. 40, 51 pp. (in Swedish, English abstract)

Staaf, H. & Berg, B. 1977. Mobilization of plant nutrients in a Scots pine forest mor in Central Sweden. – Silva fenn. 11: 210–217.

Starr, J. L., DeRoo, H. C., Frink, C. R. & Parlange, J. Y. 1978. Leaching characteristics of a layered field soil. – Soil Sci. Soc. Am. J. 42: 386–391.

Tamm, C. O. 1953. Growth yield and nutrition in carpets of a forest moss (*Hylocomium splendens*). – Medd. Statens Skogsforskn. Inst. 43, 140 pp.

Tamm, O. 1920. Bodenstudien in der Nordschwedischen Nadelwaldregion. – Medd. Statens SkogsförsAnst. 17: 49–300. (In Swedish, German summary)

Troedsson, T. 1955. Das Wasser des Waldbodens. – Kungl. Skogshögskolans Skrifter (Stockholm) 20, 215 pp. (In Swedish, German summary)

Ulrich, B., Mayer, R. & Khanna, P. K. 1979a. Fracht an chemischen Elementen in den Niederschlägen im Solling. – Z. Pflanzenernähr. u. Bodenk. 142: 601–615.

Ulrich, B., Mayer, R. & Khanna, P. K. 1979b. Deposition von Luftvereinigungen und ihre Auswirkungen auf Waldökosystemen im Solling. Frankfurt am Main: J. D. Sauerländers Verlag, 291 pp.

Vitousek, P. M. & Reiners, W. A. 1975. Ecosystem succession and nutrient retention: a hypothesis. – BioScience 25: 376–381.

361

Persson, T. (ed) 1980
Structure and Function of Northern
Coniferous Forests – An Ecosystem Study
Ecol. Bull. (Stockholm) 32: 363–372.

DECOMPOSITION RATE AND CHEMICAL CHANGES OF SCOTS PINE NEEDLE LITTER.
I. INFLUENCE OF STAND AGE

B. Berg[1] and H. Staaf[2]

Abstract

Decomposition of Scots pine needle litter, its organic components, and release of the plant nutrients N, P, K, S, Ca and Mg were followed in four pine stands on a podzolized sandy soil in Central Sweden over a period of three years. The differences in weight loss rate were generally small but significantly higher in the mature (120 years) stand than in stands aged 60 years and 20–25 years.

Decomposition was slowest in a very thin, young stand, clear-cut seven years before the investigation started. At the latter site, however, the highest leaching rate of K, Mg and P was noted, a phenomenon related to the specific climatic conditions of that site. Nitrogen and phosphorus, on the other hand, seemed to be most efficiently retained in litter when placed in the 60-year-old stand. Cellulose disappearance tended to be faster in the two old stands compared to the two young ones, but otherwise the inter-site differences in decomposition of separate organic components were small.

Additional keywords: Cellulose, lignin, litter-bag, mineralization, plant nutrient.

Background

Decomposition has been studied in the Swedish Coniferous Forest Project partly to gather more information on the process and partly to provide data for simulation models on nutrient transfers in soil (see Bosatta, 1980). At present these models have been tested in a single stand and over a short time domain. In order to extend hypotheses drawn from them in time and to a regional validity, the present and further studies on litter decomposition were started to answer specific questions. Scots pine needle litter was selected as test substrate in these studies.

Introduction

Coniferous litter is characterized by low nutrient concentration, tanned proteins, and a high content of polyphenolic substances; factors which all tend to give it a low

[1] Dept. of Microbiology, Swedish University of Agricultural Sciences, S-750 07 Uppsala, Sweden
Present address: Dept. of Ecology and Environmental Research, Swedish University of Agricultural Sciences, S-750 07 Uppsala, Sweden
[2] Dept. of Plant Ecology, University of Lund, S-223 62 Lund, Sweden

decompostion rate (Millar, 1974). The activity of soil organisms is greatly influenced by temperature (Flanagan & Veum, 1974), so that in cold temperate or boreal forests there is a considerable storage of energy and plant nutrients in litter and humus.

In coniferous forest the total release of essential plant nutrients from soil organic matter is a complex result of long-term changes in the amounts of litter and humus on the forest floor and the immediate effect of temperature, soil moisture and other environmental conditions. Both amount and structural composition of litterfall differs in Scots pine stands of different ages (Mälkönen, 1974; Flower-Ellis & Olsson, 1978). Woody litter is generally decomposed slowly (McFee & Stone, 1966), and increasing amounts of such material could be expected to be transferred to soil as forests get older. Other factors that are changed with stand age are the ground vegetation and tree density, these being factors that influence the soil micro-climate and total amount of litter formed. Tree density has an influence on soil temperature (Ångström, 1936). Increased decomposition rates of whole soil layers (Wright, 1957) and of cellulose (Piene & Van Cleve, 1978) have been found after thinnings in coniferous forests.

The aim of the present study was to investigate the net influence of the environmental factors induced by stand age of Scots pine on the decomposition rate and release of some plant nutrients from one dominant litter type. This was done by incubating an identical litter in stands of different ages close to each other and on the same soil type during a two-year period, and analyzing for weight loss and chemical composition at intervals.

Site description

The studies were made at the Swedish Coniferous Forest Project research site Ivantjärnsheden, Jädraås, in Central Sweden. The site is a plain sandy sediment area with a series of Scots pine stands of which a clear-felled and subsequently planted area of pines aged 5–10 years (Ih I), and stands aged 20–25 years (Ih III), 60 years (Ih IV), and 120 years (Ih V) were used. These stands are all characterized as dry dwarf-shrub forest type (Arnborg, 1953); the ground vegetation and stand characteristics are described in detail by Bråkenhielm (1978). The soil type is an iron podzol. Ih V differs from the others by a coarser soil structure in layers below 40 cm (Jansson, 1977) and as a whole it might be considered drier (dry – very dry dwarf-shrub forest type) than the others because of the lower water retaining capacity of the soil just below the root zone.

Material and methods

Needle collection, storage and weighing

Needle litter was sampled at Ivantjärnsheden in September 1974 from the branches of trees in a stand that was about 15 years old. Brown needles from the falling needle generation were taken at abscission from trees growing in an area of about 20×50 m and were stored at $-20°C$ until sample preparation took place.

Before weighing, the needles were air dried at room temperature to about 5–8% moisture. Dry weight was determined at 85°C and the largest difference in moisture content was less than $\pm 0.5\%$ of the average ($n = 20$).

Field incubations

The litter-bags, made of terylene net with a mesh size of about 1 mm, measured 8×8 cm. An amount of about 2 g of needle litter was enclosed in each bag.

The litter-bags were placed on the litter (L) layer in a measurement plot (1×1 m) in each of 20 blocks in a randomized block design in the different stands (1–3 ha). They were fastened to the ground by 10–15 cm long metal pins.

The experiment started in late October 1974 in all stands, and samplings were made three to six times during a three-year period; most frequently in the oldest stand. Chemical analyses were made on samples incubated for 370, 554 and 1099 days.

On each sampling occasion one sample from each of the 20 plots in each stand was collected. The litter-bags were transported directly to the laboratory and cleaned of moss, lichen and dwarf shrub remnants. After drying at 85°C they were weighed individually and then pooled to one sample for each set before the chemical analyses were carried out.

Chemical analysis

Samples were ground in a laboratory mill equipped with a 1 mm screen. The amounts of water soluble and acetone soluble substances were determined by sonicating the milled sample three times in a sonicator bath and weighing the samples after filtration and drying. The analyses for Klason lignin and solid carbohydrates (xylan, mannan, galactan, rhamnan, araban and cellulose) in the needle samples were carried out according to Betghe et al. (1971). The Klason lignin fraction was also analyzed for total nitrogen content.

The release of water soluble substances from whole needles was investigated on separate samples by allowing the needles to soak in distilled water at room temperature for 10 and 24 hours.

The milled samples were also analyzed for total contents of the elements N, P, K, S, Ca, and Mg. All analyses were in duplicate. Nitrogen was determined by a semi-micro Kjeldahl procedure (Nihlgård, 1972). After an acid wet oxidation in $HNO_3 + HClO_4$, analyses were performed for sulphur by a turbidometric analysis as $BaSO_4$-precipitate (Blanchar et al., 1965), for phosphorus by the vanadate yellow-complex method (Jackson, 1958), and for potassium by a flame photometric procedure. Calcium and magnesium were determined by atomic absorbtion spectrophotometry (Perkin-Elmer 403) in 1% LaCl-solution against acid standards (Pawluk, 1967).

Results and discussion

Methodological aspects

The litter-bags were incubated in very different forest floors. In the stands Ih III, Ih IV and Ih V the litter-bags were quickly grown through by mosses and cowberry shrub, etc. and became covered by new-fallen needle litter. The experimental litter thus had to be carefully cleaned. The litter-bag material was capable of withstanding a period of at least five years although it became brittle after this time. In the very young stand (Ih I), on the other hand, problems arose because of the relatively strong sunlight. This made the litter-bags very brittle and terminated the study earlier than in the other stands. In this area many bags were also destroyed by birds. No mosses or other vegetation grew into the bags.

There was no significant skewness in weight loss figures from the separate samplings in different stands according to statistical tests (Snedecor & Cochran, 1956). Even if replicates were few ($n = 20$), the differences between stands were analyzed by Student's t-test.

Table 1. Comparison of weight losses of needle litter in a series of very young (Ih I) to old (Ih V) Scots pine stands at Ivantjärnsheden. The weight loss measurement was run with 20 replicate samples. Start of measurement on 23 October 1974. Standard error within parentheses. * = not determined.

Date	Incubation time (days)	Weight loss (% of initial amount)			
		Ih I	Ih III	Ih IV	Ih V
23 Oct 1974	0	0	0	0	0
26 May 1975	212	13.6 (0.3)	*	*	17.7 (0.3)
12 Sept 1975	323	23.6 (0.4)	*	*	23.3 (0.4)
28 Oct 1975	370 (1 yr)	25.8 (0.4)	25.8 (0.6)	27.0 (0.5)	28.2 (0.6)
28 April 1976	554	25.8 (0.4)	27.6 (0.8)	*	32.2 (0.4)
10 Nov 1976	747 (2 yrs)	*	*	*	42.8 (0.8)
27 Oct 1977	1099 (3 yrs)	*	53.0 (1.1)	53.4 (1.5)	58.1 (1.6)

Weight loss

For most periods the weight loss rate in the mature stand (Ih V) was significantly higher than that in the very young stand (Ih I) (Table 1). This weight loss had become significantly different ($p < 0.001$) by 212 days, i.e., after the first winter. The Ih I litter caught up by a rapid weight loss in the summer of 1975. Such results suggested that only weight loss values for one-year periods ("full climate cycle") ought to be used for calculating rate constants for the different stands (Berg, 1978). After one such full-year period the difference was significant ($p < 0.01$), as well as after 554 days ($p < 0.001$).

As a rule, clear-cutting leads to a drier soil surface and increased soil temperatures with intensified diurnal variation (Odin, 1974). The general topography of the research area favoured such a development in the clear-cut plot. In spite of the relative dryness of the area there was a relative enhancement of weight loss in Ih I during the warm season. This might be partly explained by the observation that short-term fluctuations in temperature will stimulate microbial activity (Stanford et al., 1975). Due to the complexity of the interaction between environmental factors, further interpretation of the difference in weight loss is not possible.

Needle litter weight loss measured at stand Ih I gives a value for an integrated microbial activity (CO_2 release) of an introduced litter, not fully representative of the site. The further decomposed remaining litter from the old stand has a lower potential for decomposition, which can be seen from the low fungal mycelium density in the $A_{01/02}$ horizon of this stand as compared to the 120-year-old forest (Lundgren & Bååth, 1978).

One-year values for weight loss in Ih V were significantly higher ($p < 0.01$) than those of Ih III (Table 1). After three years the difference between Ih V and both Ih III and Ih IV was small but still highly significant ($p < 0.001$). There were several structural differences between these three stands which might have influenced the microclimate in the litter layer, for example, stand density, canopy cover, and field- and bottom-layer vegetation, but it is not possible to analyze how they interact to create the dynamic environment in which the litter decomposes.

The weight loss difference between Ih V and Ih IV was somewhat less pronounced than between Ih V and Ih III and appeared more difficult to explain. A higher weight loss might have been expected in Ih IV than in Ih V because of its denser canopy cover, apparently moister ground, and more luxuriant ground vegetation. It must be emphasized, on the other hand, that differences among stands as seen by the eye are not necessarily reflected by microbial activities.

Chemical changes

The differences in the decomposition pattern of organic components were small (Table 2). After one year there appeared to be a tendency for the weight loss of cellulose in the young stands (Ih I and III) to be lower than in the older ones (Ih IV and V). Later, this tendency became more marked and after 36 months the main part of the measured differences in total weight loss of the litter could be ascribed to cellulose. There was possibly also a lower weight loss for lignin in Ih IV compared to the other stands.

The similarity in organic-chemical changes indicates similar enzyme sets for the microbial populations at the different sites. This is supported by the results of Söderström & Bååth (1978), who found that in a given soil layer the species structure of microfungi was fairly equal between different podzols, including our site Ih V and a clear-cut area. On the other hand, bacterial populations changed considerably as an effect of clear-cutting (Niemelä & Sundman, 1977) as investigated by the multiple point method. However, the main change took place in the mineral soil and less in the humus layer. Differences in species composition can be reflected in the degradation patterns as indicated in a laboratory experiment by Lindeberg (1944). He showed that pure cultures of different *Marasmius* spp. degraded lignin and cellulose in spruce needle litter to varying levels, the proportion of lignin degraded being greater than that of cellulose.

The release of plant nutrients from the needle litter differed somewhat from stand to stand. However, the differences in dynamics were only minor (Fig. 1). No detectable differences were noted for nitrogen, sulphur and calcium, except for a slightly greater retention of nitrogen in litter placed in Ih IV. This was not, however, due to nitrogen fixation (T. Lindberg, pers. comm.). Phosphorus was also more efficiently retained in the Ih IV litter. The most marked phosphorus loss took place in the clear-cut area, while only small absolute net changes could be detected at the other sites during the whole incubation period (Fig. 1). Phosphorus is fairly easily leached from plant material (Tukey, 1970) and can be actively taken up into litter (Staaf & Berg, 1977). A combination of leaching and low microbial activity during the first winter might explain why the clear-cut area lost this element faster than the other stands.

Slightly higher losses of potassium and magnesium were noted in Ih I, compared to the other stands (Fig. 1). Magnesium is only partly structurally bound in plant tissue and potassium is not bound at all (Sailsbury & Ross, 1969). These two elements were subject to mechanical leaching and the initial losses were more rapid than for most other elements in pine needle litter (Staaf & Berg, 1977). In this case it seems that the physical conditions for leaching were favourable in Ih I; the larger amount of rainfall reaching the ground and the more violent temperature and moisture short-term fluctuations in this stand probably being responsible.

367

Table 2. Comparison of chemical composition in needle litter after different incubation periods. The experiment was performed in four different Scots pine stands at Ivantjärnsheden. Figures are given in mg per gram of actual weight (A) and initial weight (B). Standard error within parentheses.

	Weight loss (%)	Remaining part of components (mg g^{-1} dw)											
		Total nitrogen		Klason lignin		Total extractives		Cellulose		Hemi-celluloses		Total polymer carbohydrates	
		A	B	A	B	A	B	A	B	A	B	A	B
Initial composition		4.2	4.2	270	270	229	229	299	299	193	193	492	492
After 370 days (12 months)													
Ih I	25.8 (0.4)	4.5	3.3	332	246	118	88	350	260	181	134	525	390
Ih III	25.8 (0.6)	5.3	3.9	340	252	126	93	330	245	183	136	513	381
Ih IV	27.0 (0.5)	5.3	3.9	362	264	132	96	311	227	182	133	493	360
Ih V	28.2 (0.6)	5.3	3.8	348	250	123	88	328	236	185	133	513	368
After 554 days (19 months)													
Ih I	25.8 (0.4)	4.8	3.6	323	240	120	89	324	240	215	160	539	400
Ih III	27.6 (0.8)	5.1	3.7	312	226	141	102	349	253	185	134	533	386
Ih V	32.2 (0.4)	5.6	3.7	354	240	128	87	328	222	191	129	519	352
After 1099 days (36 months)													
Ih III	53.0 (1.1)	9.4	4.4	394	185	128	60	314	148	163	77	477	224
Ih IV	53.4 (1.5)	10.8	5.0	444	207	127	59	239	111	190	89	429	200
Ih V	58.1 (1.6)	9.9	4.1	422	177	154	65	253	106	171	72	423	177

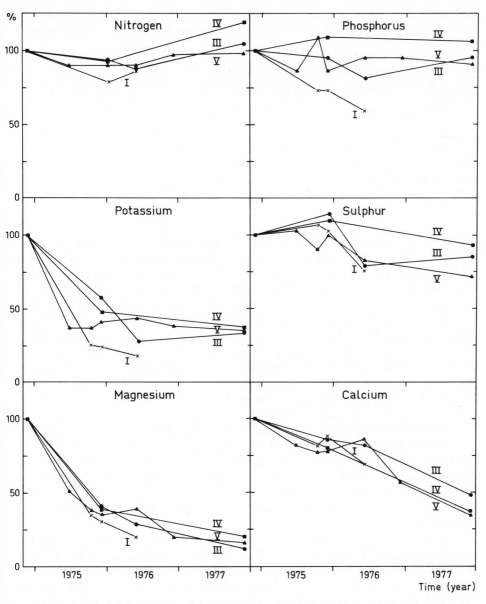

Figure 1. Amounts of nitrogen, phosphorus, potassium, sulphur, magnesium, and calcium remaining in Scots pine needle litter decomposing in stands Ih I, Ih III, Ih IV and Ih V.

Concluding remarks

Needle litter decomposed slowly and at much the same rate in the different forest stands, all of which were located in an area with the same macro-climate and soil type. As the stands all differed considerably in tree density and ground vegetation it is reasonable to believe that inherent properties of the needle litter governed the decompostion rate, rather than stand environment.

Table 3. Chemical composition of needle litterfall in three Scots pine stands at Ivantjärnsheden. Mean analysis values for the autumn of 1975. Litter samples were supplied by Dr. J. G. K. Flower-Ellis. * = not determined.

Stand	Concentration (mg g^{-1} dw)										
	Water soluble fraction	Acetone soluble fraction	Cellulose	Hemi-celluloses	Klason lignin	N	P	K	S	Ca	Mg
Ih III	134	85	269	238	271	4.0	0.21	0.51	*	4.61	0.37
Ih IV	158	97	278	202	265	3.8	0.20	0.64	0.43	3.64	0.35
Ih V	155	97	285	195	268	4.1	0.27	0.76	0.44	3.55	0.38

Chemical data on needle litterfall from Ivantjärnsheden (Table 3) show certain differences between the stands, especially in inorganic composition. The observed differences, though, were not of a kind to give rise to any significantly different weight loss rates (Berg & Staaf, 1980). Needle litter decomposes in a manner closely described by first order kinetics (Berg, 1978) and it might be concluded that the most important factor for carbon mineralization and plant nutrient release from litter is simply the amount of litter being decomposed in the stands. For release of plant nutrients their concentrations will be of importance too – even if it does not enhance weight losses (Berg & Staaf, 1980). Needles constitute the dominating component of litterfall in these stands (Flower-Ellis & Olsson, 1978) but the amount and turn-over rate of other litter fractions will of course also be important for the total nutrient supply to plants in the different stands.

In young stands, where plant seedling establishment has been delayed after clear-cutting, a lower decomposition rate of newly formed litter might have been expected. Such an effect could be due to a changed microclimate, soil biological conditions, or both. Here, on the other hand, the release rates of plant nutrients like potassium, magnesium and phosphorus, that are less firmly bound to structural parts of the litter, have a tendency to increase because of the changed physical conditions of the environment.

The effects on the decomposition process of major variations in climatic conditions and forest type are of course not seen from the present observations, all of which were made in the same locality. It is known, however, that large temperature differences between sites have a significant influence on the weight loss rate of coniferous litter (e.g., Mikola, 1960), as has the local soil water regime (Fogel & Cromack, 1977).

Acknowledgements

The skilful technical assistance of Ulla Larsson, Irene Persson and Seved Helmersson is gratefully acknowledged.

References

Ångström, A. 1936. Soil temperature in stands of different densities. – Medd. Skogsförsöksanst. Stockh. 29: 187–218. (In Swedish, English summary)

Arnborg, T. 1953. Det Nordsvenska Skogstypsschemat. Stockholm: Svenska Skogsvårdsföreningens förlag, 20 pp. (In Swedish)

Berg, B. 1978. Decomposition of needle litter in a 120–130-year-old Scots pine (*Pinus silvestris*) stand at Ivantjärnsheden. – Swed. Conif. For. Proj. Int. Rep. 80, 66 pp.

Berg, B. & Staaf, H. 1980. Decomposition rate and chemical changes in decomposing needle litter of Scots pine. II. Influence of chemical composition. – In: Persson, T. (ed.) Structure and Function of Northern Coniferous Forests – An Ecosystem Study, Ecol. Bull. (Stockholm) 32: 373–390.

Bethge, P. O., Rådeström, R. & Theander, O. 1971. Kvantitativ kolhydratbestämning – en detaljstudie. – Comm. from Swedish Forest Product Research Lab., Stockholm, 63 B. (In Swedish)

Blanchar, R. W., Remm, G. & Coldwell, A. C. 1965. Determination of sulphur in plant materials by digestion with nitric and perchloric acid. – Soil Sci. Soc. Amer. Proc. 29: 71–72.

Bosatta, E. 1980. Modelling of soil processes – an introduction. – In: Persson, T. (ed.) Structure and Function of Northern Coniferous Forests – An Ecosystem Study, Ecol. Bull. (Stockholm) 32: 553–564.

Bråkenhielm, S. 1978. Ivantjärnsheden, Jädraås – Regional physiography and description of the research area. – Swed. Conif. For. Proj. Tech. Rep. 16, 58 pp.

Flanagan, P. & Veum, A. K. 1974. Relationships between respiration, weight loss, temperature and moisture in organic residues on tundra. – In: Holding, A. J., Heal, O. W., MacLean, S. F. Jr. & Flanagan, P. W. (eds.) Soil Organisms and Decomposition in Tundra, pp. 249–277. Stockholm: Tundra Biome Steering Committee.

Flower-Ellis, J. G. K. & Olsson, L. 1978. Litterfall in an age series of Scots pine stands and its variation by components during the years 1973–1976. – Swed. Conif. For. Proj. Tech. Rep. 15, 62 pp.

Fogel, R. & Cromack, K. Jr. 1977. Effect of habitat and substrate quality on Douglas fir litter decomposition of Northern Coniferous Forests – An Ecosystem Study, Ecol. Bull. (Stockholm) 32: 553–564.

Jackson, M. L. 1958. Soil Chemical Analysis. Englewood Cliffs, N. J.: Prentice-Hall Inc., 498 pp.

Jansson, P-E. 1977. Soil properties at Ivantjärnsheden. – Swed. Conif. For. Proj. Int. Rep. 54, 66 pp. (In Swedish, English abstract)

Lindeberg, G. 1944. Über die Physiologie ligninabbauender Bodenhymenomyzeten. – Symb. Bot. Ups. 8(2): 1–183.

Lundgren, B. & Bååth, E. 1978. Fungal and bacterial investigations in a pine forest soil during two years following a clear-cutting. – Swed. Conif. For. Proj. Int. Rep. 75, 32 pp. (In Swedish, English summary)

Mälkönen, E. 1974. Annual primary production and nutrient cycle in some Scots pine stands. – Commun. Inst. For. Fenn. 84(5), 87 pp.

McFee, W. W. & Stone, E. L. 1966. The persistence of decaying wood in the humus layers of northern forests. – Soil Sci. Soc. Amer. Proc. 30: 513–516.

Mikola, P. 1960. Comparative experiment on decomposition rates of forest litter in southern and northern Finland. – Oikos 11: 161–166.

Millar, C. S. 1974. Decomposition of coniferous leaf litter. – In: Dickinson, C. H. & Pugh, G. J. F. (eds.) Biology of Plant Litter Decomposition, Vol. 1, pp. 105–128. London–New York: Academic Press.

Niemelä, S. & Sundman, V. 1977. Effects of clear-cutting on the composition of bacterial populations of northern spruce forest soil. – Can. J. Microbiol. 23: 131–138.

Nihlgård, B. 1972. Plant biomass, primary production and distribution of chemical elements in a beech and a planted spruce forest in South Sweden. – Oikos 23: 69–81.

Odin, H. 1974. Some meteorological effects of clear felling. – Sveriges Skogsvårdsförb. Tidskr. 1: 60–65. (In Swedish, English summary)

Pawluk, S. 1967. Soil analysis by atomic absorbtion spectrophotometry. – Atomic Absorbtion Newsletters 6: 53–56.

Piene, H. & Van Cleve, K. 1978. Weight loss of litter and cellulose bags in a thinned white spruce forest in interior Alaska. – Can. J. For. Res. 8: 42–46.

Sailsbury, F. B. & Ross, C. 1969. Plant Physiology. Belmont: Wadsworth Publ. Co. Inc., 747 pp.

Snedecor, G. W. & Cochran, W. G. 1956. Statistical Methods, 5th ed. Ames: The Iowa State Univ. Press, 593 pp.

Söderström, B. & Bååth, E. 1978. Soil microfungi in three Swedish coniferous forests. – Holarct. Ecol. 1: 62–72.

Staaf, H. & Berg, B. 1977. Mobilization of plant nutrients in a Scots pine forest mor in Central Sweden. – Silva Fenn. 11: 210–217.

Stanford, G., Frere, M. H. & van der Pol, R. A. 1975. Effects of fluctuating temperatures on soil nitrogen mineralization. – Soil Sci. 119: 222–226.

Tukey, H. B. Jr. 1970. The leaching of substances from plants. – Ann. Rev. Plant. Phys. 21: 305–324.

Wright, T. W. 1957. Some effects of thinning on the soil of a Norway spruce plantation. – Forestry 30: 123–133.

Persson, T. (ed) 1980
Structure and Function of Northern
Coniferous Forests – An Ecosystem Study
Ecol. Bull. (Stockholm) 32: 373–390.

DECOMPOSITION RATE AND CHEMICAL CHANGES
OF SCOTS PINE NEEDLE LITTER.
II. INFLUENCE OF CHEMICAL COMPOSITION

B. Berg[1] and H. Staaf[2]

Abstract

Decomposition of Scots pine needle litters with initially differing levels of the nutrients N, P, K, Ca, S, and Mg, as well as lignin, was studied. The initial levels of N, P, K, and S in the litter were positively correlated. The positive correlation noted between nutrient level and weight loss was restricted to weight losses less than 30%, up to which mainly solubles and some cellulose and hemicellulose were degraded. When the decomposition of lignin started, the weight-loss enhancing effect by nutrients was overrun by the slow decomposition of lignin. Lignin appeared to retard the weight loss of the components cellulose and hemicellulose.

The decomposition rate of the lignin fraction was unaffected by the plant nutrient concentrations and its decomposition started sooner in litters with much lignin than in those with little. No lignin appeared to be degraded until it had reached a concentration of about 30%.

Additional keywords: Cellulose, lignin, litter-bag, mineralization, plant nutrient.

Introduction

Decomposition rates of litters are frequently considered to be regulated by the interaction between soil organisms, environmental conditions and litter quality. Part of the latter factor might be the nitrogen content, which has been shown to influence the weight loss rate of leaf litter (Melin, 1930; Witkamp, 1966). A high percentage of lignin is considered to have a negative effect on decomposition rate (Meentemeyer, 1978), and Fogel & Cromack (1977) found it to be more rate determining than the C/N ratio or total nitrogen level in Douglas fir litter. Structural features of the litter are also important in this respect (Bocock, 1963).

In nature it is often difficult to separate the effects of individual factors. Both inter- and intra-site differences in decomposition rate could reflect a variation in several of the above-mentioned types of factors. Decomposition rates of identical Scots pine needle litter were found to be similar in stands of different ages (Berg & Staaf, 1980). However, in one stand of Scots pine different litter types exhibited

[1] Dept. of Microbiology, Swedish University of Agricultural Sciences, S-750 07 Uppsala, Sweden
   Present address: Dept. of Ecology and Environmental Research, Swedish University of Agricultural Sciences, S-750 07 Uppsala, Sweden.
[2] Dept. of Plant Ecology, University of Lund, S-223 62 Lund, Sweden

marked differences in weight loss rates (Berg, 1977). Thus, the litter quality, possibly the chemical characteristics, appears to be highly important in regulating decomposition rate.

There are differences in the chemical composition of coniferous needles, and as a rule the nitrogen content increases with the stand site index within the same climatic region (e.g., Tamm, 1964). Such a variation is likely to be reflected also in needle litter composition as is nitrogen fertilization (Miller & Miller, 1976), but chemical composition of litter seems to be less variable than that of living parts (Viro, 1956). Also organic chemical composition might be site-dependent, and Davies *et al.* (1964) found both decreased nitrogen and increased polyphenolic concentrations in Scots pine seedlings when grown under conditions with decreasing levels of available nitrogen. This indicates the complexity of changes in litter quality from site to site.

Plant nutrients are released from plant litter either by mechanical leaching or breakdown of structural organic components by soil organisms. Leaching, a process highly dependent on the litter type (Nykvist, 1963), is partly responsible for the initial release of magnesium and potassium from Scots pine needle litter (Staaf & Berg, 1977). Climatic conditions such as freeze-thaw cycles and rainfall could thus be expected to be important for the release of these elements. The release of nitrogen, phosphorus and calcium, on the other hand, which, at least in later stages of decay, are lost about proportionally to organic matter (Staaf & Berg, 1977), should be regulated by factors similar to those regulating total decomposition rate.

The aim of this investigation was to determine the influence of plant nutrient levels, mainly nitrogen, on decomposition rate and pattern of chemical changes of Scots pine needle litter. In order to reduce the chemical variability of the litter it was sampled on one forest site, but from stands given different amounts of nitrogen fertilizer. Needle litter from the Swedish Coniferous Forest Project research site was also used as a reference.

Site description

The study was conducted at the Swedish Coniferous Forest Project research site Ivantjärnsheden, Jädraås, in Central Sweden. The site is a plain sandy sediment area with an age series of Scots pine stands. A 120-year-old stand (Ih V) was used for the litter incubation. The soil type is an iron podzol and the stand is described in more detail by Bråkenhielm (1978).

Materials and methods

Needle litter (Ih) was sampled at Ivantjärnsheden in September 1975 and September 1976 as described earlier by Berg & Staaf (1980).

Needle litters with different nutrient concentrations were sampled as described above in the autumns of 1975 and 1976 from Scots pine stands, about 20 years old, at Lisselbo. This site, an optimum nutrition experiment area, described by Tamm *et al.* (1974), is situated about 50 km to the south-east of Ivantjärnsheden on a sandy soil. Samples were taken from both a control plot (N0) and three plots (N1, N2 and N3) given different doses of ammonium nitrate. The fertilization has been performed as annual additions since 1969 and since 1971 these have been equivalent to 40, 80 and 120 kg N ha^{-1} yr^{-1} for the three fertilized plots respectively (Tamm *et al.*, 1974).

Before weighing, the needles were air-dried at room temperature to about 5–8% moisture. Dry weight was determined at 85°C and the largest difference in moisture was less than $\pm 0.5\%$ of the average ($n = 20$).

Litter-bags with the five needle litter types were placed in Ih V as described by Berg & Staaf (1980) in late October 1975 (set 1) and 1976 (set 2). Samplings were made after 302, 379 and 731 days, and 212, 312, 362, 674, and 722 days, respectively. Samplings and chemical analyses were carried out as described by Berg & Staaf (1980).

Results

Initial chemical composition

The two sets of needle litter, each with five litter types, made up plant nutrient concentration gradients; initial nitrogen concentration being lowest in litter from Ivantjärnsheden (Ih) and successively higher in litter from Lisselbo trees (N0–N3), which had been given increased nitrogen fertilizer doses (Table 1). In parallel to nitrogen, litters from fertilized trees had increased levels of phosphorus, potassium and sulphur; most clearly seen in set 1. There was, on the other hand, a negative relationship between nitrogen and calcium concentrations, whereas magnesium appeared less dependent on the other plant nutrients. Concentrations of nitrogen bound to lignin and of that not bound to lignin were strongly positively correlated to the level of total nitrogen in both sets.

The organic composition of the needles varied between and within the two sets. In the first set of litter the increased nitrogen levels were accompanied by increasing percentages of lignin whereas there were inverse relations for the water and acetone extractable fractions (Table 1). There also appeared to be increasing levels of hemicellulose with increasing cellulose levels. In set 2, however, there were no significant relations between nitrogen and organic fractions, the latter having about similar percentages at all the plant nutrient levels (Table 1).

Weight loss

In both series needles initially containing most nitrogen, phosphorus, sulphur and potassium gave a significantly higher weight loss during the first year of decomposition (Table 2). During the second year this effect levelled out, but there was still a remaining influence on the accumulated weight loss (Table 2, Fig. 1). Although Fig. 1 only shows the relation between weight loss and nitrogen, similar relations were found for phosphorus, sulphur and potassium (Table 3).

In the period 12–24 months a marked difference to the first year took place. The relation between weight loss and litter type was the inverse of that in the first year (Table 2), although significant only for set 1. In this period there were no positive correlations between weight loss and initial plant nutrient concentrations (Table 3). Thus litter from the unfertilized plots at Lisselbo (N0) in set 1 had the highest weight loss rate as calculated for the separate periods and for the two years.

The litter set with an initially similar lignin level (set 2) was decomposed faster than that with an initial lignin concentration gradient (set 1) (Table 2). The difference occurred in the first year, and since the set 1 litter was incubated one year before set 2, the difference could be an effect of unfavourable climatic conditions between autumn 1975 and autumn 1976. The first-year weight losses of local needle litter (Ih) were

Table 1. Initial concentrations of major chemical components in Scots pine needle litter from Ivantjärnsheden (Ih) and from four stands at Lisselbo, one unfertilized (N0) and three (N1–N3) given different doses of nitrogen fertilizer. Litters were collected in September 1975 (set 1) and September 1976 (set 2) and incubated at Ivantjärnsheden (Ih V). Correlation coefficients (r) for linear regressions between the initial concentrations are given using total nitrogen (r_N) and cellulose (r_C) concentrations as independent variables.

Significance levels: $0.05 > p > 0.01$ (*), $0.01 > p > 0.001$ (**), $p < 0.001$ (***).

| | Concentration (mg g^{-1} dw) | | | | | N | | | | | | | |
	Water soluble	Acetone soluble	Cellulose	Total hemi-celluloses	Lignin[1]	Total	Bound to lignin	Not bound to lignin	P	K	S	Ca	Mg
Set 1													
Ih	160	100	310	190	240 (330)[1]	3.4	1.2	2.2	0.20	0.61	0.32	4.7	0.39
N0	150	90	280	210	270 (350)[1]	3.6	1.2	2.4	0.14	0.53	0.25	5.3	0.50
N1	150	100	270	210	260 (350)[1]	4.3	1.4	2.9	0.20	0.52	0.33	5.1	0.55
N2	120	90	300	200	290 (360)[1]	5.8	2.1	3.7	0.25	0.59	0.46	4.0	0.52
N3	80	60	280	230	350 (410)[1]	8.5	3.7	4.8	0.30	0.85	0.49	2.9	0.38
r_C	0.28	0.26	–	-0.74	-0.32								
r_N	-0.99**	-0.91*	-0.21	0.76	0.97**	–	0.99**	0.99**	0.91*	0.88*	0.90*	-0.95*	-0.37
Set 2													
Ih	150	90	300	200	260 (340)[1]	4.0	1.3	2.7	0.21	0.53	0.36	4.9	0.42
N0	150	100	300	190	260 (340)[1]	4.3	1.6	2.7	0.32	0.91	0.45	4.7	0.57
N1	170	90	270	220	250 (340)[1]	4.4	1.6	2.8	0.30	0.98	0.43	4.6	0.67
N2	140	90	300	210	270 (350)[1]	7.0	2.3	4.7	0.34	1.06	0.53	4.3	0.58
N3	150	80	290	210	270 (350)[1]	8.1	2.7	5.4	0.42	1.36	0.64	4.5	0.54
r_C	-0.91*	0.27	–	-0.77	0.64								
r_N	-0.46	-0.72	0.10	0.34	0.82	–	0.99**	1.00***	0.85	0.84	0.95*	-0.77	0.08

[1] Calculated both as a fraction of litter dry weight and of non-soluble material only – the latter figure within parentheses.

Table 2. Weight loss for different periods of decomposition ($n=20$) expressed as % of initial weight. The F-ratio of mean squares from analysis of variance among litter types to residual variation is given with its significance levels: $0.05>p>0.01$(*), $0.01>p>0.001$ (**), $p<0.001$ (***).

Decomposition period (months)	Litter type (set 1)					Litter type (set 2)				
	Ih	N0	N1	N2	N3	Ih	N0	N1	N2	N3
0–7										
Mean						11.1	13.8	14.0	15.5	18.3
s.e.						0.2	0.1	0.2	0.2	0.2
F-ratio						....		52.4***	....	
0–10										
Mean	14.9	14.6	16.5	15.2	17.9	21.6	26.2	26.7	28.5	30.3
s.e.	0.3	0.2	0.3	0.3	0.3	0.3	0.4	0.5	0.5	0.5
F-ratio	....		24.0***	....		....		48.6***	....	
0–12										
Mean	21.1	20.7	22.4	22.5	25.3	26.5	32.7	31.3	32.2	36.3
s.e.	0.4	0.2	0.3	0.3	0.4	0.5	0.9	0.7	0.6	0.5
F-ratio	....		28.4***	....		....		29.4***	....	
0–22										
Mean						47.0	47.4	47.6	50.0	50.7
s.e.						1.4	1.1	1.1	1.1	1.3
F-ratio						....		1.9	....	
0–24										
Mean	44.5	47.2	44.8	43.8	45.5	48.1	51.2	49.6	51.1	53.0
s.e.	0.7	1.2	1.0	0.7	1.1	1.1	1.2	1.0	0.8	0.9
F-ratio	....		1.9	....		....		3.5*	....	
7–10										
Mean						11.8	14.4	14.8	15.4	14.7
s.e.						0.4	0.4	0.5	0.5	0.5
10–12										
Mean	7.3	7.1	7.1	8.6	9.0	6.3	8.8	6.3	5.2	8.6
s.e.	0.4	0.3	0.4	0.4	0.4	0.7	0.9	0.9	0.8	0.7
12–24										
Mean	29.6	33.4	28.8	27.5	27.1	29.4	27.4	26.7	27.9	26.3
s.e.	1.0	1.5	1.3	1.0	1.6	1.6	2.3	1.8	1.4	1.6
F-ratio	....		6.0***	....		....		1.0	....	

measured in the Ih V stand (Berg, 1978) in 1974, 1975, 1976 and 1977, and were found to be 27, 28, 21 and 27% respectively. The value of 21% for 1975–76, thus, was exceptionally low, which probably can be explained by climatic differences between the years rather than by a difference in chemical composition between the two experimental litter sets. This is supported by the fact that the weight loss of set 1 Ih needles increased to a value of 30% during the second year of decomposition, while the corresponding weight loss for set 2 was 29%. Further, the chemical compositions of Ih needle litters sampled in the two consecutive years were very similar (Table 1).

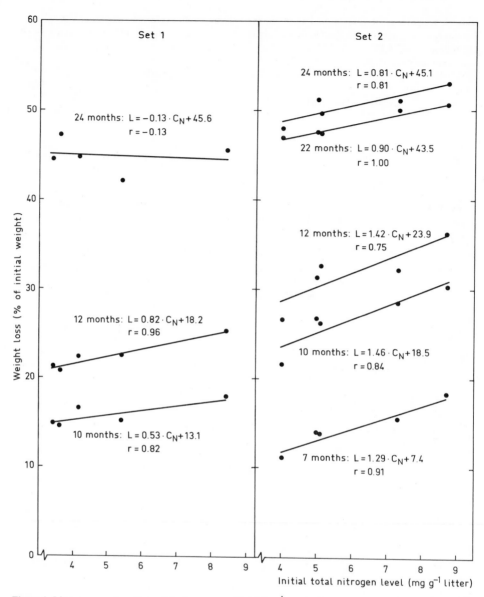

Figure 1. Linear regressions for weight loss on total initial concentration of nitrogen in Scots pine needle litter after different periods of decomposition. The left column applies to a set of litter with increasing levels of plant nutrients and lignin (set 1), and the right column to a set with increasing nutrient levels and similar lignin levels (set 2) ($n = 20$).

Decomposition of organic compounds

The weight loss of separate organic components (Table 4) followed a pattern described by Berg (1978). Water- and acetone-soluble fractions started to decompose first, followed by the hemicellulose and cellulose components, and finally lignin. For the sake of simplicity the different hemicellulose components here are lumped to-

378

Table 3. Linear correlation coefficients (r) for the regression between total initial levels of nutrients (independent variable) and weight loss (dependent variable) after different incubation periods. Two experiments with nitrogen-enriched needle litter ($n=5$). Set 1: varying initial lignin level, set 2: initially similar lignin levels.
Significance levels: $0.05 > p > 0.01$ (*), $0.01 > p > 0.001$ (**), $p < 0.001$ (***).

	Incubation period (months)	N	P	S	K
Set 1	0–10	0.82	0.76	0.65	0.75
	0–12	0.96**	0.91*	0.86	0.86
	0–24	−0.13	−0.50	−0.53	−0.03
	12–24	−0.83	−0.87	−0.70	−0.60
Set 2	0–7	0.91*	0.98**	0.99**	0.99**
	0–10	0.84	0.97**	0.93*	0.99**
	0–12	0.75	0.99**	0.91*	0.97**
	0–22	1.00***	0.85	0.95*	0.85
	0–24	0.81	0.98**	0.94*	0.92*
	12–24	−0.75	−0.91*	−0.67	−0.66

Table 4. Relative decomposition rates (% of weight) of some organic components of Scots pine needle litter of different nutrient levels in the two sets of litter (see Table 1) during the time periods 0–12 months and 12–24 months. Negative value denotes an increase in weight.

Period		Water and acetone soluble	Hemicelluloses	Cellulose	Hemicellulose and cellulose	Lignin
Set 1						
0–12 months	Ih	67.8	20.2	8.1	16.3	−12.2
	N0	57.6	18.2	10.3	13.7	1.1
	N1	64.3	27.3	3.0	13.6	−0.7
	N2	52.2	22.1	19.3	20.4	4.5
	N3	45.0	33.3	23.2	27.7	14.6
12–24 months	Ih	−5.0	45.3	42.8	38.1	18.7
	N0	26.0	45.7	41.1	42.8	21.5
	N1	11.2	58.3	33.5	42.6	15.5
	N2	29.3	34.0	36.6	35.6	19.5
	N3	10.4	33.6	39.1	36.8	19.1
Set 2						
0–12 months	Ih	46.7	33.3	21.8	26.3	7.1
	N0	58.5	29.7	37.6	34.5	4.7
	N1	57.2	35.6	32.7	34.0	−2.4
	N2	55.5	36.8	38.0	37.5	2.2
	N3	57.8	43.8	43.0	43.3	4.5
12–24 months	Ih	40.6	37.0	39.7	38.7	9.3
	N0	36.9	30.3	39.7	35.8	13.1
	N1	42.5	28.0	46.4	31.8	12.7
	N2	35.6	37.1	35.0	35.9	16.4
	N3	35.1	30.5	36.1	33.8	14.8

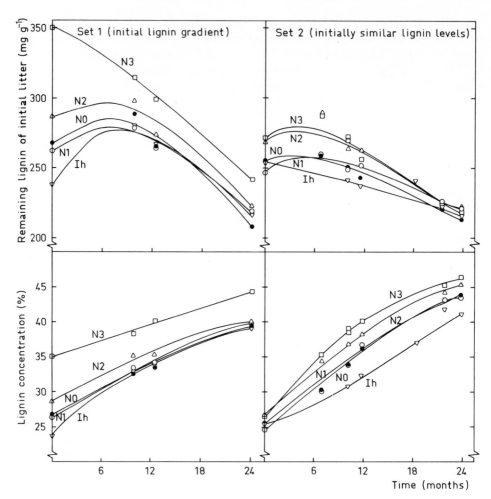

Figure 2. Changes in amounts and concentrations of lignin in litter of different plant nutrient levels. The needle litter originated from unfertilized pines (Ih and N0) and pines fertilized with different amounts of nitrogen fertilizer (N1, N2 and N3).

gether. The lignin fraction did not start to degrade until the other components had been degraded to a certain extent, meaning that its concentration increased.

For the litter set with initially similar lignin concentrations (Table 4), it appears that during the first year, part of the solubles, hemicelluloses and cellulose were degraded – also if in somewhat different proportions. After one year the lignin fraction was still mainly unaffected, and it appears that for these litter types a lignin level of at least 30% was reached before any lignin degradation took place at all (Fig. 2). After one year's decomposition lignin concentrations ranged from 32–40%, and the percentage had reached a level of 44–46% after two years (Fig. 2). In the period 12–24 months the soluble components, cellulose and hemicelluloses were degraded at about the same rate (Table 4). By now lignin had also started to degrade, but at a lower rate than the other fractions.

In the litter set with an initial lignin gradient the above mentioned decomposition pattern was mainly followed with some exceptions. The higher the lignin level the sooner the lignin degradation started. In the N3 needle litter, with a large lignin fraction (35%) and small fraction of solubles, degradation started in the 0–12 months period and after 24 months the amount of lignin degraded was in proportion to the initial level.

Plant nutrient retention and release

The pattern of plant nutrient net change in decomposing needle litter differed markedly with the element. In this respect the results from both set 1 and set 2 (Fig. 3) were similar to those found earlier for pine needle litter at Ivantjärnsheden (Staaf & Berg, 1977). A general trend was that nitrogen, phosphorus and sulphur had a lower loss rate than the organic substance or was even imported to the litter structure. Initial concentrations of these three elements were all highly correlated to weight loss (Table 3). The other elements analyzed were lost faster than, or about proportionally to, organic matter.

The nitrogen loss rate from litter increased with increasing initial concentration of the element (Fig. 3). Nitrogen was retained or accumulated in needle litter with a nitrogen level of initially about 4 mg g^{-1} or a C/N ratio of 125 or higher. On the other hand, in litter with an initial concentration of 6 mg g^{-1} (C/N ratio about 80) or below, a net loss was noted from the beginning. The earlier observed threshold point for net nitrogen release from needle litter at a C/N ratio of about 70 (Staaf & Berg, 1977) appears to be lower than that for these needles. Nitrogen accumulation in Lisselbo needles was different from that of needles from Ivantjärnsheden. In the latter case the absolute amount of nitrogen increased during the first year while this did not happen until the second year for needles of low nitrogen content from Lisselbo.

The release pattern of phosphorus was similar to that of nitrogen. The two sets had somewhat different levels of the element; initial concentrations were mostly below 0.3 mg g^{-1} in set 1 while in set 2 most initial concentrations were above this level. When the initial concentration was below 0.25 mg g^{-1}, i.e., an initial C/P ratio over 2000, the amount retained was either constant or increased whereas at C/P below 2000 there was a noticeable immediate loss of phosphorus. It was not possible, within the course of decomposition, to distinguish any threshold point for occurrence of phosphorus net loss.

Changes in sulphur amounts were similar to those of nitrogen and phosphorus. The net release was markedly increased with an increased initial sulphur concentration. In litter with a lower initial concentration than 0.030–0.035%, or a C/S ratio of about 1500, it was retained.

Potassium and magnesium were the elements most rapidly lost from the litter. After about one year of decomposition the remaining amounts were very similar in all litter types, irrespective of the initial concentrations. Thus, the initial concentrations of the elements determined their first-year release, but had no influence on concentrations or release rates in later stages of needle litter decay.

Calcium was released in amounts roughly proportional to initial concentrations of the element, and the release rate was similar for all litter types. There was a tendency for calcium to be more strongly retained during the first year in the constant lignin

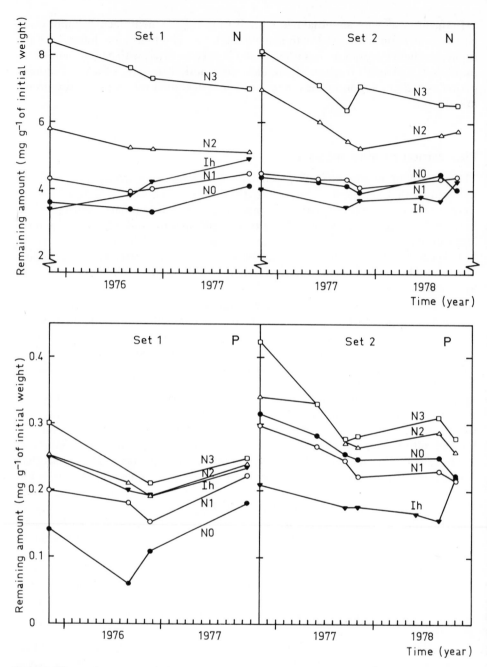

Figure 3. Changes in amounts of nitrogen, phosphorus, sulphur, calcium, potassium and magnesium in needle litter over time. The needle litter studied originated from unfertilized pines (Ih and N0) and from pines fertilized with different amounts of nitrogen fertilizer (N1, N2 and N3).

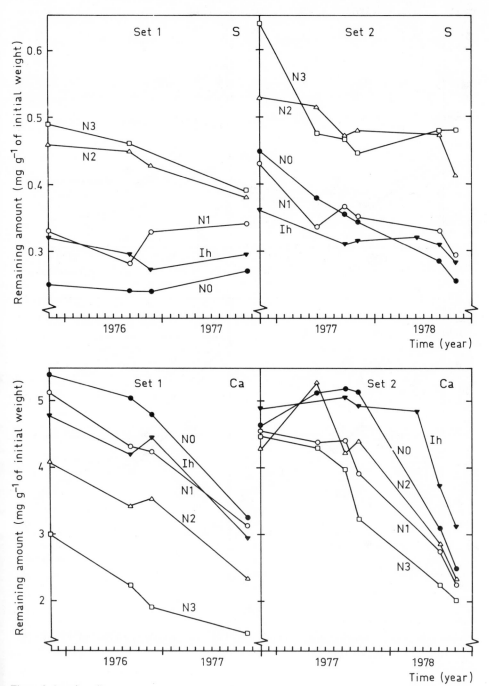

Figure 3. (continued)

383

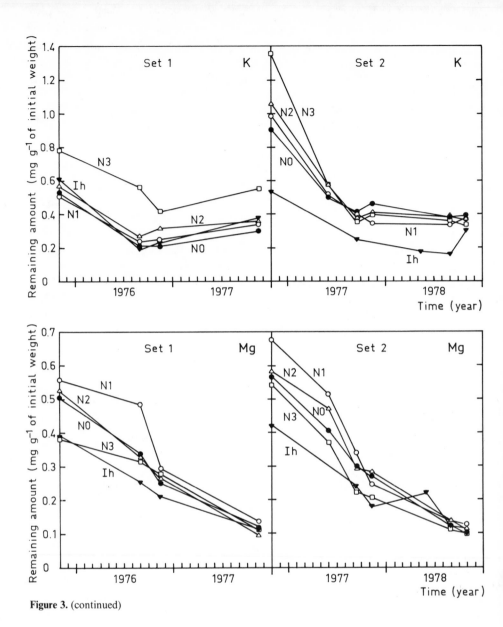

Figure 3. (continued)

level set than in the set with a lignin gradient. This was coupled to a higher decomposition rate of this set (Table 2).

Discussion

Chemical factors influencing weight loss rate

Plant nutrient elements are either structural constituents of organic compounds or are present in plant tissue as inorganic salts. Nitrogen and sulphur bound in proteins are examples of the former type, while potassium and calcium mainly occur in inorganic forms. Their total weight was only a few per cent of the total litter weight in the present material, which mainly was made up of soluble organic material, insoluble carbohydrates and lignin (see Table 1). However, the plant nutrient level in the needle litter had an obvious influence on weight loss of the organic compounds. This effect was most clearly seen in set 2 (Table 2) where the gross organic composition was very similar among the litter types.

Linear regressions of accumulated weight loss on initial plant nutrient concentrations showed significantly positive relationships up to two years of decomposition for the elements nitrogen, phosphorus, sulphur and potassium (Table 3). Calcium concentrations in litter were not closely correlated to those of nitrogen (Table 1). Further, the release pattern of potassium and magnesium indicates that these elements were in excess and thus not limiting to microbial activity. Of the elements nitrogen, phosphorus and sulphur, the latter occurs in vast amounts in throughfall of the Ivantjärnsheden forest (Bringmark, 1977) and it is not likely to be limiting. It is not possible, however, to conclude with certainty from the present material whether one or several of these three elements had any direct causal relation with litter decomposition rate. All of them are known to be needed in macroquantities for formation of microbial biomass (Alexander, 1977).

The slopes of the regressions in Fig. 1 indicate that the positive effect of an increased plant nutrient level on litter decomposition rate was most marked during the first year. In set 2 it appeared to be strongest during the first 7 months when the weight loss differentiation was greatest (Table 2), but it proceeded in the period 7–10 months. During this time a large part of the soluble fraction and minor parts of the cellulose and hemicellulose were decomposed, and the total weight loss after 10 months was in the interval of 20 to 30% of initial weight. The lignin fraction had only started to decompose.

After 12 months the regression slope was almost unchanged (Fig. 1), and weight losses between 10 and 12 months showed no clear trend with nutrient level (Table 2). The influence of initial nitrogen, phosphorus and sulphur concentrations on weight loss had thus apparently disappeared; the significant correlation found (Table 3) between plant nutrient concentrations and weight loss was therefore due to the effect exerted in earlier periods. It should be noted that during the period, when the differences in weight loss rates between needle litters disappeared, the lignin fraction had started to become degraded. Lignin concentrations, which had almost similar initial levels in set 2, were differentiated because of the varying weight loss levels (Fig. 2). Thus, concentrations became highest in litters that had decomposed fast and *vice versa*. It is possible that this, in combination with increased plant nutrient concentrations, levelled out the former weight loss differences.

In the period 12–24 months lignin was decomposed and no effect of nutrient on weight loss rate could be seen. There was, instead, a tendency for lower weight losses at higher nutrient levels. Cellulose and hemicelluloses were still decomposed during the second year, but the enhancing influence of nitrogen, phosphorus and sulphur on these components was evidently surpassed by the dampening effects of lignin. There were no positive relationships between any initial plant nutrient concentrations on the second year weight loss (Table 3).

The slopes of the regressions of weight loss on nitrogen level (Fig. 1) were 2–3 times greater for the set of needle litter without an initial lignin gradient than in that

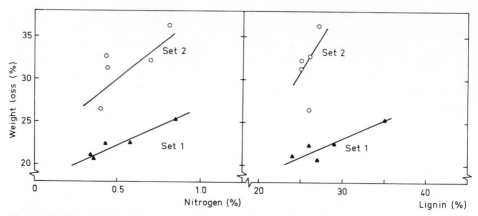

Figure 4. Relationships between initial concentrations of nitrogen and lignin in two needle litter sets and dry weight losses for the period 0–12 months. Each set consisted of five needle litter types from Ivantjärnsheden and Lisselbo with different chemical composition. Set 1 started on 28 October 1975 and set 2 started on 10 November 1976.

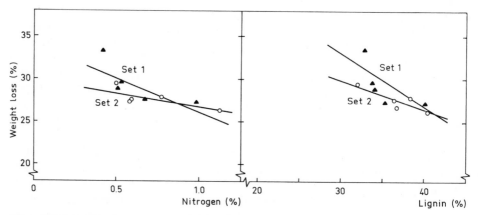

Figure 5. Relationships between concentrations of nitrogen and lignin at start of the period 12–24 months for two needle litter sets and dry weight losses during this period. Each set consisted of five needle litter types from Ivantjärnsheden and Lisselbo with different chemical composition. Set 1 started on 28 October 1975 and set 2 started on 10 November 1976.

with a gradient. The relation between the first-year weight loss and initial percentages of nitrogen and lignin in Fig. 4 shows that weight loss was less dependent on nitrogen (nutrient) level in set 1 than in set 2 whereas there was little effect of lignin level on weight loss for the set 2 needle litter. These observations support the idea of an early (first year) suppressing effect of lignin in set 1. In the second year (period 12–24 months) the relations between lignin/nitrogen and weight loss appeared to be reversed (Fig. 5), most obviously so for set 1.

The degradation of lignin started when it had accumulated to a certain concentration, and this level was reached earliest in the lignin-rich litter, but the degradation rate did not appear to be influenced by the total concentration of lignin (Table 4). There was no obvious influence of the nutrient level on the decomposition rate of the lignin component. However, a negative relation between total nitrogen level and decomposition of lignin was found in needle litter in a nearby clear-cut area (B. Berg & B. Wessén, unpubl.). In an early study, Bengtsson (1936) concluded that the presence of NH_4^+ suppressed lignin decomposition in barley litter. Keyser et al. (1978) supplied the physiological explanation to this effect in their studies on repression of the lignolytic enzyme system by NH_4^+. In the present study this was not established, but we cannot exclude the possibility of such a regulating mechanism.

Lignin will affect the total litter weight loss if it is a dominant chemical fraction. One reason for this could be the slow decrease of its own weight, and another could be a sterical interference of lignin with other components (masking) (cf. Minderman, 1968). This suppressing effect by lignin on decomposition of cellulose was investigated by Nilsson (1973), using the electron microscope. His observations strongly support the concept that lignin enclosing cellulose and hemicelluloses acts as a barrier which must be degraded to give access to the carbohydrates. Further, Fogel & Cromack (1977) found that the level of lignin in litter substrates was more rate determining than the level of nitrogen.

The following conclusions could be drawn:
(1) There are (at least) three main groups of carbon compounds: one with a fast turnover containing soluble compounds, one somewhat slower containing parts of the cellulose and hemicelluloses, and one with a slow turnover containing lignin and lignified cellulose and hemicelluloses.
(2) One or more of the elements nitrogen, phosphorus and sulphur influenced weight loss during the early decomposition stages of Scots pine needle litter (up to 20–30% weight loss) when mainly soluble material and parts of the cellulose and hemicelluloses were degraded.
(3) The influence of plant nutrients diminished as decomposition progressed, probably due to the increased lignin concentration, which retarded the decomposition rate.
(4) A high initial lignin level retarded the weight loss rate and could finally reduce or level out the initial stimulating effect of plant nutrients on litter decomposition.

Some suggestions on how chemical components regulate decomposition of Scots pine needle litter are summarized in Fig. 6.

Chemical composition of litter and plant nutrient cycling

Release from litter is an important process in plant nutrient recycling in ecosystems. The present results suggest that litter composition as given by its concentrations of nitrogen, phosphorus and sulphur has an influence on decomposition rate, and is thereby also of importance for the release of plant nutrients bound in litter. Both the rate of the process and total amount of litter in the forest floor will determine the amount of plant nutrients made available for uptake in plants.

The amount of any of the above-mentioned elements released from a given litter structure per unit of time, appears to be determined by three types of effects; a direct effect caused by its concentration, and indirect effects from changed decomposition rate and microbial retention in litter. If the element loss is proportional to total weight loss the amount released from the litter per unit of time is proportional to the concentration of the element. Thus, in the first place an increased nitrogen concentration

387

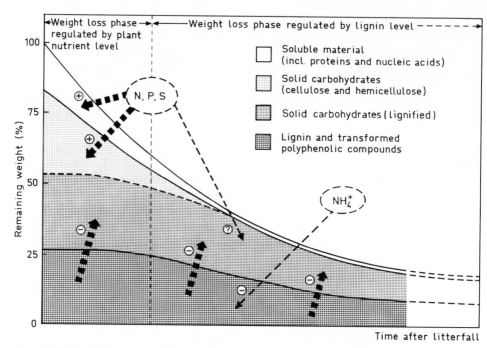

Figure 6. Schematic diagramme of the weight loss rates of some organic chemical components in Scots pine needle litter, and how these rates are influenced by increasing concentrations of nitrogen, phosphorus, sulphur and lignin. The suggested influence by NH_4^+ refers to literature data (see text).

will give a higher release rate if no additional retention mechanisms are introduced with it, even if weight loss rates are unchanged. Secondly, a higher initial weight loss is likely to result from it, the effect of which is multiplied to the first one. A third effect is the reduced retention of these elements which could be noted at higher concentrations. This will further amplify the positive effect of increased plant nutrient levels on release. The nitrogen bound to lignin (32–43% of total nitrogen) is not soluble and is retained within the structure. The amount of fungal mycelium in this type of litter is very small and probably it retains only less than 5% of the total nitrogen (Berg & Söderström, 1979). Apparently the mechanisms for this retention could be regarded as mainly unknown.

The results regarding lignin control of decomposition rate implies that lignin concentration greatly influences the plant nutrient release pattern discussed above. When lignin concentrations in litter are initially as high as in this investigation, i.e. 25%, they are likely to level out the influence of plant nutrients on decomposition rate up to a total weight loss of 25–30%. During this period very small amounts of either nitrogen, phosphorus and sulphur are lost from litter unless the initial element concentrations are exceptionally high. On the other hand the situation would be very different when considering a litter with an initial lignin concentration of, for example, only 10%, and assuming that the decomposition pattern suggested above has a general validity. The lignin influence will not appear until its concentration has reached a level of about 30%, or, in this case, when two-thirds of the original litter has been decomposed. The regulating effect of plant nutrients on decomposition rate would then extend over a period when a major part of them is released from litter. Thus, a moderate inter-site variation in the plant nutrient content of litter would have no or only a slight influence on mineralization of essential elements from it if lignin concentrations are high, but would increase with a decreasing lignin concentration.

From the statements above it appears that apart from input rate of litter, its lignin concentration is a critical factor in regulating plant nutrient transfers in soil. It might also possibly be an expression of soil fertility. Forest plants, both herbs and trees, often have an inter-site variation in mineral nutrient composition, which is sometimes related to indexes of soil fertility (Zöttl, 1960; Höhne, 1963; Tamm, 1964). A similar variation is likely to be found also in the litter they produce, but systematic investigations of this are very few in coniferous forests. Aaltonen (1955) found high lignin concentrations and only slightly variable gross organic chemical composition in needles from different sites of Scots pine and Norway spruce in Finland. The latter observation implies that a variable nitrogen or phosphorus level of needles cannot explain an inter-site variation in productive ability of Scandinavian coniferous forest sites by its influence on decomposition rate. This ought to be valid also for woody tree litter. Instead, the explanation of the regional variation should be looked for among climatic variables regulating weight loss rates, or the quantitative and qualitative variation of litter input from forest ground vegetation. Textural and geomorphological characters might also influence it by means of micro-climate and plant nutrient transports. The role of slight systematic variations in lignin concentration in tree litter together with associated variations in nutrient levels cannot be excluded, however, and should be further investigated.

Acknowledgements

We are indebted to Prof. Carl Olof Tamm for the needle litter from the nitrogen fertilized trees. The skilful technical assistance of Ulla Larsson, Irene Persson and Seved Helmersson is gratefully acknowledged.

References

Aaltonen, V. T. 1955. Die Blattanalyse als Bonitierungsgrundlage des Waldbodens. II. – Commun. Inst. For. Fenn. 45(2), 21 pp.
Alexander, M. 1977. Introduction to Soil Microbiology, 2nd ed. New York: John Wiley & Sons, 467 pp.
Bengtsson, N. 1936. Decomposition of cellulose, pentosans and lignin in soil. Experiments on barley stubbles and roots in sand. – Ann. Agr. Coll. Sweden 3: 1–48. (In Swedish, English summary)
Berg, B. 1977. Weight loss values for one year's decomposition of different litters at Ivantjärnsheden. – Swed. Conif. For. Proj. Int. Rep. 64, 16 pp.
Berg, B. 1978. Decomposition of needle litter in a 120-year-old Scots pine (Pinus silvestris) stand at Ivantjärnsheden. – Swed. Conif. For. Proj. Int. Rep. 80, 66 pp.
Berg, B. & Söderström, B. 1979. Fungal biomass and nitrogen in decomposing Scots pine needle litter. – Soil Biol. Biochem. 11: 339–341.
Berg, B. & Staaf, H. 1980. Decomposition rate and chemical changes in decomposing needle litter of Scots pine. I. Influence of stand age. – In: Persson, T. (ed.) Structure and Function of Northern Coniferous Forests – An Ecosystem Study, Ecol. Bull. (Stockholm) 32: 363–372.
Bocock, K. S. 1963. The digestion and assimilation of food by Glomeris. – In: Doeksen, J. & van der Drift, J. (eds.) Soil Organisms, pp. 85–91. Amsterdam: North-Holland Publ. Comp.

389

Bringmark, L. 1977. A bioelement budget of an old Scots pine forest in Central Sweden. – Silva fenn. 11: 201–209.

Bråkenhielm, S. 1978. Ivantjärnsheden, Jädraås – Regional physiography and description of the research area. – Swed. Conif. For. Proj. Tech. Rep. 16, 58 pp.

Davies, R. I., Coulson, C. B. & Lewis, D. A. 1964. Polyphenols in plant, humus, and soil. IV. Factors leading to increase in biosynthesis of polyphenol in leaves and their relation to mull and mor formation. – J. Soil Sci. 15: 310–318.

Fogel, R. & Cromack, K. Jr. 1977. Effect of habitat and substrate quality on Douglas fir litter decomposition in Western Oregon. – Can. J. Bot. 55: 1632–1640.

Höhne, H. 1963. Der Mineralstoff- und Stickstoffgehalt von Waldbodenpflanzen in Abhängigkeit vom Standort. – Arch. Forstw. 12: 791–805.

Keyser, P., Kirk, T. K. & Zeikus, J. G. 1978. Lignolytic enzyme system of *Phanerochaete chrysosporium:* Synthesized in the absence of lignin in response to nitrogen starvation. – J. Bact. 135: 790–797.

Meentemeyer, V. 1978. Macroclimate and lignin control of litter decomposition rates. – Ecology 59: 465–472.

Melin, E. 1930. Biological decomposition of some types of litter from North American forests. – Ecology 11: 72–101.

Miller, H. G. & Miller, J. D. 1976. Analysis of needle fall as a means of assessing nitrogen status in pine. – Forestry 49: 57–61.

Minderman, G. 1968. Addition, decomposition and accumulation of organic matter in forests. – J. Ecol. 56: 355–362.

Nilsson, T. 1973. Studies on wood degradation and cellulolytic activity of microfungi. – Stud. for. suec. 104: 4–40.

Nykvist, N. 1963. Leaching and decomposition of water-soluble organic substances from different types of leaf and needle litter. – Stud. for. suec. 3, 31 pp.

Staaf, H. & Berg, B. 1977. Mobilization of plant nutrients in a Scots pine forest mor in Central Sweden. – Silva fenn. 11: 210–217.

Tamm, C. O. 1964. Determination of nutrient requirements of forest stands. – In: Romberger, J. A. & Mikola, P. (eds.) International Review of Forestry Research, Vol. 1, pp. 115–170. New York–London: Academic Press.

Tamm, C. O., Nilsson, Å. & Wiklander, G. 1974. The optimum nutrition experiment Lisselbo. A brief description of an experiment in a young stand of Scots pine (*Pinus silvestris* L.). – Dept. of Forest Ecology and Forest Soils, Royal College of Forestry, Stockholm, Research Notes 18, 25 pp.

Viro, P. J. 1956. Investigations on forest litter. – Commun. Inst. For. Fenn. 45(6), 65 pp.

Witkamp, M. 1966. Decomposition of leaf litter in relation to environment, microflora and microbial respiration. – Ecology 47: 194–201.

Zöttl, H. 1960. Die Mineralstickstoffanlieferung in Fichten- und Kiefernbeständen Bayerns. – Forstwiss. Zbl. 79: 221–236.

390

Persson, T. (ed) 1980
Structure and Function of Northern
Coniferous Forests – An Ecosystem Study
Ecol. Bull. (Stockholm) 32: 391–400.

CHEMICAL COMPONENTS OF SCOTS PINE NEEDLES AND NEEDLE LITTER AND INHIBITION OF FUNGAL SPECIES BY EXTRACTIVES

B. Berg[1], K. Hannus[2], T. Popoff[3] and O. Theander[4]

Abstract

Differences in the composition of various groups of lipophilic extractives, low-molecular carbohydrates, cyclitols, phenolic glycosides, polysaccharides, lignin, ash and crude protein in green needles and brown needle litter from the same stand of Scots pine (*Pinus sylvestris*) were studied. There was a great drop of sugars, steryl esters and triglycerides going from green to brown needles on the tree. Some isoprenoid alcohols, sterols and some acids as well as lignin belong to the components that changed least. Tests were made on extracts for inhibition of growth of fungal strains isolated from the same site as the needles. The most commonly found strains in the litter layer were not inhibited whereas some strains frequently isolated at other sites, but uncommon at the present, were strongly inhibited.

Additional keywords: Cyclitols, isoprenoid alcohols, lignin, lipophilic extractives, low-molecular carbohydrates, phenolic glycosides, polysaccharides, sterols, steryl esters, triglycerides.

Introduction

Chemical components in litter may affect the process of soil formation. Coniferous forests in Fennoscandia generally develop a podzol whereas the common birch species (*Betula pendula* and *B. pubescens*) will support the formation of a mull type. Such differences sometimes have been suggested to depend on the level of phenolic/polyphenolic substances in the litter which could vary with the nutrient status of the soil (Gosz, 1981, Staaf & Berg, 1981). High polyphenol levels are encountered on poor soils and low levels on rich ones. A high level of polyphenolic compounds could be expected to cause a decrease in the biological activity in the soil and affect the species composition. Söderström & Bååth (1978) found that the podzol profile had a rather constant composition of fungal species at a number of different sites. Also the turn-

[1] Dept. of Microbiology, Swedish University of Agricultural Sciences, S-750 07 Uppsala, Sweden. Present address: Dept. of Ecology and Environmental Research, Swedish University of Agricultural Sciences, S-750 07 Uppsala, Sweden
[2] Institute of Wood Chemistry and Cellulose Technology, Åbo Akademi, Åbo, Finland. Present address: Raision Tehtaat OY, SF-212 00 Raisio, Finland
[3] Waters Associates AB, Sommarvägen 5, S-171 40 Solna, Sweden
[4] Dept. of Chemistry and Molecular Biology, Swedish University of Agricultural Sciences, S-750 07 Uppsala, Sweden

over of organic material in the soil is strongly affected by the litter's chemical components. Fogel & Cromack (1977) found that the lignin level was more rate determining for litter decomposition than the C/N quotient. Berg & Staaf (1980) reported an increasing rate with higher nutrient levels whereas the lignin level decreased the rate and was more rate-determining in later stages of decomposition when most of the easily degraded compounds had been decomposed.

In connection with clearcutting where large amounts of green needles are left on the forest floor, or in connection with complete tree utilization where they may be removed, a good knowledge of the chemical composition of needles and leaves in foliage is essential. A removal of needles and leaves will remove a considerable amount of nutrients such as N, P and S which are present in much higher concentrations in green needles than in litter (Viro, 1956). Other chemical components which will be removed are, for example, phenolic or other extractives which may have strong influence on the growth of microorganisms and compounds which might play a role in the formation of soil type.

Extensive studies of extractives of various types of green needles from Scots pine (*Pinus sylvestris*) have been made (see Popoff & Theander, 1976), and recently investigations of the lipophilic extractives of the so-called technical foliage of Scots pine have been reported (see Hannus, 1976). Up to about one-fourth to one-third of the needles on the tree become litter in the autumn and it is therefore of interest to compare the composition of green needles with that of the brown ones that normally make up most of the litterfall.

The present investigation was connected with the Swedish Coniferous Forest Project. Its aim was to study the organic chemical composition of green needles and needle litter from the same stand of Scots pine and to investigate possible effects of inhibiting or stimulating substances on parts of the fungal flora at the site. Part of this work has been preliminarily reported earlier (Theander, 1978).

Materials and methods

Four-year-old needles were collected from 12–15 year-old trees in the research area at Jädraås, 140 km north of Uppsala, Sweden, as green in May and as brown – from the same trees – in October 1973 just before the peak of needle litterfall.

The main lines of the procedure of analysis are indicated in Fig. 1. The nitrogen determination for estimating the crude protein value ($6.25 \times$ N) was done by Kjeldahl analysis and the ash contents by heating at 600°C for 3 h.

In a typical work-up procedure, air dried needles (200 g) were milled and extracted with acetone (3×700 ml for 30 min) in an ultra-sonic bath at room temperature. The combined extracts were evaporated to a small volume (aqueous solution/suspension) and by extractions divided into fractions comprising compounds soluble in light petroleum (b.p. 40–60°C), ethyl acetate, 2-butanone (saturated with water) and those left in the water (Popoff & Theander, 1977). All evaporations were done at reduced pressure below 40°C.

The dried residues after extraction were analysed for sulfuric acid lignin (Klason lignin) and carbohydrates by hydrolysis (12.0 M H_2SO_4 at room temperature for 2 h and reflux for 6 h after dilution to 0.358 M), and a quantitative determination of the natural sugars in the hydrolysate was performed after reduction and acetylation by gas liquid chromatography (Bethge *et al.*, 1971). The polyuronide contents were determined by a decarboxylation method (Bylund & Donetzhuber, 1968).

The light petroleum extractives were separated into neutral and acidic compounds and further into major groups (hydrocarbons, steryl esters, triglycerides, fatty and diterpene acids, sterols and diterpene alcohols) as described previously (Hannus & Pensar, 1974).

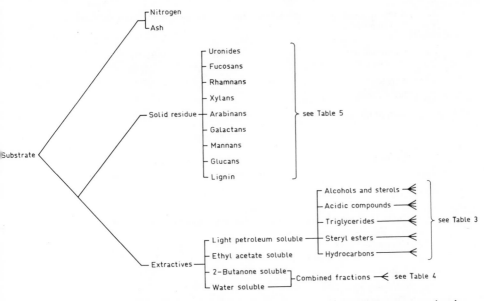

Figure 1. Survey of the procedure of analysis. The organic and inorganic components were analysed on different subsamples. The organic components were divided into one solid and one extractable part. After hydrolysis the former was analysed for polysaccharides (estimated as polymers of the individually determined carbohydrate constituents) and lignin, whereas the latter was further subdivided by chromatographic technique.

The contents of phenolic glycosides in the ethyl acetate, 2-butanone- and water-extracts were determined gravimetrically after fractionation on Sephadex LH-20 followed by silicic acid columns. Individual phenolic compounds present were identified by thin layer chromatography (TLC) as previously described (Popoff & Theander, 1977). Low-molecular carbohydrates in the two types of extracts were determined by gas liquid chromatography (GLC) after silylation (Theander & Åman, 1976).

Extracts from the samples were used for bio-assay on the following fungal strains: *Aureobasidium pullulans* (de Bary) Arnaud, *Cladosporium herbarum* (Pers) Link ex Fr., *Penicillium spinulosum* Thom, *Trichoderma polysporum* (Link ex Pers) Rifai, *T. viride* (IMI 92027 from the Commonwealth Mycological Institute, Kew, G.B.), *Oidiodendron maius* Barron and a *Hormonema* strain. The strains were mainly isolated from the top layers of the soil at the Jädraås site. For the isolation, characterization and frequency of the fungal strains, see Söderström (1974) and Bååth & Söderström (1974).

The medium used was modified from Pettersson *et al.* (1963) and contained: $NH_4H_2PO_4$, 2 g; KH_2PO_4, 0.6 g; K_2HPO_4, 0.4 g; $MgSO_4 \cdot 7H_2O$, 0.5 g; ferric citrate, 10.0 mg; $ZnSO_4 \cdot 7H_2O$, 4.4 mg; $CaCl_2$, 55.0 mg; $CoCl_2 \cdot 6H_2O$, 1.0 mg; $MnSO_4 \cdot 4H_2O$, 5.0 mg; yeast extract, 0.1 g; distilled water, 1000 ml; pH 5.8.

The extracts were dissolved or dispersed in ethanol and added to warm (about 50°C) sterilized mineral medium containing 1.5% agar and 0.3% glucose in tubes which were then shaken until a homogeneous suspension was formed. In the control series, the corresponding amounts of the ethanol were added alone (to 3%). The concentration used corresponded to the concentration of the fractions in the needles. The agar medium was poured into sterilized plastic rings placed in Petri dishes and was inoculated with pieces of fungal mycelium measuring about 1 × 1 mm cultivated on the agar medium mentioned above. Three replicates were made and the radial growth in the culture medium was measured after an incubation time of five days if not otherwise indicated.

Part of the ethyl acetate extract from the needle litter sample was fractionated on a Sephadex LH-20 column as in previous studies on the effect of spruce root extractives on *Fomes annosus* (Popoff *et al.*, 1975). Six subfractions were tested as described above on the growth of *C. herbarum*, *T. viride* and *T. polysporum*.

393

Table 1. Some main chemical components (% of dw) of live green and dead brown needles.

Component	Green	Brown
Extractives	41.1	27.2
Solid residue	65.4	73.2
Sum of fractions	106.5	100.4
Ash	2.3	2.3
Crude protein	5.3	2.4

Table 2. Composition (% of dw) of the main groups of extractives.

Component	Green	Brown
Light petroleum soluble	29.7	30.9
Ethyl acetate soluble	12.2	23.9
2-Butanone soluble	9.7	11.4
Water soluble	48.4	33.8
Sum of fractions	100.0	100.0

Results and discussion

Chemical composition of green and brown needles

The amounts of acetone-soluble extractives were considerably higher in green needles on the tree than in brown needles (Table 1), as also was the case with crude protein. It was shown by Miller & Miller (1976) that mineral nutrients in general are lower in the litter than in the green needles also if the concentration varies during the year.

The amounts of light petroleum and 2-butanone extractives were fairly similar but there was an increase in the level of the ethyl acetate extractives. The concentrations of water extractives dropped considerably from green to brown needles (Table 2). The total amounts of identified compounds in each subgroup of lipophilic extractives are given in Table 3. Monoterpenes probably disappeared during the working-up procedure used and polyisoprenyl acetates were not determined. There was a notable drop in the amount of steryl esters and triglycerides going from green to brown needles. The concentrations of free acids, especially the predominant pinifolic acid, had increased and the concentrations of alcohols and sterols were fairly similar. The level of isoabienol (identified by Ekman et al., 1977) was lower in needle litter wheras n-nonacosan-10-ol and β-sitosterol increased.

In the ethyl acetate extracts aglycones of dilignol glycosides, dihydroquercetin, quercetin and procyanidines (Popoff & Theander, 1977) were found, but the level of these identified compounds was lower in brown than in green needles on the tree. The amount of more condensed unidentified phenolic products was higher in brown

Table 3. Composition of the main constituents (% of dw) in the light petroleum fractions.

Component	Green	Brown
Hydrocarbons	2.1	2.7
Sesquiterpenes	2.0	2.7
δ-cadinene	0.7	0.9
γ-cadinene	0.5	0.7
β-carophyllene	0.1	0.2
Diterpenes	<0.05	<0.05
Steryl esters	9.8	6.5
Acids: 16:0	0.7	0.3
9–18:1	0.4	0.2
9, 12–18:2	0.3	0.4
5, 9, 12–18:3	0.8	0.2
9, 12, 15–18:3	0.8	0.1
5, 11, 14–20:3	0.4	0.2
Sterols: β-sitosterol	4.3	2.7
β-sitostanol	0.6	0.4
cycloartenol	0.2	0.3
Triglycerides	23.1	8.1
Acids: 16:0	2.5	0.8
9, 18:1	6.3	0.8
9, 12–18:2	6.7	0.8
5, 9, 12–18:3	1.4	0.1
9, 12, 15–18:3	2.9	1.1
5, 11, 14–20:3	0.9	<0.05
Acidic compounds	9.8	14.3
Fatty acids	2.0	1.6
16:0	0.4	0.4
9, 18:1	0.3	0.2
9, 12–18:2	0.5	0.2
5, 9, 12–18:3	0.1	0.1
9, 12, 15–18:3	0.6	0.1
Diterpene acids	7.6	12.7
abietinic	0.3	0.4
dehydroabietinic	1.2	2.7
pinifolic	4.8	7.3
Alcohols and sterols	7.5	6.6
isoabienol	6.4	3.6
n-nonacosan-10-ol	0.6	1.5
β-sitosterol	0.5	1.3

needles. The phenolic glycosides were enriched in the 2-butanone extract and most of the low-molecular carbohydrates, including cyclitols, were found in the water extracts. The amounts of some of the major identified hydrophilic compounds in these two extracts are given in Table 4. In earlier investigations higher levels of dihydroquercetin-3′-β-glucoside (ca 2% of the needle dry weight) have usually been found in green needles than in the present analyses (Popoff & Theander 1976).

395

Table 4. Composition of low-molecular carbohydrates and phenol glycosides (% of dw) in the water and 2-butanone fractions.

Component	Green	Brown
Pinitol	11.7	3.3
Myoinositol	1.3	0.5
Mannitol	7.5	0.8
Glucose	9.6	3.3
Fructose	6.7	4.1
Sucrose	2.9	1.6
Dilignol glycoside	2.5	1.1
Dihydroquercetin-3'-β-glucoside	2.9	0.4

Table 5. Composition (% of dw) of the solid residue fraction.

Chemical component	Green	Brown
Lignin	22.6	30.5
Neutral carbohydrate constituents	54.5	46.7
Calculated as:		
glucans	39.0	27.2
mannans	6.7	8.1
galactans	2.7	3.8
arabinans	4.0	5.5
xylans	2.0	2.9
rhamnans	0.1	0.1
fucosans	<0.05	<0.05
Acidic carbohydrate fractions[a]	5.2	6.2
Sum of fractions	82.3	83.7

[a] Calculated as hexuronides.

Besides variations in the composition of extractives from different trees this might be due to the age of the needles (only 4-year-old needles were used in the present investigation). There was a considerably lower concentration of sugars in the brown needles than in the green ones.

Among the hydrophilic compounds in green needles – mainly carbohydrates and the related cyclitols – some components such as glucose, fructose, sucrose, pinitol and shikimic acid have been isolated, each yielding 1.5–2.5% of extractives' dry weight. Also present (in the range of 0.1–1%) were arabinose, rhamnose, mannitol, melibiose, raffinose, myoinositol and sequoitol, and traces of laminaribiose and cellobiose (Assarsson & Theander, 1958). Among the hydrophilic extractives was a complex of phenolic glycosides and phenols. At elution of these on a Sephadex LH-20 column a group of monocyclic glycosides of guaiacyl- and p-hydroxyphenylglycerol was obtained (Theander, 1965) followed by a complex mixture of dilignol glycosides, which was recently fractioned and identified (Popoff & Theander, 1976, 1977), followed by dihydroquercetin-3'-β-glucosides, quercetin-3'-β-glucoside, the corresponding aglycones, and (+)-catechin (procyanidins). The latter have also been studied by Thompson *et al.* (1972) in green needles of Scots pine.

The chemical composition of the solid residue of green needles after the extraction was also investigated by recording the amount of acidic (uronic acid) and neutral polysaccharides, Klason lignin, crude protein and ash contents. The levels of polysaccharides and Klason lignin (corrected for the crude protein contents, based upon a nitrogen determination) in the residues after extraction varied to some extent between the litter types (Table 5). The proportions of polysaccharides in the samples did not differ characteristically but the increased level of Klason lignin was evident. Cellulose was clearly the predominating polysaccharide component followed by mannose-containing components. Galactans, arabinans, uronides and xylans had concentrations between 2 and 6% whereas only trace amounts were found for rhamnans and fucosans. Note that the polysaccharides in Table 5 are expressed as homoglycans, i.e., galatans, etc., although most of the main non-cellulose glycans are constituents of more than one sugar or uronic acid constituent.

Effect of pine needle extractives on fungal growth

The effect of extracts from green and brown needles was tested on the growth of several fungal species isolated at the Jädraås site. They generally gave a very similar effect with some few exceptions (Tables 6 and 7). There was an inhibition of growth compared to the control of most of the fungal strains tested, except for *Aureobasidium pullulans* which is commonly found on falling needles. The inhibition was particularly marked for the ethyl acetate extracts. The inhibitory effect of these – particularly those from the green needles (Table 6) – was very strong on the common fungi: *Cladosporium herbarum*, *Trichoderma polysporum* and the less common *Oidiodendron maius*. *Trichoderma viride*, otherwise commonly occurring in litter layers, but rather infrequently isolated at this site (Söderström, pers. comm.), was also strongly inhibited. Five subfractions of the ethyl acetate extract from brown needles, obtained after separation on a Sephadex LH-20 column were tested for their effect on the growth of the three latter fungi. The results (Table 8) indicated that unidentified components, probably tannins and condensed phenolics, which were eluted late from the column, were the most inhibiting compounds, whereas the identified phenolic glycosides and low-molecular catechins exerted smaller effect. Previously, decomposition of organic substances by mixed cultures in soil was found to be decreased by condensed tannins of the catechin type. It appears that the condensed tannins themselves are highly resistant to microbial attack (Lewis & Starkey, 1968) but apparently could be degraded, as found by Grant (1976) with a *Penicillium* sp.

Concluding remarks

The chemical changes found in the present study took place during the needles' six last months on the tree. On average the needles of Scots pine at this site can be four years old before shedding, and it is reasonable to assume that there are large changes in chemical composition between very young green needles and older ones. The rela-

Table 6. Radial growth (mm) of some fungal strains on agar medium containing crude extracts from *Pinus sylvestris* fresh green needles. Incubation time was five days with three replicates unless otherwise indicated. The concentration of extracts in medium was equal to that in the needles. $-$ = inhibited, $+$ = not inhibited.

Strain	Petroleum ether extract	Ethyl acetate extract	2-butanone extract	Control
Aureobasidium pullulans	10	5	7	4
Cladosporium herbarum	3	0	2	4
Hormonema sp.	1	6	8	5
Penicillium spinulosum	$-$[a]	$-$[a]	$+$[a]	$+$[a]
Trichoderma polysporum	10	0	10	15
Trichoderma viride	5[b]	0[b]	9[b]	10[b]
Oidiodendron maius	0 (5)[c]	0 (1)[c]	1 (5)[c]	2 (6)[c]

[a] Formation of aerial mycelium made direct measurements uncertain. Growth was apparently inhibited by the petroleum ether and ethyl acetate extracts.
[b] Growth after three days.
[c] Growth after two weeks.

Table 7. Radial growth (mm) of some fungal strains on agar medium containing crude extracts from *Pinus sylvestris* brown needles. Incubation time was five days with three replicates unless otherwise indicated. The concentration of extracts in medium was equal to that in the needles. $-$ = inhibited, $+$ = not inhibited.

Strain	Petroleum ether extract	Ethyl acetate extract	2-butanone extract	Water extract	Control
Aureobasidium pullulans	9	6	7	10	7
Cladosporium herbarum	4	2	3	5	4
Hormonema sp.	5	2	9	10	4
Penicillium spinulosum	$-$[a]	$-$[a]	$+$[a]	$+$[a]	$+$[a]
Trichoderma polysporum	5	2	3	8	7
Trichoderma viride	10[b]	5[b]	8[b]	10[b]	10[b]
Oidiodendron maius	2 (5)[c]	0 (2)[c]	2 (4)[c]	4 (6)[c]	4 (6)[c]

[a] Formation of aerial mycelium made direct measurements uncertain. Growth was apparently inhibited by the petroleum ether and ethyl acetate extracts.
[b] Growth after three days.
[c] Growth after two weeks.

Table 8. Radial growth of some fungal species on agar containing fractions of ethyl acetate extracts from brown needles separated on a Sephadex LH-20 column. Three replicates and incubation for five days.

Fraction no.	Fungal strain		
	C. herbarum (growth, mm)	T. viride (growth, mm)	T. polysporum (growth, mm)
8	4	9[a]	13
9	3	6[a]	9
10	1	2	1
11–13	1	1[a]	1
14	3	4[a]	2
Control	4	11[a]	14

[a] Growth after 3 days.

tive concentrations of lignin and solid polymer carbohydrates such as cellulose have not been found to change significantly during the development from young to old green needles (B. Berg, unpubl.).

Before the needles die there is a considerable withdrawal of nutrients to the tree, a process which is beneficial for the nutrient economy of the tree (Viro, 1956). This type of nutrient strategy has recently been discussed by Gosz (1981) and Staaf & Berg (1981). One can speculate in the possibility of whether the heavy reduction in, for example, triglycerides from green to brown needles is also a mechanism for saving valuable compounds.

Acknowledgements

The skilful technical assistance of Mrs G. Fransson and Mr S. Helmersson and the financial support from Carl Trygger's Foundation is particularly appreciated. Dr B. Söderström, who supplied us with the fungal strains, and Prof. E. Haslam, who helped us with a sample of procyanidine (B 3) are gratefully acknowledged. Part of the work was carried out within the Swedish Coniferous Forest Project.

References

Assarsson, A. & Theander, O. 1958. The constituents of conifer needles. I. Low molecular weight carbohydrates in the needles of *Pinus sylvestris*. – Acta Chem. Scand. 12: 1319–1322.

Bååth, E. & Söderström, B. 1974. Decomposition of cellulose, xylan, chitin and protein by microfungi isolated from coniferous forest soils. – Swed. Conif. For. Proj. Int. Rep. 19, 15 pp. (In Swedish, English abstract)

Berg, B. & Staaf, H. 1980. Decomposition rate and chemical changes in Scots pine needle litter. II. Influence of chemical composition. – In: Persson, T. (ed.) Structure and Function of Northern Coniferous Forests – An Ecosystem Study, Ecol. Bull. (Stockholm) 32: 373–390.

Bethge, P. O., Rådeström, R. & Theander, O. 1971. Kvantitativ kolhydratbestämning – en detaljstudie. – Comm. from Swedish Forest Product Research Lab., Stockholm, 63 B. (In Swedish)

Bylund, M. & Donetzhuber, A. 1968. Semi-micro determination of uronic acids. – Svensk Papperstidn. 15: 505–508.

Ekman, R., Sjöholm, R. & Hannus, K. 1977. Isoabienol, the principal diterpene alcohol in *Pinus sylvestris* needles. – Acta Chem. Scand. (B) 31: 921–922.

Fogel, R. & Cromack, Jr., K. 1977. Effect of habitat and substrate quality on Douglas fir litter decomposition in Western Oregon. – Canad. J. Bot. 55: 1632–1640.

Gosz, J. R. 1981. Nitrogen cycling in coniferous ecosystems. – In: Clark, F. E. & Rosswall, T. (eds.) Terrestrial Nitrogen Cycles. Processes, Ecosystem Strategies and Management Impacts, Ecol. Bull. (Stockholm) 33: in press.

Grant, W. D. 1976. Microbial degradation of condensed tannins. – Science 193: 1137–1139.

Hannus, K. 1976. Lipophilic extractives in technical foliage of pine (*Pinus sylvestris*). – Appl. Polym. Symp. 28: 485–501.

Hannus, K. & Pensar, G. 1974. Silvichemicals in technical foliage II. Nonpolar lipids in the technical foliage of Scots pine. – Finn. Chem. Letters 1: 255–262.

Lewis, J. A. & Starkey, R. L. 1968. Vegetable tannins, their decomposition and effects on decomposition of some organic compounds. – Soil Sci. 106: 241–247.

Miller, H. G. & Miller, J. D. 1976. Analysis of needle fall as a means of assessing nitrogen status in pine. – Forestry 49: 57–61.

Pettersson, G., Cowling, E. B. & Porath, J. 1963. Studies on cellulolytic enzymes I. Isolation of low-molecular-weight cellulase from *Polyporus versicolor*. – Biochem. Biophys. Acta 67: 1–8.

Popoff, T. & Theander, O. 1976. Phenolic glycosides from *Pinus sylvestris* L. – Appl. Polym. Symp. 28: 1341–1347.

Popoff, T. & Theander, O. 1977. The constituents of conifer needles. VI. Phenolic glycosides from *Pinus sylvestris* L. – Acta Chem. Scand. (B) 31: 329–337.

Popoff, T., Theander, O. & Johansson, M. 1975. Changes in sapwood of roots of Norway spruce, attacked by *Fomes annosus*, part II. Organic chemical constituents and their biological effects. – Physiol. Plant. 34: 347–356.

Söderström, B. 1974. Some microfungi isolated from different soil horizons in a 120-year-old pine forest in Central Sweden. – Swed. Conif. For. Proj. Int. Rep. 17, 7 pp. (In Swedish, English abstract)

Söderström, B. & Bååth, E. 1978. Soil microfungi in three Swedish coniferous forests. – Holarctic Ecology 1: 62–72.

Staaf, H. & Berg, B. 1981. Plant litter input to soil. – In: Clark, F. E. & Rosswall, T. (eds.) Terrestrial Nitrogen Cycles. Processes, Ecosystem Strategies and Management Impacts, Ecol. Bull. (Stockholm) 33: in press.

Theander, O. 1965. The constituents of conifer needles. III. Isolation of β-D-glucosides of guaiacyl glycerol from *Pinus sylvestris* L. – Acta Chem. Scand. 19: 1792–1793.

Theander, O. 1978. Leaf litter of some forest trees. Chemical composition and microbiological activity. – Tappi 61: 69–72.

Theander, O. & Åman, P. 1976. Low-molecular carbohydrates in rapeseed and turnip rapeseed meals. – Swed. J. Agric. Res. 6: 81–85.

Thompson, R. S., Haslam, D. J. E. & Tanner, R. J. N. 1972. Plant proanthocyanidins. Part 1. Introduction; the isolation, structure and distribution in nature of plant proanthocyanidins. – J. Chem. Soc. Perkin. I: 1387–1399.

Viro, P. J. 1956. Investigation on forest litter. – Commun. Inst. For. Fenn. 45(6), 65 pp.

Persson, T. (ed) 1980
Structure and Function of Northern
Coniferous Forests – An Ecosystem Study
Ecol. Bull. (Stockholm) 32: 401–409.

INFLUENCE OF SOIL ANIMALS ON DECOMPOSITION OF SCOTS PINE NEEDLE LITTER

B. Berg[1], U. Lohm[2], H. Lundkvist[3] and A. Wirén[3]*

Abstract

The role of the mites *Phthiracarus* spp. and *Rhysotritia ardua* and the enchytraeid worm *Cognettia sphagnetorum* for decomposition of Scots pine needle litter was studied in field and laboratory experiments. Modified litter bags enclosed litter and animals in various combinations. Needle litter with mites present was less decomposed than the control and had in one case lower amounts of lignin left at the end of the experiment. As regards weight loss, an increase or no effect at all was found with enchytraeids present, while the effect on lignin levels was the same as that found with mites. Different mechanisms for animal influence on decomposition are discussed in order to interpret the results.

Additional keywords: Acari, Enchytraeidae, lignin, weight loss.

Introduction

The soil fauna influences the process of litter decomposition which basically is carried out by microorganisms. The direction and degree of this influence is, however, strongly dependent upon the type of soil animals (e.g., Edwards & Heath, 1963; Crossley, 1977) as well as the litter's chemical composition and the season of the year. Soil animals have thus been found to increase the decomposition rate of harder tissues but not of softer ones (Heath *et al.*, 1966). The influence of soil animals resulted in a lowered decomposition rate in the autumn whereas the situation changed completely in the winter, when the animals caused an increased rate of litter weight loss (Malone & Reichle, 1973).

As the organic substance of litter is a carrier of nutrients, litter decomposition also means a release of nutrients. Malone & Reichle (1973) reported that the retention of

[1] Dept. of Microbiology, Swedish University of Agricultural Sciences, S-750 07 Uppsala, Sweden
  Present address: Dept. of Ecology and Environmental Research, Swedish University of Agricultural Sciences, S-750 07 Uppsala, Sweden
[2] Dept. of Ecology and Environmental Research, Swedish University of Agricultural Sciences, S-750 07 Uppsala, Sweden
  Present address: Dept. of Water in Nature and Society, University of Linköping, S-581 83 Linköping, Sweden
[3] Dept. of Zoology, Uppsala University, Box 561, S-751 22 Uppsala, Sweden
* Authors given alphabetically. See also Acknowledgements.

litter in the upper soil layer was greater in soil without any animals present. Such a notable difference could thus affect the total nutrient turnover rate in a forest.

The mechanisms by which soil arthropods influence litter decomposition could be many (Crossley, 1977). They may consume the dead organic material and microorganisms, produce faeces and change the chemical composition. They also could change the structure of litter by fragmentation and mix it with the soil. Such influence may also be associated with the presence of other soil animal groups.

When litter is decomposed the soluble material and part of the polymer carbohydrates are degraded before lignin (Berg & Staaf, 1980b) and the relative amount of the latter component thus increases with weight loss. Higher percentages of nutrients give initially higher weight losses whereas a high lignin level has the opposite effect. It also appears that there is a pool of non-lignified tissue which can be degraded faster than the lignified (Berg & Staaf, 1980b).

Decomposition of organic matter in field situations is often studied in different types of litter bag experiments. Litter bags can be chosen with a mesh size that makes the litter accessible only to soil fauna within a certain size range (Edwards & Heath, 1963; Bocock, 1964; Mignolet & Lebrun, 1975). It is also possible to enclose a known quantity of animals with litter and compare the decomposition rate with that in litter bags without these animals (Standen, 1978). The study presented here is of the latter kind and was carried out within the frame of a survey of the decomposition and mineralization processes in a pine forest soil. The aim of the present study was to investigate whether any of the more abundant soil animals had an influence on the litter decomposition in a nutrient-poor forest system. Two types of animals associated with litter decomposition, namely one enchytraeid (*Cognettia sphagnetorum*, Vejd.) and two phthiracarid mite species, were chosen for the experiment.

The feeding preferences of the enchytraeid worm *C. sphagnetorum* are not known in detail but it is considered to be a litter and microorganism feeder (Springett & Latter 1977; Standen & Latter, 1977). The phthiracarid mites are believed to be litter feeders, and Luxton (1972) has classified them as "macrophytophages". There are also some examples of fungal feeding in phthiracarid mites (Forsslund, 1938; Hartenstein, 1962).

Materials and methods

Site description

The site used for the experiment is a 120-year-old Scots pine (*Pinus sylvestris* L.) stand on sandy sediment at Ivantjärnsheden, Jädraås, in Central Sweden (Lat. 60°49'N, Long. 16°30'E, Alt. 185 m above M. S. L.). The ground is covered by a mosaic of mosses and lichens and the field layer of the vegetation is dominated by the dwarf shrubs heather (*Calluna vulgaris*) and cowberry (*Vaccinium vitis-idaea*) (Axelsson & Bråkenhielm, 1980). The soil type is an iron podsol. The dry weight of the humus layer is about 2 kg m^{-2}, of which 77% is dead organic material (Staaf & Berg, 1977).

Litter substrate

The litter used for the experiment was slightly degraded Scots pine needle litter of two age categories; needle litter fallen less than six months before being collected for this experiment (substrate A), and older litter, estimated to be between 1 and 2 years old (substrate B). This tentative classification of the needles was based on their colour – mainly dependent on microbial activity. The needles were dried to constant weight at room temperature and apportioned into lots of about 0.5 g.

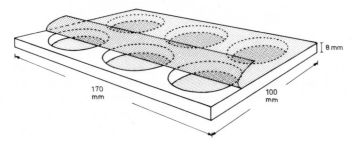

Figure 1. A set of litter chambers used in the study.

Soil animals

Two kinds of animals were tested separately in the experiment, namely mites of the families Phthiracaridae and Euphthiracaridae, in the following simply called box-mites, and the enchytraeid worm *C. sphagnetorum*, the latter being a dominant soil faunal component at the site in terms of biomass. The mites used in the experiment were extracted from the soil with Tullgren funnels and the enchytraeids with modified Baermann funnels.

Litter chambers

In a pilot study conventional litter bags of tea-bag design were found to be unsuitable as the nylon mesh became electrostatically charged, which made the bag walls stick together with the animals more or less squeezed between them. For the following experiments a new type of litter chamber was constructed. As shown in Fig. 1, plexiglass sheets, 10.5 cm × 17 cm × 0.8 cm, were provided with six holes and covered on both sides with 25 μm nylon mesh. The litter in the chamber was moistened with water from a humus suspension (1:1 of humus and tap water) before introduction of the animals. For further details see Lundkvist (1978).

Experiments and experimental periods

Two experiments were made at the field site. In these experiments a combination of 10 *Phthiracarus* spp. and 5 *Rhysotritia ardua* (C. L. Koch) were added to each 0.5 g portion of needle litter, and in another combination 15 *C. sphagnetorum* were added.

The preparation of a series of litter chambers before the start of the experiments, as well as the treatment after sampling, could be completed within two days, during which the material was stored at +5°C. Transportation of the litter chambers from the laboratory to the field and *vice versa* was done in insulated thermoboxes. The sets of litter chambers were distributed to randomly selected spots and placed in the A_{01} soil horizon. The experimental periods were 27 August – 28 October 1974 and 27 August 1974 – 3 June 1975, i.e., 62 and 280 days, respectively. Both substrates A and B were used in this series.

Another experiment was conducted in the laboratory using only substrate B. The sets of litter chambers were placed in soil blocks from the field site with field vegetation, kept in plastic pots (ca 30 × 30 × 15 cm). In this series 12 *Phthiracarus* spp. were added to 3 of the litter chambers in each set. Six sets of litter chambers were used. The experiment was run for 122 days at a temperature of 20–30°C. The soil blocks were watered at regular intervals in order to compensate the water loss through evapotranspiration.

The faeces of the box-mites were mostly found on the bottoms of the litter chambers and thus did not disturb weight loss determinations and chemical analysis. Those of the enchytraeids in all probability remained within the needles, but the extent is unknown.

After the experimental periods the following analyses were undertaken:
– All litter was examined under the stereomicroscope for remaining animals.
– Loss of dry weight of the litter was determined after drying for 24 h at 85°C.
– Content of Klason lignin was determined (Bethge *et al.*, 1971) on randomized subsamples.

Results

The number of animals recovered varied considerably between the different experiments. Of the surviving enchytraeids and box-mites in the field experiment about 75% of the box-mites were classified as vital after 62 days and about 50% after 262 days. There were no large differences between the different substrates. As regards the enchytraeids, 40% were alive on substrate B and 25% on substrate A after 62 days. Only a low percent (ca. 5%) were found alive after 262 days. Very few surviving mites (on the average 13%) were found at the end of the laboratory experiment. The experimental period lasted only 122 days but due to the high temperature this would correspond to a much longer period in the field (cf. weight loss and lignin values). Faeces and feeding marks on the needles showed that considerable animal activity had occurred during the experiment. Juvenile box-mites were found in one litter chamber only.

In both experimental periods there were significant ($p < 0.05$) differences in weight loss measures in the field experiments (Table 1). In all cases the needle litter in chambers with box-mites had a lower weight loss than those without. The differences were significant only in two of the four cases, however. In the laboratory experiment (Table 2) a decrease in weight loss was also observed with mites present. The enchytraeids in the field experiment appeared to have the opposite effect, if any, on the process. Only in one case was there a significant difference to the control.

The amount of lignin in the needles before the experiment was 35% in substrate A and 34% in substrate B. According to Berg (1978), one would expect higher percentage of lignin in the older B needles than in the A needles. The lignin level in undecomposed needle litter at this site normally is 20–25% and as the decomposition proceeds this level increases (Berg, 1978). Thus, a higher level of lignin will indicate a higher degree of decomposition. For one age bracket of pine needles at the same locality, Berg (1978) found an almost linear increase in the percentage of lignin, from 20 to 40%, for the first two years of decomposition.

The change in both percentage and weight of lignin in substrate A was affected by the presence of animals (Table 1). On the other hand, there was no significant difference for substrate B, which indicates a difference between the two litters.

In the laboratory experiment the amount of lignin had increased about 4% both with and without animals present (Table 2). The method of lignin analysis used not only gives lignin but also humification products, and the lignin fraction thus can show a net increase before its decomposition starts.

Discussion

The method used generally gave somewhat higher litter weight losses than the litter-bag method used at the site by Berg & Staaf (1980a) and Berg (1978), who used terylene litter bags with 1 mm mesh size in decomposition experiments. A similar increase in weight loss as a function of decreasing mesh sizes was noted by Berg & Rosswall (1972) when comparing the influences of mesh sizes from 10 μm to 1 mm on weight loss rate. The increased weight loss could be due to an increased moisture level caused by the fine nets used in the litter chambers.

A general draw-back for all types of bags and chambers for enclosure of litter and

Table 1. Decomposition of Scots pine needle litter (mean of 10 replicates) with controlled populations with and without enchytraeids and phthiracarids in an old Scots pine stand at Jädraås, Central Sweden. Standard error within parentheses. Initial lignin level for substrate A 35% of dry weight and for substrate B 34%. × ———— × indicates a significant difference ($p < 0.05$).

Period		Substrate A Weight loss (mg)	Substrate B Weight loss (mg)	Substrate A Lignin loss (mg)	Substrate A Lignin concentration (% of litter dry weight)	Substrate B Lignin loss (mg)	Substrate B Lignin concentration (% of litter dry weight)
27 Aug.–28 Oct. 1974	Control	61.6 (2.4)	66.0 (2.4)	17.7[1] (1.9)	35.7[1] (0.8)	15.9[1] (3.2)	35.7[1] (0.6)
	Phthiracarids	55.5 (1.1)	64.9 (3.2)	27.9[1] (1.1)	33.0[1] (0.2)	15.3[1] (2.2)	35.8[1] (0.7)
	Enchytraeids	66.7 (1.9)	63.8 (1.1)	27.9[1] (1.9)	33.3[1] (0.4)	10.1[1] (2.2)	37.1[1] (0.5)
27 Aug. 1974–3 June 1975	Control	129 (3.3)	120 (2.1)	23.5 (3.1)	40.6 (0.3)	19.5 (1.6)	40.1 (0.5)
	Phthiracarids	123 (5.0)	106 (5.4)	33.0 (2.6)	37.5 (0.5)	15.1 (2.4)	39.9 (0.5)
	Enchytraeids	128 (2.2)	124 (3.5)	34.1 (1.9)	37.7 (0.5)	23.5 (1.9)	40.0 (0.5)

[1] $n = 4$ at the lignin analysis.

Table 2. Decomposition (mean values) of Scots pine needle litter in a laboratory experiment with and without phthiracarids. Incubation at 20–30°C for 122 days. Initial level of lignin was 34%. Standard error within parentheses. ×——× indicates a significant difference ($p < 0.05$).

	Weight loss (mg)	Lignin fraction	
		(% of initial dry wt)	increase (mg)
Control	178 (8.8) ×	54.2 (0.7) ×	5.3 (2.8)
Phthiracarids	159 (10.7) ×	52.1 (1.1) ×	7.7 (2.2)

animals is that the possibility for the animals to avoid unfavourable microsites is very much reduced; a factor presumably most important during periods of drought. However, this appeared to be of minor importance in the present experiment, as the field part was run during autumn and winter months with no long dry periods.

Soil animals may influence litter decomposition in various ways, either directly through consumption of litter or indirectly through affecting the microorganisms involved in the decomposition of various components.

When consuming litter the animals would mechanically eat whole litter structures without regard to single chemical components like lignin. The direct mechanical eating by animals thus causes a higher weight loss together with opening of surfaces accessible to microorganisms. The microorganisms can only act enzymatically and dissolve chemical components. When unable to degrade lignin, fungi, for instance, will degrade just the polymer carbohydrates which are sterically available at the cell surface of a plant (cf. Nilsson, 1973).

Both a higher weight loss as well as a stimulating effect on the lignin decomposition was found in experiments with *Cognettia sphagnetorum* present. This result could be interpreted as due to a direct consumption of the substrate. It is also consistent with Standen (1978), who found that *C. sphagnetorum* increased dry weight losses of *Eriophorum*-, *Calluna*- and *Sphagnum*-litter. Standen also found that the enchytraeids affected decomposition much less in the winter than in other seasons. Thus, the result of the present experiment, where no weight loss differences were found between the enchytraeid treatment and the control during the longer period, which was dominated by the winter, also agrees with Standen's findings. But, on the other hand, the survival during this period was low, which makes the result inconclusive.

The lower amount of lignin that appeared alone, i.e., not linked to an increased weight loss, in one enchytraeid treatment could also be interpreted as the result of enchytraeid influence on the microbial decomposition of lignin (cf. the discussion below on box-mites and lignin decomposition).

Both interpretations are quite plausible, although the results of the present experiment seem to give stronger support for the former of the two.

The indeterminate results as regards the enchytraeids could be due to the litter chosen for the experiment. *C. sphagnetorum* has been shown to prefer litter in later stages of decomposition and certain litter species before others, e.g., *Eriophorum* and *Calluna* before *Sphagnum* (Standen & Latter, 1977; Latter & Howson, 1978; Standen, 1978). Pine needle litter might on the whole not be very attractive to the enchytraeids, but in this study pine needles were the major source of food available to the worms.

The lower weight loss of needle litter with box-mites present indicated that direct litter consumption was negligible. Instead, the results pointed towards an interaction with the microorganism populations.

The effects of an indirect influence through consumption of microorganisms would be highly dependent on the extent and selectivity of this consumption. A stimulating effect on the microbial activity by grazing, measured indirectly by measuring the change in respiration, has been found in laboratory experiments (van der Drift & Jansen, 1977; Addison & Parkinson, 1978). This effect would probably be reflected in higher weight loss rates. More complex soil fauna/microbial interactions have been found in a laboratory experiment (Hanlon & Anderson, 1979) from which it was concluded that the same soil animal species could either increase or inhibit a particular microorganism population depending on the density of the animal population.

The lower amount of lignin found in the field experiments with substrate A when box-mites were present suggests that these animals have a favourable effect on the lignin decomposing microorganisms, in this case basidiomycetes (B. Söderström, pers. comm.). It is not known whether this is a result of a growth stimulus on these organisms through faunal grazing on the very same microorganism population or if it is due to consumption of other sections of the microorganism community which in turn may enhance the competitive ability of the lignin decomposers.

The effect observed on substrate A was not found on substrate B. As the qualitative difference between the two substrates is not known in detail, this difference in mite influence is difficult to explain. The lignin analysis includes both lignin and humification products. The apparent increase of the lignin fraction in the laboratory experiment could be explained as the result of humification. Considering the close connection between humus synthesis and lignin degradation (Christman & Oglesby, 1971), an effect of box-mites on humification is quite possible even though no conclusion can be drawn from the present experiment.

One plausible interpretation of our results with regard to box-mites could be that they selectively ingest microorganisms decomposing carbohydrates instead of lignin, i.e., mainly fungi that are predominant on the litter surface and able to decompose different solid carbohydrates. This in turn might favour lignin-decomposing fungi which can penetrate deeper in the litter substrate. Effects of animal grazing on the competitive ability for one species of litter fungi have been shown by Parkinson et al. (1977) in a laboratory experiment with one collembolan species and two species of fungi in litter.

The results presented in this study suggest that the influence on pine needle litter decomposition by the animals studied is relatively small and the effect on the general turnover of organic material in the system could be of minor importance measured as total amounts. On the other hand, the results indicate that the animals could have an influence on the decomposition of the slowly decomposed components like lignin and lignified tissues, and as such that they might have a larger effect on long-term litter turnover than is indicated by simple weight loss.

Acknowledgements

The study was carried out within the Swedish Coniferous Forest Project. The authors were all involved in the general planning of the study and in preparation of the manuscript. The detailed planning, preparation and treatment of the field experiment was done by H. Lundkvist, whereas A. Wirén prepared the laboratory experiment.

References

Addison, J. A. & Parkinson, D. 1978. Influence of collembolan feeding activities on soil metabolism at a high arctic site. – Oikos 30: 529–538.
Axelsson, B. & Bråkenhielm, S. 1980. Investigation sites of the Swedish Coniferous Forest Project – biological and physiographical features. – In: Persson, T. (ed.) Structure and Function of Northern Coniferous Forests – An Ecosystem Study, Ecol. Bull. (Stockholm) 32: 25–64.
Berg, B. 1978. Decomposition of needle litter in a 120-year-old Scots pine (*Pinus silvestris*) stand at Ivantjärnsheden. – Swed. Conif. For. Proj. Int. Rep. 80, 66 pp.
Berg, B. & Rosswall, T. 1972. Decomposition of cellulose in pot experiments in the laboratory. – In: Sonesson, M. (ed.) Swedish IBP Tundra Project Tech. Rep. No. 14, pp. 134–141.
Berg, B. & Staaf, H. 1980a. Decomposition rate and chemical changes in decomposing needle litter of Scots pine. I. Influence of stand age. – In: Persson, T. (ed.) Structure and Function of Northern Coniferous Forests – An Ecosystem Study, Ecol. Bull. (Stockholm) 32: 363–372.
Berg, B. & Staaf, H. 1980b. Decomposition rate and chemical changes of Scots pine needle litter. II. Influence of chemical composition. – In: Persson, T. (ed.) Structure and Function of Northern Coniferous Forests – An Ecosystem Study, Ecol. Bull. (Stockholm) 32: 373–390.
Bethge, P. O., Rådeström, R. & Theander, O. 1971. Kvantitativ kolhydratbestämning – en detaljstudie. – Comm. from Swedish Forest Product Research Lab. 63B, Stockholm. (In Swedish)
Bocock, K. L. 1964. Changes in the amounts of dry matter, nitrogen, carbon and energy in decomposing woodland leaf litter in relation to the activities of the soil fauna. – J. Ecol. 52: 273–284.
Christman, R. F. & Oglesby, R. T. 1971. Microbial degradation and the formation of humus. – In: Sarkanen, K. V. & Ludwig, C. H. (eds.) Lignins: Occurrence, Formation, Structure and Reactions, pp. 769–795. New York: Wiley & Sons.
Crossley, D. A. 1977. The roles of terrestrial saprophagous arthropods in forest soils: Current status of concepts. – In: Mattson, W. J. (ed.) The Role of Arthropods in Forest Ecosystems, pp. 49–56. New York: Springer-Verlag.
Drift, J. van der & Jansen, E. 1977. Grazing of springtails on hyphal mats and its influence on fungal growth and respiration. – In: Lohm, U. & Persson, T. (eds.) Soil Organisms as Components of Ecosystems, Proc. 6th Int. Coll. Soil Zool., Ecol. Bull. (Stockholm) 25: 203–209.
Edwards, C. A. & Heath, G. W. 1963. The role of soil animals in breakdown of leaf material. – In: Doeksen, J. & van der Drift, J. (eds.) Soil Organisms, pp. 76–80. Amsterdam: North Holland Publishing Co.
Forsslund, K-H. 1938. Bidrag till kännedom om djurlivets inverkan på markomvandlingen. 1. Om några hornkvalsters (oribatiders) näring. – Medd. Statens Skogsförsöksanst. 31: 87–104. (In Swedish, German summary)
Hanlon, R. D. G. & Anderson, J. M. 1979. The effects of Collembola grazing on microbial activity in decomposing leaf litter. – Oecologia (Berlin) 38: 93–99.
Hartenstein, R. 1962. Soil Oribatei. I. Feeding specificity among forest soil Oribatei (Acarina). – Ann. Ent. Soc. Amer. 55: 202–206.
Heath, G. W., Arnold, M. K., Edwards, C. A. 1966. Studies in leaf litter breakdown. 1. Breakdown rates among leaves of different species. – Pedobiologia 6: 1–12.
Latter, P. M. & Howson, G. 1978. Studies on the microfauna of a blanket bog with particular reference to Enchytraeidae. II. Growth and survival of *Cognettia sphagnetorum* on various substrates. – J. Anim. Ecol. 47: 425–448.
Lundkvist, H. 1978. The influence of soil fauna on decomposition of pine needle litter: A field experiment. – Swed. Conif. For. Proj. Tech. Rep. 18, 15 pp.
Luxton, M. 1972. Studies on the orbatid mites of a Danish beech wood soil. I. Nutritional biology. – Pedobiologia 12: 434–463.
Malone, C. R. & Reichle, D. E. 1973. Chemical manipulations of soil biota in a fescue meadow. – Soil Biol. Biochem. 5: 629–639.
Mignolet, R. & Lebrun, Ph. 1975. Colonisation par les Microarthropodes du sol de cinq types de litière en décomposition. – In: Vaněk, J. (ed.) Progress in Soil Zoology, Proc. 5th Int. Coll. Soil Zool. pp. 261–281. The Hague: W. Junk and Prague: Akademia Publishing House.

Nilsson, T. 1973. Studies on wood degradation and cellulolytic activity of microfungi. – Stud. for. suec. 104, 40 pp.

Parkinson, D., Visser, S. & Whittaker, J. B. 1977. Effects of collembolan grazing on fungal colonization of leaf litter. – In: Lohm, U. & Persson, T. (eds.) Soil Organisms as Components of Ecosystems, Proc. 6th Int. Coll. Soil Zool., Ecol. Bull. (Stockholm) 25: 75–79.

Springett, J. A. & Latter, P. M. 1977. Studies on the microfauna of a blanket bog with particular reference to Enchytraeidae. I. Field and laboratory tests on micro-organisms as food. – J. Anim. Ecol. 46: 959–974.

Staaf, H. & Berg, B. 1977. Mobilization of plant nutrients in a Scots pine forest mor in Central Sweden. – Silva fenn. 11: 210–217.

Standen, V. 1978. The influence of soil fauna on decomposition by micro-organisms in blanket bog litter. – J. Anim. Ecol. 47: 25–38.

Standen, V. & Latter, P. M. 1977. Distribution of a population of *Cognettia sphagnetorum* (Enchytraeidae) in relation to micro-habitats in a blanket bog. – J. Anim. Ecol. 46: 213–229.

Persson, T. (ed) 1980
Structure and Function of Northern
Coniferous Forests – An Ecosystem Study
Ecol. Bull. (Stockholm) 32: 411–418.

MINERALIZATION OF NITROGEN IN INCUBATED SOIL SAMPLES FROM AN OLD SCOTS PINE FOREST

B. Popović[1]

Abstract

Nitrogen mineralization in a Scots pine forest soil was studied by incubation of soil samples for 6-week periods. Soil samples incubated in the laboratory and in the field differed in nitrogen mineralization rate, mainly because of different temperature, moisture and substrate heterogeneity. Incubation of litter, humus and mineral soil samples in the field during two consecutive years resulted in low rates of mineralization or immobilization. The mineralization rate estimated for the whole soil profile during the growing season was far too low for maintaining the plant community with mineral nitrogen. It is suggested that the low mineralization rates in the incubated samples are caused by fine-root death, which in the present soil of high C/N ratio results in initial immobilization.

Additional keywords: C/N ratio, immobilization.

Introduction

One of the central interests in the Swedish Coniferous Forest Project (SWECON) is nitrogen cycling in forest ecosystems. The Scots pine forests studied have low productivity, one of the main reasons being the limited supply of nitrogen. The inputs of nitrogen from the atmosphere in form of dry and wet deposition and nitrogen fixation are fairly small (Bringmark, 1977, 1980; Granhall & Lindberg, 1980), and the mineralization rate of the nitrogen bound in organic compounds is of importance for the nitrogen supply to the plant roots.

The aim of the present study was to estimate the amounts of soil mineral nitrogen in the field and to get an understanding of the dynamics of the nitrogen mineralization in incubated samples, where no uptake by roots and leaching occurs.

A preliminary experiment was carried out during the summer of 1973 with simultaneous storage of litter and humus samples in the laboratory (20°C) and in the field. After this pilot study only field incubations were used. The changes in concentrations of NH_4^+ and NO_3^- in incubated samples were compared with the natural concentrations in the field. The study was performed in a 120-year-old Scots pine stand (Ih V) (1973–75). The results are more extensively reported in Popović (1974, 1976, 1977).

---

[1] Dept. of Ecology and Environmental Research, Swedish University of Agricultural Sciences, S-750 07 Uppsala, Sweden

The Ivantjärnsheden research area is situated in Central Sweden, 60°49′N, 16°30′E, 185 m above M.S.L. The soil is an iron-podzol on sandy sediments. The humus type is a typical mor. Further site characteristics are given in Axelsson & Bråkenhielm (1980).

Methods

Sample treatment

Individual soil samples were collected by a specially designed auger (38.48 cm^2 surface area) with a plastic insertion. Three sample units of the humus layer (A_0-horizon) were collected from 23 spots and were separated from the mineral soil and mixed by hand to form three composite samples. Three mineral soil samples were collected from 8 spots in the 0–10 cm and 10–20 cm layers and mixed in the same way as the humus samples. In both cases roots were removed as far as possible. Litter samples ($n = 23$) of 20×20 cm were also mixed to form a composite sample, which was separated into three fractions: mosses and lichens, cones and remaining litter (Popović, 1976).

One part of each mixed sample was immediately analyzed for inorganic nitrogen and water content in the laboratory. Another part was placed in a polyethylene bag (20×32 cm) to about one-third of the bag's capacity. The bags were closed tightly and replaced in hollows made in pit walls of the soil profile at the same depth from which the material had been taken. The polyethylene bags prevented removal of inorganic nitrogen during storage, both by roots and by leaching (Runge, 1971).

The soil samples were stored for about six weeks, after which the inorganic contents in the bags were analyzed and the water content was determined. At the time of removal of the older samples, new soil samples treated in the same way as the older ones were placed in the soil profile for another period of six weeks, and these replacements continued throughout the growing season. The incubation series lasted for three years in the mature stand (Ih V). During the first year (1973) samples were also incubated in the laboratory.

Analytical procedure

Before analysis, the moist humus was passed through a 3 mm mesh sieve and the mineral soil through a 2 mm mesh sieve, and 20 g of humus or 40 g of mineral soil were placed into 500 ml polyethylene flasks together with 200 ml of 1% $KAl(SO_4)_2$ solution with pH adjusted to about 6.5 and shaken for one hour. The suspension was filtered and the filtrate was used for immediate analysis or for storage in a refrigerator.

Ammonia nitrogen was estimated colorimetrically on a Beckman spectrophotometer Model B after addition of indophenol reagent to the filtrate (Runge, 1971). Nitrate nitrogen was determined by phenoldisulphonic acid (Popović, 1971) following pretreatment of filtrate with addition of fine granulated active coal to remove interfering colour (Holz & Kremer, 1970). Determinations of loss on ignition, Kjeldahl nitrogen and pH were also made on each batch of samples.

Results and discussion

Mineral nitrogen in the field

The contents of mineral nitrogen fluctuated considerably in the humus layer of the 120-year-old stand during the frost-free periods in 1974–76 (Fig. 1), and there were differences in the average contents for each year. The peak values in Fig. 1 for July and October 1974 followed periods of extraordinarily high precipitation, when the water contents were about 170 and 300% of the humus dry weight, respectively (Popović, 1976).

The mean amounts of mineral nitrogen measured during the frost-free periods of 1974–76 are given in Table 1. The mineral soil contained the largest amounts of

412

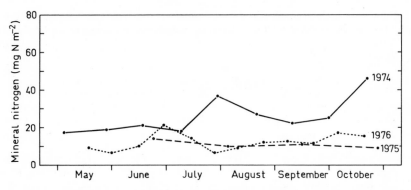

Figure 1. Content of mineral nitrogen (NH_4^+-N and NO_3^--N) in the humus layer of the 120-year-old Scots pine stand at Ivantjärnsheden during the frost-free periods in 1974–76.

Table 1. Mean amounts of mineral nitrogen (NH_4^+-N and NO_3^--N) (mg m^{-2}) in different soil layers during the frost-free periods of 1974–76 in the 120-year-old Scots pine stand at Ivantjärnsheden based on samplings indicated in Fig. 1. The dry weights of the layers (kg m^{-2}) used for conversion from concentration units are given within parentheses.

	1974	1975	1976
Litter layer	14 (1.4)	6 (1.4)	7 (1.5)
Humus layer	26 (3.7)	11 (3.0)	12 (3.5)
Mineral soil 0–10 cm	149 (96)	86 (100)	48 (97)
Mineral soil 10–20 cm	210 (117)	148 (124)	93 (117)
Total	399	251	160

mineral nitrogen, and these amounts varied pronouncedly between the years. The largest amounts of mineral nitrogen were recorded in 1974, which also had the highest precipitation, but the intermediate year 1976 as regards precipitation had, on average, smaller amounts of mineral nitrogen than the dry year 1975. However, water content is not the only factor affecting the microbial release of mineral nitrogen, and the water content in the soil may influence the intricate balance between microbial release, uptake by roots and leaching of mineral nitrogen in a non-linear way.

Preliminary comparison of laboratory and field incubations

The incubations in the laboratory and in the field in 1973 resulted in different mineralization rates (Table 2). These differences were probably caused by temperature, water content and differences in substrate quality.

The temperature in the laboratory (20°C) was considerably higher than the soil temperature in the field. The field soil temperatures at the depths of 5 and 10 cm read twice a week at 08.00 varied between 10 and 15°C from late June to early September, whereas the temperatures were lower before and after this period (Popović, 1974). Consequently, one should have expected more similar values between laboratory and

413

Table 2. Net mineralization of nitrogen (μg g^{-1} dw) in litter and humus from the 120-year-old Scots pine stand at Ivantjärnsheden incubated for 6-week periods in the laboratory (20°C) and in the field during 1973. Negative values denote immobilization and values within parentheses denote water content (% water of dw) at the end of the period.

Soil layer		May 29–July 10	June 20–July 31	July 10–Aug. 20	July 31–Sept. 13	Aug. 20–Sept. 30	Sept. 13–Oct. 25
Litter	Laboratory	−10 (150)	−11 (150)	9 (335)	24 (186)	−6 (144)	1 (144)
	Field	149 (144)	79 (37)	25 (335)	32 (170)	−11 (223)	−14 (163)
Humus	Laboratory	−2 (156)	−12 (156)	24 (156)	0 (156)	2 (156)	3 (156)
	Field	16 (203)	−14 (133)	29 (138)	22 (133)	10 (108)	6 (96)

field incubations during the warmer period (columns 1–4, Table 2) than during the colder.

The water content was usually of the same magnitude in samples incubated in the laboratory and in the field, but the large difference in nitrogen mineralization between the litter materials during June 20–July 31 may be assigned to different water contents. The different values in the litter materials during May 29–July 10 can be explained neither by temperature nor by water content. The most probable explanation seems to be different proportions of litter components, since the litter was not subdivided into homogeneous fractions in 1973. This source of error was avoided during the subsequent years (see Methods).

Nitrogen mineralization in samples incubated in the field

The results of the incubation experiments carried out within the 120-year-old Scots pine stand during the growing seasons of 1974–75 are shown in Table 3. Nitrogen net mineralization (positive values) and immobilization (negative values) appeared to be small in the litter layer, more moderate in the humus layer and large in the mineral soil layers. This is largely a consequence of the dry weights of the soil layers (see Table 1), and expressed on a per gramme basis the mineralization/immobilization figures are usually much higher in the litter and humus than in the mineral soil.

Two incubation series were made in 1974, and series 1 started earlier and ended later than series 2 (Table 3). Series 1 had lower mineralization/higher immobilization than series 2, and the difference was especially pronounced for the mineral soil layers. This difference can only partly be assigned to the different periods in time, and it is possible that the method is too crude for determining net mineralization rates in the mineral soil, where the concentrations of mineral nitrogen are very low.

It must be remembered that the incubated samples constitute artificial systems and only partly simulate the undisturbed field situation. A fundamental difference between the litter and humus layer samples is that the litter layer does not include any living plant parts when sampled, while the humus layer contains living roots. It was impossible to remove all fine roots before incubation and, therefore, the humus samples also contained root material that had recently died, and with low nitrogen content. According to unpublished analyses made within SWECON the fine root

414

Table 3. Net mineralization of nitrogen (mg N m^{-2}) in incubated samples from different soil layers in the 120-year-old Scots pine stand at Ivantjärnsheden after 6-week-periods in the field during the growing seasons of 1974–75. Negative values denote immobilization.

	Litter layer	Humus layer	Mineral soil 0–10 cm	Mineral soil 10–20 cm	Total
1974 (Series 1)					
May 3–June 17	−4	1	−29	−47	−79
June 17–July 29	2	9	−39	−70	−98
July 29–Sept. 9	−1	6	−10	−47	−52
Sept. 9–Oct. 21	3	−5	19	71	89
May 3–Oct. 21, total	0	11	−59	−93	−142
1974 (Series 2)					
May 27–July 8	9	30	58	35	132
July 8–Aug. 20	−1	23	−58	−47	−81
Aug. 20–Sept. 30	2	−4	−29	0	−31
May 27–Sept. 30, total	10	48	−29	−12	17
1975					
June 23–Aug. 4	7	12	9	10	38
Aug. 4–Sept. 15	5	14	9	−12	16
Sept. 15–Oct. 27	1	7	49	75	132
June 23–Oct. 27, total	13	33	67	73	186

(<2 nm) concentration of total nitrogen was 0.4–0.5% of the dry weight and the C/N ratio was >100. The C/N ratio was high, about 40–50 in the humus layer as a whole (Popović, 1977) which indicates that normally there should be low rates of nitrogen mineralization. Addition of easily decomposable fine roots with very high C/N ratios would probably induce immobilization since it is known that immobilization dominates over mineralization during initial decomposition (Bosatta et al., 1980; Keeney, 1980). When decomposition proceeds the total N-concentration of the incubated humus layer should increase and net mineralization start.

Temperature and moisture are important factors for nitrogen mineralization of humus material from Ivantjärnsheden (Sohlenius et al., 1976) (Figs. 2 and 3). The rate of mineralization increases with increasing temperature but, in situations with initial immobilization, increasing temperature should both increase the rate of immobilization and shorten the initial phase of immobilization. This probably explains the mineralization pattern for the humus layer samples, with higher mineralization during June–August than after this period (Table 3). The temperature during June–August was probably high enough to enable the decomposition to lower the C/N ratio with resulting net mineralization within a 6-week-period, while the temperature from September onwards was lower, resulting in net immobilization (1974, both series) or only slight mineralization (1975).

The estimates of nitrogen mineralization (Table 3) are large underestimates as

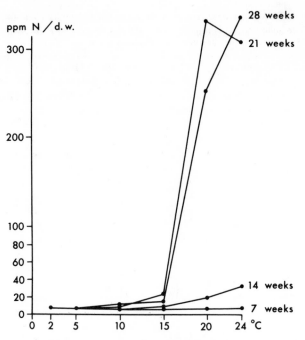

Figure 2. Concentration of mineral nitrogen (NH_4^+-N and NO_3^--N) in humus samples incubated in the laboratory up to 28 weeks at different temperatures and at a water content of 60% WHC.

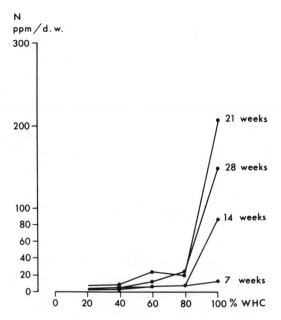

Figure 3. Concentration of mineral nitrogen (NH_4^+-N and NO_3^--N) in humus samples incubated in the laboratory up to 28 weeks at different water contents and constant temperature (15°C).

416

regards the humus layer. The estimates for the litter layer seem to be more reliable, and a fluctuation between immobilization and mineralization is quite expected for a material with a C/N ratio of 50–60 (Popović, 1977).

The reliability of the incubation experiments for simulation of the field situation was tested by an input/output analysis of the pine forest. Bringmark (1977) estimated the uptake by roots to be 3.13 g N m^{-2} yr^{-1} in the 120-year-old Scots pine stand at Ivantjärnsheden in 1976, the precipitation reaching the soil contained 0.23 g N m^{-2} during the growing season the same year (Bringmark, 1980), the nitrogen fixation was 0.03 g N m^{-2} yr^{-1} (Granhall & Lindberg, 1980) and the leaching from a depth of 27 cm in the soil was 0.01 g N m^{-2} yr^{-1} (Bringmark, 1980). Consequently, the remaining plant need of 2.5–3.0 g N m^{-2} yr^{-1} should have been produced by mineralization. The mineralization for the whole soil profile was estimated to be 0.19 g N m^{-2} during June–October in 1975 (Table 3) and, thus, about 15 times lower than the amount needed by the plant community in 1976.

Concluding remarks

The present study has provided experience on the incubation method. The concentration and the mineralization rates of mineral nitrogen were very low in the Ivantjärnsheden soil in comparison with other soils, for example, in West Germany (Runge, 1971). The accuracy of the incubation method used seems to be low for soils with low nitrogen content (high C/N ratio) because of the relative importance of immobilization. The incubation period of 6 weeks was too short to reduce the impact of initial immobilization on the final result, but very long incubation periods will probably result in artificial effects. Total elimination of fine roots from the humus material is very difficult to obtain but should increase the reliability of the incubation method. The method is probably useful for comparative purposes.

Acknowledgements

The present investigation was conducted as part of the Swedish Coniferous Forest Project. The author is indebted to Tryggve Persson for valuable discussions and constructive criticism of the manuscript. Bo Johansson, Ove Emteryd and Bengt Andersson are gratefully acknowledged for skilful technical assistance.

References

Axelsson, B. & Bråkenhielm, S. 1980. Investigation sites of the Swedish Coniferous Forest Project – biological and physiographical features. – In: Persson, T. (ed.) Structure and Function of Northern Coniferous Forests – An Ecosystem Study, Ecol. Bull. (Stockholm) 32: 25–64.

Bosatta, E., Bringmark, L. & Staaf, H. 1980. Nitrogen transformation in a Scots pine forest mor – a model analysis of mineralization, uptake by roots and leaching. – In: Persson, T. (ed.) Structure and Function of Northern Coniferous Forests – An Ecosystem Study, Ecol. Bull. (Stockholm) 32: 565–589.

Bringmark, L. 1977. A bioelement budget of an old Scots pine forest in Central Sweden. – Silva fenn. 11: 201–209.

Bringmark, L. 1980. Ion leaching through a podsol in a Scots pine stand. – In: Persson, T. (ed.) Structure and Function of Northern Coniferous Forests – An Ecosystem Study, Ecol. Bull. (Stockholm) 32: 341–361.

Granhall, U. & Lindberg, T. 1980. Nitrogen input through biological nitrogen fixation. – In: Persson, T. (ed.) Structure and Function of Northern Coniferous Forests – An Ecosystem Study, Ecol. Bull. (Stockholm) 32: 333–340.

Holz, F. & Kremer, H. 1970. Automatische Bestimmung von Nitrat in Pflanzensubstanz. – Landwirtsch. Forsch. 23: 23–25.

Keeney, D. R. 1980. Prediction of soil nitrogen availability in forest ecosystems: A literature review. – Forest Sci. 26: 159–171.

Persson, H. 1980. Death and replacement of fine roots in a mature Scots pine stand. – In: Persson, T. (ed.) Structure and Function of Northern Coniferous Forests – An Ecosystem Study, Ecol. Bull. (Stockholm) 32: 251–260.

Popović, B. 1971. Effect of sampling date on nitrogen mobilization during incubation experiments. – Plant & Soil 34: 381–392.

Popović, B. 1974. Nitrogen mineralization – a comparison between incubation experiments in the field and in the laboratory. – Swed. Conif. For. Proj. Int. Rep. 11, 17 pp. (In Swedish, English abstract)

Popović, B. 1976. Nitrogen mineralization in an old pine stand. – Swed. Conif. For. Proj. Int. Rep. 35, 16 pp. (In Swedish, English abstract)

Popović, B. 1977. Nitrogen mineralization in an old and a young Scots pine stand. – Swed. Conif. For. Proj. Int. Rep. 60, 15 pp. (In Swedish, English abstract)

Runge, M. 1971. Investigation of the content and the production of mineral nitrogen in soils. – In: Ellenberg, H. (ed.) Integrated Experimental Ecology. Ecological Studies, pp. 191–202. Berlin–Heidelberg–New York: Springer-Verlag.

Sohlenius, B., Berg, B., Clarholm, M., Lundkvist, H., Popović, B., Rosswall, T., Staaf, H., Söderström, B. & Wirén, A. 1976. Mineralisation and soil organism activity in a coniferous humus – a model building experiment. – Swed. Conif. For. Proj. Int. Rep. 40, 51 pp. (In Swedish, English abstract)

Persson, T. (ed) 1980
Structure and Function of Northern
Coniferous Forests – An Ecosystem Study
Ecol. Bull. (Stockholm) 32: 419–459.

TROPHIC STRUCTURE, BIOMASS DYNAMICS AND CARBON METABOLISM OF SOIL ORGANISMS IN A SCOTS PINE FOREST

T. Persson[1], E. Bååth[2], M. Clarholm[3], H. Lundkvist[4], B. E. Söderström[2]
and B. Sohlenius[5]*

Abstract

Simultaneous samplings of soil organisms were performed during a 14-month-period in a 120-year-old
Scots pine forest. About 50 microfungal and more than 200 animal species were identified. Abundance,
hyphal length, biomass and respiratory metabolism were estimated for bacteria, fungi, protozoans, nematodes, rotifers, tardigrades, enchytraeids, micro- and macroarthropods, which were also classified into
trophic categories.

Annual mean biomass of fungi was high (120 g dw m^{-2}) but, on average, only 2% was metabolically
active according to the FDA-method. Bacteria had a remarkably high mean biomass (39 g m^{-2}) for being
found in an acidic soil. Soil animals had a low mean biomass (1.7 g m^{-2}). FDA-active fungal biomass
reached maxima in late autumn and early spring with minima in between. Biomass peaks were estimated in
late summer for protozoans and early autumn for bacteria, while most animal groups had biomass maxima
in late autumn. In the soil profile all organism groups had biomass maxima in the upper horizons, but the
animal biomass decreased more abruptly with increasing depth than the microorganism biomass.

Annual carbon flow through the organisms was calculated on the basis of respiration values. In terms of
carbon, bacteria appeared to be more important for decomposition than fungi, and animal saprovores
had little significance. The soil fauna contributed 4% to the annual heterotrophic respiration. Despite the
low respiration, bacterivores and fungivores were estimated to remove as much as 30–60% of the annual
production of bacteria and fungi in the litter and humus layers. The consumption pressure was suggested
to reduce microorganism biomass and increase turnover and mineralization rate of mineral nutrients.
Carnivore predation was very high, while root consumption was negligible. Fungivore grazing of mycorrhizal fungi was believed to affect the roots more pronouncedly than the rhizophages did.

Additional keywords: Bacteria, carbon flow, consumption, Enchytraeidae, fungi, macroarthropods,
microarthropods, microfauna, microorganisms, Nematoda, Protozoa, respiration.

Introduction

A very significant part (30–60%) of the total ecosystem metabolism is devoted to the
activities of the heterotrophic soil organisms (Reichle, 1977). Soil organisms decom-

---

[1] Dept. of Entomology, Uppsala University, Box 561, S-751 22 Uppsala, Sweden
[2] Dept. of Microbial Ecology, University of Lund, Ecology Building, S-223 62 Lund, Sweden
[3] Dept. of Microbiology, Swedish University of Agricultural Sciences, S-750 07 Uppsala, Sweden
[4] Dept. of Zoology, Uppsala University, Box 561, S-751 22 Uppsala, Sweden
[5] Dept. of Zoology, University of Stockholm, Box 6801, S-113 86 Stockholm, Sweden
* Author responsibilities given in Acknowledgements.

pose the organic substrates under release of carbon dioxide, water and mineral nutrients. The efflux rate of carbon dioxide provides a useful denominator for comparison of different organisms (Reichle, 1977), and according to current estimates the microorganisms release 80–99% and the soil animals 1–20% of the non-root losses of carbon dioxide from various soils (Huhta & Koskenniemi, 1975; Persson & Lohm, 1977; Coulson & Whittaker, 1978). The quantitative dominance of the microorganisms is, thus, outstanding in most soils. However, the soil organism community is an interacting system with many feed-backs, and organisms at higher trophic positions may exert important regulating functions without being characterized by high metabolic rates. It is, therefore, important to distinguish between different trophic groups within the soil organism community in order to get a better understanding of what the metabolic activity really implies.

Besides their direct and indirect influences on decomposition of organic matter and mineralization of bioelements, the soil organisms have a biomass which consists of a relatively large pool of mineral nutrients. The turnover of this pool and factors influencing its size are of great importance for the supply to plant roots and for the retention of these element within the ecosystem.

Relatively few ecosystem studies include major parts of both the microbial and the animal communities in the soil (e.g., Rosswall & Heal, 1975; Heal & Perkins, 1978; Coupland, 1979). For coniferous forest soils such complete studies seem to be lacking in the literature, although biomass dynamics and respiratory metabolism of major soil animal groups have been investigated by, for example, Huhta et al. (1967), Huhta & Koskenniemi (1975) and Kitazawa (1977). The present paper, based on studies within the Swedish Coniferous Forest Project, emphasizes the trophic structure, biomass dynamics and respiratory metabolism of bacteria, fungi and major groups of soil animals to obtain an understanding of the relative importance of these groups in the carbon flow in a northern Scots pine forest soil. The nitrogen turnover was also studied but is not presented here.

This paper consists essentially of two sets of data. The first set is based on a monthly sampling series with high resolution as regards the seasonal changes, but with insufficient sampling depth for some taxa. The second set is based on complementary data obtained from deeper samples. The second set, thus, allows a correction of the annual mean values. The first set is mainly reported in "Seasonal dynamics" and the second in "Vertical distribution".

In the present study the protozoans are included in the "microfauna". The microfauna also includes Nematoda, Rotatoria and Tardigrada, which here are called metazoan microfauna when treated collectively. The microarthropods include Symphyla, Collembola, Protura and Acari, whereas all other arthropods, irrespective of size, are included in the macroarthropod group.

It was not possible to treat the microorganisms with the same detailed resolution as the soil fauna because of methodological difficulties. Therefore, the paper is somewhat unbalanced in favour of the soil fauna. Furthermore, most of the descriptive data on the fungi have been published elsewhere (e.g., Söderström & Bååth, 1978; Bååth & Söderström, 1979a; Söderström, 1979a), while only parts of the soil faunal studies (T. Persson, 1975; Sohlenius, 1977, 1979) have previously been reported.

Site description

The research area, Ivantjärnsheden, Jädraås, Gästrikland in Central Sweden, is situated at latitude 60°49′ N, longitude 16°30′ E and altitude 185 m above M.S.L. The long-term mean annual air temperature is 3.8°C with a maximum of +15.8°C in July and a minimum of −7.0°C in January. The mean annual precipitation is about 600 mm. The average duration of snow cover is November 9–April 24 (Bråkenhielm, 1978). The growing season (mean air temperature exceeding 6°C) lasts, on average, from May 2 to October 12.

The samplings were performed in a fairly thin (400 trees ha^{-1}, mean height 16 m) regular stand of 120-year-old (1974) Scots pine (*Pinus sylvestris* L.). The vegetation belongs to the *Cladonio-Pinetum boreale* association with a ground vegetation of the dry to very dry dwarf-shrub type (Axelsson & Bråkenhielm, 1980). Biomass estimates are about 200 g dw m^{-2} of field layer, mainly *Calluna vulgaris* (L.) Hull. and *Vaccinium vitis-idaea* L., and about 260 g dw m^{-2} of bottom layer, mainly *Pleurozium schreberi* (Brid.) Mitt., *Dicranum polysetum* Sw., *Cladonia silvatica* (L.) Harm. and *C. rangiferina* (L.) Web. (H. Persson, 1980a).

The soil is an iron-podzol developed in a layered glacifluvial material dominated by fine-medium sand (0.06–0.6 mm) at 0–40 cm depth overlying medium-coarse sand (0.2–2 mm). The litter layer is very loose with living mosses and lichens interwoven in it, the humus type is a typical mor, and the bleached layer is fairly weakly developed (Staaf & Berg, 1977a). The soil profile is spotwise disturbed which makes the estimates of, for example, horizon thickness, uncertain. The soil horizons are indicated in Fig. 1, and the mean characteristics of the soil are given in Table 1.

Soil temperature and moisture

The temperature and moisture conditions prevailing in the soil during the sampling period (see below) are exemplified in Fig. 2. During the annual period 5 July 1974–4 July 1975 the mean temperatures were 5.0, 5.0 and 5.1°C in the litter layer, humus layer and about 10 cm beneath the litter layer at the interface of the A_2 and B horizons, respectively. The temperature was, on average, about 1°C higher in the uppermost layer than in the deeper layer during spring and summer and about 1°C lower during winter (Fig. 2).

The soil moisture was measured gravimetrically on each sampling occasion and more frequently (Jansson, 1977) from May 1975 onwards. According to the sparse measurements in 1974 the soil water content seemed to increase from the early summer in 1974 to the late autumn (Fig. 2). This period showed unusually high precipitation in July and September–November. There was an opposite trend in the soil water values during the summer in 1975, when the soil moisture decreased more or less steadily from the time of snow melt to the middle of August when a long drought was broken. However, the main study (see below) did not cover more than the first part of the summer in 1975 and, therefore, the sampling series represents a predominantly wet period. The soil water content was at its maximum during the winter, but this was mainly caused by accumulation of ice in the soil.

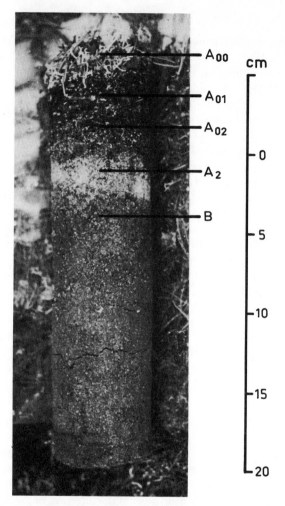

Figure 1. Soil horizons in the 120-year-old Scots pine stand at Ivantjärnsheden. A_{00} = litter layer (including mosses and lichens in the bottom layer), A_{01} = fermentation layer, A_{02} = raw humus layer, A_2 = bleached layer and B = enrichment layer. Depths (cm) in the mineral soil are indicated.

Methods

Sampling

Most of the present study is based on a monthly sampling scheme covering the period May 1974 to June 1975 with sampling dates around the 20th each month. However, owing to deep hard frost, the sampling in March 1975 was omitted. Core samples for different soil organism groups were taken close to each other in 10×10 m quadrats, randomly chosen within the research plot (100×200 m). The same sampling quadrats were used each month, the position being moved by about two meters each time. Six cores each were taken for bacteria, fungi and metazoan microfauna, 12 (including the former 6) each for micro- and macroarthropods and 18 (including the former 12) for enchytraeids. The fungal samples for total biomass were only taken every third month during the main sampling period, but complementary samplings were made monthly during 1975–77 for estimation of FDA-active biomass (see below). Protozoans were not studied quantitatively during the main sampling period, but supplementary monthly samplings ($n = 10$) were made in May–October 1978.

422

Table 1. Mean characteristics of the soil horizons in the 120-year-old Scots pine stand at Ivantjärnsheden (Ih V). * = not estimated.

	Thickness[a] (cm)	Weight[b] (kg dw m^{-2})	Organic content[b] (kg dw m^{-2})	(% of dw)	Loss on ignition[b] (% of dw)	C[b] (g m^{-2})	N[b] (g m^{-2})	C/N-ratio	pH$_{H_2O}$
Litter layer (A$_{00}$)	2	0.71	0.67	95.5[c]	95.5[c]	339	6.9	49[b]	4.4[d]
Humus layer (A$_{01}$/A$_{02}$)	3.5	1.99	1.54	77.3	77.3	687	16.2	42[b]	4.0[d, e]
Bleached layer (A$_2$)	4	21.4	0.8	3.6	5.6	*	*	33[e]	4.3[e]
Enrichment layer (B)	30	*	*	*	*	*	*	27[e]	4.9[e]
Mineral soil 0–10 cm (A$_2$ + B)		99	2.54	2.6	3.6	1470	42	35[b]	4.6[d]
Mineral soil 10–20 cm (B)		121	1.75	1.5	2.8	1010	36	28[b]	5.0[d]
Mineral soil 20–30 cm (B)		133	0.5	0.4	1.4	300	12	25[b]	*

[a] Used in the present study.
[b] From Staaf & Berg (1977a). Living mosses, lichens and roots excluded.
[c] Additional estimate from Clarholm (1977).
[d] From Popović (1977).
[e] From Söderström (1979a).

423

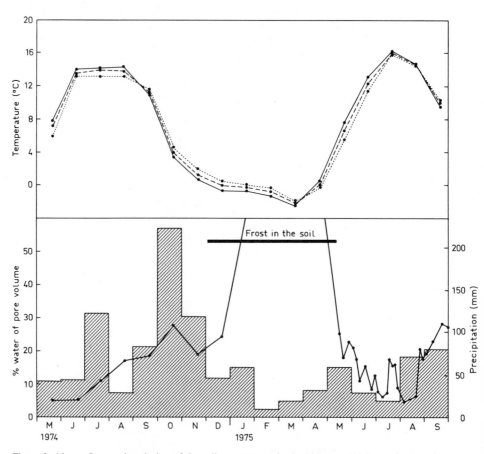

Figure 2. Above: Seasonal variation of the soil temperature in the 120-year-old Scots pine stand at Ivantjärnsheden in the litter layer (solid line), humus layer (broken line) and about 10 cm beneath the litter layer (dotted line). Since organism samplings were made on the 20th each month, it can be noted that the monthly means given concern a symmetrical period around this date, i.e., May 5–June 4, etc.
Below: Monthly precipitation (hatched columns), soil moisture in the humus layer (solid line) and duration of frost in the soil (horizontal bar) during 1974–75.

Treatment of samples

The bacterial soil cores measured 35.2 cm^2 (surface area) × 10 cm (depth) and the fungal cores 35.2 cm^2 × 18 cm. The intact cores were wrapped in plastics and brought back to the laboratory. Bacteria were processed within 3–4 hours of sampling. The cores were divided into a litter (A_{00}) layer, a fermentation (A_{01}) layer, a raw humus (A_{02}) layer, an eluvial (bleached) (A_2) layer and an illuvial (enrichment) (B) layer. Corresponding layers from the six cores were pooled to form composite samples.

The bacteria were counted directly by fluorescence microscopy after staining with acridine orange. The bacterial biomass was calculated after size determinations of approximately 30 cells per sample assuming the same size distribution throughout the sample, a density of 1.0 and a dry weight of 20% of the fresh weight. The total fungal biomass was analysed with the agar-film method (Jones & Mollison, 1948; Bååth & Söderström, 1977, 1979a). Calculation of the fungal biomass is described in Bååth & Söderström (1977, 1979b). The FDA-active fungal biomass was studied from the A_{01}/A_{02} (pooled), A_2 and B horizons with the fluorescein diacetate (FDA) method (Söderström, 1977, 1979a). The microfungal species composition was determined with the soil washing technique (Parkinson & Williams, 1961; Söderström & Bååth,

424

1978). The protozoans were only studied in 1978 in the A_{01}/A_{02} horizon using the most probable numbers method according to Darbyshire *et al.* (1974). Growth medium was a previously isolated mixed natural bacterial population grown for two days at 24°C on Tryptone Soy Broth (diluted to 1/10 strength) with modified Neff's amoeba saline (Page, 1967).

The cores for extraction of metazoan soil fauna measured 4.15 cm² (surface area) × 10 cm (depth) for the microfauna, 10.5 cm² × 20 cm for the microarthropods, 22.1 cm² × 20 cm for the enchytraeids and 125 cm² × 20 cm for the macroarthropods. The cores were divided into A_{00}, A_{01}/A_{02}, A_2 and various depths in the B layer, except for the enchytraeids, which were extracted from the pooled A_{00} and A_{01}/A_{02} horizons on most occasions. The A_{00} layer included living mosses and lichens (i.e., more properly called S-layer, *stratum superficiale*) for all faunal extractions. The macroarthropod cores also included the field layer vegetation. The microfaunal and microarthropod soil cores were brought intact to the laboratory, while the enchytraeid and macroarthropod cores were divided into appropriate layers in the field.

The metazoan microfauna was extracted by means of a modified Baermann method as described previously (Sohlenius, 1977). The animals were killed by heat and stored in 4% formaldehyde. Before counting, the suspensions with animals from each soil layer were pooled into two batches originating from three cores each. The enchytraeids were extracted according to a modified Baermann method (O'Connor, 1962) and counted alive. The microarthropods were extracted by a high gradient canister technique (Persson & Lohm, 1977). Macroarthropods as well as mobile microarthropods were extracted in Tullgren funnels equipped with lamps that increased the heat in the upper part of the inverted soil core fraction to 30°C after two days and to 50°C after four days when the extraction was ended. For enchytraeids and all arthropods the individual cores were treated separately.

The animal biomasses were determined by means of volumetric methods for nematodes, tardigrades and rotifers (Sohlenius, 1977, 1979), length/weight regressions for collembolans (Persson & Lohm, 1977) and spiders (T. Persson, in prep.), and length/width/weight regressions for small acarids (Persson & Lohm, 1977). The mean body weights of ciliates and naked amoebae were adopted from Fenchel (1974) and Band (1959), respectively, while the mean weight of flagellates (see Table 2) is an average from various references. Most arthropod species were weighed individually or collectively on a Cahn 4700 or a Cahn 25 Automatic Electrobalance. The average body weight of enchytraeids was determined on one sampling occasion (May 1977). Correction for gut content was made for enchytraeids, where the average dry gut content was estimated to be 12.3 µg which was about 50% of the average dry tissue weight (H. Lundkvist, in prep.). The fresh weight/dry weight ratios in Table 2 were adopted from Laybourn & Finlay (1976), Persson & Lohm (1977) and Lundkvist (1978).

Respiratory metabolism

The calculations of the respiratory metabolism of the soil fauna groups are based on the relations between live body weights and oxygen consumption rates according to equations of the form $Q = aW^b$, where Q denotes oxygen consumption rate per individual, W denotes live body weight and a and b are constants particular for each taxonomic group (Table 2). Most of the constants used for enchytraeids and arthropods are discussed in Persson & Lohm (1977). However, the parameters for Chilopoda (derived from Byzova, 1973) and Formicidae (from Jensen, 1978) are additions or changes as proposed by Persson & Lohm. The parameters for Protozoa were derived from the respiration rate of *Tetrahymena pyriformis* given by Laybourn & Finlay (1976) assuming a general b-value of 0.80 in close accordance to the mean regression proposed by Reichle (1971). The equation based on *T. pyriformis* should be $Q = 27 \cdot W^{0.80}$ at 10°C for active ciliates but, since respiration is largely reduced (down to 10–15%) during encystment (Pigon, 1958), half the activity respiration, i.e., $Q = 13.5 \cdot W^{0.80}$, was considered to be a more probable figure. The ciliate equation was also used for flagellates and amoebae. The equation given by Klekowski *et al.* (1972) for nematodes was also generalized to rotifers and tardigrades.

Conversion of oxygen consumption rates to carbon efflux rates assumed a RQ of 0.8 for all animals and all sampling occasions (cf. Brody, 1945). Adjustment to the field temperature was made assuming the Q_{10} values given in Table 2. Reasons for most Q_{10} values are outlined in Persson & Lohm (1977). The Q_{10} values used for low temperatures are mainly assumptions owing to lack of literature data, but higher values towards lower temperatures are in agreement with the Krogh (1941) curve. The soil temperature was measured at several depths (see Perttu *et al.*, 1980) and, depending on the animal's vertical distribution, the soil temperature used varied for each soil animal taxon and time (cf. Fig. 2). Since the soil temperature showed considerable within-day fluctuations (see above) and due to the exponential dependence of the temperature, the oxygen consumption rates were calculated for each hourly mean temperature by means

425

Table 2. Parameters used for calculation of oxygen consumption rate per individual (Q) with the live body weight W for different soil fauna taxa at Ivantjärnsheden. The parameter values of a and b in the equation $Q = aW^b$ presuppose Q as mm^3 O_2 ind^{-1} h^{-1} and W as g live body weight at the temperature given in the appropriate column below. Adjustments to other temperatures are indicated by the Q_{10} values. Below 5°C the Q_{10} was assumed to be 5, except for Protozoa and Enchytraeidae, for which a linear decrease in oxygen consumption from +5°C to a zero-value at −5°C was assumed. Except for Protozoa and Enchytraeidae, the mean body weights given here were considered too crude and were not used for calculation of oxygen consumption.

	Mean body dry wt (µg)	fw/dw ratio	a	b	Temp. (°C)	Q_{10} at 5–20°C
Protozoa						
Ciliata	0.0015	6	13.5	0.80	10	2
Flagellata	0.0004	6	13.5	0.80	10	2
Rhizopoda	0.0008	6	13.5	0.80	10	2
Metazoan microfauna						
Nematoda	0.028	5	29.25	0.72	20	3
Rotatoria	0.065	5	29.25	0.72	20	3
Tardigrada	0.22	4	29.25	0.72	20	3
Enchytraeidae	25	6.67	33.6	0.67	20	2
Microarthropods						
Symphyla	5.1	5.88	63	0.73	18	2.5
Collembola	1.6	3.33	63	0.73	18	2.5
Protura	0.41	4	63	0.73	18	2.5
Acari						
Gamasina	5.6	2.5	102	0.87	10	3
Uropodina	7.4	2.5	5.0	0.67	10	3
Prostigmata	0.24	2.5	102	0.87	10	3
Astigmata	0.73	2.5	102	0.87	10	3
Cryptostigmata, Euptyctima	10	2.5	3.5	0.69	10	3
Cryptostigmata, Aptyctima	0.87	2.5	7.2	0.69	10	3
Macroarthropods						
Diplopoda	160	2.2	18	0.73	10	2.5
Chilopoda	600	3.33	83	0.80	10	2.5
Blattodea	550	4	74	0.70	10	2.5
Psocoptera	46	3.33	63	0.73	18	2.5
Coleoptera						
Elateridae larvae	650	4	53	0.80	10	2.5
Curculionidae larvae	57	4	89	0.80	10	2.5
Other Coleoptera larvae	105	4	141	0.77	10	2.5
Coleoptera adults	570	3	113	0.74	10	2.5
Hymenoptera						
Parasitica adults	50	4	63	0.73	18	2.5
Formicidae adults	1100	3.33	146	0.85	20	2.5
Raphidioptera larvae	85	4	167	0.77	10	3
Diptera larvae	37	4	210	0.87	10	2.5
Pseudoscorpiones	80	3.7	90	0.92	10	2.5
Araneae	420	3.7	90	0.92	10	2.5

of a computer. In comparison with this way of calculation, the use of, for example, the monthly mean temperature of the litter layer in June 1975 would have meant an underestimation of 7, 12 and 17% for animals with Q_{10} values of 2, 2.5 and 3, respectively (T. Persson, in prep.). The monthly respiration (R_M) (g C m^{-2} month^{-1}) for a single species was calculated according to the equation:

$$R_M = a \cdot \frac{0.8 \cdot 12}{22.4} \cdot 10^{-6} \cdot 24 \cdot D_M \cdot k \cdot \sum_i (W_i^b \cdot N_i)$$

where W_i denotes g mean live body weight of the size class i, N_i the number per m^2 of this size class, D_M the number of days per month, and k the conversion factor calculated with regard to daily fluctuations of temperature, different Q_{10} and the temperature at which the constants a and b have been determined (see Table 2). The other figures denote volume CO_2/volume O_2 (0.8), g C per 1 CO_2 (12/22.4) l per µl (10^{-6}) and hours per day (24).

Classification into trophic categories

Many taxonomic groups consist of species with different trophic positions. Therefore, a rough classification of the organisms' trophic position was undertaken.

Most isolated fungi were able to utilize protein. A smaller number of species could decompose xylan and cellulose and a few species could degrade chitin. Almost all of the isolated *Mortierella* species belonged to the latter group (Bååth & Söderström, 1980). Bacterial strains with the ability to decompose protein, xylan, cellulose and chitin were isolated. The most developed ability to hydrolyze cellulose and especially lignin is generally found among basidiomycetes (Harley, 1971), but these fungi were not isolated. The above-mentioned fungi and bacteria were considered as saprotrophs (Swift *et al.*, 1979), as they utilize dead matter. The mycorrhizal fungi, which could not be distinguished from the other fungi, were considered as a special category since they receive carbohydrates from their hosts.

The animals were classified into five broad feeding groups, namely, saprovores, bacterivores, fungivores, carnivores and herbivores (rhizophages). The classification was based on a large number of studies, e.g., Gere (1956), Wallwork (1958), Führer (1961), Karg (1961), Bhattacharyya (1962), Hartenstein (1962), Nielsen (1962), Woodring (1963), Christiansen (1964), Müller & Beyer (1965), Raw (1967), Stout & Heal (1967), Gilmore & Raffensperger (1970), Petersen (1971), Luxton (1972), Pande & Berthet (1973), Harding & Stuttard (1974), Anderson (1975), Mitchell & Parkinson (1976), Springett & Latter (1977), Latter & Howson (1978) and Sohlenius (1979). With regard to species composition and population density, this information was generalized as follows:

(1) Saprovores: Flagellata and Enchytraeidae (50%).
(2) Bacterivores: Ciliata, Rhizopoda, Nematoda (part), Rotatoria and Enchytraeidae (25%).
(3) Fungivores: Nematoda (part), Enchytraeidae (25%), Diplopoda, Collembola, Protura, Blattodea, Psocoptera, Coleoptera (part), Diptera Nematocera (larvae) and Acari (Uropodina, Astigmata, Cryptostigmata).
(4) Carnivores: Nematoda (part), Tardigrada, Chilopoda, Coleoptera (part), Hymenoptera (Formicidae, Parasitica), Raphidioptera (larvae), Diptera Brachycera (larvae), Pseudoscorpiones, Araneae and Acari (Gamasina, Prostigmata).
(5) Herbivores: Nematoda (*Tylenchus, Geocenamus*), Coleoptera (Curculionidae larvae) and Symphyla.

Flagellates, which can feed on soluble organic matter (Stout & Heal, 1967) and, thus, resemble bacteria in feeding behaviour, and those enchytraeids which feed on dead plant remains (see below), were classified as saprovores (saprotrophs). Also other soil fauna members in the research area, such as the diplopod *Proteroiulus fuscus*, some elaterid larvae, Diptera larvae and phthiracarid mites, can consume dead organic matter (e.g., McBrayer & Reichle, 1971; Luxton, 1972), but it is doubtful whether they are also able to digest this material. As it is probable that most animals with mixed dead organic matter/microorganism diets chiefly assimilate the microorganisms, these animals were either considered to be fungivores and/or bacterivores.

The nematode fauna was primarily divided into three feeding categories, namely, root/fungal feeders, bacterial feeders and miscellaneous feeders (Sohlenius, 1979). In this study members of *Tylenchus* and *Geocenamus* are classified as rhizophages, and the other root/fungal feeders are considered as fungivores (cf. Magnusson & Sohlenius, 1980). The miscellaneous feeders are assumed to be carnivores. No obligate predators such as species of Mononchoidea were found. The enchytraeid *Cognettia sphagnetorum* probably can feed and grow on various kinds of substrate and, in lack of better knowledge, it was considered to be 50% saprovore, 25% fungivore and 25% bacterivore (cf. Latter & Howson, 1978).

427

A large variety of feeding types occurs within Coleoptera (see, e.g., Raw, 1967) and, according to the crude classification that was undertaken, a minority of species were considered as fungivores (e.g., Crypto-phagidae, Lathridiidae and Silphidae). The majority of species was classified as carnivores (e.g., Carabidae, Staphylinidae and larvae of Cantharidae). Only a few species, all belonging to Curculionidae, were classified as root feeders in their larval stage. None of the elaterid species found had larvae known to be rhizophages (Schaerffenberg, 1942; Nilsson, 1971) and are here considered as 50% carnivores and 50% fungivores in lack of more precise knowledge.

Results

The soil organism community

Except for bacteria, the soil organisms found in the samplings were primarily classi-fied into taxonomic groups and could mostly also be determined to species. The microfungal species composition was determined separately with the soil washing technique. The number of identified species within each taxonomic group is given in Table 3, in which 51 microfungal and 214 animal species are noted. The latter figure is a clear underestimate, since (1) animal species found outside the sampling programme were not included and (2) some animal groups have not been treated as regards their species composition. However, further determination can hardly change the general view that Acari is the most species-rich animal taxon.

Table 3 also summarizes the annual means of hyphal lengths, abundance, biomass and respiratory metabolism of the soil organisms. The quantitative dominance of fungi and bacteria in relation to the soil animals is evident. The abundance and bio-mass of bacteria are higher than normally found in coniferous forests with acidic soils. The total fungal biomass (calculated with the agar-film method) is considerably higher than the bacterial biomass, but the metabolically active part of the fungal biomass determined with the FDA-method constitutes only 1.8% of the total fungal biomass (see below).

The high abundance and relatively high biomass of protozoa are also remarkable, since protozoans generally have been ignored in quantitative studies of coniferous forest soils. The estimates indicate that the protozoans constitute an important element in the soil organism community in such soils. The estimates of the other soil animal groups give a general picture of normal or high (Nematoda, Rotatoria, Acari) abundances and fairly low biomasses in comparison with other forest soils.

The most commonly isolated microfungal genera were *Mortierella* and *Peni-cillium*. Other genera isolated with high frequencies were *Oidiodendron, Tolypocla-dium, Trichoderma* and *Verticillium*. The distributions of these and some other genera in the soil layers are illustrated in Fig. 3. Some genera, for example *Mortierella*, were found in high frequencies in all horizons below the litter layer. However, exam-ination of the various species within *Mortierella* showed that the individual species had distinct preferences for certain horizons in the soil profile (Fig. 4).

The most commonly isolated species in A_{00} were *Aureobasidium pullulans* (de Bary) Arnaud and *Cladosporium herbarum* (Pers.) Link ex Fr., in A_{01} *Mortierella verticillata* Linnemann and *Penicillium spinulosum* Thom, in A_{02} *M. isabellina* Oudem. and *P. spinulosum*, in A_2 *M. macrocystis* W. Gams, *M. nana* Linnemann and *Mycelium radicis atrovirens* Melin, and in B *M. nana* and *M. r. atrovirens*. For further details see Söderström (1974) and Söderström & Bååth (1978).

The macrofungal flora was only superficially studied. The most common species

Table 3. Number of identified species and annual means of hyphal lengths, abundance, biomass and respiratory metabolism of the organisms found in the 120-year-old Scots pine stand at Ivantjärnsheden according to the regular soil samplings. The annual means are calculated from Tables 4, 5 and 6 for the period July 1974–June 1975 (FDA-active fungi from 1975–77 and Protozoa from 1978 included). n.d. = not determined.

	No. of species	Abundance (no. m^{-2})	Biomass (mg dw m^{-2})	Respiratory metabolism (mg C m^{-2} yr^{-1})
Fungi (agar-film)[a]	}51[b]	–[c]	80 000	}60 000
Fungi (FDA)	}	–	1 400	}
Bacteria[a]	n.d.	16 × 10^{13}	20 000	105 000
Protozoa[a]	n.d.	130 × 10^6	90	1 700
Ciliata	n.d.	3 × 10^6	5	69
Flagellata	n.d.	40 × 10^6	16	330
Rhizopoda	n.d.	86 × 10^6	69	1 300
Metazoan microfauna[a]	34	4 950 000	166	930
Nematoda	28	4 390 000	122	740
Rotatoria	2	510 000	33	140
Tardigrada	4	49 000	11	43
Enchytraeidae	3	16 200	405	2 000
Microarthropods	118	744 000	609	1 800
Symphyla	1	35	0.2	1
Collembola	26	60 000	94	470
Protura	1	700	0.3	3
Acari	90	684 000	515	1 340
Gamasina	14	8 400	47	130
Uropodina	2	180	1.3	2
Prostigmata	20	210 000	50	210
Astigmata	2	40 000	29	110
Cryptostigmata	52	425 000	388	890
Macroarthropods	>61	1 700	313	720
Diplopoda	1	8	1.2	1
Chilopoda	1	2	0.9	4
Blattodea	1	2	1.0	4
Psocoptera	2	11	0.5	4
Coleoptera	30	440	131	390
Carabidae	2	2	5.5	33
Staphylinidae	9	49	15	69
Elateridae larvae	5	110	80	110
Cantharidae larvae	4	260	25	150
Other Coleoptera	10	25	4.6	29
Hymenoptera	>5	37	11	15
Parasitica adults	n.d.	29	1.6	6
Formicidae adults	5	8	9.0	9
Raphidioptera larvae	1	2	0.1	3
Diptera larvae	19	780	29	120
Nematocera larvae	12	700	21	89
Brachycera larvae	7	82	9	31
Pseudoscorpiones	1	1	0.1	0.1
Araneae	n.d.	330	138	180

[a] Annual means underestimated here because of insufficient sampling depths.

[b] Microfungal species (Söderström & Bååth, 1978).

[c] Average hyphal length 85 000 km m^{-2} (before correction to greater depth).

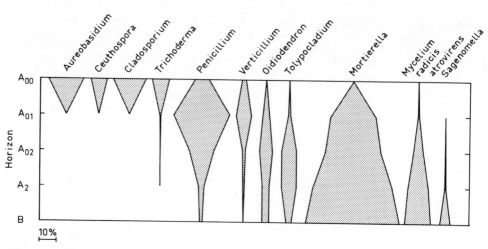

Figure 3. Distribution of some microfungal genera in different soil horizons in the 120-year-old Scots pine stand at Ivantjärnsheden (% of total number of isolates per horizon).

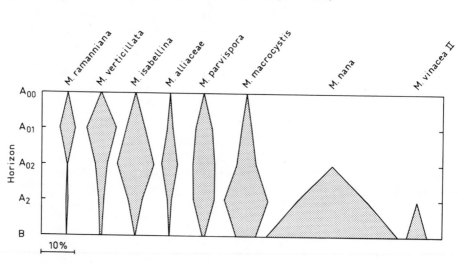

Figure 4. Distribution of some species of *Mortierella* in different soil horizons in the 120-year-old Scots pine stand at Ivantjärnsheden (% of total number of isolates per horizon).

appeared to be *Lactarius rufus* Scop. ex Fr., and a common genus was *Cortinarius*.

As indicated in Table 3 the protozoans consisted of ciliates, flagellates and amoebae, of which both naked amoebae and testate amoebae occurred. Eleven species of testate amoebae have been identified from the 120-year-old Scots pine stand (Axelsson *et al.*, 1974), while the other protozoan groups have not been determined to species.

The nematode genera *Acrobeloides*, *Plectus*, *Tylenchus* and *Aphelenchoides* were numerically important, while *Eudorylaimus*, *Aporcelaimus* and *Acrobeloides* had high biomass (Sohlenius, 1977). The totally (99.9%) dominant enchytraeid species was *Cognettia sphagnetorum* (Vejd.).

430

The microarthropods were numerically dominated by small oribatids, e.g., *Tectocepheus velatus* Mich. and various Brachychthoniidae, *Oppia* and *Suctobelba* species. Also small prostigmatids, e.g., *Tydeus* sp. and *Tarsonemus* sp., small astigmatids, such as *Schwiebea* cf. *nova* (Oudms), and small collembolans like *Tullbergia krausbaueri* Börn. were abundant. *T. velatus* and medium-sized acarids such as *Carabodes* spp. dominated the microarthropod biomass.

The most abundant macroarthropods were Cantharidae and Cecidomyiidae larvae. High biomasses were estimated for the elaterid larvae *Corymbites impressus* F., *Prosternon tesselatum* L. and *Athous subfuscus* Müll., for cantharid larvae and for some spider species.

Hand sortings revealed very low abundances of lumbricids, isopods and molluscs, and these groups were not represented in the regular samplings. Of the ants, the commonly known *Formica rufa* L. was not found. Also other taxa than those noted in Table 3 were found in the soil samples, namely, Thysanoptera, Homoptera, Heteroptera, Hymenoptera Symphyta (larvae) and Lepidoptera (larvae). The members of these groups as well as some Coleoptera species were not included in the soil fauna. Some Thysanoptera, Homoptera and Heteroptera might possibly be considered as soil animals, but true soil animals such as root-feeding aphids were so few that the total exclusion of the groups above was justified.

Seasonal dynamics

Hyphal length

The fungal hyphae estimated with the agar-film technique appeared to reach maximum length in spring and minimum length during summer and autumn followed by a recovery during late autumn (Table 4). The precision in the estimates is not known since the sample units were pooled. However, in a nearby plot the coefficient of variation ($s/\bar{x}$) was found to be about 0.5 in the A_{01}/A_{02} horizon (E. Bååth & B. Söderström, unpubl.) indicating 95% confidence intervals of $\pm 50\%$ of the regular estimates. Thus, the 95% confidence intervals of all estimates might be overlapping.

Abundance of bacteria and animals

The monthly mean abundances of bacteria and various faunal taxa in the whole soil profile investigated are given in Table 4. The bacterial numbers fluctuated in the region of $10-15 \times 10^{13}$ m^{-2} during most of the year but showed a pronounced peak in the early autumn (August–October). The lowest values were estimated in May–June 1974 when the precipitation and soil moisture was very low.

The protozoans sampled in the humus layer in 1978 had a distinct maximum in the late summer but fairly small numbers at the beginning (May) and end (October) of the sampling series.

The nematodes accounted for 89% of the annual mean number of metazoan microfauna. The nematode number increased successively from June 1974 to December the same year, after which high abundances were found during the whole winter (the soil was frozen also at the April sampling) until a sudden drop in May. The rotifers and tardigrades also had their lowest numbers during the summer of 1974, but the

431

Table 4. Lengths (km m⁻²) of fungal hyphae according to the agar-film method, and abundances (no. m⁻²) of bacteria and soil animal taxa estimated for 1974–75 (Protozoa from 1978 included). Interpolated values used for calculation of annual means in Table 3 given within parentheses. * = not estimated.

	Month													
	M	J	J	A	S	O	N	D	J	F	M	A	M	J
Fungi (agar-film) (km m⁻²)	130700	*	*	71200	*	*	56500	*	*	103000	*	*	110900	*
Bacteria (×10⁻¹³)	7.2	5.2	9.6	28.6	34.1	19.3	12.5	11.2	9.2	10.8	(12.9)	14.9	14.4	13.8
Protozoa (×10⁻⁶)	*	*	364	839	144	20	*	*	*	*	*	*	<0.8[a]	(182)
Ciliata (×10⁻⁶)	*	*	11	11	4	6	*	*	*	*	*	*	[a]	(5)
Flagellata (×10⁻⁶)	*	*	99	266	54	12	*	*	*	*	*	*	[a]	(49)
Rhizopoda (×10⁻⁶)	*	*	255	562	87	2	*	*	*	*	*	*	[a]	(128)
Metazoan microfauna, total (×10⁻³)	1980	*	2600	2783	4576	3663	5836	6770	(6697)	6623	(6880)	7135	2671	3122
Nematoda (×10⁻³)	1109	*	2340	2506	4188	3298	4912	6254	(6213)	6171	(6046)	5920	2279	2567
Rotatoria (×10⁻³)	857	*	212	268	368	337	864	419	(411)	403	(777)	1151	319	541
Tardigrada (×10⁻³)	14	*	48	9	20	28	60	97	(73)	49	(57)	64	73	14
Enchytraeidae (×10⁻³)	16.3	9.4	23.1	15.4	13.8	17.8	17.8	21.0	18.3	23.6	(16.8)	9.9	10.9	6.1
Microarthropods, total (×10⁻³)	*	*	*	*	697	*	*	*	*	*	*	*	792	*
Symphyla (×10⁻³)	*	*	0.02	0	0.14	0.02	0.01	0.01	(0.02)	0.03	(0.02)	0.01	0.08	0.06
Collembola (×10⁻³)	*	*	*	*	65	*	*	*	*	*	*	*	54	*
Protura (×10⁻³)	*	*	*	*	0.95	*	*	*	*	*	*	*	0.48	*
Acari (×10⁻³)	*	*	*	*	631	*	*	*	*	*	*	*	737	*
Macroarthropods, total	*	*	1212	1641	1530	1728	2232	2234	(1847)	1459	(1470)	1480	1789	1222
Coleoptera	*	*	333	447	387	536	813	520	(450)	380	(322)	264	583	285
Diptera larvae	*	*	433	607	587	802	1053	1187	(1026)	866	(891)	917	674	347
Araneae	*	*	320	487	360	341	333	467	(317)	167	(212)	257	313	382
Other arthropods[b]	*	*	126	100	196	49	33	60	(53)	46	(44)	42	219	208

[a] Value too low for accurate detection (<800000 ind. m⁻²).
[b] Diplopoda, Chilopoda, Blattodea, Psocoptera, Hymenoptera, Raphidioptera and Pseudoscorpiones.

increasing trends towards the winter were not as pronounced as that of the nematodes. The precision of the monthly estimates was lower for the tardigrades than for the nematodes and rotifers (Sohlenius, 1979).

The enchytraeid fluctuations were fairly moderate with the lowest numbers observed in the early summer and a long period with high values during the winter. The totally dominant species *Cognettia sphagnetorum* normally reproduces asexually by fragmentation, and numerical increases are consequently influenced by factors inducing fragmentation.

Acarids and collembolans dominated the microarthropod abundance almost totally. The September and May estimates were fairly equal but had high standard errors giving 95% confidence intervals of about ±45% around the estimated means. The magnitude of the figures are in very good agreement with those estimated in the same plot in September 1972, when the mean abundance was 58 000 m^{-2} for Collembola, 930 m^{-2} for Protura and 750 000 m^{-2} for Acari (T. Persson, 1975).

The macroarthropods seemed to have an abundance minimum in June and July and a maximum in November and December. This fluctuation pattern was mainly due to the Diptera larvae which dominated the macroarthropods numerically. High numbers of Diptera larvae were found from late autumn to early spring. The decrease in numbers from May to June probably reflects the pupation of many abundant species. A considerable number of adult dipterans (about 300 individuals m^{-2}), predominantly gall midges and sciarids, were found in the samples in July and August, indicating abundant hatching during these months. The increment in larval abundances from June and July onwards also indicates a successive larval hatching during the late summer and autumn. No distinct trends could be found in the fluctuations of total Coleoptera. Owing to the large variety of life histories and development patterns any trend in the population development of one species was probably obscured by diverging trends of others. No significant fluctuation in spider abundances could be detected. The high abundance of "other arthropods" in May and June was mainly due to psocopterans and parasitic wasps.

Biomass

The biomass of microorganisms and soil animals is indicated in Table 5. The total fungal biomass (estimated with the agar-film method) had fairly constant values around 90 g dw m^{-2} except for a lower estimate in November. On the other hand, the FDA-active biomass had seasonal fluctuations with summer and winter minima and autumn and spring maxima (Table 5, Fig. 5).

The bacteria had a pronounced biomass maximum in August–September, and probably a smaller maximum in early spring, the latter peak being uncertain due to low precision of the estimates (Table 5, Fig. 5).

The protozoans had a marked biomass peak during the late summer. The metazoan microfauna, on the other hand, had high abundance and biomass values during the late autumn and winter. The enchytraeid biomass fluctuated in pace with the abundance and had minimum values during the early summer. The microarthropods had similar biomasses in September 1974 and May 1975. The mean of these two monthly estimates was regarded as a preliminary annual mean. This value was used when monthly totals were estimated (Table 5, last line).

The total biomass of the macroarthropods reached maximum values during late

433

Table 5. Seasonal variation in estimated biomass (mg dw m^{-2}) of microorganisms and soil animal taxa during 1974–75 (FDA-active fungi from 1975–77 and Protozoa from 1978 included). Interpolated values used for calculation of annual means in Table 3 given within parentheses. The lacking figures for the microarthropods are substituted with the corresponding annual means when calculating monthly totals. * = not estimated; values for Protozoa during November–April assumed to be negligible. + = <0.5. [a] Mean of June in 1975 and in 1977. [b] Value too low for accurate detection (<0.6 mg dw m^{-2}).

	Month												
	M	J	J	A	S	O	N	D	J	F	M	A	J
Fungi (agar-film)	98 000	*	*	93 000	*	*	45 000	*	*	88 000	*	*	*
Fungi (FDA) 1975–76	*	800	460	1430	1760	*	1820	*	850	810	1370	1650	1520
Fungi (FDA) 1976–77	*	*	1450	970	900	1480	2400	1860	*	*	*	1510	1920
Fungi (FDA) 1977	*	*	1630	1640	2180	1970	1450	*	*	*	*	*	*
Fungi (FDA) monthly mean	*	*	1180	1350	1610	1730	1890	1860	850	810	1370	1650	1360[a]
Bacteria	6700	5000	17 000	45 000	49 000	20 000	14 000	9900	11 000	12 000	(16 000)	21 000	9800
Protozoa	*	*	259	573	97	16	*	*	*	*	*	*	<1[b] (130)
Ciliata	*	*	16	17	5	10	*	*	*	*	*	*	[b] (8)
Flagellata	*	*	40	107	22	5	*	*	*	*	*	*	[b] (20)
Rhizopoda	*	*	204	449	70	1	*	*	*	*	*	*	[b] (102)
Metazoan microfauna, total	*	86	87	62	150	97	181	229	(223)	218	(256)	293	91
Nematoda	*	33	65	49	129	78	119	186	(183)	179	(179)	179	49
Rotatoria	*	50	10	11	16	13	52	27	(28)	28	(62)	95	35
Tardigrada	*	3	12	2	5	6	10	16	(14)	11	(15)	19	7
Enchytraeidae	408	235	577	385	345	446	446	524	458	589	(419)	248	152
Microarthropods, total	*	*	*	*	646	*	*	*	*	*	*	572	*
Symphyla	*	*	+	0	+	+	+	+	(+)	+	(+)	+	+
Collembola	*	*	*	*	100	*	+	+	*	+	*	88	*
Protura	*	*	*	*	+	*	*	*	*	*	*	+	*
Acari	*	*	*	*	546	*	*	*	*	*	*	484	*
Macroarthropods, total	*	*	157	358	290	187	461	387	(475)	563	(354)	144	174
Coleoptera	*	*	107	204	62	85	272	115	(182)	248	(148)	47	52
Diptera larvae	*	*	6	6	10	30	68	46	(43)	40	(40)	39	13
Araneae	*	*	35	121	206	66	106	207	(233)	258	(153)	47	86
Other arthropods	*	*	9	27	12	6	15	19	(18)	17	(14)	11	23
Total fauna	*	*	1690	1990	1530	1360	1700	1750	1770	1980	(1640)	1300	1160

434

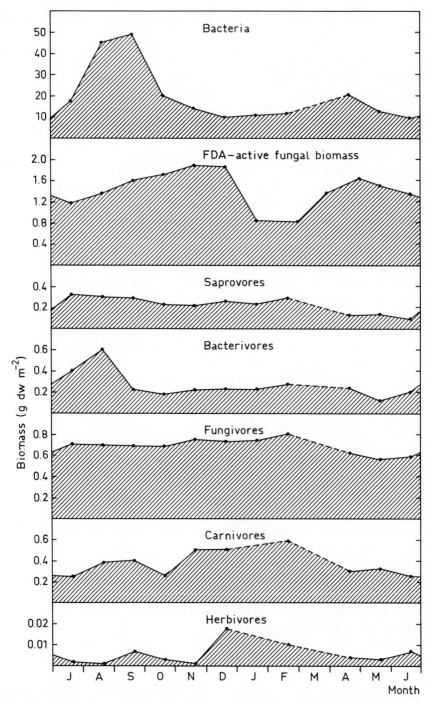

Figure 5. Seasonal fluctuations in the biomass of bacteria, FDA-active part of fungi and soil animal trophic categories in the 120-year-old Scots pine stand at Ivantjärnsheden, predominantly during 1974–75 (Protozoa from 1978 included). FDA-active fungi is represented by the monthly mean values for 1975–77 (see also Table 5).

autumn and winter. The biomass values of Coleoptera fluctuated irregularly. This was probably caused by the very aggregated distribution of late-instar elaterid larvae found in association with decaying wood. Also the occurrence or absence of adult spiders in the samples influenced the biomass estimates considerably. However, the general pattern, especially pronounced for Diptera larvae but also perceptible for Coleoptera, Araneae and others, was an increased biomass towards the late autumn.

As a whole, the fauna showed high biomasses during late summer and winter, and lower values in early autumn and especially in spring and early summer (Table 5). The late summer maximum was predominantly caused by the high protozoan biomass. The estimates of protozoan biomass are, however, uncertain since these organisms were only sampled during a limited period in 1978.

The biomass fluctuations of animal trophic categories are shown in Fig. 5 together with those of the bacteria and FDA-active fungi. The saprovore biomass reached a high level during the late summer, autumn and winter, after which the biomass in spring and early summer was reduced to about half the earlier level. This was mainly a reflection of the enchytraeid dynamics, while the flagellates contributed to the higher biomasses during the late summer. The bacterivores had a 2–3 fold elevation in biomass during the late summer owing to the large influence of naked amoebae and ciliates, while the biomass remained at a lower level during the rest of the year. The fungivores had very small biomass fluctuations over the year, the lowest value occurring in May. This constancy does not reflect the true situation because of the use of constant biomass values for Collembola, Astigmata and Cryptostigmata. The carnivores showed a two-fold increase in biomass from the early summer minimum to the winter maximum, followed by a spring decline. The herbivores probably had a late autumn maximum owing to the early autumn growth of Curculionidae larvae and increasing biomasses of the rhizophagous nematodes, but the figures have low precision because of the small populations.

Respiratory metabolism

The calculation of respiratory metabolism of fungi and bacteria presented several problems and these are outlined in the section of vertical distribution. The soil animals contributed a very small part of the soil organism respiration. However, their respiration could be calculated in much greater detail (Table 3). According to the prerequisites in Table 2 and the data on abundance (Table 4), biomass (Table 5) and size distributions (not presented in this paper), it is logical to find the highest rates of respiration per m^2 during the summer. Thus, 25% of the annual respiration occurred in August, 20% in July, 12% in September and 11% in June, leaving only 31% of the respiration to the other eight months.

The calculations indicated two opposite types of seasonal respiration (Table 6), represented by the protozoans and the Diptera larvae. The protozoans had maximum biomasses at the time of maximum soil temperature which, together with high respiration rates per unit weight (Table 2), resulted in an exceptionally high annual respiration in relation to the annual mean biomass. The Diptera larvae had high biomasses during periods of low temperature and low biomasses during warmer periods. The larger amount of respiring biomass compensated the lower respiration rate per unit weight and *vice versa*, resulting in very small fluctuations in respiratory

436

Table 6. Seasonal variation in respiratory metabolism (mg C m^{-2} month^{-1}) calculated for the soil animal taxa during 1974–75 (Protozoa from 1978 included). Interpolated respiration rates used for calculation of annual means in Table 3 are given within parentheses after adjustment to ambient temperature. * = not estimated; values for Protozoa during November–April assumed to be negligible. + = denotes a value less than 0.5.

	Month													
	M	J	J	A	S	O	N	D	J	F	M	A	M	J
Protozoa	*	*	420	915	109	12	*	*	*	*	*	*	+	(200)
Ciliata	*	*	22	23	6	6	*	*	*	*	*	*	+	(11)
Flagellata	*	*	72	191	32	4	*	*	*	*	*	*	+	(34)
Rhizopoda	*	*	325	701	71	1	*	*	*	*	*	*	+	(155)
Metazoan microfauna, total	*	110	129	99	176	48	58	50	43	37	51	66	65	104
Nematoda	*	57	106	85	159	41	44	43	37	31	38	45	48	65
Rotatoria	*	51	11	13	15	6	13	5	5	5	11	17	8	32
Tardigrada	*	2	12	1	2	1	1	2	1	1	2	4	9	7
Enchytraeidae	231	183	486	314	235	181	125	123	102	107	(33)	53	136	112
Microarthropods, total	*	*	(335)	(341)	254	(102)	(64)	(52)	(52)	(44)	(40)	(59)	160	(310)
Symphyla	*	*	+	0	+	+	+	+	(+)	+	(+)	+	+	+
Collembola	*	*	(82)	(85)	66	(27)	(17)	(14)	(14)	(12)	(11)	(17)	42	(79)
Protura	*	*	(1)	(1)	+	(+)	(+)	(+)	(+)	(+)	(+)	(+)	+	(1)
Acari	*	*	(252)	(255)	188	(75)	(47)	(38)	(38)	(32)	(29)	(42)	118	(229)
Macroarthropods, total	*	*	83	135	91	44	65	38	40	37	23	21	63	78
Coleoptera	*	*	61	82	38	26	44	18	20	20	12	8	30	29
Diptera larvae	*	*	9	9	9	11	14	10	9	7	6	9	9	15
Araneae	*	*	10	35	40	6	6	9	10	9	5	3	21	24
Other arthropods	*	*	3	9	4	1	1	1	1	1	(+)	1	3	10
Total fauna	*	*	1450	1800	870	390	310	260	240	220	150	200	420	800

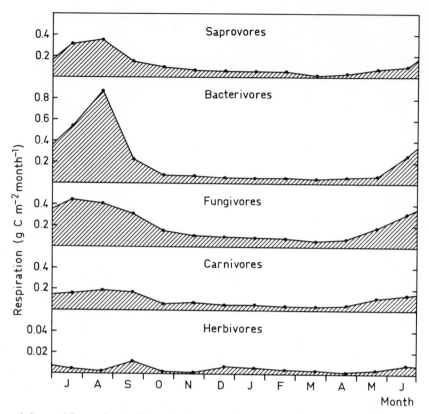

Figure 6. Seasonal fluctuations in the respiratory metabolism of soil animal trophic categories in the 120-year-old Scots pine stand at Ivantjärnsheden in 1974–75 (Protozoa from 1978 included). Interpolated respiration rates are given for January (some groups) and March (all groups) after adjustment to ambient temperature.

metabolism over the year. Apart from the protozoans and some of the macroarthropod taxa, most of the faunal groups had increased biomasses towards the winter which meant that the respiration fluctuation was somewhat levelled out over the year.

The respiratory metabolism reached high rates during the summer for all trophic categories (Fig. 6). Peak values were found for fungivores in July, for saprovores, bacterivores and carnivores in August and for herbivores in September. The contribution by carnivores to total animal respiration was relatively large during the autumn due to a high biomass at that time.

Vertical distribution

Biomass

The figures of abundance, biomass and respiratory metabolism presented above, all concern the situation in the soil profile sampled at the regular samplings. Since the sampling depth varied for various organisms, the figures given are not fully comparable. This is evident in Fig. 7 and Table 7, which show the main vertical distribu-

438

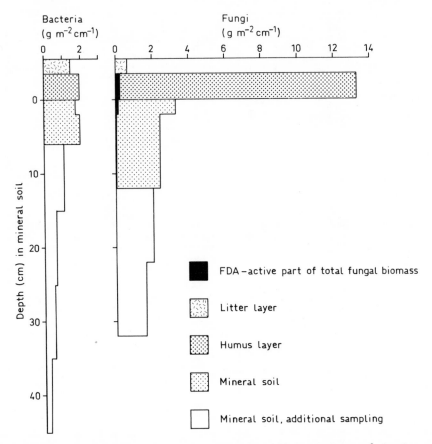

Figure 7. Annual mean vertical distribution of bacterial and fungal biomass (g dw per m² of surface area and cm of depth). The FDA-active part of the total fungal biomass is given for the humus and upper mineral soil layers. The total fungal biomass in the litter layer was only estimated for the needle litter fraction. The total fungal biomass would be 3 g m⁻² cm⁻¹ in the litter layer assuming that the other litter fractions had the same fungal density as the needle litter (see Table 7). Results from one additional sampling in the deeper mineral soil are indicated.

tion of bacterial and fungal biomass. Additional samplings to large depths (on 22 July 1975 for bacteria and 27 May 1975 for total fungi) indicated that 57 and 33% of the bacterial and fungal biomass, respectively, occurred below the depth taken at the regular samplings. This meant that the sampling depth was too shallow for a proper estimation of the microorganisms. It is obvious, however, that the largest biomass density (per volume soil) was in the upper part of the soil profile, in the humus, bleached and upper enrichment layers for bacteria, and in the humus layer for total fungi. However, as much as 82 and 60% of the bacterial and fungal biomass, respectively, was found in the mineral soil. The FDA-active fungal biomass (mean of 1975–77) had a similar distribution as the total fungal biomass, but with a relatively higher proportion in the bleached layer (in Fig. 7 considered to be 2 cm thick). It is realistic to assume presence of active fungal biomass in the litter layer as well as in the mineral soil beneath the regular sampling depth, since these layers contained fungi

Table 7. Annual mean distribution of bacterial, fungal and animal biomass (mg dw m^{-2}) in the litter, humus and mineral soil layers to a depth of 30 cm beneath the humus layer/bleached layer interface. Owing to crude assumptions for FDA-active fungi and Protozoa the values within parentheses are especially uncertain. + indicates a value below 0.5.

	Bacteria	Total fungi	FDA-active fungi	Soil animal trophic groups					Total fauna
				Sapro-vores	Bacteri-vores	Fungi-vores	Carni-vores	Herbi-vores	
Litter layer	1 500	6 000[a]	(300)[b]	36	(36)	260	226	+	559
Humus layer	6 900	46 700	680	96	148	347	120	3	714
Mineral soil 0–10 cm	15 400	26 800	720	99	(169)	88	59	3	418
Mineral soil 10–20 cm	8 500	22 200	(370)[c]	7	(19)	5	2	+	33
Mineral soil 20–30 cm	6 400	19 000	(320)[c]	0	3	1	0	0	4
Total	38 700	120 600	(2 390)	238	(374)	700	407	7	1 727

[a] Total fungal biomass was estimated at 1290 mg dw m^{-2} in needle litter which accounted for 21.5% of the total S-layer litter (Staaf & Berg, 1977a). The figure of 6000 mg dw m^{-2} assumes the same biomass density in the remaining litter fractions.

[b] Calculated as 5% of total fungal biomass.

[c] Calculated as 1.67% of total fungal biomass, i.e., the same proportion as in the 10 cm layer just beneath the bleached layer.

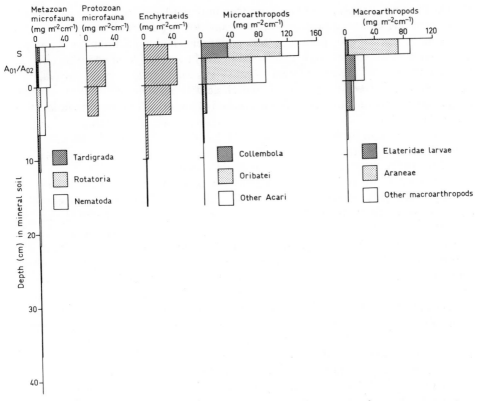

Figure 8. Annual mean vertical distribution of soil faunal biomass (mg dw per m² of surface area and cm of depth). The protozoans were not sampled in the S-layer and beneath 4 cm depth in the mineral soil, and the distribution between 0–4 cm is based on one supplementary sampling. The distribution of metazoan microfauna below 6.5 cm depth in the mineral soil is also based on one additional sampling.

according to the agar-film method. These assumptions are included (within parentheses) in Table 7.

The vertical distributions of soil animal groups are shown in Fig. 8. Additional samplings of the metazoan microfauna indicated that 18% of the biomass was found beneath the regular sampling depth. Both nematodes and rotifers occurred throughout the soil profile, while the tardigrades chiefly occurred in the litter and humus layers. When the deep distribution to a depth of 30 cm in the mineral soil was taken into account, the annual mean biomass estimate for the metazoan microfauna increased from 166 (Table 5) to 200 mg dw m^{-2}, of which 13% occurred in the litter layer, 33% in the humus layer and 55% in the mineral soil (Fig. 8).

The monthly samplings of protozoans only concerned the humus layer (Table 5), but an additional sampling to larger depths in 1978 showed numbers in the bleached soil layer of about two-thirds of that in the humus layer. If this distribution is representative for the whole year this gives an annual mean of about 60 mg dw m^{-2} in the bleached soil layer (Fig. 8). In analogy with the metazoan microfauna of similar feeding habits, the protozoans in the litter layer and in the mineral soil beneath the

441

bleached layer were assumed to account for another 10 and 40 mg dw m^{-2}, respectively, resulting in a total protozoan biomass of 200 mg dw m^{-2}.

The mean vertical distribution of the enchytraeids had a maximum in the humus layer, but high biomasses were also found in the litter and bleached layers (Fig. 8). On average, 57% of the enchytraeid biomass was found in the organic layers, 35% in the bleached layer and 8% in the enrichment layer. The distribution changed considerably from time to time with a maximum of about 80% in the organic layers in September and a minimum of about 30% in January, when as much as 20% of the biomass occurred in the enrichment layer (H. Lundkvist, in prep.). Despite seasonal variation in the vertical distribution, the sampling depth seemed to have been sufficient for proper estimates of the enchytraeid population.

The microarthropod biomass had a density maximum in the litter layer, although the thicker humus layer contained higher biomass (51%) than the litter layer (44%). On average the collembolan biomass was more superficially distributed than the acarid biomass with 75% in the litter layer, 21% in the humus layer and 3% in the mineral soil layers. The corresponding figures for the acarids were 39, 57 and 4%.

The macroarthropod biomass was predominantly (56%) found in the litter layer, while 30% was found in the humus layer and 14% in the mineral soil. Araneae were totally restricted to the uppermost layer, while the deeper layers were mainly populated by beetle larvae. Thus, nearly 50% of the biomass in the humus layer, 75% in the bleached layer and 45% in the enrichment layer was due to elaterid larvae, which seemed to have their biomass maximum near the interface between the humus and bleached layers (Fig. 8).

The biomass distribution of animal trophic categories in the soil profile is summarized in Table 7. The values are corrected according to the additional samplings to large depth. The revised figures for the metazoan microfauna and Protozoa increased the mean bacterivore biomass from 0.26 to 0.37 g dw m^{-2}, while the rest of the fauna got very small additions (<0.02 g dw m^{-2}).

The highest biomass values for bacterivores, saprovores, and herbivores were obtained in the mineral soil. For fungivores it was found in the humus layer, whereas the carnivores reached their highest biomass values in the litter layer.

As a whole, the vertical distribution of animal biomass differed considerably from the microorganism distribution (Table 7). The soil fauna generally had a much more superficial distribution than the bacteria and fungi, and only 2% of the animal biomass occurred deeper than 10 cm in the mineral soil.

Respiration

The annual mean respiration estimates in Table 3 for Protozoa and metazoan microfauna had to be corrected for respiration at greater depths. The protozoan estimate increased from 1.7 to 3.7 g C m^{-2}yr^{-1} and that of metazoan microfauna from 0.9 to 1.1 g C m^{-2}yr^{-1} and, thus, the estimate for the whole fauna increased to 9.4 g C m^{-2}yr^{-1} (Table 8).

The bacterivores had the largest respiration in the mineral soil. The saprovores, fungivores and herbivores had the largest respiration in the humus layer and the carnivores in the litter layer. Of the total faunal respiration, 21% occurred in the litter layer, 43% in the humus layer and 35% in the 0–30 cm mineral soil layers (Table 8).

The respiratory metabolism of fungi and bacteria was calculated to be 60 and 105 g

Table 8. Vertical distribution of respiratory metabolism (g C m^{-2} yr^{-1}) of bacteria, fungi and soil animals in the litter, humus and mineral soil layers to a depth of 30 cm beneath the humus layer/bleached layer interface. The values within parentheses are especially uncertain.

	Bacteria	Fungi	Soil animal trophic groups					Total fauna
			Sapro-vores	Bacteri-vores	Fungi-vores	Carni-vores	Herbi-vores	
Litter layer	(8)	(13)	0.23	(0.31)	0.90	0.53	0.002	(1.96)
Humus layer	(36)	(28)	0.77	1.73	1.06	0.40	0.029	4.00
Mineral soil 0–10 cm	(38)	(30)	0.69	(1.81)	0.32	0.22	0.022	(3.06)
Mineral soil 10–20 cm	(21)	(16)	0.06	(0.22)	0.03	0.02	0.001	(0.32)
Mineral soil 20–30 cm	(16)	(13)	0	0.02	0.005	0	0	0.03
Total	(119)	(100)	1.74	(4.09)	2.32	1.17	0.05	(9.37)

C m^{-2}yr^{-1}, respectively, according to the regular samplings. The estimate for fungi is based on studies (still in progress) on the relationship between FDA-active fungal biomass, respiration and temperature, and for bacteria on a relationship found between bacterial production and rainstorms (Clarholm & Rosswall, 1980).

These very approximate figures were underestimates because of too shallow core depths in the regular samplings. The fungal respiration in the soil horizons not studied in the regular samplings was calculated in the same way as that in the upper layers, i.e., by assuming respiration to be proportional to FDA-active biomass and adjusted for ambient temperature. In this way the FDA-active biomass in Table 7 implied a total fungal respiration of 100 g C m^{-2} yr^{-1} down to a depth of 30 cm in the mineral soil (Table 8).

The active part of the bacterial biomass was not determined in this study, but preliminary data from the same Scots pine stand indicated 39% of the total bacterial biomass to be FDA-active (B. Lundgren, pers. comm.). This proportion, however, was determined in the humus layer, and the proportion at greater depths is unknown. The bacterial respiration was, therefore, assumed to be proportional to the biomass only in the litter and humus layers, in which the annual bacterial respiration was calculated to be 8 and 36 g C m^{-2} yr^{-1}, respectively (Table 8).

The bacterial respiration at greater depths was calculated from measurements of total soil respiration on a number of occasions over the year. On average, the organic layers accounted for 40% and the mineral soil layers for 60% of the total CO_2 efflux (H. Staaf, pers. comm.). These figures include root respiration, but according to the vertical distribution of root production (H. Persson, 1980b) and, hence, evolution of root CO_2, the proportions of 40:60 are reasonable both for root respiration and heterotrophic respiration. If the heterotrophic respiration was distributed as 40% (91 g C m^{-2} yr^{-1}) in the organic layers and 60% (137 g C m^{-2} yr^{-1}) in the 0–30 cm mineral soil layers, the total heterotrophic respiration figure would be 228 g C m^{-2} yr^{-1} and the bacterial respiration 119 g C m^{-2} yr^{-1} (Table 8). According to these estimates the contribution to total heterotrophic respiration was 52% for bacteria, 44% for fungi and 4% for soil animals. However, the animal contribution differed considerably in the various soil layers. The animal share of respiration was 9% in the litter layer, 6% in the humus layer and 4%, 0.8% and 0.1% in the 0–10, 10–20 and 20–30 cm layers of the mineral soil.

Relations between annual mean biomass and carbon flow

The annual mean biomass and the annual respiration of the soil fauna were estimated to be 1.7 g dw m^{-2} and 9.4 g C m^{-2} yr^{-1} when the entire soil profile was taken into consideration. The protozoan and metazoan microfauna together made up 24%, the enchytraeids 23% and the arthropods 53% of the total biomass (Fig. 9). The proportions between the microfauna and the arthropods were nearly the reversed as regards the annual respiration, to which the protozoan and metazoan microfauna contributed 51%, the enchytraeids 22% and the arthropods 27%. The high contribution to total respiration by the microfauna was mainly caused by high respiration rate per unit weight (see Table 2) and biomass maximum during the warm season for the protozoans. The macroarthropods had a low respiration rate per unit weight and a biomass maximum during the cold season. The microarthropods were dominated by

444

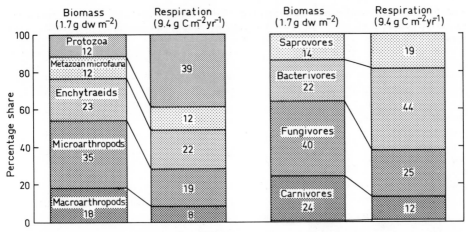

Figure 9. Contribution (%) to the annual mean biomass and annual respiration of the main taxonomic (left) and trophic (right) groups within the soil fauna. The herbivores (at the very bottom to the right) contributed 0.4% to the biomass and 0.6% to the respiration. Note that the protozoan share and the bacterivore share are very approximate (see text).

cryptostigmatid mites, which have an unusually low respiration rate per unit weight (see Table 2).

The contribution of soil faunal trophic categories to the annual mean biomass and the annual respiration is also shown in Fig. 9. The bacterivores were dominated by protozoans and nematodes which explains the high respiration in relation to the biomass. The fungivores and carnivores were dominated by arthropods, which resulted in low respiration in relation to biomass.

If the annual respiration is known, other flows of matter and energy can be approximately calculated according to the basic equations $C = P + R + F$ and $A = P + R$, where C = consumption, P = production, R = respiration, F = defecation and A = assimilation (Petrusewicz & Macfadyen, 1970), and where both equations are relevant for animals and the latter for microorganisms.

The annual flows of carbon were calculated from the estimates of respiration (Table 8) in combination with the efficiency quotients suggested by Heal & MacLean (1975) for different trophic categories. For invertebrates these quotients, P/C, R/C and F/C, were 0.08, 0.12 and 0.80 for saprovores, 0.12, 0.18 and 0.70 for microbivores, 0.16, 0.24 and 0.60 for herbivores and 0.24, 0.56 and 0.20 for carnivores, respectively, while for microorganisms P/A and R/A were 0.4 and 0.6, respectively. The carbon flows calculated in this way are summarized in Table 9 for the whole soil profile investigated. To simplify the terminology animal consumption and microbial assimilation were both called intake (I) in this table. Table 9 also shows the relation between carbon in annual production (P) and annual mean biomass ($\bar{B}$).

The bacterial and fungal intake (assimilation) was about ten times higher than the ingestion by the bacterial and fungal feeding animals. These groups ingested together 20 times more than the carnivores. The saprovores had somewhat higher intake than the fungivores.

The $P/\bar{B}$ ratios were higher than 10 yr^{-1} for bacterivores and herbivores, which

445

Table 9. Carbon in annual mean biomass ($\bar{B}$) (g C m^{-2}) and annual intake (I), production (P), respiration (R) and defecation (F) (g C m^{-2} yr^{-1}) for soil organism groups in the joint litter, humus and 0–30 cm mineral soil layers. Here, $I = P + R$ for bacteria and fungi and $I = P + R + F$ for soil animals. The $P/\bar{B}$ relations are also indicated. Carbon content assumed to be 45, 48 and 50% of dry weight of fungi, bacteria and soil animals, respectively.

	$\bar{B}$	I	P	R	F	$P/\bar{B}$
Bacteria	19	199	80	119	–	4.3
Fungi	54[a]	167	67	100	–	1.2
Saprovores	0.12	15	1.2	1.7	12	9.8
Bacterivores	0.19	23	2.7	4.1	16	14.5
Fungivores	0.35	13	1.5	2.3	9.0	4.4
Carnivores	0.20	2.1	0.5	1.2	0.4	2.5
Herbivores	0.003	0.22	0.04	0.05	0.13	10.7

[a] According to the agar-film method.

were both dominated by microfaunal forms with short generation times. Saprovores had a ratio of about 10 yr^{-1}, and all other categories had lower ratios than 5 yr^{-1}. The ratio of 1.2 yr^{-1} for fungi is low, but it is based on total fungal weight, which was probably dominated by inactive hyphae. The FDA-active fungal biomass had a $P/\bar{B}$ ratio as high as 54 yr^{-1}. If only a part of the bacterial biomass is active, the $P/\bar{B}$ of bacteria would also increase considerably from the calculated value of 4 yr^{-1}.

Discussion

Accuracy of the estimates

In studies of soil organisms there are several difficulties in obtaining the basic estimates of abundance and biomass. One difficulty is the more or less aggregated distribution of the organisms, which reduces the precision of the estimates, and another difficulty concerns the extraction of the organisms. In the present investigation the precision (95% confidence interval) of the monthly estimates for enchytraeids, microarthropods and macroarthropods was mostly in the region of ± 30–50%. The precision of the monthly estimates for the other organisms was not known since the samples were pooled.

The methods used for extraction and enumeration are well established with the exception of the FDA-technique. The recovery of the different methods used for multicellular animals was suggested to be in the order of 70–100% (Abrahamsen, 1972; Persson & Lohm, 1977; Leinaas, 1978; Sohlenius, 1979). For fungi it was obvious that at least 20% of the FDA-active hyphae were not included (Söderström, 1979b). The reliabilities of the bacterial and protozoan methods are not evaluated but the acridine orange method used for bacteria gives 100–1000 times larger estimates than the plate count method indicating high reliability.

In the monthly sampling series some organism groups (see Table 3) were underestimated because of insufficient sampling depth. This was especially evident for the bacteria and the protozoans, where more than 50% of the biomass of the former was found at greater depths than included in the regular sampling programme. The corrections based on additional samplings made the annual mean estimates for these organism groups representative for the whole soil profile but the extrapolation also resulted in reduced accuracy of the estimates.

Respiration cannot be measured directly in natural populations of soil organisms and, therefore, estimates of respiratory metabolism of field populations require extrapolation from the laboratory. This may involve serious errors (Petrusewicz & Macfadyen, 1970; Humphreys, 1977, 1978; Ågren & Axelsson, 1980). For this study some important sources of error were eliminated for a majority of soil animals, i.e., the use of weight classes instead of mean weight and the correction for within-day fluctuations in temperature, but it was not possible to correct for a number of biological factors affecting the metabolic activity. Such factors are locomotory activity, feeding, starvation, sex, moulting and reproduction, and the change in respiration due to many of these factors may be cumulative (Humphreys, 1977, 1978). The conclusion is, thus, that the respiration estimates are very approximate due to accumulation of errors. The respiration estimates of bacteria, fungi and Protozoa are still more uncertain than those of the other soil organisms.

The estimated ratio of bacterial to fungal respiration of about 55/45 is contradictory to the average ratio of 30/70 estimated by Anderson & Domsch (1975) for various agricultural and deciduous forest soils. In the latter case the respiration of either the bacteria or the fungi was inhibited by selective antibiotics after activation of the whole microbial biomass by addition of glucose. Large parts of this biomass could have been in a dormant, inactive state before the activation and, therefore, the two respiration ratios are not totally comparable.

The classification of the animals into different trophic groups is very difficult because our knowledge about what many soil animals consume and digest is far from complete. Thus, the trophic classification made is far too crude and is probably wrong in certain respects. However, trophic classification was necessary in order to study the flow of carbon within the soil organism community (see below).

Factors influencing seasonal dynamics

Fluctuations in abundance and biomass of soil organisms are generally interpreted as caused by changes in physical conditions, or food supply, or to be effects of biotic interaction such as predation. The generation times are certainly also important, and it may be suspected that organisms with short generation times are more fluctuating than organisms with longer ones.

In the present study it seems likely that the late part of July and September in 1974 and May in 1975 constituted periods with suitable temperature and moisture regimes (Fig. 2), especially where the water-dwelling organisms are concerned. From November to April the low temperatures ought to have had a retarding influence on the activity. This is evident when the dynamics of the respiratory metabolism is considered (Fig. 6). Also the low soil moisture during the dry period of June and possibly also of August might have had a depressing influence on several taxa. These effects were, however, not included when the animal metabolism was calculated, which meant that the respiration could have been overestimated for the water-dependent fauna during these periods.

Besides the rather fluctuating physical conditions, the energy and nutrient input to the soil also change seasonally. The peak litterfall occurs during autumn, mainly from early August to mid-October when 80–85% of all needle litter reaches the ground (Flower-Ellis & Olsson, 1978), but considerable amounts of litter, for example twigs and fine litter, also reach the ground in April and May in connection with snowmelt. The litter input from the roots seems to be closely related to periods of drought during which the mortality of fine roots increases (H. Persson, 1979, 1980b). Since drought may occur accidentally during the whole growing season the seasonality for root litter formation is less pronounced than for litterfall.

Although there is a more or less distinct seasonality in litter input as a whole, it is doubtful whether the decomposer organisms would have a parallel change in biomass. The organisms can only grow on palatable and chemically available substrates, and toxic substances, such as tannins and other polyphenols (cf. Berg et al., 1980), in the fresh litter may initially retard the ingrowth of microorganisms.

With few exceptions it was difficult to find seasonality in the soil organism biomass that could be attributed to either physical factors or maxima in litter inputs. However, investigations by Clarholm & Rosswall (1980) indicate that short-term fluctuations in bacterial populations are closely connected with rainstorms, and in another study at Ivantjärnsheden, M. Clarholm (in prep.) observed that rainfall induced growth of both bacteria and protozoans but with different time lag. Bacteria and flagellates reached a population peak two days after a rainfall followed by a population decline, while the bacterial feeding naked amoebae increased 20-fold in number from the day of precipitation to a maximum four days later, i.e., two days after the bacterial peak. The naked amoebae, which were the dominant protozoans, seemed to respond to bacterial growth, while the main part of the flagellates were osmotrophs reacting on precipitation in the same way as bacteria. The decrease in bacterial biomass after the peak was interpreted as an effect of consumption by the amoebae. These observations are highly relevant for the present study, in which the biomass peak of Protozoa (in August 1978) occurred at the beginning of the bacterial peak (as found in 1974), and indicate that increases in soil water may induce growth of bacterial populations which, in turn, may be regulated by protozoans. It is wellknown that many nematodes and rotifers, like many protozoans, feed on bacteria, but the increase in abundance and biomass of nematodes and rotifers occurred later during the autumn. It is possible that the nematodes and rotifers responded to the bacterial peak with high reproduction which later during the autumn was manifested in high biomass. The joint consumption by the nematodes and rotifers was, however, not large enough to explain the decline of the bacterial peak.

The FDA-active fungal biomass exerted a pattern with peaks during September to December and during April to May with lows in between, and this type of fluctuation was evident for a couple of years (Söderström, 1979a). The results obtained indicate that soil moisture may be a factor that influences the amount of FDA-active mycelium. Increases in soil moisture content always resulted in increased biomasses, except during periods of frozen soil. The fungal biomass never seemed depressed by high moisture contents in the easily drained soil. Temperature did not seem to influence the amount of active hyphae to any large extent although it certainly affected the metabolic rate and biomass turnover. However, temperature also affected the fungivore grazing. Changes in fungal biomass may be due to changes in consumption pressure, fungal death rate and fungal growth rate, and the balance of these three factors might have been dislocated in favour of the first during the summer, resulting in lower FDA-active fungal biomass. From the present material it is, however, hard to find any causal relations between the fungal and the fungivore dynamics in biomass.

A general trend among the fungivores, and among the carnivores as well, was to reach high biomass during late autumn and winter. This might be an effect of high fungal production during the early autumn, but the high autumn biomass is also a consequence of the dominant development patterns. The fungivores and carnivores mainly consisted of arthropods, and the arthropods had usually generation times of one year or more from egg to egg. Some arthropod species had extended hatching periods resulting in a number of coexisting size-classes, while others had more narrow hatching periods followed by more or less simultaneous development. The rigidity in phenological patterns and long development times indicated that the arthropods, in comparison with the protozoans and nematodes, had less ability to respond with population increase to occasional external factors such as increased food availability and optimal soil moisture. As fungivores are mainly found among the arthropods it, thus, seems plausible that the fungi/fungivore trophic system is less fluctuating than the bacteria/bacterivore system.

The dynamics of respiratory metabolism illustrated in Fig. 6 shows another aspect in the seasonality of the soil organisms. In many countries the soil organism activity is often considered to be at a maximum during spring and autumn, while summer is too dry and winter too cold. At Ivantjärnsheden the main period of high metabolic activity occurs during the summer, while spring and late atutumn are too cold for high activity. The details in Fig. 6 can be questioned since the estimates rely on crude assumptions without any attempt to correct for drought inactivity, but although water-dependent soil organisms probably are overestimated in this respect, the general picture of summer activities seems to be indisputable.

In conclusion, the simultaneous studies of soil organisms gained much information of the seasonal dynamics of individual groups. However, the causes of the biomass fluctuations were generally hard to evaluate and it was, furthermore, difficult to draw any conclusions about feeding relations from the fluctuation patterns.

Seasonality in nutrient release

It is sometimes considered that the soil organism biomass constitutes an easily available pool of essential mineral nutrients such as nitrogen. It is also considered that there is a competition between microorganisms and roots for mineral nutrients (Bååth et al., 1978). This means that decreasing amounts of nutrients are available to plant roots during periods of increase in soil organism biomass, and the reverse situation prevails when there is a decrease in biomass with a subsequent mineralization of nutrients. During 1974–75 the "active" biomass of the soil organisms largely followed the dynamics of the bacteria because of the dominance of this group. Accordingly, the bacteria and the soil organisms as a whole would have needed increased amounts of, for example, nitrogen during August and September, smaller amounts during the winter, increased amounts again during April and smaller amounts during May and June. The increased need during early autumn probably meant immobilization of, for example, mineral nitrogen, while the decrease in biomass and presumed mineralization of nutrients in May and June should have favoured the roots. This pattern of early summer mineralization and late summer/ early autumn immobilization of nitrogen is contradictory to the simulations made by Bosatta *et al.* (1980). However, analyses of litter layer leachates by Bringmark (1980) showed a net release of NH_4^+ from the litter layer during the early summer (both in 1975 and 1976) turning into net immobilization after September 1 which, thus, is in agreement with the soil organism pattern. The dynamics in fineroot biomass of Scots pine indicate vigorous growth in the early summer and a decrease in biomass between August and September in 1974 (H. Persson, 1979), which also supports the idea of early summer availability of mineral nitrogen.

Vertical distribution

The vertical distribution of the organisms was characterized by a rather sharp decline of faunal abundance and activity below the humus layer. This is partly explained by the absence of large burrowing forms, and most macro- and microarthropods did not penetrate into the mineral soil, obviously as a result of the rather small pore size. It is interesting to notice that smaller animals such as rotifers and nematodes had a relatively greater importance in the mineral soil than in the organic layers.

It is also notable that the proportions and impacts of different feeding groups differed considerably in the different soil layers. This could only partly be explained by the vertical distribution of the food sources which, however, explains the scarcity of below-ground herbivores in the litter layer where no roots occurred. The carnivores had their greatest abundance and biomass in the litter layer. This layer is passed both by animals from the above-ground system (for shelter and hibernation) and those from deeper soil layers (vertical migration). Obviously the large size of many of the arthropod predators, for example, spiders, restrict them to the uppermost soil layer.

The decline with increasing depth was also obvious for fungivores and bacterivores, and one can speculate whether the relatively large biomasses of bacteria and fungi at greater depths (see Table 7) are merely a consequence of lack of fungivore and bacterivore grazing. The significance of this grazing is discussed below in more detail.

Carbon flow through the soil system

One of the possibilities to validate the uncertain estimate of 228 g C m^{-2} yr^{-1} being the total heterotrophic respiration, is to make an input/output analysis. The main inputs of carbon to the heterotrophic part of the soil system were litterfall and root litter formation, which were studied within the project. Other inputs such as root exudation, crown drip, stem flow and drain of carbohydrates to the mycorrhiza were not studied. Hence, the input/output data have many weaknesses.

The annual mean value of total above-ground litterfall from the trees during 1973–76 was about 140 g dw m^{-2} (Flower-Ellis & Olsson, 1978). The litterfall from field and bottom layer plant species was roughly calculated to be about 100 g dw m^{-2} yr^{-1}. Fine-root litter production was about 230 g dw m^{-2} yr^{-1} (H. Persson, 1980b).

Table 10. Input (g C m^{-2} yr^{-1}) of above- and below-ground plant litter to the soil system in the 120-year-old Scots pine stand at Ivantjärnsheden. All values are converted from dry weight estimates by assuming the carbon content to be 50% of the dry matter.

	Litter input (g C m^{-2} yr^{-1})	Data source
Above-ground litter formation	120	
Pinus sylvestris	71	Flower-Ellis & Olsson (1978)
Calluna vulgaris	20[a]	H. Persson (1980a)
Vaccinium vitis-idaea	6[a]	,,
Mosses	17[b]	,,
Lichens	6[c]	,,
Below-ground litter formation	116	
Pinus sylvestris	90[d]	H. Persson (1980b)
Calluna vulgaris	12[d]	,,
Vaccinium vitis-idaea	14[d]	,,
Total input	236	

[a] Calculated as half the biomass of current-year and one-year-old shoots.
[b] Turnover rate 0.25 yr^{-1} according to Staaf & Berg (1977b).
[c] Turnover rate 0.10 yr^{-1} in accordance with a reindeer husbandry area (Ahti, 1977).
[d] Mycorrhiza sheath included.

This figure was taken as an approximation of the total root litter formation since coarse-root production is very slight (H. Persson, 1979).

The annual supplies of the major litter constituents are given in Table 10, where all estimates are converted to carbon units. The annual mean estimate of 236 g C m^{-2} yr^{-1} is remarkably close to the estimate of heterotrophic respiration of 228 g C m^{-2} yr^{-1} (Table 8). This similarity is perhaps a coincidence since both estimates are rather uncertain, but because the two estimates are totally independent, they support each other and may indicate the magnitude of the processes.

The magnitude of input of soluble organic substances is very hard to evaluate. The contribution of such substances in crown drip and stem flow was probably very small (L. Bringmark, pers. comm.). Root exudation may, on the other hand, be substantial (Rovira, 1979). Up to 39% of the carbon translocated to wheat roots has been reported to be released into the soil (Martin, 1977). Reid & Mexal (1977) found that in *Pinus contorta* about 30% of the translocated carbon was exuded. This indicates that a substantial exudation may occur also in the Ivantjärnsheden study area.

Another problem for the understanding of the carbon flow was that the proportion of mycorrhizal fungi in the total fungal biomass could not be determined with the FDA or with the agar-film method. The estimates of fungal biomass included mycorrhiza in the fine roots, and also H. Persson's (1980b) study on root production included mycorrhiza attached to the roots. Therefore, unfortunately the mycorrhiza was included in both of the estimates given above for in- and outflowing carbon.

Thus, in order to avoid confusion in the input/output analysis it was necessary to estimate the mycorrhizal biomass. Harley (1978) reported values of ectomycorrhizal sheath masses of between 30 and 45% of the dry mass of *Fagus* root tips. Observations by H. Persson (pers. comm.) indicate that probably less than 10% of the fine-root (<2 mm diameter) biomass of Scots pine roots at Ivantjärnsheden might consist of mycorrhiza. If 10% of the pine fine-root biomass is mycorrhiza, this corresponds to a weight of 12 g dw m^{-2}. With the same percentage for *Calluna* and *Vaccinium* roots with ericoid mycorrhiza, a total value of 34 g dw m^{-2} for all mycorrhiza covering and penetrating the roots was obtained. This is 28% of the total fungal biomass. With the same respiration/biomass and respiration/production ratios as above for total fungi, this means that the mycorrhizal respiration, production and assimilation (drain from the plant hosts) would be 28, 19 and 47 g C m^{-2} yr^{-1}, respectively. The real figures might be remote from this hypothetical example. Much higher values have been reported by Fogel & Hunt (1979), who estimated the mycorrhizal sheath standing crop in a Douglas fir stand to be 10 009 kg ha^{-1}, i.e., about 500 g C m^{-2}, and a turnover time of 1.64 years. This would be equivalent to a production of 300 g C m^{-2} yr^{-1}.

Under the assumptions of mycorrhiza given above it was possible to summarize the data in a carbon flow diagramme for the whole soil profile studied (Fig. 10). The diagramme does not include root exudation (see above). As 19 g C m^{-2} yr^{-1} was considered to be mycorrhizal production, the value of 116 g C m^{-2} yr^{-1} for root litter formation (Table 10) had to be reduced by the same amount to 97 g C m^{-2} yr^{-1}. Another consequence of the assumed amount of mycorrhiza was that the decomposer fungi only assimilated 120 g C m^{-2} yr^{-1}, which meant that the bacteria accounted for most of the decomposition in purely quantitative terms.

The total carnivore consumption was assumed to be distributed in proportion to the biomass of the prey groups. Therefore, the fungivores, which had a high biomass, were assumed to contribute about half of the food to the carnivores (Fig. 10).

All dead organisms that were not ingested by consumers were considered to be transferred to the large pool of dead organic matter. All faeces from the animals were also transferred to that pool. This recirculation was of the order of 150 g C m^{-2} yr^{-1}, consisting of dead animals (3%), dead microorganisms (72%) and faeces (25%).

The values used in Fig. 10 indicate an annual input of 264 g C m^{-2} yr^{-1} (i.e., 217 g C m^{-2} yr^{-1} to the organic matter pool and 47 g C m^{-2} yr^{-1} to the mycorrhizal fungi) from the above- and below-ground plant parts, while the heterotrophic soil organisms respired 228 g C m^{-2} yr^{-1}. Consequently, 36 g C m^{-2} yr^{-1} accumulated in the soil, which corresponds to an 1% increase of dead organic matter per year.

In reality the values in Fig. 10 only give the order of magnitude, and it is impossible to conclude whether the increase of carbon in dead organic matter is 0, 1 or 2% per year. The input/output analysis was, thus, a very blunt instrument in validating the data, although it strongly indicated realism in the estimates.

The quantitative dominance of bacteria and fungi is clearly illustrated in Fig. 10. However, because of different trophic positions a direct comparison between, say, bacterial and bacterivore respiration is unfair, as a bacterivore respiration of 1 (g C m^{-2} yr^{-1}) corresponds to a predation of 5.6, a loss which, in turn, needs a bacterial respiration of 8.3 to be replaced. This example illustrates that the consumption can be important despite low respiration values.

This is obvious in Table 11, where the exploitation efficiency, i.e., the proportion between the annual consumption of a certain trophic group and the biomass pro-

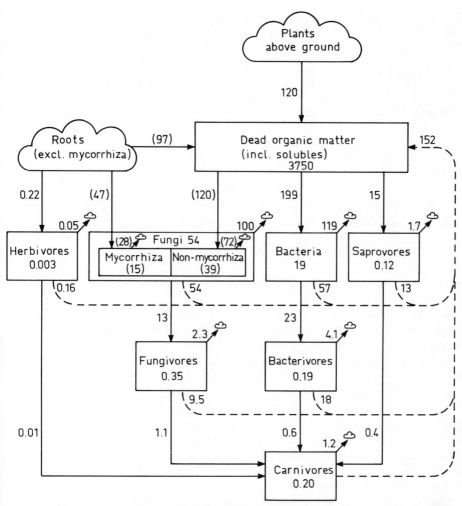

Figure 10. Carbon flow diagramme of the soil in the 120-year-old Scots pine stand at Ivantjärnsheden to a depth of 30 cm in the mineral soil. Boxes denote annual mean biomass (g C m^{-2}) and arrows denote flows (g C m^{-2} yr^{-1}), of which arrows with small clouds indicate respiration. Broken lines ending in an arrow denote transfer of dead (non-predated) organisms and faeces to the pool of dead organic matter. All values are uncertain and in particular those influenced by the assumptions of mycorrhiza (within parentheses).

duced per year by its food organisms, is given for different soil layers. Table 11 shows that the bacterivore withdrawal of bacterial production was 30–40% in the litter, humus and 0–10 cm mineral soil layers, and with decreasing percentages at larger depths. The fungivores extracted about 60% of the fungal production in the litter layer, 30% in the humus layer and steadily smaller percentages at increasing depth. The predation by carnvores was remarkably high (about 80%) in the litter layer and still evident in the humus layer (30%) and in the 0–10 cm (21%) and 10–20 cm (15%) mineral soil layers. The carnivore consumption of non-carnivorous forms was probably overestimated, since both ordinary carnivores and top-carnivores were

Table 11. Percent annual mean exploitation efficiency ($C_{consumer}/P_{food}$) for some trophic relations in different soil layers in the 120-year-old Scots pine stand at Ivantjärnsheden.

	$\dfrac{C_{bacterivores}}{P_{bacteria}}$	$\dfrac{C_{fungivores}}{P_{fungi}}$	$\dfrac{C_{carnivores}}{P_{non-carnivores}}$	$\dfrac{C_{herbivores}}{P_{roots}}$
Litter layer	33	59	82	0 [a]
Humus layer	39	31	30	0.2[a]
Mineral soil 0–10 cm	40	8.8	21	0.2[a]
Mineral soil 10–20 cm	8.5	1.7	15	0 [a]
Mineral soil 20–30 cm	1.1	0.3	0	0 [a]
Total	29	19	37	0.2

[a] Root consumers occurred sporadically in the litter layer, but since no roots were found in this layer the root consumption was assumed to have been made in the humus layer. Root production (H. Persson, 1980b) was not estimated for sublayers in the mineral soil.

lumped together in one category because of difficulty to distinguish between the two groups.

It is hard to draw any conclusions of the effects of the consumption. The bacterivore exploitation seemed to be high enough for regulation of the bacterial population at certain times (see discussion above). A similar effect of the fungivore grazing could not be detected, but it is very probable that the high exploitation efficiency depressed the fungal biomass in the litter and humus layers. The low consumption of bacteria and fungi in the deeper layers of the mineral soil could explain the high proportion of microorganism biomass found in these layers (see Table 7). Despite the high grazing intensity in the humus layer, the total fungal biomass (see Table 7) contained 3% of total carbon and as much as 11% of total nitrogen in that layer. The fungivore consumption, therefore, seems to be very important as a means of reducing the retention of, for example, nitrogen in the fungi and, thus, also increasing the turnover of this element.

Only 0.2% of the actual root production was consumed by root feeding herbivores, i.e., an extremely low degree of exploitation. The figure is probably an underestimation since, for example, some omnivorous species which can be partly rhizophages were not included in this category. However, their consumption could only have increased the percentage marginally.

The low value should be compared with a figure of about 4–8% estimated for root consumption in a grass field in Central Sweden (Persson & Lohm, 1977). However, because the large fungivore consumption in the humus layer probably also included mycorrhizal fungi, one can assume that the fungal feeders drained more carbon from the plant roots and affected nutrient uptake by roots more substantially than could ever be achieved by the true rhizophages.

Concluding remarks

The present study was restricted to one study area and, for most organism groups, one annual period which reduced the representativity of the data. However, the unusually complete coverage of soil organism groups enabled more proper comparisons between taxonomic and trophic groups than normally found in the literature. The following conclusions and general results were arrived at:

(1) The population estimates of bacteria were higher than normally found in coniferous forests with acidic soils, and the bacterial/fungal biomass ratio was higher than expected from previous studies. This is doubtless due to the direct count method which is superior to the plate count method used in earlier studies. This indicates that bacteria probably are more important in coniferous forest soils than earlier believed. This is also indicated by the high ratio of bacterial to fungal respiration.
(2) The total fungal mass was fairly large in comparison with the estimates of many other forest soils. On average, only 2% of the total mass was found to be FDA-active. The large total fungal mass emphasizes the role of fungi as immobilizers of mineral nutrients.
(3) The large estimates of the protozoans can probably be attributed to a general lack of knowledge of this group in coniferous forest soils. As a whole, the soil faunal biomass was fairly low and, except for the protozoans, in agreement with other soil faunal studies of northern coniferous forest soils.
(4) Despite the low biomass and respiration estimated for the soil fauna, a great part of the annual production of the microorganisms is consumed by the animals. This predation is probably very important for reduction of the microbial biomass in the upper soil layer, thereby enhancing the release rate of bioelements.
(5) The animal root consumers seem to be of minor importance, and it is concluded that fungivores via feeding on mycorrhizal fungi have a larger influence on the plant roots than the true rhizophages.
(6) Striking differences in species structure, biomass, metabolic activity and feeding relations were found in different soil layers. A vertical stratification is, therefore, necessary in studies of trophic interactions in podzols.
(7) The study demonstrates that it is difficult to draw definite conclusions from field data about the causes of biomass fluctuations of soil organisms. Mutual influences between different trophic categories are, thus, difficult to verify from field estimates, and controlled experiments are mostly needed as a complement.

Acknowledgements

This work was conducted within the Swedish Coniferous Forest Project. The study was coordinated by T. Persson, who also was responsible for the arthropod groups. E. Bååth and B. Söderström were responsible for fungi, M. Clarholm for bacteria and protozoans, H. Lundkvist for enchytraeids and B. Sohlenius for nematodes, rotifers and tardigrades. T. Persson and B. Sohlenius synthesized the material. We are grateful to U. Lohm for continuous support. All other colleagues who have contributed to the study will be fully acknowledged in forthcoming publications.

References

Abrahamsen, G. 1972. Ecological study of Enchytraeidae (Oligochaeta) in Norwegian coniferous forest soils. – Pedobiologia 12: 26–82.

Ågren, G. I. & Axelsson, B. 1980. Population respiration: a theoretical approach. – Ecol. Modelling 11: 39–54.

Ahti, T. 1977. Lichens of the boreal coniferous zone. – In: Seaward, M. R. D. (ed.). Lichen Ecology, pp. 145–181. London–New York–San Francisco: Academic Press.

Anderson, J. M. 1975. Succession, diversity and trophic relationships of some soil animals in decomposing leaf litter. – J. anim. Ecol. 44: 475–495.

Anderson, J. P. E. & Domsch, K. H. 1975. Measurement of bacterial and fungal contributions to respiration of selected agricultural and forest soils. – Can. J. Microbiol. 21: 314–322.

Axelsson, B. & Bråkenhielm, S. 1980. Investigation sites of the Swedish Coniferous Forest Project – biological and physiographical features. – In: Persson, T. (ed.) Structure and Function of Northern Coniferous Forests – An Ecosystem Study, Ecol. Bull. (Stockholm) 32: 25–64.

Axelsson, B., Holmberg, O., Johansson, A., Larsson, S., Lohm, U., Lundkvist, H., Persson, T., Sohlenius, B., Tenow, O. & Wirén, A. 1974. Qualitative and quantitative survey of the fauna at Ivantjärnsheden – a pine forest in Gästrikland – and some other coniferous forest sites in Central Sweden. – Swed. Conif. For. Proj. Int. Rep. 6, 44 pp. (In Swedish, English abstract)

Bååth, E. & Söderström, B. E. 1977. Mycelial lengths and fungal biomasses in some Swedish coniferous forest soils, with special reference to a pine forest in Central Sweden (Ivantjärnsheden, Ih VA). – Swed. Conif. For. Proj. Tech. Rep. 13, 45 pp.

Bååth, E. & Söderström, B. E. 1979a. Fungal biomasses and fungal immobilization of plant nutrients in Swedish coniferous forest soils. – Rev. Ecol. Biol. Sol 16: 477–489.

Bååth, E. & Söderström, B. E. 1979b. The significance of hyphal diameter in calculation of fungal biovolume. – Oikos 33: 11–14.

Bååth, E. & Söderström, B. E. 1980. Degradation of macromolecules by microfungi isolated from different podzolic soil horizons. – Can. J. Bot. 58: 422–425.

Bååth, E., Lohm, U., Lundgren, B., Rosswall, T., Söderström, B., Sohlenius, B. & Wirén, A. 1978. The effect of nitrogen and carbon supply on the development of soil organism populations and pine seedlings: a microcosm experiment. – Oikos 31: 153–163.

Band, R. N. 1959. Nutritional and related biological studies on the free-living soil amoeba, *Hartmannella rhysodes*. – J. gen. Microbiol. 21: 80–95.

Berg, B., Hannus, K., Popoff, T. & Theander, O. 1980. Chemical components of Scots pine needles and needle litter and inhibition of fungal species by extractives. – In: Persson, T. (ed.) Structure and Function of Northern Coniferous Forests – An Ecosystem Study, Ecol. Bull. (Stockholm) 32: 391–400.

Bhattacharyya, S. K. 1962. Laboratory studies on the feeding habits and life cycles of soil-inhabiting mites. – Pedobiologia 1: 291–298.

Bosatta, E., Bringmark, L. & Staaf, H. 1980. Nitrogen transformations in a Scots pine forest mor – model analysis of mineralization, uptake by roots and leaching. – In: Persson, T. (ed.) Structure and Function of Northern Coniferous Forests – An Ecosystem Study, Ecol. Bull. (Stockholm) 32: 565–589.

Bringmark, L. 1980. Ion leaching through a podsol in a Scots pine stand. – In: Persson, T. (ed.) Structure and Function of Northern Coniferous Forests – An Ecosystem Study, Ecol. Bull. (Stockholm) 32: 341–361.

Bråkenhielm, S. 1978. Ivantjärnsheden, Jädraås – regional physiography and description of the research area. – Swed. Conif. For. Proj. Tech. Rep. 16, 58 pp.

Brody, S. 1945. Bioenergetics and Growth. New York: Reinhold Publishing Corporation, 1023 pp.

Byzova, J. B. 1973. Respiration of soil invertebrates. – In: Ghilarov, M. S. (ed.) Ecology of Soil Invertebrates, pp. 3–39. Moskva: Izdatelystvo "Nauka". (In Russian)

Christiansen, K. 1964. Binomics of Collembola. – Ann. Rev. Ent. 9: 147–178.

Clarholm, M. 1977. Monthly estimations of soil bacteria at Jädraås and a comparison between a young and a mature pine forest on a sandy soil. – Swed. Conif. For. Proj. Tech. Rep. 12, 17 pp.

Clarholm, M. & Rosswall, T. 1980. Biomass and turnover of bacteria in a forest soil and a peat. – Soil Biol. Biochem. 12: 49–57.

Coulson, J. C. & Whittaker, J. B. 1978. Ecology of moorland animals. – In: Heal, O. W. & Perkins, D. F. (eds.) Production Ecology of British Moors and Montane Grasslands, pp. 52–93. Berlin–Heidelberg–New York: Springer-Verlag.

Coupland, R. T. (ed.) 1979. Grassland Ecosystems of the World: Analysis of Grasslands and Their Uses. Cambridge–London–New York–Melbourne: Cambridge University Press, 401 pp.

456

Darbyshire, J. F., Wheatley, R. E., Greaves, M. P. & Inkson, R. H. E. 1974. A rapid micromethod for estimating bacterial and protozoan populations in soil. – Rev. Ecol. Biol. Sol 11: 465–475.

Fenchel, T. 1974. Intrinsic rate of natural increase: The relationship with body size. – Oecologia (Berl.) 14: 317–326.

Flower-Ellis, J. G. K. & Olsson, L. 1978. Litterfall in an age series of Scots pine stands and its variation by components during the years 1973–1976. – Swed. Conif. For. Proj. Tech. Rep. 15, 62 pp.

Fogel, R. & Hunt, G. 1979. Fungal and arboreal biomass in a western Oregon Douglas-fir ecosystem: distribution patterns and turnover. – Can. J. For. Res. 9: 245–256.

Führer, E. 1961. Der Einfluss von Pflanzenwurzeln auf die Verteilung der Kleinarthropoden im Boden, untersucht an *Pseudotritia ardua* (Oribatei). – Pedobiologia 1: 99–112.

Gere, G. 1956. The examination of the feeding biology and the humificative function of Diplopoda and Isopoda. – Acta Biol. Hung. 6: 257–271.

Gilmore, S. K. & Raffensperger, E. M. 1970. Foods ingested by *Tomocerus* spp. (Collembola, Entomobryidae), in relation to habitat. – Pedobiologia 10: 135–140.

Harding, D. J. L. & Stuttard, R. A. 1974. Microarthropods. – In: Dickinson, C. H. & Pugh, G. J. F. (eds.) Biology of Plant Litter Decomposition, Vol. 2, pp. 489–532. London–New York: Academic Press.

Harley, J. L. 1971. Fungi in ecosystems. – J. appl. Ecol. 8: 627–642.

Harley, J. L. 1978. Ectomycorrhizas as nutrient absorbing organs. – Proc. R. Soc. Lond. B. 203: 1–21.

Hartenstein, R. 1962. Soil Oribatei. I. Feeding specificity among forest soil Oribatei (Acarina). – Ann. Ent. Soc. Amer. 55: 202–206.

Heal, O. W. & MacLean, S. F. 1975. Comparative productivity in ecosystems – secondary productivity. – In: Van Dobben, W. H. & Lowe-McConnell, R. H. (eds.) Unifying Concepts in Ecology, pp. 89–108. The Hague: W. Junk and Wageningen: Pudoc.

Heal, O. W. & Perkins, D. F. (eds.) 1978. Production Ecology of British Moors and Montane Grasslands, Ecological Studies 27. Berlin–Heidelberg–New York: Springer-Verlag, 426 pp.

Huhta, V. & Koskenniemi, A. 1975. Numbers, biomass and community respiration of soil invertebrates in spruce forests at two latitudes in Finland. – Ann. Zool. Fennici 9: 42–48.

Huhta, V., Karppinen, E., Nurminen, M. & Valpas, A. 1967. Effect of silvicultural practices upon arthropod, annelid and nematode populations in coniferous forest soil. – Ann. Zool. Fennici 4: 87–143.

Humphreys, W. F. 1977. Respiration studies on *Geolycosa godeffroyi* (Araneae: Lycosidae) and their relationship to field estimates of metabolic heat loss. – Comp. Biochem. Physiol. 57 A: 255–263.

Humphreys, W. F. 1978. Ecological energetics of *Geolycosa godeffroyi* (Araneae: Lycosidae) with an appraisal of production efficiency in ectothermic animals. – J. anim. Ecol. 47: 627–652.

Jansson, P.-E. 1977. Soil properties at Ivantjärnsheden. – Swed. Conif. For. Proj. Int. Rep. 54, 66 pp. (In Swedish, English abstract)

Jensen, T. F. 1978. Annual production and respiration in ant populations. – Oikos 31: 207–213.

Jones, P. C. T. & Mollison, J. E. 1948. A technique for the quantitative estimation of soil microorganisms. – J. gen. Microbiol. 2: 54–69.

Karg, W. 1961. Ökologische Untersuchungen von edaphischen Gamasiden (Acarina, Parasitiformes). – Pedobiologia 1: 53–98.

Kitazawa, Y. (ed.) 1977. Ecosystem Analysis of the Subalpine Coniferous Forest of the Shigayama IBP Area, Central Japan. JIBP Synthesis, Vol. 15. Tokyo: University of Tokyo Press, 199 pp.

Klekowski, R. Z., Wasilewska, L. & Paplińska, E. 1972. Oxygen consumption by soil-inhabiting nematodes. – Nematologica 18: 391–403.

Krogh, A. 1941. The Comparative Physiology of Respiratory Mechanisms. Philadelphia: Univ. of Pennsylvania Press, 172 pp.

Latter, P. M. & Howson, G. 1978. Studies on the microfauna of blanket bog with particular reference to Enchytraeidae. II. Growth and survival of *Cognettia sphagnetorum* on various substrates. – J. anim. Ecol. 47: 425–448.

Laybourn, J. & Finlay, B. J. 1976. Respiratory energy losses related to cell weight and temperature in ciliated Protozoa. – Oecologia (Berl.) 24: 349–355.

Leinaas, H. P. 1978. Sampling of soil microarthropods from coniferous forest podzol. – Norw. J. Ent. 25: 57–62.

Lundkvist, H. 1978. A technique for determining individual fresh weights of live small animals, with special reference to Enchytraeidae. – Oecologia (Berl.) 35: 365–367.

Luxton, M. 1972. Studies on the oribatid mites of a Danish beech wood soil. I. Nutritional biology. – Pedobiologia 12: 434–463.

457

Magnusson, C. & Sohlenius, B. 1980. Root consumption in a 15–20 year old Scots pine stand with special regard to phytophagous nematodes. – In: Persson, T. (ed.) Structure and Function of Northern Coniferous Forests – An Ecosystem Study, Ecol. Bull. (Stockholm) 32: 261–268.

Martin, J. K. 1977. Effect of soil moisture on the release of organic carbon from wheat roots. – Soil Biol. Biochem. 9: 303–304.

McBrayer, J. F. & Reichle, D. E. 1971. Trophic structure and feeding rates of forest soil invertebrate populations. – Oikos 22: 381–388.

Mitchell, M. J. & Parkinson, D. 1976. Fungal feeding of oribatid mites (Acari: Cryptostigmata) in an aspen woodland soil. – Ecology 57: 302–312.

Müller, G. & Beyer, R. 1965. Über Wechselbeziehungen zwischen mikroskopischen Bodenpilzen und fungiphagen Bodentieren. – Zbl. Bakt., Abt. II 119: 133–147.

Nielsen, C. O. 1962. Carbohydrases in soil and litter invertebrates. – Oikos 13: 200–215.

Nilsson, C. 1971. Wireworms (Col.; Elateridae) in Sweden. Taxonomy and Importance for Agriculture. A Literature Study. Solna: Statens Växtskyddsanstalt, 74 pp. (In Swedish)

O'Connor, F. B. 1962. The extraction of Enchytraeidae from soil. – In: Murphy, P. W. (ed.) Progress in Soil Zoology, pp. 279–285. London: Butterworths.

Page, F. C. 1967. Taxonomic criteria for limax amoebae, with descriptions of 3 new species of *Hartmannella* and 3 of *Vahlkampfia*. – J. Protozool. 14: 499–521.

Pande, Y. D. & Berthet, P. 1973. Studies on the food and feeding habits of soil Oribatei in a black pine plantation. – Oecologia (Berl.) 12: 413–426.

Parkinson, D. & Williams, S. T. 1961. A method for isolating fungi from soil microhabitats. – Plant & Soil 13: 347–355.

Persson, H. 1979. Fine-root production, mortality and decomposition in forest ecosystems. – Vegetatio 41: 101–109.

Persson, H. 1980a. Structural properties of the field and bottom layers at Ivantjärnsheden. – In: Persson, T. (ed.) Structure and Function of Northern Coniferous Forests – An Ecosystem Study, Ecol. Bull. (Stockholm) 32: 153–163.

Persson, H. 1980b. Death and replacement of fine roots in a mature Scots pine stand. – In: Persson, T. (ed.) Structure and Function of Northern Coniferous Forests – An Ecosystem Study, Ecol. Bull. (Stockholm) 32: 251–260.

Persson, T. 1975. Abundance, biomass and respiration of the soil arthropod community in an old Scots pine heath stand on Ivantjärnsheden, Gästrikland (Central Sweden) – a preliminary investigation. – Swed. Conif. For. Proj. Int. Rep. 31, 35 pp. (In Swedish, English abstract)

Persson, T. & Lohm, U. 1977. Energetical significance of the annelids and arthropods in a Swedish grassland soil. – Ecol. Bull. (Stockholm) 23, 211 pp.

Perttu, K., Bischof, W., Grip, H., Jansson, P.-E., Lindgren, Å., Lindroth, A. & Norén, B. 1980. Micrometeorology and hydrology of pine forest ecosystems. I. Field studies. – In: Persson, T. (ed.) Structure and Function of Northern Coniferous Forests – An Ecosystem Study, Ecol. Bull. (Stockholm) 32: 75–121.

Petersen, H. 1971. The nutritional biology of Collembola and its ecological significance. A review of recent literature with a few original observations. – Ent. Meddr 39: 97–118. (In Danish, English summary)

Petrusewicz, K. & Macfadyen, A. 1970. Productivity of Terrestrial Animals – Principles and Methods. IBP Handbook No. 13. Oxford–Edinburgh: Blackwell Scientific Publications, 190 pp.

Pigon, A. 1958. Respiration of *Colpoda cucullus* during active life and encystment. – J. Protozool. 5: 303–308.

Popović, B. 1977. Nitrogen mineralisation in an old and a young Scots pine stand. – Swed. Conif. For. Proj. Int. Rep. 60, 15 pp.

Raw, F. 1967. Arthropoda (except Acari and Collembola). – In: Burges, A. & Raw, F. (eds.) Soil Biology, pp. 323–362. London–New York: Academic Press.

Reichle, D. E. 1971. Energy and nutrient metabolism of soil and litter invertebrates. – In: Duvigneaud, P. (ed.) Productivity of Forest Ecosystems. Ecology and Conservation 4, pp. 465–477. Paris: Unesco.

Reichle, D. E. 1977. The role of soil invertebrate in nutrient cycling. – In: Lohm, U. & Persson, T. (eds.) Soil Organisms as Components of Ecosystems, Ecol. Bull. (Stockholm) 25: 145–156.

Reid, C. P. P. & Mexal, J. G. 1977. Water stress effects on root exudation by lodgepole pine. – Soil Biol. Biochem. 9: 417–421.

Rosswall, T. & Heal, O. W. (eds.) 1975. Structure and Function of Tundra Ecosystems. – Ecol. Bull. (Stockholm) 20, 450 pp.

Rovira, A. D. 1979. Biology of soil-root interface. – In: Harley, J. L. & Scott Russell, R. (eds.) The Soil-Root Interface, pp. 145–160. London–New York–San Francisco: Academic Press.

Schaerffenberg, B. 1942. Die Elateridenlarven der Kiefernwaldstreu. – Z. angew. Ent. 29: 85–115.

Söderström, B. E. 1974. Some microfungi isolated from different soil horizons in a 120-year-old pine forest in Central Sweden. – Swed. Conif. For. Proj. Int. Rep. 17, 7 pp. (in Swedish, English abstract)

Söderström, B. E. 1977. Vital staining of fungi in pure culture and in soil with fluorescein diacetate. – Soil Biol. Biochem. 9: 59–63.

Söderström, B. E. 1979a. Seasonal fluctuations of active fungal biomass in the horizons of a podzolized pine forest soil in Central Sweden. – Soil Biol. Biochem. 11: 149–154.

Söderström, B. E. 1979b. Some problems in assessing the fluorescein diacetate active fungal biomass in the soil. – Soil Biol. Biochem. 11: 147–148.

Söderström, B. E. & Bååth, E. 1978. Soil microfungi in three Swedish coniferous forest soils. – Holarctic Ecology 1: 62–72.

Sohlenius, B. 1977. Numbers, biomass and respiration of Nematoda, Rotatoria and Tardigrada in a 120-year-old Scots pine forest at Ivantjärnsheden, Central Sweden. – Swed. Conif. For. Proj. Tech. Rep. 9, 40 pp.

Sohlenius, B. 1979. A carbon budget for nematodes, rotifers and tardigrades in a Swedish coniferous forest soil. – Holarctic Ecology 2: 30–40.

Springett, J. A. & Latter, P. M. 1977. Studies on the micro-fauna of blanket bog with particular reference to Enchytraeidae. I. Field and laboratory tests of microorganisms as food. – J. anim. Ecol. 46: 959–974.

Staaf, H. & Berg, B. 1977a. A structural and chemical description of litter and humus in a mature Scots pine stand at Ivantjärnsheden. – Swed. Conif. For. Proj. Int. Rep. 65, 30 pp.

Staaf, H. & Berg, B. 1977b. Mobilization of plant nutrients in a Scots pine forest mor in Central Sweden. – Silva fenn. 2: 210–217.

Stout, J. D. & Heal, O. W. 1967. Protozoa. – In: Burges, A. & Raw, F. (eds.) Soil Biology, pp. 149–195. London–New York: Academic Press.

Swift, M. J., Heal, O. W. & Anderson, J. M. 1979. Decomposition in Terrestrial Ecosystems. Oxford–London–Edinburgh–Melbourne: Blackwell Scientific Publications, 372 pp.

Wallwork, J. A. 1958. Notes on the feeding behaviour of some forest soil Acarina. – Oikos 9: 260–271.

Woodring, J. P. 1963. The nutrition and biology of saprophytic Sarcoptiformes. – Adv. in Acarology 1: 89–111.

THEORETICAL APPROACHES TO FOREST FUNCTIONING

Persson, T. (ed) 1980
Structure and Function of Northern
Coniferous Forests – An Ecosystem Study
Ecol. Bull. (Stockholm) 32: 463–503.

MICROMETEOROLOGY AND HYDROLOGY OF PINE FOREST ECOSYSTEMS. II. THEORY AND MODELS

S. Halldin[1], H. Grip[1], P-E. Jansson[1] and Å. Lindgren[1]*

Abstract

A modulized system of physically based models for abiotic processes in a Scots pine forest ecosystem was constructed within the Swedish Coniferous Forest Project. Composite models built of process modules were used to define the forest microclimate for models of tree growth, soil nutrients and photosynthesis. Semi-empirical formulas for regional forest evapotranspiration were found not to work properly without description of turbulent roughness and surface resistance. Snow dynamics and frost in the soil were successfully simulated by use of the specific energy concept. Snow melt was horizontally heterogeneous and was shown to infiltrate through the frost zone. Capillary rise to the lower frost boundary could be substantial. Soil water flow was simulated both in heterogeneous and, with limited amounts of soil data, in homogeneous soils. It was shown that resistances to water uptake cannot be separated into root and soil parts but must be treated in bulk. Soil heat flow was most sensitive to the insulating humus layer and a proper description of the soil surface temperature presented difficulties.

Additional keywords: Evapotranspiration formulas, frost in soil, radiation interception, root water uptake, snow, soil heat flow, soil water flow, thermal conductivity, unsaturated conductivity.

Introduction

The interdisciplinary Swedish Coniferous Forest (SWECON) Project was started in 1972 with a major objective to understand and predict forest ecosystem productivity. The initial years of the project were mainly mensurational, and the abiotic measurements are reported in the first part (Perttu et al., 1980) of this study. At a later stage when modelling work had progressed, an abiotic research group was established, dealing only with nonbiotic aspects of water and energy turnover in the coniferous forest ecosystem.

This paper is mainly a state of the art report from the modelling activities in this group around 1977. The aims of this modelling activity were (1) to supply biotic researchers in the SWECON project with proper and reliable information about the microclimate in different parts of the forest ecosystem, and (2) to forward the knowledge about processes which govern this climate. It has been an operational goal to keep modelling and measuring activities closely connected.

The paper discusses in some detail a number of abiotic processes in a pine forest.

---

[1] Dept. of Ecology and Environmental Research, Swedish University of Agricultural Sciences, S-750 07 Uppsala, Sweden
* Author responsibilities given in Acknowledgements.

Simulation results refer to sites at the Jädraås Ecological Research Station, described by Axelsson & Bråkenhielm (1980). Since most sections are fairly comprehensive on their own, they can be read separately.

Organization of abiotic models within SWECON

Application of classical physics to forest ecosystems has only recently gained impetus, but it is still safe to say that most of the basic abiotic processes are well identified. Whereas modelling of, for example, species competition, productivity and photosynthesis of a forest, can be based on a multitude of hypotheses (often contradictory), the laws that govern soil heat conduction, long-wave radiation, evaporation, etc., are well known. The abiotic modelling in SWECON could, thus, be structured slightly differently from the biological modelling.

Three groups of simulation models were distinguished. Basic modules treated only single processes. Composite models were constructed from the basic modules to fulfil certain goals. Special purpose models with a temporal or spatial resolution differing from the above categories, were constructed on the basis of special hypotheses.

Basic modules

The intention with the basic modules (Table 1) was to describe separate abiotic processes in the forest ecosystem. The modules were written as subroutines in such a way that they could easily be assembled into composite models of larger parts of the ecosystem. In order to function as self-sustained models these subroutines, therefore, had to be supplied with a main programme of their own.

Temporal and spatial resolution are closely connected in all models of this kind. A high spatial resolution calls for a high temporal resolution to avoid numerical instabilities in the simulation. A low spatial resolution allows numerical solutions with low temporal resolution. Still, it must be emphasized that the numerical time-step and the time-step of the input data of a model seldom coincide. If a model should simulate diurnal behaviour it requires input data with diurnal resolution, and the same is true for a time resolution of one day even if numerical requirements will reinforce a simulation time-step less than this.

Many of the modules in Table 1 describe processes with time constants of much less than one day, or with highly variable time constants. Nevertheless, all modules – excepting EVAPOR and INTERC – work with both diurnal and one-day resolution. This is achieved by describing the process with a diurnal resolution. The "diurnal" model is then presumed linear such that a daily average input will produce a daily average output (RADIAT, SNOW, SOILE, SOILW).

If the time constant of a process is small this necessitates a short numerical time-step in simulation. A short simulation time-step in combination with a long simulation time span is often prohibited by inconceivable simulation times. Many of the modules are, therefore, supplied with different techniques to overcome this limitation. Besides an analytical solution provided by the INTERC module, these techniques are based on different conditional bypassing of "slow" processes or on

Table 1. Basic modules and processes described.

Module	Processes included	Temporal resolution*		Time span		
		< day	≥ day	Few days	Season	Years
EVAPOR	Latent and sensible heat exchange within and between forest canopy and atmosphere above it	×		×	×	
INTERC	Interception of rain precipitation	×		×	×	
RADIAT	Absorption, emission and transmission of long- and short-wave radiation within and between forest canopy and atmosphere above it	×	×	×	×	×
SNOW	Accumulation and melting of snow	×	×		×	×
SOILE	Heat conduction, heat storage, and frost in soil	×	×	×	×	×
SOILW	Infiltration, redistribution, and and percolation of soil water	×	×	×	×	

* Required resolution of climatic input data.

variable time-steps. A special analytical solution used by the ENERGY model is discussed in the last section of the paper.

In the following sections results are presented from simulations with some of the modules utilized as self-sustained models. Simulation of the single modules was seen as a possible way of "validation" before a model became too complex to allow this. The EVAPOR and INTERC modules have been discussed elsewhere (Halldin *et al.*, 1979a). The RADIAT module is described as part of the ENERGY model. The section about snow dynamics is based on the SNOW module, the sections about frost in the soil on the complete SOIL model, the section about soil water flow on the SOILW module, and finally the section about soil heat flow on the SOILE module.

Composite models

When computer modelling first made its way into the ecological sciences, the models were often thought of as general tools for solving all varieties of problems. The more complex the model, the better it was regarded. During the last few years there has been a strong reaction against the very complex models and it has been realized that a simulation model can only be beneficial as long as it is developed in response to a single well-defined goal (or hypothesis). With this distinction as a starting-point, the basic modules were developed to form a "library" of abiotic process-descriptions. Based on the modules and complementary process descriptions, three different

465

Table 2. Composite (C) and special (S) purpose abiotic models.

Model	Type	Modules used/ processes involved	Purpose	Time span		
				Days	Season	Years
CANOPY	C	EVAPOR, INTERC, RADIAT, SNOW, soil heat flow	Explain and predict direct measurements of latent and sensible heat flux from a rough forest canopy. Guide development of semi-empirical formula for evapotranspiration from such a canopy	×	×	
ENERGY	C	RADIAT, SNOW, SOILE	Calculate radiation regimes and soil temperature profiles from standard meteorological data for the benefit of biotic forest models		×	×
SOIL	C	SOILE, SOILW, evapotranspiration, ground water flow, interception, snow, water uptake	Explain and predict heat and mass transfer processes in different types of homogeneous or layered soil profiles	×	×	×
ROOT	S	Root water uptake	Explain location of resistances in soil and root to water uptake	×		
RUNOFF	S	Evapotranspiration, interception, soil water flow, ground water flow, runoff	Predict runoff from a small catchment area		×	

composite models were constructed (Table 2). The modules listed for each model in Table 2 can be substituted by any subroutine simulating the same process. The CANOPY model uses a very simplified soil temperature routine. Simplified routines for snow dynamics, precipitation, interception and ground water flow are used in the SOIL model. The modulization has made it possible to test the sensitivity of the different models to more or less complex process formulations.

The direct measurement of latent and sensible heat made at a micrometeorological mast at Jädraås is reported in the first part (Perttu et al., 1980) of this abiotic study. One objective of these measurements was to gain an understanding of the exchange processes above the rough forest surface. Another objective was to guide the development of a simple formula to predict evapotranspiration from standard meteorological network measurements (discussed in the following section). The CANOPY model was developed to fill both these objectives. Since mast measurements were not continuous, the model was used to interpolate between measurement periods, thus enabling a comparison to be made between the energy balance (Bowen ratio) and water balance estimates of seasonal evapotranspiration (Grip et al., 1979).

Table 3. Climatic input variables of the composite and special purpose models.

Model	Time resolution		Preci-pita-tion	Radiation			Wind speed	Air tempe-rature	Rela-tive humi-dity	Comments
	<day	≥day		Net	Global	Sky				
CANOPY	×		×		×	×	×	×	×	Sky radiation can be estimated from global radiation and air temperature
ENERGY		×	×		×	×	×	×	×	
SOIL	×	×	×	×	(×)		×	×	×	Global radiation is used if net radiation is not available. If only information about cloudiness is available, radiation is calculated from this
ROOT	×									Water potentials inside the root and in bulk soil are boundary conditions, which can be given arbitrarily
RUNOFF	×		×							Precipitation is needed every two hours during the simulated period. Diurnal course of evapotranspiration is esti-mated from runoff time series during a calibration period

The behaviour and construction of the CANOPY model have been described in detail by Halldin et al. (1979a).

The ENERGY model is presented in the last section of this paper. It should be emphasized that it was constructed from the SNOW and SOILE modules as reported by Halldin et al. (1977), whereas these modules together with the RADIAT module, as presented below, have been further developed.

The SOIL model attempts to deepen our knowledge of the physical processes in the soil and is designed to cover different types of soils. It was used to evaluate the importance of feedback mechanisms between water and heat flows in the soil, and to predict possible consequences of soil management practices (Halldin et al., 1979b). It has also simulated time series of water content, water flow and temperature for calculations of nutrient transport (Bringmark, 1980) and nitrogen transformation in the soil (Bosatta et al., 1980). The SOIL model has been presented in detail by Jansson & Halldin (1979).

Special purpose models

The runoff from a water catchment is the integrated result of many different processes over a large area. Simulation of runoff requires a much lower spatial resolution than the models described above. Since it is sometimes necessary to predict runoff from information only about precipitation (Table 3) it seems clear that the RUNOFF model (Grip, 1973) falls into another category than the models mentioned above. It has, nevertheless, been intended that this model should be the basis of a future model where the basic modules could be used. This would be possible by developing RUNOFF into a distributed model conceptualizing the catchment as a number of homogeneous areas within each of which the basic modules would be applicable. Such a model could be used to predict effects of different management practices or disturbances on the forest ecosystem.

Another special purpose model was designed to study the root water uptake process. The ROOT model has been reported in detail by Halldin (1977) and a brief description of its results is given below in the section on water uptake.

Formulas for evapotranspiration

Of all elements involved in the hydrological balance, evapotranspiration is the most difficult both to estimate and measure. The balance of precipitation and evapotranspiration basically determines the humidity of a region. In ecosystem studies, productivity is commonly assumed to be linearly related to evapotranspiration (e.g., de Wit, 1958).

For specific sites it has been possible to directly measure the evapotranspiration (e.g., Perttu et al., 1980). Since such measurements have required expensive and sophisticated equipment there has been a need to construct formulas which utilize standard meteorological data. Such formulas and their applicability to forest areas have recently been reviewed by Grip (1978).

Penman (1948) proposed the now commonly used formula for "potential" evaporation:

$$E_p = \frac{\Delta(R_n - G) + \gamma E_t}{\Delta + \gamma} \tag{1}$$

where

$$E_t = [a_1 + a_2 u(z)]\delta e \tag{2}$$

and R_n is net radiation, G heat storage flux, γ psychrometric "constant", Δ slope of saturated vapour pressure function, a_1, a_2 constants, $u(z)$ wind speed at measurement height z, and δe vapour pressure deficit. Penman's equation is a combination of an energy balance equation and an equation for turbulent exchange. It is semi-empirical because the turbulent term (E_t), which expresses the potential "atmospheric demand", relies on empiricism. Since Penman's equation does not explicitly account for surface roughness it tends to underestimate the impact of turbulence on evapotranspiration in several cases. Penman & Long (1960) have, therefore, attempted to describe the turbulent term free from empiricism, by explicitly introducing a surface roughness (z_0) into the equation:

$$E_t = \frac{L_v M}{RT} \frac{\delta e}{r_a} \tag{2'}$$

with aerodynamic resistance defined as:

$$r_a = \frac{\ln^2[(z - d)/z_0]}{k^2 u(z)} \tag{3}$$

where d is displacement length and k von Karman's constant. L_v is latent heat of vapourization, M molecular weight of water, R the universal gas constant, and T the temperature in Kelvin. In order to find the actual transpiration (TR_a), Monteith (1965) introduced the concept of surface resistance (r_s):

$$TR_a = \frac{\Delta(R_n - G) + \gamma E_t}{\Delta + \gamma(1 + r_s/r_a)} \tag{4}$$

Monteith maintained the surface resistance for a closed canopy to basically equal all stomatal resistances in parallel, although Philip (1964) provided theoretical arguments against this view.

The influence of surface resistance and roughness on evapotranspiration from the sparse Jädraås forest was examined by using a constant surface resistance $r_s = 200$ s m^{-1} and the aerodynamic resistance of Eq. (3) with $k = 0.41$, $d = 0.75h$ and $z_0 = 0.1h$ (Rutter et al., 1971–72) where h denotes stand height. For June 1976 evaporation calculated by Penman's formula was about twice the amount of the transpiration given by Monteith's formula (Fig. 1). The turbulent part ranged from 10 to 50% of the total in Penman's formula, but from 55 to 90% in Monteith's. Low evapotranspiration and small turbulent exchange was connected with high relative humidity, and the peak in evapotranspiration on June 28 was caused by relatively strong winds. Measurements during dry conditions indicated that Monteith's equation gave the best estimate of the two. Importance of turbulent exchange over rough surfaces and the influence of high surface resistance of this forest was clearly demonstrated.

When Penman (1948) stated evaporation to be "potential", he implied it to be fully determined by meteorological factors, and that soil and vegetation had no influence. As seen from Fig. 1, this is obviously not applicable for a dry forest canopy.

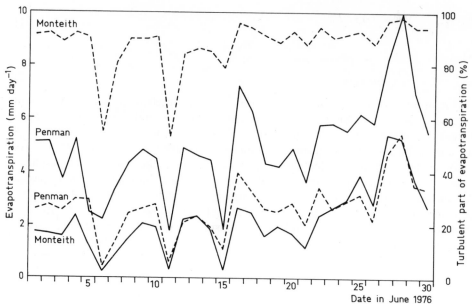

Figure 1. Total (solid line) and turbulent part (broken line) of evapotranspiration calculated with Penman's and Monteith's equations.

If, as suggested by Stanhill (1973), evaporation is explicated as "water loss to the atmosphere from soil or free water including water intercepted by, condensed on, and exuded from plant surfaces", evaporation from a wet forest canopy will always be potential, and for this situation Eq. (1) may be applicable.

As Stanhill (1973) also proposed, evapotranspiration will be used only for "total water loss to the atmosphere per unit ground surface", and transpiration will be used only for "loss of water vapour to the atmosphere through plant surfaces".

Since forest evaporation and transpiration are mainly controlled by different factors, and since evaporation normally exceeds transpiration under equal conditions, it is clear that forest evapotranspiration (ET) must be described as a combined sum of the two, with their relative weights given by the dynamics of intercepted water:

$$ET = w_1 E_p + w_2 TR_a \qquad (5)$$

Contrary to the case for a short-cut grass, it is not meaningful to elaborate the concept of potential evapotranspiration for a forest. However, it may be useful to define a potential transpiration (TR_p) as the transpiration controlled mainly by stomatal resistance of a forest canopy not short of soil water. The usefulness of this concept depends on the possibility to relate stomatal closure to plant and weather conditions.

T. Lohammar (see Lohammar et al., 1980) have suggested the following momentary equation for stomatal conductance:

$$k_s = \left(\frac{R_{is}}{a_1 + R_{is}} \right) \frac{a_2}{a_3 + \delta e} \qquad (6)$$

470

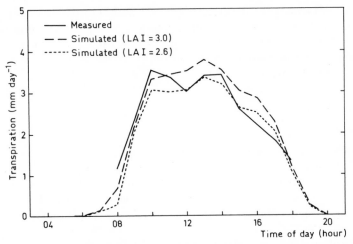

Figure 2. Potential transpiration from a mature pine stand in Jädraås on 10 August 1977 calculated as the sum of potential transpiration from ground vegetation and tree crowns. Leaf area index (*LAI*) was equally shared between trees and ground vegetation.

where R_{is} is global radiation, and a_1, a_2, a_3 are constants. In accordance with Monteith, the surface resistance is defined as:

$$r_s = (k_s \cdot LAI)^{-1} \tag{7}$$

where *LAI* is the projected (single-sided) leaf area index. To account for changes in soil moisture a reduction factor must be introduced. Actual transpiration under soil water stress can then be defined as:

$$TR_a = f(w)\, TR_p \tag{4'}$$

where w is soil water content (or possibly potential, cf. Eq. 29) in the root zone. Calculating actual evapotranspiration from potential has usually concerned only this latter reduction and the literature abounds in methods for it.

T. Lohammar estimated values for the parameters in Eq. (6) which yielded high correlation coefficients. The estimates were based on single shoot measurements by means of porometers (E. Mattson-Djos, unpubl.) and permanent assimilation chambers (Linder *et al.*, 1980) from several days during 1976, when soil water was not limiting. These estimates were then used together with Eq. (7) and Monteith's formula to predict the diurnal variation of transpiration for a slightly overcast day in August 1977 (Fig. 2). This day followed a long period of rain and, therefore, the vegetation was dry but the soil was moist. The Bowen ratio-energy balance measurements (Perttu *et al.*, 1980) could, thus, be regarded to represent potential transpiration. The values of leaf area index in the very sparse Jädraås forest was probably between the limits given in Fig. 2 (J. Flower-Ellis, pers. comm.).

The suggested conceptualization of forest evapotranspiration showed that no single formula in the literature was sufficient. An optimal compromise between data availability, physically realistic description and simplicity in handling will probably end up in a simple model. Such a model could be based on Eq. (5), where Penman's

(Eqs. 1, 2' and 3) and Monteith's (Eqs. 2', 3, 4, 6 and 7) formulas yield evaporation and transpiration, but where also interception and soil water budgets must be accounted for. The Lohammar equation (6) must be shown to work also with daily average input, and much work remains to relate the model parameters to data independently available from the field.

Snow dynamics

The start of the growing season is triggered by the time of snow melt, and plant available soil water during the spring is a function of the amount of snow melt infiltrate. Starting time for snow accumulation and the amount of snow are important factors influencing frost penetration. Snow acts as a sink and seasonal storage for air pollutants. The radiation balance is strongly dependent on type and quantity of snow.

The precipitation phase is determined by the temperatures in the air masses between the clouds and the ground, and for intercepted snow also by vegetation temperature. Snow Hydrology (1956) states the phase of precipitation (snow-rain) to be determined mainly by air temperature at ground level.

Interception of snow is a very complex process. It depends on the type of vegetation, wind, radiation, temperature, amount, age and structure of the intercepted snow (Miller, 1966). Since it is difficult to model, it is commonly assumed to slide off the vegetation immediately after a storm (e.g., Solomon et al., 1976). This simplification can usually be justified since interception losses (evaporation) are low in winter. On the other hand, vegetation albedo is drastically altered in the presence of intercepted snow. Another serious problem when modelling a snow pack for a specific site is the wind transport of snow. Besides the effects of areally heterogeneous snow depth, dune formation, accumulation and packing in edges, wind-blown snow evaporates rapidly (Schmidt, 1972; Tabler, 1975).

The major source of energy for snow melt is radiation (Granger et al., 1977) and the major determinant of radiation balance is snow albedo. If the snow is old or melting, albedo is lowered (Snow Hydrology, 1956). Albedo also depends on grain size and density of the snow (Bergen, 1975) and on cloudiness (Petzold, 1977). Melt is also caused by latent and sensible heat exchange and heat flow from the ground. The latter can often be disregarded but the influence of the former two can sometimes be considerable (Kuz'min, 1972).

Once the energy balance of the snowpack has been determined the melt of the snowpack depends on its depth and water conductivity. Melting and subsequent refreezing of meltwater in the pack gives rise to a layered structure. The layered structure strongly affects the permeability and drainage characteristics of the snow (Colbeck, 1975). For a homogeneous snowpack, permeability and water retention can probably be related to density (Rachner & Grasnick, 1975) but grain size also has a large effect (Colbeck, 1976). The density also determines thermal conductivity (Snow Hydrology, 1956).

The correlation between snow depth and water equivalent is given by snow density. Changes in density are caused by snow melt processes and snow metamorphism, i.e., morphological changes in dry snow structure. Measurements in various Swedish climatic regimes (Nord & Taesler, 1973) suggest that the metamorphism has a minor

472

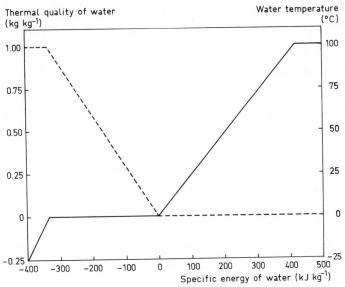

Figure 3. Thermal quality (broken line) and temperature (solid line) of water as functions of their specific energy.

influence on density changes. Since metamorphism can be seen primarily as a growth of selected crystal grains (de Quervain, 1973) it may, however, affect permeability, retention capacity and albedo.

It is easy to observe that melting of a snowpack does not proceed homogeneously in a horizontal direction. Some patches melt quicker, thereby decreasing albedo and retentivity which further accelerates melting. This may be an important mechanism when predicting melt, but since few investigations (e.g., Kopanev, 1976a, b) of cover depth distributions have been performed, this problem requires further study (Kuz'min, 1972).

Snow dynamics in forest *vs.* open field has attracted much interest, and even though it is generally agreed that melt is more rapid in the open, no such consensus is found with regard to accumulation.

A simple model was constructed based on firm physical ground. The central concept of the model is specific energy, to which temperature and thermal quality of snow are uniquely related (Fig. 3). Specific energy is (by definition) the ratio of energy to mass. When changes in both energy and mass are determined the change in specific energy is computed. By assuming vertical homogeneity of the snowpack, temperature, free water content and net freezing are obtained. If free water exceeds the retention capacity, it is released from the pack. In the present study, retention is equal to a fixed fraction of the total water equivalent.

The fraction of the ground covered by snow is a function of mean areal snow depth (V):

$$f = 1 - e^{-aV} \tag{8}$$

All energy and mass flows (except precipitation) only concern this fraction.

Precipitation to the pack can be either rain or snow. The negative latent heat of

473

snow is the major energy source for accumulation. With a knowledge of only amount and not phase of precipitation its thermal quality must be determined:

$$f_{prec} = \begin{cases} 1 & T_a < T_{min} \\ (T_a - T_{max})/(T_{min} - T_{max}) & T_{min} \leq T_a \leq T_{max} \\ 0 & T_{max} < T_a \end{cases} \tag{9}$$

Air temperatures (T_a) above T_{max} generate rain only and below T_{min} snow only. Between these limits proportions vary linearly with temperature. T_{max} around 1–2°C and T_{min} from about -2°C to -3°C has been found to give satisfactory results. Interception of snow is neglected by presuming it to slide off vegetation immediately following the storm. Energy in precipitation is calculated from air temperature and amounts of snow and rain.

Absorbed short-wave radiation is determined by the albedo. Albedo is a function of age and change in thermal quality. Following Snow Hydrology (1956):

$$\alpha_s = \begin{cases} 0.80 - 0.138t^{0.38} & \text{accumulating phase} \\ 0.60 - 0.045t^{0.59} & \text{melting phase} \end{cases} \tag{10}$$

where time (t) is counted in days.

Long-wave radiation balance is established by postulating the snow to be a perfect black-body, radiating at mean snow temperature. Sky radiation is either measured or calculated from:

$$R_{il} = \varepsilon_{app} \sigma T_a^4 \tag{11}$$

σ is Stephan-Boltzmann's constant and the apparent sky emissivity (ε_{app}) is a function of cloudiness, estimated as the ratio of actual to potential global radiation:

$$\varepsilon_{app} = 0.949 - 0.185 \, R_{is}/R_{is}^* \tag{12}$$

Latent (E_p) and sensible (H) heat exchanges are given by:

$$E_p = (\varrho c_p/\gamma) K_E[e_s(T_{snow}) - RHe_s(T_a)] \tag{13}$$

$$H = (\varrho c_p K_H(T_{snow} - T_a) \tag{14}$$

where the turbulent exchange coefficients K_E and K_H have the same linear dependency on wind speed. ϱ is air density, c_p specific heat of air, γ psychrometric constant, RH relative humidity and e_s saturated vapour pressure. The mass flow associated with latent heat exchange is taken into consideration even though it is minor.

Heat conduction between soil and snow, although small, is given by:

$$q_h = k_h(T_{snow} - T_b)/(d/2) \tag{15}$$

where snow thermal conductivity is:

$$k_h = a\varrho_s^2 \tag{16}$$

and the boundary temperature (T_b) is an average of soil and snow temperatures weighted by thermal conductivity and depth (d) of snow, a is a constant and ϱ_s snow density.

The aim of the model was to describe accumulation and melt of the snowpack in the forest and in the open. In the form presented here it was only assumed to give a

474

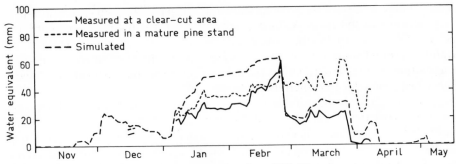

Figure 4. Water equivalent of snowpack during the winter 1975–76.

proper description of an open snow field. Detailed modelling of the differences between the forest and the open would put high requirements on the measured data and further analysis could possibly reveal the influence of local wind-drift on the measured water equivalents (Fig. 4). Simulation of snow dynamics of the winter 1975–76 stressed the importance of accumulation relative to melt. This winter was fairly uncommon on account of the frequently alternating melting and accumulation periods. Since the major energy source of accumulation is latent heat of melt and a single storm may involve a large fraction of total winter precipitation, it follows that an erroneous prediction of the precipitation phase may completely spoil both simulated energy and mass balance. Contemporary models of similar structure (e.g., Bengtsson, 1976) have shown good behaviour when only melting has been considered, but also melting is seriously affected by precipitation, especially rain.

Regarding the cumulated energy flows during the winter it was shown that mainly two flows gave rise to the annual balance. Latent heat of snow precipitation acted as a large negative storage which was consumed by the global radiation during a short period in the beginning of spring. In the middle of the winter with low radiation and short days, radiation flux played a small role. The change in day length should be seen in relation to the integration time step of the model. Due to the turn-over rate of sensible and latent heat exchange this was by necessity less than a day. Even so, the input climate was regarded as constant during the day. Possible errors involved in this presumption have yet to be evaluated. The average snow temperature used for shorter periods could not be representative for the surface temperature which determined heat radiation and sensible heat balance.

The most sensitive parameters of the model were T_{min} and T_{max} determining precipitation phase, a multiplicative parameter determining the turbulent exchange coefficients for latent and sensible heat exchange, and the retention capacity. Since all of these parameters were based on several simplified assumptions, this gave a suggestion as to where further research should be directed.

Frost in the soil

Soil freezing has severe impact on water uptake by the plant-root system. Early spring "freezing" injuries on trees can probably be explained as a drought phenomenon when the soil is still frozen but transpiration has already begun. It is also generally accepted that the start of the growing season is "triggered" by a soil heat sum which is very sensitive to soil frost. A third effect of soil frost is the release of nutrients which may be transported to the ground water by snow melt infiltration. This may be harmful to ground water quality as well as negative to the nutrient requirement of the vegetation. For these reasons it is crucial to include soil freezing in any ecological water balance model for northern latitudes.

Beskow (1932) laid the foundations for modern research into soil freezing phenomena. His studies were intended for civil engineering purposes and included relations between frost heaving and soil type, and degree-day methods for predicting frost depth. His view of freezing point depression relied on classical thermodynamic theory. Due to the concentration on road building problems, further research into the basic processes did not gain impetus until the sixties and some of the findings are still disputed (Anderson & Morgenstern, 1973).

Soil freezing, as well as snow, cannot be described without touching aspects of both mass and energy. Neglecting mass and heat transfer in vapour form, the two basic equations for capillary water flow (Darcy's law) and heat conduction (Fourier's law) in the soil are (in one dimension):

$$q_{\mathrm{w}} = k_{\mathrm{w}}(\theta_{\mathrm{w}}, T)\left[\frac{\partial \psi(\theta_{\mathrm{w}}, T)}{\partial z} + \varrho_{\mathrm{w}}g\right] \tag{17}$$

$$q_{\mathrm{h}} = k_{\mathrm{h}}(\theta_{\mathrm{w}}, \theta_{\mathrm{i}})\frac{\partial T}{\partial z} - C_{\mathrm{w}}Tq_{\mathrm{w}} \tag{18}$$

where h, w, and i are for heat, liquid water, and ice, q denotes flux, k conductivity, T temperature, C heat capacity, θ volumetric water content, z depth in the soil, ψ matric potential, ϱ density, and g gravitation.

The dependence on temperature of the conductivities and soil water potential above freezing point is minor and can be well explained by the variation in viscosity (Haridasan & Jensen, 1972). Below freezing point this situation is drastically changed because of the change of phase of the soil water. The second term in the heat flow equation stands for convective heat flow associated with water and this term is normally neglected, but in cases of snow melt infiltration it can reach significant levels. When combining the flow and continuity equations the following two partial differential equations are obtained:

$$\frac{\partial \theta}{\partial t} = \frac{\partial}{\partial z}\left[k_{\mathrm{w}}\left(\frac{\partial \psi}{\partial z} + \varrho_{\mathrm{w}}g\right)\right] + s_{\mathrm{w}}(T) \tag{19}$$

$$\frac{\partial(CT)}{\partial t} - L\varrho_{\mathrm{i}}\frac{\partial \theta_{\mathrm{i}}(T)}{\partial t} = \frac{\partial}{\partial z}\left(k_{\mathrm{h}}\frac{\partial T}{\partial z}\right) - C_{\mathrm{w}}\frac{\partial(q_{\mathrm{w}}T)}{\partial z} \tag{20}$$

where s means source/sink, and L latent heat of fusion. The source term s_{w} refers to water uptake by the root system and is strongly temperature dependent for low temperatures, partly due to viscosity, partly to metabolic effects.

In the energy equation the second term on the left designates the latent heat of the phase change. The temperature dependence of this term has a number of implications. This dependence constitutes the freezing point depression and is a capillary phenomenon. It is, thus, dependent on the type of soil. The finer the soil, the larger the depression (Beskow, 1932). For a sandy soil, as at Jädraås, the depression is small and consequently a frost front is fairly well defined, but in cases of very clayey soils

476

the frost boundary cannot be equated with the zero degree isotherm. For all soils a minor proportion of the soil water is left unfrozen even well below zero. The smaller this proportion the higher its tension. A frost-induced potential gradient towards the frost zone and a water flow towards the zone are obtained. For clays and silts this flow becomes concentrated to specific spaces in the soil because of the large water flux relative to the frost boundary velocity. This phenomenon is called ice lensing and is of importance for agricultural practices on clayey soils (Czeratzki, 1971) since it improves aggregation and water conductivity. Ice lensing is the major cause of frost heaving, and thus a concern for civil engineers (Beskow, 1932). It is mainly found in saturated soils but may also occur under unsaturated conditions (Loch & Miller, 1975).

The presence of unfrozen water also means that a transport of water can take place within the frost zone. It was previously believed that this transport was negligible but several sources (e.g., Hoekstra, 1966) confirm that large quantities of water (especially snow melt) can be transported through the frost zone. Miller *et al.* (1975) have shown that this transport is not restricted to the liquid phase, but that also vapour transport may play a significant role. It is also important to note the hysteresis effect of the freezing-thawing cycle (Koopmans & Miller, 1966).

The major climatic influence on soil freezing is the snow cover. Snow has a very low thermal conductivity and thus acts as an insulator. Snow also produces melt water that coincides with the frost, especially at the end of the winter. When snow does not cover the ground in winter the frost penetrates very deeply. Since the thermal conductivity of ice is almost four times that of water, the frost penetration may be quite fast. Calculation of thermal conductivity can either be made with empirical equations (Kersten, 1949) or with the theory of de Vries (1963) (see Penner, 1970).

As for the model formulation of the snow, the frost description is based on the concept of specific energy, but differs with respect to the freezing point depression. Since most field soils have a more or less pronounced freezing point depression, accounts are given of this. The temperature of a completely frozen soil is related to the soil water content at wilting point (15 atm.):

$$T_f = -a\theta_{\text{wilt}} \tag{21}$$

where T_f = temperature of a completely frozen soil, θ_{wilt} = volumetric water content at wilting point and a = constant.

The degree of freezing point depression is related to the pore size distribution index. The relative fraction of latent heat is expressed by:

$$f_r = (1 - Q/Q_f)^{a\lambda} \tag{22}$$

where Q = energy, Q_f = energy at T_f, a = constant and λ = pore size distribution index (cf. Eq. 26).

The energy is partitioned between latent and sensible heat for temperatures above T_f (Fig. 5). The freezing-melting is considered as a drying-wetting process. The freezing of water causes an increase in tension of the unfrozen water. This change in soil water potential causes water to flow towards the frost boundary in a similar way as water uptake causes a capillary rise towards the root zone during dry and unfrozen conditions.

The liquid conductivity in the partly frozen soil is calculated as the capillary conductivity corresponding to the amount of unfrozen water, i.e., the influence of the

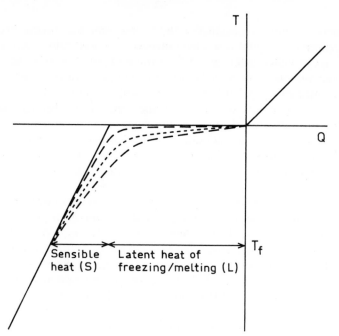

Figure 5. Temperature (T) as a function of specific energy (Q) in a soil for different degrees of freezing point depression. Note that both axes are distorted for sake of clarity. With a completely frozen soil temperature (T_f) of $-5°C$ the ratio between sensible (S) and latent (L) heat is approximately 1:24.

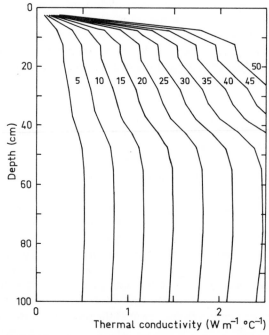

Figure 6. Thermal conductivity for a frozen Jädraås soil where a medium sand is covered by a 2–5 cm humus layer and underlain by a coarser sand layer at 40 cm. The set of curves represents water contents in % vol. (unfrozen equivalent).

478

liquid-ice interface is considered equal to the liquid-air interface. In fine-textured soils upward flow often creates ice lenses and frost heaving but no account to structural changes is taken in this model since it is intended mainly for sandy soils.

Thermal conductivity for a frozen soil (Fig. 6) given by Kersten (1949) is used in the model (cf. Eq. 33):

$$k_\text{h} = a_1 10^{a_2 \varrho_\text{s}} + a_3 \theta 10^{a_4 \varrho_\text{s}} \tag{23}$$

where a_i are constants and ϱ_s the dry bulk density of the soil. Another linear relation given by de Vries (1975) is used for the humus.

Daily values of air temperature, humidity, wind speed, precipitation and either of net radiation, global radiation or cloudiness are necessary climatic inputs to the model. The upper boundary condition to the heat flow is calculated with a gradient of temperature between soil surface and the uppermost soil layer. During conditions when snow occurs, the soil surface temperature is calculated from thickness and thermal conductivity of the snowpack and the uppermost soil layer. If liquid water is present in the snow the soil surface temperature is put equal to $0°C$. The only driving variable for the heat conduction is the air temperature, the other variables are used for the snow dynamics and the water flow equation.

The model in this context was applied only to the layered soil of a sparse pine stand at Jädraås. If it should be used for denser stands or other radiation regimes, the assumption of equality between air temperature (1.5 m above soil surface) and surface temperature (at soil or snow) should be replaced by a more realistic relation.

Two different winters with different climatic conditions were chosen to illustrate the behaviour of the model. The first winter (1975–76) was cold with little snow and consequently the frost penetrated to a considerable depth. The second winter (1976–77) was also cold but a snowpack of almost 1 m was developed which protected the soil from a deep frost. The model was run during three years, starting in the summer prior to the first winter. This was necessary in order to obtain the appropriate initial conditions before the winter. A soil temperature profile down to 10 meters was considered.

Simulated snow and frost depths (Fig. 7) showed the model to be reasonable for the two winters. A frost boundary was defined as a zero degree isotherm. This level was calculated with the assumption of a linear gradient in temperature between the middle of two adjacent layers. Since the assumption of linearity is not valid during conditions with frost in the soil, the levels were a little confusing and the calculated frost boundaries would have a smoother pattern if it were not for the finite difference approximation of equations (19) and (20). The deviation between predicted and measured frost boundaries was partly due to the evaluation of measurements. Measured frost boundaries were based on observations at four frost tubes (Perttu et al., 1980) from which a mean value was calculated. When frost occurred at some of the stations only, the mean value was still calculated from all frost tubes, but with zero depth representing tubes without frost. This ambiguity is clearly seen at the end of the first season, where the measured frost boundaries seemed to thaw from the bottom. A less ambiguous comparison between measured and simulated values of the time when frost disappeared showed good prediction capacity of the model.

Another deviation occurred during the thawing of the second season. Both the measured and simulated soil profiles became completely thawed in close association with the melting of snow. The temporal discrepancies when soil was completely

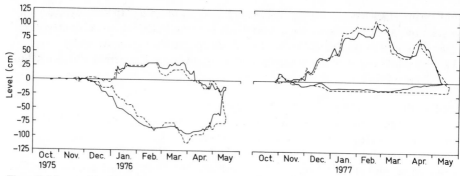

Figure 7. Measured (solid line) and simulated (broken line) snow depths and frost boundaries during two winters in the mature Scots pine stand at Jädraås. Measured values are means of four observations.

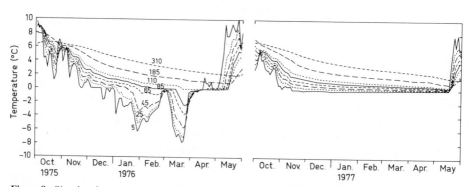

Figure 8. Simulated temperatures at different depths (cm) during two winters.

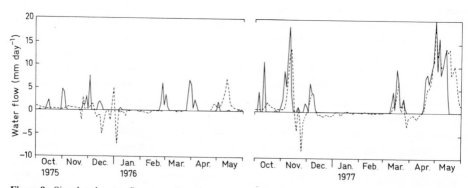

Figure 9. Simulated water flows at soil surface (solid line) and below the frost (broken line) during two winters.

thawed were consequently effects of the differences in snow melt. The simulated frost depth was due to temperatures only slightly below 0°C (Fig. 8) due to a heavy infiltration of melted snow (Fig. 9). The main factor besides air temperature in controlling penetration of frost in the soil was the thickness of snowpack. Both simulated and measured snow depths (Fig. 7) showed strong dependence of the insulation effect on the frost.

Temperature patterns in the soil profile (Fig. 8) were rather different during the two seasons. The autumn of 1975 was warmer than 1976 which gave a higher initial temperature before the winter. Spring started much earlier during the first season due to the absence of snow. The variation with time of temperature was quite irregular during 1975–76 and very smooth during 1976–77. It was interesting to note the different patterns in spring. The first winter, with a deep frost, had a delay in temperature rise, between different levels, in contrast to the second, when the rise of temperature was almost simultaneous for all levels. A less pronounced difference between the two seasons was the lowering of temperature at greater depths due to infiltration of melted snow. This effect could be seen only during the second season when the snowpack contained a lot of water (ca. 240 mm).

The water flows at soil surface and below the frost (Fig. 9) showed rather different patterns during the two seasons. The first period was fairly dry with low rates of infiltration water, whereas the opposite held true for the second period. During both seasons an upward water flow to the frost occurred, especially in the beginning of the freezing period. During the second season water flows penetrated the frost on nearly all occasions when high infiltration rates occurred. The first season showed the opposite result, with water which infiltrated and remained in the frozen soil until thawing occurred in spring. This could be explained by the thickness of the frost and the temperatures well below 0°C.

These results indicated that a mechanistic, physically based model could successfully be used for predictions of soil freezing and thawing. The model should be applied to more sites with different soil types and climatic conditions for evaluation of its predictive and explanatory value.

Soil water flows

Flow and amount of soil water are important climatic influences on microbial life in soil. As regards forest productivity, soil water is normally not limiting in the Jädraås area, but may well be during dry summers. Most aspects of water quality management also require good understanding of unsaturated soil water dynamics.

This study of unsaturated soil water was limited to the treatment of capillary water flow. Problems of spatial variability (Nielsen *et al.*, 1973) were disregarded although Freeze (1975) suggested that deterministic models would not yield results equivalent to the expectation of stochastic models with proper distribution of soil characteristics. The study concentrated on modelling the effects of vertical heterogeneity of the soil profile and the possibilities to realistically model soil water, based on limited information about site characteristics. Evaluation of field data from a layered soil profile (Perttu *et al.*, 1980) showed that a coarse layer below 40 cm depth acted as a barrier to percolation, an effect that was well reproduced by the model.

Water in an unsaturated soil is affected by gravitational, capillary, adsorptive and molecular forces. Gravitational forces are important only in the very wet range and adsorptive in the dry range. Molecular forces can usually be disregarded. Thus, it is almost only in the capillary range that the unsaturated conductivity is of interest.

The conductivity of a saturated soil (k_{sat}) was first realistically explained by Kozeny (1927):

$$k_{sat} = \frac{p^3}{a\eta s^2}$$

(24)

where p = (volumetric) porosity, s = areal porosity, η = viscosity and a = a material constant. The determination of this constant has not yet been successfully performed and, consequently, the unsaturated conductivity of a soil is usually given as a relative conductivity (k_r), being the ratio between the unsaturated conductivity at an arbitrary soil moisture level and the conductivity at a specified level, usually at saturation. At this reference level k_r is adjusted to a measured conductivity to give the final expression.

Three groups of theories for k_r may be distinguished. The first two of these use either a simple analytical or a measured relationship for the potential-relative water content function. They both rely on the fundamental equation suggested by Childs & Collis-George (1950) and Burdine (1953):

$$k_r(\theta) = S_e^a \int_0^\theta d\theta/\psi^2 \bigg/ \int_0^p d\theta/\psi^2$$

(25)

where S_e is effective saturation, and a is a constant. This equation has been further refined by Marshall (1958), Millington & Quirk (1961), Kunze et al. (1968), Green & Corey (1971) and finally Mualem (1976). In the final form it reads:

$$k_r(\theta) = S_e^n \left[\int_0^\theta d\theta/\psi \bigg/ \int_0^p d\theta/\psi \right]^2$$

(25')

where n is a material constant accounting for the correlation between pores and flow path tortuosity.

The third type of theory has been proposed by Farrel & Larson (1972). They utilize an analogy with the classical theory of electromagnetism parallel to that of de Vries (1963) for heat conductivity (cf. Eq. 34).

In the model all coupled heat and water flows, vapour fluxes, freezing phenomena, and root water uptake are neglected. Therefore, equations (17) and (19) can be simplified to:

$$q_w = k_w(\theta) \left[\frac{\partial \psi(\theta)}{\partial z} + \varrho_w g \right]$$

(17')

$$\frac{\partial \theta}{\partial t} = \frac{\partial}{\partial z} \left[k_w(\theta) \left(\frac{\partial \psi(\theta)}{\partial z} + \varrho_w g \right) \right]$$

(19')

Hydraulic properties required for the model are moisture characteristics and unsaturated conductivity as functions of water content. Measured retention data for undisturbed field cores (when available) are fitted to the functional relation given by Brooks & Corey (1964):

$$S_e = (\psi/\psi_a)^{-\lambda}$$

(26)

482

where ψ_a = air entry tension and λ = pore size distribution index. The effective saturation is written as:

$$S_e = \frac{\theta - \theta_r}{p - \theta_r} \tag{27}$$

where θ_r = residual water content.

Based on the theory of Burdine (1953) (Eq. 25) in the form of Mualem (1976) (Eq. 25′) the analytical expressions in Eqs. (26) and (27) yield the following equations for the unsaturated conductivity:

$$k_w = k_{sat} \cdot S_e^{n + 2 + 2/\lambda} \tag{28}$$

or

$$k_w = k_{sat}(\psi_a/\psi)^{2 + (2 + n)\lambda} \tag{28'}$$

Brooks & Corey (1964) had the value of n inherently equal to one. Mualem (1976) suggested $n = 1/2$ to be an optimal value, but also stated that it could vary with different soil types.

Equations (26) to (28) together with the six parameters k_{sat}, λ, ψ_a, p, n and θ_r give a complete description of hydraulic properties for each soil layer.

The model applies to a soil partly covered with mosses and lichens which can be considered as capillary systems with supplies and demands at the boundaries. Water is lost only from the uppermost layer. Potential transpiration (Eq. 4) calculated for a forested area with a constant surface resistance of 300 s m^{-1} is, in this case, reduced to a constant fraction (f_{pot}) to obtain values proper for a clear-cut area. Reduction from potential to actual transpiration is done according to Eq. (4′) but by using soil water potential in each layer rather than total water content. Earlier works (Denmead & Shaw, 1962; Cowan, 1965; Zahner, 1967) have shown that a critical potential (ψ_c) exists where the reduction in transpiration begins. Reduction also depends on the rate of potential transpiration (Denmead & Shaw, 1962; Cowan, 1965). The following reduction factor is used:

$$f = \min[1, (\psi_c/\psi)^{aT\overline{R}_p}] \tag{29}$$

This function is rather general in form but it is clear that the parameters must be determined empirically since they depend on site factors such as type of vegetation, root densities and soil type.

A unit head gradient is assumed for unsaturated conditions at the bottom of the profile. A simplified assumption about net horizontal ground water flow is adopted when ground water level (z_{gr}) is above the bottom (z_{min}) of the profile considered:

$$q_{gr} = (1 - z_{gr}/z_{min}) q_{max} \tag{30}$$

"Maximal" ground water flow (q_{max}) is estimated from measured ground water levels.

Equation (19′) is solved with an explicit forward differencing scheme (Euler integration) and discretization of the soil profile. A special routine calculates soil characteristics in the middle of each compartment and at the interface between them. The number and size of compartments can be varied almost arbitrarily in accordance with demands for numerical stability, correct representation of morphology, and position of transducers in the soil.

483

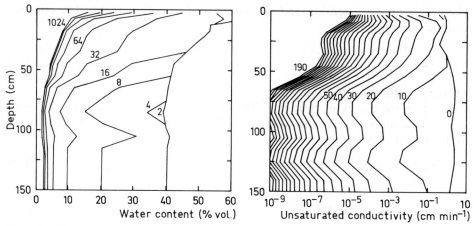

Figure 10. Water content and unsaturated conductivity at different tensions (cm water) for the same soil as in Fig. 6.

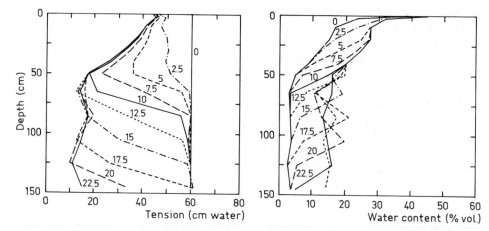

Figure 11. Simulated values of soil water tensions and water contents during 22.5 hours of infiltration. Original tension was 60 cm water, and 200 mm were precipitated on the surface during the experiment.

The model was applied to two different soil profiles with great differences in their hydraulic properties. Basic information about the properties also differed between the two profiles. One plot was cleared for a conductivity experiment (Perttu *et al.*, 1980) and had a layered soil profile with fine-medium sand in the upper and coarse sand in the lower part. The other plot was situated at a clear-felling, where the soil profile was rather homogeneous, consisting of fine sand. This plot had a fairly shallow ground water level. Both plots were covered with a 2–5 cm thick humus layer.

Soil moisture characteristics for the conductivity experiment plot were obtained from undisturbed soil cores taken in a pit about 100 meters from the plot (Fig. 10). Cores were taken with 5 cm deep steel cylinders down to 20 cm depth and with 10 cm cylinders below that to 120 cm depth. When computing the conductivity, Eq. (28′)

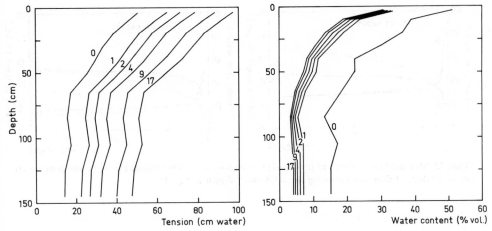

Figure 12. Simulated values of soil water tension and water content during 17 days of drainage after the infiltration shown in Fig. 11.

and $n = 1$ were used according to Brooks & Corey (1964).

Only texture and dry bulk density were measured in the soil profile at the clear-felling. Direct fitting to the expression used by Brooks & Corey could not be done. Moisture characteristics were taken from a mineral soil with similar texture presented in a detailed survey of Swedish soils (Andersson & Wiklert, 1972). These moisture characteristics were then used to evaluate parameters required in Eqs. (26) and (27). Porosity values were given by dry bulk densities. The upper 5 cm of the soil profile consisted of a humus layer with properties similar to those of the conductivity experiment plot. Saturated conductivity was unknown and had to be assumed.

Simulations of the conductivity experiment were simplified by submitting the experimental setup to simple boundary and initial conditions. Tensions in the soil profile were initially set to a value corresponding to an approximate field capacity. Irrigation of 200 mm was enough to get the whole profile in equilibrium (Fig. 11). The water contents increased by about 10% in the whole profile and the tensions decreased from 60 to 10–30 cm water. The profile was then allowed to drain and evapotranspiration was prohibited by a plastic cover (Fig. 12).

When comparing measured and simulated results one should be observant of:

(1) Soil water flows at specified levels during the drainage period which have been given both as accumulated and momentary values.
(2) Absolute tensions at different times and at specified level or differences in tensions obtained during part of, or the whole period.
(3) Absolute water contents at specified levels and at different times.

These comparisons are important to interpret the behaviour of water in the profiles. If agreement is obtained in only one case then different moisture characteristics in the model and in reality can be expected and the comparison is irrelevant. The different representativity of the model and the field measurements must also be considered. Deviation in water content may, for example, be due to errors in neutron

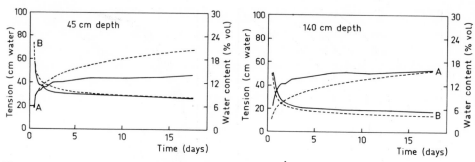

Figure 13. Measured (solid line) and simulated (broken line) soil water tensions (A) and water contents (B) during 17 days of drainage following the infiltration shown in Fig. 11.

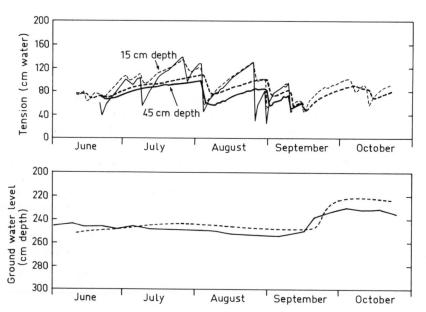

Figure 14. Measured (solid line) and simulated (broken line) soil water tensions and ground water level in 1976. The soil is a homogeneous sand covered with a 2–5 cm humus layer.

probe measurements. Deviation in water flow must be regarded as more serious since the neutron probe measures changes more accurately than it measures absolute water contents.

Simulations were also performed with different choices of n in the conductivity expressions of Eqs. (28) and (28′). The best agreement between measured and calculated variables was obtained when n was given to be 1.5 for the upper layers and 0.5 for the coarse deeper layers (Fig. 13). The agreement was better with regard to water content than with regard to tension which indicated that the soil water characteristics in the model did not perfectly represent reality.

For the homogeneous soil profile at the clear-felling, reasonable agreement was obtained after adjustment of parameters which control the amount of evapo-transpiration over the clear-felled area, the saturated conductivity and the n in the equations (28) and (28'). Changes in the three parameters (f_{pot}, k_{sat}, n) were sometimes working in the same direction but they could be separated since the measured data were of good quality. An increase in evapotranspiration had a similar effect on tension at 15 cm depth as a decrease in conductivity, but the effect on ground water level was different. The rise of ground water level (Fig. 14) was very sensitive to varia-tions of the saturated conductivity. The best agreement with measured data was obtained when f_{pot} was 0.16, k_{sat} was 1 cm h^{-1}, and n was 1.5. The very low evapotranspiration (equivalent to an apparent surface resistance of about 2000 s m^{-1}) from the clearing could be explained by an almost total absence of living vegetation and a humus layer protecting the soil from evaporation.

It was found preferable to test this complex, physically based model for soil water flows on a system where root water uptake and interactions with heat flows were absent. In doing so one could feel assured that the treatment of pure soil water flows in a more complete model would be working well. It was also demonstrated that the model could be used even where limited amounts of data about the soil were present.

Water uptake by roots

Under normal conditions, soil water is seldom a limiting factor for the productivity of forest trees in Sweden. However, a drought can have fatal and long-lasting effects (Bengtson, 1978), and it is valuable to understand the mechanism of water uptake under limiting conditions. Plant nutrient uptake usually follows water uptake and a realistic description of soil water dynamics for hydrological and other purposes also requires a sound description of root water uptake.

The scientific study of water uptake has historically followed two main courses. Scientists concerned with soil water availability have been interested in the uptake of whole root-systems mainly from a hydrological point of view. Those concerned with water flow resistance in the plant or the rhizosphere have been concentrated on plant physiological or soil physical descriptions.

The classical aspect of soil-water availability was that the soil water was equally available from the upper limit (field capacity) to the lower (the permanent wilting point) (see Veihmeyer, 1972). Even if these limits were never clearly defined, Wadleigh (1946) found it evident that "as a plant removes water from a soil, the water stress upon the soil is continually increasing". These ideas were generally accepted until fairly recently, and today they are used mainly in large-scale hydrological run-off models and in practical forest management.

In the soil-plant-atmosphere continuum (Philip 1966), the greatest resistance to water flow is in the stomata. This resistance is governed by plant water potential which in turn depends on the resistance to water flow from bulk soil to the leaf. It has generally been accepted (e.g., Boyer, 1969, 1971; Jarvis, 1975) that within the plant, the major resistance is found in the root. It is, hence, natural to enquire about the relative size of resistances in the root and in the soil immediately surrounding it, the rhizosphere. Since it is practically inconceivable to measure the two resistances *in situ*, this problem has long been controversial. Cowan (1965), in agreement with

Gardner (1964), stated the belief, then common, that root resistance was negligible. Newman (1969a, b) stated the reverse, except under conditions of extreme drought or very low root density, but in 1976 Rose *et al.* realized that "current models... and presently available data do not permit allocation of the dominant liquid phase resistance to the soil or the plant ...".

In this study the microscopic approach is adopted and only one unit length of an idealized cylindrical root in perfect contact with the soil is considered. Rewriting Eqs. (17) and (19) in cylindrical coordinates and neglecting gravitational flow will yield:

$$q_w(r) = 2\pi r k_w \frac{\partial \psi}{\partial r} \qquad (17'')$$

$$\frac{\partial \theta}{\partial t} = \frac{1}{r} \frac{\partial}{\partial r} \left(2\pi r k_w \frac{\partial \psi}{\partial r} \right) \qquad (19'')$$

Equation (19″) has been analyzed in some detail but has been given analytical or quasi-analytical solutions only for the cases when conductivity is constant and/or when the solution refers to steady state or steady rate (see, e.g., Philip, 1957; Gardner & Mayhugh, 1958; Passioura, 1963; Miles, 1964). To get a general solution with arbitrary initial and boundary conditions simulation technique must be used.

The soil around the root is divided into seven compartments. The outer boundary of each compartment is described by:

$$r_i = a^i \cdot r_{root} \qquad i = 1,7 \qquad (31)$$

where r_{root} = root radius and a = a constant. Eq. (19″) is then solved with an explicit forward differencing scheme:

$$q_i = 2\pi r_i k_{i, i+1} (\psi_i - \psi_{i+1})/r_{i, i+1} \qquad i = 0,6 \qquad (19'')$$

The calculation of $k_{i, i+1}$ is very sensitive and follows the technique given by Halldin *et al.* (1977). Conductivity and matric potential of the soil is discussed above (Eqs. 28 and 26).

Earlier attempts to simulate water uptake according to the microscopic approach has always used the root surface potential or water content as a boundary condition (e.g., Lambert & Penning de Vries, 1973; Jacobsen, 1974). In this way a crucial coupling mechanism has been overlooked, namely the continuity of water flux and potential over the soil-root interface. In the present study the water potential inside the root is used as a boundary condition. The solution to the continuity conditions at the interface is given in detail by Halldin (1977).

Simulation results indicated that neither the root nor the rhizosphere resistance fully governed the uptake. Instead, interaction between the two seemed to be the important process. Researchers who have favoured the rhizosphere resistance as the largest of the two have done so on the assumption of a rapid desiccation in the vicinity of the root due to a high transpirational pull. However, root resistance opposed such high pulls and therefore prevented rapid desiccation. This feedback mechanism would always set up a given equilibrium ratio between the two resistances which depended on the uptake rate. It was concluded that the resistance to water uptake should preferably be regarded as a bulk resistance common to both soil and plant.

488

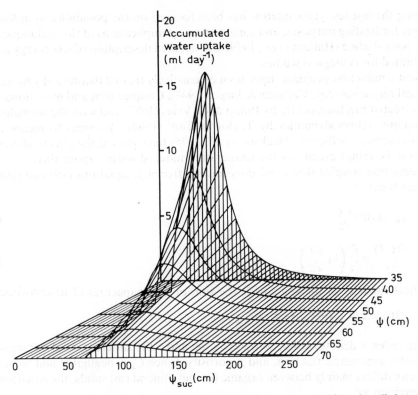

Figure 15. Accumulated water uptake as a function of initial soil water potential (ψ) and applied constant vacuum (ψ_{suc}) at 55 cm depth for the same soil as in Fig. 6.

As mentioned previously, field measurements of root water uptake are difficult. One possible way to avoid the problem has been to work with an "artificial root" (Briggs & McCall, 1904). Such a "root" could be a commonly used cylindrical porous cup for soil water sampling. When using a cup of this kind it has generally been presumed that the quickest sampling would result from a maximal vacuum applied (i.e., a "high transpirational pull"). This strategy has failed to work in many situations where the soil around the cup has dried out. In order to find remedies to this situation a multiple simulation with different constant vacuum and initial soil water potentials was run, each run covering one (simulated) day. It could be seen (Fig. 15) that in order to get a maximum efficiency of the sampling, applied vacuum should only slightly exceed the soil water suction. It should not be overlooked that the self-regulatory plant root would probably have followed this strategy automatically.

Soil heat flows

Low soil temperature is a major limiting factor for plant growth and water uptake by roots. In soil biology many processes are profoundly influenced by temperature.

During the last few years interest has been focused on the possibility to utilize soil energy for heating purposes, and some ecological implications of this technique have now been studied (Halldin et al., 1979b). A detailed description of soil energy is thus warranted for ecological studies.

Heat conduction problems have been exhaustively treated theoretically by mathematical physicists (e.g., Carlslaw & Jaeger, 1947). Coupled heat and mass flows have been treated mechanistically by Philip & de Vries (1957) and with the formalism of irreversible thermodynamics by Taylor & Cary (1964). Attempts to measure the cross-coupling coefficients (Jackson et al., 1975) have proved the effects of coupled flows to be minor except for the temperature induced water vapour flux.

Neglecting coupled flows and disregarding freezing, equations (18) and (20) can be simplified to:

$$q_h = k_h(\theta) \frac{\partial T}{\partial z} \tag{18'}$$

$$\frac{\partial (CT)}{\partial t} = \frac{\partial}{\partial z} \left(k_h \frac{\partial T}{\partial z} \right) \tag{20'}$$

The heat capacity of the soil equals the sum of heat capacities of its constituents:

$$C(\theta) = \sum_i f_i C_{si} + \theta C_w + (p - \theta) C_a \tag{32}$$

where index s denotes solid, w water, a air and i the different solid constituents, f denotes volumetric fraction, and p porosity. Since C_a is negligible and solid heat capacity differs mainly between organic (o) and mineral (m) solids, the equation can be rewritten as:

$$C(\theta) = f_m C_{sm} + f_o C_{so} + \theta C_w \tag{32'}$$

The heat capacities are found in several handbooks, and the volumetric fractions can easily be determined from field samples.

Based on extensive measurements, Kersten (1949) derived empirical thermal conductivity relations for various mineral soils. For unfrozen sand (cf. Eq. 23) he stated:

$$k_h(\theta) = (a_1 \log \theta + a_2) \, 10^{a_3 \varrho_s} \tag{33}$$

where a_1, a_2 and a_3 denote constants and ϱ_s dry bulk density of the soil.

Water has a thermal conductivity 30 times that of air but considerably less than that of minerals. The thickness and the geometric arrangement of the water around the soil particles should thus have a major influence on the soil thermal conductivity. Since the arrangement of water in the soil is related to its matric potential, al-Nakshabandi & Kohnke (1965) proposed, at least in the first approximation, the conductivity to be uniquely determined by the water tension irrespective of soil type.

A third expression has been proposed by de Vries (1963). In analogy with the theory of electric conductivity of a granular media he postulated:

$$k_h = \sum_i x_i f_i k_i / \sum_i x_i f_i \tag{34}$$

where i denotes soil constituents, f_i volumetric fractions, k_i constituent thermal conductivities, and x_i a proportionality factor:

490

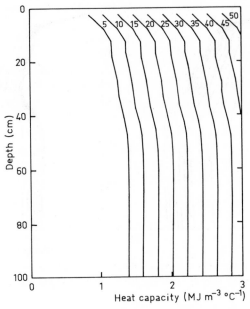

Figure 16. Heat capacities at different water contents (% vol.) for the unfrozen sandy soil in Fig. 6.

$$x_i = \frac{1}{3} \sum_{j=x, y, z} \left[1 + \left(\frac{k_i}{k_0} - 1 \right) g_j \right]^{-1} \tag{35}$$

where x, y, z are principal axes of the soil particles and g_j are shape factors defined for different idealized geometries of the particles. k_0 is the conductivity of the continuous medium.

De Vries' theory has often been advocated because of its strong physical foundation but, since both determination of the g-factor and choice of continuous medium in the dry range are based on calibration measurements, the theory can only be regarded as semi-empirical. Nevertheless, it has gained widespread acceptance, and a number of researchers have found good agreement between the theory and laboratory or field measurements (e.g., Wierenga *et al.*, 1969; Hadas, 1977). Good agreement has also been found by using simulation technique (Wierenga & de Wit, 1970).

For simulation of soil heat flow the water content was treated as a parameter. Site and simulated period were the same as those used for heat flow calculations in Perttu *et al.* (1980), and water contents from field measurements were used.

Volumetric heat capacity (Eq. 32) in the soil profile was calculated from measured porosity data at different water contents. The lower levels had larger heat capacities than the upper at equal water contents (Fig. 16). The soil was layered with a medium sand underlain by a coarse sand and water content was higher at the upper levels. The heat capacity at different depths was, thus, fairly equal.

Kersten's equation (33) of thermal conductivity rather than de Vries' (Eq. 34) was preferred because of its simplicity and also since no data were available for the

491

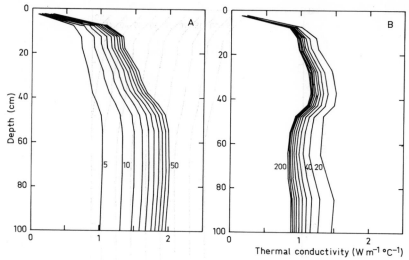

Figure 17. Thermal conductivities (A) at various soil water contents (steps of 5% vol.) and (B) at various soil water tensions (steps of 20 cm water). The soil is the same as in Fig. 6.

relative fraction of quartz in the profile. When the thermal conductivity was expressed as a function of volumetric water content and depth (Fig. 17A), an increase with depth was seen. The very small conductivity near the soil surface was due to the humus layer. For this a separate conductivity function was used (de Vries, 1975). When expressed as a function of water tension (cf. Fig. 10) it could be seen that thermal conductivity in the mineral soil varied less with depth for a given tension compared to a given water content (Fig. 17B). This supported to some degree the assumption of al-Nakshabandi & Kohnke (1965) that thermal conductivity can be treated as a unique function of water tension independent of soil type.

A difficult problem in simulating soil heat flux is to properly describe the upper boundary condition. This condition can either be given as a temperature or as a heat flux. When (net) radiation (R_n) reaches the ground it is partitioned to evapotranspiration (ET), sensible heat flux (H) and heat conduction in the soil (q_h):

$$R_n = ET + H + q_h (z = 0) \tag{36}$$

The partitioning of this energy is governed by exchange processes in the vegetation and atmosphere and is very difficult to describe. Spatial variability of heat flux in the upper soil layer may, furthermore, be substantial (Fritton et al., 1976; Scharringa, 1976), thus preventing a unique definition of the upper boundary in one dimension. In this study these pitfalls were avoided by using a measured temperature near the soil surface as the upper boundary condition.

Simulated heat flows at different levels (Fig. 18) showed a smoother pattern than calculated heat flows (Perttu et al., 1980). This was partly due to different time resolution in the two cases. For the measured profile a difference between two values measured hourly was obtained, while in the model time resolution was one minute, and a linear interpolation was used between the measured hourly temperatures driving the model. The simulated heat flows were then averaged over each hour. It should be noted that the heat flow was almost completely out of phase at about 40 cm

492

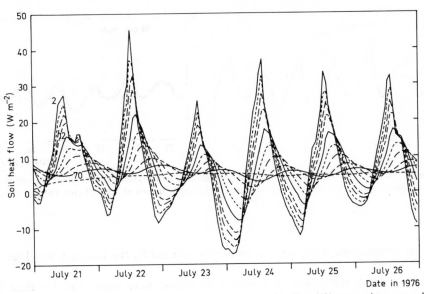

Figure 18. Simulated heat flows at depths of 2, 4, 6, 8, 12, 17, 23, 33, 44 and 70 cm on six summer days.

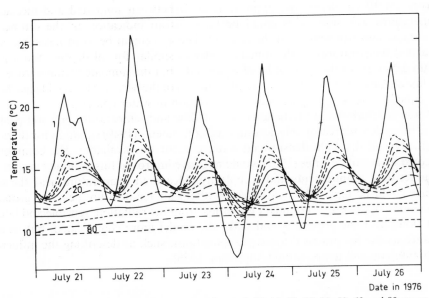

Figure 19. Simulated soil temperatures at depths of 3, 5, 7, 10, 15, 20, 28, 38, 50, 63 and 80 cm on six summer days. Measured temperature at 1 cm was used as the upper boundary condition.

depth compared to the surface. This indicated that the profile could be treated with an apparent damping depth of about 13 cm, if an analytic solution to equation (20′) should be preferred (Kniebe & Koepf, 1970).

Simulated temperatures (Fig. 19) showed a pattern similar to that of the heat flows. Damping of heat flows with depth showed almost no correlation with soil structure,

493

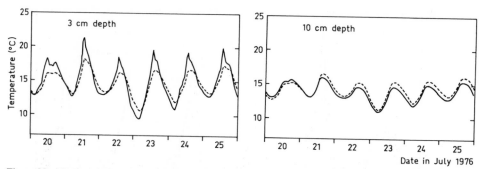

Figure 20. Measured (solid line) and simulated (broken line) temperatures at two different levels in the mineral soil on six summer days. Measured values are hourly means of three (3 cm) and two (10 cm) sensors.

whereas temperature damping was primarily affected by the humus layer (Figs. 18 and 19).

At 3 cm depth the measured temperature varied more within the day than the simulated (Fig. 20). This could either have been an effect of a too low thermal conductivity in the model or an error in the position assignment of temperature sensors. At 10 cm depth, the opposite relation between simulated and measured temperatures was seen. This could be taken as an indication of the erroneous position assigned to sensors in the top soil. The agreement between measured and simulated temperatures in the mineral soil was similar for all depths. Variations within days were of the same order of magnitude, but the simulated temperatures all became a little higher than the measured at the end of the period. This could have been due either to thermal properties or to a variation in water content.

It was concluded that predictions of heat flow and temperature in a soil profile could be made with reasonable accuracy using Kersten's (1949) equation for thermal conductivity if dry bulk density and water content was available. The commonly accepted theory of de Vries (1963) would not have improved this accuracy in spite of its larger data requirements and complexity. Measured temperature near the soil surface could be replaced by information about air temperature near the ground. Calculation of the upper boundary condition from net radiation, sensible and latent heat flows near the ground would make the model more complicated, but would enhance its use for practical forestry applications, such as describing the influence of thinning on soil temperature (Ångström, 1936).

A crude model of energy flows in a pine forest ecosystem

The development of ecosystem models describing the kind of pine forests studied within the SWECON project called for a low resolution submodel of the distribution of heat and water in the system.

As a first attempt to fill this need the crude ENERGY model was constructed with the intention to deliver climatic input variables to the biotic models within SWECON, mainly the tree growth model (Ågren & Axelsson, 1980) and the nutrient model (Bosatta et al., 1980). These input variables were: total daily incoming short-wave

494

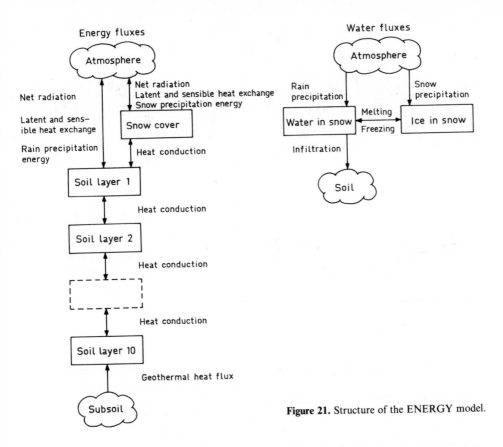

Energy fluxes

Atmosphere

Net radiation

Net radiation
Latent and sensible heat exchange
Snow precipitation energy

Latent and sens-
ible heat exchange

Snow cover

Rain precipitation
energy

Heat conduction

Soil layer 1

Heat conduction

Soil layer 2

Heat conduction

Heat conduction

Soil layer 10

Geothermal heat flux

Subsoil

Water fluxes

Atmosphere

Rain
precipitation

Snow
precipitation

Melting

Water in snow

Ice in snow

Freezing

Infiltration

Soil

Figure 21. Structure of the ENERGY model.

radiation, day-time temperature, night-time temperature, humidity, soil temperature profile, and light intensity at the ground level, all with a time resolution of one day.

Submodels describing snow dynamics and soil temperature profiles were used as building-blocks. These had been developed earlier as parts of a rather detailed energy model (Halldin et al., 1977). Since the model was supposed to be crude and to cover a longer period, it does not simulate the daily course of latent and sensible heat fluxes within the forest canopy. The latent heat flow within the canopy is disregarded since it is not essential in determining the daily change of heat storage. Consequently, the energy content of the crowns is not included in the model as a state variable and daily evapotranspiration is calculated with Penman's (1948) semi-empirical formula. Radiation exchange of the canopy is taken into consideration, but not explicitly in the energy balance of the model. The model contains 13 state variables, two for water and 11 for energy (Fig. 21).

The model uses six driving variables, namely, temperature, precipitation, vapour pressure, wind speed, incoming short-wave radiation and incoming long-wave radiation, all with a time-resolution of one day (Fig. 22). Stability requirements make it necessary to use a somewhat shorter simulation time-step of 0.2 or 0.33 days, which still gives rise to acceptable execution times.

Given the incoming short-wave and long-wave radiation, calculation of the other terms of the radiation balance are based on a simplified view of the forest canopy

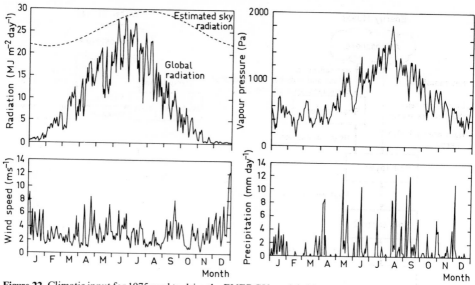

Figure 22. Climatic input for 1975 used to drive the ENERGY model. Air temperature is shown in Fig. 24.

(Fig. 23). The canopy is supposed to cover a fraction d_c of the sky. This fraction of the radiation hits the canopy, and is then either absorbed, transmitted or reflected. The remainder $(1 - d_c)$ passes the canopy undisturbed. There is a slight difference between the behaviour of the short-wave and long-wave radiation. Only long-wave radiation is emitted and only short-wave radiation is transmitted through the covered part of the canopy. The different terms of the short-wave radiation is deduced by adding their separate components (Fig. 23):

$$R_{osa} = R_{osb}(1 - d_c) + R_{isa}d_c\alpha_c + R_{osb}d_c(1 - \alpha_c)e^{-kLAI/d_c} \tag{37a}$$

$$R_{isb} = R_{isa}(1 - d_c) + R_{osb}d_c\alpha_c + R_{isa}d_c(1 - \alpha_c)e^{-kLAI/d_c} \tag{37b}$$

$$R_{osb} = R_{isb}\alpha_g \tag{37c}$$

Here R denotes radiation, o outgoing, i incoming, s short-wave, a above canopy and b below canopy. Reflectance (albedo) of canopy and ground are denoted α_c and α_g, respectively. The light extinction coefficient for light passing through the covered part of the canopy is denoted by k, and LAI is projected leaf area index. The explicit solution to this system of linear equations with R_{isa} as independent variable is easily given.

For the long-wave radiation, transmitted components are replaced by emitted and the formulas turn out as:

$$R_{ola} = R_{olb}(1 - d_c) + R_{ila}d_c(1 - \varepsilon_c) + d_c\varepsilon_c\sigma T_c^4 \tag{38a}$$

$$R_{ilb} = R_{ila}(1 - d_c) + R_{olb}d_c(1 - \varepsilon_c) + d_c\varepsilon_c\sigma T_c^4 \tag{38b}$$

$$R_{olb} = R_{ilb}(1 - \varepsilon_g) + \varepsilon_g\sigma T_g^4 \tag{38c}$$

The index 1 denotes long-wave, ε_c and ε_g are emissivities of canopy and ground. T_c and T_g are temperatures of canopy and ground and σ is Stefan-Boltzmann's

496

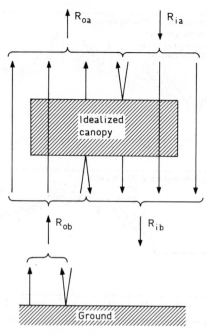

Figure 23. Components of incoming (i) and outgoing (o) radiation above (a) and below (b) the canopy.

constant. As for short-wave radiation, the explicit solution of the system is easily given.

Energy flows to the snowpack depend, among other things, on the temperatures of the air, snow and soil. The heat flow between snow and soil is proportional to the difference in temperature. Occasionally the snowpack is very small and with the simple kind of integration procedure normally used (Euler integration), a too small compartment is always a source of numerical instability. To avoid this instability an analytical solution of the energy flow equations for the snowpack is inserted into the model. The solution is complicated by possible phase transitions. If the snowpack contains both ice and water, its temperature is always $0°C$, and a change in the energy content only influences the amount of liquid water in the snow. There are three flows proportional to a temperature difference and hence potential sources of instability, firstly, the sensible heat flow between air and snow, secondly, the heat conduction between ground and snow, and thirdly, the exchange of heat radiation between snow and sky.

Heat radiation reaching the snow (R_{ilb}) is associated with a temperature, T_R, of a black body emitting radiation of the same intensity. There are two surfaces facing each other and exchanging heat radiation, the snow surface radiation at snow temperature and the source of the incoming radiation at temperature T_R. Net long-wave radiation is taken proportional to the difference between the temperatures of these two surfaces. This is the basis of a different formulation of some of the long-wave terms to that given by equations (38). When a snow cover is present, these formulations are replaced by the analytical solution outlined above.

497

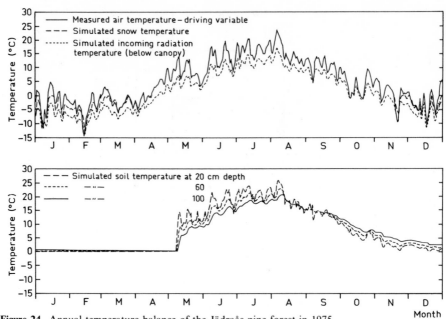

Figure 24. Annual temperature balance of the Jädraås pine forest in 1975.

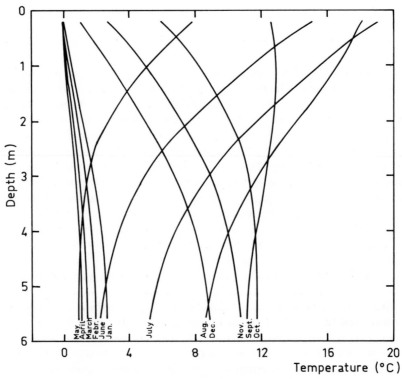

Figure 25. Simulated mean monthly soil temperatures during 1975.

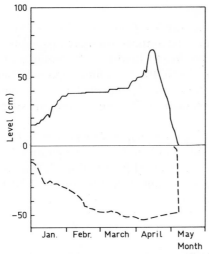

Figure 26. Simulated snow and frost depths in 1975.

The heat flows in the soil are given by a simple difference approximation of the heat-conduction equation (Eq. 20). The flows between the different soil layers are proportional to the temperature difference. Euler integration applied this way has a potential for numerical instability and this is a critical point in the model, setting an upper limit to the simulation time-step.

The model was tested with climatic data from 1975 (Figs. 22 and 24). Formulation of energy flux to the uppermost soil layer was not fully satisfactory, as could be seen from the too high soil temperatures (Fig. 25). The too rapid disappearance of the soil's frost layer in the spring was also connected with this problem (Fig. 26). This indicated that use should be made of a soil surface temperature higher than the mean temperature of the first layer to calculate energy flows to and from the soil. The attempt to get numerical stability of the snow temperature was successful and simulated snow depths (Fig. 26) compared favourably with field data.

Concluding remarks

This paper has given a brief theoretical treatment of some major abiotic processes in the coniferous forest ecosystem. Whereas much of the theoretical background to these processes is well known, the model syntheses and applications to a specific forest soil and canopy are new. Especially the treatment of winter conditions allows an understanding of processes on an annual scale which is seldom found in other integrated ecosystem research studies.

Acknowledgements

The abiotic research in the Swedish Coniferous Forest Project has primarily been carried out as a teamwork. The authors are therefore greatly indebted to the other members of the abiotic group. A. Lindroth, B. Norén and K. Perttu have been especially involved in the CANOPY modelling reported elsewhere (Halldin *et al.*, 1979a). The authors are also greatly indebted to T. Lohammar without whose simulation package (Lohammar, 1979) and continuous support this paper would never have been written.

The responsibilities in the present paper were primarily: H. Grip: Evapotranspiration formulas and snow; P-E. Jansson: Evapotranspiration formulas, frost and heat in soil and soil water; Å. Lindgren: ENERGY modelling. S. Halldin coordinated the work and took part in all sections except the one on ENERGY modelling.

References

Ågren, G. I. & Axelsson, B. 1980. PT – a tree growth model. – In: Persson, T. (ed.) Structure and Function of Northern Coniferous Forests – An Ecosystem Study, Ecol. Bull. (Stockholm) 32: 525–536.

Anderson, D. M. & Morgenstern, N. R. 1973. Physics, chemistry and mechanics of frozen ground. A review. – In: North American Contribution, Proc. 2nd Int. Conf. Permafrost, pp. 257–288. Washington D.C.: National Academy of Sciences.

Andersson, S. & Wiklert, P. 1972. Water-holding properties of Swedish soils. – Grundförbättring 2–3: 53–143. (In Swedish, English summary)

Ångström, A. 1936. Soil temperature in stands of different densities. – Medd. Statens Skogsforskn. Anst. 29(3): 187–218.

Axelsson, B. & Bråkenhielm, S. 1980. Investigation sites of the Swedish Coniferous Forest Project – biological and physiographical features. – In: Persson, T. (ed.) Structure and Function of Northern Coniferous Forests – An Ecosystem Study, Ecol. Bull. (Stockholm) 32: 25–64.

Bengtson, C. 1978. Effects and After-effects of Water Stress on Transpiration Rate. Ph. D. Dissertation. Dept. of Plant Physiology, University of Göteborg, 50 pp.

Bengtsson, L. 1976. Snow melt estimation from energy budget studies. – Nordic Hydrology 7: 3–18.

Bergen, I. D. 1975. A possible relation of albedo to the density and grain size of natural snow cover. – Water Resour. Res. 11: 745–746.

Beskow, G. 1932. Soil freezing and frost heaving with special application to roads and railroads. – Sveriges Geologiska Undersökning, serie C, No. 375, Årsbok 26(3), 242 pp. (In Swedish, transl. to English in 1947 by N. Western Tech. Inst., Evanston)

Bosatta, E., Bringmark, L. & Staaf, H. 1980. Nitrogen transformations in a Scots pine forest mor – model analysis of mineralization, uptake by roots and leaching. – In: Persson, T. (ed.) Structure and Function of Northern Coniferous Forests – An Ecosystem Study, Ecol. Bull. (Stockholm) 32: 565–589.

Boyer, J. S. 1969. Free-energy transfer in plants. – Science 163: 1219–1220.

Boyer, J. S. 1971. Resistances to water transport in soybean, bean and sunflower. – Crop Sci. 11: 403–407.

Briggs, L. J. & McCall, A. G. 1904. An artificial root for inducing capillary movement of soil moisture. – Science 20: 566–569.

Bringmark, L. 1980. Ion leaching through a podsol in a Scots pine stand. – In: Persson, T. (ed.) Structure and Function of Northern Coniferous Forests – An Ecosystem Study, Ecol. Bull. (Stockholm) 32: 341–361.

Brooks, R. H. & Corey, A. T. 1964. Hydraulic properties of porous media. – Hydrology Paper No. 3, Colorado State University, Fort Collins, Colorado, 27 pp.

Burdine, N. T. 1953. Relative permeability calculations from pore size distribution data. – Petroleum Trans. Am. Inst. Mining Metallurgical Eng. 198: 71–78.

Carslaw, H. S. & Jaeger, J. C. 1947. Conduction of Heat in Solids. London: Oxford University Press, 386 pp.

Childs, E. S. & Collis-George, N. 1950. The permeability of porous materials. – Proc. Roy. Soc. Lond. A 201: 392–405.

500

Colbeck, S. C. 1975. A theory for water flow through a layered snowpack. – Water Resour. Res. 11: 261–266.

Colbeck, S. C. 1976. An analysis of water flow in dry snow. – Water Resour. Res. 12: 523–527.

Cowan, I. R. 1965. Transport of water in the soil-plant-atmosphere system. – J. Appl. Ecol. 2: 221–239.

Czeratzki, W. 1971. Die Bedeutung des Bodenfrostes für den Ackerbau und speziell für die Bodenbearbeitung. – Landbauforschung Völkenrode 21(1): 1–12.

Denmead, O. T. & Shaw, R. H. 1962. Availability of soil water to plants as affected by soil mosture content and meteorological conditions. – Agr. J. 54: 385–390.

Farrel, D. A. & Larson, W. E. 1972. Modeling the pore structure of porous media. – Water Resour. Res. 8: 699–706.

Freeze, R. A. 1975. A stochastic-conceptual analysis of one-dimensional ground water flow in nonuniform heterogeneous media. – Water Resour. Res. 11: 725–741.

Fritton, D. D., Martsolf, J. D. & Busscher, W. I. 1976. Spatial distribution of soil heat flux under a Sour Cherry tree. – Soil Sci. Soc. Am. J. 40(5): 644–647.

Gardner, W. R. 1964. Relation of root distribution to water uptake and availability. – Agr. J. 56: 41–45.

Gardner, W. R. & Mayhugh, M. S. 1958. Solutions and tests of the diffusion equation for the movement of water in soil. – Soil Sci. Soc. Am. Proc. 22: 197–201.

Granger, R. J., Chanasyk, D. S., Male, D. H. & Norum, D. I. 1977. Thermal regime of a prairie snowcover. – Soil Sci. Soc. Am. J. 41: 839–842.

Green, R. E. & Corey, J. C. 1971. Calculation of hydraulic conductivity: A further evaluation of some predictive methods. – Soil Sci. Soc. Am. Proc. 35: 3–8.

Grip, H. 1973. A deterministic parametric water balance model. – Nordic Hydrology 4: 191–205.

Grip, H. 1978. Semiempirical formulas for estimating evapotranspiration – a preliminary review. – Swed. Conif. For. Proj. Int. Rep. 71, 18 pp. (In Swedish, English abstract)

Grip, H., Halldin, S., Jansson, P-E., Lindroth, A., Norén, B. & Perttu, K. 1979. Discrepancy between energy and water balance estimates of evapotranspiration. – In: Halldin, S. (ed.) Comparison of Forest Water and Energy Exchange Models, pp. 237–255. Copenhagen: International Society for Ecological Modelling.

Hadas, A. 1977. Evaluation of theoretically predicted thermal conductivities of soils under field and laboratory conditions. – Soil Sci. Soc. Am. J. 41: 460–466.

Halldin, S. 1977. Water uptake – but how? ROOT – a model for testing different uptake hypotheses. – Swed. Conif. For. Proj. Tech. Rep. 14, 53 pp.

Halldin, S., Grip, H., Jansson, P-E., Lindgren, Å. & Perttu, K. 1977. E1 – A model of the annual course of energy flows in a pine forest. – Swed. Conif. For Proj. Int. Rep. 53, 148 pp.

Halldin, S., Grip, H. & Perttu, K. 1979a. Model for energy exchange of a pine forest canopy. – In: Halldin, S. (ed.) Comparison of Forest Water and Energy Exchange Models, pp. 59–75. Copenhagen: International Society for Ecological Modelling.

Halldin, S., Jansson, P-E. & Lundkvist, H. 1979b. Ecological effects of longterm soil heat pump use. – Proc. Nordic Symp. Earth Heat Pump Systems, Suppl., pp. 14–23. Gothenburg: Chalmers University of Technology.

Haridasan, M. & Jensen, R. D. 1972. Effect of temperature on pressure head – water content relationship and conductivity of two soils. – Soil Sci. Soc. Am. Proc. 36: 703–708.

Hoekstra, P. 1966. Moisture movements in soils under temperature-gradients with the cold-side temperature below freezing. – Water Resour. Res. 2: 241–250.

Jackson, R. D., Kimball, B. A., Reginato, R. I., Idso, S. B. & Nakayama, F. S. 1975. Heat and water transfer in a natural soil environment. – In: de Vries, D. A. & Afgan, N. H. (eds.) Heat and Mass Transfer in the Biosphere. I. Transfer Processes in Plant Environment, pp. 67–78. Washington D.C.: Scripta Book Co.

Jacobsen, B. F. 1974. Water and phosphate transport to plant roots. – Acta Agric. Scand. 24: 55–60.

Jansson, P-E. & Halldin, S. 1979. Model for annual energy and water flow in a layered soil. – In: Halldin, S. (ed.) Comparison of Forest Water and Energy Exchange Models, pp. 145–163. Copenhagen: International Society for Ecological Modelling.

Jarvis, P. G. 1975. Water transfer in plants. – In: de Vries, D. A. & Afgan, N. H. (eds.) Heat and Mass Transfer in the Biosphere. I. Transfer Processes in Plant Environment, pp. 369–394. Washington D.C.: Scripta Book Co.

Kersten, M. S. 1949. Thermal properties of soils. – Inst. of Technology, Eng. Exp. Station, Bull. No. 28, 226 pp. Minneapolis: Univ. Minnesota.

Kniebe, G. & Koepf, H. 1970. Theoretischer Beitrag zur Tagesrythmik der Bodentemperaturen. – Z. Pflanzenernähr. Bodenk. 125(3): 211–217.

Koopmans, R. W. R. & Miller, R. D. 1966. Soil freezing and soil water characteristic curves. – Soil Sci. Soc. Am. Proc. 30: 680–685.

Kopanev, I. D. 1976a. Variations in the duration of stable snow cover in the USSR. – Soviet Hydrology 15(4): 270–275.

Kopanev, I. D. 1976b. Probability estimate of snow depth and distribution. – Soviet Hydrology 15(4): 281–287.

Kozeny, J. 1927. Über die Kapillare Leitung des Wassers im Boden (Aufstieg, Versickerung und Anwendung auf die Bewässerung). – Ber. Akad. Wiss. Wien 136: 271–306.

Kunze, R. J., Uehara, G. & Graham, K. 1968. Factors important in the calculation of hydraulic conductivity. – Soil Sci. Soc. Am. Proc. 32: 760–765.

Kuz'min, P. P. 1972. Melting of Snow Cover. Jerusalem: Israel Program for Scientific Translations Ltd., 290 pp.

Lambert, J. R. & Penning de Vries, F. W. T. 1973. Dynamics of water in the soil-plant-atmosphere system: A model named Troika. – In: Hadas, A., Swartzendruber, D., Rijtema, P. E., Fuchs, M. & Yaron, B. (eds.) Physical Aspects of Soil Water and Salts in Ecosystems, Ecological Studies 4, pp. 257–273. Berlin–Heidelberg–New York: Springer-Verlag.

Linder, S., Nordström, B., Parsby, J., Sundbom, E. & Troeng, E. 1980. Gas exchange system for field measurements of photosynthesis and transpiration in a 20-year-old stand of Scots pine. – Swed. Conif. For. Proj. Tech. Rep. 23, 34 pp.

Loch, J. P. G. & Miller, R. D. 1975. Tests of the concept of secondary frost heaving. – Soil Sci. Soc. Am. Proc. 39: 1036–1041.

Lohammar, T. 1979. SIMP – Interactive mini-computer package for simulating dynamic and static models. – In: Halldin, S. (ed.) Comparison of Forest Water and Energy Exchange Models, pp. 35–43. Copenhagen: International Society for Ecological Modelling.

Lohammar, T., Larsson, S., Linder, S. & Falk, S. O. 1980. FAST – simulation models of gaseous exchange in Scots pine. – In: Persson, T. (ed.) Structure and Function of Northern Coniferous Forests – An Ecosystem Study, Ecol. Bull. (Stockholm) 32: 505–523.

Marshall, R. J. 1958. A relation between permeability and size distribution of pores. – J. Soil Sci. 9: 1–8.

Miles, J. W. 1964. Diffusion into a slender growing root. – Proc. Roy. Soc. Lond. A 284: 137–145.

Miller, D. H. 1966. Transport of intercepted snow from trees during snow storms. – U.S. Forest Service Research Paper PSW-33, Pacific Southwest Forest and Range Exp. Station, Berkley, California, 30 pp.

Miller, R. D., Loch, J. P. G. & Bresler, E. 1975. Transport of water and heat in a frozen permeameter. – Soil Sci. Soc. Am. Proc. 39: 1029–1036.

Millington, R. J. & Quirk, J. P. 1961. Permeability of porous solids. – Trans. Faraday Soc. 57: 1200–1206.

Monteith, J. L. 1965. Evaporation and environment. – In: Fogg, G. E. (ed.) The State and Movement of Water in Living Organisms, 19th Symp. Soc. Exp. Biol., pp. 205–234. Cambridge: The Company of Biologists.

Mualem, Y. 1976. A new model for predicting the hydraulic conductivity of unsaturated porous media. – Water Resour. Res. 12: 513–522.

al-Nakshabandi, G. & Kohnke, H. 1965. Thermal conductivity and diffusivity of soils as related to moisture tension and other physical properties. – Agric. Meteor. 2: 271–279.

Newman, E. I. 1969a. Resistance to water flow in soil and plant. I. Soil resistance in relation to amounts of root: Theoretical estimates. – J. Appl. Ecol. 6: 1–12.

Newman, E. I. 1969b. Resistance to water flow in soil and plant. II. A review of the experimental evidence of the rhizosphere resistance. – J. Appl. Ecol. 6: 261–272.

Nielsen, D. R., Biggar, J. W. & Ehr, K. T. 1973. Spatial variability of field-measured soil-water properties. – Hilgardia 42: 215–259.

Nord, M. & Taesler, R. 1973. Density and weight of snow cover in Sweden. – National Swedish Building Research Summaries R21, 124 pp. (In Swedish, English summary)

Passioura, J. B. 1963. A mathematical model for the uptake of ions from the soil solution. – Plant & Soil 18: 225–238.

Penman, H. L. 1948. Natural evaporation from open water, bare soil and grass. – Proc. R. Soc. Ser. A 193: 120–145.

Penman, H. L. & Long, I. F. 1960. Weather in wheat: an essay in micrometeorology. – Quart. J. R. Met. Soc. 86: 1650.

Penner, E. 1970. Thermal conductivity of frozen soils. – Can. J. Earth Sci. 7: 982–987.

502

Perttu, K., Bishof, W., Grip, H., Jansson, P-E., Lindgren, Å., Lindroth, A. & Norén, B. 1980. Micrometeorology and hydrology of pine forest ecosystems. I. Field studies. – In: Persson, T. (ed.) Structure and Function of Northern Coniferous Forests – An Ecosystem Study, Ecol. Bull. (Stockholm) 32: 75–121.

Petzold, D. E. 1977. An estimation technique for snow surface albedo. – Climatol. Bull., McGill Univ., Montreal, Canada, Dept. of Geography 21: 1–11.

Philip, J. R. 1957. The physical principles of soil water movement during the irrigation cycle. – Int. Comm. Drain. Irr., 3rd Congr. 8: 125–154.

Philip, J. R. 1964. Sources and transfer processes in the air layers occupied by vegetation. – J. Appl. Meteor. 3: 390–395.

Philip, J. R. 1966. Plant water relations: Some physical aspects. – Ann. Rev. Plant Physiol. 17: 245–268.

Philip, J. R. & de Vries, D. A. 1957. Moisture movements in porous materials under temperature gradients. – Trans. Am. Geophys. Union 38: 222–238, 594.

de Quervain, M. R. 1973. Snow structure, heat, and mass flux through snow. – In: The Role of Snow and Ice in Hydrology, Proc. Banff Symp. Sept. 1972, Vol. 1, pp. 203–226. Geneva–Budapest–Paris: UNESCO–WMO–IAHS.

Rachner, M. & Grasnick, H-J. 1975. Ein Versuch zur Berücksichtigung des Speichervermöges der Schneedecke für freies Wasser bei der Modellierung des Schmelzprocesses des Schneedecke. – Z. Meteorol., Berl. 25: 286–291.

Rose, C. W., Byrne, G. P. & Hansen, G. K. 1976. Water transport from soil through plant to atmosphere: A lumped-parameter model. – Agric. Met. 16: 171–184.

Rutter, A. J., Kershaw, K. A., Robins, P. C. & Morton, A. J. 1971–72. A predictive model of rainfall interception in forests. I. Derivation of the model from observations in a plantation of Corsican pine. – Agric. Met. 9: 367–384.

Schmidt Jr., R. A. 1972. Sublimation of wind-transported snow – A model. – USDA Forest Service Research Paper RM-90, 24 pp.

Sharringa, M. 1976. On the representativeness of soil temperature measurements. – Agric. Meteor. 16: 263–276.

Snow Hydrology 1956. Summary report of the snow investigations. Portland, Oregon: North Pacific Division, Corps of Engineers, U.S. Army, 437 pp.

Solomon, R. M., Ffolliott, P. F., Baker Jr., M. B. & Thompson, J. R. 1976. Computer simulation of snowmelt. – USDA Forest Service Research Paper RM-174, 8 pp.

Stanhill, G. 1973. Evaporation, transpiration and evapotranspiration: A case for Ockham's razor. – In: Hadas, A., Swartzendruber, D., Rijtema, P. E., Fuchs, M. & Yaron, B. (eds.) Physical Aspects of Soil Water and Salts in Ecosystems, Ecological Studies 4, pp. 207–220. Berlin–Heidelberg–New York: Springer Verlag.

Tabler, R. D. 1975. Estimating the transport and evaporation of blowing snow. – In: Snow Managem. on Great Plains Symp. Proc. Great Plains Agric. Counc. Publ. 73: 85–104.

Taylor, S. A. & Cary, J. W. 1964. Linear equations for the simultaneous flow of water and energy in a continuous soil system. – Soil Sci. Soc. Am. Proc. 28: 167–172.

Veihmeyer, F. J. 1972. The availability of soil moisture to plants: Results of empirical experiments with fruit trees. – Soil Sci. 114: 268–294.

de Vries, D. A. 1963. Thermal properties of soils. – In: van Wijk, W. R. (ed.) Physics of plant environment, pp. 210–235. Amsterdam: North-Holland Publishing Co.

de Vries, D. A. 1963. Thermal properties of soils. – In: van Wijk, W. R. (ed.) Physics of Plant Environment, Transfer in the Biosphere. I. Transfer Processes in Plant Environment, pp. 5–28. Washington D. C.: Scripta Book Co.

Wadleigh, C. H. 1946. The integrated soil moisture stress upon a root system in a large container of saline soil. – Soil Sci. 61: 225–238.

Wierenga, P. J., Nielsen, D. R. & Hagan, R. M. 1969. Thermal properties of a soil based upon field and laboratory measurements. – Soil Sci. Soc. Am. Proc. 33: 354–360.

Wierenga, P. J. & de Wit, C. T. 1970. Simulation of heat transfer in soils. – Soil Sci. Soc. Am. Proc. 34: 845–848.

de Wit, C. T. 1958. Transpiration and crop yields. – Versl. Landbouwk. Onderz. 646, 88 pp.

Zahner, R. 1967. Refinement in empirical functions for realistic soil-moisture regimes under forest cover. – In: Sopper, W. E. & Lull, H. W. (eds.) Forest Hydrology, pp. 261–274. Oxford: Pergamon Press.

503

Persson, T. (ed) 1980
Structure and Function of Northern
Coniferous Forests – An Ecosystem Study
Ecol. Bull. (Stockholm) 32: 505–523.

FAST – SIMULATION MODELS OF GASEOUS EXCHANGE IN SCOTS PINE

T. Lohammar[1], S. Larsson[1], S. Linder[1] and S. O. Falk[2]

Abstract

A simulation model for the carbon dioxide and water exchange of Scots pine has been developed. The carbon dioxide exchange pertains only to the foliage. Two model versions are described: one complex model called FAST-P (physiological) and one simplified model, called FAST-S (simple), which is derived from FAST-P. FAST-P has a high resolution in both time and structure, whereas FAST-S has a lower resolution, appropriate to growth models. FAST-S uses daily mean values for driving variables, and provides analytical expressions for the daily carbon dioxide and water exchange. A short description of structures and functions of the two FAST models is given, together with comparisons between simulations and measured field data, as well as comparisons between the models. The main outputs from the FAST models are the amounts of carbon fixed and water transpired.

Additional keywords: Mesophyll conductance, photosynthesis, stomatal conductance, transpiration.

Introduction

The gas exchange of Scots pine is subjected to a large seasonal variation attributable both to a large annual variation in climatic factors, and to a seasonal variation in biological processes, which are adapted to the "normal" climatic pattern of the specific site. Since the aim of the FAST modelling is to provide a good biological background for the modelling of growth, and not to provide a detailed description of photosynthesis as such, the concept of gross photosynthesis has been excluded. The model presented here is, thus, a semi-empirical attempt to describe net photosynthesis without consideration of the respiratory component in light, which in practice is very hard to study under field conditions.

FAST-P is a model of within-day resolution. The model has a time step of 5 minutes, which means that state variables having a short time constant (less than 10 minutes) are eliminated and calculated algebraically.

However, existing growth models have a low resolution in both time and structure. Thus, to provide a submodel for both photosynthesis and transpiration in growth models, a second model, FAST-S, was derived from FAST-P equations. The

[1] Dept. of Ecology and Environmental Research, Swedish University of Agricultural Sciences, S-750 07 Uppsala, Sweden
[2] Dept. of Plant Physiology, University of Göteborg, Carl Skottsbergs Gata 22, S-413 19 Göteborg, Sweden

FAST-S model provides a set of instantaneous equations from which time integrals of both net photosynthesis and transpiration may be calculated analytically, appropriate to growth models (Fig. 1).

FAST-S includes some of the most important variables from FAST-P. The simplifications have been made in a stepwise manner so that it is possible to assess the effects of each simplification. In order to achieve analytical solutions to FAST-S, the driving variables have to be approximated either by constants or by sine forms for each day.

At present, a number of important mechanisms have been omitted from the model and its use should therefore be restricted to situations where these simplifications have a minor influence on the model outputs. Examples of such "ignored" mechanisms are hardening, temperature adaptive changes, after-effects of water- and temperature stress, feed-back from assimilates on the rate of net photosynthesis and seasonal changes in photosynthetic efficiency or mesophyll conductance. Some of these mechanisms will be included in the next generation of FAST models.

Abbreviations and symbols

Abbreviations with ′ represent concentrations of CO_2 or resistances and conductances for CO_2 transfer

c_a	Concentration of water vapour in ambient air
c_i	Concentration of water vapour in intercellulars
c_i'	Concentration of CO_2 in intercellulars
c_0'	Concentration of CO_2 at the carboxylation site
E	Transpiration
I	Irradiance (300–3000 nm)
$I_{1/2}$	Half light saturation point for g_m'
I_0	Light compensation point for g_m'
g	Conductance $= 1/$resistance, subscripts denoting location
g_a	Boundary layer diffusion conductance
g_c	Cuticular conductance
g_g	Total gas phase diffusion conductance (from intercellular to ambient air)
g_l	Leaf conductance $= g_s + g_c$
g_m'	Mesophyll conductance ("residual conductance")
g_r	Root conductance for water uptake
g_s	Stomatal conductance
g_x	Xylem conductance for water transport
p_{index}	Parameter (i.e., constant in the context at hand)
PN	Net photosynthesis
r	Resistance $= 1/$conductance, subscripts denoting location
R	Dark respiration (of foliage)
RH	Relative air humidity
RWC	Relative water content
TA	Air temperature
TN	Needle temperature
TS	Soil temperature
VCD	Water vapour concentration deficit in air
WS	Wind speed
α	Maximum value of g_m'
Ψ_n	Needle water potential
Ψ_r	Water potential in roots, stem and branches
Ψ_s	Soil water potential (at root surface)

506

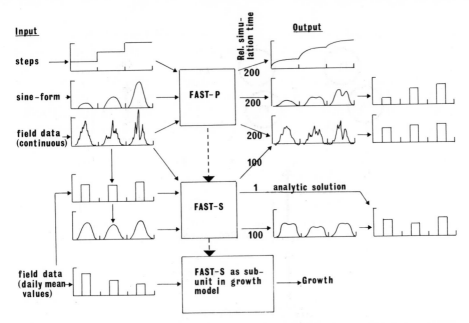

Figure 1. Strategy of the FAST modelling. First a physiological model called FAST-P was developed, from which a simplified model called FAST-S was derived. Both these models can be driven by within-day resolution field data, but FAST-S was developed primarily for use with daily mean values of climatic variables. The assumption is made here that some of these variables approximate a diurnal cut sine-form, enabling FAST-S to be solved for daily outputs in terms of daily mean values of climatic data. This renders FAST-S suitable as a submodel in a growth model.

FAST-P model

The program of the FAST-P model is listed in Lohammar *et al.* (1979). The only state variables in the model are compartments for water in different parts of the tree (Fig. 2). Water in branches, stem and roots is considered as one compartment (state variable). Each of the four age-classes of needles has its own compartment of water. All other variables are calculated algebraically from driving variables, parameters and state variables. The model structure is the same for each of the four needle age-classes. The only differences between the age-classes are photosynthetic efficiency and biomass, which are given as parameters.

There are six driving variables in the model: air temperature, TA; soil temperature, TS; short wave radiation (300–3000 nm), I; relative air humidity, RH; wind speed, WS; and soil water potential, Ψ_s; CO_2 concentration in ambient air is set constant.

Three different types of input have been used (Fig. 1):

(1) a step input, used to calculate steady state values of different output variables,
(2) a sine formed input, used as a "standardized" daily climate,
(3) an input of measured climatic variables.

Water status and transport in the tree

The various resistances to water conduction within and outside the tree (Fig. 3) and the water flow through the xylem ducts effects a water potential, Ψ, gradient from

507

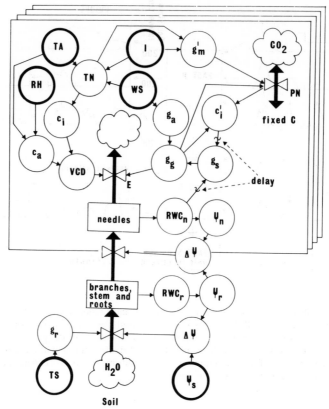

Figure 2. Model structure of FAST-P. State variables are represented by boxes and material flows by thick arrows. Thin arrows are informational flows and thin circles represent intermediate variables. Driving variables are represented by thick circles. The frame encloses one age-class of needles and is repeated for four age-classes.

the needles to the roots. Ψ becomes increasingly negative with "down-stream" transfer in the conduction pathway.

Very few data are available on xylem resistances, r_x, in trees. By way of avoiding an additional complexity to the model structure, all needles are allocated the same needle water potential, Ψ_n. To achieve this, different resistances are calculated between the single compartment for water in the xylem and the different needle age-class compartments. These resistances are chosen such that they are inversely proportional to the needle surface area and hence to the transpiration loss of the different age-classes.

To derive water potential, Ψ, values in the model from the actual water content in the different compartments, a relationship between Ψ and relative water content, RWC, is used (see Parameters below):

$$\Psi = RWC - 100 \tag{1}$$

$$RWC = \frac{\text{Actual water content}}{\text{Saturated water content}} \times 100 \tag{2}$$

508

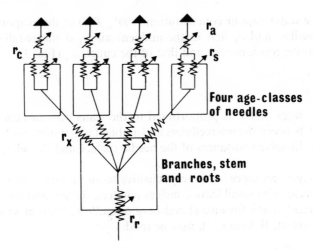

Figure 3. The various resistances to water conduction in FAST-P. Resistances with arrows are variable. The different compartments in the model are represented by squares.

The actual water contents are state variables and the saturated water contents are calculated from structural parameters.

Water uptake

The driving force for the conduction of water across the root surface is the difference in Ψ:

$$\text{Water uptake} = \frac{\Psi_s - \Psi_r}{r_r} \tag{3}$$

The soil water potential, Ψ_s, is given at the root surface (not in bulk soil), and Ψ_r is the water potential in the compartment for roots, stem and branches. The root resistance, r_r, is dependent on soil temperature, TS:

$$r_r = \frac{1}{g_{r_{max}}} \cdot f(TS) \tag{4}$$

where $g_{r_{max}}$ is the maximum root permeability and $f(TS)$ the relative effect of TS on root permeability (Fig. 5) (see also Parameters below).

Transpiration

Transpiration, E, depends upon the same external factors as the process of evaporation. E rises with increased I and the associated warming of the needles, and it also is dependent on RH and WS. When the air is in motion the boundary layer resistance, r_a, is lowered. However, E, is usually controlled mainly by the leaf resistance, r_l:

$$E = \frac{c_i - c_a}{r_l + r_a} = \frac{VCD}{r_l + r_a} \tag{5}$$

where c_i is the water vapour concentration (100% RH) at the evaporating surfaces within the needles, and c_a that in the ambient air. r_1 is the parallel coupling of stomatal diffusive resistance, r_s, and that of the cuticle, r_c (Fig. 3):

$$r_1 = \frac{r_s \cdot r_c}{r_s + r_c} \qquad (6)$$

Equation (5) states that E is proportional to the water vapour concentration difference, VCD, between the intercellulars and ambient air, and inversely proportional to the sum of diffusive resistances of the needle surface and the adjacent boundary layer.

Boundary layer resistance, r_a, is very sensitive to air motion, size and form of the leaves. For species with small leaves, such as conifers, the size and form of the leaves are less important, and a formula (Landsberg & Ludlow, 1970) in which r_a depends only on wind speed, WS (m s^{-1}), may be used:

$$r_a = p_{47} + \frac{p_{48}}{\sqrt{WS}} \qquad (7)$$

The r_s changes with internal factors in the needle, such as water stress and CO_2 concentration in the intercellulars (Raschke, 1975). The internal factors control the stomatal conductance, g_s, by regulating the stomatal pore width. Water stress in the needles tends to close the stomata. A high CO_2 concentration in the intercellulars also tends to close the stomata, and a low concentration tends to open them. During high levels of irradiance and correspondingly high photosynthetic activity, the CO_2 control system initially counteracts the tendency of closure due to water stress. If water balance is severely impaired, the water stress control system predominates over the effect of a low CO_2 concentration, and the stomata will close.

Taking into account the above interactions, a response surface has been constructed for the g_s, as a function of RWC in the needles and CO_2 concentration in the intercellulars, c_i' (Fig. 4). In order to account for the inertia in stomatal movement, both RWC and c_i' are filtered through a first order delay before they affect stomatal conductance.

Photosynthesis

Net photosynthesis, PN, is calculated in a manner similar to that used in calculating E, but with an additional resistance to CO_2 transfer in the pathway between the intercellulars and the carboxylation sites (Rabinowitch, 1951). This so-called mesophyll resistance, r_m', may be conceived as a series of resistances comprising a large number of rate limiting processes. Due to problems in separating the processes of gross photosynthesis and respiration, all needle respiration is neglected in the definition of r_m', i.e., $r_m' = (c_i' - c_0')/PN$. Thus:

$$PN = \frac{c_a' - c_0'}{r_g' + r_m'} \qquad (8)$$

where c_a' and c_0' are the CO_2 concentrations in ambient air and at the carboxylation sites, respectively. The total gas phase resistance to CO_2 transfer, r_g', is given by:

$$r_g' = r_a' + r_1' = 1.6 \cdot (r_a + r_1) \qquad (9)$$

510

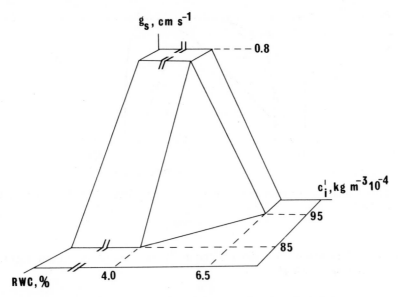

g_s, cm s^{-1}

0.8

c_i', kg m^{-3}10^{-4}

95

85

4.0   6.5

RWC, %

Figure 4. Response surface for stomatal conductance, g_s, as a function of relative water content, RWC, and CO_2 concentration in the intercellulars, c_i' (see Jarvis, 1976 and Running, 1976).

where r_a' and r_1' are boundary layer and leaf resistance to CO_2 transfer and the factor 1.6 is the ratio of the diffusion coefficients for water vapour and CO_2 in air. In the model the CO_2 concentration in ambient air, c_a', is assumed constant, and the CO_2 concentration at the carboxylation sites, c_0', is set to zero. Then, rewriting Eq. (8) in terms of conductance:

$$PN = \frac{c_a' \cdot g_g' \cdot g_m'}{g_g' + g_m'} \tag{10}$$

where g_g' and g_m' are total gas phase and mesophyll conductances, respectively. The mesophyll conductance, g_m', is light and temperature dependent:

$$g_m' = \alpha \cdot \frac{I - I_0}{I + I_{1/2}} \cdot f(TN) \tag{11}$$

where, α is the maximum value of g_m' (α decreases with increasing needle age), I is the irradiance, I_0 is the light compensation point, $I_{1/2}$ is the irradiance at which g_m' is approximately equal to $\alpha/2$ and $f(TN)$ denotes the needle temperature dependence of g_m', shown in Fig. 5.

Since the definition of g_m' is based on PN, g_m' has a negative value if I is below the compensation point, I_0 (as during dark periods). Then, the calculation of CO_2 exchange from Eqs. (10) and (11) may be problematic. If g_g' assumes a small value of the same magnitude as g_m', than PN as calculated from Eq. (10) assumes very large (positive or negative) values. This would be the case during dark periods, when the needles are water-stressed. Therefore, a different description of PN is used at I below the I_0:

$$PN = R \cdot (I - I_0)/I_0 \tag{12}$$

511

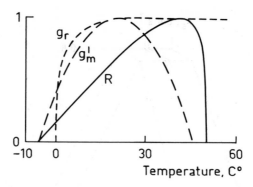

Figure 5. Relative influence of temperature on mesophyll conductance, g'_m, dark respiration, R, and root permeability, g_r.

where R is the dark respiration, determined as the product of maximum respiratory rate and a function of TN (Fig. 5).

Needle temperature

Needle temperature, TN, is derived from the heat budget of a hypothetical leaf, whose surface area tends to infinity. Then:

$$\frac{dH}{dt} = a \cdot I + b \cdot [(273 + TA)^4 - (273 + TN)^4] + \frac{c}{r_a} \cdot (TA - TN) - e \cdot E \qquad (13)$$

$$\underset{\text{wave)}}{\text{(short-}} \quad \underset{}{\text{(net long-wave radiation)}} \qquad \underset{\text{tion)}}{\text{(convec-}} \quad \underset{\text{heat)}}{\text{(latent}}$$

where:

H = sensible heat per unit leaf area,
a = absorption coefficient for short wave radiation,
b = Stephan–Boltzmann's constant,
c = heat convection constant, and
e = heat of evaporation of water.

The long-wave radiation term may be linearized in TN, i.e.:

$$b \cdot [(273 + TA)^4 - (273 + TN)^4] \approx 4b \cdot (273 + TA)^3 \cdot (TA - TN) \qquad (14)$$

Thus:

$$\frac{dH}{dt} = \frac{dTN}{dt} \cdot \text{const} \approx \left[4b \cdot (273 + TA)^3 + \frac{c}{r_a} \right] \cdot (TA - TN) + a \cdot I - e \cdot E \qquad (15)$$

$$\frac{dTN}{dt} = -TN/\tau + TA/\tau + (a \cdot I - e \cdot E)/\text{const} \qquad (16)$$

From this differential equation the time constant, τ, of response of TN to a step change in TA or I may be calculated. Typically, τ, is in the order of one minute. Thus, the dynamics of TN may be ignored and TN may be calculated algebraically from $dTN/dt = 0$, i.e.:

512

$$TN = TA + \frac{a \cdot I - e \cdot E}{4b \cdot (273 + TA)^3 + c/r_a} \qquad (17)$$

Since transpiration, E, depends non-linearly on TN, Eqs. (5) and (17) must be solved for both TN and E. To date, this has been done by an iteration technique, although a better way to obtain this solution would be to linearize E in TN (in Eq. (5)).

Driving variables

With the above model structure and functions, numerical values for a large number of inputs are required. These comprise driving variables (the physical environment of the tree) that may exhibit a substantial diurnal variation, and parameters (mostly plant characteristics) that are considered constant for each day or several days, but which probably vary slowly during the year.

FAST-P uses six driving variables. Four of these define the above-ground environment of the tree: TA, RH, I, and WS. Two driving variables define the below-ground environment: TS, and Ψ_s.

A homogeneity for each of the above-ground driving variables (except I), may be assumed for a young, open stand. Thus values measured above the stand are used (Perttu et al., 1977). Incident short-wave radiation is attenuated considerably (Troeng & Linder, 1978) but, for validation purposes, the values of light intensity measured at the cuvette from which the gas exchange data are obtained, are applied to all parts of the tree (i.e., all needle ages). In order to simulate the gas exchange of the whole crown using the "above-crown" short-wave radiation intensity, a model for radiation interception would also be required.

The soil water potential is equated with that of the root surface, thus neglecting any "rhizosphere resistance". There is evidence (E. Mattson-Djos, unpubl.) that for the site at Jädraås total resistance to water flow from bulk soil to the needles decreases with increasing E. This is contrary to what would be expected if there were any appreciable rhizospere resistance caused by soil water depletion at the root surface. Thus, in this instance, the equating of Ψ_s with that of the root surface is probably valid.

Parameters

All parameter values are listed in Appendix A.

The present model simulates PN and E over short time spans (days), such that growth and mortality processes may be ignored. Thus the biomass structure of the tree is specified on a parameter basis.

The parameters which specify the properties of the various biomass components comprise both resistance and capacitance. Resistance parameters affect steady state values for flow and state variables, and in conjunction with capacitance parameters, affect the dynamics of steady state attainment. Capacitance parameters do not affect steady state values. Since all time constants in the model are much less than one day, the effect, for example, of a morning value on any night value of a state variable, is negligible.

Values for resistance parameters have been estimated from field data pertaining to a 20-year-old Scots pine stand at Jädraås. In this data analysis, steady state conditions have been assumed. Parameters determining PN, g'_m and R were estimated from CO_2 data measured with chamber techniques (cf. Linder & Troeng, 1980) pertaining to the first half of July 1977. The estimated temperature responses (cf. Fig. 5) are rather uncertain for temperatures outside the field temperature range.

Parameters in the formulation of g_s (Fig. 4) were estimated from porometer measurements (June–August 1976) (E. Mattson-Djos, unpubl.) and from chamber measurements of E (July 1977) (S. Linder & E. Troeng, unpubl.). The five parameters of the response surface (Fig. 4) were estimated largely by trial and error, since simultaneous estimation tends to give variable and sometimes unrealistic values.

The relationship between Ψ_n and RWC was estimated at Jädraås 1977 (S. Larsson, unpubl.). Maximum root permeability was taken from Andersson et al., 1974. Total r_x to water flow from roots to needles was chosen such that the sum of r_x and minimum r_r equaled the resistance value derived from simultaneous measurements of g_s and Ψ_n, at high E rates (E. Mattson-Djos, unpubl.)

It must be noted that some of the parameters for g'_m and g_s are probably invalid outside the time period from late June to August.

Simulation with FAST-P

Measured and simulated PN and E of a one-year-old shoot are shown in Fig. 6 for the three days 17–19 July 1977. This period provided variable light conditions and chamber measurement series (sampled at 45 minute intervals).

The measurements of PN are not corrected for the feed-back effect of shoot modification of the CO_2 environment in the chamber, as this effect is very small in the measurement system used. Because of the design and functioning of the measurement system, the chamber E data have to be corrected for the sometimes large difference between RH within the chamber and that of ambient air (Linder & Troeng, 1980). The value of g_s is considered to be the same for both enclosed and unenclosed shoots. 'Measured' E is thus calculated as the product of g_s (as calculated from chamber E) and the VCD of the ambient air (cf. Linder & Troeng, 1978).

The r^2 values for linear regression of simulated values on measured values were 0.94 for PN and 0.90 for E (for the period 12–31 July 1977). These values do not reflect very well the fact that PN is much better simulated than E (Fig. 6). This difference is better conveyed by the index 1 – (mean of squared residual)/(variance of data), which gives the values 0.94 and 0.80 for PN and E, respectively.

Two circumstances (besides inadequacies of the model) may explain the rather large differences between measured and simulated E. In the calculation of measured E, TN is assumed to equal TA. Also, there is a substantial variation in g_s (but not in PN) between comparable shoots of different tree individuals (Linder & Troeng, 1978).

FAST-S model

One of the primary aims of the FAST-S model is to furnish growth models with a means of obtaining daily integrals or averages of PN, E, and Ψ, of a tree, such that

514

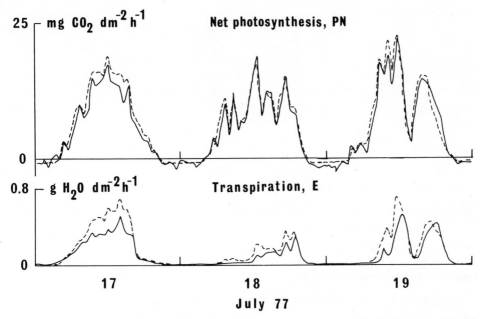

Figure 6. Net photosynthesis, *PN*, and transpiration rate, *E*, of a one-year-old shoot, measured (solid line) and simulated (broken line) by FAST-P.

they may be calculated from not too complicated analytical expressions, provided a set of biotic parameters and climatic (driving) variables.

In the main, two properties of the above described FAST-P model prevent its analytical integration with time for that purpose:

(1) The flow description for E is non-linear with respect to the state variables on which it depends. This renders the system of differential equations non-linear, and hence (analytically) insoluble.
(2) Also if all the differential equations were linear with respect to the state variables, serious problems would arise because most of the driving variables enter the flow expressions non-linearly.

There exist two alternatives for deriving the appropriate time integrals:

(1) Numerical solution (integration) of the FAST-P model using a computer.
(2) Analytical solution, by introducing a number of simplifying assumptions to the FAST-P model. Analytical solution here means firstly, solution for (analytical) expressions for (instantaneous values of) PN and E, and secondly, the (analytical) integration over a day of these flow expressions.

This latter approach is followed here.

For analytical solution of the model, two kinds of approximation are necessary. Firstly the model structure has to be simplified. Secondly, to allow analytical integration over time of the simplified model, the driving variables must also be approximated by some simple mathematical function, e.g., a sine-form.

515

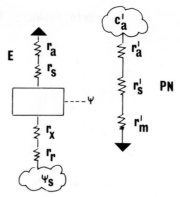

Figure 7. The various resistances to water (left) and CO_2 (right) transfer within and outside the tree (cf. Fig. 3).

Simplification of model structure

Simplification of the FAST-P model may be categorized as:

(1) Steady state approximation, i.e., all state variables are assumed to respond instantaneously to any change in driving variables. This reduces the problem of finding the instantaneous value of any model variable to that of solving a system of algebraic equations.

(2) Simplification of process descriptions, most of which will lead to change in steady state values (as well as in the dynamics of state variable responses, if state variables are retained).

Combination of all the state variables for water (Fig. 3) into one compartment, leads to the diagram in Fig. 7 for water and CO_2 flows of the tree.

The responses of the model shown in Fig. 7 to driving variables may be described in terms of its component resistances and Ψ (Eqs. (3) and (5)):

$$\frac{dx}{dt} = \text{Uptake} - \text{Transpiration} = \frac{\Psi_s - \Psi}{r_r + r_x} - \frac{VCD}{r_g} \qquad (18)$$

With the steady state approximation ($dx/dt = 0$), E must always equal the uptake term. Then:

$$E = \frac{\Psi_s - \Psi}{r_r + r_x} = \frac{VCD}{r_g} \qquad (19)$$

$$PN = \frac{c_a'}{r_g' + r_m'} \qquad \text{(see Eq. 10)}$$

In order to solve Eq. (19) in terms of driving variables alone, relationships between the resistances and other variables are required. To this end, the following simplifications of the resistance descriptions were made, at first resulting in an oversimplified model: Cuticular conductance, g_c, and boundary layer resistance, r_a, (Eq. 7) are set to zero. The mesophyll conductance, g_m', (Eq. 11) is made light dependent only, and TN is approximated by TA. The stomatal conductance, g_s, is approximated to be

516

Table 1. Average values of $\int PN \, dt$ and $\int E \, dt$ for the eleven-day period 9–19 July 1977. The numbers to the left indicate the approximation steps. The change of value in relation to the former is given in percent.

Approximations	$\int PN \, dt$ (kg CO_2 m^{-2} day^{-1})		$\int E \, dt$ (kg H_2O m^{-2} day^{-1})	
FAST-P	0.0287		1.27	
1. g'_m (I only)	0.0313	$+ 9\%$	1.29	$+ 2\%$
2. $TN = TA$	0.0317	$+ 1\%$	1.17	$- 10\%$
3. g_s (Ψ only)	0.0326	$+ 3\%$	1.42	$+ 22\%$
4. g_s (Ψ) linear	0.0332	$+ 2\%$	1.50	$+ 2\%$
5. $r_a = 0$	0.0339	$+ 2\%$	1.61	$+ 7\%$
6. $I_0 = 0$	0.0375	$+ 10\%$	1.61	0%
7. Steady state	0.0372	$- 1\%$	1.56	$- 3\%$
8. Sine-formed climate	0.0390	$+ 5\%$	1.43	$- 9\%$

linearly related to Ψ, $g_s = a + b\Psi$. This approximation corresponds to the area in Fig. 4, where g_s depends only on RWC and not on the intercellular CO_2 level. This is equivalent to neglecting stomatal closure at low levels of irradiance.

Using the above approximation, Eq. (19) can be solved for Ψ, and thus for E and PN in terms of the driving variables, thus giving the required instantaneous flow expressions:

$$g_s = \frac{g_r(a + b \cdot \Psi_s)}{g_r + b \cdot VCD}, \text{ where } g_r = \frac{1}{r_r + r_x} \tag{20}$$

$$E = g_s \cdot VCD \tag{21}$$

$$PN = c'_a \cdot \frac{g'_s \cdot g'_m}{g'_s + g'_m} \tag{22}$$

Approximation of driving variables

In the model simplifications to date, it is possible to include "smooth diurnal variation" in only two of the driving variables. The remaining driving variables have to be represented by a constant for each day. The two driving variables whose normal diurnal variations have the strongest influence on PN and E are I and VCD. VCD is not listed as a driving variable of FAST-P, but is calculated from TA and RH. For these two variables a cut cosine function max $(0, d_1 + d_2\cos(t))$ is used, such that its mean diurnal value equals some specified mean value, and such that its value is greater than zero for a specified day length.

Test of the approximation steps

In order to determine which of the approximations contributed most to the differences in daily PN and E between the models, a number of test runs were made (Table 1). In these runs the model approximations were introduced one by one into FAST-P until the only difference between the models was the presence of state

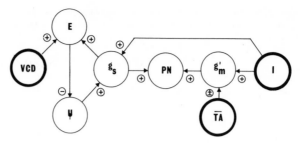

Figure 8. The structure of FAST-S. On a seasonal basis daily mean values of soil water potential and soil temperature are also driving variables.

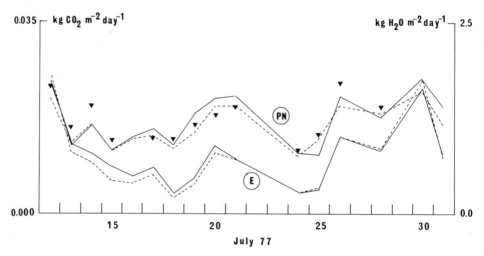

Figure 9. Daily photosynthesis, *PN*, and transpiration, *E*, in one-year-old shoots, simulated by FAST-S (———) and by FAST-P (– – – –). Estimates of daily *PN* from chamber measurements (▼).

variables for water in FAST-P. Driving variables were measured climatic data from 9–19 July 1977, a period during which a gradual change occurred from clear and dry to cloudy and wet conditions.

A comparison of the over-simplified model (run with sine-formed climate approximation) with the FAST-P model shows the former over-estimated both *PN* (36%) and *E* (13%) as calculated by FAST-P for the eleven-day period.

The two model simplifications contributing most to the difference in $\int PN \mathrm{d}t$ between the models are the omission of a temperature influence on g'_m, and the choice of light compensation point $I_0 = 0$. However, neither of these simplifications are strictly necessary in order to guarantee an analytical solution of FAST-S.

A further source of error in $\int PN \mathrm{d}t$ is the sine approximation of light and the nonlinear relationship between *PN* and light. This error should decrease if $I_{1/2}$ (Eq. 11) is given a higher and more realistic value than the low (125 W m^{-2}) value used in these simulations.

518

The model simplifications contributing most to the differences in $\int E dt$ between the models were the omission of stomatal closure at low light intensities, and of the temperature differences between needles and the ambient air. A simple light dependency in g_s had to be included in FAST-S, although it is not directly derivable from the more detailed formulations in FAST-P.

The effect of approximating VCD by cut sine form leads to a decrease in daily E, contrary to what would be expected if the VCD fluctuations around the sine form were purely random. Thus, in this approximation there is an error in the form that is difficult to eliminate.

Taking into account the factors that can be handled analytically, the over-simplified model was modified to give the present FAST-S model (Fig. 8).

(1) g_m' is made dependent on mean TA, according to Eq. (11). The use of mean TA in the function for instantaneous values gives too low values of g_m' (and PN) at low mean TA and too high g_m' at high TA. With this modification to g_m' FAST-S still overestimates PN by 6% when compared with FAST-P over the period 12–31 July 1977 (Fig. 9).

(2) g_s is made dependent on I by multiplying the maximum g_s-value by a reduction factor, so that:

$$g_s = \frac{a \cdot (I + I_{s0})/(I + I_{s1}) + b \cdot \Psi_s}{1 + \dfrac{b}{g_r} \cdot VCD} \tag{23}$$

where $I_{s0} = 5$ W m^{-2} and $I_{s1} = 75$ W m^{-2}. This reduces g_s at low light levels, so that the steady state response to light of g_s in FAST-P is approximated. With this modification to g_s, FAST-S overestimated E by 4% when compared with FAST-P.

Note, however, that this new g_s formulation may be used in the expression for E in Eq. (21), but not in the expression for PN (Eq. 22) for reasons explained in Appendix B. It may be noted from Table 1 that the simplification $g_s (\Psi)$ had a very small influence on daily PN.

From the data shown in Fig. 9, the r^2 values for the linear regression between FAST-S, FAST-P and field data are calculated (Fig. 10).

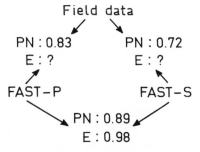

Figure 10. r^2 values for linear regression of the daily integrals of PN and E between FAST-P, FAST-S and field data.

Concluding remarks

The simplified FAST-S model appears to be useful as a submodel for simulating photosynthesis input in growth models over long-term periods. Although the FAST-S model itself is not very mechanistic, it is derived from a more mechanistic one, from which some of the most important parameters have been retained. The most advantageous use of the FAST-S model, however, would be in studying possible interactions between growth mechanisms and photosynthesis.

Acknowledgement

This description of the FAST models is a revised version of a recently published Technical Report in the SWECON project (Lohammar et al., 1979).

References

Andersson, L. Å., Falk, S. O. & Larsson, S. 1974. A simulation model for the water relations of pine seedlings (*Pinus silvestris*). – Swed. Conif. For. Proj. Int. Rep. 3, 34 pp. (In Swedish, English abstract)

Dwight, H. B. 1961. Tables of Integrals and Other Mathematical Data. New York: The MacMillan Comp.

Jarvis, P. G. 1976. The interpretation of the variations in leaf water potential and stomatal conductance found in canopies in the field. – Phil. Trans. R. Soc. Lond. B 273: 593–610.

Landsberg, J. J. & Ludlow, M. M. 1970. A technique for determining resistances to mass transfer through the boundary layer of plants with complex structure. – J. appl. Ecol. 7: 187–192.

Linder, S. & Troeng, E. 1978. Gas exchange in a 20-year-old stand of Scots pine. III. A comparison of net photosynthesis and transpiration of eight different pine trees. – Swed. Conif. For. Proj. Int. Rep. 82, 19 pp. (In Swedish, English abstract)

Linder, S. & Troeng, E. 1980. Photosynthesis and transpiration of 20-year-old Scots pine. – In: Persson, T. (ed.) Structure and Function of Northern Coniferous Forests – An Ecosystem Study, Ecol. Bull. (Stockholm) 32: 165–181.

Lohammar, T., Larsson, S., Linder, S. & Falk, S. O. 1979. FAST – A simulation model for the carbon dioxide and water exchange of Scots pine. – Swed. Conif. For. Proj. Tech. Rep. 19, 33 pp.

Perttu, K., Lindgren, A., Lindroth, A. & Norén, B. 1977. Micro- and biometeorological measurements at Jädraås. Instrumentation and measurement technics. – Swed. Conif. For. Proj. Tech. Rep. 7, 67 pp.

Rabinowitch, E. I. 1951. Photosynthesis and Related Processes, 2(1). New York: Interscience.

Raschke, K. 1975. Stomatal action. – Ann. Rev. Plant Physiol. 26: 309–340.

Running, S. W. 1976. Environmental control of leaf water conductance in conifers. – Can. J. For. Res. 6: 104–112.

Troeng, E. & Linder, S. 1978. Gas exchange in a 20-year-old stand of Scots pine. IV. Photosynthesis and transpiration within the crown of the tree. – Swed. Conif. For. Proj. Int. Rep. 83, 20 pp. (In Swedish, English abstract)

Appendix A

Parameters

*	Parameters retained in FAST-S		
g_c	Cuticular conductance of needles	(m min^{-1})	$5 \cdot 10^{-3}$
p_{02}	Time constant of delay state variables	(min)	25
* R_{max}	Max dark respiration of needles	(kg m^{-2} min^{-1})	$3 \cdot 10^{-6}$
p_{06}	Fine-root area per weight at saturation	(m^2 kg^{-1})	2.2
p_{07}	Slope of $\Psi(RWC)$-relation	(bar)	100
p_{09}	Ratio of diff. coeff. of CO_2 and H_2O vapour	$(-)$	0.623
* $g_{r_{max}}$	Max permeability to water uptake to roots	(kg min^{-1} bar^{-1} m^{-2})	$6.0 \cdot 10^{-4}$
* $I_{1/2}$	Irradiance at half max g_m' all needles	(W m^{-2})	225
* I_0	Light compensation point for g_m' all needles	(,,)	10
c_a'	CO_2 concentration in canopy air	(kg m^{-3})	$6.0 \cdot 10^{-4}$
p_{21}	Proj. area per dry weight of current needles	(m^2 kg^{-1})	3.2
p_{22}	,, C+1 ,,	(,,)	3.2
p_{23}	,, C+2 ,,	(,,)	3.2
p_{24}	,, C+3 ,,	(,,)	3.2
p_{29}	Dry weight of current needles	(kg)	0.35
p_{30}	,, C+1 ,,	(,,)	0.35
p_{31}	,, C+2 ,,	(,,)	0.18
p_{32}	,, C+3 ,,	(,,)	0.09
p_{33}	,, branches, stem and roots	(,,)	2.36
p_{36}	,, fine roots	(,,)	0.26
* p_{37}	Low Ψ break-point in $g_s(\Psi)$-relation	(bar)	-15
* p_{38}	High Ψ break-point in $g_s(\Psi)$-relation	(,,)	-5
p_{41}	Low CO_2 break-point in $g_s(CO_2)$-relation	(kg m^{-3})	$4.0 \cdot 10^{-4}$
p_{42}	High CO_2 break-point in $g_s(CO_2)$-relation	(,,)	$6.5 \cdot 10^{-4}$
* $g_{s_{max}}$	Max stomatal conductance	(m min^{-1})	0.48
p_{47}	Boundary layer resistance parameter, min.	(min m^{-1})	$6.5 \cdot 10^{-2}$
p_{48}	Boundary layer resistance parameter	$(-)$	0.21
p_{56}	Fraction water of saturated weight of current needles	(,,)	0.65
p_{57}	,, C+1 ,,	(,,)	0.50
p_{58}	,, C+2 ,,	(,,)	0.50
p_{59}	,, C+3 ,,	(,,)	0.50
p_{60}	,, branches, stem, roots	(,,)	0.53
p_{63}	,, fine roots	(,,)	0.80
* p_{65}	Max g_m' of current needles, α	(m min^{-1})	0.12
p_{66}	,, C+1 ,,	(,,)	0.12
p_{67}	,, C+2 ,,	(,,)	0.10
p_{68}	,, C+3 ,,	(,,)	0.06
* r_x	Total xylem resistance to water flow	(bar min kg^{-1})	400

Appendix B

Analytical expressions for daily PN and E

The equations for the instantaneous flow rates E and PN are taken from Eqs. (21) and (22):

$$E = g_s \cdot VCD$$

$$PN = c_a' \cdot \frac{g_s' \cdot g_m'}{g_s' + g_m'}$$

where:

521

$$g_s = \frac{a \cdot (I+I_{s0})/(I+I_{s1}) + b \cdot \Psi_s}{1 + \dfrac{b}{g_r} \cdot VCD} \qquad \text{from Eq. (23)}$$

$$g_s' = \frac{a + b \cdot \Psi_s}{1.6 \cdot \left(1 + \dfrac{b}{g_r} \cdot VCD\right)} \qquad \text{from Eq. (20)}$$

$$g_m' = \alpha \cdot \frac{I - I_0}{I + I_{1/2}} \cdot f(\overline{TA}) \qquad \text{from Eq. (11)}$$

Substitution into Eqs. (21) and (22) yields expressions in terms of only driving variables and parameters:

$$E = \frac{a \cdot (I+I_{s0}) + b \cdot \Psi_s \cdot (I+I_{s1})}{I + I_{s1}} \cdot \frac{VCD}{1 + \dfrac{b}{g_r} \cdot VCD} \qquad (B1)$$

$$PN = c_a' \cdot \frac{(a + b\Psi_s) \cdot (I - I_0) \cdot \alpha \cdot f(\overline{TA})}{(a + b\Psi_s) \cdot (I + I_{1/2}) + 1.6 \cdot (I - I_0) \cdot \alpha \cdot f(\overline{TA}) \cdot \left(1 + \dfrac{b}{g_r} VCD\right)} \qquad (B2)$$

Now, substituting $I = l_1 + l_2 \cos t$ and $VCD = d_1 + d_2 \cos t$ in Eqs. (B1) and (B2) will give expressions for PN and E having the form of quotients between polynomials in $\cos t$:

$$E = \frac{a' + b' \cos t + c' \cos^2 t}{d' + e' \cos t + f' \cos^2 t} \qquad (B3)$$

$$PN = \frac{a'' + b'' \cos t}{d'' + e'' \cos t + f'' \cos^2 t} \qquad (B4)$$

where, for each day, $a', a'', \ldots, f', f''$ are constant algebraic expressions, depending on the model parameters, "constant driving variables" $\overline{TA}$, $\overline{TS}$, Ψ_s and the constants l_1, l_2, d_1, d_2 that describe I and VCD each day.

Next, in order to enable integration over time, we perform partial fraction expansion:

$$E = \frac{c'}{f'} + \frac{h'}{\cos t - r_1'} + \frac{k'}{\cos t - r_2'} \qquad (B5)$$

$$PN = \frac{h''}{\cos t - r_1''} + \frac{k''}{\cos t - r_2''} \qquad (B6)$$

where $h', h'', k', k'', r_1', r_1'', r_2', r_2''$ are new constant expressions for each day.

We need to integrate these expressions only over the light part ($|t| < \arccos(-l_1/l_2)$) of the day ($|t| \leq \pi$). During night time VCD is assumed to vanish, making E zero, and PN is assumed to equal a constant dark respiration. When both Ψ_s and I are low enough, stomatal closure will occur, i.e., $g_s = 0$, thus inhibiting both E and positive PN for times $|t| > t_1$, $t_1 = \min [t_c, \arccos(-l_1/l_2)]$, where t_c is determined from $g_s = 0$. The time integrals of PN and E over the light part of the day may now be written as:

$$\int_{-t_1}^{t_1} E \, dt = 2 \frac{c'}{f'} t_1 + 2 \int_0^{t_1} \frac{h'}{\cos t - r_1'} \, dt + 2 \int_0^{t_1} \frac{k'}{\cos t - r_2'} \, dt \qquad (B7)$$

$$\int_{-t_1}^{t_1} PN \, dt = 2 \int_0^{t_1} \frac{h''}{\cos t - r_1''} \, dt + 2 \int_0^{t_1} \frac{k''}{\cos t - r_2''} \, dt \qquad (B8)$$

If the flows E and PN are expressed per minute, we will also have to multiply the integrals by $1440/2\pi$. It is possible to evaluate the above integrals according to the formula (Dwight, 1961):

$$\int_0^{t_1} \frac{dt}{p + q \cos t} = \frac{2}{\sqrt{p^2 - q^2}} \operatorname{arctg}\left(\frac{p - q}{\sqrt{p^2 - q^2}} \operatorname{tg} \frac{t_1}{2}\right) \qquad (B9)$$

However, when p becomes complex-valued and when $p^2 < q^2$ it is necessary to use the relationship:

$$\operatorname{arctg} z = \frac{1}{2i} \ln\left(\frac{i - z}{i + z}\right) \qquad (B10)$$

Although the resulting integrals $\int PN \, dt$ and $\int E \, dt$ are real-valued, some calculations are advantageously

522

carried out using complex variables. Only two of the driving variables have been approximated by the cut cosine-form. However, dependence on other diurnally varying driving variables may be included, if the new variables do not produce higher powers of $\cos t$ than the second, in the denominators of the new equations corresponding to Eqs. (B3) and (B4). Where this limitation is not met, other driving variables must be approximated by constant values for each day.

Persson, T. (ed) 1980
Structure and Function of Northern
Coniferous Forests – An Ecosystem Study
Ecol. Bull. (Stockholm) 32: 525–536.

PT – A TREE GROWTH MODEL

G. I. Ågren[1] and B. Axelsson[1]

Abstract

The model describes the growth of a Scots pine, about 15 years old, with a time step of one day. The tree has been subdivided into eight different organs: (1–4) four age-classes of needles, (5) branches, (6) stem, (7) large roots, and (8) fine roots. In addition, the entire resources of labile carbohydrates, nitrogen, and water are defined as state variables. The dynamics of the carbon module is established by considering photosynthesis, growth, respiration, and losses of structural material. Each of the nitrogen and water modules contains only one uptake and one loss process. Throughout the model it is assumed that the combined effect of several factors on a process can be described in a multiplicative way. Wherever possible, physiological information has been used for process descriptions, but in many cases only qualitative guesses have been possible. Driving variables are only expressed through their daily means. The results of some simulations are reported. One conclusion derived from the simulation is that the handling of the dynamics of the labile carbohydrate requires great care.

Additional keywords: Carbon, nitrogen, simulation, water.

Introduction

The simulation model described here should be seen as a step towards a causal model for stand growth of conifers. The model was built with the aim of explaining phenomena rather than obtaining high accuracy of prediction. To reach this objective it was considered necessary that in addition to the natural carbon modules the model should contain both water and nitrogen as state variables, the latter two, however, being given a much more perfunctory treatment. Today the model describes the growth of one tree (*Pinus sylvestris* L.) throughout one year, and the results of the model are only qualitative. The model is described in full detail by Axelsson & Ågren (1976).

Model structure

The structure of the model reflects a compromise between a desire to keep the model as simple as possible and the necessity of making it comprehensive. The model tends to increase in complexity as further information about the different processes

[1] Dept. of Ecology and Environmental Research, Swedish University of Agricultural Sciences, S-750 07 Uppsala, Sweden

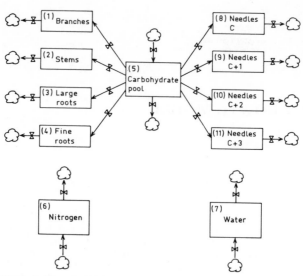

Figure 1. Flow chart of the PT-model.

is collected and judged indispensable for the proper behaviour of the model. However, at the same time the lack of knowledge required to piece this information together imposes simplifications upon the model. In this case the outcome of these expansions and contractions is a model with 11 state variables, 9 of which refer to the carbon module of the model and one for each of the nitrogen and water modules. A diagrammatic presentation of the model is given in Fig. 1. Eight of the carbon state variables represent structural units and any transfer out of these state variables means the death of that organ. The last of the carbon state variables, slightly incorrectly named the carbohydrate pool because it also includes substances like fats and proteins, contains all the mobile and metabolizable substances in the trees. Due to the fairly high mobility of the carbohydrates, nitrogen and water, it was estimated that the model should not require several state variables to describe their distribution within the trees but they could all be lumped into one state variable each.

Mathematically the model has been formulated as a difference equation of flows T_{ij} from state variable X_i to state variable X_j. The time step is one day and all simulations start on January 1.

Driving variables

Climatic measurements in 1974 at Ivantjärnsheden formed the basis for the driving variables. Since the model operates with a time step of one day, all driving variables have been expressed as daily means. To facilitate climatic manipulations in the model, simple analytical functions have generally been used instead of measured data. The driving variables used in the model are:

$D_1 =$ Air temperature, light part of the day. D_1 has been approximated with a sine function.

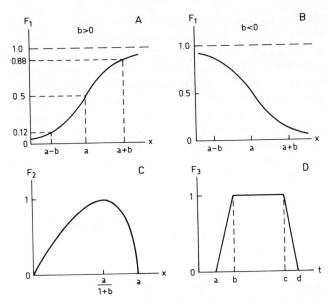

Figure 2. Special functions used in the PT-model: (A and B) $F_1(x, a, b) = \dfrac{1}{1 + \exp[-2(x-a)/b]}$;

(C) $F_2(x, a, b) = x \dfrac{1+b}{a} \left[\dfrac{(a-x)(1+b)}{ab} \right]^b$; (D) $F_3(t, a, b, c, d)$ is defined by the figure.

$D_2 =$ Soil temperature. D_2 has been approximated with a sine function.

$D_3 =$ Soil water potential. D_3 has been constructed to give constant soil water potential during most of the year except for a drought around midsummer.

$D_4 =$ Soil nutrient status. D_4 is essentially the product of D_3 and D_2.

$D_5 =$ Radiation. D_5 has been approximated with a sine function to the radiation in the interval 300–4000 nm.

$D_6 =$ Relative humidity. D_6 has been approximated with a sine function.

$D_7 =$ Day length. D_7 has been approximated with a sine function.

$D_8 =$ Air temperature, dark part of the day. D_8 has been approximated with a sine function.

$D_9 =$ Daily air temperature. D_9 is the mean value of D_1 and D_8.

Description of flows

All flows, except the flow through the water module, are built up as multiplicative functions of the regulating variables. Quite often these functions vary only between 0 and 1, thus only indicating the effects of a certain control variable on a relative scale. For this purpose it was found convenient to define three special functions representing three classes of effects that a control variable could have. These three functions are shown in Fig. 2. A complete list of the flows is given in Appendix A. More details are given in the original report (Axelsson & Ågren, 1976).

The water module required special treatment since it might encounter a turnover where almost the entire supply is renewed during one time step (a day). Consequently, it was necessary to calculate the flows of water from a continuous description and then integrate analytically to give the daily flows. Several approximations were required to make these calculations feasible, the most serious probably being the assumption that the stomatal conductance is a linear function of tree water potential.

The nutrient uptake is given a very simple formulation and all the difficulties are placed in the formulation of the driving variable soil nutrient status. In the uptake process the influence of competing vegetation is included by allowing the tree to take up nutrients only proportionally to its fraction of the total root biomass. Nutrient losses are modelled even more simply as they are assumed to occur when some structural part of the tree is lost, that part assumed to contain a fixed fraction, 0.8%, of nitrogen.

The varying stomatal conductance during the day is explicitly included in the description of the photosynthesis. The different photosynthetic efficiencies of different age-classes of needle were easy to incorporate in the model, but no attempts were made to account for the effects of the varying light intensity in different parts of the crown. A photosynthetic efficiency varying with time was only included in the current needles since when the model was formulated no experimental data for the older needles were available. Although fairly perfunctory, the description of the photosynthesis is adequate for the purpose of the model. A more detailed treatment, but of net photosynthetic production, is given by Lohammar et al. (1979).

The respiration of the tree consists of two parts, maintenance respiration and respiration associated with growth. Maintenance respiration is calculated with the method of Penning de Vries (1975) which takes into account the costs of maintaining proteins, lipids and ion concentrations. This method also requires an estimate of the living biomass, which is made according to the method suggested by Yoda et al. (1965). The growth respiration is calculated from biochemical consideration about costs involved in building certain complex molecules from glucose (Penning de Vries, 1974).

All growth processes are modelled in a similar fashion. The flows are built up as multiplicative functions of temperature, available carbohydrates, water potential in the tree, nutrient status of the tree, and a function containing the time of the year explicitly. In general, very little information was available about these processes and generally it only concerns the cumulated result of these processes over long time periods. Fairly reliable estimates were only found for the effect of temperature on growth and the order in which different organs should start their growth, i.e., stem, branches, and large roots start growing when the average daily temperature exceeds 6°C for 5 consecutive days, and growth begins to slow down when the days get shorter than 18.5 h, or a fixed time thereafter, and then fades out during a fixed time period. The only organ to differ in growth is the fine roots, which grow whenever the soil temperature exceeds 2°C.

Losses of structural material have been given very simple formulations; either the losses are a constant fraction of the biomass or zero (stem and large roots). The exception is the oldest needles, all of which are forced to fall from the tree during the autumn.

Initial values for a pine aged 15–20 years growing at Ih II are given in Appendix B and corresponding parameter values in Appendix C.

Simulations

Several simulations were made with the model. In its present development stage it was not judged capable of making any quantitative evaluations but only qualitative ones. One simulation, corresponding to the parameter and initial values given by Appendix B and C, was therefore assigned as a standard run against which the other simulations were evaluated. This standard run assumed that stem and branches increase their biomass approximately by 10%, current needles and fine roots only slightly whereas nitrogen and carbohydrate concentrations should be approximately the same at the end of the year as at the beginning. The dynamics of the state variables are displayed in Fig. 3.

The model was generally run with the smooth driving variables described under 'Driving variables'. This approximation was tested using measured climatic variables for 1974 whenever possible and, failing this, the analytically defined driving variables. As could be expected, the exact form of the driving variables had little importance. The main difference being an increase in current needle production of 8% and concurrently an increase in the yearly photosynthesis of 5%.

An important variable is the soil temperature and particularly the day of thawing, since with the model's present formulation no photosynthesis can take place in the spring until after thawing. In one simulation the thawing was delayed from April 10 to May 7, resulting in a 15% decrease in the yearly photosynthesis. As a consequence, all growth processes were greatly reduced, branch growth by 50% and stem growth by 30%. The current needles reached 92% of the previous year's growth compared to 104% in the standard run. Moreover, this would also result in important effects on the growth of the coming year, because the carbohydrate pool at the end of the year was reduced to only half of its value in the standard run.

The growths of stem and current needles are shown in Fig. 4. As can be seen there is a pronounced dip in the growth in the middle of the summer, which essentially can be attributed to the low soil water potential during this period. One simulation was performed where this summer drought was removed and the soil water potential was held at a constant -0.1 bar throughout the year. For the current needles the dip during the summer then disappeared, while there was still a slight depression in the growth curve for the stem, which can be traced back to a shortage of carbohydrates. The annual growth of stem and branches was 50% higher than in the standard run. The current needles increased by as much as 64% over the standard run, which was sufficient to compensate through increased photosynthesis for the higher utilization of carbohydrates in growth with the result that the carbohydrate concentration at the end of the year was the same as in the standard run. In addition, the fine roots were able to increase the nitrogen uptake by 44%, which is more than sufficient to maintain the nitrogen concentration in the tree which increased to 0.72% compared to 0.64% in the standard run.

Discussion

One recurrent problem with this model has been an incorrect matching between production and use of carbohydrates. In certain simulations a severe shortage has occurred while in others the tree has almost taken the aspect of a sugar beet. One

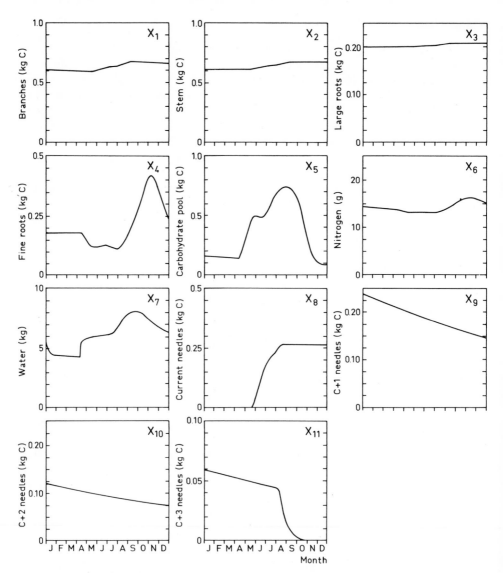

Figure 3. Time course of state variables for a 15-year-old Scots pine.

fundamental reason why these imbalances occur is the high turnover of carbo-hydrates. The annual fluxes through the carbohydrate pool are summarized in Fig. 5. Of the fluxes, only the growth (and consequently the growth respiration) has been coupled to the available amount of carbohydrates, while there is no feed-back from the carbohydrate pool to neither the photosynthesis nor the maintenance respiration. Since the maintenance respiration is approximately twice the carbohydrate pool and the photosynthesis 16 times, it is clear that even small variations in these flows will drastically influence the size of the carbohydrate pool. One question is how large a part of the tree is alive and respiring and what is its seasonal variation?

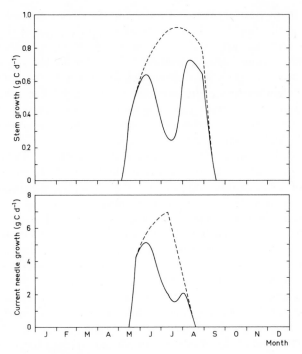

Figure 4. The effect of soil water potential on stem growth and current needle growth in a 15-year-old Scots pine. Solid line = standard run, broken line = no summer water stress.

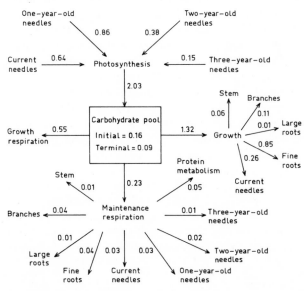

Figure 5. Annual fluxes through the carbohydrate pool in the standard run. All values in kg C or kg C yr^{-1} for a 15-year-old Scots pine.

531

Possibly, the living part of the tree is related to the size of the carbohydrate pool, which included in the model would have a stabilizing influence. This will guarantee that the tree does not die early in the growing season. Moreover, it is also necessary to introduce either some negative feed-back from the carbohydrate pool to the photosynthesis or a stronger positive feed-back to growth. In spite of several experiments aimed at demonstrating the existence of a feed-back mechanism between photosynthesis and the carbohydrate pool in the leaves, the results are not conclusive. Therefore, the use of such a feed-back, which is a common solution in order to stabilize physiological growth models, is not well supported and although the model will behave reasonably it may be the result of a false hypothesis. A plausible alternative to maintain balance is to let the growth of the fine roots be strongly dependent on the amount of carbohydrates. At present, all growth processes become independent of carbohydrate resources, already at moderate levels (cf. Fig. 2 B). The alternative is to take away the ceiling for fine root growth rate and instead increase their growth rate with increasing carbohydrate resources. Such a relation should be efficient in reducing the carbohydrate level in late summer. Since the fine roots metabolize around 65% of annual photosynthesis (cf. Ågren et al., 1980) they should be able to absorb seasonal variations in photosynthesis.

Another improvement to be made in the model is to extend the process of thawing over a longer period, thereby allowing the tree get a smoother start in the spring. This will require a more detailed description of the soil and the root distribution. In the one-year perspective of this model the nitrogen dynamics has been found to be of little importance except for the growth of current needles. However, this would probably be different if the model was run over several years and the bud initiation was included. Ågren & Axelsson (in prep.) have found that bud size can be positively correlated with either average needle length or total needle length of the parent shoot. If this coupling was introduced into the model, the requirements of correct prediction of current needle biomass would be increased, since fluctuations in the current needle biomass would propagate over several years. Thus, in a model running over several years the nitrogen dynamics seems to require greater attention.

This work should be seen in the context of the general goals of the Swedish Coniferous Forest Project, where understanding and predicting changes in different plant biomasses are specific objectives. However, models intended for prediction are not always optimal for understanding, and *vice versa*. In this model understanding has been emphasized and, as it stands, the model is probably useless for quantitative predictions. On the other hand, the model can be a very useful tool for testing alternative hypotheses about tree growth. As regards the one-year perspective at least, we believe that we are close to this objective.

References

Ågren, G. I., Axelsson, B., Flower-Ellis, J. G. K., Linder, S., Persson, H., Staaf, H. & Troeng, E. 1980. Annual carbon budget for a young Scots pine. – In: Persson, T. (ed.) Structure and Function of Northern Coniferous Forests – An Ecosystem Study, Ecol. Bull. (Stockholm) 32: 307–313.
Axelsson, B. & Ågren, G. I. 1976. Tree growth model (PT1) – a development paper. – Swed. Conif. For. Proj. Int. Rep. 41, 79 pp.
Lohammar, T., Larsson, S., Linder, S. & Falk, S. O. 1979. FAST – a simulation model for the carbon dioxide and water exchange of Scots pine. – Swed. Conif. For. Proj. Tech. Rep. 19, 38 pp.

Penning de Vries, F. W. T. 1974. Substrate utilization and respiration in relation to growth and maintenance in higher plants. – Neth. J. agric. Sci. 22: 40–44.
Penning de Vries, F. W. T. 1975. The cost of maintenance processes in plant cells. – Ann. Bot. 39: 77–92.
Yoda, K., Shinozaki, K., Ogawa, H., Hozumi, K. & Kira, T. 1965. Estimation of the total amount of
respiration in woody organs of trees and forest communities. – J. Biol. Osaka City Univ. 16:
15–26.

Appendix A

Formulation of the flows in the model

Tij denotes a flow from state variable *i* to state variable *j*. $i(j) = 00$ menas a source (sink). State variables
are denoted by *X*, parameters by *P*, and driving variables by *D*.

Transpiration

$$T0700 = \left(A_3 + \frac{A_4}{B_{dw}} \alpha_1 \right) D_7 + \frac{A_4}{A_2 + A_4} (X_7 - \alpha_1) \left(1 - \exp\left\{ -\frac{A_2 + A_4}{B_{dw}} D_7 \right\} \right)$$

Water uptake

$$T0007 = \left(A_1 - \frac{A_2}{B_{dw}} \alpha_1 \right) D_7 - \frac{A_2}{A_2 + A_4} (X_7 - \alpha_1) \left(1 - \exp\left\{ -\frac{A_2 + A_4}{B_{dw}} D_7 \right\} \right) +$$
$$+ [\alpha_2 - X_7(D_7)] \left[1 - \exp\left\{ -\frac{A_2}{B_{dw}} (1 - D_7) \right\} \right]$$

where:

$A_1 = P_3 (D_3 - P_1) [1 - \exp\{ -[P_4 \max (0, D_2)]^{0.4}\}] X_4$

$A_2 = P_2 P_3 [1 - \exp\{ -[P_4 \max (0, D_2)]^{0.4}\}] X_4$

$A_3 = P_7 \Delta e (X_8 + X_9 + X_{10} + X_{11}) (1 + P_1 P_6)$

$A_4 = P_7 \Delta e (X_8 + X_9 + X_{10} + X_{11}) P_6 P_2$

B_{dw} (total carbon content) $= X_1 + X_2 + X_3 + X_4 + X_7 + X_8 + X_9 + X_{10} + X_{11}$

$\alpha_1 = B_{dw}(A_1 - A_3)/(A_2 + A_4)$

$\alpha_2 = A_1 B_{dw}/A_2$

$X_7(D_7)$ (water content at dusk) $= [X_7 - (A_1 - A_3)B_{dw}/(A_2 + A_4)] \times$
$$\times \exp\left\{ -\frac{A_2 + A_4}{B_{dw}} D_7 \right\} + \frac{A_1 - A_3}{A_2 + A_4} B_{dw}$$

Δe (water vapour pressure deficit) $= P_8 (\exp\{ -P_9/(T_N + 273)\} - \exp\{ -P_9/(D_1 + 273)\} D_6)$

T_N (needle temperature) $= P_5 D_5 + D_1$

Nitrogen loss
$$T0600 = P_{11} (T0800 + T0900 + T1000 + T1100) + P_{12} (T0100 + T0400)$$

Nitrogen uptake
$$T0006 = D_4 \frac{X_4}{X_4 + P_{10}}$$

Carbohydrate loss

$T0500 = A_1 + A_2 + A_3 + A_4$

where:

A_1 (protein metabolism) $= P_{61} X_6 \exp\{P_{62} D_9\}$

A_2 (above-ground maintenance respiration) $= P_{75} \exp\{P_{62} D_9\} [(P_{76} X_1 + P_{77} X_2) \times$
$\times F_3(t, Y_1, Y_1 + P_{50}, Y_2 + P_{51}, Y_2 + P_{52}) + X_8 + P_{16} X_9 + P_{17} X_{10} + P_{18} X_{11}]$

A_3 (below-ground maintenance respiration) $= P_{75} \exp\{P_{62} D_2\} [P_{78} X_3 F_3(t, Y_1, Y_1 +$
$+ P_{50}, Y_2 + P_{51}, Y_2 + P_{52}) + X_4]$

A_4 (growth respiration) $= P_{63} (T0501 + T0502 + T0503 + T0504) + P_{64} (T0508 + T0509 +$
$+ T0510 + T0511)$

Photosynthesis

$T0005 = P_{13} [X_8 F_3(t, Y_1 + P_{14}, Y_1 + P_{15}, 366, 367) + P_{16}X_9 + P_{17}X_{10} + P_{18}X_{11}] \times$
$\times B_1 F_2(T_N + P_{21}, P_{22}, P_{23}) D_5$

$Y_1 =$ daynumber when daily mean temperature (D_9) during P_{24} consecutive days is $\geq P_{25}$

$Y_2 =$ daynumber when daylength gets shorter than P_{40}

$F(X_7, D_7)$ (average stomatal conductance) $= \left(1 + P_1 P_6 + \dfrac{A_1 - A_3}{A_2 + A_4} P_2 P_6\right) D_7 +$

$+ P_2 P_6\left(\dfrac{X_7}{B_{dw}} - \dfrac{A_1 - A_3}{A_2 + A_4}\right)\left(1 - \exp\left\{-\dfrac{A_2 + A_4}{B_{dw}} D_7\right\}\right) / [(A_2 + A_4) D_7]$

$B_1 = D_7 F(X_7, D_7)/[1 + P_{19} F(X_7, D_7)]$

Current needle growth

$T0508 = P_{26} F_2(D_9 - P_{27}, P_{28}, P_{29}) F_1(X_5/B_{dw}, P_{30}, P_{31}) [1 - P_{32} + P_{32} F_1(\Psi, P_{33}, P_{34})] \times$
$\times F_1(\Psi, P_{73}, P_{74}) F_1(X_6/B_{dw}, P_{35}, P_{36}) F_3(t_1, Y_1 + P_{37}, Y_1 + P_{38}, Y_2, Y_2 + P_{39})$

Ψ (tree water potential) $= P_1 + P_2 X_7/B_{dw}$

C+1 needle growth

$T0509 = 0$

C+2 needle growth

$T0510 = 0$

C+3 needle growth

$T0511 = 0$

Branch growth

$T0501 = P_{44} X_1 F_2(D_9 - P_{45}, P_{46}, P_{47}) F_1(X_5/B_{dw}, P_{48}, P_{49}) [1 - P_{32} + P_{32} F_1(\Psi, P_{33}, P_{34})] \times$
$\times F_1(\Psi, P_{73}, P_{74}) F_1(X_6/B_{dw}, P_{35}, P_{36}) F_3(t_1, Y_1, Y_1 + P_{50}, Y_2 + P_{51}, Y_2 + P_{52})$

Stem growth

$T0502 = P_{53} X_2 F_2(D_9 - P_{45}, P_{46}, P_{47}) F_1(X_5/B_{dw}, P_{48}, P_{49}) [1 - P_{32} + P_{32} F_1(\Psi, P_{33}, P_{34})] \times$
$\times F_1(\Psi, P_{73}, P_{74}) F_1(X_6/B_{dw}, P_{35}, P_{36}) F_3(t, Y_1, Y_1 + P_{50}, Y_2 + P_{51}, Y_2 + P_{52})$

Large root growth

$T0503 = P_{54} X_3 F_2(D_2 - P_{55}, P_{56}, P_{57}) F_1(X_5/B_{dw}, P_{48}, P_{49}) [1 - P_{32} + P_{32} F_1(\Psi, P_{33}, P_{34})] \times$
$\times F_1(\Psi, P_{73}, P_{74}) F_1(X_6/B_{dw}, P_{35}, P_{36}) F_3(t, Y_1, Y_1 + P_{50}, Y_2 + P_{51}, Y_2 + P_{52})$

534

Fine root growth

$T0504 = P_{58} X_4 F_2(D_2 - P_{55}, P_{56}, P_{57}) F_1(X_5/B_{dw}, P_{48}, P_{49}) [1 - P_{32} + P_{32} F_1(\Psi, P_{33}, P_{34})] \times$
$\quad \times F_1(\Psi, P_{73}, P_{74}) F_1(X_6/B_{dw}, P_{59}, P_{60})$

Branch death

$T0100 = P_{65} X_1$

Stem death

$T0200 = 0$

Large root death

$T0300 = 0$

Fine root death

$T0400 = P_{66} X_4$

Current needle death

$T0800 = 0$

C + 1 needle death

$T0900 = P_{67} X_9$

C + 2 needle death

$T1000 = P_{68} X_{10}$

C + 3 needle death

$T1100 = P_{69} X_{11} + P_{70} X_{11} F_3(t, P_{71}, P_{72}, 365, 366)$

Appendix B

Initial values for a 15-year-old pine

$X_1 = 0.61$ kg C
$X_2 = 0.61$ kg C
$X_3 = 0.20$ kg C
$X_4 = 0.18$ kg C
$X_5 = 0.16$ kg C
$X_6 = 0.0145$ kg N

$X_7 = 5.7$ kg H$_2$O
$X_8 = 0$ kg C
$X_9 = 0.24$ kg C
$X_{10} = 0.12$ kg C
$X_{11} = 0.06$ kg C

535

Appendix C

List of parameter values

Para-meter	Value	Dimension	Flow[1]	Para-meter	Value	Dimension	Flow
P 1	-100	bar	$T0700$	P 39	40	d	$T0508$
2	37	bar	,,	40	0.77		$T0500$
3	2.2	$bar^{-1} d^{-1}$	,,	44	0.012	d^{-1}	$T0501$
4	0.8	$°C^{-1}$	,,	45	6.0	°C	,,
5	$6.4 \cdot 10^{-3}$	$°C W^{-1} m^2$	,,	46	39.0	°C	,,
6	0.04	bar^{-1}	,,	47	1.05		,,
7	3353	$bar^{-1} d^{-1}$	,,	48	0.06		,,
8	$1.96 \cdot 10^6$	bar	,,	49	0.036		,,
9	5350	K	,,	50	10	d	,,
10	0.51	kg	$T0006$	51	50	d	,,
11	0.01	$kg\ kg^{-1}$	,,	52	70	d	,,
12	0.01	$kg\ kg^{-1}$	,,	53	$7.0 \cdot 10^{-3}$	d^{-1}	$T0502$
13	$1.3 \cdot 10^{-3}$		$T0005$	54	$2.1 \cdot 10^{-3}$	d^{-1}	$T0503$
14	15	d	,,	55	2.0	°C	,,
15	45	d	,,	56	43.0	°C	,,
16	0.9		,,	57	1.39		,,
17	0.8		,,	58	0.045	d^{-1}	$T0504$
18	0.7		,,	59	$2.47 \cdot 10^{-3}$	$kg\ kg^{-1}$	,,
19	4.0		,,	60	$2.5 \cdot 10^{-3}$	$kg\ kg^{-1}$	,,
21	7.0	°C	,,	61	$6 \cdot 10^{-3}$	kg C $(kg\ N)^{-1} d^{-1}$	$T0500$
22	47	°C	,,	62	0.0693	$°C^{-1}$	,,
23	1.14		,,	63	0.42		,,
24	5.0	d	,,	64	0.42		,,
25	6.0	°C	,,	65	$2.5 \cdot 10^{-4}$	d^{-1}	$T0100$
26	0.035	$kg\ d^{-1}$	$T0508$	66	0.015	d^{-1}	$T0400$
27	6.0	°C	,,	67	$1.4 \cdot 10^{-3}$	d^{-1}	$T0800$
28	39.0	°C	,,	68	$1.4 \cdot 10^{-3}$	d^{-1}	,,
29	1.05		,,	69	$1.4 \cdot 10^{-3}$	d^{-1}	,,
30	0.053		,,	70	0.051	d^{-1}	,,
31	0.036		,,	71	214	d	,,
32	0.55		,,	72	228	d	,,
33	-12.0	bar	,,	73	-15.0	bar	$T0508$
34	3.0	bar	,,	74	3.0	bar	,,
35	$6.3 \cdot 10^{-3}$	$kg\ kg^{-1}$	,,	75	$3.7 \cdot 10^{-4}$	d^{-1}	$T0500$
36	$3.7 \cdot 10^{-3}$	$kg\ kg^{-1}$	,,	76	0.6		,,
37	10	d	,,	77	0.2		,,
38	20	d	,,	78	0.6		,,

[1] Denotes the flow where the parameter is first used.

Persson, T. (ed) 1980
Structure and Function of Northern
Coniferous Forests – An Ecosystem Study
Ecol. Bull. (Stockholm) 32: 537–545.

CONSUMPTION AND PINE GROWTH – HYPOTHESES ON EFFECTS ON GROWTH PROCESSES BY NEEDLE-EATING INSECTS

A. Ericsson[1], J. Hellkvist[2,3], K. Hillerdal-Hagströmer[2], S. Larsson[4], E. Mattson-Djos[2] and O. Tenow[4]

Abstract

In connection with field experiments on the effects of insect grazing on growth of young Scots pine (*Pinus sylvestris* L.) trees some tentative hypotheses on the effect of defoliation on growth and carbohydrate dynamics in the pine are presented. The hypotheses are supported by preliminary results from artificial defoliation experiments performed at Ivantjärnsheden, Central Sweden, in 1976–77. Compensating mechanisms, *viz.* improved water status, increased rate of photosynthesis and increased mobilization of starch reserves seem to occur, delaying growth reduction until a high degree of defoliation has been attained. The compensation is more effective when trees are defoliated early in summer than later in the season.

Additional keywords: Artificial defoliation, compensating mechanisms, photosynthetic rate, starch content, stomatal conductance, tree growth, water potential.

Introduction

It has long been known that a reduction of the needle biomass decreases the growth rate of the tree. The defoliation may affect growth in different ways according to the time and degree of defoliation and to the fraction of foliage removed (e.g. Kulman, 1965, 1971; Rook & Whyte, 1976).

A plant is an integrated system of sources and sinks (Wareing & Patrick, 1975; Moorby, 1977) with regard to the production and utilization of, e.g., carbohydrates, nitrogen compounds and plant hormones. The sink strength as well as the source strength of the different organs changes during the growing season, and it is therefore not surprising that defoliations occurring at different times of the year or removal of different needle age-classes, result in quantitatively different effects on growth.

In the present paper tentative hypotheses are presented concerning growth and carbohydrate dynamics in Scots pine (*Pinus sylvestris* L.) following a defoliation. Some preliminary empirical data from defoliation experiments in a 15–20 year old stand (Ih II) at Ivantjärnsheden are presented as support for the hypotheses.

[1] Dept. of Plant Physiology, University of Umeå, S-901 87 Umeå, Sweden
[2] Dept. of Physiological Botany, Uppsala University, Box 540, S-751 21 Uppsala 1, Sweden
[3] Present address: National Swedish Food Administration, Box 622, S-751 26 Uppsala, Sweden
[4] Dept. of Entomology, Uppsala University, Box 561, S-751 22 Uppsala 1, Sweden

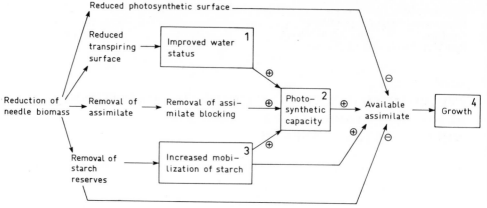

Figure 1. Schematic representation of hypothetic connections between defoliation, carbohydrate dynamics and growth. Tested hypotheses are framed and numbered as in the text.

Hypotheses

The hypothetic connections between defoliation and its effects on tree growth are schematically shown in Fig. 1. The different hypotheses are discussed below.

Water relations and photosynthesis

In a tree in a closed stand the water transporting system of roots, sapwood and needles are in a well-established balance, so that the sapwood cross-sectional area is a function of leaf biomass (Jarvis, 1975). During growth a tree is evolving towards this balance. A reduction in needle biomass by defoliation reduces the transpirating area, which means that the balance between needle area, sapwood area and root area changes to the benefit of the water-uptaking and water-transporting tissues. If the resistances against water transport in the tree could be presumed to remain fairly constant, this would result in a smaller total transpiration. As a result, water uptake would diminish, leading to a higher water potential in the soil-root interface and in the soil in the vicinity of the root. The higher soil water potential together with the large root area and the large sapwood cross-sectional area compared to needle area will result in higher water potential in remaining needles.

Hypothesis 1

The changed balance between root area, sapwood cross-sectional area and needle area after a defoliation results in higher needle water potential in the remaining shoots. Hence, the stomata of remaining needles will, during dry periods, to a higher degree remain open for longer periods of the day. This is valid at least up to a certain degree of defoliation, where the defoliation is strong enough to cause injury or negative effects to the remaining parts of the tree, for example, lack of photosynthate leading to retarded root activities.

Hypothesis 2

As an effect of the improved water status it may be presumed that the stomatal conductance of defoliated trees during dry weather periods will not limit the rate of

538

photosynthesis to the same degree as the stomatal conductance in non-defoliated trees. Thus, photosynthetic capacity of remaining needles under these conditions will increase.

Starch dynamics

It is well-known that evergreen conifers accumulate starch during the later part of the spring (e.g. Kozlowski, 1971). These reserves are later mobilized when the growth of the tree starts (Ericsson, 1978, 1979). Investigations at Ivantjärnsheden have shown that the starch content can reach levels of 25–30% of dry weight of the needles as well as of the living parts of the stem bark (Ericsson, 1979). A defoliation in early summer, when the starch reserves are at a high level, will probably result in a more intense utilization of the reserves in the remaining needles.

A reduction of the needle biomass in the later part of the summer reduces the photosynthetic area and thus the possibilities for photosynthetic production the following spring. A large reduction will probably result in low levels of starch reserves in the remaining needles, since the production of current photosynthate during the spring only will be enough to satisfy the sink demand of the different growth regions. During the most intense growth period of the summer, this reduced photosynthetic capacity of the tree, as well as the small amounts of starch reserves, will result in limited availability of carbohydrates for growth.

A further consequence of the increased mobilization of starch probably will be an increased rate of photosynthesis (cf. hypothesis 2), since high levels of assimilate, especially starch, are considered to decrease the rate of photosynthesis (Neals & Incoll, 1968; Nafziger & Koller, 1976).

Hypothesis 3
Defoliation in early summer, when the starch content of the needles is at a high level, will result in an increased rate of utilization of the starch reserves in the remaining needles to compensate for decreased availability of photosynthate. Defoliation in the later part of the summer will decrease the possibility for the tree to accumulate large amounts of carbohydrate reserves in the remaining needles during the following spring and the reserves will be used very rapidly.

Growth effects

In earlier studies it has been shown that defoliation of older needles during the intense growth period will not cause drastic growth losses (Craighead, 1940; Kulman, 1965). This seems to be contradictory to the general opinion that wood production is proportional to the needle biomass in Scots pine (e.g. Albrektson et al., 1977). However, the formation of new shoots is independent of defoliation of the older shoots earlier in the same season (cf. Kulman, 1965). Furthermore, according to hypotheses 1–3, there are compensating mechanisms acting to increase the availability of carbohydrates after the defoliation.

A late summer defoliation of current-year needles has a more deleterious effect on growth (cf. O'Neil, 1962) probably since the formation of new shoots early in the following season requires carbohydrate reserves, which have been built up during the spring and stored in the older needles (Ericsson, 1978, 1979). Hence, after the

539

defoliation of these needles, growth may be limited by shortage of carbohydrates. The compensating mechanisms in the remaining old needles probably are not of sufficient magnitude to compensate for the decreased needle biomass.

Hypothesis 4

Defoliation interferes with the formation of assimilate, and thus tree growth, by two counteracting effects: the reduction of the amount of needle biomass available for carbohydrate production and the compensatory physiological processes. Reduced tree growth will occur at a critical degree of defoliation where the latter effect will not be able to balance the former.

Empirical support

Defoliation experiments were performed at Ivantjärnsheden by two different methods: consumption by controlled populations of larvae of the European pine sawfly (*Neodiprion sertifer* Geoffr.) and by removal of needles by hand. In both types of experiments the same growth variables were measured, thus enabling the reliability in the results from the artificial defoliation experiment to be estimated. The most intensive studies, including the plant physiological measurements, were made within the artificial defoliation experiment where complete systematical sampling was possible. Some preliminary results from this study are presented here.

The artificial defoliations were performed on about 18-year-old pine trees on two occasions: once in early summer (15–16 June 1976) and once in late summer (16–18 August 1976). On both occasions either the youngest age-class or the two youngest age-classes of needles were removed. Five degrees of defoliation were used: 0, 25, 50, 75 and 100% for each defoliated age-class of needles. The effects on stem girth, shoot length, needle length, number of buds and number of needles were studied as well as the effects on starch content, water potential, stomatal conductance and photosynthetic rate of the remaining needles.

Results from the early summer defoliation are shown in Tables 1–2 and Figs. 2–3. It was found that water potential, stomatal conductance and rate of photosynthesis of needles of all studied age-classes increased due to the defoliation treatments (Table 1).

The starch content on the date of defoliation (before the defoliation treatment) varied between the different treatments (Table 2), and the values in Fig. 2 are therefore presented as percentages of the starch content at defoliation. The results indicated a more rapid decrease of starch in the defoliated trees than in the control trees (Fig. 2). No effect could be found on the starch reserves of the current year's needles.

The number of buds, needle length and number of needles per unit length appeared to be unaffected, as was the growth of lateral shoots, except at the highest degree of defoliation. The only variables showing a significant growth retardation were the leading shoot and the stem girth (Fig. 3).

In the late summer experiment, no studies were made on water status and photosynthesis. However, it can be assumed that the results of the defoliation should be in accordance with the results obtained in the early summer experiment, with an increased photosynthesis due to an improved water balance.

Table 1. Water potential, stomatal conductance and rate of photosynthesis in pine trees for various degrees of early summer defoliation. Measurements are from 21 July 1976. Pre-dawn = measurement at 03.00 p.m. (0 μE m^{-2}, 12.5°C), pre-noon = measurement at 07.00 p.m. (800 μE m^{-2} s^{-1}, 18°C) and noon = measurement at 12.00 (1600 μE m^{-2} s^{-1}, 24°C).

Degree[a] of defoliation	Age-class of studied needles	Water potential[b] (bar), mean ±s.e.		Stomatal conductance[c] (cm s^{-1})		Rate of photosynthesis[c] (mg CO$_2$ dm^{-2} h^{-1}), mean ±s.e.	
		pre-dawn	noon	pre-noon	noon	pre-noon	noon
0/0	1976	-10.5 ± 2.0	*	0.34	0.23	18.9 ± 0.6	12.8 ± 1.1
25/0	1976	-7.1 ± 1.4	*	*	*	*	*
50/0	1976	-6.9 ± 0.6	*	*	*	*	*
75/0	1976	-8.3 ± 0.6	*	*	*	23.3 ± 4.4	16.7 ± 1.1
75/75	1976	-7.7 ± 0.6	*	0.40	0.27	*	*
0/0	1975	-10.0 ± 1.4	-14.6 ± 0.6	0.41	0.24	20.0 ± 1.1	17.2 ± 1.1
25/0	1975	-7.7 ± 0.9	-14.0 ± 0.6	*	*	*	*
50/0	1975	-8.0 ± 0.6	-12.9 ± 0.3	*	*	26.1 ± 0.6	18.3 ± 2.2
75/75	1975	*	*	0.83	0.49	*	*
0/0	1974	-10.3 ± 1.4	-18.0 ± 1.1	0.37	0.20	24.4 ± 1.1	15.0 ± 0.6
75/0	1974	-7.1 ± 0.6	-11.1 ± 0.9	*	*	28.5 ± 1.7	24.2 ± 2.2
100/0	1974	-6.9 ± 0.3	-14.0 ± 0.6	*	*	23.9 ± 1.7	25.0 ± 1.7
75/75	1974	*	*	1.00	0.54	*	*

[a] The first value represents the defoliation degree (in %) of one-year-old needles and the second value the defoliation degree of two-year-old needles.
[b] Water potentials are given at ψ_{max} (pre-dawn) and at ψ_{min} (noon), that is, the highest and the lowest values respectively of the diurnal variation of water potential are given.
[c] Stomatal conductance and rate of photosynthesis are shown at $g_{s_{max}}$ (pre-noon) and at noon.
* No measurements made.

Table 2. The effect of early summer defoliation during 1976 on the starch content (% of dw) of one-year-old and two-year-old needles. Each value is the mean of two determinations (differences less than 1% of dw). Initial samples were taken at the date of defoliation: June 15 (50/50%), June 16 (25/25%), and June 17 (0/0%), 1976. For symbols, see Table 1.

	Age-class of studied needles					
	1975			1974		
Date	0/0	25/25	50/50	0/0	25/25	50/50
June 15–17	25.0	19.7	22.3	21.4	18.1	21.5
June 24	26.6	22.8	20.2	23.8	22.2	21.2
July 5	22.2	16.3	16.7	20.0	16.0	17.7
July 15	19.6	13.4	13.0	18.2	14.0	13.2
July 26	15.9	12.4	10.0	15.1	11.3	13.4
August 5	19.3	15.4	15.0	17.8	13.7	16.9

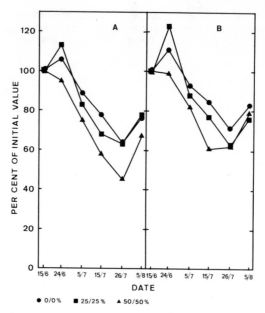

Figure 2. The effect of early summer defoliation on the starch content of one-year-old (A) and two-year-old (B) needles in 1976. The data are presented as percentages of the starch content on the defoliation date. For the symbols, see also Table 1.

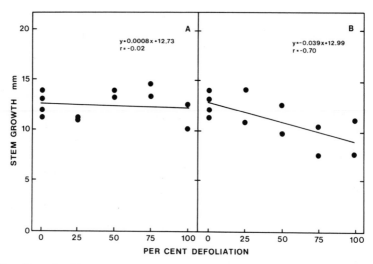

Figure 3. The effect of early summer defoliation on growth of stem girth in 1977. (A) Defoliation of one-year-old needles, (B) defoliation of both one-year-old and two-year-old needles.

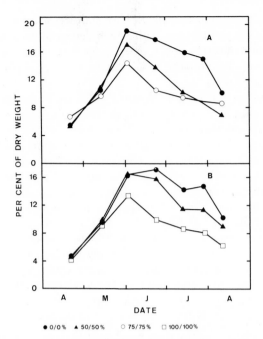

Figure 4. The effect of late summer defoliation on the starch content of one-year-old (A) and three-year-old (B) needles in 1977. The defoliation treatments were made on 16–18 August 1976, and included current and one-year-old needles. The first value of 0/0, 50/50, etc. represents the defoliation degree of current-year needles, the second value the defoliation degree of one-year-old needles.

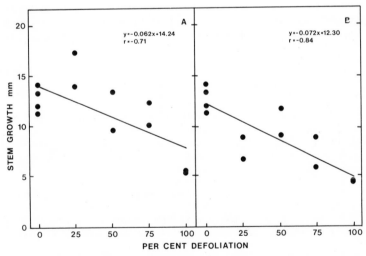

Figure 5. The effect of late summer defoliation on growth of stem girth in 1977. (A) Defoliation of current-year needles, (B) defoliation of both current-year and one-year-old needles.

The effects of the late summer defoliation on starch content in needles are shown in Fig. 4. The figure shows that trees with a high degree of defoliation never obtain the same concentration of starch as the control trees. The small reserves that are built up disappear very rapidly, probably since nearly all current photosynthate is immediately needed for growth.

Most growth variables studied were negatively affected by the late summer defoliation (e.g., stem girth in Fig. 5). In trees with the highest degrees of defoliation some of the current year's shoots and the new buds even died during the first season after defoliation. As stated above, the drastic growth reduction might be a result of insufficient amounts of carbohydrates. However, nitrogenous compounds, which are stored in the older needles, have also been suggested to be important for shoot growth (Krueger, 1967). The impact on nitrogen economy and canopy growth in Scots pine following shoot defoliation by *Blastophagus piniperda* L. has been discussed by Fagerström *et al.* (1978).

In conclusion, the results of our experiments support the hypothesis on compensating mechanisms in Scots pine after defoliation of needles. These compensating mechanisms, together with the effect of the predetermined shoot development, seem to be enough to maintain a more or less normal growth after an early summer defoliation. The more drastic effect on tree growth observed after the late summer defoliation probably is due to the removal of the needles most important for bud formation and the following years' shoot growth.

Acknowledgements

This work was carried out within the Swedish Coniferous Forest Project. Theoretical and practical problems have been discussed with Drs. Aron Aronsson, Jeremy Flower-Ellis and Sune Linder, working within the SWECON project. Many persons have contributed to field and laboratory data which will be reported and acknowledged in full length elsewhere. Our thanks are due to all these persons.

References

Albrektson, A., Aronsson, A. & Tamm, C. O. 1977. The effect of forest fertilisation on primary production and nutrient cycling in the forest ecosystem. – Silva fenn. 11: 233–239.

Craighead, F. C. 1940. Some effects of artificial defoliation on pine and larch. – J. For. 38: 885–888.

Ericsson, A. 1978. Seasonal changes in translocation of ^{14}C from different age-classes of needles on 20-year-old Scots pine trees (*Pinus silvestris* L.). – Physiol. Plant. 43: 351–358.

Ericsson, A. 1979. Effects of fertilization and irrigation on the seasonal changes of carbohydrate reserves in different age-classes of needle on 20-year-old Scots pine trees (*Pinus silvestris* L.). – Physiol. Plant. 45: 270–280.

Fagerström, T., Larsson, S., Lohm, U. & Tenow, O. 1978. Growth in Scots pine (*Pinus silvestris* L.). A hypothesis on response to *Blastophagus piniperda* L. (Col., Scolytidae) attacks. – For. Ecol. Mgmt. 1: 273–281.

Jarvis, P. G. 1975. Water transfer in plants. – In: de Vries, D. A. & Afgan, N. H. (eds.) Heat and Mass Transfer in the Biosphere. I. Transfer Processes in Plant Environment, pp. 370–394. Washington, D.C.: Scripta Book Co.

Kozlowski, T. T. 1971. Growth and Development of Trees, Vol. 1. New York & London: Academic Press, 443 pp.

Krueger, K. W. 1967. Nitrogen, phosphorus and carbohydrate in expanding and year-old Douglas-fir shoots. – For. Sci. 13: 352–356.

Kulman, H. M. 1965. Effects of artificial defoliation of pine on subsequent shoot and needle growth. – For. Sci. 11: 90–98.

Kulman, H. M. 1971. Effects of insect defoliation on growth and mortality of trees. – Ann. Rev. Ent. 16: 289–324.

Moorby, J. 1977. Integration and regulation of translocation within the whole plant. – In: Jennings, D. H. (ed.) Integration of Activity in the Higher Plant, Symp. Soc. Biol. 31, pp. 425–454. Cambridge: Cambridge University Press.

Nafziger, E. D. & Koller, H. R. 1976. Influence of leaf starch concentration on CO_2 assimilation in soybean. – Plant Physiol. 57: 560–563.

Neals, T. F. & Incoll, L. D. 1968. The control of leaf photosynthesis rate by the level of assimilate concentration in the leaf: A review of the hypothesis. – Bot. Rev. 34: 107–125.

O'Neil, L. C. 1962. Some effects of artificial defoliation on the growth of Jack pine (*Pinus banksiana* Lamb.). – Canad. J. Bot. 40: 273–280.

Rook, D. A. & Whyte, A. G. D. 1976. Partial defoliation and growth of 5-year-old radiata pine. – N. Z. J. For. Sci. 6: 40–56.

Wareing, P. F. & Patrick, J. 1975. Source-sink relations and the partition of assimilates in the plant. – In: Cooper, J. P. (ed.) Photosynthesis and Productivity in Different Environments, IBP 3, pp. 481–499. Cambridge: Cambridge University Press.

Persson, T. (ed) 1980
Structure and Function of Northern
Coniferous Forests – An Ecosystem Study
Ecol. Bull. (Stockholm) 32: 547–551.

COEXISTENCE OF PLANT SPECIES: A THEORETICAL INVESTIGATION

G. I. Ågren[1] and T. Fagerström[1]

Abstract

This paper discusses the possibilities for coexistence of plant species competing for the same growth-limiting resources in spatially homogeneous environments. It is found that differentiation with respect to (i) temporal average, (ii) temporal variance, (iii) phenology of diaspore production can ensure coexistence, whereas differentiation solely with respect to (iv) longevity does not. The possible effects upon the equilibrium populations of the two species when an increase in phenological separation also results in an increased seed production, assumed due to a decreased competition for pollinators, is discussed.

Additional keywords: Competition, diaspore production, phenology.

Introduction

Current theory on resource partitioning (e.g., Schoener, 1974) predicts that two species cannot co-exist in a homogeneous environment unless they are limited by quantitatively or qualitatively different factors. Phrased differently, the theory states that co-existence requires the niches of the species not to overlap too much. In the case of animal communities one can fairly easily envisage that the resources of the environment, whether be it nesting sites, food quality or foraging habitats, are usually sufficiently diverse for competition to be relaxed through differential utilization by the different animal species. In the case of plant communities, on the other hand, the situation is different. Autotrophic plants all need light, carbon dioxide and essentially the same mineral nutrients. It seems unlikely, for example, that all the grass species in a meadow could occupy different niches with respect to these resources; yet they can apparently co-exist.

Grubb (1977) emphasized the importance of the regeneration niche for the maintenance of species richness in plant communities. That is, different species can co-exist, even if they compete for the same limiting factors in the sessile stage, by being differentiated with respect to regeneration properties, such as the amount of seeds produced, or the dispersability of seeds.

The purpose of the work summarized here was to analyze some routes of differentiation that are theoretically possible to exploit by an inferior competitor, as

[1] Dept. of Ecology and Environmental Research, Swedish University of Agricultural Sciences, S-750 07 Uppsala, Sweden

well as the extent of differentiation required in order to survive. A detailed account is available in three papers (Fagerström & Ågren, 1979, 1980; Ågren & Fagerström, 1980).

Theory

Consider an environment inhabited by two plant species that reproduce only by dispersing diaspores once a year. Let this environment consist of a fixed number of sites, each site supporting only one adult plant and let species 1 be a superior competitor in the sense that a diaspore of species 2 that falls at a given empty site will develop into an adult if and only if there are no diaspores of species 1 present. Diaspores falling on already occupied sites will not develop into adult individuals. Let the number of viable diaspores produced per individual of species i in the year t be a normally distributed stochastic variable with mathematical expectation a_i and variance σ_i^2 and let λ_i be the (constant) death rate of adults of species i ($i = 1, 2$). Let further the year-to-year variations in diaspore production have auto-correlation zero and cross-correlation ϱ.

It can then be shown (Fagerström & Ågren, 1979) that species 1 (the superior competitor in the sessile stage) will survive indefinitely if:

$$\frac{\lambda_2 a_1}{\lambda_1 (1 - e^{-a_2 + \frac{1}{2}\sigma_2^2})} > 1 \tag{1a}$$

and species 2 (the inferior competitor) if:

$$\frac{\lambda_1 (a_2 - \varrho\sigma_1\sigma_2)}{\lambda_2 (e^{a_1 - \frac{1}{2}\sigma_1^2} - 1)} > 1 \tag{1b}$$

Hence, if both inequalities (1) are satisfied indefinite coexistence prevails; the region in parameter space where the inequalities are valid thus defines the amount of differentiation with respect to regeneration properties required in species 2 in order to compensate for the inferior competitive ability in this species when in the sessile stage.

Results and discussion

The implications of the inequalities (1a and 1b) in terms of differentiation in species 2 solely with respect to a, σ, λ and ϱ, are shown in Fig. 1. As seen from the figure, differentiation solely with respect to average (a), variance (σ), or cross-correlation (ϱ) of diaspore production suffices, whereas differentiation with respect to death rate (λ) of the sessile stage does not.

With regard to empirical evidence, it is a trivial notion that coexisting plant species often differ considerably with respect to the average number (taken over time) of viable diaspores produced per individual (a). It is well known that diaspore production may vary considerably from year to year (σ), e.g., an annual weed such as *Chenopodium album* L. may produce from four to 100 000 seeds depending on the nutrient and water status of the soil (Harper, 1967). It is, perhaps, less well

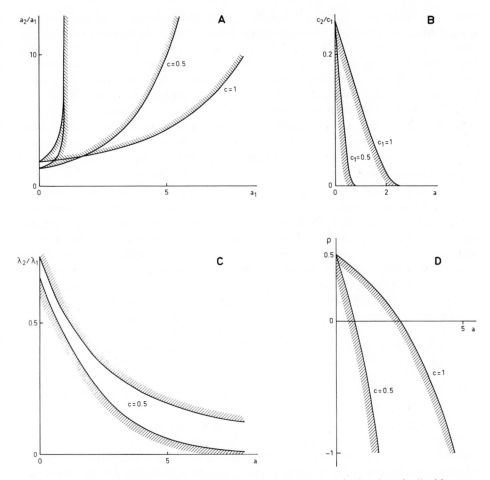

Figure 1. The amount of differentiation (expressed as a ratio between species 2 and species 1) with respect to (A) average seed production per plant; (B) variance in seed production per plant; (C) longevity of the sessile plant; (D) phenology of flowering, required in species 2 for survival given that it is identical with species 1 in all other respects. Hatching indicates areas where co-existence is possible. $c = \sigma^2/a$. (From Fagerström & Ågren, 1979)

known that coexisting species may also be differentiated with respect to the magnitude of this temporal variation as predicted above. However, several studies (reviewed by Grubb, 1977) support this prediction, e.g., for forest trees in Prussia (Schwappach, 1895) and New Zealand (Beveridge, 1973). Grubb (1977:123) identified three main patterns of time variation in seed production, *viz.* (i) moderate production in most years, (ii) fruiting rather irregular, and (iii) abundant fruiting strongly periodic. Regarding these patterns as alternative strategies, our results show that either (i) or (ii) may be advantageous depending on the signs of the pairwise correlations between the diaspore productions of the involved species, while (iii) is not covered by our analysis.

It is well established that coexisting species may be differentiated with respect to phenology of flowering or fruiting (e.g., Snow, 1965, 1968). This phenomenon is

549

frequently interpreted as being a result of competition for pollinators (Mosquin, 1971; Stiles, 1975) or seed dispersal agents (Snow, 1965). However, as further explained in Fagerström & Ågren (1980), $\varrho < 1$ can be interpreted as the two species being phenologically separated, and hence our analysis suggests that phenological spread in itself makes for coexistence, without the assumption that it serves as a partitioner of, e.g., pollinators. This result may explain the observations that phenological spread occurs also among apomictic species and species pollinated by wind (e.g., Pemadasa & Lovell, 1974). Also, it suggests an answer to the doubts raised by Harper (1977:719): "It is not easy to see the relevance of differentiation between flowering periods unless the plants are competing for pollinators or for seed dispersal agents – both these interpretations seem improbable."

The idea that competition for pollinators should be a force promoting phenological separation has been discussed by several authors (Levin & Anderson, 1970; Mosquin, 1971; Straw, 1972; Stiles, 1975; Wissel, 1977; Waser, 1978a, b), their idea being that the decreased competition should increase the seed production and consequently the fitness of the involved species. However, it is not certain that an increased seed production is beneficial because the increased seed production will also lead to an increased competition between seedlings. The situation can be summarized as: increased phenological separation as such decreases competition between seedlings and decreases competition for pollinators with a subsequent increased seed production. Both these two effects taken separately should be advantageous to the involved species. But a third, counter-acting, effect is the increased competition between seedlings due to the increased seed production. We have analyzed with the present two-species model the balance between these opposite forces (Ågren & Fagerström, 1980) and found that depending upon the strength in the coupling between the changes in phenological separation and seed production, as well as the position in parameter space of the species, there are three possible outcomes: (i) species 1 loses and species 2 gains, this happens when a change in phenological separation is accompanied by only a small change in seed production; (ii) both species gain, this is the case when a_1 and a_2 are small: (iii) species 1 gains and species 2 loses, this occurs when there is a strong coupling between changes in phenological separation and seed production or a_1 and a_2 are large.

If we assume, according to, e.g., Roughgarden (1976), that differentiation with respect to either of the parameters discussed in this analysis imposes a cost on the differentiating population, we should expect an inferior competitor to differ from its competitors by just the minimum amount required for survival, i.e., by the amounts obtained if the inequalities (1) are replaced by equalities. The limit to similarity thus obtained is equivalent to that of the celebrated theory of limiting similarity in the context of resource partitioning (MacArthur & Levins, 1967). However, as seen from the above equalities, we find no correspondence with the robust "$d/w \approx 1$" prediction of the latter theory (May, 1973); instead our analysis suggests that the limits to similarity in plants differing in regeneration properties are highly dependent on where in parameter space a given species is represented. Thus, it follows from the inequalities (1) that the minimum amount of differentiation required in species 2 with respect to a_2, σ_2 and ϱ, respectively, depends strongly on all other parameters.

It is important to point out that the possibilities for coexistence are enhanced through the variable environment. The interesting consequence is thus that variability of the environment should not necessarily be seen as a stress that an organism should attempt to buffer against, but as something which could be taken advantage of and utilized. These ideas are expanded in some recent articles (Levins, 1979; Ekbohm *et al.*, 1980; P. Chesson & R. Warner, unpubl.).

Acknowledgements

This work was carried out within the Swedish Coniferous Forest Project.

References

Ågren, G. I. & Fagerström, T. 1980. Increased or decreased separation of flowering times? The joint effect of competition for space and pollination in plants. – Oikos 35: 161–164.

Beveridge, A. E. 1973. Regeneration of podocarps in central North Island forest. – N. Z. J. For. 18: 23–35.

Ekbohm, G., Fagerström, T. & Ågren, G. I. 1980. Natural selection for variation in offspring numbers: Comments on a paper by J. H. Gillespie. – Am. Nat. 115: 445–447.

Fagerström, T. & Ågren, G. I. 1979. Theory for coexistence of species differing in regeneration properties. – Oikos. 33: 1–10.

Fagerström, T. & Ågren, G. I. 1980. Phenological spread in plants: a result of adaptations to environmental stochasticity. – Vegetatio 43: 83–86.

Grubb, P. J. 1977. The maintenance of species-richness in plant communities: the importance of the regeneration niche. – Biol. Rev. 52: 107–145.

Harper, J. L. 1967. A Darwinian approach to plant ecology. – J. Ecol. 55: 247–270.

Harper, J. L. 1977. Population Biology of Plants. London–New York–San Francisco: Academic Press, 892 pp.

Levin, D. A. & Anderson, W. A. 1970. Competition for pollinators between simultaneously flowering species. – Am. Nat. 104: 455–467.

Levins, R. 1979. Coexistence in a variable environment. – Am. Nat. 114: 765–783.

MacArthur, R. H. & Levins, R. 1967. The limiting similarity, convergence and divergence of coexisting species. – Am. Nat. 101: 377–385.

May, R. M. 1973. Stability and Complexity in Model Ecosystems. – Princeton, N. J.: Princeton Univ. Press, 235 pp.

Mosquin, T. 1971. Competition for pollinators as a stimulus for the evolution of flowering time. – Oikos 22: 398–402.

Pemadasa, M. A. & Lovell, P. H. 1974. Factors controlling the flowering time of some dune annuals. – J. Ecol. 62: 869–880.

Roughgarden, J. 1976. Resource partitioning among competing species – a coevolutionary approach. – Theor. Pop. Biol. 9: 388–424.

Schoener, T. W. 1974. Resource partitioning in ecological communities. – Science 185: 27–39.

Schwappach, A. 1895. Die Samenproduktion der wichtigsten Waldholzarten in Preussen. – Z. Forst- u. Jagdw. 27: 147–174.

Snow, D. W. 1965. A possible selective factor in the evolution of fruiting seasons in tropical forest. – Oikos 15: 274–281.

Snow, D. W. 1968. Fruiting seasons and bird breeding seasons in the New World tropics. – J. Ecol. 56: 5P–6P.

Stiles, F. G. 1975. Ecology, flowering phenology, and hummingbird pollination of some Costa Rican *Heliconia* species. – Ecology 56: 285–301.

Straw, R. M. 1972. A Markov model for pollinator constancy and competition. – Am. Nat. 106: 597–620.

Waser, N. M. 1978. Competition for pollination and sequential flowering of two Colorado wildflowers. – Ecology 59: 934–944.

Waser, N. M. 1978b. Interspecific pollen transfer and competition between co-occurring plant species. – Oecologia (Berl.) 36: 223–236.

Wissel, C. 1977. On the advantage of the specialization of flowers on particular pollinator species. – J. theor. Biol. 69: 11–22.

Persson, T. (ed) 1980
Structure and Function of Northern
Coniferous Forests – An Ecosystem Study
Ecol. Bull. (Stockholm) 32: 553–564.

MODELLING OF SOIL PROCESSES – AN INTRODUCTION

E. Bosatta[1]

Abstract

Two models developed within the Swedish Coniferous Forest Project are presented. The first model, N1NIT, was used to simulate the seasonal and annual variations in nitrogen mineralization, uptake by roots and leaching in the mor layer of a pine forest soil. The second model, N1EXCH, was aimed to simulate the dynamics in soil (mor + mineral layers) of different ions after nutrient addition. A description of the structure of both models is given. Finally an outline of the experience acquired in modelling is given by discussing how these models, considered as a collection of existing knowledge, have been used to stimulate more original research.

Additional keywords: Decomposition, ion exchange, leaching, nitrogen mineralization, uptake by roots.

Introduction

The main topic of this paper is to describe the structure and to discuss some predicaments of two soil models developed in order to analyze two different problem-areas. The general purpose of both models is to simulate, or in other words, to describe the dynamics of some nutrients present in the soil system. If $x(t)$ denotes the concentration of a nutrient in some soil compound at time t, some processes will produce an increase in x, i.e., an inflow at the rate of the processes, while the others will produce an outflow, and in this way the rate of change, $\dot{x}$, of x can be expressed as:

$$\dot{x} \equiv dx/dt = (\text{sum of rates of processes in}) - (\text{sum of rates of processes out}) \quad (1)$$

It is by means of solving a system of differential equations of this form, normally with the aid of a computer, that the dynamics of the nutrients are simulated by both models.

It is known that the best way of dealing with complex models is to construct them starting with submodels covering more delimited problem-areas (see for example Goodall, 1976). Submodels correspond, in this way, to the subprograms or modules linked together in a program by the computer. The two models here are constructed around three main categories of submodels with the main purpose to formulate and calculate the rates of different processes with a time resolution of one day. These submodels are:

[1] Dept. of Ecology and Environmental Research, Swedish University of Agricultural Sciences, S-750 07 Uppsala, Sweden

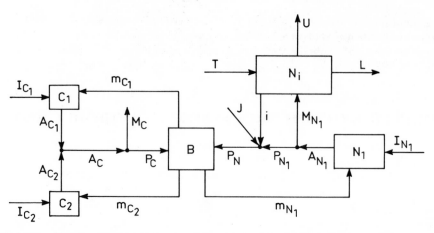

Figure 1. Flow diagram of nitrogen and carbon in the soil. N_1, N_i = organic and inorganic nitrogen pools, C_1 = organic carbon bound to organic nitrogen, C_2 = organic carbon not bound to nitrogen, B = decomposer biomass. I_{C_1}, I_{C_2}, I_{N_1} = rate of input of each element through litterfall and root litter formation. A_{C_1}, A_{C_2}, A_{N_1}, A_C = assimilation rate of each element and of total carbon. P_C, P_N, P_{N_1} = incorporation rate in biomass of total carbon, total nitrogen and organic nitrogen. M_C, M_{N_1} = mineralization rate of carbon and nitrogen. m_{C_1}, m_{C_2}, m_{N_1} = decomposer mortality rate in terms of carbon and nitrogen. J = nitrogen fixation rate, i = nitrogen inmobilization rate. T, L, U = rates of throughfall, leaching and uptake by roots, respectively, in terms of nitrogen. The sums of flows going out from one point must equal the sum of flows coming in; so, for example, $A_C = A_{C_1} + A_{C_2}$ must apply all the time.

(1) DECOM – deals with processes such as mineralization, decomposition, assimilation, production of decomposer biomass, immobilization, etc.
(2) INORG – deals with adsorption of nutrients to soil particles, exchange, leaching, etc.
(3) ROOT – deals with uptake of nutrients by the root system.

As a means of testing different hypotheses, however, alternative versions of a module have sometimes been used.

The space available in a report of this kind is usually too restricted for detailed discussions to be given of applications, results as well as mathematical details of a model. This paper attempts to give proper consideration to the mathematical details and, thus, only few results (mainly with illustrative purposes) will be presented together with the description of the models. More exhaustive discussions on these results and applications will be the subject of forthcoming papers.

Description of the models

N1NIT – a carbon-nitrogen model

A great deal of knowledge exists on separate nitrogen transfer processes in soil. This model is an attempt to synthesize some of the existing hypotheses on how nitrogen mineralization, transport, adsorption, and uptake by plant roots are regulated. The model (see Bosatta et al., 1980) was applied to the soil mor layer of a forest site from which a reasonably complete set of empirical data exists on climate, soil processes, and components over several years. The aims were to study whether such an integrat-

554

ed model can give a realistic view of nitrogen transfers, to and from the soil solution, as far as it can be tested from measured data, and to identify possible functions in the system which are less satisfactorily described at present. The basic objective was thus to get an improved background for further studies of how soil factors regulate the plant nutrient uptake by plants.

The simplest possible structure was chosen with respect to the level of knowledge about the included processes, biotic and abiotic components in relation to time scale and the type of problem to be analyzed. Fig. 1 shows the compartments and processes concerning nitrogen and carbon transformation in the model. The litter (L) and humus (FH) layers are combined to one functional structure. Decomposers are considered to utilize this structural substrate, which is made up of the three chemical substrates: C_1 = organic carbon in C–N compounds (substances, such as proteins, which contain nitrogen as a molecular constituent), C_2 = organic carbon in C–C compounds (such as cellulose) and N_1 = organic nitrogen in C–N compounds.

In previous versions of DECOM (Berg & Bosatta, 1976), the organic matter was partitioned in several organic substrates but it was found that variables of interest, such as total nitrogen mineralization, transport and uptake by plants were insensitive to this partition. The inorganic nitrogen compartment, N_i, includes adsorbed ammonium ions and ammonium in the soil solution. The driving variables, on which the rates of processes depend, are provided by external sources (Halldin *et al.*, 1980). These are:

D_1 = soil temperature (°C), D_4 = water content (fraction of volume), D_7 = water infiltration (l m^{-2} day^{-1}) and D_8 = water percolation (l m^{-2} day^{-1}).

The rates of inputs I_{C_2}, I_{C_2} and I_{N_1} (see Fig. 1) are also driving variables. They are generated by the model by defining for chosen time periods of the year a certain daily amount of litterfall and root litter formation. The compartments are expressed in units of g m^{-2} and hence, all rates are in g m^{-2} day^{-1}.

DECOM module

The theory of Parnas (1975) on the substrate exploitation strategy of decomposers has been adopted. The basic idea is that either carbon or nitrogen may be suboptimal in the substrate in relation to decomposer needs, and that an optimal composition exists. If nitrogen is the limiting nutrient element, decomposers use nitrogen compounds primarily as a nitrogen source and the non-nitrogen compounds as the main carbon source. If, on the other hand, carbon is limiting, the simple hypothesis is used that both nitrogen and non-nitrogen compounds serve equally well as carbon sources. The whole substrate is then looked upon as one unit. When its effective C/N ratio is lower than that for optimal production rate there will be a nitrogen surplus and nitrogen mineralization will occur. This optimal or "critical" C/N ratio can be calculated from knowledge of the chemical composition of the decomposer biomass and the efficiency of carbon utilization in their biomass production. In N1NIT the critical C/N ratio is a parameter which, compared to the C/N ratio of a certain substrate, determines whether decomposition calculations are to be made on the assumption of carbon or nitrogen as the limiting substance. The parameters are: G_m = specific production rate of decomposers in a reference state (day^{-1}), f_C = C-fraction of decomposer biomass (in dry weight), f_N = N-fraction of decomposer biomass (in dry weight), e = production/assimilation ratio for carbon, d_B = specific

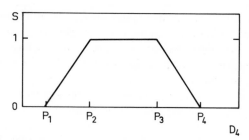

Figure 2. The moisture scale function, $S(D_4)$, regulating decomposer specific production rate. As seen, four parameters are needed in order to define the function.

mortality rate of decomposers (day^{-1}), φ = fraction of decomposer biomass fixing nitrogen, $Q = Q_{10}$ factor of temperature response of decomposer production rate, and r_c = "critical" carbon-nitrogen ratio $= f_C/(f_N e)$.

Two auxiliary variables are:

$r(t) = (C_1 + C_2)/N_1$ i.e., the carbon-nitrogen ratio of the decomposing substrate

and

$r_1(t) = C_1/N_1$ i.e., the carbon-nitrogen ratio of the C–N compounds in the substrate.

The specific production rate of decomposers is:

$$G = \begin{cases} G_m S(D_4) Q^{(D_1 - 20)/10} \\ 0 \quad \text{(if carbon or nitrogen are exhausted)} \end{cases} \tag{2}$$

where $S(D_4)$ is shown in Fig. 2. According to Eq. (2) the specific rate will be equal to G_m when $D_1 = 20°C$ and D_4 is in the optimal range ($P_2 - P_3$ in Fig. 2).

In a changing substrate the specific production rate of decomposers might also be affected by the developing substrate quality. Parnas (1975) described the dependence on carbon and nitrogen concentrations and the C/N ratio in addition to temperature and moisture. However, when whole soil layers are regarded as one single morphological substrate, the gross substrate quality is not likely to change during the course of one year. Besides, the concentration concept is difficult to apply to terrestrial environments. Certainly there is a dependence of concentration on a micro-scale level in the soil solution, which is not described here, when using a rough substrate definition suitable for the ecosystem level.

The biomass production rate, P, is defined as $P = GB$ and, thus, the incorporation rate of carbon (P_C) and the incorporation rate of nitrogen (P_N) are given by $P_C = f_C GB$ and $P_N = f_N GB$.

The nitrogen fixation rate is defined as $J = \varphi f_N GB$, i.e., as the required amount of nitrogen, P_N, times the fraction, φ, of the nitrogen fixed. The remaining nitrogen, $P_N - J$, must partially be supplied by the inorganic pool, N_i. Thus, nitrogen immobilization rate is calculated as:

$i = (P_N - J)N_i/(N_i + N_1 D_4)$

Note that not all N_1 is assumed equally available as N_i, and that the factor defining this availability has been assumed as equal to D_4, i.e., the fraction of the volume filled with water. The incorporation rate of organic nitrogen is (see Fig. 1):

556

$$P_{N_1} = P_N - J - i$$

The assimilation rate of carbon is:

$$A_C = P_C/e = f_C GB/e$$

and the respiration rate:

$$M_C = A_C - P_C = (1-e)f_C GB/e$$

The C_1 assimilation (decomposition) rate is given by:

$$A_{C_1} = \begin{cases} r_1 P_{N_1} & \text{if } r > r_c & \text{(3a)} \\ A_C C_1/(C_1 + C_2) & \text{if } r \leq r_c & \text{(3b)} \end{cases}$$

i.e., in the first case, when nitrogen is limiting, C_1 is decomposed according to the requirements of nitrogen for production. In the second case – the energy limited system – C_1 is decomposed according to the requirements of carbon. The C_2 assimilation rate is:

$$A_{C_2} = A_C - A_{C_1}$$

N_1 assimilation rate is given by:

$$A_{N_1} = A_{C_1}/r_1 \tag{4}$$

and the nitrogen mineralization rate is:

$$M_{N_1} = A_{N_1} - P_{N_1}$$

If now A_{C_1} is given by Eq. (3a), one can see that according to Eq. (4), $A_{N_1} = P_{N_1}$ and thus $M_{N_1} = 0$. On the other hand, if the system is energy limited, M_{N_1} will be greater than zero.

The mortality rate of decomposers is: $m = d_B B$, where d_B is the specific mortality rate (day^{-1}). If the carbon-nitrogen ratio of the C–N compounds in the biomass of decomposers is 4 g g^{-1}, the transfers of carbon and nitrogen to organic matter due to decomposer mortality are given by: $m_{C_1} = 4f_N m$; $m_{C_2} = (f_C - 4f_N)m$; $m_{N_1} = f_N m$.

INORG module

The parameters in the INORG module are: c_0 = concentration of inorganic nitrogen at throughfall, g_0 = amount of ammonium adsorbed to soil particles when the soil complex is in a given reference state, μ_0 = chemical potential at the reference state, k = slope of the adsorption isotherm curve, and c_r = remaining ion concentration.

The throughfall input rate is defined as $T = D_7 c_0$, where c_0 is defined above (g l^{-1}). Similarly, the rate of leaching is:

$$L = D_8 c \tag{5}$$

where c is the nitrogen concentration in the soil solution (g l^{-1}) which is, in part, controlled by the exchange processes between ammonium and the remaining ions occurring at the adsorption sites in the soil particles.

The exchange phenomenon is handled as follows: let $g(t)$ be the amount of inorganic nitrogen adsorbed to soil particles; the following relation between N_i, c and g (all three, henceforth, expressed in meq l^{-1}) must be fulfilled:

$$N_i(t) = D_4(t)c(t) + g(t) \tag{6}$$

If $g(t)$ is known, $c(t)$ can be determined from this expression since $N_i(t)$ is already calculated by the model. One way to determine $g(t)$ could be to formulate an explicit equation like (1), i.e.,

$$\dot{g} = f(g, c, c_r)$$

where $\dot{g}$, the net adsorption rate, is assumed to be a function of g, c and c_r. The disadvantages of this procedure are twofold; the complexity of the model is increased by the addition of the extra compartment g, and some knowledge is required about the kinetics of the exchange processes. To avoid this, $\dot{g}$ is set to zero, and the adsorbed amount obtained as a function of both concentrations, i.e., $g = g(c, c_r)$.

This approximation, known as the adiabatic elimination hypothesis (see e.g., Haken, 1977), can be used if the relaxation times involved in the exchange processes are much shorter than those in the remaining processes. The approximation $\dot{g} = 0$ can also be interpreted as a "steady state approximation", meaning that, at each time step, g immediately adjusts to the steady state value imposed on it by the remaining system, i.e., all transient effects in g are ignored. Equation (6) is now written as:

$$N_i = D_4 c + g(c, c_r) \tag{7}$$

and can be used to calculate the concentration c if $g(c, c_r)$ is explicitly defined. The function $g(c, c_r)$, known as the adsorption isotherm, is obtained by measuring the changes in the adsorbed amount with respect to a reference state, as a function of the chemical potential in the equilibrium solution. Under conditions of chemical equilibrium the adsorption rate equals desorption rate, i.e., the net rate of adsorption is zero, in agreement with the approximation introduced above. According to Bringmark (1977) the isotherm is given by:

$$g = g_0 + k(\mu - \mu_0) \tag{8}$$

where g_0 (meq 1^{-1}), μ_0 (J meq^{-1}) and k(meq^2 J^{-1} 1^{-1}) are defined as above and the chemical potential, μ, is given by:

$$\mu = RD_1 \left(3 \ln c^a - 2 \ln \frac{c_r^a}{3}\right) \tag{9}$$

where R is the universal gas constant (J meq^{-1} K). D_1 is temperature (here in °K) and c^a and c_r^a are the chemical activities (dimensionless) of ammonium and remaining ions. These are defined as:

$$c^a = f^a c \, 10^{-3}; \quad c_r^a = f_r^a c_r \, 10^{-3}$$

where f^a and f_r^a, henceforth assumed equal to one, are the activity coefficients (1 eq^{-1}).

Since the logarithm term makes it difficult to obtain c directly from Eq. (7), this equation is differentiated as:

$$dN_i = (D_4 + \partial g/\partial c)dc = \beta dc \tag{10}$$

which gives the change induced in the concentration, dc, by a change dN_i produced in the time interval dt under the assumption that D_4 is kept constant during this interval. In simulations with the model, a value is defined for c at the start and the successive increments are calculated with an equation similar to Eq. (10) (for more details see Bosatta & Bringmark, 1976).

558

A useful quantity is obtained by taking the average of β over an interval (c_1, c_2) of concentrations, namely, the linear buffering power of the soil, b. According to this and using equations (8), (9) and (10):

$$b = D_4 + \frac{3kRD_1}{c_2 - c_1} \ln \frac{c_2}{c_1} = D_4 + b_g \qquad (11)$$

In this range of concentrations Eq. (7) can be approximated by:

$$N_i = (D_4 + b_g)c = bc$$

and the rate of leaching can be expressed as:

$$L = D_8 N_i / (Vb) = k_L N_i \qquad (12)$$

where V is the volume (l) of the soil layer, k_L is the specific rate of leaching (day^{-1}) and N_i the inorganic nitrogen pool (g m^{-2}). It can be seen from equations (11) and (12) that the rate of leaching will reach a maximum if the ion is not adsorbed to the soil, i.e., if k (and hence b_g) is equal to zero.

ROOT module

The parameters are: $\varrho =$ root density or specific root length (cm cm^{-3}), $a =$ root radius (cm), $d_2 =$ diffusion coefficient of the ammonium ion in free solution (cm^2 day^{-1}), $b_g =$ a term in the linear buffering power of the soil (see Eq. 11). According to Baldwin (1975), the amount of nitrogen taken up by the roots in a time interval Δ_t is given by:

$$U = \left[1 - \exp \left\{ \frac{-2\pi d_2 D_4{}^2 \Delta_t \varrho}{b \ln(a_e/1.65a)} \right\} \right] \cdot N_i = k_U N_i \qquad (13)$$

where $b = b_g + D_4$ and $a_e = (\pi\varrho)^{-1/2}$ is the effective radius of the soil cylinder surrounding the root (cm), and N_i is the ammonium pool (g m^{-2}). If Δ_t is one day, the term in brackets, k_U, can be interpreted as the specific rate of nitrogen uptake (day^{-1}) and, in this way, U is the daily rate of nitrogen uptake by the roots (g m^{-2} day^{-1}).

Application of the model

In order to find out the degree to which the model represents the natural situation, attempts were made to falsify the submodels and the integrated N1NIT. It was considered that qualitative properties of the model were more appropriate to test than quantitative ones, since the present aim was to clarify mechanisms. This meant that time sequences and relative magnitudes of processes were considered more important than absolute figures.

Field data on inorganic nitrogen, decomposer biomass, carbon and nitrogen mineralization and leaching from different years, mainly obtained from 1976 from a mature stand, were used to test the validity of the model outputs (see Bosatta et al., 1980). One example is shown in Fig. 3.

N1EXCH – a model for ion exchange

The N1EXCH model simulates the dynamics of the mineral fraction of different ions after nutrient addition to the soil (Bosatta & Bringmark, in prep.). The added nutrients are assumed to move only downwards and to be subjected to exchange

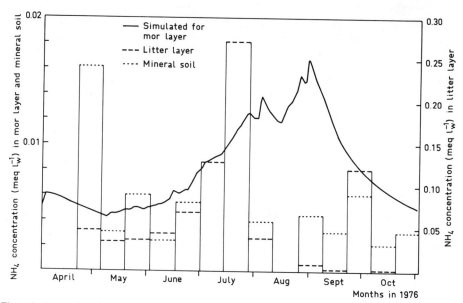

Figure 3. Comparison between measured and simulated NH₄ concentrations in the soil solution in 1976. The simulated concentrations are daily values for the mor layer, while the measurements were made every fourteen days in lysimeter leachates from the litter layer and in the mineral soil 6 cm below the mor layer. (From Bosatta *et al.*, 1980)

processes and to uptake by the root systems. Furthermore, it was assumed that the fate of the nutrients "normally" produced by the system is irrelevant here and, thus, no DECOM module is included. The soil was divided into three compartments: (1) the L + FH layer plus 0–10 cm of the mineral soil, (2) 10–40 cm of the mineral soil and (3) 40–90 cm of the mineral soil.

The external driving variables, temperature and water, are now defined for each soil layer. The input of nutrients is also a driving variable.

Two compartments are considered for each soil layer, *viz.*, x = the amount of a given ion, and x_r = the amount of remaining ions. Thus the parameters in the INORG module are as before, except that

– c_0, g_0, μ_0 and k are given the values corresponding to the ion chosen for the simulation and/or the layer of the soil, and

– c_r is no longer a parameter (see below) and a new parameter is introduced, namely, E, the cation exchange capacity of the soil (meq l⁻¹).

The flows are defined through equations similar to Eq. (5), so the concentration of x in solution, c (meq l⁻¹), and the corresponding one for the remaining ions, c_r, must first be calculated.

To this end two equations must be solved for each soil layer for c and c_r:

$$x = D_4 c + g(c, c_r) \tag{14a}$$

$$x_r = D_4 c_r + [E\text{-}g(c, c_r)] \tag{14b}$$

560

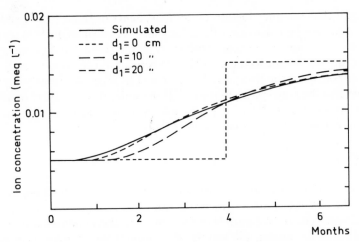

Figure 4. The propagation of a concentration front through a homogeneous soil column at a depth of 95 cm as simulated with the three compartments of N1EXCH and as given by the solution of equation (16) for three values of the dispersion coefficient d_1. At time zero the concentration at the top of the soil is raised to 0.015 meq. l^{-1} and afterwards is kept constant. $D_8 = 0.16$ cm d^{-1}, $b = 0.20$. Under these conditions, the numerical dispersion is approximately equivalent to the 20 cm hydrodynamic dispersion.

Thus, the adsorbed amount of remaining ions is defined as the difference between the cation exchange capacity, E, and the adsorbed amount, g, of the ion x. Introducing the variables $x_t = x + x_r$ and $c_t = c + c_r$, equations (14a) and (14b) can be transformed to:

$$x = D_4 c + g(c, c_t) \tag{15a}$$

$$x_t = D_4 c_t + E \tag{15b}$$

In this way c_t can be obtained directly from Eq. (15b) and, after inserting it in Eq. (15a), one equation is left with the unknown c, which can be solved with the methods used before (see Eq. 10 and onwards).

It can be seen that by using the definition of c_t, Eqs. (15b) and (10), and assuming D_4 constant, one gets:

$$dc_r = dx/D_4 - dx/\beta = dx \ \frac{\beta - D_4}{\beta D_4}$$

which means that as a result of the exchange interaction formulated by equations (15a) and (15b), and the fact that $\beta \geq D_4$, c_r (and thus, leaching) will increase if x is increased.

Uptake of both x and x_r in the root system is assumed to occur only in the first soil layer and, thus, the parameters in the ROOT module are as before, except that b_g and d_2 must now be specified for the ion x and for the remaining ions x_r. The specific and the daily uptake rates are then calculated as before (see equation 13 and onwards).

A simplified version of N1EXCH (with only one ion x and no ROOT module) has also been used to analyze the numerical dispersion caused by the introduction of finite soil layers.

561

It is known that the introduction of compartments of finite size to simulate the transport of an ion by convection flow, i.e., such as given by Eq. (5), can lead to considerable distortion (numerical dispersion) of the simulated concentration profile (see e.g. de Wit & van Keulen, 1972). Dispersion, on the other hand, is an additional component of the transport flow, caused by variable water velocity in the different parts of the pore system in the soil. If the water flow, D_8 (here in dm day^{-1}), and the buffering power, b (see Eq. 11), are assumed constant, the equation describing the dynamics of a concentration front is:

$$\frac{\partial c}{\partial t} = -\frac{D_8}{b}\frac{\partial c}{\partial z} + \frac{d_1|D_8|}{b}\frac{\partial^2 c}{\partial z^2} \tag{16}$$

where d_1 (dm) is the coefficient of hydrodynamic dispersion, z (dm) is depth in the soil and $|D_8|$ is the absolute value of the water flow.

In order to estimate the magnitude of the numerical dispersion caused by the finite compartments in the model, the simulated concentration profiles were compared with analytical solutions of Eq. (16) obtained for different values of d_1 and given boundary conditions (see Fig. 4).

Discussion

From the descriptions given above it is evident that both models can be looked upon as a well organized collection of already existing knowledge. This first stage in the modelling has fulfilled two important purposes. It has provided a number of people with a common language to discuss a certain area of problems and it has influenced the organization of data collected in field or laboratory experiments.

Even if it is known that no general recipes can be given to generate new theories (see e.g., chapter 8 in Bunge, 1967), it seems natural to ask, in a second stage, whether these models can be used to create new knowledge. In some cases, discrepancies between the actual and the expected behaviour of parts of a model (see, for example, Fig. 3) may imply that more delimited but more original problems should be looked for. The analysis of some structural properties of a model may sometimes also lead to the acquisition of new results. For example, using a modified version of N1NIT, the stability properties of the root-decomposer system have been analyzed under varying conditions for positive or negative net mineralization of nitrogen to occur. This analysis, which has only been possible through the use of simplifying hypotheses and approximations, resulted in the following conclusions:

– If decomposers are energy limited (nitrogen net mineralization positive), the system is asymptotically stable, thus permitting persistent coexistence of roots and decomposers;
– if decomposers are nitrogen limited (net mineralization negative), microorganisms "outcompete" the roots;
– if the system oscillates between both states (energy and nitrogen limited), dynamic stability can prevail, permitting persistent coexistence (see Fig. 5).

The influence that several factors such as mortality rates, rate of leaching, etc., have on this state of dynamic stability, has also been analyzed (E. Bosatta, in prep.).

From a more practical point of view, it may also be convenient to simplify a model

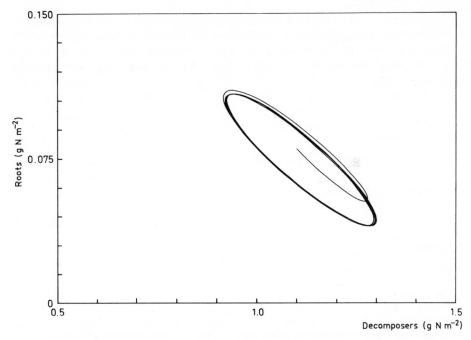

Figure 5. Trajectory described after ten years by the decomposer-root system. When decomposers are nitrogen-limited and thus nitrogen net mineralization is negative, the root concentration decreases. When decomposers are energy limited (net mineralization positive), roots recover and their concentration increases. In this example, decomposers are nitrogen-limited during, approximately, 20% of the year. The system is stable since decomposers and roots are both greater than zero.

so that it yields simpler relations between a reduced number of variables. This new, simpler model may be more suitable for generalizations than the former one.

The example of N1NIT, which is a model representing a system in approximately steady state, can be considered. Using this assumption, *viz.*, that the system approximately returns to its original state after a year, a simple relation can easily be established between the annual nitrogen input, I_N (here in g m^{-2} yr^{-1}) and the annual nitrogen uptake in the roots, U (here also in g m^{-2} yr^{-1}), namely:

$$U = \frac{k_U}{k_U + k_L} I_N \tag{17a}$$

where k_L and k_U are defined in equations (12) and (13), respectively. Similarly, the annual leaching, L (g m^{-2} yr^{-1}) is

$$L = \frac{k_L}{k_U + k_L} I_N \tag{17b}$$

Equations (17a) and (17b) are, thus, the new model. If the amount of input at throughfall can be neglected, I_N in the above expressions can be replaced by the amount of nitrogen mineralized during the year. Giving numerical values to the parameters, and taking mean values for D_4 and D_8 appearing in k_L and k_U, one finds that approximately 96% of the mineralized nitrogen will go to the roots and approximately

4% to leaching. This result is in agreement not only with the values predicted by NINIT but with the calculated annual budget for the system (Staaf & Berg, 1977).

Simplified models built in this way have a greater resolution time than the original model and, thus, they may be useful in a third stage, i.e., in the description of long-range phenomena.

Acknowledgement

I wish to acknowledge the support of many members of the Swedish Coniferous Forest Project and particularly those in the soil process group who patiently put up with my unlearned chatter.

References

Baldwin, J. P. 1975. A quantitative analysis of the factors affecting plant nutrient uptake from some soils. – J. Soil Sci. 26: 195–206.

Berg, B. & Bosatta, E. 1976. A carbon-nitrogen model of a pine forest soil ecosystem – development paper. – Swed. Conif. For. Proj. Int. Rep. 42, 61 pp.

Bosatta, E. & Bringmark, L. 1976. A model for transport and adsorption of inorganic ions in a pine forest soil ecosystem. – A development paper. – Swed. Conif. For. Proj. Int. Rep. 43, 42 pp.

Bosatta, E., Bringmark, L. & Staaf, H. 1980. Nitrogen transformations in a Scots pine forest mor–model analysis of mineralization, uptake by roots and leaching. – In: Persson, T. (ed.) Structure and Function of Northern Coniferous Forests – An Ecosystem Study, Ecol. Bull. (Stockholm) 32: 565–589.

Bringmark, L. 1977. Cation adsorption in a sandy pine forest soil. – Swed. Conif. For. Proj. Int. Rep. 52, 29 pp.

Bunge, M. 1967. Studies in the Foundations Methodology and Philosophy of Science. Scientific Research I. The Search for System. Vol. 3/1. New York–Heidelberg–Berlin: Springer-Verlag, 536 pp.

Goodall, D. W. 1976. The hierarchical approach to model building. – In: Arnold, G. W. & de Wit, C. T. (eds.) Critical Evaluation of Systems Analysis in Ecosystems Research and Management, pp. 10–21. Wageningen: Pudoc.

Haken, H. 1977. Synergetics. An Introduction. Berlin–Heidelberg–New York: Springer-Verlag, 320 pp.

Halldin, S., Grip, H., Jansson, P-E. & Lindgren, Å. 1980. Micrometeorology and hydrology of pine forest ecosystems. II. Theories and models. – In: Persson, T. (ed.). Structure and Function of Northern Coniferous Forests – An Ecosystem Study, Ecol. Bull. (Stockholm) 32: 463–503.

Parnas, H. 1975. Model for decomposition of organic material by microorganisms. – Soil Biol. Biochem. 7: 161–169.

Staaf, H. & Berg, B. 1977. Mobilization of plant nutrients in a Scots pine forest mor in Central Sweden. – Silva fenn. 11: 210–217.

de Wit, C. T. & van Keulen, H. 1972. Simulation of Transport Processes in Soils. Wageningen: Centre for Agricultural Publishing and Documentation, 99 pp.

Persson, T. (ed) 1980
Structure and Function of Northern
Coniferous Forests – An Ecosystem Study
Ecol. Bull. (Stockholm) 32:565–589.

NITROGEN TRANSFORMATIONS IN A SCOTS PINE FOREST MOR – MODEL ANALYSIS OF MINERALIZATION, UPTAKE BY ROOTS AND LEACHING

E. Bosatta[1], L. Bringmark[2] and H. Staaf[2]*

Abstract

The dynamic interaction between nitrogen mineralization, immobilization, leaching, and uptake by roots in the plant-soil system of an old Scots pine (*Pinus sylvestris* L.) forest in Central Sweden was analyzed by means of a mechanistic model, N1NIT. Submodels on decomposition, uptake by roots and ion exchange were joined into an integrated model. Outputs from it were thereafter compared to measured processes and state variables.

The simulations depict a system with a very tight nitrogen circulation. Mineralization is on most occasions immediately balanced by root uptake. The level of mineral nitrogen resulting from this balance is determined by water content and root density, which thereby have direct influence on the leaching. A mineralization maximum is always reached in early autumn as result of a successive growth of the decomposer biomass during summer. Temperature and moisture conditions in soil have a great effect on the annual accumulated mineralization and uptake by roots. Furthermore, in summer the climate influences the build-up of a microbial biomass, and in early autumn the immediate effect on its activity is most pronounced.

Field observations support, to some extent, the image given by the model, but there are important contradictions. The seasonal development of the inorganic nitrogen compartment in the model appears, for example, less realistic, and the possibility of an imperfect representation of nitrogen transfers in immobilization and humification are indicated. The difficulty in predicting the between-year variation of decomposer biomass suggests a formulation of mineralization for long-term models, which should be less dependent on organism properties than in the present model.

Additional keywords: Decomposition, humus, litter, microorganisms.

Introduction

All soil processes coupled to decomposer activity, including weight loss of litter and humus (Witkamp, 1966; Wood, 1974) and mineralization of nitrogen (Zöttl, 1960 etc.), are known to be temperature and moisture dependent. As the physical processes generally are less temperature dependent than the biological, the climatic influence on nutrient transports in soil is mainly affected by the water conditions. Nutrient uptake by plants is often regarded to be regulated by a combination of factors determining the supply rate, transport in soil, root

[1] Dept. of Ecology and Environmental Research, Swedish University of Agricultural Sciences, S-750 07 Uppsala, Sweden
[2] Dept. of Plant Ecology, University of Lund, S-223 62 Lund, Sweden
* Authors given alphabetically. See also Acknowledgements.

geometry and uptake efficiency of plants for the specific element (see e.g. Baldwin *et al.,* 1973). In boreal coniferous forests nitrogen is normally a limiting nutrient element for primary production (Tamm, 1975), and thus it needs particular attention.

Annual ring increments in wood of Scots pine have been found to be related to climatic variables of both current and preceding years (Eklund, 1954; Jonsson, 1969). Both direct plant responses on climate and indirect ones via the nutrient supply from soil can be expected to be involved in this phenomenon. In northern European soils climatic conditions which improve decomposition and nitrogen mineralization might be considered analogous to small additions of inorganic nitrogen fertilizer and the maximum tree growth response to fertilization has a time delay of about three years (Tamm & Carbonnier, 1961; Fagerström & Lohm, 1977). In a variable climate this results in a complicated year to year variation in productivity of a forest, which can be explained only from a fundamental knowledge of both soil and plant responses to climate.

It is evident from the statements above that it is an important task to understand the mechanisms that regulate nitrogen uptake into forest trees. In a natural soil this requires an integrated treatment of the whole soil-root system, since the uptake is simultaneously influenced by all other processes coupled to the soil water phase. They are in turn more or less affected by environmental conditions. The complexity of interaction make such studies difficult to perform and the validity of the resulting predictions is basically determined by the depth and congruity of the knowledge of separate soil processes.

Aims of the study

A great deal of knowledge exists on separate nitrogen transfer processes in soil. This paper is an attempt to synthesize some of the existing hypotheses on how nitrogen mineralization, transport, adsorption, and uptake by plant roots are regulated. They were combined to a single model, N1NIT (see Bosatta, 1980), which was applied to a forest site from which a reasonably complete set of empirical data exists on climate, soil processes, and components over several years. The aims were to study whether such an integrated model can give a realistic view of nitrogen transfers, to and from the soil solution, as far as it can be tested from measured data. A further aim was to identify possible functions in the system which are less satisfactorily described at present. The basic objective was thus to get an improved background for further studies of how soil factors regulate the plant nutrient uptake.

Field site

The study object was the mor layer of a mature Scots pine stand (Ih V) at Ivantjärnsheden in Central Sweden. The soil is an iron podzol and the mor is made up of a litter (L) layer, mixed with living mosses and lichens, and a humus (FH) layer, 5–8 cm and 3–6 cm thick respectively. The soil has been described in more detail by Jansson (1977) and Staaf & Berg (1977b).

Scots pine (*Pinus sylvestris* L.), heather (*Calluna vulgaris* L.), and cowberry (*Vaccinium vitis-idaea* L.) are the three most important vascular plants of the site, and the field and bottom vegetation layers are well developed. The biomass structure of the latter has been described by Persson (1975). Fine roots (< 2 mm diameter) are mainly distributed in the FH layer and in the uppermost mineral soil layer (Persson, 1980), and plant nutrient budget calculations (Staaf & Berg, 1977a) indicate that the main part of nitrogen mineralization and uptake into plants occurs here too.

From the stand history (see Bråkenhielm, 1978) and the high age of the stand (120–130 years old), the soil is considered approximately balanced regarding energy and nutrient flow, and in this study it is treated as a system in a dynamic steady state.

The model

Transports and adsorption of NH_4 in soil

The transports in the soil solution consist of three components: diffusion, dispersion, and mass flow (Boast, 1973). Diffusion is often the most important factor for the flow to the roots (Olsen & Kemper, 1968; Ballard & Cole, 1974), while mass flow and dispersion flow are the most important factors for the ion distribution in the soil profile.

Diffusion is the result of molecular movement. According to Fick's law the flow is proportional to the concentration gradient. The proportionality factor (D) is dependent on the diffusivity in free solution (d_2), the length of the diffusion path in the soil, the water content (D_4), and the viscosity in the thin layers of solution (Olsen & Kemper, 1968). A simple empirical expression given by Baldwin (1975) based on Porter *et al.* (1960) is used in N1NIT:

$$D = d_2 D_4{}^2$$

Mass flow is expressed as the product of water flow and concentration in the solution. Dispersion, however, is an additional component of the mass flow, caused by variations in water velocity in the different parts of the pore system (Boast, 1973). This, as well as diffusion (except to the roots), is not included explicitly in the present model version. Hence, the nitrogen losses by leaching were obtained by multiplying the daily amounts of percolating water with the NH_4 concentration in the soil solution.

Changes of the NH_4 concentration in the soil solution are buffered by adsorption. This is empirically described by means of adsorption isotherms, in which exchange with other cations on the adsorption sites is considered (Khanna & Ulrich, 1973). With the assumption of an instantaneous equilibrium between the ion exchanger and the solution, the adsorption isotherm can be used for calculating the adsorbed quantity. After this operation the NH_4 transports can be dealt with separately (Bosatta, 1980). However, the equilibrium assumption may not always be appropriate because of incomplete mixing of the solution in the pore system of the soil (Nielsen & Biggar, 1962).

In N1NIT the adsorption isotherm of NH_4 is defined as:

$$g = g_0 + k(\mu - \mu_0) \qquad \text{and} \qquad \mu = 3\,RT \ln c - 2\,RT \ln (c_r/3)$$

where g is the adsorbed amount (meq 1^{-1}), g_0 is the adsorbed amount at "equilibrium" (meq 1^{-1}), μ is the relative chemical potential (J meq^{-1}), μ_0 is the chemical potential at "equilibrium" (J meq^{-1}), k is the isotherm slope (meq^2 1^{-1} J^{-1}), c and c_r are the chemical activities of NH_4 and remaining cations, respectively, R is the universal gas constant and T the absolute temperature. In the formulation of μ, exchange with K, Ca, and Mg ions has been considered. The relative chemical potential may be written:

$$\mu = 3\,RT \ln c_{NH_4} - RT \ln c_K - 0.5\,RT \ln c_{Ca} - 0.5\,RT \ln c_{Mg}$$

This has been transformed into the previous expression, in which c_r is treated as a constant characteristic of the soil and g_0 and μ_0 are parameters defining an "equilibrium" state of the system. This is identical with the initial state of the soil in the experimental determinations of the adsorption isotherm. The formulation of the isotherm in the model allows changes of the slope (k) to be made, when g_0 and μ_0 are kept constant.

Decomposition and nitrogen mineralization

Satchell (1974) defines decomposition as "the breakdown of complex organic molecules to carbon dioxide, water and mineral nutrients". Of these, only carbon dioxide and mineral nitrogen are considered in the N1NIT model. A decomposer biomass, B(g m^{-2}), is supposed to utilize litter and humus (soil organic matter, SOM) for its need of energy and nutrients in proportion to its specific rate of biomass production, G (day^{-1}). Thus, the production rate of carbon, P_C (g m^{-2} day^{-1}), is:

$$P_C = f_C\, G\, B$$

where f_C is the fraction of carbon in the biomass. The production rate of nitrogen, P_N (g m^{-2} day^{-1}), is similarly obtained as:

$$P_N = f_N\, G\, B$$

where f_N is the fraction of nitrogen in the biomass. The amount of carbon assimilated (decomposed), A_C (g m^{-2} day^{-1}), by decomposers is the sum of P_C and the amount of carbon used for respiration. The production/assimilation ratio, e, is here considered as a constant, and thus:

$$A_C = P_C/e \qquad \text{or} \qquad A_C = G\,B\,f_C/e$$

A specific production rate, G_m (day^{-1}), realized under optimal environmental conditions (reference state) must be determined for each type of substrate. Morphological and anatomical substrate structure as well as its spatial distribution and chemical composition determines G_m.

Temperature and moisture regulates the specific production rate of decomposers according to:

$$G = G_m\, S\, Q^{(D_1 - 20)/10}$$

where S is a reduction factor, numerically between 0 and 1, and determined by the functional response of the substrate's respiration rate to moisture. S has the shape of a trapezoid: a maximum and a minimum value of D_4 define the interval of moisture over which S is different from zero and two further values define the optimal interval over which S is equal to one. Q is the Q_{10} factor of the temperature response and D_1 is the soil temperature (°C). In this way, G is defined to be equal to G_m at optimal moisture and 20°C. When either nitrogen or carbon are exhausted G immediately becomes zero.

In a changing substrate the specific production rate of decomposers might also be affected by the developing substrate quality. Parnas (1975, 1976) described the dependence on carbon and nitrogen concentrations and the C/N ratio in addition to temperature and moisture. A similar formulation as hers was used by Berg & Bosatta (1976) in a model version preceding the present N1NIT. However, when whole soil layers are regarded as one single morphological substrate, the gross substrate quality is not likely to change during the course of one year. Besides, the concentration concept is difficult to apply to terrestrial environments. Certainly there is a dependence of concentration on a micro-scale level in the soil solution, which is not described here, when using a rough substrate definition suitable for the ecosystem level.

When the decomposers die, carbon and nitrogen are transferred to SQM. The nitrogen transfer, m_N (g m^{-2} day^{-1}) is, for example:

$$m_N = f_N \, d_B \, B$$

where f_N is the fraction of nitrogen in biomass and d_B is the specific mortality rate (day^{-1}).

The theory of Parnas (1975) on the substrate exploitation strategy of decomposers has been adopted. The basic idea in it is that either carbon or nitrogen may be suboptimal in the substrate in relation to decomposer needs, and that an optimal composition exists. If nitrogen is the limiting nutrient element, decomposers use nitrogen compounds primarily as a nitrogen source and non-nitrogen compounds as the main carbon source. In this case the assimilation of nitrogen, A_N, is determined by the nitrogen required for decomposer growth.

If, on the other hand, carbon is limiting, the simple hypothesis is used that both nitrogen and non-nitrogen compounds serve equally well as carbon sources. Then the nitrogen assimilation is determined by the carbon need of the decomposers. The whole substrate is looked upon as one unit. When its effective C/N ratio is lower than that for optimal production rate there will be a nitrogen surplus and nitrogen mineralization will occur. This optimal or "critical" C/N ratio can be calculated from knowledge of the chemical composition of the decomposer biomass and the production/assimilation efficiency (e). In N1NIT the critical C/N ratio is a parameter which, compared with the C/N ratio of a certain substrate, determines whether decomposition calculations are to be made on the assumption of carbon or nitrogen as the limiting substance.

In principle, immobilization is thought to function as proposed by Parnas (1975). This means that NH$_4$ ions and organic nitrogen are considered equally available as a nitrogen source for decomposers, and that they are used in proportion to their relative concentrations. We have made the additional specification that only the part of organic nitrogen corresponding to the soil water volume fraction competes with inorganic nitrogen as a nitrogen source. The rest of the organic nitrogen is considered unavailable for spatial reasons. NH_4, on the other hand, is easily supplied to decomposers because of its water solubility. The immobilization (g N m^{-2} day^{-1}) is then described as:

$$i = P_N N_i/(N_i + N_1 D_4)$$

where N_1 and N_i denote the organic and mineral nitrogen amounts (g m^{-2}) and D_4 is the water content of the soil (fraction of volume). Lignin decomposes slowly (Minderman, 1968) and accumulates in litter, especially in the initial stages (Millar, 1974). Berg (1978) found that after 2.5 years of pine needle decomposition a considerable absolute decrease of lignin started. Staaf & Berg (1977b) found a low content in humus in the litter layer, meaning that a rapid decomposition or transformation of lignin occurs in the final stages of coniferous litter decay. For this reason the lignin fraction with associated nitrogen is considered available to decomposers in litter, but stable in humus, seen in a one-year perspective.

Uptake by roots

A formulation of uptake given by Baldwin (1975) was used here. The uptake by roots is a function of the concentration at the root surface (c_a), and for low concentrations the uptake (U) can be regarded as proportional to c_a:

$$U = \alpha c_a$$

where α is the physiological absorption power of the root. c_a depends on the balance between transports to the root surface and withdrawal by the root. By allotting each root within a certain soil volume a separate soil cylinder as nutrient source and assuming steady state flow through this cylinder, it is possible to relate c_a to the mean concentration in the soil solution (Baldwin et al., 1973). The uptake at the time interval Δ_t can then be expressed as a function of the total inorganic amount (N_i) in the soil layer or:

$$U = N_i [1 - \exp\{-2\pi \varrho D \Delta_t/b \ln(a_e/1.65 \, a)\}]$$

$$a_e = 1/\sqrt{\pi \varrho} \quad \text{and} \quad D = d_2 D_4{}^2$$

where:

N_i is total amount of mineral nitrogen (g m^{-2}),
ϱ is root density or specific root length (cm cm^{-3}),
D is effective diffusivity (cm^2 day^{-1}),
a_e is radius of the soil cylinder (cm),
a is mean radius of the roots (cm),
b is linear adsorption power of the soil,
d_2 is diffusivity in free solution (cm^2 day^{-1}), and
D_4 is water content (fraction of volume).

If Δ_t is one day the term in parentheses can be interpreted as the specific rate of nitrogen uptake (day^{-1}) and U is the daily rate of nitrogen uptake by roots (g m^{-2} day^{-1}).

To arrive at the formulation above, certain approximations have to be made.

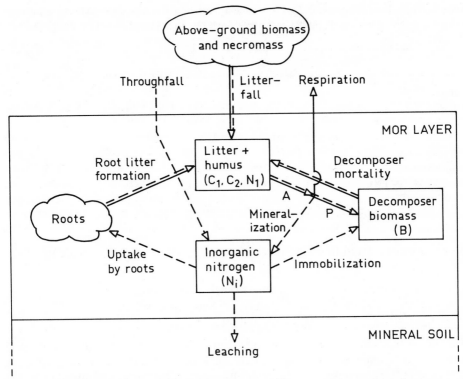

Figure 1. The structure of the N1NIT model, represented by some components and processes of carbon (solid line) and nitrogen (broken line). A = assimilation (decomposition), P = production (incorporation into decomposer biomass).

The conditions for these are that a_e^2 is much greater than a^2, that $\alpha\, a\, D^{-1}$ is much greater than 1, and that the mass flow component of transports to the root is negligible (see Baldwin, 1975), all of which is reasonable for the investigated site at Ivantjärnsheden. An important consequence of the approximations is that α disappears, leaving the geometrical variables of the root as the only plant factors for uptake. The reason for this is that roots with a high absorption ability reduce the concentration around themselves to such a level that uptake rate is limited entirely by movement through the soil. Unfortunately, the root geometry in forests is very laborious to determine, especially as the variability over time is very great (Persson, 1978). Mycorrhiza is frequent at the studied site and probably important as a geometrical extension of the root systems (Bowen, 1973).

Model structure

The simplest possible structure was chosen with respect to the level of knowledge about the included processes, biotic and abiotic components in relation to time scale and the type of problem to be analyzed. Fig. 1 shows the compartments and processes concerning nitrogen and carbon transformation in the model. The litter (L) and humus (FH) layers are combined to one functional structure. Decom-

Table 1. Annual litter influxes (g m⁻² yr⁻¹) and initial values of soil components (g m⁻²) in simulations with the N1NIT model. C_1 = carbon in C-N compounds, C_2 = carbon in C-C compounds, N_1 = nitrogen in C-N compounds and N_i = mineral nitrogen.

	Dry weight	C_1	C_2	N_1	N_i
Influxes					
Litterfall	190	29	68	0.63	–
Root litter formation	250	38	90	1.50	–
Soil components					
Soil organic matter	2 210	218	659	22.6	–
Decomposer biomass	5	0.8	1.7	0.2	–
Inorganic nitrogen	–	–	–	–	0.025

posers are considered to utilize this structural substrate, which is made up of the three chemical substrates C_1, C_2 and N_1, where:

C_1 = organic carbon in C-N compounds (such as protein),
C_2 = organic carbon in C-C compounds (such as cellulose) and
N_1 = organic nitrogen in C-N compounds.

The quantification of carbon and nitrogen in C-C and C-N compounds and nitrogen associated to lignin was made on analytical data from Staaf & Berg (1977b) and Berg (unpubl.). In the litter all organic nitrogen was included in N_1. In the humus, however, nitrogen associated with lignin was considered stable and was not included in the model. Start values on decomposer biomass are transformed data from Clarholm (1977) for bacteria summed with those for microfungi (Bååth & Söderström, 1977). Soil animals were not included as a compartment.

The inorganic nitrogen compartment (N_i) includes adsorbed ammonium ions and ammonium in the soil solution. Both fractions are thus considered equally available to decomposers. Only very small amounts of nitrate are present in soil and are neglected here. When entered into the expression for immobilization, N_i was averaged for the whole soil layer. Roots were assumed only to occur in the

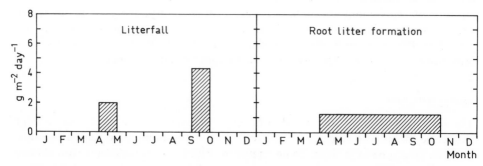

Figure 2. Litterfall and root litter formation rates used as driving variables of N1NIT for 1966, 1975, 1976 and 1977.

FH layer, and only a part of N_i, proportional to the volume fraction of this layer compared to total volume, was used in the inorganic submodel. This gives ion concentrations that correspond to those of the soil layer where ion exchange and uptake in roots really prevail. Data on state variables, which are used as start values in the model, are compiled in Table 1.

Detailed mathematical descriptions of processes and component updating are given by Bosatta (1980). All process calculations were made with a time step of one day, and the Euler method of integration was used.

Driving variables

Litter formation

Annual figures for the root litter formation and litterfall (Staaf & Berg, 1977a; Flower-Ellis & Olsson, 1978; Persson, 1980) and chemical analysis of different litter types (Bringmark, 1977; Berg & Staaf, unpubl.) were the basis for calculating a mean annual influx of chemical substrates to the soil (Table 1). A litterfall regime simplified from Flower-Ellis & Olsson (1978) was used; one-third of the total annual litterfall transferred in spring and two-thirds in early autumn (Fig. 2). The dynamics of root litter formation is poorly known, and a mean figure for daily input during the period May – October was used.

Nitrogen in throughfall

A mean concentration of inorganic nitrogen in throughfall from the tree canopy (c_0) was calculated from the amounts of water and nitrogen deposited during 1976 (Bringmark, 1977). The nitrogen deposition on the ground was then obtained by multiplying this concentration with amounts of infiltrating water during each time step (day).

Soil temperature, water content and water flow

The soil temperatures (Fig. 3) as well as infiltration, percolation (Fig. 4) and soil water data (Fig. 5) were taken from SOILW, another SWECON model (Halldin *et al.*, 1980). Soil water data were tested against manual measurements of soil water content from 1976.

Parameters

Parameters concerning carbon and nitrogen ratios of different litter inputs (Table 2) are based on chemical analyses of a large number of field samples on different litter components from the Ih V site. Figures from Bååth & Söderström (1977) on nutrient concentration in fungi were used for the decomposer biomass composition. Parameters describing the moisture and temperature response of biomass production rate were adopted from the corresponding data for respiration from different substrates in controlled environments (Clarholm, 1977; Rosswall, unpubl.).

Microorganisms are considered to have a high production/assimilation ratio (e), and 0.4 has been suggested for mixed populations on a long-term basis (Heal & MacLean, 1975) or sometimes higher than 0.5 (see Kaszubiak *et al.*, 1977). Introduction of more than one trophic level, however, will decrease the total

573

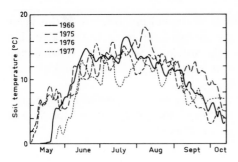

Figure 3. Daily means of soil temperatures in the FH layer used as driving variables for N1NIT.

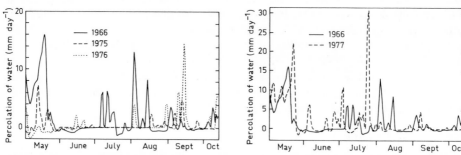

Figure 4. Percolation of soil water through an imaginary horizontal surface in the middle of the FH layer, the values used as driving variables for N1NIT.

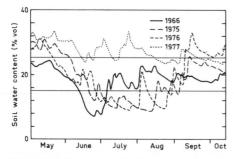

Figure 5. Daily means of soil water contents in the FH layer used as driving variables for N1NIT. Horizontal lines indicate optimal range for decomposer production.

efficiency ratio, since each additional level includes respiration losses. Considering this effect, the effective production/assimilation ratio was estimated to 0.2.

No measurements exist on optimal production rate (G_m) or mortality rate (d_B) of decomposers. Instead, it was necessary to determine them from the model behaviour. Climatic data from 1966 were applied on the model and the two parameters were adjusted to achieve a steady state over one year in the carbon,

Table 2. Numerical values and denotations for parameters used in the N1NIT model. Parameters of a purely technical character are not included in the list.

Module	Symbol	Meaning	Value	Dimension
DECOMP				
	f_C	Fraction carbon in decomposer biomass	0.5	
	f_N	Fraction nitrogen in decomposer biomass	0.04	
	e	Production/assimilation ratio	0.2	
		Fraction nitrogen in litterfall	0.003	
		Fraction nitrogen in root litter formation	0.006	
		Fraction C_1 in litterfall	0.15	
		Fraction C_1 in root litter formation	0.15	
		Fraction C_2 in litterfall	0.36	
		Fraction C_2 in root litter formation	0.36	
	G_m	Specific production rate of decomposers at 20°C and optimum moisture conditions	0.08	day^{-1}
	d_B	Specific mortality rate of decomposers	0.017	day^{-1}
	Q_{10}	Response of decomposer production rate on a temperature increase of 10°C	3.0	
	p_1	Moisture scale parameter for decomposer production rate	0	cm^3 cm^{-3}
	p_2	Moisture scale parameter for decomposer production rate	0.15	cm^3 cm^{-3}
	p_3	Moisture scale parameter for decomposer production rate	0.25	cm^3 cm^{-3}
	p_4	Moisture scale parameter for decomposer production rate	0.40	cm^3 cm^{-3}
INORG				
	c_0	Input concentration of inorganic nitrogen	0.05	meq l$^{-1}_{\text{water}}$
	g_0	Adsorbed NH_4 at equilibrium	0.03	meq l$^{-1}_{\text{soil}}$
	μ_0	Chemical potential at equilibrium	−38	J meq^{-1}
	k	NH_4 adsorption isotherm slope	0.017	meq^2 l$^{-1}_{\text{soil}}$ J^{-1}
	c_r	Remaining ion concentration	0.14	meq l$^{-1}_{\text{water}}$
ROOT				
	ϱ	Root density	4.5	cm cm^{-3}
	a	Root radius	0.03	cm
	d_2	Diffusion coefficient	1.3	cm^2 day^{-1}
	b_g	Buffer power	4	

nitrogen and decomposer biomass components. The year 1966 was selected as the one corresponding best to mean monthly temperature and precipitation data from the period 1965–76.

Adsorption parameters g_0, μ_0, and k have been determined experimentally by equilibration of mor samples with weak salt solutions of different composition. The concentration of other cations (c_r) has been given a value to make ($c_r/3$) equal to the mean value of $c_K \sqrt{c_{Ca}} \sqrt{c_{Mg}}$ measured in water collected from the litter layer by tension lysimeters during 1976. The diffusion coefficient for NH_4(d_2) has been taken from chemical standard literature. The linear buffering power of the soil (b) has been estimated from the adsorption isotherm by calculating the average of dN_i/dc over an interval (c_1, c_2) of concentrations (Bosatta, 1980). Thus:

Table 3. Mean values of some climatic soil variables in the mor layer for the period May 1–October 31 in the years 1966 and 1975–77. All values are derived from the SOILW model.

Variable	1966	1975	1976	1977
Soil temperature (°C)	9.5	11.2	9.3	8.0
Water content (% of volume)	18.1	18.7	19.2	27.5
Infiltration (mm day^{-1})	2.4	0.9	1.3	2.5
Percolation (mm day^{-1})	1.6	0.3	0.4	2.3

$$b = D_4 + \frac{3kRT}{c_2 - c_1} \ln \frac{c_2}{c_1} = D_4 + b_g$$

If c_2 and c_1 are put to 0.15 and 0.0005 meq l^{-1} respectively, then $b_g \sim 4$. For values of c lesser than c_1, $g(c)$ has been put to zero.

Root density (ϱ) and root radius (a) are calculated as the mean of data from three root samplings at Ih V (H. Persson, unpubl.). The obtained root density (< 1 mm diameter) for Scots pine has been multiplied with a factor 3 to get an estimate of total root density, also including heather and cowberry.

Model application

The model was driven with climatic data from the years 1975–1977. Each simulation covered the period May 1 – October 13, using a time step of one day. Characteristic climatic features of these three periods and the "standard year" 1966 are given in Table 3. Other conditions as litter formation and the initial size of soil components as given in Table 1 were considered identical for all simulated years. The inorganic deposition, however, varied in proportion to the amount of infiltrating water in a certain year. Thus, no information produced by one simulation was transferred to a simulation of another year.

Results and discussion

Model performance

Sensitivity to parameter changes

In order to analyze the dependence of the model output on some parameters, the numerical values of the parameters were changed one by one keeping the remaining parameters unaltered. Driving variables valid for 1976 were used for the repeated simulations. The resulting relative changes in annual nitrogen mineralization, leaching, and uptake in roots are shown in Fig. 6.

In the simulations, the solute concentrations were calculated from the total mineral nitrogen amount (N_i) by using the adsorption isotherm. The slope (k) of the latter was found to determine the leachable portion of N_i in a manner almost inversely proportional to k. With increasing concentration of cations other than NH$_4$ (c_r) the adsorption power of the soil decreased, and this was reflected in the

576

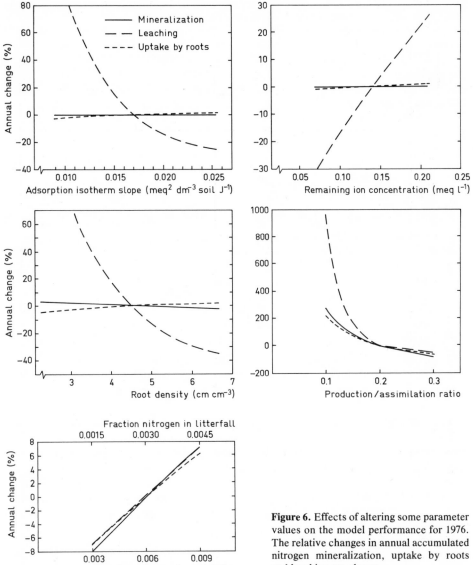

Figure 6. Effects of altering some parameter values on the model performance for 1976. The relative changes in annual accumulated nitrogen mineralization, uptake by roots and leaching are shown.

response to c_r. The changes directly imposed on leaching affected uptake only to a small extent, since the latter process is by far the greatest of them.

Root density (ϱ) might be regarded as a measure of the importance of the whole product $\varrho\, d_2\, D_4{}^2\, b^{-1}$ in the uptake expression. Surprisingly, the uptake is almost unaltered after a change of ϱ, meaning that there must be a counteracting effect from a changing N_i. Thus, with otherwise constant conditions, the root density regulates the level of mineral nitrogen in soil, a low density meaning a large mineral pool and a high density a minor one. An increased concentration of mineral nitrogen in soil will in turn increase decomposer immobilization, but will

577

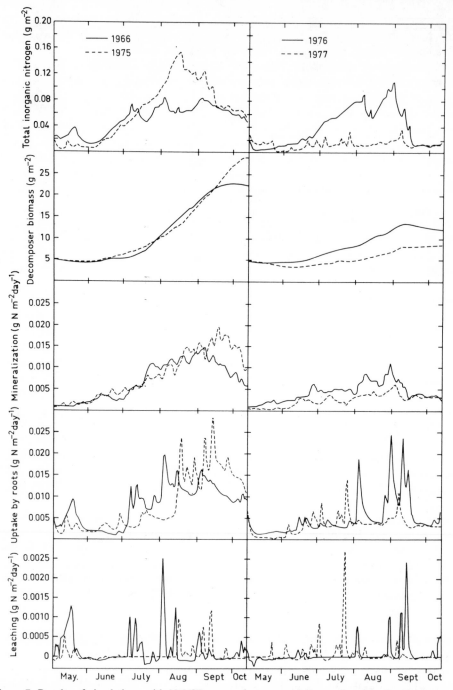

Figure 7. Results of simulations with N1NIT concerning seasonal fluctuations of mineral nitrogen component, decomposer biomass, nitrogen mineralization, uptake by roots and leaching for 1966 and 1975 (left) and 1976 and 1977 (right).

578

only to a very small extent affect mineralization. Nutrient losses by leaching, however, are highly sensitive to the efficiency of the root systems.

Another parameter tested was the production/assimilation efficiency of decomposers (e). The amount of carbon that has to be assimilated (A_C) to maintain a certain production rate is proportional to $1/e$ since $e = P_C/A_C$. In a carbon-limited system the utilization of C-N and C-C compounds is directly determined from their relative composition in the substrate. This will make also nitrogen assimilation and mineralization proportional to the inversion of e. Of the tested parameters the model was most sensitive to changes in the latter. It influences leaching via the mineral nitrogen compartment, N_i. The logarithmic form of the adsorption isotherm makes leaching extra sensitive in the low range of e, where N_i is high.

The nitrogen content of litter input has a moderate effect on mineralization as the addition is small compared to the large resident pool. Within the realistic range of the between-year variation of the parameter its effect is probably negligible at this site.

Seasonal dynamics

The seasonal development of the simulations with driving variables from 1966, 1975, 1976 and 1977 and the resulting variation in soil components, mineralization, uptake by roots and leaching are given in Fig. 7. The "normal" development of all years is a rather steady increase in nitrogen mineralization and respiration rate from spring during summer up to a top level in August or September. In the first part of this period it is caused by rising soil temperatures, but later mainly from the successive build-up of the decomposer biomass. After September the decreasing temperature lowers the decomposer rate of production with a resulting biomass decrease, which combines with the direct effect of lowered temperatures in retarding mineralization. The seasonal development is closely connected with the growth of the microbial biomass (GB), while the almost constant soil components C_1, C_2 and N_1 (Table 4) as well as the parameters e, f_N and f_C (Table 2) constitute a static matrix determining the outcome of the simulations.

The link between mineralization and uptake by roots is the mineral nitrogen component (N_i). For numerical reasons an expression of the type $U = N_i[1 - \exp(-x)]$ can be regarded as approximately identical to $U = N_i x$ when $x < 0.3$. The value of the exponent in the uptake expression is about 0.22 for a water content of 0.2 cm³ cm⁻³ using the parameter values in Table 2. The simplification, thus, would be justified here and the uptake rate given the form:

$$U = p \, N_i \, \varrho \, d_2 \, D_4^2 \, b^{-1}$$

where p is a proportionality factor. From this expression it is evident that an increase of N_i leads to an increased uptake rate, and a build-up of a mineral nitrogen pool is counteracted. On the other hand, a dynamic balance between mineralization with increasing rate and uptake in roots must be accompanied by an increase of mineral nitrogen (N_i). This is what occurs during the summer period of all years.

The uptake expression includes a factor D_4^2, indicating a strong dependence of water content in soil. Great changes in N_i are a necessary result of a decreased water content in order to retain the balance between influx and outflux of the

579

inorganic nitrogen pool. This is a second reason for the build-up of N_i during dry summer periods as in July 1975 (Fig. 7). But on the first rain occasion thereafter, the balance is rapidly restored by a sharp peak in uptake. The dynamic effect of D_4 and N_i on the uptake is controlled by the static framework created by the root density (ϱ), the ion diffusivity (d_2) and the buffer power (b).

Another consequence of the simplified uptake expression above is that in a soil with mixed root systems, each plant gets a share of the total uptake proportional to its share of the total root density. A high density of adsorbing roots, thus, will be favourable in the competition for nitrogen between different plant species, even if the total uptake, as already mentioned, is rather insensitive to changes in ϱ.

Leaching is another transfer from the mineral nitrogen pool, but quantitatively about two orders of magnitude lower than mineralization and uptake by roots. The limited leaching indicates a soil system with a tight internal nutrient circulation. Losses are prevented by the effectivity of root uptake in keeping concentrations in the soil solution low but also by the adsorption of NH_4 on humus particles. The level of N_i and the water flow determine the amount leached, so that the highest losses are in the late season. Sudden rains after dry periods, when N_i has been increased, are the most effective. Leaching is usually low after periods of rain because of lowered concentrations from a facilitated uptake into plants. Throughfall input, being a water-borne transport, is simultaneous with the leaching and roughly tenfold in magnitude.

Decomposer immobilization (i) of nitrogen does not affect the level of N_i in a carbon-limited system. With denotations used in Fig. 1 immobilization can be written as:

$$i = M_N + P_N - A_N$$

meaning that a change in i will result in a compensating change in mineralization (M_N), as the other terms, production (P_N) and assimilation of nitrogen (A_N), are unaffected. This means that competition between decomposers and plants will not occur unless the former are nitrogen-limited. In that case mineralization is turned to zero while immobilization continues, thus consuming the mineral nitrogen store. Such a situation never occurred in the present simulations, but would have arisen if a separate litter component had been distinguished in the model. The high C/N ratio of litter input would have made the litter system nitrogen-limited.

The sizes of the chemical substrate components (C_1, C_2 and N_1) are rather constant throughout the year (Table 4), as well as the C/N ratio which is kept in the interval 38–40. This means that the system is carbon-limited during the whole year, which ensures an uninterrupted nitrogen mineralization. It must be noted that even if the incoming litter has a relatively high C/N ratio (~ 90), the C/N ratio of dead decomposers is low (~ 10), which keeps the overall value relatively constant.

Annual differences

The simulations of four different years using climatic driving variables give very striking differences (Fig. 7, Table 4), the outcome of decomposer development being the central issue. The water content and the temperature in the soil have

Table 4. Simulated size of components and nitrogen transfers from May 3 to October 13 of different years.

	1966			1975			1976			1977		
	min	mean	max	min	mean	max	min	mean	max	min	mean	max
Components ($g\ m^{-2}$)												
C_1	218	230	243	218	229	238	218	232	253	218	235	259
C_2	659	680	700	659	679	687	659	687	732	659	697	751
N_1	22.2	22.7	23.0	22.0	22.6	22.9	22.6	22.9	23.3	22.6	23.2	23.7
N_i	0.02	0.05	0.08	0.004	0.06	0.15	0.004	0.04	1.07	0.002	0.01	0.03
Decomposer biomass	4.3	11.4	22.6	4.5	12.0	28.6	4.5	8.51	13.6	3.3	5.5	8.5
Processes ($g\ N\ m^{-2}\ yr^{-1}$)												
Throughfall		0.26			0.11			0.15			0.29	
Mineralization		1.13			1.33			0.72			0.42	
Uptake by roots		1.30			1.43			0.84			0.70	
Leaching		0.03			0.01			0.01			0.03	

their greatest immediate effect at the end of the summer, when the microorganisms are most abundant. This was evident for 1975, as favourable conditions in September caused a continued growth to a biomass of 29 g m^{-2} (Fig. 7). In 1976, when the conditions were less favourable in the late summer, a top level of only 13 g m^{-2} was reached already one month earlier than in 1975. The early summer climate is fundamental for the microbial growth later in summer. A very weak biomass development in 1977 was a result of early environmental conditions, and decomposer biomass reached only 9 g m^{-2} in spite of a favourable climate from August to October.

Temperature is the superior environmental variable for the microbial growth, while the water content only deviates slightly from the optimal range (see Fig. 5). Effects of the water conditions are noticeable as modifications of the temperature-determined seasonal biomass development. Temperature and water content are often inversely related to each other, which may lead to counteracting effects during dry periods (beginning of August 1975) or a combined negative effect during wet periods (early summer 1977). During the latter period low temperatures were combined with a supra-optimal soil water content (Fig. 5).

Mineralization is proportional to the growth of the decomposers, and the resulting ratio between the highest and the lowest annual figure of mineralization was as much as three times (Table 4). On a yearly basis, the uptake by plant roots was always balancing the input to the inorganic nitrogen pool by throughfall and mineralization. For shorter periods of low water content the N_i may be unbalanced, as discussed previously. The annual differences in throughfall produced by the model happen to counteract the differences in mineralization, making the greatest annual uptake only twice the size of the smallest (Table 4). The great variations in leaching between the years is explained by the great differences in water flow and mineralization.

Table 5. Mean amounts of mineral nitrogen (mg N m^{-2}) in the mor layer for the snow-free periods in 1974–76 as simulated by N1NIT and measured by KA1(SO$_4$)$_2$ extraction (Popović, 1976, 1977, 1978).

Year	Simulated	Measured			No. of measurement occasions
		min	mean	max	
1974	31	27	40	67	9
1975	62	15	17	22	4
1976	40	12	19	24	12

Realism of the model

In order to find out to what degree the model represents the natural situation, attempts were made to falsify the submodels and the integrated N1NIT. It was considered that qualitative properties of the model were more appropriate to test than quantitative ones, since the present aim was to clarify mechanisms. This meant that time sequences and relative magnitudes of processes were considered more important than absolute figures.

Field data on inorganic nitrogen, decomposer biomass, carbon and nitrogen mineralization and leaching from different years, mainly obtained from 1976 from the mature stand at Ivantjärnsheden (Ih V), were used to test the validity of the model outputs. Unfortunately, direct measurements of uptake in roots of a stand cannot be performed with the techniques existing today.

The NH$_4$ concentrations measured in lysimeter leachates during 1976, collected 6 cm below the humus layer (Bringmark, 1980), were of the same magnitude as the ones produced by the model for concentrations in water within the mor layer (Fig. 8). However, the simulated seasonal development of concentrations could not be detected in these lysimeters. Water percolating from the litter to the humus layer, on the other hand, showed a very pronounced NH$_4$ concentration peak in June–July, followed by low concentrations in the period of simulated maximum values (Fig. 8). This latter discrepancy might be attributed to immobilization in the litter layer.

The total amount of inorganic nitrogen (N$_i$), measured in the field 1974–76 by Popović (1976, 1977, 1978), was of the same magnitude as the model output. However, the seasonal trend with high peaks in July–August produced by the model was not obvious in the field data on N$_i$ (Fig. 9). Thus, different measurement methods have provided contradictory results regarding the seasonal dynamics of the inorganic nitrogen. The annual differences in Popović's determinations of N$_i$ are not in agreement with the outcome of the model simulations (Table 5).

The balance between NH$_4$ deposited by rain and percolating out of the litter layer is the net result of mineralization and immobilization going on in the litter layer. Immobilization is of greater importance in this layer than in the total system considered in N1NIT, indicating that this layer is, at least partly, nitrogen-limited. Measurements in lysimeters demonstrate net losses from the litter layer in summer periods (Table 6), while there are net gains or diminished losses in

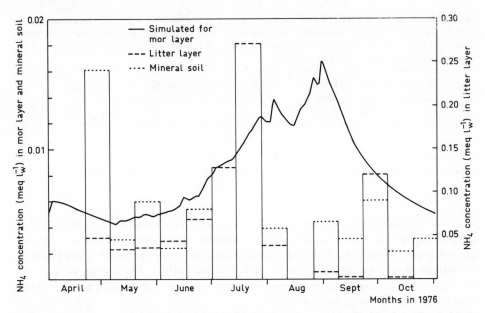

Figure 8. Comparison between measured and simulated NH_4 concentrations in the soil solution in 1976. The simulated concentrations are daily values for the mor layer, while the measurements were made biweekly in lysimeter leachates from the litter layer and in the mineral soil 6 cm below the mor layer.

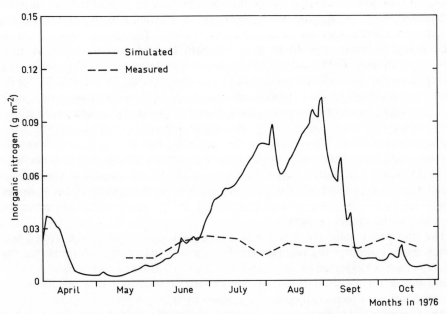

Figure 9. Total amount of mineral nitrogen in the mor layer as simulated by N1NIT and measured after extraction by 1% $KAl(SO_4)_2$ of mor samples. Field data from Popović (1978).

Table 6. Measured flows of NH_4 (mg m^{-2}) in percolating water of the litter and humus layers during the snow-free period. Monthly differences between input and output are given for the litter layer. Negative differences mean net mineralization, positive differences mean net immobilization, since there is no uptake by roots in the litter layer.

	Depo-sition	Litter layer output	Humus layer output	Litter layer input minus output						
				May	June	July	Aug	Sept	Oct	Nov
1975	59	75	23	−3	−5	−5	−15	−3	−1	+9
1976	100	109	19	−16	−17	−14	−14	+30	+6	+26

autumns. This increase in immobilization can be taken as support for the idea that there is higher microbial activity in the autumn, although there are also living mosses in the lysimeters. The greater part of the net mineralization takes place in the humus layer, where also the plant roots are active. The model as well as lysimeter measurements depict a tight soil-root system with small leaching losses from the humus layer (Tables 4 and 6).

The regulation of decomposer biomass in the model is highly simplified, since no mechanistic formulation of consumption is included in it; instead a constant specific mortality rate is assumed. A simulated regular biomass increase from May onwards to a maximum during September–October followed by a decrease is the general result (Fig. 7). Clarholm (1977) reports from 1974 that the highest bacterial biomass was estimated in July–September, as apparent from monthly determinations in the A_{01} and the A_{02} horizons. A maximum of 10 g m^{-2} was found in September and a minimum of about 2 g m^{-2} in May. During the same period the total fungal biomass was 20–40 g m^{-2} (Bååth & Söderström, 1977). A main problem with these field results is to determine how large a part of the biomass is active. Söderström (1979) found that at 21 samplings during 1975–77, 2–4 % of the total biomass (stained with fluorescein diacetate, FDA) was in an active state. The seasonal course of change in active fungal biomass also confirms, in a very rough sense, the model output (Fig. 10), while differences between years are in less good accordance. There seems to be two important divergences between the two data sets. (1) At the onset of the snow-free period (about May 1) there were great differences in active fungal biomass, while in the modelling work equal initial values were used. (2) Biomass depressions in the middle of the summer, which are especially marked during 1976 and 1977, were underestimated or put too early in the model outputs.

The first point indicates that a biomass growth can occur in the frozen soil, which might influence the biomass level as the soil thaws. It is obvious that this effect, which is neglected in the model, has a great influence on biomass development during the vegetation period, and it can be assumed that the difference between different years is largely determined by it.

The second point indicates some inaccuracies in the formulation of soil climate on decomposer rate of production, possibly the influence of soil moisture. Dry periods often occur in June–July, and Söderström (1979) considered soil moisture to be highly important in regulating the active fungal biomass. On the other hand,

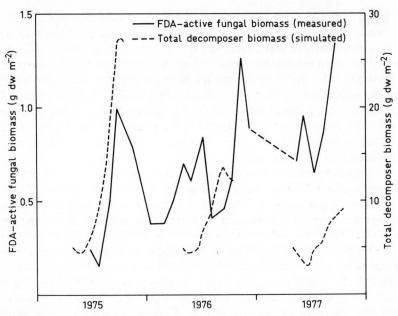

Figure 10. Total decomposer biomass in the mor layer for 1975–1977 as simulated by N1NIT and measured FDA-active fungal biomass (Söderström, 1979) for the same period.

he also suggested the possibility of a changed consumption rate during such periods. Finally, it must be admitted that it is difficult to validate the decomposer biomass change, since the annual and seasonal variations of active bacterial biomass are not known.

Realistic field measurements on nitrogen mineralization have proved difficult to perform. Popović (1976, 1977) incubated humus samples from Ih V for six weeks at different points of time during the years 1974 and 1975. He found the highest capacity of inorganic nitrogen accumulation in June–July, while the model puts it somewhat later (Fig. 7). The net mineralization was measured to be less than 30 mg N m^{-2} (6 weeks)$^{-1}$ compared to the mean model output of 6–7 mg N m^{-2} day^{-1}, and it was difficult to establish with good accuracy. The methodological problems with field measurements of this process makes the data a weak validating instrument.

When summarizing the experimental validation of N1NIT it seems as if several variables roughly exhibit the same seasonal trends in the model as in the real system. The size of the mineral nitrogen component (N_i) is of central importance for the regulation of uptake in vegetation, and here is a critical conflict between measured and simulated data. This component is simultaneously regulated by mineralization, leaching and uptake by roots.

Of these processes leaching is only a minor transfer and although it has an influence on the soil mineral nitrogen component during high water flow period, it could not be expected to reduce the build-up of high concentrations during dry periods. Thus, errors in the description of this process are not likely to explain the seasonal variation of N_i, which was found in the model output. Further, it is too

585

small to give any major annual differences in nitrogen amounts supplied to plants.

There were almost no possibilities to test the functioning of the root uptake formulation. Root density was concluded above to have only a minor influence on total annual nitrogen uptake by roots, and in that respect it seems reasonable to have a constant value for it in the model. It is known, however, that there is a considerable seasonal root biomass dynamics in a nearby stand (Persson, 1978). The root density has a direct influence on the size of N_i via an influence on the uptake rate, and describing it as a variable in the model might give a more realistic picture of the seasonal variation of N_i. This has not been done so far owing to the lack of detailed root biomass data.

Finally, and most probably, the discrepancies found should be looked for in the decomposition/mineralization part of the model. Two specific points of malfunction were found in this analysis. The first of them has to do with the dynamics of the decomposer biomass component, a variable of primary importance in the present model. There are definite inaccuracies in the formulation of decomposer growth, and a first attempt could be to reconsider its temperature and moisture dependence in more long-term measurements. It is also necessary to extend the simulations to the whole year, since there seems to be microbial activity in the frozen soil of importance to the situation later in the year. A second problem is to deal with the situation of sudden change from a negative to a positive net mineralization, which is encountered in the litter layer in the autumn of 1976 (see Table 6). Periods of rapid nitrogen immobilization are known to occur in early stages of litter decomposition (see Staaf & Berg, 1977). They would be realized by N1NIT if a separate litter component were dealt with, as the higher C/N ratio of litter input makes this subsystem nitrogen-limited. At present, the rough substrate division used in the model precludes the working of such a mechanism that, if put in function, would also make immobilization to be a process regulating the size of the mineral nitrogen pool. In view of the considerable dynamics of the root biomass observed in the field, newly formed root litter in the humus layer might act as a periodic sink for the mineral nitrogen. This is one probable reason for the divergence in the sequences of soil mineral nitrogen amounts between model and reality.

Possible development

The discussion above indicates some critical points in the validation of the integrated N1NIT. A major problem is that actual measurements of seasonal variation in nitrogen uptake by root populations of whole forest stands are not feasible with present-day techniques. Mechanisms of plant nutrient recycling in the field, proposed by the model, are thereby rendered more difficult to evaluate. Testing as many aspects as possible of the model appears to be the only way of approaching a reasonably safe conclusion about them. The present results indicate three main lines to follow in the further work:

(1) Improvement of quantitative characteristics of the model. Especially parameters in the decomposition module, e.g., the production/assimilation ratio and the parameters regulating the decomposer response to climatic variables are crucial for the final output of the model. Their values and status as constants should be reconsidered in further experiments.

(2) Trying alternative formulations on immobilization of the mineral nitrogen pool. Microbial immobilization is a less satisfactorily known process, and further studies on substrate utilization are desirable. Progress might be achieved both by testing the mechanisms for a carbon-limited substrate or by treating the humus layer as a mixture of carbon- and nitrogen-limited subsystems. Investigation of the significance of abiotic humification processes in transferring mineral nitrogen to an organic form would also be valuable. The root module of the model might be developed separately on well-defined experimental conditions.
(3) Development of models with a longer time-scale. Here it appears necessary to enter the decomposer organism activity in a simpler way, and possibly use more empirical data from litter weight loss studies, etc. In such modified models humification and the turn-over of the slowly mineralized nitrogen pool in soil should be considered.

Acknowledgements

H. Staaf provided the scientific background for the decomposition submodel, and L. Bringmark did likewise for submodels of uptake by roots and ion exchange. Both authors are responsible for the discussion of the results. E. Bosatta performed mathematical and computer work. This study was made in the Swedish Coniferous Forest Project, and we want to express our gratitude to many persons in this project, notably P-E. Jansson, H. Persson and J. G. K. Flower-Ellis for making important data available.

References

Bååth, E. & Söderström, B. E. 1977. Mycelial lengths and fungal biomasses in some Swedish soils, with special reference to a pine forest in Central Sweden. – Swed. Conif. For. Proj. Tech. Rep. 13, 45 pp.

Baldwin, J. P. 1975. A quantitative analysis of the factors affecting plant nutrient uptake from some soils. – J. Soil Sci. 26: 195–206.

Baldwin, J. P., Nye, P. H. & Tinker, P. B. 1973. Uptake of solutes by multiple root systems from soil. III. A model for calculating the solute uptake by a randomly dispersed root system developing in finite volume of soil. – Plant & Soil 38: 621–635.

Ballard, T. M. & Cole, D. W. 1974. Transport of nutrients to tree root systems. – Can. J. For. Res. 4: 563–565.

Berg, B. 1978. Decomposition of needle litter in a 120-year-old Scots pine (Pinus silvestris) stand at Ivantjärnsheden. – Swed. Conif. For. Proj. Int. Rep. 80, 66 pp.

Berg, B. & Bosatta, E. 1976. A carbon-nitrogen model of a pine forest soil ecosystem – a development paper. – Swed. Conif. For. Proj. Int. Rep. 42, 61 pp.

Boast, C. W. 1973. Modelling the movement of chemicals in soils by water. – Soil Sci. 115: 224–230.

Bosatta, E. 1980. Modelling of soil processes – an introduction. – In: Persson, T. (ed.) Structure and Function of Northern Coniferous Forests – An Ecosystem Study, Ecol. Bull. (Stockholm) 32: 553–564.

Bowen, G. D. 1973. Mineral nutrition of ectomycorrhizae. – In: Marks, G. C. & Kozlowski, T. T. (eds.) Ectomycorrhizae – Their Ecology and Physiology, pp. 151–205. New York–London: Academic Press.

Bråkenhielm, S. 1978. Ivantjärnsheden, Jädraås – regional physiography and description of the research area. – Swed. Conif. For. Proj. Tech. Rep. 16, 58 pp.

587

Bringmark, L. 1977. A bioelement budget of an old Scots pine forest stand in Central Sweden. – Silva fenn. 11: 201–257.

Bringmark, L. 1980. Ion leaching through a podsol in a Scots pine stand. – In: Persson, T. (ed.) Structure and Function of Northern Coniferous Forests – An Ecosystem Study, Ecol. Bull. (Stockholm) 32: 341–361.

Clarholm, M. 1977. Monthly estimations of soil bacteria at Jädraås and a comparison between a young and a mature pine forest on a sandy soil. – Swed. Conif. For. Proj. Tech. Rep. 12, 17 pp.

Eklund, B. 1954. Variations in the widths of the annual rings in pine and spruce due to climatic conditions in northern Sweden during the years 1900–1944. – Medd. Stat. Skogsforskn.-inst. 44: 140–150. (In Swedish, English summary)

Fagerström, T. & Lohm, U. 1977. Growth in Scots pine. Mechanism of response to nitrogen. – Oecologia 26: 305–315.

Flower-Ellis, J. G. K. & Olsson, L. 1978. Litterfall in an age series of Scots pine stands and its variation by components during the years 1973–1976. – Swed. Conif. For. Proj. Tech. Rep. 15, 62 pp.

Halldin, S., Grip, H., Jansson, P-E. & Lindgren, Å. 1980. Micrometeorology and hydrology of pine forest ecosystems. II. Theory and models. – In: Persson, T. (ed.) Structure and Function of Northern Coniferous Forests – An Ecosystem Study, Ecol. Bull. (Stockholm) 32: 463–503.

Heal, O. W. & MacLean, S. F. Jr. 1975. Comparative productivity in ecosystems – secondary production. – In: Van Dobben, W. H. & Lowe-McConnell, R. H. (eds.) Unifying Concepts in Ecology, pp. 89–108. The Hague: Junk and Wageningen: Pudoc.

Jansson, P-E. 1977. Soil properties at Ivantjärnsheden. – Swed. Conif. For. Proj. Int. Rep. 54, 66 pp. (In Swedish, English abstract)

Jonsson, B. 1969. Studies of variations in the widths of annual rings in Scots pine and Norway spruce due to weather conditions in Sweden. – Dept. of Forest Yield Research, Royal College of Forestry, Stockholm, Research Notes 16, 297 pp. (In Swedish, English summary)

Kaszubiak, H., Kaczmarek, W. & Pedziwilk, Z. 1977. Comparison of different methods for estimating the productivity of microorganisms in soil. – Ekol. pol. 25: 289–296.

Khanna, P. K. & Ulrich, B. 1973. Ion exchange equilibria in an acid soil. – Gött. Bodenk. Ber. 29: 211–230.

Millar, C. S. 1974. Decomposition of coniferous leaf litter. – In: Dickinson, C. H. & Pugh, G. J. F. (eds.) Biology of Plant Litter Decomposition, Vol. 1, pp. 105–128. London–New York: Academic Press.

Minderman, G. 1968. Addition, decomposition and accumulation of organic matter in forests. – J. Ecol. 56: 355–362.

Nielsen, D. R. & Biggar, J. W. 1962. Miscible displacement: III. Theoretical Considerations. – Soil Sci. Soc. Amer. Proc. 26: 216–221.

Olsen, S. R. & Kemper, W. D. 1968. Movements of nutrients to plant roots. – Adv. Agron. 20: 91–151.

Parnas, H. 1975. Model for decomposition of organic material by microorganisms. – Soil Biol. Biochem. 7: 161–169.

Parnas, H. 1976. A theoretical explanation of the priming effect based on microbial growth with two limiting substrates. – Soil Biol. Biochem. 8: 139–144.

Persson, H. 1975. Dry matter production of dwarf shrubs, mosses and lichens in some Scots pine stands at Ivantjärnsheden, Central Sweden. – Swed. Conif. For. Proj. Tech. Rep. 2, 25 pp.

Persson, H. 1978. Root dynamics in a young Scots pine stand in Central Sweden. – Oikos 30: 508–519.

Persson, H. 1980. Death and replacement of fine roots in a mature Scots pine stand. – In: Persson, T. (ed.) Structure and Function of Northern Coniferous Forests – An Ecosystem Study, Ecol. Bull. (Stockholm) 32: 251–260.

Popović, B. 1976. Nitrogen mineralisation in an old pine stand. – Swed. Conif. For. Proj. Int. Rep. 35, 16 pp. (In Swedish, English abstract)

Popović, B. 1977. Nitrogen mineralisation in an old and a young Scots pine stand. – Swed. Conif. For. Proj. Int. Rep. 60, 15 pp. (In Swedish, English abstract)

Popović, B. 1978. Nitrogen mineralization during the early phase after clear-cutting. – In: Granhall, U. (ed.) Nutrient Turnover in the Early Phase after Clear-cutting. Results from Introductory Investigations. – Swed. Conif. For. Proj. Int. Rep. 70: 40–46. (In Swedish, English abstract)

Porter, L. K., Kemper, W. D., Jackson, R. D. & Stewart, B. A. 1960. Chloride diffusion in soils as influenced by moisture content. – Soil Sci. Soc. Amer. Proc. 24: 460–463.

588

Satchell, J. E. 1974. Litter – interface of animate/inanimate matter. – In: Dickinson, C. H. & Pugh, G. J. F. (eds.) Biology of Plant Litter Decomposition, Vol. 1, pp. 13–44. London–New York: Academic Press.

Söderström, B. E. 1979. Seasonal fluctuations of active fungal biomass in horizons of a podzolized pine forest soil in Central Sweden. – Soil Biol. Biochem. 11: 149–154.

Staaf, H. & Berg, B. 1977a. Mobilization of plant nutrients in a Scots pine forest mor in Central Sweden. – Silva fenn. 11: 210–217.

Staaf, H. & Berg, B. 1977b. A structural and chemical description of litter and humus in a mature Scots pine stand. – Swed. Conif. For. Proj. Int. Rep. 65, 31 pp.

Tamm, C. O. 1975. Plant nutrients as limiting factors in ecosystem dynamics. – In: Reichle, D. E., Franklin, J. F. & Goodall, D. W. (eds.) Productivity of World Ecosystems, pp. 123–132. Washington, D. C.: US National Academy of Sciences.

Tamm, C. O. & Carbonnier, C. 1961. Plant nutrients and forest yields. – Kungl. Skogs- o. Lantbruksak. Tidskr. 100: 96–124.

Witkamp, M. 1966. Decomposition of leaf litter in relation to environment, microflora and microbial respiration. – Ecology 47: 194–201.

Wood, T. G. 1974. Field investigations on the decomposition of leaves of *Eucalyptus delegatensis* in relation to environmental factors. – Pedobiologia 14: 343–371.

Zöttl, H. 1960. Methodische Untersuchungen zur Bestimmung der Mineralstickstoffanlieferung des Waldbodens. – Forstwiss. Cbl. 79: 72–88.

Persson, T. (ed) 1980
Structure and Function of Northern
Coniferous Forests – An Ecosystem Study
Ecol. Bull. (Stockholm) 32: 591–596.

EXPERIENCES OF ECOSYSTEM RESEARCH IN THE SWEDISH CONIFEROUS FOREST PROJECT

G. I. Ågren[1], F. Andersson[1] and T. Fagerström[1]

Abstract

The experiences of letting models play an important role in the research of a large ecological project are summarized. The development of the modelling within the Swedish Coniferous Forest Project from large complex models towards a more problem oriented approach is described. The possibilities of using systems analysis as a tool in basic research are examined. Finally, some possible lines of development of the modelling are outlined.

Additional keywords: Models, simulation, systems analysis.

Retrospect

Project philosophy

In the early applications for research grants of the Swedish Coniferous Forest Project (SWECON) "systems analysis" and "systems approach" were recurrent words. In these two expressions a scientific method as well as a scientific paradigm were implicit. Systems analysis as a method was inherited from engineering and management theory and also from its application within American ecology. It was hoped to provide a tool for setting priorities between and coordination of the different subprojects. The scientific paradigm was the belief in the ecosystem as a fundamental unit which could be made the object of scientific theories.

One of the important tools for implementing the systems analysis was the utilization of models, particularly large simulation models. Much effort has therefore been invested in building and analysing such models. Roughly, 10% of the effort of the project in terms of time has been devoted to these activities. This figure can be compared with 0% for the period 1920–35 and 0.4% for the period 1945–65 as calculated by Watt (1966) for some major American ecological projects. In this paper we will try to analyse the experiences of our attempt to promote this way of thinking in Swedish ecological research.

The primary aim initially formulated for SWECON was to analyse the most im-

---

[1] Dept. of Ecology and Environmental Research, Swedish University of Agricultural Sciences, S-750 07 Uppsala, Sweden

portant sub-systems of the coniferous forest in terms of simulation models. It was hoped that such models would lend themselves to prediction of effects of various kinds of perturbations to the forest ecosystem, e.g., acid precipitation or clear-cutting. Important spin-offs were also expected with regard to educational effects and experience in interdisciplinary research.

The early project development

Modelling efforts were made already in the preparatory stage of the project in 1971 and 1972. However, it soon became evident that this exercise was too abstract for several of the scientists involved. The reasons might have been that the overall objectives were not fully understood and, furthermore, that the biologists were not accustomed to this type of deskwork. The modellers, on their side, had obviously underestimated the difficulties in obtaining the basic facts necessary in the model building. Therefore, when the biologists examined the models, these were often believed to be too speculative and too void of biological realism to be perceived as important research tools.

An examination of the project plans was done in May 1973, resulting in a re-organization and the establishing of an investigation system where the field and laboratory work dominated over the modelling efforts (Andersson, 1980). Andersson (1977) discusses this and subsequent reorganizations in more detail.

There are several reasons why the field work in most cases started independently of the model development and not as a result of extensive analysis of a model telling which areas were worth studying. One is the purely psychological one, what Van Dyne has called "the getting started syndrome", i.e., the eagerness of most people to "really" get something done once the resources are available and not just discussing what should be done. This wish is, however, also based on the fact that many biological studies require a long time span and it is therefore often necessary to start as soon as possible in order to obtain the results before the project is ended. These sometimes very slow processes must also be kept in mind when considering the possibilities of managing and planning ecological research. Whereas testing a hypothesis in a model by simulation might take five minutes the field experiment to falsify the hypothesis might require five years. The ideal situation sketched in so many books about systems analysis in ecology where model studies initiate field studies which in turn give rise to new model studies, etc., can therefore often be impossible to carry out in practice.

Finally, the system of funding research forces large research projects to build up the scientific staff rapidly in an early stage of the project. The possibilities of changing research directions are then, of course, limited by the interests and knowledge of this staff.

The model family 1975–79

The situation prevailing until 1975 was that the practical field and laboratory work went in parallel with some modelling attempts. It was, however, found that the organizational "problem areas" did not correspond to the actual ecosystem problems that were identified. In particular, the different time scales operating in the eco-system had no counterparts in the organization. Therefore, it became necessary to identify a number of models or submodels connecting the research performed in the different problem areas. Models of different components and time scales were identified and can be grouped as follows (cf. Andersson, 1980):

- The FAST, PT, and DEVS (later STAND) models for primary production of pine or a pine forest with a time domain of 1 day, 1–10 years, and 100 years, respectively.
- The N-model for the turnover of nutrients (nitrogen) in the soil.
- The WATER and ENERGY models for the physical processes pertaining to turnover of water and energy in the forest ecosystem.

While these models have subsequently become split up into sub-models that are developed more or less independently, they still remain the central theme for the modelling efforts. Characteristic of these models are their large number of state variables and parameters. Sometimes they also demand relatively large amounts of precise information.

In a later stage of the project, and partly as an anti-thesis to the work on these large models, the interest of some of the modellers turned towards hypothesis formulation, which can be defined as working with small and less complicated (in terms of the number of state variables and parameters) models, and which could be seen as hypotheses on specific phenomena rather than descriptions of large systems. There has also been some work on more abstract models (e.g., Ågren & Fagerström, 1980).

One important factor to keep in mind when evaluating the modelling efforts, is the very different premises existing in the different areas of modelling. The best starting-point was, of course, in the abiotic area where the modelling mainly concerned flows of energy and water obeying well-known physical laws. The modellers who had to deal with biological problems had larger difficulties, because these areas have so few basic principles from which one naturally can start the development of models, although certain parts of these models could also be based on more well-established grounds. Thus, the FAST model had gaseous diffusion as an important element and the inorganic part of the nutrient model was based on theories of physico-chemical reactions. More or less along the same scale a willingness can be found among the modellers to leave the large-scale models and turn towards formulation of hypotheses. Also in the cooperation between modellers and the other scientists in the project a gradient can be found. Within the abiotics group there was not even a clear division into field scientists and modellers, only a continual shift from full-time field work to full-time modelling. Therefore, the feed-back between field work and modelling has also been intensive, which is also quite natural in a field so closely related to physics and where the use of mathematics to express the ideas has long been the normal way of work (e.g., Halldin, 1979). At the other extreme one can take the work on plant growth. The separation into field workers and modellers has here been almost total. There has also been very little coupling between the field work and the models, mainly because the field work was planned long ahead of the start of the modelling work. A feed-back has developed only during the very last years.

Systems analysis and basic research

The idea of using systems analysis for managing SWECON came from the success of the method in projects like the Apollo project. However, important distinctions never made were the inherent differences between applied projects and basic research projects as well as between technological and biological problems. An important aspect of systems analysis often stressed is that the systems analysis should result in recommendations about which decisions should be taken in a given situation. Consequently, it is necessary that alternative courses of action can be evaluated and expressed in terms of costs and benefits. Many long but unsuccessful discussions about these problems have taken place within SWECON. The reason why so little has come out of these discussions is probably inherent in the problem approached – one of basic research analysis. Calculation of the costs and benefits of *understanding* a specific process, or even answering the fundamental question of how to define what understanding the process meant, appeared too difficult. Particularly difficult is, of course, the evaluation of what understanding will mean in benefits, because we cannot actually evaluate the benefits before we have the understanding. As a result the assessments of different actions, e.g., whether understanding plant growth would gain most from studying soil processes or photosynthesis, could therefore not rely upon the formal machinery of systems analysis but had to be done subjectively. This contrasts to the problems of synthesis, e.g., the construction of a rocket of specified capacity, where one essentially deals with known pieces which should be assembled in the optimal way. Still, systems analysis can possibly be used in basic research as a tool for structuring problems and maybe in small groups also as an instrument for setting priorities.

A side of the modelling that now and then has been criticized is that the models have not been built in such a way that they could be falsified, which is ordinarily required in scientific work, but mainly intended to describe a segment of the ecosystem or maybe only to summarize current knowledge. As such they had, of course, a didactic value and could serve as a basis for discussions within the project, but for the scientific community outside the project and for the scientific meriting of the modellers they were of questionable value. We do not deny the value of synthesizing knowledge but resist the idea that such synthesis always should be in the form of a model. In SWECON the knowledge was too often forced into the strait-jacket of mathematics whether this was suitable or not. Another weakness in letting the model serve as an assembler of data (induction) is that the strongest side of the use of mathematical models, deduction, is not utilized. A reason for this (mis)use of models is probably the strong tradition of descriptions existing in ecology, and many ecologists therefore only regarded the models as a sophisticated (or complicated) means of describing collected data, rather than as deductive tools which could anticipate structures or relationships (sometimes counterintuitive) in data to be collected.

Among the benefits derived from the extensive use of models are on one hand, of course, the direct outputs from the models. Some of these concern variables that otherwise would be very hard to obtain information about, e.g., the dynamic aspect of mineralization (Bosatta *et al.*, 1980). In other cases more abstract questions have been addressed, e.g., the amount of differentiation in the regeneration niche required for coexistence of plant species (Fagerström & Ågren, 1979). While these benefits are directly measurable as the number of publications they give rise to, there are also other more intangible benefits. Most important of these has been the possibility for investigators with a background in the "hard" sciences, physics and mathematics, to work within the project over a long period. Hopefully they have been able to instill in the ecologist some of their problem-oriented thinking and their experiences of handling problems deductively. At the same time they should have learnt from the contacts with ecologists to adopt a critical attitude towards the use of the tools they offer to ecology. If these two last statements are true, the investment in the modelling has certainly been worthwhile and will for a long time after SWECON's termination be rewarding to Swedish ecology.

Prospect

In the past the SWECON project has been dominated by information-gathering and organization of information into complex models. During this period we have learnt much, not least about our ignorance. In particular the work on the complex models within the plant growth (Ågren, in press) and soil processes has given a good overview of the situation in these areas. In the abiotic area the view upon the world has been much more coherent from the beginning and most of the time spent has therefore more been directed towards filling the known lacunae in knowledge rather than identifying them. As a consequence we have now a substantial amount of data concerning a specific ecosystem and quite a lot of knowledge of the same system, and not least, we have a much better appreciation of our areas of ignorance.

One thing we have learnt is that time is not yet ripe (if it will ever be) for the complex models we started out with. However, during the work with these models we have identified quite a number of specific problems that should be possible to analyse and perhaps solve. In particular this applies to the area of plant growth and soil nutrient dynamics. Examples of such problems are:

- carbon budgets for trees and forests of arbitrary age and site index
- coupling between soil nutrient dynamics and tree growth
- importance of interaction between soil organisms for mineralization
- stability of production and turnover processes.

Another line of development must be towards more long-term perspectives. So far the work has been dominated by investigations covering only a few years. However, the real interest lies of course in what can happen over, say one hundred years. For the proper understanding of events over such a long period the use of models is imperative. The models developed until now are in general far too complex and will require considerable simplification. This process of simplification is most important, because the crucial processes for the operation of the ecosystem will thereby be sorted out. A good example of such a simplification is given in the FAST model (Lohammar et al., 1979, 1980) where the description of the photosynthesis and transpiration is simplified step by step until an analytically treatable model results.

Results from the SWECON project will probably also be important in discussions about environmental problems and forest utilization. An important current problem is the effect of acid deposition upon the forest ecosystem. By adding pieces together from various subprojects it has been possible to establish a nitrogen budget for a forest, and with knowledge of decomposition rates it should be possible to trace the effects of the acid deposition. In a similar way it should be possible to analyse the effects upon the long-term fertility of forest soils from whole tree utilization.

The SWECON project has presented itself as believing in the ecosystem concept.

So far most of the efforts have been concentrated upon fairly distinct subsystems or ecosystem processes but very little work has pertained to the ecosystem as a unit. It is now of interest to try to establish some form of coupling between these subsystems or submodels in order to analyse properties of higher level systems. Our knowledge of ecosystem processes has increased, but so far we have not explored the possibility of deriving or testing new theories pertaining to the ecosystem level. In combination with our information on physiologically based processes there exists a challenge to advance towards ecosystem theories.

Acknowledgements

The views presented in this paper are the result of many stimulating discussions with our colleagues in the SWECON project.

References

Ågren, G. I. in press. Problems involved in modelling tree growth. – Stud. for. suec.

Ågren, G. I. & Fagerström, T. 1980. Coexistence of plant species: A theoretical investigation. – In: Persson, T. (ed.) Structure and Function of Northern Coniferous Forests – An Ecosystem Study, Ecol. Bull. (Stockholm) 32: 547–551.

Andersson, F. 1977. Development, coordination and administration of the SWECON project. – In: Training in Research Programme, Planning and Administration, pp. 36–47, Joint Committee of the Research Councils, Natural Science Research Council, Stockholm.

Andersson, F. 1980. Ecosystem research within the Swedish Coniferous Forest Project. – In: Persson, T. (ed.) Structure and Function of Northern Coniferous Forests – An Ecosystem Study, Ecol. Bull. (Stockholm) 32: 11–23.

Bosatta, E., Bringmark, L. & Staaf, H. 1980. Nitrogen transformations in a Scots pine forest mor–model analysis of mineralization, uptake by roots and leaching. – In: Persson, T. (ed.) Structure and Function of Northern Coniferous Forests – An Ecosystem Study, Ecol. Bull. (Stockholm) 32: 565–589.

Fagerström, T. & Ågren, G. I. 1979. Theory for coexistence of species differing in regeneration properties. – Oikos 33: 1–10.

Halldin, S. (ed.) 1979. Comparison of Forest Water and Energy Exchange Models. Copenhagen: International Society for Ecological Modelling, 258 pp.

Lohammar, T., Larsson, S., Linder, S. & Falk, S. O. 1979. FAST – A simulation model for the carbon dioxide and water exchange of Scots pine. – Swed. Conif. For. Proj. Tech. Rep. 19, 38 pp.

Lohammar, T., Larsson, S., Linder, S. & Falk, S. O. 1980. FAST – simulation models of gaseous exchange in Scots pine. – In: Persson, T. (ed.) Structure and Function of Northern Coniferous Forests – An Ecosystem Study, Ecol. Bull. (Stockholm) 32: 505–523.

Watt, K. E. F. 1966. Ecology in the future. – In: Watt, K. E. F. (ed.) Systems Analysis in Ecology, pp. 253–267. New York–London: Academic Press.

Percolation, 15, 16, 42
Phenolic substances, 391, 396:
  glycosides, 393, 396
Phenology, 272, 300, 301, 302, 549, 550
Phosphate, 344
Phosphorus, 14, 15, 221, 227, 233, 234, 291, 299,
  369, 374, 375, 376, 379, 382, 385, 387, 388
  see also under Fertilizer
Photon flux densities, 174, 175, 187, 190, 309
Photosynthate, 137, 246, 247, 538, 539
Photosynthesis, 15, 125, 165–78, 183–203, 205–6,
  209–12, 215, 247, 298, 307, 312, 505, 506,
  510–12, 521–3, 528, 529, 530, 531, 532, 539,543:
  rate of, 186–7, 188, 189, 190, 193–4, 308–10,
  515, 540, 541
  water stress and, 193–4, 205, 206, 209, 211,
  212, 216, 217
Phthiracarids, 402, 403, 405, 406
Phthiracarus, 403 see also Box-mites and
  Phthiracarids
Picea abies, 28, 62, 144, 325
Picea sitchensis, 247
Pine loopers, 43
Pine moth, 43
Pinifolic acid, 394, 395
Pinitol, 396
Pinus banksiana, 301
Pinus cembra, 166, 307
Pinus contorta, 451
Pinus echinata, 150
Pinus radiata, 205
Pinus resinosa, 205, 291
Pinus sylvestris, 13–567 passim
Plagiothecium, 145
Plant species, coexistence of, 547–51
Plectus, 430
Pleurozium schreberi, 54, 62, 145, 148, 149, 155,
  157, 158–9, 421
Podzol, 32, 55, 341–60 et passim
Pohlia nutans, 145, 148, 155
Pollinators, 550
Polyphenols, 160, 363, 391
Polysaccharids, 397
Polytrichum commune, 145
Polytrichum juniperinum, 145, 146, 155
Polytrichum piliferum, 146, 155
Populus tremula, 144
Potassium, 14, 15, 220, 227, 231, 233, 234, 235,
  291, 299, 347, 349, 350, 351, 352, 354, 355–6,
  359, 367, 369, 374, 375, 376, 379, 382, 385 see
  also under Fertilizer
Precipitation, 37, 39, 57, 77, 108 et passim, see
  also Interception, Snow, Stem flow,
  Throughfall
Procyanidines, 394
Prosternon tesselatum, 431
Proteins, 363, 384
Proteroiulus fuscus, 427

Protozoans, 420, 425–38 passim, 441, 442,
  446–9 passim, 455
Protura, 420, 426, 429, 432, 434, 437
Prunus serotina, 297, 301
Pseudoscorpiones, 426, 429
Pseudotsuga menziesii, 257, 302
Psocoptera, 426, 429
Ptilidium ciliare, 145
Ptilidium pulcherrimum, 145
Ptilium crista-castrensis, 48, 145, 155

Quantum yield, 174
Quercetin, 394
Quercus rubur, 27–8, 31

Radiation, 16, 527:
  global, 55, 83, 90–9, 471, 475
  long-wave, 97–9, 474, 495, 496, 512
  short-wave, 36, 59, 83, 96, 494–5, 496, 507
Radiation shield, 80, 81, 84, 85
Raffinose, 396
Raphidioptera, 426, 429
Regeneration niche, 547
Resource partitioning, 547
Respiration, 14, 15, 16, 166, 167, 176–7, 310–11,
  425–7, 437–8, 442–4, 510, 512:
  branch, 310–11, 312
  growth, 167, 528, 534
  maintenance, 167, 528, 530, 531, 534
  root, 311, 312
  stem, 176–7, 310, 311, 312
Rhamnans, 396, 397
Rhizopoda, 426, 429, 432, 434, 437
Rhysotritia ardua, 403
Ring increments, 566
Roe deer, 49, 52
Roots:
  biomass, 132, 133, 134, 135, 256, 319, 320, 321
  consumption of, 261–7, 454
  grafting, 256
  growth of, 256, 257, 534
  litter production, 355, 451, 452, 573
  live-to-dead ratios, 257–8
  nitrogen content, 232
  production of, 255–6, 307, 312
  resistance in, 487, 488
  starch content, 240
  temperature, 233
  tips, 243, 244, 246, 452
  uptake, 353, 355, 570–1, 586
  water uptake, 487–9
  weight distribution, 253–5
  see also following entry
Roots, fine, 126, 134, 135, 137, 235, 337:
  biomass, 253
  death of, 239, 251–8, 535
  growth of, 239–48, 252–8 passim, 534
  turnover, 252, 253

602

Rotatoria, 420, 425, 426, 428, 429, 431, 432, 434, 437, 441
Rotifers, *see* Rotatoria
Rotylenchus, 263
Rubus idaeus, 222
Run-off, 15
Rutter drainage function, 110

Sagenomella, 430
Sawflies, 43, 280, 284, 287, 301, 540
Schwiebea, 431
Sciarids, 433
Scots pine, *see Pinus sylvestris*
Semiothisa liturata, 281, 300
Sensors, 80, 81, 83
Sequoitol, 396
Shikimic acid, 396
Siljansfors, 37, 39, 55–62
S-layer, 335, 346, 348, 351, 352, 356, 425
Snow:
　accumulation, 111–13
　density, 77, 88, 111
　depth, 77, 111
　dynamics, 472–5, 495
　measurement of, 88
　melt, 111–13, 474, 475
Sodium, 221, 291, 347, 348, 349, 351, 354, 355
Soil:
　animals and, 261–7, 401–7, 419–55
　electric charge balance, 348–50
　frost in, 475–81
　heat conduction in, 16, 474,476, 477, 478, 479, 490, 491, 492, 494
　heat flow in, 116–19, 489–94, 499
　microflora, 261, 419–55
　pH, 358, 423
　processes of, 23, 553–64
　temperature, 77, 81, 118, 160, 171, 335, 421, 424. 481, 495, 499, 507, 527, 529, 555, 573 580
　water, measurement of, 88
　water flow in, 113
　water potential, 507, 518, 527, 529
　see also following entry
Soil organisms, 17, 419–55:
　biomass of, 433–6, 438–42, 445, 447, 448, 455
　carbon flow and, 444–6
　distribution of, 450
　respiration of, 442–4, 445, 446, 447
　trophic categories of, 427–8, 438
Soil-root resistance, 199–200
Solidago virgaurea, 144, 155
Solling project, 12
Sonicator bath, 365
Sphagnum, 62, 334, 335, 338, 406
Sphingidae, 275, 276, 280, 281, 282, 283, 285–6 290, 291
Spruce, 325, 334, 337:

Norway, 28, 62, 325
　sitka, 166
Stand:
　age and needle litter decomposition, 363–70
　development, 325–6
　structural properties and dynamics of, 125–37
Starch, 539, 542, 543, 544:
　reserves of, 239–48
Stem:
　bark, 240, 245, 246
　biomass, 319, 323, 324
　death of, 535
　diameter, changes in, 184–5, 187, 194–7
　flow, 87, 111, 450, 451
　growth of, 529, 531, 534, 542, 543
Stefan-Boltzmann's constant, 97, 474
Sterols, 395
Steryl esters, 394, 395
Stomata:
　closure of, 175, 211, 216, 517
　conductance, 172, 175, 176, 185, 186, 188, 189 190, 192–3, 208, 209, 211, 470–1, 516, 539, 540, 541
　regulation, 184, 201
　resistance, 167, 206, 469, 510
Strophosomus, 280
Stumps, 319, 320, 321, 334, 336, 337, 338
Sucrose, 396
Suctobelba, 431
Sugar beet, 529
Sulphate, 233, 234, 344, 347, 348, 349
Sulphur, 221, 230, 291, 359, 367, 369, 375, 376, 379, 381, 382, 384, 385, 387, 388
Surface resistance, 471
SWECON:
　biometeorological measurements, 80–4
　data handling, 65–71
　ecosystem research, 11–20
　instrumentation and measurement programme, 79–90
　investigation sites, 25–62, 76
　micrometeorological measurements, 84–6
　objectives of, 12–13, 329–32
　organization and management, 13–17
　problem areas, 13–17
　simulation techniques, 65–71
Swedish Natural Research Council, 11
Symphyla, 262, 420, 426, 429, 432, 434, 437
Symphylids, *see* Symphyla

Tannin, 301, 397
Tardigrada, 420, 425, 426, 429, 431, 432, 434, 437
Tarsonemus, 431
Tectocepheus velatus, 431
Tensiometers, 89, 90, 115, 116
Tetrahymena pyriformis, 425
Throughfall, 15, 87, 108, 342, 343, 557, 573, 581
Tilia cordata, 28

Tolypocladium, 428, 430
Tomicus piniperda, 43
Toxic materials, 248
Transducers, 81, 83, 100–1, 187
Transmissivity, 92, 93, 94
Transpiration, 14, 15, 165–78, 198, 201, 206,
 217, 470, 471, 472, 483, 505, 506, 513, 516,
 521–3:
 rate, 191, 201, 515
Trees:
 complete utilization of, 392
 height of, 35, 324
Trichoderma, 428, 430:
 polysporum, 393, 397, 398
 viride, 393, 397, 398
Trientalis europaea, 144
Triglycerides, 394, 395, 399
Tullbergia krausbaueri, 431
Turbidometric analysis, 365
Twigs, 334
Tydeus, 431
Tylencholaimus, 262, 263:
 mirabilis, 262, 263, 264, 266
 stecki, 262, 263, 264, 265
Tylenchus, 263, 264, 266, 427, 430

Ulmus glabra, 28
Uronic acid, 397

Vaccinio-Pinetum (boreale), 43
Vaccinium spp., 158, 222:
 myrtillus, 28, 48, 62, 143, 144, 149, 154, 155,
  157, 158
 uliginosum, 144, 149
 vitis-idaea, 54, 133, 134, 136, 141, 143–9

passim, 154–8 *passim,* 161, 253, 254–5, 256,
 266, 421, 451, 567
Vanadate method, 276, 365
Vegetation dynamics, 139–50
Vegetation temperature, 82
Velen project, 107
Verticillium, 428, 430
Virelles project, 12

Water:
 balance, 77, 99, 103–6, 540
 conductivity, 477, 490
 exchange, 15
 flows, 344–6, 351–2, 481–7, 573
 plant-available, 31–2
 relations, field studies of, 183–203
 reserves, 184
 stress, 175, 185, 187, 193–4, 195, 201, 205–12,
  510 *see also* Photosynthesis
 transport, 15, 16, 215–17, 353–4, 507–9, 538
 turnover, 14, 21–2, 463
 uptake, 15, 166, 487, 488, 509–10, 516, 533, 538
Weathering, 353, 354, 355, 359
Wheat, 451
Wind, 37, 40, 57, 58, 83–4, 108, 495, 507
Winter-hardening, 215–7, 232, 233
Wood lemming, 28

Xylans, 396, 397
Xylem radius, 195
Xylem resistance, 508

Yponomeutidae, 281

Zinc, 221

604

LIST OF INTERNAL AND TECHNICAL REPORTS FROM THE SWEDISH CONIFEROUS FOREST PROJECT

Results obtained within the Swedish Coniferous Forest Project are primarily reported in two types of publications, *viz.* internal reports and technical reports. Internal reports contain contributions, necessary to the current progress of the project. Technical reports are intended for more elaborate contributions, which are not sufficiently complete for inclusion in the open literature. The internal and technical reports are listed below, whereas the open literature publications are frequently referred to in the ordinary reference lists of this volume.

Technical reports are in English while most of the internal reports are in Swedish (S) but contain an English abstract. Figures as well as tables have legends in English. Reports and copies of publications can be obtained from the author and requests can be sent to the project secretariat with the address:

Swedish Coniferous Forest Project
Dept. of Ecology and Environmental Research
Swedish University of Agricultural Sciences
S-750 07 UPPSALA, Sweden

Internal reports

1. SWECON-seminar 1973-05-14–1973-05-21, 1974. Summaries of group activities. 76 pp.
2. Tenow, O. 1974. Development of forested landscape and forest use in Fennoscandia up to the 20th century – an outline. 60 pp. (S)
3. Andersson, L.-Å., Falk, S. O. & Larsson, S. 1974. A simulation model for the water relations of a young pine seedling (*Pinus silvestris* L.). 34 pp. (S)
4. Glanz, F. 1974. Data gathering, storage and retrieval within SWECON. 65 pp. (S)
5. Andersson, L.-Å., Falk, S. O. & Larsson, S. 1974. Cultivation of young pine seedlings in climate chambers. 20 pp. (S)
6. Axelsson, B., Holmberg, O., Johansson, A., Larsson, S., Lohm, U., Lundkvist, H., Persson, T., Sohlenius, B., Tenow, O. & Wirén, A. 1974. Qualitative and quantitative survey of the fauna at Ivantjärnsheden – a pine forest in Gästrikland – and some other coniferous forest sites in Central Sweden. 44 pp. (S)
7. Söderström, B. 1974. Microfungi in the different soil horizons in a planted Norway spruce forest in Scania, Southern Sweden. 14 pp. (S)
8. Mortensen, U. & Staaf, H. 1974. Evolution of heat and carbon dioxide from soil samples – a comparison of two methods for measuring the total activity of organisms in soil. 18 pp.
9. Clarholm, M. 1974. Daily direct countings of bacteria in soil as a method for estimating biomass and productivity. 12 pp.
10. Hast, R. 1974. The total activity of microorganisms in the soil – an evaluation of some methods. 37 pp. (S)
11. Popović, B. 1974. Nitrogen mineralization – a comparison between incubation experiments in the field and in the laboratory. 17 pp. (S)
12. Lindberg, T. 1974. Pre-investigation of nitrogen fixation in a coniferous forest ecosystem. 21 pp. (S)
13. Granhall, U. (ed.) 1974. Research notes on soil processes. 21 pp.
14. Unpublished.
15. Bååth, E. & Söderström, B. 1974. An estimation of fungal biomass in a 120-year-old pine forest at Jädraås, Gästrikland (Central Sweden). 8 pp. (S)
16. Söderström, B. & Bååth, E. 1974. Collection of pure cultures of microfungi isolated in a 120-year-old pine forest at Jädraås, Gästrikland (Central Sweden). 8 pp. (S)

17. Söderström, B. 1974. Some microfungi isolated from different soil horizons in a 120-year-old pine forest in Central Sweden. 7 pp. (S)
18. Bråkenhielm, S. 1974. The vegetation of Ivantjärnsheden. 51 pp. (S)
19. Bååth, E. & Söderström, B. 1974. Decomposition of cellulose, xylan, chitin, and protein by microfungi isolated from coniferous forest soils. 15 pp. (S)
20. Statskontoret. 1974. Report on the computer equipment of the Swedish Coniferous Forest Project. (S)
21. Bringmark, L., Bååth, E., Clarholm, M., Granhall, U., Lindberg, T., Lohm, U., Magnusson, C., Persson, T., Petersson, G., Rosswall, T., Sohlenius, B. & Söderström, B. 1975. Simultaneous analysis of activity and biomass of soil organisms in a 120-year-old pine forest at Jädraås, Gästrikland (Central Sweden). 14 pp. (S)
22. Bosatta, E., Lohm, U. & Tenow, O. 1975. An outline of a dynamic model of interaction between *Pinus silvestris* and *Blastophagus piniperda* L. (Col., Scolytidae). 19 pp.
23. Bringmark, L. & Petersson, G. 1975. Downward transport of mineral solutes through the soil of a pine forest on sand in Gästrikland (Central Sweden). 17 pp. (S)
24. Sohlenius, B., Lagerlöf, J. & Magnusson, C. 1975. Studies on feeding ecology of nematodes from a pine heath soil. 23 pp. (S)
25. Wirén, A. 1975. Quantitative data on Collembola at Ivantjärnsheden, Gästrikland (Central Sweden), and some other Scots pine stands. 13 pp. (S)
26. Lindroth, A. & Perttu, K. 1975. Routines for collecting, processing and reporting of standard climate data. 28 pp. (S)
27. Bringmark, L. & Petersson, G. 1975. Some chemical soil variables in a 120-year-old Scots pine forest growing on glacifluvial sand (Jädraås, Central Sweden). 40 pp. (S)
28. Hellkvist, J., Hillerdal, K. & Parsby, J. 1975. Studies of water potential and photosynthesis in Scots pine. 23 pp. (S)
29. Hellkvist, J., Hillerdal, K. & Parsby, J. 1975. Measurement of stem-diameter changes with a strain gage transducer. 10 pp. (S)
30. Svensson, J. 1975. ECODAC – ECOlogical DAta Collection system. System description. 22 pp. (S)
31. Persson, T. 1975. Abundance, biomass and respiration of the soil arthropod community in an old Scots pine heath stand on Ivantjärnsheden, Gästrikland (Central Sweden) – a preliminary investigation. 35 pp. (S)
32. Larsson, S. & Tenow, O. 1975. Frass-drop from needle-eating insect larvae in a Scots pine forest in Central Sweden. 23 pp. (S)
33. Bergqvist, E. & Grip, H. 1975. The Gusselbäck station – construction of a gauging station for accurate and continuous discharge measurement. 23 pp. (S)
34. Lohm, U. & Nihlgård, B. 1975. "Elemental Cycling Conference" Estes Park, Colorado, USA, 15–19 December 1975 – travel report. 21 pp. (S)
35. Popović, B. 1976. Nitrogen mineralisation in an old pine stand. 16 pp. (S)
36. Staaf, H. 1976. Carbon dioxide evolution from soil in a 120-year-old Scots pine stand at Ivantjärnsheden, Gästrikland – preliminary results from summer and autumn periods in 1974. 27 pp. (S)
37. Schütt, T. 1976. Research project methodology. 156 pp. (S)
38. Albrektson, A. 1976. The amount and the distribution of tree biomass in some pine stands (*Pinus silvestris*) in northern Gästrikland. 26 pp. (S)
39. Lohm, U. (ed). 1976. Soil processes, progress report 1974 and 1975. 42 pp. (S)
40. Sohlenius, B., Berg, B., Clarholm, M., Lundkvist, H., Popović, B., Rosswall, T., Staaf, H., Söderström, B. & Wirén, A. 1976. Mineralisation and soil organism activity in a coniferous humus – a model building experiment. 51 pp. (S)
41. Axelsson, B. & Ågren, G. Tree growth model (PT 1) – a development paper. 79 pp.
42. Berg, B. & Bosatta, E. 1976. A carbon-nitrogen model of a pine forest soil ecosystem – a development paper. 61 pp.
43. Bosatta, E. & Bringmark, L. 1976. A model for transport and adsorption of inorganic ions in a pine forest soil ecosystem – a development paper. 42 pp.
44. Bringfelt, B. & Orrskog, G. 1976. Recording the heat storage in a forest in the Velen representative basin. 38 pp.
45. Bischof, W. & Odh, S.-Å. 1976. CO_2-measurements within and above a Scots pine stand. Part 1: Installation. 18 pp. (S)
46. Hellkvist, J., Hillerdal, K. & Parsby, J. 1977. Influence of fertilization and irrigation on the water potential of young pine trees. 23 pp. (S)
47. Hellkvist, J., Hillerdal, K. & Karlsson, G. 1977. Field studies of photosynthesis and stomatal con-

ductance in Scots pine. 16 pp. (S)

48. Hellkvist, J. & Hillerdal, K. 1977. The relation between water potential and stem circumference change in 20-year-old Scots pine. 16 pp. (S)

49. Wiman, B. & Nihlgård, B. 1977. Aerosol separation by pine needles. The design of a wind tunnel system, tests of its applicability by two methods and a tentative outline of a simulation model. 85 pp.

50. Staaf, H. 1977. Below-ground biomass respiration of pine, heather, and cowberry in an old Scots pine stand. 19 pp.

51. Fagerström, T. 1977. Effect of acid precipitation on growth and nitrogen turnover in a pine forest – a systems analysis approach. 14 pp. (S)

52. Bringmark, L. 1977. Cation adsorption in a sandy pine forest soil. 29 pp. (S)

53. Halldin, S., Grip, H., Jansson, P.-E., Lindgren, Å. & Perttu, K. 1977. E1 – a model of the annual course of energy flows in a pine stand. 148 pp.

54. Jansson, P.-E. 1977. Soil properties at Ivantjärnsheden. 66 pp. (S)

55. Linder, S. 1977. The diurnal and seasonal changes in net photosynthesis in seedlings of Scots pine. 26 pp. (S)

56. Linder, S. & Troeng, E. 1977. Gas exchange in a 20-year-old stand of Scots pine. I: The seasonal change of net photosynthesis in current and one-year-old needles. 14 pp. (S)

57. Linder, S. & Troeng, E. 1977. Gas exchange in a 20-year-old stand of Scots pine. II. The variation in stem respiration during the growing season. 14 pp. (S)

58. Perttu, K. (ed.), Bringfelt, B., Engelbrecht, B., Grip, H., Jansson, P.-E., Lindgren, Å., Lindroth, A., Norén, B. & Odin, H. 1977. Seminar 770302–03: Measurements of energy exchange in Sweden. Modelling, methods and results. 97 pp. (S)

59. Bringmark, L., Jansson, P.-E. & Staaf, H. 1977. Seminar on mineral nutrients in the soil, especially ion uptake by roots. – Lund 770329–30. 10 pp. (S)

60. Popović, B. 1977. Nitrogen mineralisation in an old and a young Scots pine stand. 15 pp. (S)

61. Odö, E. 1977. Arthropods in stumps and branches of Scots pine in a clear-cut area in central Sweden. 21 pp. (S)

62. Tamm, C. O. 1977. How should ecosystem functions be studied and is there a special need for research on the ecosystem level? 33 pp. (S)

63. Berg, B. 1977. Research notes on decomposition 1–4. 22 pp.

64. Berg, B. 1977. Weight loss values for one year's decomposition of different litters at Ivantjärnsheden. 17 pp.

65. Staaf, H. & Berg, B. 1977. A structural and chemical description of litter and humus in a mature Scots pine stand. 31 pp.

66. Ågren, G., Axelsson, B. & Troeng, E. 1977. A simple estimate of carbon budgets for one day of two Scots pines, one fertilized and one control, in August 1977, 9 pp.

67. Bååth, E. & Söderström, B. 1977. An estimation of the annual production of basidiomycete fruitbodies in a 120-year-old pine forest in central Sweden (Ivantjärnsheden, Ih VA, Gästrikland). 11 pp.

68. Mattson-Djos, E. & Hellkvist, J. 1977. Stomatal conductance and water potential of Scots pine – Introductory field studies. 33 pp. (S)

69. Larsson, S., Tenow, O., Ericsson, A., Hellkvist, J., Hillerdal, K. & Mattson-Djos, E. 1978. Effects of artificial early summer defoliation on growth of Scots pine (Pinus silvestris L.). 41 pp. (S)

70. Granhall, U. (ed.). 1978. Nutrient turnover in the early phase after clear-cutting. Results from introductory investigations. 64 pp. (S)

71. Grip, H. 1978. Semiempirical formulas for estimating evapotranspiration – a preliminary review. 18 pp. (S)

72. Persson, H. 1978. Data on root dynamics in a young Scots pine stand in central Sweden. 13 pp.

73. Albrektson, A. 1978. Tree biomass in some Scots pine stands (Pinus silvestris L.). 19 pp. (S)

74. Albrektson, A. & Andersson, B. 1978. Estimates of litterfall in pine stands (Pinus silvestris L.). 17 pp. (S)

75. Lundgren, B. & Bååth, E. 1978. Fungal and bacterial investigations in a pine forest soil during two years following a clear-cutting. 32 pp. (S)

76. Gemmel, P. & Perttu, K. 1978. Short wave radiation within a pine stand. Comparison between measured radiation and radiation calculated for fish-eye photographs. 18 pp. (S)

77. Axelsson, B. 1978. The effect of moose (Alces alces L.) browsing on Scots pine (Pinus sylvestris L.) stands. I. Inventory of Smedspåret (Gästrikland). 44 pp. (S)

78. Lindberg, T. & Popović, B. 1978. Quantities of inorganic nitrogen in a clear-cut area (Ih 0), 1977. 9 pp.

79. Albrektson, A. & Andersson, B. 1978. Biomass in an old mixed coniferous forest in Dalarna. 40 pp. (S)
80. Berg, B. 1978. Decomposition of needle litter in a 120-year-old Scots pine (*Pinus silvestris*) stand at Ivantjärnsheden. 66 pp.
81. Lindroth, A. 1978. Calibration of radiation meters. 17 pp. (S)
82. Linder, S. & Troeng, E. 1978. Gas exchange in a 20-year-old stand of Scots pine. III. A comparison of net photosynthesis and transpiration of eight different pine trees. 19 pp. (S)
83. Troeng, E. & Linder, S. 1978. Gas exchange in a 20-year-old stand of Scots pine. IV. Photosynthesis and transpiration within the crown of one tree. 20 pp. (S)
84. Perttu, K., Grip, H., Halldin, S., Jansson, P.-E., Lindgren, Å., Lindroth, A. & Norén, B. 1979. Abiotic research in the Swedish Coniferous Forest Project. I. Activities during the latest years. 46 pp. (S)
85. Grip, H., Halldin, S., Jansson, P.-E., Lindgren, Å., Lindroth, A., Norén, B. & Perttu, K. 1979. Abiotic research in the Swedish Coniferous Forest Project. II. Preliminary results from a IUFRO-workshop on heat and mass transfer models. 55 pp.
86. Persson, A. & Sohlenius, B. 1979. Influence of clear-cutting on nematodes, rotifers and tardigrades in pine forest soil. 29 pp. (S)
87. Söderström, B. 1979. Fourth North American Conference on Mycorrhiza June 24 to July 14, 1979 – travel report. 14 pp. (S)
88. Lindroth, A. 1979. The specific heat of wood from mature Scots pine. 18 pp. (S)
89. Söderström, B. 1979. Ectomycorrhiza; identification of the fungal partner. A short review. 10 pp. (S)
90. Lohm, U. (ed.). 1979. A seminar on nitrogen fertilization in forests. 23 pp. (S)
91. Troeng, E., Linder, S. & Långström, B. 1979. Gas exchange in a 20-year-old Scots pine. V. Pilot study on the effects on gas exchange during the attack of pine shoot beetle (*Tomicus piniperda* L.). 16 pp. (S)
92. Staaf, H. 1979. Effects of increased biomass removal on nutrient cycling and productivity in forests. – Problems and present knowledge. 68 pp. (S)
93. Lindroth, A. & Norén, B. 1980. A travel report from a visit to Institute of Hydrology, England. 16 pp. (S)
94. Linder, S. 1980. Photosynthesis and respiration in conifers. A classified reference list. 17 pp. (S)
95. Berg, B. & Lindberg, T. 1980. Is litter decomposition retarded in the presence of mycorrhizal roots in forest soil? 10 pp.
96. Hillerdal-Hagströmer, K. & Stjernquist, I. 1980. Rate of photosynthesis in dominating species in tree, field and bottom layers of an old and a young stand of Scots pine at varying water and nutrient status. 44 pp. (S)
97. Lindberg, T. & Popović, B. 1980. Quantities of inorganic nitrogen in a clear-cut area (Ih 0), 1978 and 1979. 12 pp.
98. Gaud, W. S. 1980. Preliminary analysis of nitrogen dynamics in Scots pine. 20 pp.

Technical reports

1. Dyne, G. M. van, Gay, L. W., Stewart, J. B., Eriksson, E., Bischof, W., Waring, R. H., Heal, O. W., Ulrich, B., Khanna, P. K., Mayer, R. & Prenzel, J. 1975. Procedures and examples of integrated eco-system research. – Papers presented to the SWECON seminar in May 1973. 163 pp.
2. Persson, H. 1975. Dry matter production of dwarf shrubs, mosses and lichens in some Scots pine stands at Ivantjärnsheden, Central Sweden. 25 pp.
3. Flower-Ellis, J., Albrektson, A. & Olsson, L. 1976. Structure and growth of some young Scots pine stands: (1) Dimensional and numerical relationships. 98 pp.
4. Sohlenius, B., Persson, H. & Magnusson, C. 1977. Root-weight and nematode numbers in a young Scots pine stand at Ivantjärnsheden, Central Sweden. 22 pp.
5. Andersson, L.-Å., Bengtson, C., Falk, S. O. & Larsson, S. 1977. Cultivation of pine and spruce seedlings in climate chambers. 17 pp.
6. Jensén, P. & Pettersson, S. 1977. Effects of some internal and environmental factors on ion uptake efficiency in roots of pine seedlings. 19 pp.
7. Perttu, K., Lindgren, Å., Lindroth, A. & Norén, B. 1977. Micro- and biometeorological measurements at Jädraås. Instrumentation and measurement technics. 67 pp.
8. Lindgren, Å. 1977. A random climatic data generator. 22 pp.
9. Sohlenius, B. 1977. Numbers, biomass and respiration of Nematoda, Rotatoria and Tardigrada in a 120-year-old Scots pine forest at Ivantjärnsheden, Central Sweden. 40 pp.

10. Aronsson, A., Elowson, S. & Ingestad, T. 1977. Elimination of water and mineral nutrition as limiting factors in a young Scots pine stand. I. Experimental design and some preliminary results. 38 pp.
11. Granhall, U. & Lindberg, T. 1977. Nitrogen fixation at coniferous forest sites within the SWECON project. 39 pp.
12. Clarholm, M. 1977. Monthly estimations of soil bacteria at Jädraås and a comparison between a young and a mature pine forest on a sandy soil. 17 pp.
13. Bååth, E. & Söderström, B. E. 1977. Mycelial lengths and fungal biomasses in some Swedish coniferous forest soils, with special reference to a pine forest in central Sweden (Ivantjärnsheden, Ih VA). 45 pp.
14. Halldin, S. 1978. Water uptake – but how? ROOT – a model for testing different uptake hypotheses. 53 pp.
15. Flower-Ellis, J. G. K. & Olsson, L. 1978. Litterfall in an age series of Scots pine and its variation by components during the years 1973–1976. 62 pp.
16. Bråkenhielm, S. 1978. Ivantjärnsheden, Jädraås – regional physiography and description of the research area. 58 pp.
17. Engelbrecht, B. & Svensson, J. 1978. Data collection, storage, retrieval and analysis of continuous measurements. 48 pp.
18. Lundkvist, H. 1978. The influence of soil fauna on decomposition of pine needle litter; a field experiment. 15 pp.
19. Lohammar, T., Larsson, S., Linder, S. & Falk, S. O. 1979. Fast – A simulation model for the carbon dioxide and water exchange of Scots pine. 38 pp.
20. Larsson, S. 1979. Water stress as a regulating factor for transpiration of plants. 40 pp.
21. Bengtson, C. 1979. Effects and after-effects of water stress on transpiration rate. 36 pp.
22. Larsson, S. 1979. Climate as growth regulating factor in trees. I. A review of the literature. 53 pp.
23. Linder, S., Nordström, B., Parsby, J., Sundbom, E. & Troeng, E. 1980. A gas exchange system for field measurements of photosynthesis and transpiration in a 20-year-old stand of Scots pine. 34 pp.
24. Larsson, S. & Bengtson, C. 1980. Effects of water stress on growth in Scots pine. 19 pp.
25. Linder, S. 1980. Understanding and predicting tree growth. Poster proceedings from a SWECON workshop, September 2–8, 1979. 155 pp.
26. Jansson, P.-E. & Halldin, S. 1980. Soil water and heat model. Technical description. 94 pp.

ECOLOGICAL BULLETINS

Published by:

Swedish Natural Science Research Council,
Editorial Service,
Box 23136,
S-104 35 Stockholm,
Sweden

in cooperation with the

Commission for Research on Natural Resources,
Swedish Council for Planning and Coordination of Research,
Box 6710
S-113 85 Stockholm,
Sweden

Editor-in-Chief:

T. Rosswall,
Department of Microbiology,
Swedish University of Agricultural Sciences,
S-750 07 Uppsala,
Sweden

Starting with Vol. 29, the **Ecological Bulletins** series is published by the Swedish Natural Science Research Council (NFR) and the Commission for Research on Natural Resources of the Swedish Council for Planning and Coordination of Research (FRN).

The Swedish Natural Science Research Council, NFR, is the central governmental agency responsible for the promotion of basic research in the natural sciences in Sweden. The research council has several special committees to support activities in fields, such as ecology, hydrology, and oceanography.

In 1977, a new research-promoting body – the Swedish Council for Planning and Coordination of Research, Forskningsrådsnämnden (FRN) – was established in Sweden. The council includes representatives from research councils, research funding bodies, the parliament, and the labour unions. One of its main purposes is to plan, initiate and coordinate projects of special importance to society. In early 1978, the council established a Commission for Research on Natural Resources, which is responsible for integrated research in relation to natural resources and environmental problems. The commission is acting as the Swedish Committee for Unesco's MAB Programme.

Copies of the bulletins can be ordered from the Editorial Service of NFR, Box 23136, S-104 35 Stockholm, Sweden. The Editorial Service, which provides financial and practical assistance for the publication of scientific works, is responsible for the distribution of all NFR publications.

Available Ecological Bulletins (December 1980)